The Impacts of Lasting Occupation

Series in Political Psychology

Series Editor
John T. Jost

Editorial Board
Mahzarin Banaji, Gian Vittorio Caprara, Christopher Federico, Don Green, John Hibbing, Jon Krosnick, Arie Kruglanski, Kathleen McGraw, David Sears, Jim Sidanius, Phil Tetlock, Tom Tyler

Image Bite Politics: News and the Visual Framing of Elections
Maria E. Grabe and Erik P. Bucy

Social and Psychological Bases of Ideology and System Justification
John T. Jost, Aaron C. Kay, and Hulda Thorisdottir

The Political Psychology of Democratic Citizenship
Eugene Borgida, Christopher Federico, and John Sullivan

On Behalf of Others: The Psychology of Care in a Global World
Sarah Scuzzarello, Catarina Kinnvall, and Kristen Renwick Monroe

The Obamas and a (Post) Racial America?
Gregory S. Parks and Matthew W. Hughey

Ideology, Psychology, and Law
Jon Hanson

The Impacts of Lasting Occupation: Lessons from Israeli Society
Daniel Bar-Tal and Izhak Schnell

Representing Red and Blue: How the Culture Wars Change the Way Citizens Speak and Politicians Listen
David C. Barker and Christopher Jan Carman

The Impacts of Lasting Occupation

Lessons from Israeli Society

Edited by Daniel Bar-Tal and Izhak Schnell

OXFORD
UNIVERSITY PRESS

Oxford University Press is a department of the University of Oxford. It furthers the
University's objective of excellence in research, scholarship, and education by publishing
worldwide.

Oxford   New York
Auckland   Cape Town   Dar es Salaam   Hong Kong   Karachi
Kuala Lumpur   Madrid   Melbourne   Mexico City   Nairobi
New Delhi   Shanghai   Taipei   Toronto

With offices in
Argentina   Austria   Brazil   Chile   Czech Republic   France   Greece
Guatemala   Hungary   Italy   Japan   Poland   Portugal   Singapore
South Korea   Switzerland   Thailand   Turkey   Ukraine   Vietnam

Oxford is a registered trade mark of Oxford University Press in the UK and certain other
countries.

Published in the United States of America by
Oxford University Press
198 Madison Avenue, New York, NY 10016

© Oxford University Press 2013

All rights reserved. No part of this publication may be reproduced, stored in a retrieval
system, or transmitted, in any form or by any means, without the prior permission in
writing of Oxford University Press, or as expressly permitted by law, by license, or under
terms agreed with the appropriate reproduction rights organization. Inquiries concerning
reproduction outside the scope of the above should be sent to the Rights Department,
Oxford University Press, at the address above.

You must not circulate this work in any other form
and you must impose this same condition on any acquirer.

Library of Congress Cataloging-in-Publication Data
   The impacts of lasting occupation : lessons from Israeli society /
      edited by Daniel Bar-Tal and Izhak Schnell.
   p. cm.—(Series in political psychology)
   Includes bibliographical references and index.
   ISBN 978-0-19-986218-4 (hardback)
   1. Israel-Arab War, 1967—Occupied territories   2. Arab-Israeli conflict—1993-
   3. Israel—Social conditions—21st century.
   I. Bar-Tal, Daniel.   II. Shnell, Itzhak.
   DS127.6.O3I47 2012
   956.9405'4—dc23   2012003477

9 8 7 6 5 4 3 2 1
Printed in the United States of America on acid-free paper

Contents

Foreword: On Occupations *by Michael Walzer*   vii

Preface   xi

Introduction: Occupied and Occupiers—The Israeli Case
—Daniel Bar-Tal and Izhak Schnell   1

I. Fundamentals of Occupation   29

1 The Law of Belligerent Occupation as a System of Control: Dressing Up Exploitation in Respectable Garb—*David Kretzmer*   31

2 Is There a Controversy Concerning the Morality of the Occupation and Its Implications?—*Marcelo Dascal*   61

3 Geographical Ramifications of the Occupation for Israeli Society—*Izhak Schnell*   93

4 Psychological Legitimization—Views of the Israeli Occupation by Jews in Israel: Data and Implications
—Tamir Magal, Neta Oren, Daniel Bar-Tal, and Eran Halperin   122

II. Political Effects of Occupation   187

5 The Occupation and Israeli Democracy—*Yaron Ezrahi*   189

6 The Occupation and Its Effect on the Israel Defense Forces—*Reuven Pedatzur*   208

7 Intradomestic Bargaining Over the Lands and the Future: Israel's Policy Toward the 1967 Occupied Territories
—Gideon Doron and Maoz Rosenthal   250

8   The Impact of the Occupation of the West Bank and the
    Gaza Strip on the Political Discourse of the Palestinians
    in Israel—*Muhammad Amara and Mohanad Mostafa*   273

III. Societal Effects of Occupation   297

9   The Wallkeepers: Monitoring the Israeli-Arab Conflict
    —*Dan Caspi with Danny Rubinstein*   299

10 Economic Cost of the Occupation to Israel—*Shir Hever* 326

11 Gendering the Discourse on Occupation: A Sociological
    Perspective—*Hanna Herzog*   359

12 The Psychological and Moral Consequences for Israeli
    Society of the Occupation of Palestinian Land
    —*Charles W. Greenbaum and Yoel Elizur*   380

IV. Cultural Effects of Occupation   409

13 Appealing to Enlightened Self-Interest: The Impact of
    Occupation on Human Rights within Israel
    —*Edward (Edy) Kaufman*   411

14 The Occupation as Represented in the Arts in Israel—*Dan Urian*   438

15 Vocabulary and the Discourse on the 1967 Territories
    —*Nadir Tsur*   471

Conclusion: The Occupied Territories as a Cornerstone in the
Reconstruction of Israeli Society—*Izhak Schnell
and Daniel Bar-Tal*   507

Contributors   540

Index   549

Foreword

ON OCCUPATIONS

I have put my title in the plural, although this is a book about only one occupation. I mean to suggest that people reading this book should think comparatively, not only about the Israeli occupation of the Palestinian territories, but also about other occupations and about their character and consequences, historically and in the contemporary world. One day, I hope, we will also be able to undertake a comparative study of withdrawals: how occupations have ended, in Israel/Palestine and in other places, too. The Israeli withdrawals from the Sinai and the Gaza Strip will be part of the history that needs to be studied, but there are critically important installments still to come.

This occupation began, in my view, with a just war. Israel's preemptive strike in June 1967 has become for many theorists and lawyers the paradigmatic case of a justified preemption—and one that makes very clear the difference between preemptive and preventive wars: the second of these is still commonly regarded as unjust and illegal. But the justice of the Six Day War does not justify what came afterward. The decision to hold the territories that the Israeli army had seized in the war (which then included the Sinai, the Golan Heights, Gaza, and the West Bank) might have been defensible if the land had simply been "held" until Arab rejectionists were replaced, as they eventually were, by Arab negotiators. But that is not what happened.

Instead, there was an organized effort by religious radicals and right-wing nationalists, with government support, to turn the occupation into a conquest—not just to hold the territories but to settle them and incorporate them into Israel proper. The settlement movement is the great wrong of the occupation because it involved the illegal taking of land and water and because it brought into the occupied territories a large (and growing) number of people who had to be "protected" by the Israeli army—and this required, in turn, a radical intervention in Palestinian society and an often cruel repression.

The intervention and the repression have received wide and highly critical publicity. Throughout the Arab world, and in Europe also, the badness of the occupation, which is bad enough, has been elaborated and exaggerated in efforts to call into question the legitimacy of the State of Israel itself. I think of these efforts as a unique feature of the Israeli occupation. People who are, like me, critics of the occupation alone need to distinguish themselves from those other critics who are aiming at a larger target. Comparisons are helpful here. The French occupation of Algeria, which also included a policy of settlement extended over many years, drew (and deserved) harsh criticism, but none of the critics ever thought to call the legitimacy of the French state into question. Chinese rule in Tibet, which the Tibetans regard as an occupation and which includes a concerted effort to bring Han Chinese in large numbers into the province, has justly been condemned around the world, but no one thinks that China is an illegitimate state.

So, Israel is a special case, and the sense that this is so, and not for good reasons, makes many Israelis defensive even in the face of "occupation alone" criticism. But this latter kind of criticism is justified and necessary. The occupation has been a disaster for the Palestinian people, denying them the possibility of civic development and self-determination and subjecting them to an autocratic, often lawless, and systematically humiliating regime. The regime was not entirely new: before 1967, it was Egypt and Jordan that denied civic development and self-determination to the Palestinians. But all this, or at least the Israeli part of it, is well known. What is less well known, and rarely discussed by Israel's external critics, is that the occupation has also been a disaster for Israel.

This second disaster is the subject of this book. Once again, the subject invites comparisons, and I want to describe very briefly some other cases before saying something about how the editors and authors represented here have approached the Israeli case. The blowback of military/political occupations is especially consequential when the occupying power is a democracy. If the occupation is very far away and doesn't include a policy of settlement, as in the case of the United States in the Philippines, for example, the consequences may be minor. The United States even managed to sustain strong hostility to colonialism while ruling a colony of its own. But if the occupation is close by, and if the occupying power has produced a settler population, as in the case of French Algeria, the consequences are huge. In France, the occupation brought fierce political strife, the strengthening of the far Right, the fall of the Third Republic, an attempted military coup d'etat, state terror and revolutionary and then counterrevolutionary terror, and finally, the return to France of a million or more angry and alienated settlers. It is (and, one might say, it should be) a terrible strain for a democratic state to rule undemocratically over a nearby country where many of its own citizens are living in the midst of a subject population.

By contrast, occupations are much easier for authoritarian states. The post–World War II military occupation of Eastern Europe by the Soviet Union produced no internal difficulties for the Stalinist state. Nor, for many years, did the occupation or, better, the incorporation of the Baltic countries and the republics of the Caucuses. More recently, repression in Chechnya (which most Chechens regard as an occupied country) has probably strengthened President and then Prime Minister Putin's hand. In China, the occupation of Tibet is not a politically divisive issue (outside of Tibet). Few Chinese dissidents are concerned to protest the government's policy—even the massive settlement policy (which far Right Israelis must look at with envy). Of course, if the costs of occupation are high enough, even authoritarian governments may not be able to sustain them, as the example of the Soviet Union in Afghanistan makes clear.

Does the American presence in Iraq or NATO's in Afghanistan count as an occupation? As of this writing, I do not think that either country has yet been effectively occupied. A full-scale effort to achieve that level of control would indeed produce severe strains on American and European democracy. And for that reason, there is not going to be an effort of that sort. These are very partial occupations that will soon be brought to a (probably inglorious) end.

The Israeli occupation of Palestinian lands has now lasted for over forty-five years, and the cost to Israel and to Israeli democracy has been very high. The focus here is on the domestic costs, but it is worth noting that there are international costs, too. The movement of hundreds of thousands of settlers into the occupied territories and the rise of political forces determined to hold the territories forever has made the "peace process" even more difficult than it otherwise would have been—and this has greatly damaged Israel's standing in the world. The sometimes legitimate Israeli complaint that there is no reliable Palestinian partner has now been seconded by a similar Palestinian complaint: given the power of the settler movement and its supporters, there is no reliable Israeli partner. So, the creation of a Palestinian state alongside Israel becomes harder and harder to imagine, and the prospect of a one-state solution looms larger. And for Israel's Jews that prospect should be frightening, for that one state could not be both Jewish and democratic.

The occupation is a threat to Israel's future, but this is a speculative threat since the future is often a surprise. By contrast, the effects of the occupation on Israel's present are not a matter for speculation but for concrete analysis. They range over every aspect of political, social, economic, and cultural life. The effects are structural, involving the legal system, the practice of democracy, the effectiveness of the army, economic costs, the design of school curricula, and much else. But they are also intimate and personal, affecting individual psychology and both individual and collective ideas of identity—because the geographic and social distances are so small and so many Israelis now live in the territories, or have relatives there, or serve in the occupying army, or deal every day with Palestinian workers coming from the territories.

All this is analyzed in these chapters. It is analyzed harshly; the writers are, all of them, enemies of the occupation. There are degrees of harshness; I suspect some political differences among these writers, but they belong to the same political camp. It is the camp with which I sympathize, though I also have some disagreements with some of the authors. But theirs is a camp in which disagreement is allowed and criticism encouraged. It is a credit to Israeli democracy that it has produced these critics, and it is important to note that this book will appear simultaneously in English and in Hebrew. The citizens of Israel are its first audience, because they are the ones who must decide to seek an end to the occupation.

Michael Walzer

Preface

The idea of publishing a book about occupation evolved a long time ago, as we considered this issue to be an important one that warrants thorough examination. Although the issue is regarded by many Israelis as controversial, we feel strongly that it cannot be neglected, as it concerns a real-life problem that preoccupies human beings not only in this region but also in other parts of the world. Occupation as war, exploitation, or discrimination exists in the world, and in most cases it is viewed as a problem. The subject of occupation demands a multifaceted perspective not only in terms of its analysis, but also in terms of interdisciplinary perspectives that can illuminate its various aspects. Finally, occupation can be analyzed not only from the perspective of the occupied society, but also from the perspective of the occupying society. While the former analysis is more prevalent, we focus on the latter.

The occupation analyzed in this book is the Israeli occupation of the Palestinian land and its residents, which has attracted great interest from the international community. But for us, as Israelis, it constitutes the focal problem that not only determines all intergroup relations in the region, but also profoundly affects every aspect of life for the two societies involved—the Palestinians and the Israelis. Nonetheless, the case of occupation with which we contend is extremely controversial in Israeli society. This controversy begins with the manner in which the situation is identified within at least four main positions, not mutually exclusive, that characterize the Israeli public discourse: The first of these rejects any definition of the situation as an occupation. According to this view, the West Bank and the Gaza Strip are part of the Promised Land, liberated in a war that was forced upon us. The second view recognizes the status of the territories as occupied but stresses the fact that the occupation is needed to create a controlled security zone. This is required because of the grave existential threat posed to the small and vulnerable State of Israel by the Arab world, including the Palestinian people, whose real goal is Israel's destruction. The third view regards the occupied territories as a possible asset that could be exchanged for peace upon the emergence of a trusted and capable partner, which does not currently exist. The force behind this position is mainly the fear that Israel will lose its Jewish and/or democratic nature should the occupation continue. The fourth position, with which we, the editors, identify, perceives the territories as being occupied and urges Israeli society to make the compromises necessary to reach an agreement with the present Palestinian leaders. It also recognizes the moral and practical consequences that Israel's policies of occupation have for both the occupied Palestinian society and the occupying Israeli society. We choose to discuss these consequences critically in order to unravel their impacts on Israeli society.

We also evaluate the situation of occupation from a moral perspective, believing that occupation, in most cases, inherently and fundamentally causes injustice, inequality, human rights violations, and restriction of freedom. We are well aware that in taking this view we become both observers and participants in the controversy. Many members of our Jewish society in Israel and abroad, and even some members of the international community, may reject our premise that the territories are occupied.

In this political-socio-psychological climate, some liberal Jews critically evaluate China's occupation of Tibet, attack the Sudanese atrocities in Darfur, and castigate at least some Arab states for their violation of human rights. But they can hardly bring themselves to look at the Israeli occupation and the massive violation of human rights that takes place from this perspective. Even some of the Jewish champions of human rights look the other way so as not to see Israel's violations. Moreover, some of them even view the critical evaluation of the Israeli occupation as an attempt to undermine the existence of the State of Israel.

We believe that the differing viewpoints stem from different experiences, knowledge, values, and moral convictions that shape the prism through which social scientists, like all human beings, view reality, process information, and arrange priorities of judgments. These are the roots of individual and group differences. Both of us are greatly preoccupied with the lasting Israeli-Palestinian conflict and specifically with the ongoing occupation. First and foremost, the occupation goes against our moral values. In addition to its devastating effects on Palestinian society, we are convinced that it has had a disastrous effect on the State of Israel and its society. The latter subject is the focus of our book. We love our country and our society; we grew up in Israel, have fulfilled our duties, and have reared our children in Israel. We worry tremendously about the implications of the prolonged occupation, which, slowly but surely, is approaching the point of no return.

It is this concern that has led us to launch a serious academic investigation of the effects of the occupation on Israeli-Jewish society. It is the duty of an academic scholar not only to express evaluative opinions, but also to pose research questions and launch serious, comprehensive, and systemic studies capable of shedding light on issues that are part of the public debate. Although the selection of research questions depends on the researchers' prism, the answers must be provided in accordance with scientific standards. Thus, we believe that despite our position and involvement, we have succeeded in editing a book that meets scientific criteria, just as past social scientists with strong moral convictions were able to provide major contributions to the understanding of racism, poverty, anti-Semitism, and war.

This is also a place to express our special indebtedness to the Slifka Foundation, which provided us with a grant that allowed us to carry out and complete the translations of the chapters, as well as to present the initial ideas in a conference. Great thanks go to Naomi Paz, who translated some of the chapters from Hebrew into English and then edited other chapters that were written in English. Her dedication and skills contributed to the quality of the final versions.

We hope that the book will instigate a vivid, courageous, and comprehensive debate over its premises. Additionally, we hope that the book will be understood in more general terms, as a contribution to the understanding of the processes that take place in any occupying society. In any event, we hope that the book will make a contribution to both the understanding of Israeli society and the comprehension of the phenomenon of occupation in occupying societies in general—an oft-neglected perspective. Even though we recognize that the occupied people suffer more from the occupation than do the occupiers, we dedicate this book to all the Palestinian and Israeli children who suffer because of the occupation—they all deserve a better future.

Daniel Bar-Tal
Izhak Schnell

Introduction: Occupied and Occupiers–The Israeli Case

Daniel Bar-Tal and Izhak Schnell

We begin our introduction with two quotations that reveal much about the nature of the occupation and the relationship between the occupied and the occupiers.

In a speech that attempted to explain the rationale of his "disengagement plan," the former Prime Minister of Israel, Ariel Sharon, said that he had reached the conclusion that "it is impossible to hold 3.5 million Palestinians under occupation" and that "the occupation cannot last indefinitely" (Likud party meeting at the Knesset, May 25, 2003).[1] About five years later, Sharon's successor, Ehud Olmert, said to soldiers serving in the occupied territories of the West Bank:

> We have to understand that a very large population of Palestinians lives here and we need to find the smartest and boldest mechanism so that before it happens [the withdrawal from the territories], we still achieve maximal security. But we shall not create such breaches with them that will darken the continuation of our life for the coming generations ... take for example a 50-year-old man who lives here—a man who has spent most of his life—40 years of it from age 10—under the control of the Israeli soldier. This soldier justifiably holds a gun. But this is the narrative of this man. Take those who were made to undress at the checkpoints because there may have been terrorists among them. Take those who stand for hours at the checkpoints because a vehicle packed with explosives might go through that checkpoint. It could be a boiling pot that can explode and cause terrible burns and could be something else—that depends only on your understanding and your ability to act with wisdom and boldness. (*Haaretz*, 2008, p. 3)

These two quotations indicate the realization of two Israeli Prime Ministers, both of whom are political hawks, of the problems that necessarily occur in interactions between occupier and occupied and their serious repercussions. Both quotations focus on the negative effects of the occupation on the occupied population, but the subtext also indicates that the speakers are aware of the negative effects on the occupying society. This is as far as they went. In this book, we will investigate these latter effects.

This book focuses on protracted occupation, which is viewed as both attention-grabbing and puzzling in the twenty-first century—an era in which long-term occupation has become exceptional and rare. The analysis begins with a viewpoint suggesting that occupation, by its very nature, usually acquires negative connotations because it is usually carried out coercively, against the will of the occupied population (Edelstein, 2008).[2] In the discussion of occupation, therefore, the focus is frequently on the occupied society, because it bears the very heavy tangible and intangible burdens of the occupation. There is a growing literature on this issue (e.g., Bornstein, 2008; Carlton, 1992; Edelstein, 2008; Playfair, 1992). We are also obliged to analyze the relatively neglected effects of the occupation on the occupying society, effects that are not always explicit or easily observed.

There are two major reasons for this neglect. First, those who study occupations tend to focus on those who are regarded as the primary victims of the occupation—the occupied society. The occupied society, which suffers the major physical and mental costs of the occupation, tries to bring attention to itself to obtain material and moral support and end its own suffering. In turn, the international community, which in the postcolonial era has become more sensitive to oppression and the violation of human rights, focuses on those cases in which occupation still persists, attempting to help the occupied and end the subjugation (Arangio-Ruiz, 1979). Second, the occupying society tries to hide and minimize the costs of the occupation and to focus instead on its justification and legitimization (cf. Jost & Major, 2001). In addition, analysis of the costs requires a critical self-examination, which is very painful and seldom done (Bar-Tal, Oren, & Nets-Zehngut, in press). Analysis of the effects on the occupying society is thus rare, even though it can provide important information on the political, sociological, psychological, legal, cultural, and educational processes in that society, all of which are aspects of the prolonged occupation. These processes have an imprinting and lasting effect on the occupying society, even if that society is not aware of them, ignores them, and/or tries to deny and hide them. We thus believe that it is important to shed light on these processes and to relocate them to the center of academic debate and future research, as well as in public discourse.

This book focuses on a particular case of prolonged occupation—that of the West Bank and the Gaza Strip by Israel following the Six Day War in 1967. The causes of this war and its particular context have been well presented in various books, and we shall not rehash them here (e.g., see Lesch, 2008; Morris, 2001; Oren, 2003; Segev, 2007). We shall also ignore the history of the Israeli-Arab conflict in general and the Israeli-Palestinian conflict in particular, because these are presented in detail elsewhere (e.g., see Ben-Yehuda & Sandler,

2002; Caplan, 2009; Dowty, 2005; Morris, 2001; Tessler, 1994; Wasserstein, 2003). Of importance for us is the fact that since 1967 Israel has been occupying Palestinian territories, and the Palestinian population has been living for over four decades under this occupation. In the summer of 2005, Israel withdrew unilaterally from the Gaza Strip and from four settlements on the West Bank; otherwise, it continues to control many aspect of life in Gaza.

As noted above, we will not address the effects of the occupation on Palestinian society because so many publications have been written from this perspective (e.g., Abu-Harthieh, 1993; Aruri, 1989; Gordon, 2008; Khalidi, 1997; Makdisi, 2008). Rather, we will focus on what has been omitted from an interactive analysis of the context of occupation: the effects of the Israeli occupation of the West Bank and the Gaza Strip on the State of Israel and its entire society.

CONCEPTUAL FRAMEWORK: THE OCCUPIER AND THE OCCUPIED

The fundamental assumption guiding this book is that a prolonged occupation as a military-political-societal-economic-cultural system, which includes both the occupied and occupying societies, has interactive features that influence both societies. Memmi (1990), in his seminal book on colonialism, noted that the colonizers, too, are affected by the system of colonialism. We seek to apply and extend this insight to the situation of occupation and suggest that occupiers are greatly influenced by the system of occupation, focusing on the Israeli occupation. This analysis applies to all those cases in which the occupation is prolonged and unacceptable to the occupied society. These are two necessary conditions for the unfolding of the deleterious effects of occupation that will be described.

We believe that an occupation cannot operate separately from the occupying society, which cannot seal itself off from the occupation and its effects. This connection becomes especially pronounced when the occupier not only penetrates the spaces of the occupied territories but also settles in these spaces, which are perceived as a continuation of the homeland territory, as in the Israeli case. Following the occupation by the military forces, the boundaries expand, albeit mainly for the occupiers; a continuous process of interaction between occupiers and occupied begins. Although the occupying force believes that it can control the occupied society and its territory, in reality it begins to lose its grip, and processes gradually evolve in the occupied society that exceed the control of the occupying force. These processes first of all touch upon every aspect of the collective life of the occupied society, including political, economic, cultural, and security aspects. Moreover, these processes also affect the occupying society, because once the occupation begins, a multifaceted and continuous interaction between occupier and occupied occurs, usually starting with resistance to the occupation (see Bar-Tal, in press).

From the beginning, an occupied society is not a passive entity. Instead, it develops forms of action in response to the developing situation, to which the occupying society believes it has the responsibility to react. Some of these forms of action may be explicit; others are not always easily detectable. That is, the occupying force, which is usually not familiar with the culture and customs of the occupied society, finds it difficult to perceive some of these actions and/or attribute the correct meaning to them. In any event, such actions have an effect on the occupying force in the occupied territories and subsequently on the occupying society as a whole. These effects may not appear overnight, but they will gradually penetrate the occupying society and change its nature.

Focusing here on only one example that reflects the cycles of resistance and oppression, we suggest that signs of resistance lead the occupying forces to exert greater control over the occupied society. The occupying society may redirect security forces and resources to the new mission, construct narratives to rationalize the new situation, develop new diplomacy to justify the struggle against resistance, and so on (e.g., see Halperin, Bar-Tal, Sharvit, Rosler, & Raviv, 2010; Jost, Kay, & Thorisdottir, 2009). These moves slowly lead to changes in the occupying society, changes that are not always observable at first; as the resistance gains strength, however, they become salient. The occupier's reactions, in turn, provoke counterreactions by members of the occupied society, with both sides entering into an intensive, ongoing, mutual interaction, including vicious cycles of violence that quickly extend into other domains (see also Bar-Tal, 2011). Such violent exchanges are only one example of the complex mutual interactions between the occupied and the occupiers that become a natural and inherent part of the occupation.

Prolonged occupation requires many different activities by both societies in many different domains, such as providing the services needed for daily life; establishing a legal system; opening schools, clinics, and hospitals; providing religious services; developing a system of surveillance and control; and so on. The occupying society initiates well-planned and unplanned series of acts in various areas, beginning with the military but also the legal, political, economic, and more—and these, in turn, trigger new processes that lead to intended or unintended consequences. Moreover, these effects do not stop at the border but influence the occupying society as well, particularly in the case of Israel, where spatial continuity between the homeland and the occupied territories exists and the occupied territory is settled as part of the homeland.

Under such conditions, boundaries become blurred and interactive processes permeate the two territories, initiating long-term changes in every aspect of the occupying society's life. New goals, interests, needs, trends, and developments appear at all levels of the society. New dogmas arise to justify the continuing occupation; new interest groups emerge; new norms, language, and moral standards develop to support the occupation; economic investments are made; the desire arises to seize resources, exploiting the occupied territories and their populations; a new political culture evolves to maintain the occupation; new security needs and new military strategies are developed; new trade markets appear; and groups emerge that object to the occupation and carry out a political struggle against it, reflecting the evolving sociopolitical polarization, and so on. These processes are well demonstrated in this book.

An analysis of the mutual influences, however, does not depend only on the formal and informal policies and the derivative actions of both societies. The individuals who make up the occupying military and civil forces that are stationed in the occupied territories and enforce the occupation are part of the larger occupying society, and they think and act in a particular way when they are in the occupied territories. They accumulate information, experiences, and political views as well as needs and aspirations. Later, they return to their original milieu with a new behavioral and ideological repertoire that affects their lives. This new repertoire becomes a new motivating force in their thoughts, feelings, and actions. In this respect, the norms, codes of behavior, morals, and practices that develop in the treatment of the occupied population and the occupied territories do not stop at the border. They permeate, even unwittingly, the occupying society and leave their mark on its system of beliefs, values, and patterns of behaviors (Bar-Tal & Halperin, in press).

It is important to remember that the occupied society frequently carries its resistance into the home territory of the occupying forces. It makes every effort to harm the occupying society and strike the most sensitive targets. These acts of violence, including terror, often have a profound effect on the occupying society in many areas of its personal and collective life. Finally, in many cases, members of the occupying society may have contact, either direct or indirect, with members of the occupied society in contexts such as workplaces, personal meetings, and media representations. These contacts eventually affect the occupying society.

These dynamics greatly intensify when the occupying society decides to annex de facto the occupied territories and when it decides to settle in them, bringing new populations that require ideological justification, security and defense, material resources, a legal system, and so on. In these cases, the occupying society tries to differentiate its treatment of the occupied and the occupiers (i.e., the settlers). These decisions greatly accelerate the effects of lasting occupation on the occupying society and eventually produce deep changes that are very difficult to reverse. The occupying society has to adapt to accommodate, contain, deal with, and live with the evolving context of prolonged occupation. But not all the effects are intended; many are unintended and undesirable. Nevertheless, they become part of the dynamic processes of societal change in the occupying society.

Our main contention is that due to the problematic nature of an occupation—especially a prolonged occupation in which members of the occupying society settle in the occupied territories—it generally leads to violence, oppression, exploitation, domination, and discrimination. The costs on the occupying society thus override the benefits. We go even further in suggesting that an occupying society, when it violates the fundamental principles of justice, morality, and human rights, is condemned to deterioration, degeneration, and decline—at least in regard to its democratic, humane, and moral qualities, which leads to a corresponding political degeneration. We believe that the above analysis is general and can be applied to various societies that carry out lasting occupations to which the occupied resist. We elaborate on this issue in the concluding chapter. In the meantime, we focus on Israeli society, which is the subject of our book.

From the beginning of the occupation Israeli society has been greatly affected by the occupation, not only because of its prolonged nature with all of the implications, including ongoing violence, but especially because the State of Israel has carried out an extensive Jewish settlement of the occupied territories. The objective of this book is to delineate the continuing effects of the Israeli occupation on various aspects of life in Israeli society. Before describing these effects, however, we summarize the legal considerations regarding the nature of occupation in general and prolonged occupation in particular. We then describe the implications of the prolonged occupation before considering the nature of the Israeli occupation. This is followed by a brief outline of the physical costs of the occupation to Palestinian society as well to Israeli society. Finally, we discuss the structure of the book and its constituent chapters.

Occupation: The Legal View

Most current definitions of the term "occupation" are found in the field of international law (e.g., Carlton, 1992). We learn from them that occupation is the temporary control of a territory by another state that claims no right to permanent sovereign control over that territory. An occupying power must intend at the onset of the occupation to vacate the occupied territory and return its control to the indigenous population. A precise date for the return need not be specified, but the occupying power's intention must be clear about terminating this situation. This view is well reflected in the definition proposed by the international legal scholar Eyal Benvenisti, who defined occupation as "effective control of a certain power (be it one or several states or an international organization), over a territory which is not under the formal sovereignty of that entity, without the volition of the actual sovereigns of that territory" (Benvenisti, 1993, p. 4). Edelstein (2004) adds that occupation refers to temporary control of a territory by a state that does not claim the right to permanent sovereignty over that territory. This distinguishes occupation from colonialism or annexation, in which the occupant does not necessarily intend to vacate the territory in the future (see Lustick, 1993).

This definition shows that international law considers occupation to be a formal procedure that has implications for the relationship between the occupying force and the occupied population. The main characteristic of occupation, according to these definitions, is its temporary nature. Hence, the occupant is forbidden to take actions that would introduce permanent changes to the occupied territory (see Benvenisti, 1993; Playfair, 1989, 1992; Roberts, 1985, 1990). In addition, legal definitions reveal that occupation is usually seen as a potential (unplanned) by-product of military activities, which result in the conquering party ruling a territory that is recognized as belonging to the defeated party. Such a situation is usually regarded as "belligerent" or "military" occupation (McCarthy, 2005; Rivkin & Bartram, 2003).

However, the history of the last two centuries has demonstrated that occupation can also be the long-term outcome of a threat to use force made by a party, either because of the status quo or a formal agreement, including a peace agreement (e.g., the German occupation of Bosnia in 1939 and of Denmark in 1940). These options have shifted the emphasis from studying occupation as the result of a war-like act to attempting to understand occupation and its mechanisms.

Roberts (1985) distinguishes among 17 types of military occupation that vary in terms of the circumstances in which they occur, the degree of consent of the occupied to the action, the identity of the occupying entity, and the previous status of the occupied territory. The aspect most relevant to the present discussion is the duration of the occupation, which may reflect its essence as well as the goals of the occupant. If the occupation is perceived—by both occupier and occupied—as temporary from the outset, intended to protect the military interests of the occupier and to prevent the occupied territory from becoming a source of instability, then both the occupier and the occupied will likely strive to end it as quickly as possible (Edelstein, 2004).

Roberts (1990) argued that "prolonged occupation" must be regarded as a category that is entirely distinct from temporary military occupation. He defined the former as lasting for more than five years and continuing even when military hostilities have subsided or ceased. In addition, prolonged occupation raises legal questions concerning the aims of the occupier, who may intend to change the status of the occupied territory. This situation usually has very clear implications for both the occupied and the occupying societies.

In any event, it is important to note that since the early twentieth century, the international community has attempted to regulate and control the behavior of occupying powers. The first important convention concerning moral codes in occupied territories was the Hague Convention of 1907, which stated that concerning "[a] territory that has in fact passed into the hands of the occupant, this authority will take all the measures in its power to restore, and ensure, as far as possible, public order and safety, while respecting, unless absolutely prevented, the laws in force in the country" (Article 43, Hague Regulations, 1907). The Hague Regulations also forbid the occupying state from introducing permanent changes into the occupied territory unless these changes emanate from military needs, in the narrow sense, or are intended to benefit the local population. Later, in 1949, the Geneva Conventions were drafted. They have achieved universal acceptance, with amended protocols reinforcing the codification of moral principles regarding occupation. The Fourth Geneva Convention (Article 49) prohibits the occupying state from transferring civilians from its own territory to the occupied territory. Thus, the occupying power should be seen as a trustee of the occupied territory and is responsible for protecting the territory and ensuring the rights of the occupied population (Playfair, 1992).

Another key document setting out the basis for moral principles regarding war and occupation is the Rome Statute of the International Criminal Court, which was adopted by the United Nations Diplomatic Conference in 1998 and to which 104 countries were signatories as of the beginning of 2007. According to the Rome Statute, grave violations of the Geneva Conventions of 1949 are considered to be war crimes, and they can be judged and punished by the International Criminal Court.

Implications of the Occupation

The implications of the occupation are reflected in three different perspectives: those of the occupied society, the international community, and the occupying society (cf. Simon & Klandermans, 2001).

The Occupied Society

From the viewpoint of the occupied society, occupation in most cases is an oppressive experience. Very few societies accept occupation willingly. (We do recognize that there are such cases—sometimes by part of the population, such as Turkish Cypriots, who welcomed Turkey's invasion of the eastern part of Cyprus.) Resistance can be manifested in political action, civil disobedience, and other forms of peaceful protest. In many cases, however, resistance may also involve violent acts, such as attacks against the occupying military forces as well as the occupying civilian population. The occupier naturally attempts to prevent the resistance and punish its initiators. Preventive measures take the form of surveillance, forced collaboration, imposed curfews, and the restriction and prevention of free movement by means of roadblocks and checkpoints, as well as extensive arrests, expulsions, and even killings (Bornstein, 2008). If the preventive measures are also designed to punish the resisting occupied groups, this can lead to other harsh measures, such as imprisonment without trial, torture, deportation of individuals, and/or mass forced transfer, destruction of property, and the use of excessive force against the civilian population, including collective punishments, which can lead to mass killings and even ethnic cleansing.

During prolonged occupations, the occupying power often takes various direct actions that serve its ideological, political-economic, military, and social interests (Gordon, 2008). These may include confiscation of land, settlement by civilians from the occupying state in the occupied territory, use of natural and economic resources of the occupied land, economic exploitation of the occupied population, institutionalized discrimination against the occupied population, and more. In addition, the occupying force may strive to maintain its superiority and domination by exercising continuous control and surveillance over the local population. To accomplish this, the occupier may seek to control the occupied population's political, social, economic, educational, health, and other systems, and their movement and migration. It may also try to prevent their social, economic, and cultural development. These actions cause humiliation to the occupied population both as a collective and as individuals. On the collective level, in addition to the physical harm resulting from the continuous oppression, these acts often greatly damage the societal infrastructure, causing demographic changes, destroying the economic foundations, and damaging the cultural heritage (Aruri, 1983). On the individual level, members of the society living under prolonged occupation, with its vicious circle of coercion, resistance, and violence, not only suffer physically but may also suffer from complex chronic posttraumatic stress disorder, as well as a pessimistic personal and national vision of the future (Lavi & Solomon, 2005).

The International Community

Occupation in general is not acceptable in the normative code of today's world. If it takes place, the occupying state must provide convincing reasons to justify such an extreme and unacceptable act, especially if the state wishes to be part of the democratic international community. The contemporary liberal discourse, with its emphasis on equality and personal and collective civil and human rights (such as the right to self-determination), significantly influences moral positions on occupation (Howe, 2002). Occupation contradicts the principles of self-determination, collective rights, political independence, and territorial integrity that have gained worldwide acceptance as basic moral principles concerning states and other collectives. Occupation violates those moral principles that constitute the basis of universal human rights, such as the dignity of human life, equality, and the right of the individual and the collective to freedom and independence (Rosler, Bar-Tal, Halperin, Sharvit, & Raviv, 2009). All of these principles are firmly anchored in various international declarations, agreements, and conventions. An example can be found in the first Geneva protocol (1977), which applies to situations in which nations fight for their right to self-determination against "colonial domination, foreign occupation and ... racist regimes," all of which are treated as equivalents (see also Roberts, 1985). Occupation also violates internationally protected human rights as listed in the Universal Declaration of Human Rights (UDHR), subsequently developed in the Covenant on Civil and Political Rights and the Covenant on Economic, Social and Cultural Rights. Thus, it is not surprising that both the international community and public opinion have condemned prolonged occupation. Occupation in itself, and especially prolonged occupation, is criticized in international forums, and the occupying states and societies are condemned (see Roberts, 1990). Moreover, in many societies in which notions of human and collective rights are of concern, public opinion and the mass media express their opposition to occupying states and societies. Finally, the occupying states and societies are under close watch and subjected to criticism by various nongovernmental organizations (NGOs) concerned about human rights, by intellectual and cultural elites with progressive and liberal views, and by the public in many states in general.

The Occupying Society

We suggest that over the last few decades, when at least the well-established democracies have been guided by the liberal values and norms that have developed since the end of World War II, occupation in general and prolonged occupation in particular have become almost totally unacceptable. Occupation has thus acquired a deeply negative meaning, and every occupying society must necessarily confront this (Halperin et al., 2010). The need to view one's own group positively, including its perception as moral, is based on the well-established finding that members of a society draw their personal self-esteem from the esteem of the groups to which they belong (Tajfel, 1978, 1981). All this adds to the social, cultural, political, and (sometimes) financial cost that prolonged occupation inflicts on the occupying society. We also need to add the cost of the human loss and destruction that usually accompany an occupation, in part because of the violent resistance of the occupied population.

It is clear that in the current international climate, in order for an occupation to persist, the occupying society must be driven by deep and significant motives to attempt it and even more seriously to maintain it. The longer the occupation continues, the more it confronts occupants with difficulties relating to their own morality and legitimacy in their relationship both with the occupied population and with the international community. Members of such a society must thus construct a convincing rationale for the act of occupation or else deny its existence (Bar-Tal, Oren, & Nets-Zehngut, in press).

Many different rationales are given for occupation (Bar-Tal, in press). Sometimes the occupiers believe that the occupation serves an important superordinate (sometimes international) goal, and that occupation is necessary to prevent a higher-level disaster or to achieve another highly valued goal (e.g., the occupation of Iraq by the United States). In other cases, the occupiers believe that the occupation is necessary to achieve existential goals, without which they believe their society cannot survive (e.g., the occupation of Manchuria by Japan). Sometimes the occupiers believe that it is necessary to punish the occupied nation for its wrongdoing (e.g., the occupation of Afghanistan by the United States). In yet other situations, occupying societies may refuse to accept their action as an occupation and define it instead as a "liberation" (e.g., the occupation of certain regions of Georgia by the Russians, the occupation of Kuwait by Iraq, or the occupation of Tibet by China). In all cases the occupants try to provide, even if only superficially, a normal life to the occupied society, and in most cases the occupying society forces openly declare the occupation to be temporary. In very few cases of prolonged occupation, the occupying states make an effort to create fully normal conditions that do not resemble an occupation; even in Tibet the Tibetans officially enjoy the same civil rights as the Chinese population.

We turn now to a discussion of one of the few prolonged cases of occupation today: the Israeli occupation of the Palestinian territory.

THE ISRAELI OCCUPATION

While many countries were moving to end colonialism and occupation, Israel paradoxically moved in the opposite direction. Most analysts of Israeli policy following the 1967 war, when the territories of the West Bank, the Gaza Strip, and the Golan Heights were seized, believe that the prolonged occupation, rather than being the result of a well-considered decision-making process, is the product of an inability to decide or a "decision not to decide" (Gazit, 1999). An alternative view, described by Pedatzur (1996) and others, maintains that the prolonged occupation is an accurate reflection of Israel's aims and interests (Segev, 2007; Zertal & Eldar, 2007).

A meeting between Chief of Staff Yitzhak Rabin and Minister of Defense Moshe Dayan that took place about six weeks after the end of the 1967 war is highly illuminating (see Segev, 2007). The original protocol referred to one of the topics on the agenda of the meeting as "occurrences in the occupied territories." A few days later, an "invisible hand" amended the protocol in writing and replaced the term "occupied territories" with the term "liberated territories"—which had acquired more favorable sociopolitical connotations even at this early stage. Already in the historical decision by the Israeli government on June 19, 1967, in which it was decided by one vote to exchange the Golan Heights and Sinai for peace and, if possible, to unite Jerusalem and incorporate the Gaza Strip into Israel, the ministers could not reach an agreement with regard to the West Bank. Many of them hoped to create an autonomous Palestinian entity adjoining the State of Israel (Oren, 2003). There are also several accounts of how the Israeli political and military leadership decided that the new lines of defense that were established with the conquest of the territories during the 1967 war would become defensive borders (see the chapters by Pedatzur and Magal et al., this volume).

Finally, there are profound discrepancies between Israel's formal legal position and the stance in forums of international law (Benvenisti, 1993; Roberts, 1985). Since June 1967 the Israeli government has in general maintained in all international forums that the territories do not constitute occupied territories and, therefore, that the Fourth Geneva Convention is not applicable to this case. This argument has been based on the supposition that the territories had never been under either Jordanian (in the West Bank) or Egyptian (in Gaza) sovereignty. Thus, the Israel Defense Forces (IDF) cannot be seen as an occupier that has usurped the territories from their legal owners (Playfair, 1989; Roberts, 1985). Israel has preferred to regard the territories as being "under dispute," which, it was believed, provided room to maneuver in future negotiations. This position has been rejected by many scholars as well as by many states and international organizations. In reality the territories were not annexed; therefore, legally, the Palestinians in the West Bank are not citizens of Israel and they are not allowed to exercise the rights that a sovereign representative government should provide (see the chapter by Kretzmer, this volume).

Nonetheless, some ambivalence has slipped into Israeli policy making, because in practice it has complied with some of the laws pertaining to an occupying force (Roberts, 1990). Shortly after the end of the 1967 war, then Attorney General Meir Shamgar decided that the Israeli military administration of the territories would obey the rule of international law, "of its own good will," in any case that concerned the treatment of Palestinians in the territories and would even agree to be subjected to the scrutiny of the Supreme Court of Israel. In September 1967, the legal counsel to the Israeli Foreign Ministry, Justice Theodor Meron, issued a legal opinion (classified as top secret) that Jewish settlement in the occupied territories would constitute a violation of the Fourth Geneva Convention (Gorenberg, 2006). However, as the years went by and the influence of this legal viewpoint on Israel's conduct in the territories weakened, many previously self-imposed restrictions were ignored, Jewish settlements prospered, and violations of Palestinian human rights increased dramatically (Ben-Naftali, Gross, & Michaeli, 2006; Gordon, 2008).

Over time, the Israeli leaders, the political elites, and Israeli society in general have developed a national ideology that provides well-based arguments for remaining in the occupied territories. The foundations of this ideology, which lie in Zionism and Judaism, served well the initial return of Jews to their homeland and eventually the establishment of the State of Israel. The 1967 war, with the occupation of new territories and with its unintended results, led to a reconstruction of the ideology, which aimed at presenting a new view of the emergent situation. Basically, this ideology reformulated the "ethos of conflict" that had dominated Jewish society prior to the 1967 war (see Bar-Tal, 2007). In principle, it provided a system of organized societal beliefs to justify continuing to hold the occupied territories for various reasons—including religious, historical, national, and security-based reasons. Moreover, these beliefs served as the epistemic basis for the extensive Jewish settlement in the occupied territories. In general, they provide ideological justification for continuing the occupation and its accompanying actions, as well as facilitating the construction of a positive collective self-image of the occupying group and the delegitimization of the occupied nation (Halperin et al., 2010; Jost & Major, 2001; Levy, 2006; Kelman, 2001).

In contrast to the dominant view in Israel, it is our contention that both societies are paying a heavy cost for the prolonged occupation. These costs are incomparable, however, because the costs to the occupied society are not only higher, but are also of a different, harsher quality. Because this book focuses on the costs to the occupying society, we shall just briefly mention some of the tangible costs to Palestinian society of the continuing occupation up to 2010.

These costs are directly related to the serious violations of Palestinians' human rights. We leave out of this description an analysis of the societal, political, economic, cultural, and environmental costs, for these are presented in depth elsewhere (Abu-Harthieh, 1993; Aruri, 1989; Gordon, 2008; Khalidi, 1997; Makdisi, 2008; Ophir, Givoni, & Hanafi, 2009).

Costs of the Occupation to Palestinian Society[3]

In order to evaluate the extent of the damage done to the Palestinian people, we should note that in 1967, after the war, there were about 600,000 Palestinians residing in the West Bank and about 355,000 in the Gaza Strip (http://israeli-palestinian.procon.org/view.resource.php?resourceID=000636#chart5). As of 2010, according to the *World Factbook of the CIA,* there are 2,514,845 Palestinians residing in the West Bank and an additional 209,000 in East Jerusalem in an area of 5,860 km². There are currently about 1,600,200 Palestinians in the Gaza Strip in an area of 360 km² (https://www.cia.gov/library/publications/the-world-factbook/geos/gz.html). In addition, in 2010 there were about 313,000 Jewish Israeli settlers in the West Bank and more than 197,000 living in East Jerusalem, annexed by Israel (http://www.cbs.gov.il).

We were unable to obtain any systematic and reliable information concerning the effects of the Israeli occupation on Palestinian society since June 1967. Rather, there are various reports that provide a partial description of the various costs, and we refer to some of them.[4]

The first twenty years after the Six Day War constituted a relatively quiet period in the occupied territories, with economic progress and some broadening of individual liberties as compared with the era of Jordanian rule that had preceded it. This period was even viewed by liberal Israeli Jews as a "benign occupation." Israel invested in developing a more sophisticated form of agriculture, and several colleges were opened. Close to 100,000 registered Palestinian workers and 70,000 unregistered workers commuted to Israel as manual workers, and their standards of living rose. Moreover, as a result of the development during the 1970s and the open border policy, a negative migration balance was replaced by a positive one, and the Palestinian population began to grow rapidly. Finally, with the occupation, the three Palestinian communities in the West Bank, the Gaza Strip, and Israel were reconnected after nineteen years of separation. The ensuing communication among them contributed to the crystallization of a Palestinian national identity (see Gazit, 2003; Portugali, 1996).

This picture dramatically changed in the late 1970s, however, when the Israeli governments began to alter their policies regarding the occupied territories. For example, an extensive and heavily subsidized Jewish settlement was initiated there, with the aim of disrupting Palestinian territorial continuity in order to implement the ideology of a "Greater Israel" (Gorenberg, 2006; Zertal & Eldar, 2007). Parallel to this development, during the 1980s the occupied Palestinians moved from an attitude of *summud* (steadfastness) to one of *intifada* (eliminate occupation) or rebellion, leading to massive attempts by Israel to contain it through various means of control, oppression, and collective punishment. In the following discussion of the effects of the occupation on the occupied Palestinian society, we begin with a description of the Jewish settlement.

Jewish Settlement

The United Nations report notes that Israel built, and continues to expand, Jewish settlements in the occupied territories in violation of the Fourth Geneva Convention (Dugard, 2006). According to B'tselem, Israel has expropriated 50% of all West Bank territories, mostly by declaring and registering these lands as state lands (B'Tselem, *Taking control of the land in the West Bank*, 2010) and building Jewish settlements on them (B'Tselem, 1997a). Moreover, according to a report by the Israeli Civil Administration, over one-third of all West Bank settlements have for decades been constructed on private Palestinian lands expropriated for "security needs" via temporary military injunctions (Rapoport, 2008). By March 2010, there were over 120 settlements in the territories (excluding East Jerusalem) and about 100 outposts,[5] officially unrecognized by the authorities, containing 283 permanent homes and 1,865 caravans (Arieli, 2010).

Land Expropriation

According to B'Tselem, the procedure by which the State of Israel declares lands to be state lands circumvents the land registration process that is anchored in Jordanian law and international law. Two-thirds of all West Bank lands have thus not been appropriately registered, and their ownership derives from long-term possession (B'Tselem, 1997a). East Jerusalem is just one area in which this procedure has been utilized. Following the 1967 war, Israel annexed to the municipality over 70 km^2 of land bordering on West Jerusalem, which was part of the State of Israel. About 24 km^2 of the annexed area, most of which is privately owned by Arabs, was later expropriated by the state. By the end of 2001, 46,978 housing units had been constructed on the lands expropriated in East Jerusalem for the city's Jewish population, while not a single one had been built for Palestinians, who constitute about 33% of the city's residents (B'Tselem, *Revocation of residency in East Jerusalem*, 2010).

Casualties

At present, there are no sources of reliable and comprehensive data on the total number of Palestinians killed throughout the period of occupation. It is especially difficult to obtain information regarding the first two decades of the occupation. Nonetheless, various organizations do provide partial data on the later periods.

According to data compiled by the B'Tselem, between 1989 and 2009 Israeli security forces killed 7,398 Palestinians in Israel and the occupied territories, including at least 1,537 minors[6] (Yahav, 2009). Various collections of data relate to the decisive moments in the occupation, such as the first and second *intifadas* (the two Palestinian uprisings). Thus, for example, from December 1987, when the first *intifada* started, to the end of December 1993, 997 Palestinians were killed by the Israeli army (IDF) and 16,839 were injured by the IDF[7] (B'Tselem, 1994). Subsequently, according to information provided by Amnesty International, between 2000 and 2005, during and following the second *intifada*, over 3,200 Palestinians were killed by the Israeli forces, including 600 children and over 150 women (Amnesty International, 2005). To these statistics we must add the number of Palestinians who were injured, which probably involves many thousands, but we were unable to find reliable data.

Imprisonment

An estimated 700,000 Palestinians were imprisoned in Israel between 1967 and 2007 (Dugard, 2008), and many thousands of others were tried by the Israeli military courts. Between 1990 and 2006, for example, over 150,000 Palestinians were tried in the military courts (Yesh Din, 2007). At the end of February 2010, 6,759 Palestinians were being held by the Israeli security forces, including 297 minors (B'Tselem, *Detainees and prisoners*, 2010).

Some of the detainees are held by means of administrative detention, which is carried out by an administrative order alone, with no judicial ruling, indictment, or trial. A person detained in this way does not know why he or she has been detained or on what charges. Nor is the individual given an opportunity to question witnesses or challenge the truth of the accusations in any way. Between December 1987 and December 1997, over 18,000 administrative detention orders were issued against residents of the occupied territories (B'Tselem, 1998). According to the Israel Prison Service, of 548 administrative detainees held by the army in January 2009, 42 had been held for over two consecutive years and 23 for over two and a half years (B'Tselem, 2008).

Various interrogation and torture methods are used against some of the detainees. According to Physicians for Human Rights, 1,000–1,500 Palestinians are interrogated by the Shin Bet (security service) annually, and 85% of them are subjected to methods that fall under the definition of torture (Physicians for Human Rights, 2000). According to B'Tselem (1996), approximately 23,000 Palestinians were interrogated by the Shin Bet between 1987 and 1994. The 1987 Landau Commission, which was headed by Supreme Court Justice Moshe Landau, was appointed to examine the interrogation methods of the General Security Service (GSS). It exposed a widespread practice of torture and coverup. The commission outlawed torture but also noted that "the exertion of a moderate degree of physical pressure cannot be avoided." Nevertheless, a 1994 State Comptroller's Report (released in summary form in February 2000) found that the GSS interrogation methods continued to violate the law, the Landau Commission guidelines, and the internal guidelines formulated by the service itself.

House Demolitions

The demolition of Palestinian houses is carried out for various reasons: as a form of punishment, in response to the failure to obtain a building permit, due to military needs, to make way for the separation barrier, and to facilitate the detention of wanted individuals (Dugard, 2006). House demolitions may be carried out completely, partially, or by sealing off the property. According to the Israel Committee Against House Demolitions (ICAHD), Israel demolished over 24,100 Palestinian houses between 1967 and April 7, 2009, leaving 70,000 Palestinians homeless (ICAHD, *Campaign against house demolitions*, 2010).

Movement Restrictions

Upon occupying the territories in 1967, Israel declared the West Bank and Gaza Strip to be restricted territories, with all movement into or out of them requiring permits. Roadblocks and curfews are special means of restricting the movement of Palestinians in the occupied territories. Some of the roadblocks are permanent; others are movable. As of late August 2009, the IDF regularly maintained 60 West Bank roadblocks; 28 of these were continuously manned, some 24 hours a day and others only during daylight or other hours. Thirty-nine additional roadblocks—all permanent and continuously manned—constitute the entrance checkpoints between the West Bank and the State of Israel. Additionally, the IDF operates movable roadblocks and physical obstructions such as earth mounds (B'Tselem website, Movement Restrictions). According to reports by the United Nations Office for the Coordination of Humanitarian Affairs in the Occupied Palestinian Territory (OCHA), in April 2010 there were 504 movement obstacles (65 checkpoints, 22 partial checkpoints, 107 road gates, 68 roadblocks, 168 earth mounds, 10 trenches, 44 road barriers, and 20 earthen walls). Two years earlier, there were 607 movement obstacles.

Deportations, Revocations of Residency, and Family Reunifications

According to data compiled by B'Tselem (1993), over 1,000 Palestinians were deported from the territories between 1967 and 1987. From December 1987 to the end of 1992, 481 Palestinian residents of the territories were deported as a form of punishment (B'Tselem, 1998). Of special interest is the revocation of residency and family separation in East Jerusalem after its annexation. Following a census taken by Israel, 66,000 Palestinians who were found in their residences during the census lost their right to obtain Israeli identity cards. Their family members had to request family reunification and Israeli identity cards on their behalf (B'Tselem, 1997b). Between 1984 and 1993 only a few hundred of these permits were issued (B'Tselem, 1999b).

This review of the costs does not take into account the humiliation, cruel treatment, psychological violence, and trauma, which exist on a very large scale and are a continuous part of daily life for much of the occupied Palestinian population (see Hobfoll, Hall, & Canneti, 2012 Punamaki, Komproe, Qouta, Elmasri, & de Jong, 2005). In the context of the occupation, some Palestinians have continuously carried out violent acts of various types, including terrorist attacks that have led to severe losses for the Israeli-Jewish population. In order to see the full picture of the relationship between the occupied and the occupiers, we next provide information on the costs to Israeli-Jewish society.

The Costs to Israeli-Jewish Society

Just as there is a paucity of data regarding harm to the Palestinians, there are no reliable data on the harm caused to Israelis as a result of Palestinian terrorism throughout the years of occupation. The Israel Intelligence Heritage & Commemoration Center (IICC) states that no reliable, comprehensive database exists on the victims of suicide attacks (IICC, 2006). Nonetheless, some data are available for different periods.

According to the Ministry of Foreign Affairs, 987 people were killed in Israel in Palestinian terrorist attacks between 1967 and 1999 (Israel Ministry of Foreign Affairs, 2010)., More specifically, between 1990 and 1999, 344 people were killed in such attacks (Shin Bet Security Service, 2010). According to B'Tselem, between 1989 and 2009 Palestinians killed 1,483 Israelis, including 139 minors; 488 of those killed were security personnel and 995 were civilians (Yahav, 2009). Data provided by B'Tselem, the Yesha Settlements Council, the Shuvi organization, the Organization of Families Victims, the IDF, and *Haaretz* reveal that 230 Israelis were killed in the Gaza Strip between 1967 and 2005 (Regular & Gottlieb, 2005).

Reports by the Shin Bet and the IICC provide detailed information on Palestinian terrorism in the twenty-first century. According to Shin Bet data, between September 29, 2000, and December 31, 2009, 1,178 people were killed as a result of Palestinian terrorism, including 790 Israeli civilians, 328 security personnel, and 60 foreign nationals. In total, 146 suicide attacks took place in this period (Shin Bet [Security Service], 2010). According to IICC data, 24,247 attacks were carried out between September 28, 2000, and February 8, 2005; 0.54% of these were suicide attacks that were responsible for 49% of all Israeli fatalities (502 killed). Also in this period, 3,528 long-range fire incidents took place, comprising 3,096 mortar attacks and 432 rocket attacks (IICC, 2005).

One of the most common attack methods in the region in the last decade has been rocket fire from the Gaza Strip. This began in 2001 and has gradually become one of the central threats posed by Palestinians. In total, 2,383 rockets and 2,543 mortars landed in the western Negev between 2001 and 2007 (as of the end of November 2007), with the town of Sderot, a prime target, absorbing 45% of all rockets landing in residential areas. As a result of this rocket fire, 10 civilians were killed and 10 others (including 8 civilians) died as a result of mortar shelling. These experiences and previous ones clearly have caused severe psychological damage, expressed as posttraumatic stress disorder and other effects (e.g., see Bleich, Gelkopf, & Solomon, 2003; IICC, 2007).

THE BOOK

This book elaborates on the effects that an occupation has on the occupying society in different spheres of public life. It begins with a description of the nature of occupation as perceived from different angles.

The first chapter, by David Kretzmer, describes the way laws have been used and, in effect, misused as a system of control, discrimination, and exploitation of the occupied territories and their Palestinian residents. Thus, in establishing settlements and exploiting the resources in the occupied territories for the good of Israel and Israeli Jews, formal legal norms have been ignored. However, in justifying restrictions on the rights and liberties of the Palestinian residents, the formal norms of belligerent occupation have been cited time and again. Kretzmer calls this situation "legal hypocrisy," because the territories themselves are not regarded by Israel as occupied; their *Palestinian* residents are, however, subjected to the laws of occupation.

The chapter by Marcelo Dascal examines the nature of the relationship between morality and occupation. It considers the possibility that the relationship is bidirectional. Dascal presents an open-ended, innovative, eclectic, and multidisciplinary approach that could pave the way for progress in resolving a conflict that has been described as "an ostensibly intractable ethno-national conflict." (Rouhana & Bar-Tal, 1998, p. 761).

The next chapter, by Izhak Schnell, explores how the State of Israel has related with duplicity to the occupied territories. On the one hand, it has preserved their legal status as occupied territories; on the other hand, it has used a wide variety of practices designed to include the territories within an area that is identified with the Jewish nation. In effect, the state and the settlers developed many practices that were intended to annex the land to the national territory. These included rebuilding the territories through their Judaization and reconstructing the territories' awareness of the nation in a way that incorporates them into the Israeli homeland, all in contradiction to the recognized status of the territories as occupied.

The chapter by Tamir Magal, Neta Oren, Daniel Bar-Tal, and Eran Halperin explains how the psychological legitimization of the occupation emerged. They do this by describing the various ideological orientations regarding the status of the occupied territories and the perceptions of the Palestinian nation that have prevailed among Israeli Jews from 1967 to the present. It focuses on the platforms of the political parties, the beliefs of the leaders, and public opinion (cf. Kelman, 2001). Views of the territories as being liberated because they are part of the Jewish homeland and belong exclusively to Jews, and claims that these territories are of supreme importance for securing the future existence of the State of Israel, have shaped the determination of borders, the removal of settlements, and the division of Jerusalem, as well as the establishment of a Palestinian state. This ideology was a marginal one before the 1967 war, but with the conquest of the West Bank and the Gaza Strip, it has become a dominant view among many Jewish-Israeli leaders and citizens.

The remaining chapters elucidate the various effects that the occupation has had on the State of Israel and its society. The chapter by Yaron Ezrahi discusses the political effects of the occupation, describing its imprinting on the structure and political culture of the Israeli regime, which endangers the state's democratic character in the future. The chapter describes the destructive impact of the occupation on the Israeli political system, educational system, legal structure, and military, as well as on social perceptions of legitimate internal and external uses of force, norms and practices of the bureaucracy, the status of Israeli Arabs, the relationship between religion and politics, and the international legitimacy of Israel as a democracy.

The chapter by Reuven Pedatzur focuses on the effects that the occupation has had on the Israeli army. He argues that the army has naturally played a major role in the management of the occupied territories but that in fulfilling this role, it has been responsible for encouraging, initiating, realizing, and supporting Jewish settlement in the West Bank and the Gaza Strip. This has produced illegal acts, the legitimization of illegal acts, the political involvement of the army, and the disregarding of violations of Palestinians' human rights. It has also weakened the military's ability to fight a conventional war, insofar as it has preoccupied itself with managing the resistance of the Palestinians and combatting terrorism.

The chapter by Gideon Doron and Maoz Rosenthal concerns the policy of settling Jewish populations in the occupied territories. The authors believe that this policy was derived from the ability of radical right-wing parties to maneuver between the needs of their constituencies and strong ideological commitments.

The chapter by Muhammad Amara and Mohanad Mustafa describes the impact of the Israeli occupation on the Palestinian-Arab citizens of Israel. It focuses on political discourse in the organization of the Palestinians and Arabs in Israel, and their relationship to the state, and how these have changed since the occupation. The main thesis of the chapter is that since the 1970s, a collective attitude has crystallized in which civil equality is sought alongside a solution to the national question.

The next part of the book addresses societal effects of the occupation. The chapter by Dan Caspi and Danny Rubinstein describes the ways in which the mass media have handled the occupation. It suggests that Israel has concentrated on building an "Information Wall" that separates Arab and Israeli societies, blocking information on what is happening in Palestinian society—and thus perpetuating mutually held stereotypes.

The chapter by Shir Hever describes the economic costs of the occupation to Israeli society. It concludes that funding the occupation has been the most expensive project undertaken by Israel since 1967. The financial outlay to maintain security forces in the occupied territories and to carry out the activities entailed by the occupation, together with the building and defense of Jewish settlements, is taking an ever-increasing toll on the State of Israel in a way that may undermine economic growth in the near future.

Hanna Herzog's chapter suggests that the prolonged conflict and the occupation have become a social mechanism that institutionalizes a narrow understanding of the concept of human security, excluding issues of personal and economic security. In particular, it replicates the gendered division of social roles and has contributed to a gendered hierarchy as well as discrimination and even violence against women.

The chapter by Charles Greenbaum and Yoel Elizur examines the effects of the occupation on moral thinking, mental health, and violence in Israeli society. It suggests that the occupation has exposed Israelis of all ages to trauma, leading to a variety of stress-related reactions, including increasingly violent behavior both within Israeli society and by Israeli soldiers and settlers in the occupied territories toward Palestinians.

The final part of the book explores the cultural effects of the occupation. The chapter by Edy Kaufman analyzes the impact of the occupation on the violation of human rights within Israel. It shows how the political culture that has developed ignores issues of human rights, with severe consequences for Israeli society.

The chapter by Dan Urian reveals how Israeli theater artists since the early 1980s have introduced into their works the problem of "divided reality" and the need for a critical examination of the Zionist ideology that created the State of Israel and subsequently enabled the policy of occupation.

The chapter by Nadir Tsur examines the link between prolonged occupation and the language of public discourse that has evolved in the State of Israel. It demonstrates the close relationship between the two and identifies how the use of language has been transformed from that of religious belief to a discourse of national rights, including discourse about security, including the language of conciliation and peace as well as separation and disengagement.

In the Conclusion, Izhak Schnell and Daniel Bar-Tal integrate the collective insights derived from the individual chapters of the book. Three major themes emerge: (1) the development of an Israeli national identification and its relationship to the emerging regime; (2) the life domains in which the occupation has brought about transformative, largely deleterious effects on the occupying society; and (3) the psychological and ideological mechanisms that have facilitated "ethnicization" in the occupied territories. Each of these themes is deeply deserving of political psychological analysis (e.g., Sears, Huddy, & Jervis, 2003; see also Jost & Sidanius, 2004)—not only in the context of Israel, but around the world.

NOTES

1. Also of interest is a report by the Attorney General of Israel, Elyakim Rubinstein, who protested to the Prime Minister against use of the word "occupation" and argued that the official position of every Israeli government since 1967 has been that the territories are "under dispute" and not "occupied" (Zertal & Eldar, 2007).
2. We recognize that occupation, according to its legal definition, can be willingly accepted in some cases by the occupied population (or part of it) when it is

viewed as congruent with other aspirations, goals, and needs. One example is the acceptance of Turkish occupation of northern Cyprus by Turkish Cypriots.
3. The information on costs to the Palestinians and Israelis was compiled with the assistance of Hadar Biran.
4. We are aware that the Israeli government, IDF, part of the media and various NGOs attempt to delegitimize sources that monitor the Israeli violations of human rights in the occupied territories. We have thus tried to use only those sources that we believe to be reliable.
5. An **outpost** ("a stronghold") refers to a community built within the West Bank (excluding Jerusalem) that was constructed without the authorization of the Israeli government but very often with its help. Some of these are illegal because they are built on privately owned Palestinian land.
6. Additional detailed information indicates that from December 1987 to the end of February 1999, the Israeli security forces killed 1,472 Palestinians in the territories, 1,341 of whom were civilians and 18 of whom were members of the Palestinian security forces. 113 Palestinians were killed by Israeli civilians, mostly Jewish settlers. Of those killed, 302 were children under the age of 17 (B'Tselem 1999).
7. Between the end of September 2000 and the end of December 2008, the Israeli security forces killed 4,792 Palestinians in the West Bank and Gaza Strip, 952 of whom were under the age of 18. At least 2,222 of those killed were not engaged in armed struggle at the time, and 233 were targets of assassination (B'Tselem website, fatalities).

REFERENCES

Abu-Harthieh, M. (1993). *The right to the development under occupation: The case of Palestine*. Unpublished doctoral dissertation, University of Essex, Great Britain.

Amnesty International. (2005). *Israel: Conflict, occupation and patriarchy—Women carry the burden*. London: Amnesty. Retrieved March 31, 2010, from http://www.amnesty.org/en/library/info/MDE15/016/2005

Arangio-Ruiz, G. (1979). *The UN declaration on friendly relations and the system of the sources of international law*. Alphen aan den Rijn, The Netherlands: Sijthoff & Noordhoff.

Arieli, S. (2010). *All the data on all the settlements*. Retrieved March 29, 2010, from http://www.shaularieli.com/77951/%D7%94%D7%AA%D7%A0%D7%97%D7%9C%D7%95%D7%99%D7%95%D7%AA (in Hebrew)

Aruri, N. A. (Ed.). (1983). *Occupation, Israel over Palestine*. Belmont, MA: Association of Arab-American University Graduates.

Aruri, N. A. (Ed.). (1989). *Occupation: Israel over Palestine* (2nd ed.). Belmont, MA: Association of Arab-American University Graduates.

Bar-Tal, D. (2007). *Living with the conflict: Socio-psychological analysis of the Israeli-Jewish society*. Jerusalem: Carmel (in Hebrew).

Bar-Tal, D. (Ed.). (2011). *Intergroup conflicts and their resolution: Social psychological perspective.* New York: Psychology Press.

Bar-Tal, D. (in press). *Intractable conflicts: Socio-psychological foundations and dynamics.* Cambridge: Cambridge University Press.

Bar-Tal, D., & Halperin, E. (in press). The psychology of intractable conflicts: Eruption, escalation and peacemaking. In L. Huddy, D. Sears, & J. Levy (Eds.), *Oxford handbook of political psychology* (2nd ed.). New York: Oxford University Press.

Bar-Tal, D., Oren, N., & Nets-Zehngut, R. (in press). Socio-psychological analysis of conflict-supporting narratives. *American Psychologist.*

Ben-Naftali, O., Gross, A. M., & Michaeli, K. (2006). Illegal occupation: Framing the occupied territory. *Berkeley Journal of International Law, 23,* 551–613.

Benvenisti, E. (1993). *The international law of occupation.* Princeton, NJ: Princeton University Press.

Ben-Yehuda, H., & Sandler, S. (2002). *The Arab-Israeli conflict transformed: Fifty years of interstate and ethnic crisis.* Albany: State University of New York Press.

Bleich, A., Gelkopf, M., & Solomon, Z. (2003). Exposure to terrorism, stress-related mental health symptoms, and coping behaviors among a nationally representative sample in Israel. *JAMA: Journal of the American Medical Association, 290,* 612–620.

Bornstein, A. (2008). Military occupation as carceral society: Prisons, checkpoints, and walls in the Israeli-Palestinian struggle. *Social Analysis, 52,* 106–130.

B'Tselem website. *Movement restrictions.* http://www.btselem.org/

B'Tselem. (1993). *Deportation of Palestinians from the occupied territories: The mass deportation of December 1992.* Jerusalem: B'Tselem.

B'Tselem. (1994). *Bi-annual report 1992/1993: Violations of human rights in the occupied territories.* Jerusalem: B'Tselem.

B'Tselem. (1996). *Legitimizing torture: The High Court's rulings on Bilbisi, Hamdan and Mubarak—sources and comments.* Jerusalem: B'Tselem (in Hebrew).

B'Tselem. (1997a). *Israeli settlement in the occupied territories as a violation of human rights: Legal and conceptual aspects.* Jerusalem: B'Tselem.

B'Tselem. (1997b). *The silent transfer: Revocations of residency from Palestinians in east Jerusalem.* Jerusalem: B'Tselem.

B'Tselem. (1998). *1987–1997: A decade of human rights violations.* Information Sheet, January 1998. Jerusalem: B'Tselem.

B'Tselem. (1999a). *Quarterly for human rights in the occupied territories, second issue.* Jerusalem: B'Tselem.

B'Tselem. (1999b). *Family reunifications—separation of Palestinian families in the territories.* Jerusalem: B'Tselem.

B'Tselem. (2008). *2008 annual report: Human rights in the occupied territories.* Jerusalem: B'Tselem.

B'Tselem. *Detainees and prisoners.* Retrieved March 31, 2010, from http://www.btselem.org/english/statistics/detainees_and_prisoners.asp

B'Tselem. *Fatalities*. Retrieved March 31, 2010, from http://www.btselem.org/english/statistics/casualties.asp

B'Tselem. *Restrictions on movement*. Retrieved March 31, 2010, from http://www.btselem.org/english/freedom_of_movement/statistics.asp

B'Tselem. *Revocation of residency in East Jerusalem*. Retrieved March 31, 2010, from http://www.btselem.org/english/jerusalem/revocation_statistics.asp

B'Tselem. *Taking control of the land in the West Bank*. Retrieved March 31, 2010, from http://www.btselem.org/english/settlements/taking_control.asp

Caplan, N. (2009). *The Israeli-Palestine conflict: Contested history*. Malden, MA: Wiley-Blackwell.

Carlton, E. (1992). *Occupation: The policies and practices of military conquerors*. London: Routledge.

Dowty, A. (2005). *Israel/Palestine*. Cambridge: Polity Press.

Dugard, J. (2006). *Report of the special rapporteur on the situation of human rights in the Palestinian Territories occupied since 1967*. Retrieved March 31, 2010, from http://documents-dds-ny.un.org/doc/UNDOC/GEN/G06/138/12/pdf/G0613812.pdf?OpenElement

Dugard, J. (2008). *Human rights situation in Palestine and other occupied Arab territories*. Retrieved March 31, 2010, from http://www.unhcr.org/cgi-bin/texis/vtx/refworld/rwmain?docid=47baaa262

Edelstein, D. M., (2004). Occupational hazards: Why military occupations succeed or fail. *International Security, 29*, 49–91.

Edelstein, D. M. (2008). *Occupational hazards: Success and failure in military occupation*. Ithaca, NY: Cornell University Press.

Gazit, S. (1999). *Trapped fools*. Tel-Aviv: Zmora-Bitan (in Hebrew).

Gazit, S. (2003). *Trapped fools: Thirty years of Israeli policy in the Territories*. London: Frank Cass.

Gordon, N. (2008). *Israel's occupation*. Berkeley, CA: University of California Press.

Gorenberg, G. (2006). *The accidental empire: Israel and the birth of the settlements: 1967–1977*. New York: Times Books.

Haaretz. (2008, April 11).

Halperin, E., Bar-Tal, D., Sharvit, K., Rosler, N., & Raviv, A. (2010). Social psychological implications for an occupying society: The case of Israel. *Journal of Peace Research, 47*, 59–70.

Hobfoll, S. E., Hall, B. J., & Canneti, D. (2012). Political violence, psychological distress, and perceived health: A longitudinal investigation in the Palestinian authority. *Psychological Trauma: Theory, Research, Practice, and Policy, 4*, 9–21.

Howe, S. (2002). *Empire: A very short introduction*. Oxford: Oxford University Press.

ICAHD (Israeli Committee Against House Demolitions). (2010). *Campaign against house demolitions*. Retrieved May 6, 2010, from http://icahd.org/eng/campaigns.asp?menu=4&submenu=2

IICC (Israel Intelligence Heritage & Commemoration Center). (2005, February 8). *Summary of data on Palestinian terrorism during the present confrontation with Israel up to the Sharm al-Sheikh summit, September 28, 2000–February 8, 2005*. Retrieved May 15, 2010, from http://www.terrorisminfo.org.il/hebsite/html/search.asp?sid=9&pid=97&numResults=4&isSearch=yes&isT8=no

IICC (Israel Intelligence Heritage and Commemoration Center). (2006, January 1) ,*Suicide terrorism in the during the Israeli-Palestinian confrontation (September 2000—December 2005)*, 2nd ed. Retrieved May 15, 2010, from http://www.terrorism-info.org.il/malam_multimedia/Hebrew/heb_n/pdf/suicide_terrorism.pdf (in Hebrew).

IICC (Israel Intelligence Heritage and Commemoration Center). (2007, December 14). *Rocket threat from the Gaza Strip, 2000–2007*. Retrieved May 15, 2010, from http://www.terrorism-info.org.il/malam_multimedia/Hebrew/heb_n/pdf/rocket_threat.pdf (in Hebrew)

Israel Ministry of Foreign Affairs. (2010). *Terrorism deaths in Israel 1920–1999*. Retrieved May 15, 2010, from http://www.mfa.gov.il/MFA/MFAArchive/2000_2009/2000/1/Terrorism%20deaths%20in%20Israel%20-%201920–1999

Jost, J. T., Kay, A. C., & Thorisdottir, H. (Eds.). (2009). *Social and psychological bases of ideology and system justification*. New York: Oxford University Press.

Jost, J. T., & Major, B. (Eds.). (2001). *The psychology of legitimacy: Emerging perspectives on ideology, justice, and intergroup relations*. New York: Cambridge University Press.

Jost, J. T., & Sidanius, J. (Eds.). (2004). *Political psychology: Key readings*. New York: Psychology Press/Taylor & Francis.

Kelman, H. C. (2001). Reflections on social and psychological processes of legitimization and delegitimization. In J. T. Jost & B. Major (Eds.), *The psychology of legitimacy: Emerging perspectives on ideology, justice, and intergroup relations* (pp. 54–73). New York: Cambridge University Press.

Khalidi, R. (1997). *Palestinian identity: The construction of modern national consciousness*. New York: Columbia University Press.

Lavi, T., & Solomon, Z. (2005). Palestinian youth of the Intifada: PTSD and future orientation. *Journal of American Academy of Child and Adolescent Psychiatry, 44*, 1176–1183.

Lesch, D. W. (2008). *The Arab-Israeli conflict: A history*. New York: Oxford University Press.

Levy, G, (2006). On the day that Israeli society will really know. In H. Herzog & K. Lahad (Eds), *Knowledge and silence: On mechanisms of denial and repression in Israeli society* (pp. 75–82). Tel Aviv: Hakibutz Hameuchad (in Hebrew).

Lustick, I. S. (1993). *Unsettled states, disputes lands*. Ithaca, NY: Cornell University Press.

Makdisi, S. (2008). *Palestine inside out: An everyday occupation*. New York: W. W. Norton.

McCarthy, C. (2005). The paradox of the international law of military occupation: Sovereignty and the reformation of Iraq. *Journal of Conflict & Security Law, 10*(1), 43–74.

Memmi, A. (1990). *The colonizer and the colonized*. London: Earthscan.
Morris, B. (2001). *Righteous victims: A history of the Zionist-Arab conflict 1881–2001*. New York: Vintage Books
Ophir, A., Givoni, M., & Hanafi, S. (Eds.). (2009). *Power of inclusive exclusion: Anatomy of Israeli rule in the occupied Palestinian territories*. New York: Zone Books.
Oren, B. M. (2003). *Six days of war: June 1967 and the making of the modern Middle East*. New York: Random House.
Pedatzur, R. (1996). *The triumph of embarrassment: Israel and the territories after the Six-Day War*. Tel-Aviv: Yad-Tabenkin-Galili Research Institute and Bitan Publishers (in Hebrew).
Physicians for Human Rights. (2000). *Rights under detention—the human rights of people in custody*. Tel Aviv: Physicians for Human Rights (in Hebrew).
Playfair, E. (1989). Legal aspects of Israel's occupation of the West Bank and Gaza: Theory and practice. In N. H. Aruri (Ed.), *Occupation: Israel over Palestine* (2nd ed., pp. 101–126). Belmont, CA: Association of Arab-American University Graduates.
Playfair, E. (Ed.). (1992). *International law and the administration of occupied territories*. Oxford: Clarendon Press.
Portugali, J. (1996). *Implicated relations: Society and space in the Israeli-Palestinian conflict*. Tel Aviv: Hakibutz Hameuchad (in Hebrew).
Punamaki, R.-L., Komproe, I. H., Qouta, S., Elmasri, M., & de Jong, J. V. M. (2005). The role of peritraumatic dissociation and gender in the association between trauma and mental health in a Palestinian community sample. *American Journal of Psychiatry, 162*, 545–551.
Rapoport, M. (2008, February 17). Third of settlements built on land seized for "security purposes." *Haaretz*. Retrieved March 31, 2010, from http://www.haaretz.com/print-edition/news/third-of-settlements-built-on-land-seized-for-security-purposes-1.239485
Regular, A., & Gottlieb, Z. (2005, August 23). 230 Israelis and about 2600 Palestinians have been killed in the Gaza Strip since its occupation. *Haaretz*. Retrieved April 14,2010, from http://www.haaretz.co.il/hasite/pages/ShArtPE.jhtml?itemNo=616042&contrassID=2&subContrassID=21&sbSubContrassID=0 (in Hebrew).
Rivkin, D. B., & Bartram, D. R. (2003). Military occupation: Legally ensuring a lasting peace. *The Washington Quarterly, 26*(3), 87–103.
Roberts, A. (1985). What is a military occupation? *British Yearbook of International Law 1984, 55*, 249–305.
Roberts, A. (1990). Prolonged military occupation: The Israeli-occupied territories since 1967. *The American Journal of International Law, 84*, 44–103.
Rosler, N., Bar-Tal, D., Halperin, E., Sharvit, K., & Raviv, A. (2009). Moral aspects of prolonged occupation: Implications for an occupying society. In S. Scuzzarello, C. Kinnvall, & K. Monroe (Eds), *On behalf of others: The morality of care in a global world* (pp. 211–232). New York: Oxford University Press.

Rouhana, N., & Bar-Tal, D. (1998). Psychological dynamics of intractable conflicts: The Israeli-Palestinian case. *American Psychologist, 53*, 761–770.

Sears, D. O., Huddy, L., & Jervis, R. (Eds.). (2003). *Oxford handbook of political psychology*. New York: Oxford University Press.

Segev, T. (2007). *1967: Israel, the war, and the year that transformed the Middle East*. New York: Metropolitan Books.

Shin Bet Security Service. (2010). *Distribution of fatalities of Palestinian terror since the beginning of the present conflict*—December 31, 2009–September 29, 2010. Retrieved May 15, 2010, from http://www.shabak.gov.il/English/EnTerrorData/decade/Fatalities/Pages/default.aspx

Simon, B., & Klandermans, B. (2001). Politicized collective identity. *American Psychologist, 56*, 319–331.

Tajfel, H. (1978). Social categorization, social identity and social comparison. In H. Tajfel (Ed.), *Differentiation between social groups* (pp. 61–76). London: Academic Press.

Tajfel, H. (1981) *Human groups and social categories*. Cambridge: Cambridge University Press.

Tessler, M. (1994). *A history of the Israeli-Palestinian conflict*. Bloomington: Indiana University Press.

Wasserstein, B. (2003). *Israelis and Palestinians: Why do they fight ? Can they stop?* New Haven, CT: Yale University Press.

Yahav, N. (2009, January 22). *B'Tselem: 8881 Israeli and Palestinian fatalities*. Retrieved May 7, 2010, from http://news.walla.co.il/?w=/2689/2518463

Yesh Din. (2007). *Backyard proceedings—The implementation of due process rights in the military courts in the occupied territories*. Tel Aviv: Author.

Zertal, I., & Eldar, A. (2007). *Lords of the land: The war over Israel's settlements in the occupied territories, 1967–2007*. New York: Nation Books.

I

Fundamentals of Occupation

CHAPTER 1

The Law of Belligerent Occupation as a System of Control: Dressing Up Exploitation in Respectable Garb

David Kretzmer

> No military government may create in its area facts for its military purposes that are intended from the very start to exist even after the termination of military rule in that area, when the fate of the territory after the termination of the military rule is unknown.
> —*Elon Moreh case, 1979, p. 22*

> The considerations of the military commander are, on the one hand, ensuring his security interests in the [occupied] area, and, on the other hand, ensuring the interests of the civilian population in the area. Both of these considerations are directed toward the [occupied] area itself. The commander is not allowed to consider the national, economic or social interests of his own state, to the extent that they do not have implications for his security interests in the area or the interests of the local population. Even military needs are his military needs in the area, and not national security interests in the wide sense. An area subject to belligerent occupation is not a field open to economic or other exploitation
> —*Jamait Ascan case, 1983, p. 794*

INTRODUCTION

The above quotations are not taken from a textbook on the law of belligerent occupation, from the writings of an academic expert in the field, or from a nongovernmental organization (NGO) report. They appear in two judgments of the Supreme Court of Israel, handed down in 1979 and 1983, respectively, that are still regarded as leading precedents on issues relating to the legal situation in the Occupied Territories (OT). Yet, anyone who has even a cursory knowledge of government policies and actions in those territories will be aware that the statement of the law in these quotations does not reflect the norms that have guided the authorities in their actions in the OT. There is then obviously a glaring disparity not only between government action in the OT and the norms of international law, as interpreted by international institutions such as the UN Security Council and the International Court of Justice, but also between such action and the formal applicable legal norms that apply according to the jurisprudence of the Supreme Court of Israel. The disparity between the professed norms and those applied in practice is part of a system of control under which the government resorts to the formal norms of belligerent occupation when it serves its political purposes and ignores them when it does not. In establishing settlements and exploiting the resources in the OT for the good of Israel and Israelis, the formal legal norms have been ignored. However, in justifying restrictions on the rights and liberties of the Palestinian residents, the formal norms of belligerent occupation have been cited time and again.

The system of control over the OT may be characterized as "legal hypocrisy." In practice, it rests on a dichotomy between the status of the OT and that of the Palestinians who reside there. The *territory* itself is not regarded as occupied; its *Palestinian* residents are, however, subjected to the law of occupation (Gordon, 2008).

In describing the way law has been used as a system of control, I shall briefly describe the beginnings of the legal system in the OT and then demonstrate how it has been manipulated. In doing so, I shall refer to the following issues: settlements, highway construction, the separation barrier, and security measures.

THE LEGAL SYSTEM IN THE OT: BEGINNINGS

On the day the Israel Defense Forces (IDF) took over the West Bank and Gaza in 1967, the military commanders issued proclamations stating that they had assumed all governmental powers in the area and that the prevailing law would remain in force subject to any orders that the military commanders would promulgate (Proclamation Regarding the Taking of Power by the I.D.F, 1967).[1] Attached to this proclamation was the Security Provisions Order that contained detailed provisions for IDF rule in the occupied areas. This order included provisions relating to the establishment of military courts and the procedure before them, the definition of security offenses, powers of arrest and search by soldiers, and the granting of security powers to the military commanders, such as the power to impose a curfew or to close an area. It included the following provision:

[A] military tribunal and the administration of a military tribunal shall observe the provisions of the Geneva Convention of August 12, 1949 Relative to the Protection of Civilian Persons in Time of War with respect to legal proceedings, and in the case of conflict between this Order and the said Convention, the provisions of the Convention shall prevail. (Security Provisions Order, 1967)

Not long after the 1967 war ended, it became clear that the perception of the territories taken by the IDF in that war as "occupied" territories was incompatible with the political stance of many Israeli politicians, especially those who were soon referring to "liberated" territories.[2] This was probably the reason that the provision mentioning the Geneva Convention was revoked soon after the war ended. An order enacted by the military commander of the area simply replaced the section in which this provision appeared with another section that had absolutely nothing to do with the Geneva Convention (Rubinstein, 1988). In this way, the formal legislative adoption of the Geneva Convention as the supreme norm of military law in the OT was repealed.

The departure of the military authorities from the legislative adoption of Geneva Convention IV (apparently in response to emerging political attitudes toward the OT) was soon supported by legal argument. Doubt was raised whether Geneva Convention IV, referred to in the Security Provisions Order cited above, actually applied to the situation on the West Bank and in Gaza (Blum, 1968). The government latched on to this argument and contested formal application of the Geneva Convention to the situation in the West Bank and in Gaza. The official position of the government became that while Geneva Convention IV did not formally apply, the IDF would abide by its humanitarian provisions (Bar-Yaacov, 1988; Shamgar, 1971). Which provisions of the Convention would not be regarded as humanitarian provisions was never explained, but from subsequent developments it appears that the intention was to avoid application of Article 49 (6) of the Convention, which is discussed below.

The Supreme Court of Israel never expressly ruled on whether Geneva Convention IV formally applies to the West Bank and Gaza or not.[3] It managed to avoid doing so in two ways. In some cases—both early cases, such as the *Christian Society* case (1971), and later cases, such as the *Ajuri* case (2002) and cases dealing with the separation barrier—the authorities expressly or implicitly agreed that their actions could be judged according to the standards of the Convention. The Court simply went along with this without ruling that the Convention formally applied. In other cases, in which petitioners attempted to rely on provisions in the Convention, especially Article 49, which prohibits both deportation of protected persons from the occupied territory and transfer of the civilian population of the occupying power to the occupied territory, the Court applied the principle that international treaties would not be enforced by domestic courts unless the norms of those treaties had been incorporated in Knesset legislation or were part of customary international law. It ruled that the norms in Article 49 of Geneva Convention IV were not part of customary international law and, as they had not been incorporated in domestic legislation, they could not be enforced by Israel's courts (*Beth El* case, 1978; *Elon Moreh* case, 1979; *Kawasme* case, 1980).

In some of the first cases to reach the Supreme Court, not only did the authorities seek to avoid a ruling on the application of Geneva Convention IV, they also attempted to leave open the very status of the West Bank and Gaza. When petitioners relied on the law of belligerent occupation, the authorities declared that they were prepared for the Court to examine their actions under this law without ruling on its formal applicability. Some of the judges were prepared to go along with this procedure. In both the *Rafah Approach* case (1972) and the *Beth El* case (1978), Justice Moshe Landau examined arguments based on customary law relating to belligerent occupation while accepting the government's reservation that "it was not going into the legal question of the actual application of the rules of international law in the area occupied by the IDF since 1967." (*Beth El* case, p. 127). As time passed, these caveats were no longer included in the judgments and the Court began relying on customary international law relating to belligerent occupation as a matter of course. Eventually, in the *Jamait Ascan* case (1983), Justice Aharon Barak pushed the caveats aside and ruled categorically that the legal regime in both the West Bank and Gaza was one of belligerent occupation.

Following Justice Barak's decision and that of Justice Meir Shamgar in the *Vat* case (1981) the framework of belligerent occupation became the accepted discourse in issues connected with the OT. Hence, in a joint judgment of 10 justices in the case dealing with the legality of the Gaza disengagement plan, the Court was able to describe the legal status of the West Bank and Gaza thus:

> According to the legal outlook of all Israel's governments as presented to this court—an outlook that has always been accepted by the Supreme Court—these areas are held by Israel by way of belligerent occupation.... The legal regime that applies there is determined by the rules of public international law and especially the rules relating to belligerent occupation. (*Gaza Beach Regional Council* case, 2005, p. 514)

In recent years, the Court has also taken to referring to Geneva Convention IV as a matter of course and accepting central concepts of that Convention, such as the definition of all Palestinian residents of the West Bank (but not Israeli citizens who reside there) as protected persons (*Alram* case, 2005; *Bir Nabala* case, 2005; *Halua* case, 2004). It is clear then that not only is the West Bank regarded as occupied territory by the whole international community; it is regarded as such by the highest judicial body in Israel, whose statement of the law is binding on all lower courts and on the Israeli government too.

BELLIGERENT OCCUPATION AS A SYSTEM OF CONTROL

Two factors led the authorities to formal acceptance of the idea that the legal status of the West Bank (excluding East Jerusalem) and Gaza (before the disengagement) was one of occupied territory. The first was the entry into the arena by the Supreme Court of Israel, before which the government was required to defend many of its actions in the OT. In the absence of any other framework in international law to define Israel's status in those territories, and given the political decision not to apply Israeli law in the OT (with the exception of East Jerusalem), the only available framework was that of the powers of an occupying army in occupied territory. As we have seen above, in the first cases to reach the Court the authorities attempted to hedge their bets: stating that they were prepared to accept that the Court would assess their actions according to this framework without deciding whether it formally applied.

The second, and possibly more important, factor that led the authorities to accept the legal framework of belligerent occupation was that it provided the government with a highly convenient system of control that allowed Israel to hold on to the territory itself without extending political rights to its inhabitants. This requires some explanation.

The international law of belligerent occupation is a two-edged sword. Because it is part of the law of armed conflict, the name of the game is military rule, which allows for broad restrictions on the liberties and rights of persons in the occupied territory. The fundamental assumption behind the law of belligerent occupation, as it developed from the late nineteenth century, was that an occupation would be a short-term, provisional situation. At the end of this period, normalcy would be restored and the inhabitants of the occupied territory would enjoy the rights and liberties recognized by their own domestic legal system (Benvenisti, 1993; Dinstein, 2009). While acknowledging the dominance of the occupying power's military needs, the law of occupation places restrictions on the powers of the occupying power; those restrictions reflect its status as a temporary regime whose authority rests on force rather than legitimate authority.[4]

As it developed before the rise of modern liberal democracies, the law of belligerent occupation was originally more concerned with protecting the interests of the ousted sovereign power than those of the people living in occupied territory. Since the end of World War II, with the spread of democracy, the development of international human rights law, and recognition of the principle of self-determination of peoples as a central political and legal doctrine, this situation has changed, and the emphasis has shifted to protecting the rights, individual and collective, of persons in the occupied territory. This change was first manifested in the 1949 Geneva Convention IV, which is concerned solely with protecting civilians rather than the political interests of the belligerent parties. In recent years, the change has taken a more radical turn; treaty bodies and international tribunals now state that the human rights obligations of occupying powers bind them in their actions in occupied territory. This approach was confirmed by the International Court of Justice both in its Advisory Opinion on *Legal Consequences of the Construction of a Wall* (2004) and its judgment in the case relating to Uganda's military operations in the territory of the Democratic Republic of the Congo (*Armed Activities on the Territory of the Congo*, 2005).

Despite their initial reluctance to consider the West Bank and Gaza as occupied territories, the Israeli authorities realized early on that the regime of belligerent occupation offered them tremendous advantages. They could maintain control over these areas by the use of military force without extending political or civil rights to the Palestinian residents. Under the guise of protecting military needs, they could focus on their own political interests without bothering too much about the interests of the local population. The regime of belligerent occupation does indeed place serious restrictions on the powers of the occupying power. However, the authorities sought ways to circumvent those restrictions that blocked the promotion of their political agenda, and in doing so they generally gained the support, tacit or express, of the Supreme Court.

At the heart of Israeli policies relating to the OT lies the issue of settlements. For it is this issue, more than any other, that exposes the fundamental clash between the regime of belligerent occupation as a temporary, provisional regime based purely on military exigencies and the political agenda of successive Israeli governments that sought to make Israeli control over all or much of these territories permanent and irreversible. This agenda involved harnessing resources in the OT for the benefit of Israel and the Israeli settlers and making a clear distinction between the rights and liberties of Israelis living in the OT and those of the Palestinians. These policies made the Israeli regime there much closer to a colonial regime than to a temporary military occupation.

SETTLEMENTS AND THE LAW

Establishment of Israeli settlements on the West Bank and in Gaza has been the most controversial policy of successive Israeli governments since 1967, both domestically and internationally. The international community has stated almost unanimously that establishment of settlements by the government is incompatible with Israel's international obligations as an occupying power. There have been numerous resolutions of the UN General Assembly and the UN Security Council on this issue (UNSC Resolutions 446 and 452, 1979, and 465, 1980; UNGA Resolutions 64/93, 2009 and 65/104, 2010). The International Court of Justice also stated that the settlements were established in violation of international law (*Legal Consequences of the Construction of a Wall*, 2004). In this section, I shall briefly discuss how the Israeli authorities coped with the legal aspects of the settlement policy.

Opinion of the Legal Adviser to the Foreign Ministry

Pressures to allow settlement of Israelis on the West Bank began shortly after the hostilities ended in 1967 and Israel found itself in control of the West Bank, the Golan Heights, and northern Sinai (Eldar & Zartal, 2004; Gorenberg, 2006). This pressure came from a number of directions: family members of persons who had lived in villages destroyed in 1947–1948; groups in the Labor movement who had always regarded settlement in areas of the Land of Israel (*Eretz Yisrael*) as a major Zionist project; religious Zionists who regarded settlement in all parts of the historic Land of Israel as a religious duty; and followers of the revisionist branch of Zionism, which had opposed accepting the 1947 partition plan and had even hoped for Jewish sovereignty on the east bank of the Jordan River (Gorenberg, 2006).

The government was well aware that settlement of Israelis in the newly occupied territories could raise legal problems. The legal adviser of the Foreign Ministry, Theodor Meron, was discreetly asked for an opinion on the subject. In a top-secret memorandum written in September 1967, Meron explained that settlement of Israelis on the West Bank or the Golan Heights would be regarded as a violation of Article 49 (6) of Geneva Convention IV He added that if "steps toward Jewish settlement in the occupied territories are decided on, it seems to me, therefore, that it is essential that the settlement be carried out by military, and not civilian, bodies. It is also important, in my opinion, that such settlement should be in camps and should outwardly have a temporary and not permanent character" (Meron Legal Opinion, 1967).

Meron's legal opinion had only a minimal cosmetic effect on government decision making. The first settlements were ostensibly established as settlements of the *Nachal*, a unit of the army that combines agricultural work with military service. At times this was pure fiction; at others, settlements were indeed originally set up as *Nachal* outposts, manned by military *Nachal* units, and were later converted into civilian settlements. However, within a short time this policy was abandoned and settlements were established without any pretense of either temporariness or military character (Gorenberg, 2006).

Despite Meron's legal opinion, over the years the Foreign Ministry has attempted to find legal arguments in favor of settlements (MFA, 2001).[5] The government has also always prided itself on the fact that the legality of its actions in the OT has been subject to review by the Supreme Court of Israel (Amit-Kohn, Jarach, Glick, & Biton,1993). Hence, when Meron's memorandum was exposed, the spokesman for the Israel Foreign Ministry claimed that Meron's view had been rejected by the Supreme Court of Israel (Macintyre, 2006). This claim is not accurate.

Settlements Before the Supreme Court

The Supreme Court's approach to settlements is reflected in a long line of judgments, beginning with that in the *Rafah Approach* case, delivered in 1972, continuing through the *Beth El* and *Elon Moreh* cases, decided in the late 1970s, and culminating for the moment in the separation barrier cases and the disengagement case. I have discussed the original approach of the Court elsewhere (Kretzmer, 2002) and shall not repeat the details here. The salient points in the Court's approach until the separation barrier cases have been the following:

1. The Court has steadfastly refused to rule on the legality of settlements under international law. It has based this refusal, which may be quite understandable in political terms, on the view that the prohibition on transfer of civilians of the occupying power into occupied territory that appears in Article 49 (6) of Geneva Convention IV is not part of customary international law. It has also ruled that the general issue of settlements, as opposed to arguments relating to the legality of taking land for a specific settlement, is nonjusticiable (*Bargil* case, 1992; *Beth El* case, 1978; *Elon Moreh* case, 1979; *I'ad* case, 1998). It has thus left open the question of the settlements' legality under international law.
2. In two early decisions, the Court ruled that a settlement could fulfill a security function, and that requisition of private land needed for a settlement could be lawful, if the security grounds were proven (*Beth El* case, 1978; *Amira* case, 1979).
3. The Court declined to examine the legality of building a settlement on public land. It based its refusal on lack of standing of an individual to

challenge the use made of public land (*Ayreib*, 1984) and lack of justiciability of a challenge mounted by Peace Now (*Bargil*, 1991).
4. The Court has ruled that since belligerent occupation is a temporary regime, if a political decision is made to withdraw from occupied territory, the settlers have no right to remain in that territory (*Beth El* case, 1978; *Gaza Beach Regional Council* case, 2005; *Kiryat Arba* case, 1992).

In light of this attitude of the Supreme Court, there is no basis for the claim by government spokesmen that the Court has rejected Meron's opinion and *expressly* upheld the legality of settlements under international law. In fact, the Court has refrained from ruling on the most important legal arguments against settlements. However, by its refusal to deal with these loaded questions, its decisions in cases in which it accepted that some settlements may be justified on security grounds, and its decisions in cases in which it simply refused to consider the use of public land for settlements, the Court has provided legal legitimization for the establishment of settlements.

Use of Public Land

In the famous *Elon Moreh* case, the Supreme Court held that requisition of private land for the Elon Moreh settlement was based on political rather than military considerations; furthermore, as the declared intention was to establish a permanent settlement, the requisition order met an "insuperable obstacle."

While the decision did not entirely rule out use of private land for settlements, it certainly restricted such use to cases in which the authorities proved that the settlement would fulfill a specific and defined military purpose. The authorities consequently abandoned the requisition of private land for settlements themselves and embarked on a land grab of "public land" and its widescale use for settlements (Forman, 2009)

From a legal perspective, there were two problems with this new policy. The first relates to the system of declaring land to be public land; the second relates to the use of such land for the benefit of the civilians of the occupying power.

Declaration of land as "state lands" or "government lands" was based on a military order promulgated soon after the occupation began (Order Relating to Governmental Property, 1967). Under this order, the Custodian of Government Property appointed by the military governor is empowered to take possession of government property and regulate its use.[6] Later, a crucial section was added to the order stating that if the Custodian certified property as government property, it would be so deemed unless proved otherwise. In other words, once land is certified, the onus is on those who claim land rights to prove that the land is not state land. Claims are heard by a special appeals committee, which deals with appeals against various decisions or actions of the military government.

During the 1970s, a survey was completed of land registered in the name of absentees or of the government and the Custodian of Government Property took possession of this land (Benvenisti, 1984). Following the *Elon Moreh* decision, the Cabinet decided that all uncultivated rural land would be declared state land (Benvenisti, 1984).[7] The onus would then be placed on individuals to prove their rights in the land. This could be done only by producing a *koushan* (certificate of title) or by proving both possession and cultivation of the land for a period of at least 10 years.[8] This legal structure paved the way for a policy of taking possession of large areas of land declared to be state lands. Plia Albeck, the government attorney then in charge of checking whether land could be regarded as state land, estimated that approximately 40% of the land in the West Bank is state land (Albeck, 1985)

The connection between widening the scope of state land and the settlement policy of the Likud government was quite explicit. The Drobles Plan of 1978, which formed the basis for the original settlement policy of the Likud government, declared:

> State land and uncultivated land must be seized immediately in order to settle the areas *between* the concentrations of minority population and *around* them, with the object of reducing to the minimum the possibility for the development of another Arab state in these regions. (Drobles, 1980, p. 3)

Writing in 1985, Plia Albeck stated that approximately 90% of the Jewish settlements in the OT had been built on state land. While purporting to fulfill the occupying power's duty to preserve the right of the public in state land, the government regarded such land as a resource to be used for settlement of nationals of the occupying power.[9]

The manner in which land was declared to be public land was manipulated so as to serve government interests in creating a reserve of land for settlements. Rather than abiding by the interpretation of land law that had prevailed during the British Mandate period, and had not been abandoned during the period in which the Jordanians ruled the West Bank, the authorities used an interpretation that had originally been adopted to allow them to lay their hands on large tracts of land in the Galilee (Forman, 2009).[10] It has been argued that in adopting a controversial, and self-serving, interpretation of the prevailing land law on the West Bank that had not been part of the law before the occupation began, Israel failed to comply with its obligation to respect the local law unless absolutely prevented from doing so (Forman, 2009). Attempts to challenge the system of declaring land to be state land were unsuccessful (*Al-Naazer*, 1981).[11]

The declaration of land to be state land, and especially the policy regarding uncultivated *miri* land, were closely connected to the government's settlement policies. The Israeli authorities assumed that public or state land was at their disposal to serve the political interests of Israel and Israelis. This is totally incompatible with Article 55 of the Hague Regulations, which obligates an occupying power to administer public property as a trustee. That trusteeship is supposed to benefit the public to which the land belongs, namely, the residents of the occupied territory, and not the public of the occupying power.

The approach of the Supreme Court when efforts were made to challenge the policy of declaring land to be state land and the policy of using such land for Israeli settlements is highly revealing. In the *al-Naazer* case, Justice Shamgar mentioned the duty of an occupying power under Article 55 of the Hague Regulations to safeguard the capital of public properties and to administer them in accordance with the rules of usufruct. He presented the system as one aimed at fulfilling the duty of the occupying power to protect public property against intrusion. However, in a later case, a person unsuccessfully challenged the declaration of land that had been in his possession as state land. He also challenged the use of that land for a settlement, but Justice Shamgar held that he lacked the standing to challenge the use of public land (*Ayreib*, 1984).[12] Finally, when the Peace Now movement attempted to challenge the legality of the whole settlement enterprise, including the issue of land use, the petition was dismissed as nonjusticiable (*Bargil* case, 1991; *I'ad* case, 1998).

The use of the legal system, with the backing of the Court, to take over large tracts of land that belong to the Palestinian public, is one of the most glaring examples of the way the law has been manipulated to serve the political goals of the Israeli government. Legal powers that make the occupying power a trustee for the public in the OT are exploited to expropriate land for the benefit of Israelis. I return to the implications of this policy below.

Settlements and the Separation Barrier

A great deal has been written about the decisions of the Supreme Court of Israel and the Advisory Opinion of the International Court of Justice relating to the separation barrier being built on the West Bank (Agora, 2005; *Israel Law Review*, 2005). It is not my intention here to repeat what has already been written on the topic. I will confine my remarks to the issue of settlements in the two opinions.

The International Court of Justice stated that the settlements on the West Bank had been established in violation of Article 49 of Geneva Convention IV. It concluded that since the decision to build the separation barrier in the West Bank, rather than on the Green Line or in Israel itself, had been largely determined by the desire to protect settlements, the construction of the barrier was unlawful. More generally, it opined that "the route chosen for the wall gives expression *in loco* to the illegal measures taken by Israel with regard to Jerusalem and the settlements" and should therefore be seen as severely restricting the right of the Palestinian people to self-determination (*Legal Consequences of the Construction of a Wall*, 2004, para. 122).

When the issue of settlements arose before the Supreme Court of Israel in cases connected with the separation barrier, the Court was faced with a dilemma. It could have taken issue with the International Court of Justice on the legality of the settlements, but it was obviously reluctant to do so. On the other hand, accepting the International Court's view would have meant ignoring the Supreme Court's own role in legitimizing settlements and would probably have led to a major confrontation with the government. The Court's solution was to attempt to skirt the issue by holding that the lawfulness of the settlements was irrelevant in judging the legality of the separation barrier. The Court held that even if the settlers, as citizens of the occupying power, were not protected persons under Geneva Convention IV, the military commander had a duty to protect their lives and security. The Court's conclusion was that

> the military commander is authorized to construct a separation fence in the *area* for the purpose of defending the lives and safety of the Israeli settlers in the area. Whether this settlement activity conforms to international law or defies it, as determined in the Advisory Opinion of the International Court of Justice at the Hague, is not relevant For this reason, we shall express no position regarding that question. The authority to construct a security fence for the purpose of defending the lives and safety of Israeli settlers is derived from the need to preserve "public order and safety" (Regulation 43 of the Hague Regulations). It is called for, in light of the dignity of every human individual. It is intended to preserve the life of every person created in God's image. The life of a person who is in the area illegally is not up for the taking. Even if a person is located in the area illegally, he is not outlawed. (*Mara'abe* case, 2004, para. 19)

The Supreme Court was clearly correct in stating that the military commander has a duty to protect the lives of persons who are present in the OT, whether they are protected persons under the Geneva Convention or not. However, one cannot jump to the conclusion that the commander may use any means to fulfill this duty. The fact that persons are unlawfully in a certain location does not turn them into outlaws; but when we examine how to protect such persons against threats posed by their very presence there, the first measure to be considered must surely be their removal. In all events, if it is determined that persons are unlawfully in a location, one would assume that measures to protect them should be temporary until they can be removed.

Rather than questioning the authority of the military commander to protect settlers by including them on the western side of the barrier, the Supreme Court of Israel subjected each section of the barrier's route to a test of proportionality, weighing the harm to Palestinians against the security benefit to settlers of the particular route chosen. Even if one accepts this method of analysis, it is hard to understand how the unlawfulness of the settlements could be regarded as irrelevant. When balancing the hardship caused by the barrier to Palestinians lawfully in their villages or towns against the security of Israelis in the settlements, the unlawful nature of those settlements should surely be a relevant factor. Why should people living in lawful settlements have to face considerable hardship because of the need to protect persons in settlements that should not be there in the first place? The obvious solution is to remove the unlawful settlements, thus avoiding the need to protect their inhabitants. However one looks at the issue, the legality or illegality of the settlements should be a relevant factor in judging the lawfulness of a barrier built to protect persons in those settlements, especially when the location of the barrier infringes on the rights of others.

Settlements and the Settlers in the OT

While avoiding the restrictions in international law on transfer of Israeli citizens to the occupied territory, the authorities never attempted formally to change the legal status of the West Bank (with the exception of East Jerusalem). It remains occupied territory. This created a dilemma: how were Israeli settlements and settlers to be regarded? What legal regime would apply to them? Would they be subject to the local law that applies in the West Bank?

The answer to the above questions should have been fairly clear. The law that applies on the West Bank—namely, the law that was in force when Israel occupied the area and the military legislation enacted since then—has territorial application. It should apply in all towns and villages in the area and to all persons who reside there. Adopting this position would have meant that Israelis who took up residence in the West Bank would, for all intents and purposes, be like Israelis who took up residence in a foreign country. This would not have been compatible with the policy behind the settlements, namely, extension of Israel's control over areas of *Eretz Yisrael* that were beyond the borders of the state.

One way of solving the dilemma would have been to apply Israeli law on the West Bank, as was done in East Jerusalem and the Golan Heights. This would, however, have met with international condemnation. It would also have meant that the Palestinians on the West Bank and Gaza would have had to be offered the option of Israeli citizenship. The way out was to avoid formal application of Israeli law to the territory itself, while at the same time applying it on a personal basis to Israelis who were resident there, as well as recognizing the settlements as "Israeli enclaves" in which Israeli law would apply. This was achieved by a combination of Israeli legislation, which states that for the purpose of a series of laws Israelis living on the West Bank are to be regarded as if they were living in Israel itself (Law for Extension of Emergency Regulations [Judea, Samaria and Gaza—Jurisdiction Over Offences and Legal Assistance], 1967), and military orders that applied the substantive arrangements of Israeli law in Israeli settlements (Order Relating to Administration of Municipal Councils [Judea and Samaria] [No. 892], 1982; Order Relating to Administration of Regional Councils [Judea and Samaria] [No. 783], 1979).

The colonial aspects of the above system are self-evident. The natives living in the OT are subject to the full power of the law of belligerent occupation. The citizens of the colonial power live a privileged life, relieved of the burdens of living in a territory that is subject to a regime of belligerent occupation. They are ruled by a different legal order; the mechanism for enforcing the law against them is different, and has proved time and again to be wanting;[13] and they are tried before different courts.[14]

The legal situation caused by the Israeli enclaves has come before the Supreme Court on a number of occasions. The Court has recognized the existence of these enclaves and has had to contend with some of the issues that the distinction between the applicable territorial law and the law applied to Israelis living in the enclaves has caused. (Paz-Fuchs & Ronen, in press). On one occasion, it held that the Israeli law of torts applied to an action between a Palestinian worker who was injured in a work accident in a factory in an Israeli settlement and her Israeli employer (*Yanon* case, 2003). In another case, it held that Palestinian workers employed in Israeli settlements should enjoy the rights of Israeli labor law enjoyed by Israeli workers there rather than the local labor law that applies on the West Bank (*Kav Le'oved* case, 2007).

Attempts by the Court to mitigate the implications of a distinction between the law of the land and settlers' law have helped to illustrate how the system works. It is little wonder that the parallels between this system and the apartheid regime of South Africa have been noted (Aloni, 2007; Farsakh, 2003; Greenstein, 2006).

HIGHWAY CASES

Establishment of settlements did not mean only that land for the settlements was expropriated from private individuals or from the Palestinian public for the use of Israeli citizens. An infrastructure was required to support the settlements. A major part of this infrastructure involved building new highways throughout the West Bank as well as providing access roads from highways to the settlements. Land was expropriated for these highways and access roads.

The connection between the new highways planned for the West Bank and the settlements planned or established there was explicit. Thus, a plan for highways prepared by the World Zionist Organization (WZO) states:

> There would seem to be no need to say too much about the importance of an adequate net of highways in Samaria and Judea.... Although the matter is clear, the net of highways today (fifteen years after the Six-Day War) does not reflect the special character of the area as a central part of the country, nor help to exploit the enormous settlement potential of the area. Furthermore, it does not increase awareness of the area nor reduce the reluctance toward it of the majority of the Jewish population. (WZO Master Plan, 1983, p. 27)

Expropriation of land for highways and access roads created a problem for the authorities. According to the legal framework of occupation, the military commander may expropriate land only if it is carried out under the local law for the good of the local population. The military commander in occupied territory also has the power to *requisition* land for the needs of the army of occupation. However, requisition is supposed to involve temporary use of land, and ownership in the land remains unchanged.

As in the settlement cases, the authorities sought a way to pursue their political aims in the OT without being hindered by the law or the Supreme Court. This involved squeezing the facts into the legal framework of occupation. Roads and other projects that were being built as part of the grand design for the West Bank were presented as projects designed to benefit the local Palestinian population. This tactic, first adopted in a case dealing with connecting Hebron to the national electricity grid (*Electricity Corporation for East Jerusalem* case, 1972), enjoyed the support of the Court.

The most glaring case in which this tactic was used relates to Highway 443, which was built to connect northern Jerusalem to the Jerusalem-Tel Aviv

Highway. The highway provides the main access route to a number of towns that were built along the Israeli side of the Green Line as well as to settlements built on the West Bank.[15]

In order to build part of this highway, land was expropriated from Palestinians. The landowners challenged the expropriation on several grounds, including the argument that the highway was being built for the good of Israel and Israelis rather than for the benefit of the local population. Expropriation of private land in occupied territory for this purpose is clearly illegal.

The authorities did not contest the argument that private land could be expropriated only for the good of the local population. Although the plan to build the road dated back to the mid-1970s and was closely connected to the government's settlement policy,[16] the authorities argued that the highway was being built to cater to the needs of the local population, as the existing network of highways was inadequate and the number of cars had grown enormously. The Supreme Court swallowed this argument and stated as follows:

> From examination of the materials presented to us we see a picture of professional planning, which takes into account the conditions and needs of the area, and not only the conditions and needs of Israel.
>
> As I have mentioned, we are satisfied that the considerations that guided the respondents were considerations concerning the area, and not considerations concerning Israel. (*Jamait Ascan* case, 1983, p. 795).

In reaching its conclusion, the Court relied on the evidence presented by the authorities, which, it stated, the petitioners had not been able to refute. Even if this was indeed the case, it is hard to avoid the impression that the Court was simply ignoring the political reality. This impression is reinforced by a remark of the Court that it was surprised that the authorities had not tried to argue that the highway would also fulfill an important security function, since in a previous highway case this is exactly what they had done (*Tabeeb* case, 1981).[17] This disparity between the authorities' arguments in similar cases did not lead the Court to question the sincerity of their arguments.

The insincerity of the authorities' argument, which was accepted lock, stock, and barrel by the Supreme Court, became apparent years after Highway 443 was built. After the second *intifada* started, there were a number of drive-by shootings and attacks on the highway. The military commander concluded that he could not protect the security of Israelis if they and Palestinians traveled on the same highway. As Highway 443 had been built for the good of the local population, and not for that of Israel or Israelis, his conclusion should, of course, have been that Israelis could no longer use the highway. Not surprisingly, however, he reached the opposite conclusion and prohibited the travel of Palestinian vehicles on the highway. Despite its previous judgment that the highway was being built for the benefit of the local Palestinians, the Court was at first unwilling to interfere in the matter and asked for details from the authorities regarding alternative roads that were being built for Palestinian vehicles. As in the case of the separation barrier, the security of Israelis, whether located in unlawful settlements or traveling on roads that were built for the Palestinians, was preferred to the vital interests of the Palestinians. Eventually, three years after the petition had been submitted, the Court declared that the order prohibiting the travel of Palestinians on the highway was unlawful. It gave two reasons for its decision: (1) since the commander had no power to expropriate land for a highway that would only serve Israeli vehicles, he did not have the power to limit use of the highway to such vehicles, and (2) the harm done to Palestinians by totally preventing them from using the highway was disproportionate to the security benefit gained by that prohibition. However, the Court did not rule that the commander must allow unlimited access to Palestinian vehicles and make other provisions to protect the security of Israeli vehicles. On the contrary, the Court delayed implementation of its judgment for five months to allow the commander time to arrange the use of the highway in a manner that would regulate access for Palestinian vehicles while allowing free access to Israeli travelers (*Abu Tzefia* case, 2009). At the time of writing, the authorities have agreed only to severely limited use of the highway by Palestinian vehicles (ACRI, 2010). This casts doubt on the meaningfulness of the judicial process.

SECURITY MEASURES

Since the occupation began in 1967, security considerations have been pervasive in the actions of the military authorities. The authorities have cited security grounds for taking the private property of Palestinians, broad restrictions on their freedom of movement, refusal to allow family unification with Palestinians who live outside the OT, closure of universities, destruction of property, and a host of other actions. In their attempt to control the Palestinian population, the authorities have also used a wide variety of security measures. These have included measures directed against specific persons—deportations, house demolitions, administrative detentions, assigned residence—and measures that indiscriminately affect the whole Palestinian population or large sections thereof—curfews, roadblocks, and other restrictions on movement. This section will be devoted to such security measures.

Two of the measures targeting individuals are generally regarded as incompatible with Israel's international obligations. Deportation of protected persons from occupied territory is expressly prohibited under Article 49 (1) of Geneva Convention IV, regardless of the motive. Despite the clear language of this provision, the Supreme Court held that the prohibition does not apply to deportation of individuals on security grounds (*Afu* case, 1987). I have dealt elsewhere with the fallacies of the Court's approach and will not repeat the arguments here (Kretzmer, 2002). Suffice it to say that the approach is baseless and has been severely criticized (Dinstein, 1988). The Court also held that even if there were an absolute prohibition on deportations, it would not be part of customary international law and would therefore not be enforced by the Court (*Kawasme* case, 1980). It is difficult to believe that the Court's refusal to enforce the prohibition on deportations contributed significantly to protecting security. It did, however, lead to a fiasco—the deportation to Lebanon in late 1992 of 400 alleged members of Hamas and Islamic Jihad, many of whom later became actively involved in terrorist activities. (B'Tselem, 2011). This deportation shows that bending the law to meet the demands of the security services does not necessarily serve the security interests of society.

Even more than on the issue of deportations, the Supreme Court's approach on the issue of punitive house demolitions indicates the relaxation of legal values and standards when it comes to the OT. The formal legal basis for such demolitions is a provision in the Emergency Regulations (Defense) of 1945 that had been castigated by leaders of the Jewish Bar Association when the regulations were promulgated by the British. The provision originally found its way into British colonial legislation to provide a legal basis for retaliatory actions carried out by British soldiers in South Africa and Ireland. One only has to read the provision itself, which allows the military commander to order the forfeiture and destruction of any house "in any area, town, village, quarter or street the inhabitants or some of the inhabitants of which" have committed an act of violence to realize that this was its real function. Be this as it may, there is no way that such a provision could be enacted in a modern legal system. Had the provision itself not been on the law books in 1967, it is hard to believe that the military authorities would have been prepared to promulgate military legislation containing such a radical provision.

It is clear that use of house demolitions to demolish the family home of an inhabitant of the house who was involved in a terrorist attack (often a suicide attack) when the family was not party to the attack is totally incompatible with international law. It involves a glaring element of collective punishment; destruction of property not rendered absolutely necessary by military operations; cruel and inhuman punishment; and arbitrary interference with home and family. Furthermore, Article 78 of Geneva Convention IV provides that administrative detention and assigned residence are the most extreme measures that an occupying power may use for security reasons. House demolitions are incompatible with this provision.

Given the nature of the sanction and the overwhelming arguments that it is incompatible with international law, one would have expected the Supreme Court to prohibit its use. But it did nothing of the sort. In the first cases in which the Court approved the use of the sanction, it did not even consider the compatibility of the measure with international law or with general legal values. Rather, it went out of its way to adopt a fairly liberal interpretation of the provision in the Defense Regulations so as to give effect to "the legislative policy that lies behind it" (*Khamri* case, 1982, p. 442). Only much later did the Court strictly limit the use of house demolition by holding that it would be unreasonable to destroy a house if people other than the nuclear family of the bomber were living there. (*Turkmahn* case, 1993) Implied in this decision, of course, is that it is perfectly reasonable to destroy the home of a bomber's nuclear family even when its members had no prior knowledge of the bomber's planned actions.

With one exception, the Supreme Court has failed to address the argument that punitive house demolitions are incompatible with international law. The exception was a feeble attempt to address the argument that demolishing the family home of a bomber is a form of collective punishment (*Dajalis* case, 1985). The Court's answer to this argument is one of its more embarrassing decisions. The Court mentioned that the measure was used so that a potential bomber would know that his family would pay a price for his actions. This involved an admission that collective punishment is involved, as the very idea of collective punishment is to punish persons who were not involved in the act itself in order to deter potential perpetrators from committing similar acts.

While refusing to outlaw the use of punitive house demolitions, the Court has displayed discomfort with the measure. In one case, one of the judges remarked:

> Notwithstanding, and despite the legal reasons, it is morally distressing that the crime of the terrorist is paid for by the members of his family, who as far as we know did not assist him and did not know about his actions. This distress derives from the ancient principle of the Jewish tradition according to which "the fathers shall not be put to death for the sons, neither shall the sons be put to death for the fathers; every man shall be put to death for his own sin" (Deutr. XXIV, 16).... The sages even complained that King David had violated this principle by not showing mercy for the seven sons of Saul.... However, the chance that destruction or sealing of a

house will in the future prevent spilling of blood requires us to harden our hearts and to spare the living, who are likely to become victims of horrific acts of terrorists, more than we should spare the tenants of the house. This cannot be avoided. (*Saada* case, 2003, p. 294)

This statement reveals the extent to which the Court has internalized the idea that Israel's situation is so different from that of other democratic societies that one must overcome moral distress and cast aside fundamental legal principles in order to prevent spilling of blood—without any proof that using this sanction will indeed prevent bloodshed and some indication that it may even be counterproductive. (Harel, 2005; Shalev, 1990). The statement reflects the corruption of the legal system, for all civilized legal systems take the chance that upholding fundamental legal values—such as the prohibition on punishing persons for the acts of others, the presumption of innocence, and the principle of providing a fair trial—may involve some risk, in the short term at least. It is difficult to believe that with the rise in the number of murders in Israel, the Supreme Court would accept the argument that the presumption of innocence in murder cases should be relaxed in order to increase the deterrent effect of the criminal law. But what is the real difference between this argument and the argument that the houses of innocent persons may be demolished to deter others from committing acts of terror? When it was argued that house demolitions should be used against the families of Jewish terrorists, the Court explained that this was not justified, as cases of Jewish terror were isolated incidents, which were condemned by the Jewish public, while cases of Palestinian terror enjoyed wide public support. This is a somewhat damming explanation, as it seems to indicate that house demolition is meant to punish the public rather than deter individuals from carrying out terrorist attacks. Be this as it may, the fact is that the sanction has only been used against the houses of Palestinians.

In allowing deportations and punitive house demolitions, the Supreme Court has enabled the authorities to circumvent the restrictions placed on the powers of an occupying power. In the case of administrative detention, the Court has relied on the international law of belligerent occupation to legitimize this measure.

It would seem that the dynamics of suppression demand a never-ending search for new measures that will enable an occupying power to control a hostile population. The authorities had tried deportations, house demolitions, and administrative detention, and were still faced with a growing number of suicide bombings. In response, in 2002 a few ministers raised the idea of deporting the families of suicide bombers or expelling them from the West Bank to Gaza. Given the Supreme Court's license to use house demolitions, this proposal was not totally preposterous. However, the attorney general stated that it would be unlawful to deport persons who had no personal involvement in terrorist activities. He also opined that even though the Supreme Court had ruled that deportations on security grounds are not unlawful, such deportations would be condemned by the international community. Little was left then of the original proposal except the idea of expelling family members who had been involved in the bombers' activities from the West Bank to Gaza. And this is what the authorities decided to do. They issued an order allowing them to require West Bank residents to live in Gaza and argued that this was a legitimate form of "assigned residence" expressly permitted under Article 78 of Geneva Convention IV. The Supreme Court upheld the measure but ruled that it could only be used when the evidence of support for terrorist activities by the family member targeted by the order was strong. It found that in two of the cases before the Court the evidence met this test, but that in the third it did not (*Ajuri* case, 2002).

When it comes to general restrictions on freedom of movement, the Supreme Court has been extremely reluctant to interfere with the authorities. Thus, for example, it refused to interfere with severe restrictions on public access to stores in Beit Hadassah in Hebron after the building had been taken over by Israeli settlers (*Al Natashe* case, 1981; *Kawasme* case, 1980; *Zalum* case, 1986); with a nightly curfew that was imposed in Gaza during the first *intifada* (*Shawe*, 1990); and in cases in which Palestinians complained of severe restrictions on their right of movement to and from their towns or villages (*Alayona* case, 2003; *Al Adra* case, 2001; *Al Arja* case, 2003).

The pattern that emerges from the Supreme Court's decisions in security matters is quite clear. The Court has generally refused to interfere with the power of the authorities to employ the measures it chooses even when there are persuasive arguments that the measures are incompatible with international law. The issues of deportations and house demolitions are the most glaring examples. The Court's approach on these issues has not brought it much credit. On the other hand, the Court has on occasion interfered in the use of the measure in a particular case. And in one case, the Court did prohibit a practice adopted by the military despite the claim that it helped saved lives. This was the case of "prior warnings," in which the Court held that it was unlawful for the military to ask neighbors of Palestinians who were about to be arrested to go to their house in order to inform them of the impending arrest (*Adallah* case, 2005).

It is not difficult to find reasons for the Court's reticence in security matters. Domestic courts are generally reluctant to interfere with the discretion of the executive branch of government in security matters, especially in times of crisis. The Supreme Court of Israel is under attack from right-wing elements in the country despite its record on matters related to the OT. One can imagine what would have been the situation if the Court had been more activist in its approach. Nevertheless, the Court's attitude on security matters provides support for out main thesis: the Palestinians are subjected to the full force of occupation law. Measures that are inconceivable in Israel itself (although not in East Jerusalem, which, for these purposes, is still regarded by the authorities as part of the OT) are employed in the OT. Values that have become an integral part of Israel's legal system are abandoned when it comes to security threats from Palestinian residents of the OT.

CONCLUSIONS

What effect have the legal manipulations described in this chapter had on Israel's legal system? It is difficult to answer this question if one accepts its basic premise—that there are two separate legal systems that operate side by side. It seems to me, however, that this premise must be challenged. Rather than having two separate legal systems, since the occupation began Israel has in fact had one schizophrenic legal system. When the system is applied in Israel proper, it has a fairly liberal character and employs the rhetoric of rule of law, human rights, and democratic values. When it is applied to the Palestinians in the OT, its character has little connection to the rule of law, only minimal connection to human rights, and no connection to democratic values. It allows the Supreme Court to ignore moral distress and legal values in order to legitimize repressive measures that the authorities claim are needed to protect the public.

The legal elites like to maintain a clear separation between these two faces of the system even though they are applied by the same Supreme Court, whose precedents provide the definitive statement of law in Israel. They regard "OT law" as a temporary constraint. But in truth, after 45 years of occupation the two faces of the system cannot be separated. Just as the whole area of Mandatory Palestine (Israel and the OT) must be seen as the area of control of the State of Israel (Azoulay & Ophir, 2008), the whole legal system that applies in this area must be seen as one.

In deciding on the legality of the route of the separation barrier, the Court has taken the position that the lawfulness in international law of Israeli settlements on the West Bank is irrelevant, even though the barrier's route in many segments was determined by the existence of settlements. This did not stop the Court from relying on the powers of the military commander under international law to requisition the land needed for the barrier. Hence, in the *Beit Sourik* case the Court declared:

> Regarding the central question raised before us, our opinion is that the military commander is authorized—by the international law applicable to an area under belligerent occupation—to take possession of land, if this is necessary for the needs of the army: articles 23(g) and 52 of the Hague Convention; article 53 of the Fourth Geneva Convention. (*Beit Sourik* case, 2004, p. 831)

The approach of the Court in this and subsequent separation barrier cases—ignoring the law of occupation when it comes to settlements but using this same law to legitimize violating the rights of Palestinians—provides a perfect illustration of the theme of this chapter. Rather than serving as the legal regime that regulates the conduct of an occupying power that has temporary control over territory conquered in the course of a war, the law of belligerent occupation is used as a convenient system of control over the population in the territory, enabling the authorities to exploit this regime in order to further its political purposes.

Soon after the occupation began, Professor Yehuda Blum argued that the territories should not be regarded as occupied, although the residents should enjoy the benefits of the law of occupation (Blum, 1968). Ostensibly, Blum's view was rejected since, as we have seen, the Supreme Court has ruled time and again that the legal regime that applies in the OT is that of belligerent occupation. In fact, however, the regime created resembles that proposed by Blum. A dichotomy has been forged between the status of the territory itself and that of its Palestinian residents. The territory is not regarded as occupied; the Palestinians are subject to occupation law. Rather than protecting their rights, however, this regime is used to justify serious infringements on those rights. Belligerent occupation law has become no more than a convenient legal system of control over a population that has no political rights in the state that controls them.

In Israel the ethos of law and the rule of law are still strong. Given this ethos, it would have been inconceivable to admit that the authorities have plundered the OT by systematically exploiting its resources for the benefit of Israelis rather than their Palestinian residents. Thus, legal mechanisms have been found to justify all forms of plunder, exploitation, and control.

How unique is the Israeli system of occupation? In the post–World War II era there have been no other cases of long-term occupation of territory by democratic states. Hence, if one takes other formal situations of occupation as a measure, it is not possible to answer this question. However, if we ignore the formal legal and political framework and place control over the OT in a wider context, we can find some interesting parallels. In his seminal work *Conquest* (2008), historian David Day describes how societies overwhelm others. The mechanisms he describes include many of the policies and practices of Israel in the OT: making a legal claim to the territory, peopling it with its own citizens, and building a wall to prevent infiltration of residents of the conquered territory. Most telling when it comes to the subject of this chapter—the legal regime applied and the way law is used to legitimize taking of land and other actions—is the way Day describes the modus operandi of such societies:

> Although the dispossession of others is mostly driven by greed, such a motive is rarely regarded as sufficient justification for robbing people of their land. It is usually seen as necessary to dress up the dispossessing urge in a more respectable garb that could allow those doing the dispossession to feel legally and morally justified in their actions. (Day, 2008, p. 71)

NOTES

1. This order relates to the West Bank. A similar order was promulgated relating to Gaza and Northern Sinai, which was in Israeli hands until handed over to Egypt under the terms of the Peace Treaty between the two countries.
2. Speaking in the *Knesset* three weeks after issue of the said order, Minister of Justice Yaakov Shimshon Shapira spoke of the liberation of main parts of the Land of Israel from the burden of foreigners and the legal outlook of the State of Israel that the law, jurisdiction and administration of the state applies to parts of the Land of Israel that are in actual fact in its sphere of sovereignty: (27.6.67) 49 *Divrei Haknesset* 2420.
3. In a dictum in one case Justice Witkon did, however, express the unequivocal opinion that "it is a mistake to think ... that the Geneva Convention does not apply to Judea and Samaria." (*Elon Moreh* case, 1979, p. 29).
4. Thus, article 43 of the Hague Regulations Respecting the Laws and Customs of Law on Land, 1907, regarded as the "mini-constitution" of belligerent occupation law, speaks of the "authority of the *legitimate* power having in fact passed into the hands of the occupant ..." (emphasis added).
5. The arguments that establishment of settlements is illegal does not rest solely on the provision in article 49 (6) of Geneva Convention IV. For a concise presentation of the arguments see Program on Humanitarian Policy and Conflict Research 2009.
6. Government property is defined in the order and includes any property that belongs to the Hashemite Kingdom of Jordan or to any corporation in which the said kingdom has rights.
7. The Ottoman Land Law that was in force on the West Bank when the IDF entered in 1967 distinguishes between five categories of land: *mulk, miri,*

mukafa, *mawat* and *matrouk*. (Zamir, 1985). Rights by prescription can only be acquired in *miri* land, in which nominal ownership remains in perpetuity in the hands of the sultan. All land in which there was no proof of ownership by a *koushan* or registration was to be regarded as state land, unless it was *miri* land in which rights had been acquired through prescription. Albeck(1985), p. 8

8. The requirement of possession and cultivation for ten years is based on article 78 of the Ottoman Land Law. According to this provision, if a person has been in possession of and has cultivated *miri* land for a period of ten years, he or she is entitled to demand that the land be registered in his or her name.
9. For a comprehensive study of the land taken for settlements see B'Tselem (2002b).
10. In interpreting article 78 of the Ottoman Land Law, which enables one to gain title by cultivation of *miri* land for ten years, how does one treat cultivation of land which is partly cultivatable and partly not? During the British Mandatory period the answer was based on "reasonable cultivation." While this interpretation was adopted in an early decision of a military appeals committee, the appeals committees later adopted the interpretation that the authorities and courts had taken in Israel itself in the early nineteen fifties according to which the person who claimed title had to show that at least 50% of the land had been cultivated. This "50% rule" obviously greatly favors the government. It means that if a person held a large tract of land, patches of which were cultivatable, but the majority of which was not cultivatable, he would only gain title to the patches that he had cultivated, even if he made use of the other parts of the land for such purposes as building a house.
11. The argument in this case against the change in local law was not based on adoption of the "50% rule," but on removal of land cases from the local courts and handing jurisdiction to the military appeals committees. Justice Shamgar held that this did not effect a change in the substantive law.
12. When seen in the context of its general jurisprudence relating to standing, the above attitude of the Court is rather remarkable. According to this general jurisprudence, the Court will decide on issues relating to legality of government action, even when the petitioner has no direct and personal interest in that action, if this is required in order to ensure the rule of law. The philosophy behind this jurisprudence is that the rule of law cannot be guaranteed without judicial review. Apparently, ensuring the rule of law is not required when the issue is establishment of settlements.
13. A number of official reports have complained about the lack of law enforcement against Israelis resident on the West Bank. See Karp report, 1984; Sasson Report, 2005. Also see B'Tselem, 2002a; B'Tselem, 2002c. .
14. According to the Law for the Extension of Emergency Regulations, 1967, the courts in Israel have the jurisdiction to try Israeli citizens charged with crimes committed in the OT. While such citizens are also subject to the jurisdiction of the military courts in practice they are always tried before the courts in Israel,

whereas Palestinians charged with the same or similar offences are tried before the military courts.
15. The main towns on the Israeli side of the Green Line are Maccabim, Reut and Modi'in, now united in one common municipal authority. On the other side of the Green Line lie the settlements Mattityahu, Modi'in Elite and Hashmonaim.
16. Two documents in government archives points clearly to the connection between the decision to build the road and the settlement policy. The one is an undated memorandum from the period of Shimon Peres as minister of defense (1974–77) which mentions a new highway to Jerusalem from the Lod area that would largely follow the old Latrun—Ramallah road: Settlement plan for Judea and Samaria areas ,1976; the other is a memorandum of a meeting of the ministerial committee on settlement of June 29, 1976, in which the committee was informed of a government decision to build a new highway to Jerusalem connecting Horon to Ataraot: *Memorandum of a meeting of the ministerial committee on settlement of June 29, 1976*
17. The Court was not prepared to assume that the highway under review was being built solely for the benefit of the local population. It stated: "One must assume that the security and military authorities who undertook the task of planning and implementing this network of highways, the cost of which reaches huge sums, did not do so only in order to ease civilian transport and ecology, and that the main consideration from their point of view was military." Tabeeb case (1981), p. 634. The Court added that the fact that the highway would serve a planned settlement was "minor and secondary." Ibid., p. 635.

REFERENCES

Books and Articles

Agora. (2005). ICJ advisory opinion on construction of a wall in the occupied Palestinian territory. *American Journal of International Law, 99*(1), 1–141.

Albeck, P. (1985). *Lands in Judea and Samaria*. Tel Aviv-Jaffa: District Committee of Israel Bar Association.

Amit-Kohn, U., Jarach, R., Glick, C. B., & Biton, N.., (1993). *Israel, the "intifada" and the rule of law*. Tel-Aviv: Israel Ministry of Defense Publications.

Azoulay, A., & Ophir, A. (2008). *This regime which is not one: Occupation and democracy between the sea and the river*. Tel Aviv: Resling.

Bar-Yaacov, N. (1988). The applicability of the laws of war to Judea and Samaria (the West Bank) and to the Gaza Strip. *Israel Law Review, 24*, 485–506.

Benvenisti, E. (1993). *The international law of occupation*. Princeton, NJ: Princeton University Press.

Benvenisti, M. (1984). *The West Bank Data Project: A survey of Israel's policies*. Washington, DC: American Enterprise Institute.

Blum, Y. (1968). The missing reversioner: Reflections on the status of Judea and Samaria. *Israel Law Review, 3*, 279–301.

Day, D. (2008). *Conquest: How societies overwhelm others.* Oxford: Oxford University Press.

Dinstein, Y. (1988). Deportations from occupied territories. *Tel Aviv University Law Review, 13*, 403–416.

Dinstein, Y. (2009). *The international law of belligerent occupation.* Cambridge: Cambridge University Press.

Eldar, A., & Zartal, I. (2004). *Adonei ha'aretz (Lords of the land).* Jerusalem: Rubin Mass.

Forman, G. (2009). A tale of two regions: Diffusion of the Israeli "50% Rule" from the Galilee to the occupied West Bank. *Law and Social Inquiry, 34*(3), 671–711.

Gordon, N. (2008). *Israel's occupation.* Berkeley: University of California Press.

Gorenberg, G. (2006). *The accidental empire: Israel and the birth of the settlements, 1967–1977.* New York: Times Books.

Greenstein, R. (2006). Citizenship and political integration: Can we draw lessons from the rise and demise of apartheid? *Mishpat Umimshal, 10*, 117–150.

Israel Law Review, 38(1–2), 2005, special double issue: Domestic and international judicial review of the construction of the separation barrier.

Kretzmer, D. (2002). *The occupation of Justice: The Supreme Court of Israel and the Occupied Territories.* Albany: State University of New York Press.

Paz-Fuchs, A., & Ronen, Y. (in press*).* Occupational hazards: Labor law in the occupied territories. *Berkeley Journal of International Law, 30*(2).

Rubinstein, A. (1988). The changing status of the "Territories" (West Bank and Gaza): From escrow to legal mongrel. *Tel Aviv Studies in Law, 8*, 59–80.

Shalev, A. (1990). *The intifada: Causes and effects.* Tel Aviv: Papyrus.

Shamgar, M. (1971). The observance of international law in administered territories. *Israel Yearbook on Human Rights, 1*, 262–271.

Zamir, E. (1985). *State land in Judea and Samaria—Legal survey.* Jerusalem: Jerusalem Institute for Israel Studies.

Judicial Decisions

Abu Ita v. IDF Commander in Judea and Samaria (Vat case), HCJ 69/81 (1981) 37 PD II 197.

Abu Khelou v. Government of Israel (Rafah case), HCJ 302, 306/72 (1972) 2 PD II 169.

Abu Tzefia v. Minister of Defence, HCJ 2150/07, 2009 Dinim 130, 950.

Adallah v. Officer Commanding Central Command, HCJ 3799/02, 2005 Dinim 61, 305.

Afu v. IDF Commander on West Bank, HCJ 785/87 (1987) 42 PD II 4.

Ajuri v. IDF Commander in Judea and Samaria, HCJ 7015/02 (2002) 56 PD VI 352.

Al Adra v. ID Commander in Judea and Samaria, HCJ 32/01 (2001), available at http://elyon1.court.gov.il/verdictssearch/HebrewVerdictsSearch.aspx.

Al Arja v. IDF Commander in Judea and Samaria, HCJ 2410/03 (2003), available at http://elyon1.court.gov.il/verdictssearch/HebrewVerdictsSearch.aspx

Al Natashe v. Minister of Defense, HCJ 175/81 (1981) 35 PD III 361.
Alayona v. IDF Commander in Judea and Samaria, HCJ 2847/03 (2003), Retrieved May 14, 2012, from http://elyon1.court.gov.il/files/03/470/028/G04/03028470.g04.pdf
Al-Naazer v. IDF Commander in Judea and Samaria, HCJ 285/81 (1981) 36 PD I 701.
Alram Local Council v. Government of Israel, HCJ 5488/04, 2006 Dinim Elyon 69, 964.
Amira v. Ministry of Defense, HCJ 258/79 (1979) 34 PD I 90.
Armed Activities on the Territory of the Congo (Democratic Republic of the Congo v. Uganda), Judgment, I.C.J. Reports 2005, p. 168.
Ayreib v. Appeals Committee, HCJ 277/84 (1984) 40 PD II 57.
Ayyub v. Minister of Defense (Beth El case), HCJ 606, 610/78 (1978) 33 PD II 113.
Bargil v. Government of Israel, HCJ 4481/91 (1991) 47 PD IV 210.
Beit Sourik Local Council v. Government of Israel, HCJ 2056/04 (2004) 58 PD V 807.
Bir Nabala Local Council v. Government of Israel, HCJ 4289/05, 2006 Dinim Elyon 66, 1249.
Christian Society for the Holy Places v. Minister of Defense, HCJ 337/71 (1971) 26 PD I 574.
Dajalis v. IDF Commander on West Bank, HCJ 698/85 (1985) 40 PD II 42.
Dweikat v. Government of Israel (Elon Moreh case), HCJ 390/79, (1979) 34 PD I 1.
Electricity Corporation for East Jerusalem v. Minister of Defense, HCJ 256/72 (1972) 27 PD I 124.
Gaza Beach Regional Council v. Knesset of Israel, HCJ 1661/05 (2005) 59 PD II 481.
Halua v. Prime Minister, HCJ 6451/04 (2004), 2006 Dinim Elyon (26) 329.
I'ad v. IDF Commander, HCJ 3125/98 (1998), 58 PD II 913.
Jamait Ascan v. IDF Commander in Judea and Samara, HCJ 393/82 (1983) 37 PD IV 785.
Kav Le'oved v. National Labour Court, HCJ 5666/03, 2007 Takdin-Elyon (4) 109.
Kawasme v. Minister of Defense, HCJ 698/80 (1980) 35 PD I 617.
Kawasmi v. IDF Commander in Judea and Samaria, HCJ 7007/03, 2005 Dinim-Elyon (26) 1497.
Khamri v. IDF Commander in Judea and Samaria, HCJ 361/82 (1982), 36 PD III 439.
Kiryat Arba Local Council v. Government of Israel, HCJ 4400/92 (1992), 48 PD V 587.
Legal Consequences of the Construction of a Wall in the Occupied Palestinian Territory, Advisory Opinion, I.C.J. Reports 2004, p. 136.
Mara'abe v. Prime Minister of Israel, HCJ 7957/04 (2004) 60 PD II 477.
Saada v. Officer Commanding the Home Front, HCJ 6288/03 (2003), 48 PD II 289.
Shawe v. IDF Commander in Gaza, HCJ 1113/90 (1990) 44 PD IV 590.
Tabeeb v. Minister of Defense, HCJ 202/81 (1981) 36 PD II 622.
Turkmahn v. Minister of Defense, HCJ 5510/92 (1993) 48 PD I 217.
Yanon v. Kra'an, C.A. 1432/03 (2003) 49 PD I 345.
Zalum v. IDF Commander on West Bank, HCJ 372/86 (1986) 41 PD I 528.

Legislation

Law for Extension of Emergency Regulations (Judea, Samaria and Gaza—Jurisdiction Over Offences and Legal Assistance), 1967.

Order Relating to Administration of Municipal Councils (Judea and Samaria) (No. 892), 1982.
Order Relating to Administration of Regional Councils (Judea and Samaria) (No. 783), 1979.
Order Relating to Government Property (Area of Judea and Samaria) (No. 59), 1967.
Proclamation Regarding the Taking of Power by I.D.F (June 7, 1967).
Security Provisions Order (West Bank, 1967).

Reports and Other Sources

49 *Divrei Haknesset* 2420 (June 27, 1967).
ACRI (2010). *Route 443: Fact sheet and timeline*. Retrieved May 13, 2012, from http://www.acri.org.il/en/2010/05/25/route-443-fact-sheet-and-timeline/
Aloni, S. (2007, January 8). Yes, there is apartheid in Israel. *Counter-Punch*. Retrieved May 12, 2012, from http://www.counterpunch.org/2007/01/08/yes-there-is-apartheid-in-israel/
B'Tselem. (2002a). *Foreseen but not prevented: The Israeli law enforcement authorities handling of settler attacks on olive harvesters* (Case Study No. 16). Retrieved May 14, 2012, from http://www.btselem.org/sites/default/files2/publication/200211_olive_harvest_Eng.pdf
B'Tselem. (2002b). *Land grab: Israel's settlement policy in the West Bank*. Retrieved May 14, 2012, from http://www.btselem.org/English/Publications/Summaries/200205_Land_Grab.asp
B'Tselem. (2002c). *Standing idly by: Non-enforcement of the law on settlers: Hebron, 26–28 July 2002* (Case Study No. 15). Retrieved May 14, 2012, from http://www.btselem.org/download/200208_standing_idly_by_Eng.pdf
B'Tselem. (2011). *The mass deporation of 1992*. Retrieved May 13, 2011, from http://www.btselem.org/deportation/1992_mass_deportation
Declaration of Principles on Interim Self-Government Arrangements, September 13, 1993, 32 ILM 1525 (1993).
Drobles, M. (1980). *Settlement in Judea and Samaria: Policy and Planning*. Jerusalem: WZO Settlement Division.
Farsakh, L. (2003, November). Israel—an apartheid state? *Le Monde diplomatique*, English edition. Retrieved May 14, 2012, from
mondediplo.com/2003/11/04apartheid
Harel, A. (2005, February 17). Committee appointed by Chief of Staff: Stop demolishing houses of terrorists—it causes more harm than benefit. *Haaretz*
Israeli-Palestinian interim agreement on the West Bank and the Gaza Strip. (1995, September 28). 36 ILM 551 (1997).
Karp report: An Israeli government inquiry into settler violence against Palestinians on the West Bank. (1984). Washington, DC: Institute for Palestine Studies.
Macintyre, D. (2006, March 11). Israelis were warned on illegality of settlements in 1967 memo. *Independent*. Retrieved May 14, 2012, from http://www.

independent.co.uk/news/world/middle-east/israelis-were-warned-on-illegality-of-settlements-in-1967-memo-469443.html

Master Plan for Settlement in Judea and Samaria and Development Plan for the Area for the Years 1983–1986. (1983). Prepared by the Planning Team for Judea and Samaria of the Settlement Division of the WZO in Association with the Ministry of Agriculture.

Memorandum of a meeting of the ministerial committee on settlement of June 29, 1976. ( ). IDF Archive, 1510/89/498/55. Retrieved May 14, 2012, from http://southjerusalem.com/wp-content/uploads/2008/09/1976-june-29-settlement-committee-meeting-including-decision-to-build-road-to-northern-jerusalem.pdf

Meron, T. (1967, September). *Legal opinion on civilian settlement in the Occupied Territories*. Retrieved May 14, 2012, from http://southjerusalem.com/wp-content/uploads/2008/09/theodor-meron-legal-opinion-on-civilian-settlement-in-the-occupied-territories-september-1967.pdf

Ministry of Foreign Affairs (MFA). *Israeli settlements and international law*. (2001, May). Retrieved June 21, 2012 from http://www.mfa.gov.il/mfa/peace%20process/guide%20to%20the%20peace%20process/israeli%20settlements%20and%20international%20law

Opinion on unauthorized outposts presented to Prime Minister Ariel Sharon by Advocate Talia Sasson (Sasson Report). (2005). Retrieved May 14, 2012, from www.pmo.gov.il/NR/rdonlyres/0A0FBE3C-C741–46A6–8CB5-F6CDC042465D/0/sasson2.pdf

Program on humanitarian policy and conflict research, Harvard University. (2009). *International humanitarian law and the settlements, policy brief undated and reissued*. Retrieved May 14, 2012, from http://opt.ihlresearch.org/_data/n_0013/resources/live/briefing9999.pdf

Settlement plan for Judea and Samaria areas (1976). IDF Archive, 1510/89/498/89, Retrieved May 14, 2012, from http://southjerusalem.com/wp-content/uploads/2008/09/1976-spring-settlement-proposal-including-road-from-latrun-to-northern-jerusalem.pdf

UNGA Resolution 64/93 of December 10. 2009.

UNGA Resolution 65/104 of December 10, 2010.

UNSC Resolution 446 of March 22, 1979.

UNSC Resolution 452 of July 20, 1979.

UNSC Resolution 465 of March 1, 1980.

CHAPTER 2

Is There a Controversy Concerning the Morality of the Occupation and Its Implications?[1]

Marcelo Dascal

> Even conquerors who excelled in oppression, well beyond what Moshe Dayan is capable of doing, sat on thorns and scorpions in most conquered places until they were eradicated. Not to mention the total moral destruction prolonged occupation inflicts on the occupier. Even inevitable occupation is a corrupting occupation.
> —Amos Oz, *Davar*, August 22, 1967.

INTRODUCTION

Arguably, the title question of this chapter might be read as a rhetorical question, that is, as a way of asserting that the answer is obvious and there can be no doubt about it. Thus interpreted, those who "ask" this question simply affirm emphatically that the answer is "No," meaning that there is no room for controversy concerning the speaker's judgment of the morality of Israel's occupation of the Palestinian territories and its implications. When they ask the rhetorical question of the title, these speakers are not making a factual statement about the actual existence of disagreement or debate about the issue in question. They are, rather, ruling out the very possibility that their position on the topic is incorrect and therefore liable to controversy. Their reasons for this exclusion may differ, as do the kind of support and the content of the belief that their rhetorical question expresses. Whatever their reasons, however, they provide—from their point of view—sufficient evidence for assuring the indisputability of the belief they hold, hence its noncontroversial character.

For example, Palestinians living in the occupied territories may be absolutely convinced that the occupation and its implications are unquestionably immoral because of the inhuman suffering they cause them. Muslims living elsewhere may hold the same belief due to empathy and religious solidarity with their brothers and sisters in faith. Left-wing political activists may derive their staunch belief in the immorality of the occupation from their allegiance to ideological principles. Orthodox Jewish settlers in the territories may draw their certainty of the morality of their occupying actions from religious obligations and a sense of mission, while nonreligious settlers may ground the same belief on security reasons. Some sectors of the Israeli Jewish population may condemn the immorality of the occupation due to its violation of basic human rights, while other segments may do so due to what they take to be the occupation's role in the deterioration of morality in Israel. Regardless of how these groups ground their beliefs, and regardless of the fact that members of other groups hold opposite beliefs based on other reasons, the beliefs of each of them are—in the view of those who hold them—invulnerable to questioning.

Fortunately, the rhetorical interpretation of our title is not the only possible one. The title can also be read literally, that is, as a real interrogation about possible and factual controversies on the relationship between morality and occupation. As such, rather than limiting itself to repeating the assertion of an established, entrenched belief, the title can express an interest in the reasons supporting that assertion, in the evidence justifying the corresponding belief, in the counterarguments to one's position that one should or might be prepared to face in order to defend one's belief, and in opposing beliefs and their justifications, as well as alternatives to one's own position as well as the opponent's.

If read in this way, the title indicates that the main concern of the chapter is to elucidate the nature of the interrelation between morality and occupation. It also suggests that such an elucidation can benefit significantly from the identification and careful examination of controversies focusing on this interrelation. Moreover, it leaves open the possibility that the implications it mentions are not one-way causal relations, but perhaps two-way interactions. Furthermore, controversies reveal not only the strengths and weaknesses of the concepts and positions in confrontation, but also their complexity and flexibility, leading to a better understanding and exploration of what is at stake. This, in turn, allows for the emergence of hybrid concepts and alternatives resulting from the combination of elements from the polar positions. Together, the features briefly mentioned amount to an open-ended, innovative, multiperspective and multidisciplinary approach that might also pave the way for advancing toward a resolution to a conflict that has been described as "an ostensibly intractable ethno-national conflict" (Rouhana & Bar-Tal, 1998, p. 761). In the following sections, details of this approach will be presented and their implications discussed.

Although focusing on the Israeli occupation of the Palestinian territories as *the* case study for a critical analysis, and although drawing practical and moral conclusions that suggest innovative approaches to the resolution of the Palestinian-Israeli conflict derived from that occupation, this chapter is more ambitious. The considerations here proposed and the conclusions that can be drawn from an analysis that takes them into account are broad enough in scope, in philosophical grounding, and in historical evidence to apply to a wide variety of conflicts and circumstances and eventually help their resolution.

Pragmatic and moral issues, as well as controversies between the contenders on virtually all such issues, are *constitutive* components of those political conflicts that lead to occupation. The attempt by the contenders to deal separately with the practical and moral aspects of the conflict, albeit in different ways, underlies the different kinds of justification for the occupation, as well as for the resolution of the conflict, by each side: whereas one of them—usually the occupied side—emphasizes the moral damage and demands the full-fledged restoration of its rights as a sine qua non condition for settling the conflict, the other—usually the occupier side—tends to focus on a narrow range of its own moral rights and overlooks in general the significance of the moral issues in the conflict, particularly as regards the blatant flaws in its own moral behavior; instead, the occupier highlights the solution of the territorial and other pragmatic problems as the only fundamental requirements for the settlement of the conflict.[2] The consequences of the occupation, for both sides, are not only pragmatic but also moral: they deepen and expand the animosities between the adversaries through their daily contact; they reinforce the most heinous features of the stereotypic perception of each other; and they reciprocally delegitimize their moral, intellectual, and cultural value as human beings. As a result, a double-standard morality emerges, which justifies humiliation and violence from each side vis-à-vis the other and renders the problematic relationship between them more difficult—if at all possible—to overcome in the effort to resolve the conflict. Moreover, emphasizing the "pragmatic" approach at the expense of the overall moral issues prevents public debate of the latter and ultimately leads to a vicious circle of self-righteousness, which turns out to be counterproductive at the pragmatic level itself.

The "pragma-morality" here proposed, instead of dismissing the harmful factors mentioned above and keeping the pragmatic and moral components of a conflict separated, acknowledges their interdependence and seeks to create a framework wherein their interaction leads to a radical modification of the presumptions that each of them relies upon. Recent work in ethics, discussed in this chapter, suggests a model that takes into account the role of context in shaping a community's moral presumptions. Lists of moral commandments or rights are thus no longer the absolute standards of morality to be followed. The "other," therefore, can and must now be respected and appreciated not only by reference to their universalistic virtues, but also their particularistic ones, without fear of slipping down to relativism. If this approach to morality is employed in the pragmatic setting of a negotiations table, coupled with a framework of argumentative debate that does not privilege either the *dispute model*, where the aim is victory, or the *discussion model*, where one side alone possesses the truth, but rather adopts a *controversy model*, where the contenders are aware of each other's needs and presumptions, are willing to make reasonable concessions, and argue their cases with the sole aim of rationally persuading the opponent, then perhaps many of the violent and apparently unsolvable conflicts that plague the planet today will have a reliable pattern to follow toward their resolution. Hopefully, even the "intractable" Israeli-Palestinian conflict may move toward a solution.

BETWEEN PRAGMATIC AND MORAL CONSIDERATIONS

Most of the Israeli, Palestinian, and international public discourse on the Israeli-Palestinian conflict that is not easily recognizable as part of the ongoing psychological warfare between the parties and their allies deals in one way or another with the problem of finding a nonviolent way to end this prolonged conflict or at least reduce the violence of its outbursts. Although moral issues occasionally arise in this "conflict resolution-" and "conflict management"-oriented discourse, they rarely constitute its focus. Presumably this is the case because the parties believe that their positions on moral matters are so divergent that it is impossible to bridge the gap between them. Furthermore, these moral issues tend to be perceived by both parties not only as not directly relevant to the pressing pragmatic issues (e.g., creating fruitful negotiation, determining the agenda, devising plans acceptable to both sides, identifying and overcoming unnecessary clashes that create tension, improving the living conditions of the population in the occupied areas), but even as diverting attention to controversial claims that, unlike urgent pragmatic questions, can be postponed due to their speculative and ultimately irresolvable nature (e.g., Can a just solution satisfying both sides be found? Is reconciliation possible after so much suffering caused to both populations?). As a result, a sharp dissociation between the pragmatic and moral aspects of the conflict is established and generally accepted, as if they were indeed entirely disconnected. In this section I will argue that this is a grave mistake, whose consequences can no longer be overlooked.

On the face of it, the pragmatic/moral dissociation seems to be justified as far as the occupation is concerned. An occupation is primarily an anomalous military, geographic, humanitarian, and political situation that requires, first and foremost, appropriate practical measures in these domains for the restoration of normality. Though immediate moral needs must be taken into account in choosing and implementing such measures in the short run, in the long run it is strategic rather than moral principles that are considered to be decisive in tackling successfully the causes of the malady—causes that are themselves understood as essentially pragmatic, that is, as serving the parties' or their mentors' interests.

The interest-driven pragmatic-strategic approach has accompanied the Israeli-Palestinian conflict from its beginning. Consider the Palestine Partition Plan approved by the UN General Assembly in November 1947. Although undoubtedly influenced by the effects of the recently ended World War II, especially by the moral consideration of the Holocaust and the Jewish survivors' fate, the General Assembly translated these moral concerns into political, territorial, economic, and stability terms. Nevertheless, the translation proved to be insufficient in capturing the moral complexity of the problem that the General Assembly was trying to solve. According to the Palestinians and part of the Jewish Left, the rights of the Arab majority in Palestine were not given due weight; the foreseeable consequences of the inevitable military clashes between Jews and Arabs were not fully taken into account; and the long-term moral implications of the pragmatic decision adopted were overlooked and, rather than disappearing over time, are with us today. Indeed, the parties themselves relegated the moral dimension to a secondary level. On the political level, the Palestinians rejected the Partition Plan, arguing that it was unjust; the Jewish leadership accepted it, although in their view too it was unjust, and in May 1948 they declared the establishment of the State of Israel. The Palestinians, along with the Arab states, launched a military campaign against the newborn State of Israel, believing this would succeed in restoring their alleged rights to the whole land. In the course of the war Israel expanded the territory assigned to it by the Partition Plan, destroyed Palestinian villages, caused a large number of Palestinians to flee, prevented their return after the cease-fire, and submitted the remaining Palestinian population to military rule for several years. The occupation was thus launched two decades before the Six Day War. Ever since 1948, finding a solution to the practical and political problems concerned with the management of the occupation has monopolized the attention of the Israeli government, and that of the Palestinian leaders, and has taken up a large share of the public discourse. The moral issues were largely marginalized, and only recently have a number of Palestinians and Israelis begun to admit their mistake in not having realized earlier the harm caused to both sides by this distorted order of priorities and the urgent need to alter it.[3]

Since the moral issues are at least as important for the Palestinians as the territorial ones, from 1949 to 1967 Israel avoided discussing both the former and the latter, sticking to the purely pragmatic territorial arrangements of the 1949 cease-fire and taking advantage of the fact that the Palestinians sternly refused to acknowledge their 1948 mistake. Israelis' readiness to view the occupied territory as a negotiable asset in peace negotiations emerged only in the wake of the Six Day War. It became a main issue in the current conflict resolution agenda only after the Palestinians realized that, at the military level, they were not capable of defeating Israel. Two powerful pragmatic obstacles were nonetheless raised against the actual use of this asset. First, a long period elapsed before the two sides recognized each other and began to negotiate. Second, evacuation of the Israeli settlements in the West Bank occupied territories, erected with the approval of various Israeli governments, became over time virtually impossible. This major practical obstacle is sustained by an even stronger one, allegedly grounded in the moral dimension: the settlers' religious conviction that the "Land of Israel," especially Judaea and Samaria, is God's legacy to the Jewish people and must be retained and colonized by believers as an unquestionable religious commandment. To this must be added, on both sides, the pragmatic-religious issue of the sacred city of Jerusalem and, on the Palestinian side, the moral issue of the right of return of the Palestinian refugees. The Israelis see this right as equivalent to dismantling the Jewish state, whose existence is for the Jews an equally fundamental moral right. This combination of pragmatic and moral obstacles prevents or at least delays indefinitely the peaceful withdrawal of Israeli forces and the end of the occupation, which is crucial for the end of the conflict.

It is perhaps this discouraging conclusion that led the Zionist Left to endorse the dissociation of the moral and pragmatic factors as the only hope for a negotiated solution. After serious attempts to pursue a strand of the failed Taba official negotiations in Geneva (2000)—namely, the formulation by the Zionist Left together with their Palestinian counterparts of a shared narrative concerning the 1948 events that led to the creation of the Palestinian refugee problem—the hope of reaching an agreement on this crucial moral issue was abandoned. The Israeli leftists, as well as the Palestinian moderate pragmatists, opted for the dissociation model. They also admitted that it was wiser to set aside the two sides' irreconcilable positions on the key moral issues at stake and focus on feasible pragmatic moves, trusting that the success of such moves would at long last override the moral dissent.[4] In adopting this line, they were perhaps inspired by the success of the Egyptian-Israeli peace negotiations. Unfortunately, the Palestinian-Israeli conflict is not similar enough to the Israeli-Egyptian conflict for the latter to provide a model. The

Israeli-Egyptian conflict ultimately made room for a peace treaty by focusing exclusively on pragmatic territorial issues—except for Sadat's moving rhetorical appeal, "No more bloodshed!," which was certainly morally relevant for his listeners in the two countries that had suffered so much loss of life in several wars. However, the Israeli-Egyptian conflict was not *primarily* moral and could be successfully dealt with at the pragmatic level. This is hardly the case in the Israeli-Palestinian conflict, in which the occupation of the West Bank involves intense daily hardship and personal confrontation.

There is a further reason for questioning the moral/pragmatic dissociation either as corresponding to the facts or as offering a path toward a solution to the conflict and overcoming the implications of the occupation. The occupation has become after so many years a form of colonization. As such, it affects not only the physical and social environments where it takes place, but also—and quite deeply—the minds of the occupied as well as of the occupiers. Wherever morality is to be located, it is certainly part of our mental life. Throughout the world, although the most visible forms of political colonialism had generally disappeared by the end of the twentieth century, several of its consequences remain. Accordingly, postcolonial thought has focused on colonialism's most subtle and damaging components, particularly what has come to be known as the colonization of the mind, and on how to achieve the mind's "decolonization."[5]

The metaphor of "colonization of the mind" highlights the following characteristics: (1) an external source—the "colonizer"—intervenes in the mental sphere of a subject or a group of subjects—the "colonized"; (2) this intervention affects central aspects of the mind's structure, mode of operation, and contents; (3) its effects are prolonged and not easily eradicated; (4) there is a marked asymmetry of power between the parties involved; (5) the parties can be aware or unaware of their role of colonizer or colonized; and (6) both parties can participate in the process voluntarily or involuntarily. These characteristics are shared by various processes of mind colonization, regardless of whether or not they occur in sociopolitical situations that are literally categorized as colonial. Therefore, colonization of the mind may take place by means of social systems other than the colonial structure: for example, via the family, traditions, cultural practices, religion, science, language, fashion, ideology, political regimentation, the media, education, and other sources.

Consider education, for example. The Brazilian educator Paulo Freire has analyzed a typically mind-colonizing educational paradigm, which he suggestively dubbed the "banking" model. In this paradigm, a commodity (knowledge) is "deposited" by those who have it (the teachers) in the minds of those who don't have it (the pupils); the task of both is basically passive: that of the former to transmit "knowledge" and that of the latter to absorb it.[6] The banking model displays the characteristic *epistemic* nature of mind colonization. What grants the colonizer (in this case the teacher) the right to intervene in the pupil's mind, thereby colonizing it, is the fact that the former possesses *knowledge* and the latter lacks it. Likewise, moral authority rests on the alleged knowledge of the good by the parents, the preacher, the philosopher, or the ideologue.

In order for epistemic or moral authority to become an effective means of mind colonization, it must also obtain the support of power structures capable of transforming them into *social* authority and thereby ensuring its enforcement. These means range from displays of authority, through overrating some sources of epistemic or moral authority and devaluing others, up to appealing to overt and covert forms of discrimination, making use of socioeconomic reward or punishment, and sheer violent coercion. Needless to say, the Israeli occupation uses several of these means.

Of course, colonization of the mind does not always lead to acceptance and resignation by the colonized, although its rate of success has been surprisingly high throughout history. Frequently, the colonized react to the colonization of the mind by all-out rejection and resistance; this reaction is typical of the relatively recent decolonization movement. These two reactions are not the only ones, but they deserve special attention because, in spite of their contrast, they are widespread and equally instinctive or natural. Prima facie, the two reactions are radically opposed. The reaction of acceptance and resignation acknowledges the epistemic or moral superiority of the colonizer and adopts it as a principle of colonized belief formation. By contrast, the reaction of rejection and resistance denies the colonizer's alleged superiority, argues that it is groundless because it is based on a biased comparison procedure, and therefore refuses to adopt the presumption of epistemic or moral inferiority of the colonized. The former assumes that adopting the colonizer's conceptual framework is compatible with the preservation of the colonized identity. The latter stresses the incompatibility between these two attitudes, arguing that the adopted or adapted colonizer's mind ultimately expels the original mind of the colonized and thereby obliterates the latter's true or authentic identity. As far as the political consequences are concerned, the resigned acceptance reaction does not recognize that adopting the colonizer's beliefs and forms of thinking is one of the ways that colonizers enhance their control over the behavior of the colonized. By contrast, the resistance reaction denounces it as a means of gaining control over the will of the colonized, thus becoming a powerful tool of oppression, which must be combated.

Decolonization of the mind is not an easy task; it may require sustained effort whose success is far from guaranteed. Getting rid of the epistemic or moral authority implanted in one's mind by the colonizer may take many years, because one is often unaware of the beliefs, principles, and modes of thinking and acting acquired in the process of colonization. The colonization of minds is, therefore, an "invasion" that takes over our thinking apparatus and may survive long after political, social, or physical colonization is overcome. Insofar as freedom—especially freedom of thought and of decision—is a fundamental characteristic of morality (cf. Raz, 1986), mind colonization is clearly a violation of a basic moral right that is essential, among other things, to active membership in a democratic society.

The moral harm caused by mind colonization affects both the occupied and the occupiers.[7] The occupiers become believers in the beliefs they implant in the minds of the colonized—for example, the belief in their epistemic or moral superiority, the belief that truth and justice are always on their side, and the belief that this grants them a moral right to impose their beliefs on the colonized mind. Albert Memmi, who grew up in French-controlled Tunisia, describes vividly the mutual effects of colonization on both colonized and colonizer in his book *The Colonized and the Colonizer*, first published in French in 1957. He depicts the colonizer and colonized as living in the grip of a "colonial relationship" that chained them "into an implacable dependence, which molded their respective characters and dictated their culture" (Memmi, 1967, p. ix). Reaffirming his belief that colonialism is primarily an economic enterprise, with no "moral or cultural mission" whatsoever (ibid., p. xii), he stresses, however, that the "colonial system" determines and controls the mental attitudes of both colonized and colonizer. Nevertheless, disenchanted by the postcolonial reality he had witnessed nearly 50 years later, he did not realize that the destructive viruses of "corruption, tyranny, use of force, restriction of intellectual growth, adherence to long-standing tradition, violence toward women, xenophobia, and the persecution of minorities" (Memmi, 2006, p. xi) had been implanted in the colonized minds by the colonizers; these traits amounted to prolonged moral damage that should not have been expected to disappear with the latter's withdrawal.

Though the asymmetry of power of an occupation justifies attributing to the occupier most of the responsibility for the moral and mental effects of the occupation, one should not forget that the occupied side also has its share. This share is particularly important in the mind's colonization, which is not merely a function of the power relationship. Colonized and occupied minds are not prevented from developing their own perception and interpretation of the occupation; their own narrative of the events that led to it; their assessment of the consequences of actions performed by the occupied as well as by the occupiers; their evaluation of the two sides' responsibilities in the past, present, and future; and their expectations. From a moral point of view, the occupied can still make use of the "balance of reason" in forming their moral judgments, rather than attributing all the guilt to the occupier.

As we shall see below, the capacity to see things from two perspectives rather than only one is a fundamental characteristic of moral life. Sometimes the pragmatic and the moral are the two complementary and necessary perspectives. Had he realized this, Memmi might perhaps have concluded that the harm of colonization or occupation cannot be limited to its pragmatic effects or motives. Rather, pragmatic *and* moral factors are intertwined, rather than dissociated, in a pragmatism that has moral implications and an "effective morality" that has practical consequences. Understanding and taking into account the nature of this pragma-moral interaction and the human need to cope with it may help to explain the derailments of a conflict management conception that overlooks the role of one or the other of its basic components.

FOUNDATIONS OF PRAGMA-MORALITY

The term "pragmatic," which I have been employing so far in the broad sense of "practical" (i.e., doing rather than theorizing) as well as in the narrower sense of "realpolitik" (i.e., policy primarily concerned with material needs rather than with moral ideals), seems to imply a gap that dissociates what it refers to from morality. This gives the impression that pragma-morality is an oxymoron devoid of sense. In this section, I accept the burden of proof and intend to show that this is not the case. It will become apparent—I trust—that the combination of the concepts "pragmatic" and "moral" is far from being an artificial conceptual hybridization; to the contrary, pragma-morality draws its sense and value from the shared roots of its two components. In this respect, the hyphenated term introduced here is somewhat redundant. However, it does have value: by highlighting what the components share, it enables one to realize what connects rather than disconnects the pragmatic and the moral and to see the importance of this connection for our topic. I restrict the discussion to those facets of the connection that seem to me particularly important for our concerns.

It should not be surprising to find some of the shared roots in Aristotle, especially in the interrelations between *Nichomachean Ethics*, *Politics*, and *Rhetoric*. The link between politics and ethics is clearly established in the first of these books, where Aristotle claims that the aim of both is the good and that politics is a special application of ethics. What he has in mind is spelled out in *Politics* (Book I, Chap. 2), where he defines the *polis* as a community that, though originating in the urgent needs of life, has as its ultimate aim living well (in the moral sense). He further argues that a city is a community of families and villages whose end is a perfect and auto-sufficient life (*Politics*, Book III, Chap. 9), that is, accomplishing both its moral and subsistence purposes. The combination of the pragmatic and moral aims is further stressed by pointing out that the city is not merely a shared territory with the sole purposes of ensuring self-defense and promoting trade (ibid.). Communities of gregarious animals, Aristotle says, are "natural societies" capable of meeting pragmatic needs; by contrast, only human cities can also fulfill moral needs and are, therefore, full-fledged societies. The difference stems from the characteristics of human language, which "exists for expressing, besides pain and pleasure, what is beneficial and what is harmful, as well as the just and the unjust" and grants man the "exclusive sense of good and evil, of just and unjust" (*Politics*, Book I, Chap. 2).

Language also gives humans the ability to run their collective and individual affairs rationally thanks to the capacity of *deliberation* it affords.[8] Deliberation plays a key role in the three treatises mentioned above, where Aristotle applies this term to the debates that take place in a political assembly seeking to make a collective decision, to the special kind of rhetoric practiced in such debates, and to the internal debates that individuals have with themselves about the proper ethical or practical course of action to take in particular circumstances. Aristotle's choice of this term is thus not casual, for it reflects essential traits shared by these three domains.[9] The analogous deliberative processes share a rational procedure whose aim is to persuade others or oneself to choose the best option among those under discussion based on the evaluation of its pros and cons.[10] The typical result of this evaluation, in spite of its reasonableness, is not reducible to precise measuring methods using uniform criteria. It produces, therefore, a variety of results when performed by different individuals in different contexts; consequently, it involves considerable uncertainty. Nevertheless, it is this kind of rationality and persuasion—which Aristotle calls "calculative," in contrast to the "demonstrative" rationality of science—that occurs in deliberative decision making in pragmatic as well as moral affairs, and a fortiori in situations involving pragma-morality.

For the balance of reason in deliberation to function reliably, even though not demonstratively, its mechanism as well as the reasons considered must be, as far as possible, unbiased (see Dascal, 2005a, pp. 29–32). In other words, they must come from competent and trustworthy sources. These can be our own cognitive resources, provided that our natural trust in their reliability is untainted by emotive interference, careless reasoning, faulty observation, wrong methodological procedures, lack of competence, lack of attention, wishful thinking, self-deception, intentional bias, or other causes of epistemic distortion. Generally, however, our principal sources of information are our fellow humans. To be sure, they may be subject to failures like the ones that impair our own reliability. Just as each of us criticizes our own cognitive (and other) defects, we must be ready to criticize others. Yet, just as we naturally trust our abilities except in unusual circumstances, we also presume that most of the persons we interact with in normal circumstances are trustworthy unless there are good reasons to doubt this. In other words, as a rule, we accept others' reliability as we do our own.[11]

Presumptions such as this are indispensable for social life in its moral as well as its pragmatic dimensions. In general, we are unaware of the dense texture of presumptions we rely upon in virtually all areas of life in which they contribute to guiding our behavior and creating justified expectations concerning the behavior of others. Consider, for instance, the behavior of drivers. In Israel and other countries, it is common to complain about their uncivilized, aggressive, and careless driving. To be sure, some of these complaints refer to the punishable violations of traffic laws. Most of them, however, refer to deviations from the way drivers are supposed to act, presuming they are aware that driving is essentially a cooperative activity. Similarly, communication's cooperative nature presumes that speaker and addressee make the necessary effort to be understood and to understand each other. This presumption is the cornerstone of the ethics of communication, although the sole punishment for its disobedience is the failure of the communication. The legal system uses many presumptions of different kinds—the most famous of which is the presumption of innocence. Unlike laws, however, presumption-based inferences are not compelling, for every presumption comprises a "coda" warning its user that the conclusion drawn from it is reliable only if no (good) reasons override it. That is why the reliance on presumptions, though it allows us to expect a certain reasonable behavior from a driver, or a speech in a language that is understandable to the audience, should not surprise us too much if we face an unexpected road maneuver or choice of language. Furthermore, we should not be under the illusion that the pragmatic and the moral are always in harmony concerning the presumptions they generate. From a moral point of view, for example, in many societies there is a presumption of gender equality of rights (often legally based); pragmatically, however, the ruling presumption is often one of inequality. Needless to say, across societies and cultures, presumptions may vary considerably even in the moral sphere. Nevertheless, presumptions are extremely important precisely because of their flexibility, which guides without compelling, infers without deductively proving, and thereby suggests reasonable though modifiable possible courses of action that take into account the variable environment in which our pragmatic behavior and moral thinking occur.[12]

The use everywhere of presumptions is one of the ways in which human variability and difference are tolerated, valued, and expressed in terms of a reasonableness whose "soft" rationality is stable enough for the needs of practical and moral life.[13] In this respect, it is just one of the components of the readiness to receive and respect the other, however different, as a human being like us—a readiness that is the basic condition for interhuman moral behavior as well as for cooperative pragmatic interaction. This readiness is explicitly formulated in an encompassing moral principle, the ubiquitous "golden rule," which expresses the respect for the other in terms of the classical rules of conduct: "Do not do unto others what you would not have them do unto you"; "Do unto others what you would have them do unto you."[14] Formulated this way, the principle might suggest an ego-centered point of view; but it can also be expressed so as to stress not the role of the *ego* but rather that of the *other*. This is the approach adopted by Gottfried Wilhelm Leibniz, the seventeenth-century German philosopher, who calls the principle the "other's place." It is worthwhile to quote his brief but pregnant text before stressing its contribution to our discussion:

> The *other's place* is the true point of view both in politics and in morals. Jesus Christ's precept of putting oneself in the other's place is not only good for the end our Lord speaks of, i.e., morals, in order to know our duty with respect to our neighbour, but also for politics, in order to know what designs our neighbour may harbour against us. One's best access to these designs is obtained by putting oneself in his place, or when one pretends to be counsel and State minister of an enemy or suspect prince. This fiction stimulates our thoughts, and has served me more than once to guess with utmost precision what was concocted elsewhere. In all truth, it can happen that our neighbour is not so ill-meaning or even so clear-sighted as I suppose, but it is safest to assume the worst in political matters, i.e., when it is a question of taking precautions and being on the defensive; just as it is necessary to assume the best in moral affairs, i.e., when what is at stake is harming or offending the other.... Thus, it may be said that the other's place is an appropriate place, both in morals and in politics, to make us discover thoughts, which would otherwise not occur to us. In particular, that everything we would consider unjust, if we were in the other's place, must seem to us suspect of injustice; and even that everything we would not desire if we were in that place must make us hold on and examine it more maturely. Thus, the sense of the principle is: do not do or refuse with ease what you would not like to be done or refused to you. Think more

maturely about it, after having put yourself in the other's place, as that will provide you with the appropriate considerations for better knowing the consequences of your acts.[15]

Leibniz not only states in the first sentence the "true point of view" shared by morality and that most pragmatic of activities, politics. He also explains its rationale, modus operandi, and implications. The rationale is basically our epistemic weakness. Alone, limited to our individual perspectives, each one of us has a very limited capacity to obtain adequate knowledge of our complex universe, and we can hardly change our entrenched beliefs. Only by sharing our perspectives with those of other individuals can we improve our knowledge, either by getting rid of incorrect beliefs or by discovering and adding better ones. Hence, the difference between us and the other, and our capacity to put ourselves mentally in his or her place, play a decisive role in the epistemic enterprise. Our mental horizon is thereby challenged, purged of mistakes, and expanded, allowing us to "discover thoughts which would otherwise not occur to us." The new path thus opened is not limited in scope; it applies to theoretical and epistemic as well as to practical and moral issues. What it teaches is simple: in the light of significant differences between what you think based on your own viewpoint and what you think based on others' viewpoints, consider the possibility that your ideas, opinions, principles, or behavior are perhaps mistaken and should be carefully reexamined.

It is important to be aware of the fact that the whole process of using the moral-pragmatic principles of respecting the other and viewing things from the other's viewpoint is, like the process of deliberation, heavily context-dependent. There are no fixed procedures that ensure the successful application of these principles. In this respect, they offer no recipes but, at best, heuristic suggestions. In both cases, the identification, interpretation, and relevance of the other's circumstances are essential for successfully accessing the other's place and making proper use of it. These operations may, however, fall prey to misidentification, misinterpretation, and irrelevance, as may any other context to which we resort. No set of rules for this purpose is available, other than relatively vague recommendations such as attentiveness to the other rather than to your own perception of the other, avoiding stereotypes and other prejudices, paying attention to differences without automatically rejecting them, and so on. In fact, the other too has no privileged self-access and often needs the context for self-identification and self-interpretation, individually or collectively and, in both cases, only approximately. Since pragma-morality's principles are neither absolute nor detachable from the context of their use,[16] should we reject it as a disguised form of relativism, question its reliability, and look for a solid, absolutely reliable moral system, an anchor for handling the moral implications of the occupation? In the next section these questions are addressed.

CONTEXT-SENSITIVE MORALITY AND THE MORAL CONSEQUENCES OF OCCUPATION

Many alternatives to the kind of morality outlined above reject its emphasis on the context sensitivity of moral principles, reasons, and judgments. Generally, they favor universalistic models in which unquestionable moral principles, rights, or values are systematically ordered and function as a sort of axiomatic ground for moral judgments and the resolution of moral conflicts. This "hard" rationality approach to morality—let us call it "moral absolutism"—seeks to combat its supposed nemesis, "moral relativism," allegedly fostered by the acknowledgment of the context sensitivity of morality.

Opposition to the absolutist approach does not necessarily stress context sensitivity, but it does tend to attack directly the claim that a set of basic, unquestionable moral principles is a condition for moral thought. A case in point worth mentioning at least briefly for the reader to realize the complexity of the debate, especially concerning the role of context sensitivity, is "particularism," an ethical theory currently in evidence. One of particularism's definitions claims that "the possibility of moral thought and judgment does not depend on the provision of a suitable supply of moral principles" (Dancy, 2004, p. 7). It thus opposes "generalism," defined as the doctrine according to which "the very possibility of moral thought and judgment depends on the provision of a suitable supply of moral principles" (ibid.). Particularism is based on an analysis of the roles played by different types of moral reasons. This theory has been criticized, among other things, for incorrectly associating itself with "holism," an ethical position that emphasizes the context sensitivity of moral reason, arguing that "a feature that is a reason in one case may be no reason at all, or an opposite reason in another" (Dancy, 2004, p. 73). McKeever and Ridge (2005), for example, contend that moral reason holism cannot be associated with particularism, which they characterize as defending a total opposition to the "codification of morality," which is equivalent to the "search for a set of principles."[17] Another critic of particularism is Joseph Raz. Contrary to McKeever and Ridge, who defend holism, in his critique of Dancy's version of particularism Raz (2006) is less concerned with holism than with particularism, the two theses held by Dancy. For Raz, the former is "less radical" than the latter, and in case it is true, this "makes no difference to wider issues" (Raz, 2006, p. 118). Particularism, on the other hand, although criticized by Raz because of Dancy's lack of arguments in its support, is "a more radical thesis" (ibid.), which renders it more attractive: "One may be attracted by its rejection of absolute, nonoverridable moral principles, by its rejection of codifiable morality" (ibid.). For him, "these are sound motives," for it is clear that "morality cannot be codified, and many decisions call for contextually sensitive judgment" (ibid.). Nevertheless, these motives "do not require particularism to vindicate them" (Raz, 2006, p. 118).

As far as the occupation is concerned, moral absolutism assumes the existence of an absolute, general moral standard by which the morality of the parties in conflict ought to be judged. In principle, were this standard available and universally agreed upon, and were it applied objectively to the parties' actions, it might become a useful tool for discussing and overcoming some of the moral obstacles to the resolution of the conflict. It might, for example, permit at least some convergence rather than the habitual divergence concerning the opponents' evaluations of each other's claims or actions as justified, moral, or even true. Unfortunately, the divergence on such issues persists. Probably the reason is that what is at stake is not the absolute moral standard and its interpretation in each particular case, but rather the opponents' mutual mistrust, lack of mutual respect, incapacity to regard things from the other's point of view, lack of appropriate deliberative practices, lack of sensitivity to different presumptions, and disregard for the ever-present relevance of context.

Obviously, taking into account the above-mentioned factors would amount to accepting key tenets of the kind of morality that the defenders of moral absolutism reject because they believe it would fatally lead to moral relativism. This belief, however, stems from unjustified fear. It simply exaggerates the abysmal nature of the slippery slope that leads all the way down to moral relativism once one takes the first steps of admitting the context sensitivity of morality. Such exaggeration leads to preventive measures against the presumed danger. These measures range from public warnings by authoritative figures against any deviation from total obedience to the absolute moral norms, to their actual institutionalization—including codification and eventually punishment in case such norms are violated. Moral behavior thus becomes virtually a legal matter, to be controlled by the formal legal system rather than by the free and responsible judgment of autonomous citizens. None of these measures is justified. This should be clear from the fact that the slippery slope argument on which their requirement is based is valid only if between the heights of the plateau and the bottom of the abyss there is no tree, no rock, no salience whatsoever that could stop the slide. Yet, this is not the case. The polarization of absolute versus relative, in the case of morality as in many other cases, does not necessarily imply a strict dichotomy that does not admit any alternative between the poles. The following example of a controversy closely related to the debate on the nature of morality under discussion demonstrates this.

The Strauss-Stern confrontation that took place in the mid-twentieth century concerns a basic issue in the philosophy of history. This debate is a variant of the absolutism versus relativism debate, which in this case deals with the alleged contradiction between the idea of ahistorical natural right and the historicist critique of ahistorical universalism. Leo Strauss defends the former and Alfred Stern the latter. The following quotations succinctly present the two poles of the dichotomy:

> Historicism is an antithesis; in order to understand it, one has to know the thesis which it denies; namely, natural right, and its presupposition, the concept of a human nature or a human reason considered as unchangeable, eternal, identical throughout the ages, the nations, the civilizations, the social classes. (Stern, 1962, p. 139)

> Natural right isn't possible if all that men can know about it is that the question about the principles of justice allows for a variety of answers none of which can be proved as better than the others. Natural right is not possible if human thought, though imperfect, is unable to solve the problem of the principles of justice in a true way, hence in a universally valid way. (Strauss, 1953, p. 26)

In these statements, each of the protagonists defines his position as incompatible with and antithetical to that of his opponent. Furthermore, no third possibility is mentioned by either. Therefore, both seem to unquestionably accept the dichotomous nature of the issue, as well as its consequence: namely, that one has no option but to adopt one position or the other. Under these conditions, both try to exploit particularities of the dichotomous positions as arguments in their favor or against the adversary.

Strauss, for example, makes use of alleged self-defining features of historicism to demonstrate its absurd consequences—namely, its self-defeating character:

> Historicism claims that all human thoughts or beliefs are historical and therefore bound to die; but historicism itself is a human thought; therefore historicism can only have limited validity, or else it cannot be true. To assert the historicist thesis means to doubt it and, thus, to transcend it....Historicism thrives on the fact that it inconsistently exempts itself from its own verdict on all human thought. (Strauss, 1953, p. 26)

The same is the case in the slippery slope argument by which Strauss claims that historicism leads to nihilism (ibid.). Both arguments underrate the value of the opponent's position, and hence of the opponent himself as unworthy of serious discussion. The dichotomy is thus tendentiously presented as unbalanced; rather than a difficult problem to be solved, it is in fact predecided in favor of the arguer's party.

Stein, on the other hand, replies in a spirit of moderation, albeit without giving up the dichotomy that is the axis of the debate. He begins by conceding Strauss' point that historicism's claim to validity cannot be universal:

> [L]et us rather admit that historicism cannot claim timeless validity without violating its very principle.... By virtue of the categories at our disposal at this moment of history, human thoughts, belief and values appear historically conditioned.... Since, besides the categories of our epoch, we have no others at our disposal ... we must say that, in our epoch, historicism appears to be a well established theory. The fact that we cannot affirm the eternal, timeless, trans-historical validity of historicism does not exclude the possibility of its being valid for the present historical epoch which gave birth to it. (Stern, 1962, pp. 182–183)

He then points out that Strauss is in fact not arguing against his position, for the "extreme" historicism that Strauss attacks does not correspond to the version of "moderate" historicism that Stern actually defends. According to Stern, extreme historicism is merely a construct that opponents of historicism, like Strauss, designed for simplistically treating the issue dichotomously and thus easily winning the battle, rather than seriously engaging in resolving a thorny problem.

The moral absolutist position denies the context sensitivity of morality by depicting the latter as entailing "extreme relativism"—an easy way to defeat a scarecrow, like many other extremist adversaries. Pragma-morality, however, is neither extreme relativism nor extreme absolutism. It acknowledges the indispensable role of context in moral judgments without reducing morality to complete contextual determination; it also recognizes the role of stable moral maxims and presumptions, albeit without reducing morality to a set of fixed principles. In this respect, this kind of morality is similar to the account of meaning that, though pointing out that only in the context of use can the meaning of a linguistic expression be adequately recognized, does not deny that such recognition relies also on the lexical, literal meaning of the expression. Such an account reduces meaning neither to pragmatics nor to semantics; it is neither extreme contextualism nor extreme literalism, but lies somewhere in the middle, as one of the variants to which the adjective "moderate" might qualify, as in "moderate contextualism" or "moderate literalism."[18]

Such an intermediate alternative account of alleged polarities demonstrates, as in the cases of morality, historicism, and meaning, as well as of other generally admitted and widely used polar oppositions, that dichotomies are attractive due to their simplicity and logical pedigree, but it shows that they are context-sensitive too. According to Plato, for whom dichotomies are the cornerstone of the theory of ideas, they correspond to the conceptual structure of reality, regardless of how they can be used. There is evidence, however, that in the context of controversies, for example, polar oppositions may be presented as dichotomies or not, depending on the choice that fits better the position of the arguer. In many cases, therefore, what is decisive is not the fact that an opposition is a "true dichotomy" in the logical sense or that the arguer decides to "dichotomize" or "de-dichotomize" it in his or her argumentative strategy, but both.[19] Dichotomies and their various possible uses thus provide further evidence that the pragmatic-strategic and the logical-principled components of pragma-morality can and should work together in various ways precisely because of their context sensitivity, that is, without the risk of extreme relativism. As we will see below, context sensitivity and the other features of the kind of morality we have been elucidating play a crucial role in accounting for the moral consequences of the occupation.

A situation such as the occupation comprises a natural polarization of the adversaries as enemies. During the occupation in the course of the conflict, the polarization may be radicalized or softened, depending on the circumstances and the dichotomization or de-dichotomization strategies adopted by the parties. If the former occurs, for example, military actions may exacerbate the fear and revenge feelings that divide the opponents emotionally; the erection of checkpoints and barriers may trace this line physically; and the occupying authorities' use of special regulations and identifying documents may legally and semiotically codify and enforce a strict separation between the parties.[20] Since the compartmentalization of the occupied territories can hardly be foolproof, and since administrative, economic, or other interaction across the border is mandatory, the authorities must issue permits for this purpose. Such permits thus legitimize specific exceptions to the rule of strict separation. The pattern of a codified formal presumption emerges clearly in the thus softened version of that rule.

The occupation arena, however, includes informal—hence more context-sensitive—presumptions such as "Do not trust the enemy," "Be tough with the enemy," "It is safer to treat a suspected enemy as guilty than as innocent," and so on. These and other moral presumptions, which are part of the pragma-morality texture of the occupation, are steadily packed and shipped to the other side of the Green Line, ready to adapt themselves and be seamlessly embedded, with or without major changes, into a surrogate but familiar context—the pragma-morality core of Israeli culture. It is this ceaseless transfer that, I submit, accounts for one of the most serious moral consequences of the occupation: the self-inflicted distortion of moral presumptions.

Let us suppose that the transferred presumption is "Do not trust the enemy" as it is used in the occupied areas. Obviously, this sentence is ambivalent, since each of the groups who use it refers to different enemies and to different ways of mistrusting and treating them. Israeli soldiers presumably refer to Palestinians, settlers to Palestinians and sometimes to Israeli soldiers, and Palestinians to Jews in general, and particularly to soldiers and settlers. The presumption may thus recommend mistrusting Palestinians, or Jews, or the Israeli army, or settlers, or specific subgroups of any of these. Once the formula is exported to Israel, it carries with it all these possible readings. For the sake of the argument, let us restrict them to two—Palestinians and Israeli-Jews. Buying the formula, an Israeli can take advantage of a Buy One/Get Two savings offer. The presumption's guidance is to mistrust both Palestinians and Israeli-Jews. In the context of use, this can undoubtedly be disambiguated. Nevertheless, as general advice, it applies to these two broad categories of people without restriction. Furthermore, the preventive measures adopted against terrorist attacks in airports, restaurants, theaters, schools, and other public places, where everybody is checked (most of the time discriminating against "nonstandard"-looking or -sounding Israelis), as well as the constant reminders that one must be alert to suspicious objects, vehicles, persons, and so on, force us to be constantly tuned to our mistrust mental mode. No wonder that the various references of the absorbed ambivalent presumption merge, and mistrust becomes the basic presumption concerning virtually anyone in any context. This unified attitude toward the other replaces the traditional trust presumption. It is also reinforced by its adoption by government agencies and their advertisements, which keep reminding the citizens that they belong to an officially mistrusted population, which must be threatened in order for these citizens to fulfill their civil duties. The presumption thus becomes "Mistrust everybody" unless you have good reasons to trust them. Everyone is thus required either to feel surrounded by dangerous enemies or to be convinced that they are one of them. Having assimilated this presumption, Israelis are effortlessly put in the place of the other—of the Palestinians who have to live mistrusting even their kin as potential collaborators of the Israeli secret services.

Living in an environment where one is not presumed to trust and be trusted, but rather to mistrust and be mistrusted, no doubt implies a corrosive and exhausting shift to an attention- and energy-consuming pattern of behavior. Morally, it implies much more than the use of additional physical and psychological resources. For it affects not only a single presumption but a whole family of presumptions. Indeed, it is a fundamental part of the texture of morality—that having to do with the presumption that we owe respect to each other—that is called into question and damaged. Mistrust is closely connected to denial, disrespect, humiliation, devaluation, invidiousness, misanthropy, guilt, and dehumanization—of the other as well as of oneself. It is not difficult to see how the entire fabric of morality is shattered by the demise of a key presumption that carries with it the demise of many others. In this sense, the occupation can be condemned as responsible for moral deterioration.

The transfer of moral presumptions may be more complex than simple copying, as in the case analyzed above. The context sensitivity of presumptions may require certain modifications for ensuring their adaptation to the new environment. There may even be cases in which the implanted presumption is rejected due to its incompatibility with other existing presumptions. One usual modification has to do with the "strength" of the presumption, that is, how difficult it is to dismiss its recommendation, and its "status," that is, its importance relative to other presumptions. For instance, in traditional societies the presumption is that the elders' experience grants high value to their advice on any issue. By contrast, in modern societies, this presumption may be overridden by the presumption that updated information should prevail in decision making.

A particularly relevant example of a clash of presumptions in the Israeli-Palestinian conflict underlies the often used phrase "just peace" in discussions of the conditions for a solution. The question that naturally arises is, which of the two, justice or peace, is presumed to be morally more important than the other?—a key question for negotiating a solution acceptable to both sides. Avishai Margalit (2009, Chap. 3) addresses this question and argues that a "strong presumption of peace" overrides the presumption of justice in the attempts to reach a reasonable compromise. However, it seems to me that, although Margalit considers the presumption of justice mainly from a Palestinian viewpoint, he compares the relative strength and status of the two presumptions mostly from an Israeli perspective without attempting to consider the balance of reasons for each side.

This may well be a reason for the Palestinians' probable refusal to accept Margalit's proposal, not only in light of the fact that they have refused to give up what they view as the main component of a just solution (i.e., the right of return) or subordinate it to other conditions (e.g., all sorts of compensations, however enticing they may be), but also in light of the fact that they consider the *Naqba*, the traumatic event that generated the refugee problem, as their collective identity-forming episode. The weakening of the presumption that justice is a necessary condition for a solution to the conflict and the subordination of its status to another aim, desirable as it may be, would therefore amount to challenging the validity of an even stronger presumption embodied in over sixty years of a painful identity development process. For this reason, Margalit's suggestion seems to be as unacceptable to the Palestinians as the Uganda proposal was to the Zionist movement. Nevertheless, the proposal has the merit of opening a discussion on the validity of the thus-far-taken-for-granted crucial pragma-moral presumptions and their relative weights, both within each camp and across them. The moral controversies likely to arise as a sequel, though certainly tough, will at least refresh the debate by bringing to the fore long untouched taboos.

Whatever the route through which the moral presumptions are transferred and adopted or rejected by the Israeli or Palestinian citizenship, and whatever transformations they are subjected to on the way, the process of implantation and transmission follows a remarkably constant boomerang path. The morality that develops in the occupied side, largely influenced by the occupier's presence and aims, bounces back to the occupier's side; the fruits of colonization thus colonize back the minds of those who have planted them. Whatever original morality managed to remain in these minds during decades of occupation is doomed either to vanish or to be overridden by the superior power of presumptions so harshly tested in the boomerang trail.

CONTROVERSY, MORALITY, AND CONFLICT RESOLUTION

In the Introduction to this chapter I proposed a literal reading of its title, according to which controversies are part of conflicts and play a decisive role in enabling their resolution. If this is correct—and I will try to show that it is—the absence of substantial controversies on the moral aspects of occupation may be a major reason for the scarcity of progress in resolving the Palestinian-Israeli conflict. It is now time to conclude the chapter by returning to the claims made in the Introduction. Most of the chapter has dealt with the nature of morality, its relationship with pragmatic activity, and the moral consequences of the occupation. Here I discuss the role of controversies in conflict resolution on a more theoretical level while connecting this discussion with points touched on in the preceding sections. I hope that one of my aims, which is to promote actual controversy over the moral issues raised throughout the chapter, has already been discerned by the readers who have reached this concluding section.

I have elaborated and applied, in the last two decades, a typology of debates or "polemic exchanges" that distinguishes between three ideal types, which I have technically called "discussion," "dispute," and "controversy" (cf., for example, Dascal, 1998). This typology has proved to be very effective, and I summarize it below to serve as our reference here.

A *discussion* is the idealized form of a scientific debate. Its aim is to determine which of the positions in confrontation is true, while the other is perforce mistaken; it is a procedure accepted by the (community of) discussants that is presumably capable of yielding an unquestionable decision, to whose truth winner and loser, qua rational debaters, are committed in advance; and the privileged argumentative move in this procedure is logical, mathematical, or experimental proof. A *dispute*, at the other pole, is the idealized form of a battle of wits. Its aim is victory over the adversary; no procedure capable of deciding the issue so as to fully and decisively convince the (community of) disputants is available; and no constraints limit the kinds of argumentative stratagems designed to lead to the desired victory, however momentary it may be. Several polarities underlie and support the dichotomization of the pair *discussion/dispute*, both on the theoretical level and in its use in actual debates: *the* truth (Discussion) versus *my* truth (Dispute), the issue *can* be decided (Disc.) versus the issue *cannot* be decided (Disp.), logic (Disc.) versus rhetoric (Disp.), rational (Disc.) versus irrational (Disp.), debate about content (Disc.) versus debate about attitude (Disp.), leads to opinion change (Disc.) versus does not lead to opinion change, and so on.

Once contenders perceive the concepts of discussion and dispute as radically opposed on so many grounds, that is, as mutually exclusive and exhaustively covering all possible debates, they are compelled to view the particular debate in which they are engaged as *either a discussion or a dispute*; and this choice will determine their expectations, interpretations, and behavior in the debate. A contender may stick to his or her initial choice of category or, in the light of eventual violations by the adversary of his or her expectations or interpretations of the adversary's moves, shift to the other pole and react accordingly. This flip-flop effect that admits no intermediate alternative is not unusual in the conduct of debates that are perceived as dichotomous. Besides the descriptive inadequacy of this dyadic scheme and the unnatural flip-flop effect it forces upon debaters, what prompted my search for at least one additional ideal type to add to the taxonomy was the encounter with a different approach to controversy in the work of G. W. Leibniz—an approach virtually ignored by a tradition that highlighted instead his project of developing an algorithmic procedure for solving all controversies as if they are typical scientific *discussions*.[21] His hitherto overlooked approach suggests instead a type of controversy where the decision (either the determination of the truth or of the winner) is not the primary goal, but rather the construction or emergence of a solution through the dialectic cooperation of the debaters. This encounter with "another" Leibniz led me to the elaboration and utilization of a new ideal type of debate and to the transformation of an earlier dyadic taxonomy into a triadic one. I termed this new type "controversy." What defines it is the set of substantial differences that distinguish it from both discussion and dispute. Its justification and value must be judged by its descriptive and explanatory power.

In a controversy, unlike in a dispute, the objective is not victory but rational persuasion; each contender does not assume a priori that the adversary is entirely wrong while he or she is entirely right, thus abandoning from the outset any hope of rationally persuading the other to change his or her mind. External intervention (e.g., by a tribunal) can dissolve the dispute, but it usually does not change the contenders' belief in the correctness and justification of their positions. On the other hand, controversy differs from discussion in that, while it is based upon the possibility of rational persuasion, it does not assume that this can only be achieved if the contenders accept the unquestionable results of the application of a method they unconditionally accept. In controversy, the questioning of assumptions of all sorts is always permitted and even encouraged. This leads to a wide range of disagreements that can be quite radical—including doubts about the alleged certainty of the decision-making procedures. Hence, rational persuasion in controversy does not have the power of the dramatic revelation of the truth that it is supposed to have in discussion.

From the point of view of this chapter, the fundamental difference between controversy and its counterparts is that its nondichotomous parameters grant it a flexibility, an open-endedness, a challenging attitude vis-à-vis established beliefs and practices, a nondogmatic rationality, and a potential for innovation—all of which, together, explain its relevance to dealing with conflicts appropriately and with justified expectations for their resolution. Needless to say, the properties of controversy just listed are particularly relevant for handling moral conflicts, provided that the controversies are not conducted dogmatically in a dichotomous framework such as that opposing extreme moral absolutism to extreme moral relativism. For it is those properties that are needed to fully take into account the context sensitivity of morality and take advantage of its benefits. Furthermore, of the three types of debate, controversy is the only one that really complies with the presumption of respecting the other. In dispute, where one only wishes to demonstrate that one's view is the correct one, the opponent's view is devoid of interest and does not deserve much attention. In discussion, which of the contenders is correct is determined by a decision-making procedure that at best takes into account their relevant arguments but disregards their relevance as persons intellectually committed to clarifying the issues under discussion. It is in controversy, where the contenders engage in joint work through which each can contribute his or her knowledge to the resolution of the problem, that mutual learning, respect, and utilization of both contenders' knowledge occurs. In conducting negotiations capable of advancing the resolution of conflicts, the controversy pattern provides the conditions of mutual respect needed for the development and application of the required moral attitudes of the participants (cf. Dascal, 2008b) and the shaping of shared interests and "we-intentions" to seriously engage in purposeful negotiations (cf. Dascal, 2003, chap. 5; Dascal, 2007, pp. 84–86).

Besides its direct use as an argumentative pattern where disagreement between opponents is debated and sometimes resolved, controversy's pattern parallels similar patterns in psychological phenomena as well as in the evolution of conflicts. A psychological phenomenon close to controversy is deliberation (cf. above), which is an example of what may be called "inner debate" (cf. Dascal, 2005b). In the wake of the pioneering work of Festinger (1957), the phenomenon he called "cognitive dissonance" has been intensively investigated. According to him, cognitive dissonance occurs when there is a "nonfitting relation" among one's cognitions. For example, one may be a convinced antiracist and yet withdraw one's children from school as soon as Muslims enroll in it. Dissonance is thus an inconsistency within an individual's set of cognitions in a given domain. One may thus say that whenever one deliberates, cognitive dissonance occurs, since deliberation consists in weighing the pros and cons for doing or believing something. Similarly, when different opinions held in a public debate are brought to our attention, we may face a situation of cognitive dissonance. Festinger does not conceive dissonance in formal terms and points out that he introduced the term "dissonance" rather than "inconsistency" because the former "has less of a logical connotation" (ibid., p. 2); furthermore, he stresses that "follows from" should not be invariably interpreted as a strict logical relation (ibid., p. 14). Logical inconsistency is but one of the possible sources of dissonance; others include a variety of contextual elements, such as motivation and desired consequences, cultural conventions, past experience, and so on. Assuming, however, that "an individual strives toward consistency within himself," the theory claims that dissonance is "psychologically uncomfortable"; consequently, its presence motivates the individual to act in order "to try to reduce the dissonance and achieve consonance" (ibid., pp. 1–3).

Research in cognitive dissonance has devoted particular attention to the kind of dissonance that arises after a decision between mutually exclusive options has been made. Experimental data (cf. Festinger, 1964) show that immediately after a decision has been made, a process of rationalization of the decision begins; the attractiveness of the nonchosen option is reduced and that of the chosen alternative is increased, thus reducing the dissonance between the two options. Obviously, the unfavorable elements must remain cognitively available after the decision; otherwise, they could not cause postdecision dissonance. Furthermore, even though the aim of the rationalization is to support the decision, it amounts to a new deliberative process regarding the issue at stake. Hence, it may be the case that once this process is initiated and the reasons are reevaluated, this may lead one to override the preceding decision rather than endorse it.[22]

Postdecision dissonance, therefore, is a rather surprising phenomenon, at least insofar as it does not conform to the intuitive belief that a decision "puts an end" to doubt and inner debate by adopting one of the alternatives and removing the others, along with their supporting arguments, from the decider's cognitive horizon. Instead, the ubiquity of postdecision dissonance suggests that, as a rule, the predecision debate goes on beyond the decision point. Perhaps to preserve at least part of the intuitive belief in question, Festinger emphasizes the singularity of the moment in which a decision "is made." This singularity, according to him, creates a discontinuity in the cognitive process between what precedes and what follows it. For this purpose, he posits a sharp distinction between predecision conflict and postdecision dissonance:

> The person is in a conflict situation before making the decision. After having made the decision he is no longer in conflict; he has made his choice; he has, so to speak, resolved the conflict. He is no longer being pushed in two or more directions simultaneously. He is now committed to the chosen course of action. It is only here that dissonance exists, and the pressure to reduce this dissonance is *not* pushing the person in two directions simultaneously. (Festinger, 1957, p. 39)

This description suggests that the stage of cognitive deliberation resembles a fierce battle between opposing forces, each trying to win the deliberator's acquiescence; by contrast, the stage of dissonance reduction after the choice is made is a rather quiet process of suppressing the remaining resistance by regrouping and redeploying the apparently victorious forces after the battle. It is as if the first stage is a dispute or perhaps a discussion, while the second is closer to a controversy. In spite of the difference, they seem to be stages of a continuous debate in which roughly the same issue constantly returns without ever reaching a final solution.²³ If this is indeed the case, it turns out that in our deliberative life we hardly ever cease to be engaged in nonstop debates,²⁴ the "balance of reason" is in endless action, and decisions are ephemeral, always in the course of being reshaped, and never final.²⁵

Finally, it is worth remembering that a large percentage of conflicts are recurrent. This means that the agreements, peace treaties, or other steps that allegedly resolved them had also merely a provisional effect and did not put an end to the conflict once and for all. The reopening of the supposedly resolved conflict, much like the postdecision cognitive dissonance, indicates that the main problem is not that of finding some miraculous formula that will finalize the conflict. It is, rather, that of initiating a process of improvement and maintenance of the achieved results without delay, that is, immediately after their achievement.²⁶

Peacemaking in intractable conflicts must be acknowledged as what it really is: a very demanding and complex ongoing dialectic process. Whoever expects a prompt solution is the victim of an illusion; and whoever asks what is the use of promoting controversies in spite of their admitted inability to yield a perfect solution (i.e., capable of eliminating all controversies) to a conflict like the Palestinian-Israeli one is invited to put his or her proposal on the table. The continuing dialectical process suggested constitutes a permanent forum in which the contenders will be able to pursue the discussion of the always remaining or arising questions—including pragmatic as well as moral issues—not yet resolved by whatever formula of agreement they have already reached. That this will help rather than hamper the slow process of overcoming ever more obstacles to peace seems to be a reasonable presumption supported by the history of controversies. In any case, it should be preferred to the doubtful presumption that a complex—hence prolonged—conflict can be satisfactorily, quickly, and completely resolved by a lasting pragmatic-strategic agreement that both sides will pragma-morally accept once and for all.

NOTES

1. I wish to thank Amnon Knoll for the strong interest he has shown in this text since its inception. He located relevant material, provided information I was not aware of, corrected some of my mistakes, made numerous suggestions, and was incredibly generous with the time he spent discussing the key ideas with me. I am also grateful to Varda's courageous sharing with me the moral criticism of occupation as expressed in this chapter.
2. As examples of both, the separation of moral and pragmatic issues as well as of their joint consideration, albeit with each contender emphasizing one of them, see Gans, 2008, sections 3.1 and 4.1.

3. This does not mean, of course, that the vast majority of Palestinians did not soon realize and stress the moral significance of the 1948 events they called the *Naqba* ("catastrophy").
4. The report of one of the participants in the Geneva talks clearly points in this direction: "The remaining points of disagreement after the Taba negotiations had to do with the 1948 'narrative,' namely, with who was responsible for the creation of the refugee problem and, consequently, with what will be the nature of the agreement and its title ...the two sides learned from the failure of the official negotiations that attempted to reach an agreement on a shared narrative about what happened in the 1948 war. The Geneva initiative entrusts this task to the civil societies, supported by the two governments. There was no serious disagreement on this matter. The decision included also the issue of Israel's apology for its part in the creation of the refugee problem" (Klein 2006, 66). "Entrusting civil society with this issue is better than the attempt made in the official talks to reach a shared narrative, for no formal decision can change the public perception in both sides. Changing the perception is a long-term matter and, if it comes about at all, it will be as the result of complex long-term reconciliation processes" (ibid, 68).
5. For further details and discussion of colonization and decolonization of minds, see Chinweizu (1987), Memmi (1967, 2006), Bodei (2002), Freire (2004), Dascal (2009a).
6. "Education thus becomes an act of depositing, in which the students are the depositories and the teacher is the depositor. Instead of communicating, the teacher issues communiqués and makes deposits which the students patiently receive, memorize, and repeat. This is the 'banking' concept of education, in which the scope of action allowed to the students extends only as far as receiving, filing, and storing the deposits....In the banking concept of education, knowledge is a gift bestowed by those who consider themselves knowledgeable upon those whom they consider to know nothing....The teacher presents himself to his students as their necessary opposite; by considering their ignorance absolute, he justifies his own existence. The students, alienated like the slave in the Hegelian dialectic, accept their ignorance as justifying the teacher's existence—but, unlike the slave, they never discover that they educate the teacher" Freire (2004: 72).
7. "It is worth knowing—even if it is hard to swallow—that an occupying people, even if an unwilling one, is occupied from the inside by the occupation and its friends: the people's qualities undergo change, its character is distorted, its values make room for other values." Abraham Burg, Speaker of the Knesset, in a special session commemorating the 53th anniversary of the Israeli parliament, February 28, 2002.
8. Aristotle considered the notion of deliberation sufficiently important on its own to write a special treatise devoted to it, *Peri Symboulías*. This work is listed in Diogenes Laertius' catalog but has not yet been reconstructed.

9. Stuart Hampshire, who elaborates the Aristotelian notion of deliberation as the cornerstone of his moral theory, puts to use the external-internal debate analogy in this vivid passage: "The picture of the mind that gives substance to the notion of practical reason is a picture of a council chamber, in which the agent's contrary interests are represented around the table, each speaking for itself. The chairman, who represents the will, weighs the arguments and the intensity of the feeling conveyed by the arguments, and then issues an order to be acted on. The order is a decision and an intention, to be followed by its execution. This policy is the outcome of the debate in the council chamber" (Hampshire 1991: 51).
10. On this model of deliberation, see Dascal (2005a).
11. The obvious exceptions to this rule are cases in which either one is over-critical of oneself, over-appreciative of others, or vice-versa.
12. Interest in presumptions and their role in cognition, jurisprudence, social relations, and other domains, as well as in the history of this until recently rather overlooked concept, is steadily growing. A very useful recent work devoted to presumptions as a tool of "tentative cognition" is Rescher (2006). I myself have been attracted by Leibniz's emphasis on the fundamental importance of this concept, which he views as paradigmatic of the "soft" rationality we need in addition to the familiar logic-mathematic "hard" rationality (cf. the subject indexes of Leibniz (2006) and of Dascal (Ed.) (2008)). In the following quotation Leibniz characterizes presumption as one of the types of "probable argumentation" and stresses that most moral reasoning is presumptive: "*Probable argumentation* comes from either the *nature of things* or from *people's opinions*. The former is, in turn, either *presumption* or *conjecture*. It is a *presumption* if the proposed statement follows from what is surely true, without any requirement other than the negative one, namely that no impediment [for its truth] obtains. Therefore we will always have to declare ourselves in favor of he who has the presumption unless someone else demonstrates the contrary. Such are most moral reasonings" (Leibniz 2006, 86–87).
13. On the pragmatics of variability, the valuation of difference, and tolerance, see, respectively, Lloyd (2007), Dascal (2009b), Dascal (2005c), and Dascal (2008b).
14. The New Testament versions are in Luke 6:31 and Matthew 7:12.
15. Leibniz (2006: 164–165). The translation of the complete manuscript, which includes also legal remarks, along with my introductory comments and notes, is on pages 163–166. For further discussion of this and related Leibnizian texts, see Dascal (1993: 401–404, 1995), de Gaudemar (2008), Laerke (2010: 310–3145), and Zauderer-Naaman (2008).
16. For a typology of the different ways in which context interacts with semantic meaning in linguistic communication, see Dascal (2003, Chapter 8).
17. McKeever and Ridge point out that even Kant, famous for his principle-based ethics and codification of morality, admits several cases of context sensitivity

of moral reasons. This shows—they argue—that holism of reasons is compatible with both context sensitivity and principle-morality and, therefore, is inconsistent with particularism. Still, McKeever and Ridge believe that particularism is an interesting challenge for traditional moral philosophy to face.

18 On this still raging debate in linguistics and the philosophy of language, see Dascal (2003, Chapters 25–26), Recanati (2004), Borg (2004).

19 These concepts are defined as follows: "DICHOTOMIZATION: radicalizing a polarity by emphasizing the incompatibility of the poles and the inexistence of intermediate alternatives, by stressing the obvious character of the dichotomy as well as of the pole that ought to be preferred. DE-DICHOTOMIZATION: showing that the opposition between the poles can be constructed as less logically binding than a contradiction, thus allowing for intermediate alternatives; actually developing or exemplifying such alternatives" (Dascal 2008a, 34–35).

20. There may also be other reasons for the occupied or the occupier side to enhance the polarization, i.e., to adopt a dichotomization strategy. Barghouti (2005), for example, argues that in the situation of occupation there is a fundamental moral reason for this choice of strategy: the preservation of Palestinian identity.

21. For details of Leibniz's hitherto overlooked approach, see the Introductory Essay of Leibniz (2006).

22. This may be due, for instance, to some mistake made in the pre-deliberation phase, such as a miscalculation of the weight of some negative reason or simply forgetting to put it in the negative plate of the balance of reason.

23. Most of the *controversies* I have studied rarely end with a definitive, unquestionable "solution"—which is why I employ the term "resolution" when referring to the typical conclusion mode of *controversies*. This does not mean that they are mere dialectical exercises, for the serious and well-intentioned effort to rationally persuade an opponent yields a substantial "cognitive gain," e.g., the clarification of the controversial issues, which in turn may lead to innovative steps toward their *resolution*.

24. Presumably more akin to *controversies* than either *discussions* or *disputes* precisely because of their never ending character as well as of the uncertainty of the decision.

25. Although they mention cognitive dissonance as a central psychological predicament of occupiers that they attempt to overcome through a series of well-known psychic maneuvers, Rosler et al. (2009) do not devote special attention to the persistence of dissonance at the post-decisional stage, which suggests that the psychic devices in question have at best an ephemeral provisional effect and that the moral and psychological effects of the occupation cannot be definitively removed from our minds.

26. The establishment of a procedure for such a follow up should be part of the achieved results.

REFERENCES

Barghouti, O. (2005). Ethical implications of de-dichotomization of identities in conflict. In P. Barrotta & M. Dascal (Eds.), *Controversies and subjectivity* (pp. 325–336). Amsterdam: John Benjamins.
Bar-Tal, D. (2009). Coping psychologically with the occupation. In E. Lavi (Ed.), *Forty years of occupation: The effects on Israeli society* (pp. 217–229). Tel Aviv: Tami Steinmetz Center for Peace Research, Tel Aviv University (in Hebrew).
Bodei, R. (2002). *Personal destinies: The age of the colonization of minds*. Milan: Feltrinelli (in Italian)
Borg, E. (2004). *Minimal semantics*. Oxford: Clarendon Press.
Chinweizu, I. (1987). *Decolonising the African mind*. Lagos: Pero Publishers.
Dancy, J. (2004). *Ethics without principles*. Oxford: Oxford University Press.
Dascal, M. 1993. One Adam and many cultures: The role of political pluralism in the best of possible worlds. In M. Dascal & E. Yakira (Eds.), *Leibniz and Adam* (pp. 387–409). Tel Aviv: University Publishing Projects.
Dascal, M. (1995). Strategies of dispute and ethics: *Du tort* and *La place d'autruy*. In H. Breger (Ed.), *Proceedings of the VI Internationaler Leibniz-Kongress* (pp. 108–115). Hanover: Lebniz Gesellschaft.
Dascal, M. (1998). Types of polemics and types of polemical moves. In S. Cmejrkova, J. Hoffmannova, O. Mullerova, & J. Svetla (Eds.), *Dialogue analysis VI* (Vol. 1, pp. 15–33). Tübingen: Max Niemeyer.
Dascal, M. (2003). *Interpretation and understanding*. Amsterdam: John Benjamins.
Dascal, M. (2005a). The balance of reason. In D. Vanderveken (Ed.), *Logic, thought and action* (pp. 27–47). Dordrecht: Springer.
Dascal, M. (2005b). Debating with myself and debating with others. In P. Barrotta & M. Dascal (Eds.), *Controversies and subjectivity* (pp. 31–73).. Amsterdam: John Benjamins.
Dascal, M. (2005c). The challenge of human difference and the ethics of communication. In Y. Yovel & I. Menuchin (Eds.), *Can tolerance prevail? Moral education in an adverse world* (pp. 94–102). Jerusalem: Magnes Press (in Hebrew).
Dascal, M. (2007). Traditions of controversy and conflict resolution: Can past approaches help to solve present conflicts? In M. Dascal & Han-liang Chang (Eds.), *Traditions of controversy* (pp. 281–295). Amsterdam: John Benjamins.
Dascal, M. (Ed.). (2008a). *Leibniz: What kind of rationalist?* Dordrecht: Springer.
Dascal, M. (2008b). Dichotomies and types of debate. In F. van Eemeren & B. Garssen (Eds.), *Controversy and confrontation* (pp. 27–49). Amsterdam: John Benjamins.
Dascal, M. (2008c). Towards a dialectic of tolerance. *L'Analisi Linguistica e Letteraria*, 16, 529–541.
Dascal, M. (2009a). Colonizing and decolonizing minds. In I. Kuçuradi (Ed.), *Papers of the 2007 World Philosophy Day* (pp. 308–331). Istanbul: Philosophical Society of Turkey.

Dascal, M. (2009b). Mental diversity and unity: A pragmatic approach to the debate. *Pragmatics & Cognition, 17*(2), 403–420.
Festinger, L. (1957). *A theory of cognitive dissonance.* Stanford, CA: Stanford University Press.
Festinger, L. (Ed.). (1964). *Conflict, decision, and dissonance.* London: Tavistock.
Freire, P. (2004). *Pedagogy of the oppressed.* New York: Continuum Press.
Gans, C. (2008). *A just Zionism: On the morality of the Jewish state.* New York: Oxford University Press.
de Gaudemar, M. (2008). Leibniz and moral rationality. In M. Dascal (Ed.), *Leibniz: What kind of rationalist?* (pp. 343–354). Dordrecht: Springer.
Hampshire, S. (1991). *Innocence and experience.* Cambridge, MA: Harvard University Press.
Klein, M. (2006). *The Geneva initiative: An inside view.* Jerusalem: Carmel.
Laerke, M. (2010). The golden rule: Aspects of Leibniz's method for religious controversy. In M. Dascal (Ed.), *The practice of reason: Leibniz and his controversies* (pp. 297–319). Amsterdam: John Benjamins.
Leibniz, G. W. (2006). *Leibniz: The art of controversies.* Ed. M. Dascal. Dordrecht: Springer.
Lloyd, G. E. R. (2007). *Cognitive variations: Reflections on the unity and variation of the human mind.* Oxford: Oxford University Press.
Margalit, A. (2009). *On compromise and rotten compromises.* Princeton, NJ: Princeton University Press.
McKeever, S., & Ridge, M. (2005). What does holism have to do with moral particularism? *Ratio, 18,* 93–103.
Memmi, A. (1967). *The colonizer and the colonized.* Boston: Beacon Press.
Memmi, A. (2006). *Decolonization and the decolonized.* Minneapolis: University of Minnesota Press.
Raz, J. (1986). *The morality of freedom.* Oxford: Clarendon Press.
Raz, J. (2006). The trouble with particularism (Dancy's version). *Mind, 115,* 99–120.
Recanati, F. (2004). *Literal meaning.* Cambridge: Cambridge University Press.
Rescher, N. (2006). *Presumption and the practices of tentative cognition.* Cambridge: Cambridge University Press.
Rosler, N., Bar-Tal, D., Sharvit, K., Halperin, E., & Raviv, A. (2009). Moral aspects of prolonged occupation: Implications for an occupying society. In S. Scuzzarello, C. Kinnvall, & K. Monroe (Eds.), *On behalf of others: The psychology of care in a global world.* New York: Oxford University Press: 211–232.
Rouhana, N. N., & Bar-Tal, D. (1998). Psychological dynamics of intractable ethnonational conflicts. *American Psychologist, 53*(7),761–770.
Stern, A. (1962). *Philosophy of history and the problem of values.* The Hague: Mouton.
Strauss, L. (1953). *Natural right and history.* Chicago: University of Chicago Press.
Zauderer-Naaman, N. (2008). The place of the other in Leibniz's rationalism. In M. Dascal (Ed.), *Leibniz: What kind of rationalist?* (pp. 315–327). Dordrecht: Springer.

CHAPTER 3

Geographical Ramifications of the Occupation for Israeli Society

Izhak Schnell

INTRODUCTION

This discussion on the geographical influence of the occupation on Israeli society focuses on the connection between society and territory. This connection lies at the heart of the national ideology that unites the members of a common ethnic group around a territory for which a sense of solidarity has developed in regard to this group and its unique culture (Anderson, 1991). The emphasis here is on understanding the processes of emotional connection to certain territories in the construction of a national identity, self-determination, and social, political, and cultural autonomy (Brown, 1987; Buttimer, 2001; Chisholm & Smith, 1976, 1990; Knight, 1982; Newman, 2001; Schnell, 2001). *Territoriality* is defined as a delimited spatial unit to which people feel a bond of identification. According to this definition, territory influences one's identity on two complementary levels. One is the symbolic dimension, which charges the national territory with symbolic meaning; the other is the territory as a container for constructing one's daily life (Paasi, 1999). In accordance with the national ideology, each ethnic group or community is entitled to self-determination in a defined territory. The territory functions as a concrete source for constructing an identity with the imagined abstract community, with which it is problematic to identify directly (Anderson, 1991; Bar-Tal, 2000). Consequently, the state uses a series of territorial and other mechanisms to establish the dialectic process of constructing an identity that connects the community with the territory. This process is a dynamic political one, part of the daily experiences and worldview of the individual (Sarup, 1996).

Consequently, in addition to the demographic principle—according to which the majority of the imagined community are meant to adopt a single culture whose source lies in the nation's common territorial origin—the nation also tends to use aesthetic practices in regard to space as a central tool in creating monuments charged with symbolic meanings. The constructed spaces thereby become concrete reminders that objectify the national narrative. This practice has become an important tool used by elite groups to establish their hegemony across society as a whole in the name of the national ideology (Redfield, 2003). Anderson (1991) provides as examples the population survey as a symbol of population control, the museum as a symbol of the cultural and historical heritage of the imagined nation, and the map that brands the territory in general as a concrete image, on the one hand, while enabling control of the territory, on the other hand, as central tools in the construction of national identity. Redfield (2003) sees in the grave of the unknown soldier an archetype of a monument that charges the territory with significances that oblige civilians to enlist in the cause of the imagined community; and in accordance, countries have striven to broaden the overlap between the dispersal of the population across the national territory as a means of reducing interethnic tensions while charging that space with symbolic significances identified with the nation, and shifting to the fringes those minorities that do not fit in with the unified national identity.

In addition to the elite groups' activities in constructing a national identity, territoriality and other means, such as education, the daily reality too functions as an important mechanism by building a grassroots national identity. Many researchers in the social sciences have emphasized that the state is a central agent in constructing the practices of daily life, but to the same extent, social practices also become established from within the realities of ordinary people's daily lives (de Certeau, 1984; Giddens, 1991; Lefevre, 1971; Soja, 1996). Moreover, de Certeau emphasizes the insidious power of daily life in creating autonomous practices beyond the state's mechanisms. Memmi (1985) shows how the daily practices that develop under the conditions of colonial occupation create an unavoidable conflict between the conqueror, who wishes to establish his privileges, and the conquered, in a way that obliges the conqueror to adopt practices of oppression toward the conquered. At a certain stage, an enormous gap arises between settlers and society, a gap that can lead to a conflict created when the general population does not identify with the mechanisms of oppression that have become extremist.

Against this background, the central contention of this chapter is that the State of Israel has related with duplicity to the occupied territories. On the one hand, it has preserved their legal status as occupied territories (hereafter "territories"); on the other hand, it has developed a wide variety of practices whose purpose is to include the territories within an area identified with the nation. Both formally and legally, the state declared its intention to maintain the status of the areas as occupied territory, to act in them according to the rules of international law, and to treat the Palestinian population as subjects of the military government. While the Palestinian people were kept under occupation, the territory and the settlers were de facto annexed by the state (see the chapter by Kretzmer, this volume). Thereby, the state succeeded in suppressing international objections to the de facto annexation of the territories by the State of Israel, a step forbidden under international law regarding occupied territory, while activating a mechanism of suppression that prevented the Palestinians from expressing any effective objection to their dispossession from the land. In fact, the state and the settlers established a wide variety of practices intended to annex the land to the national territory. These included rebuilding the territories through their Judaization and reconstructing the territorial awareness of the nation in a way that incorporates the area within the homeland; all of these practices contradict the declared status of the territories as occupied. This chapter presents examples of the use of state and daily life practices to reconstruct the territories as an integral part of the national territory while ignoring their declared status as occupied territory. Because of the wide variety of mechanisms used by the state, I will provide only a few examples illustrating the extent and force of the process. I will also present my contention that this is neither a random nor a sporadic process, but a consistent and methodical one.

The methodological framework presenting the mechanisms for reconstruction of the territories as part of the national territory is summarized in the following Figure 3.1.

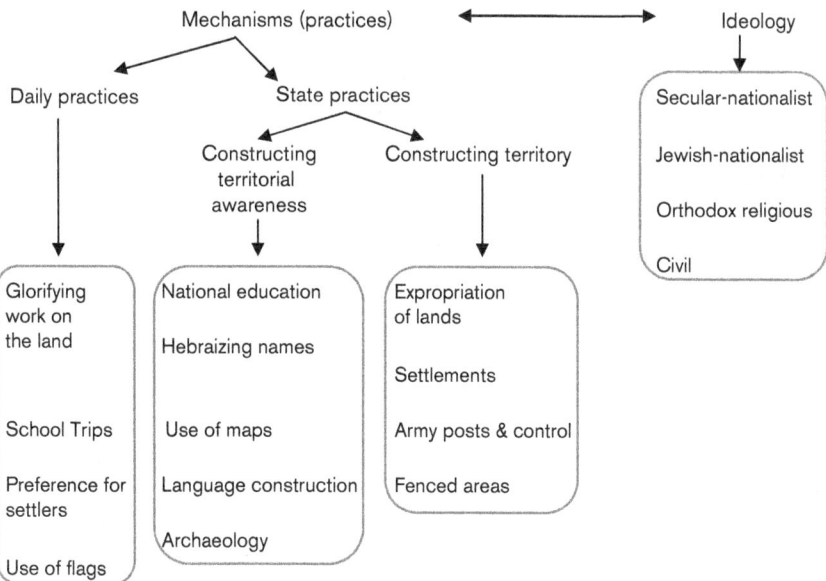

FIGURE 3.1 Constructing the occupied territories as a national territory.

Nationalism as an ideology is manifested in different ways; four main approaches can be identified in Israeli society. The first approach is that of the Jewish and Arab left wing in Israel, which calls for the establishment of a civil state that will include all of its inhabitants as citizens with equal rights, regardless of nationality. The second approach is that of many Orthodox Jews, who perceive the state as a secular one, much like many others, with no connection between the state and Jewish identity. In their minds, as commanded by the Rambam (Rabbi Moses Maimonides), the sanctity of the land does not apply to the present territory, as the people of Israel do not sanctify the land by their deeds (Shilhav, 2001). These two standpoints remain at the margins of the discourse on Israeli nationalism. The dominant standpoint in the State of Israel prior to the occupation was that of secular nationalism, which aspired to establish a national, democratic Jewish society in the Land of Israel. Its proponents believed that the creation of a Jewish majority in the land and an independent life would bring together once more the Jewish people as a nation like any other nation. A virtuous nation was defined by David Ben-Gurion as a Jewish obligation to promote progress in the Third World based on the successful experience of the Zionist movement. The Jabotinsky approach, the third one, sees the national aim as being achieved by conquering the land and cooperating with the Arab population in developing the land and society for the good of all its inhabitants. The approach of the labor movements was to settle areas of the land inhabited by a Jewish majority and to work those areas as a means of creating a territorial and productive bond with the land. The fourth approach, adopted by the more prominent religious-Zionist sector, saw the process of settlement, advocated by the workers' parties, as part of a process that would completely unite the people of Israel with the Torah and the Land of Israel. Regarding occupation of the territories, the national-religious discourse focused on the commandment to settle the land as a mechanism for reinforcing the triple union of nation, people, and Torah. Moreover, following the Yom Kippur War, Rabbi Zevi Jehuda Kook, Jr., ruled that a national-religious movement of awakening should be developed in the territories, reestablishing the Israeli identity on strict religious grounds at the expense of the now degenerate secular identity (Ravitzky, 1993; Sheleg, 2000). Even though Gush Emunim, the national religious settlers' political movement, remained only a small minority of the population, it succeeded in achieving social leverage by identifying to varying degrees with right-wing movements and broad sectors of the ultra-Orthodox population of Israel, who increasingly emphasized the specific Jewish-nationalist identity, as well as with the secular right- wing parties and even segments of the left-wing labor party (Schnell, 2009).

The mechanisms that made the territories part of the state derived from both establishment and daily practices in the same way as they became established by the daily practices of the settlers. The state mechanisms act to directly control the territories, mainly by annexing lands; constructing settlements, camps, and military installations; and creating separate roads for Jews in the area; other mechanisms consist of constructing territorial awareness by erasing the borders of the Green Line, Hebraicizing place names, selectively managing information that incorporates the territories within the homeland in the education system, and building memorials to those who died in the wars that liberated the Land of Israel. Archaeology has a central role in Judaicizing the territories, both in shaping the territories themselves and in shaping territorial awareness. This chapter focuses on the activity patterns of several mechanisms that contributed to the construction of the territories as an integral part of the national territory and as an important incubator for the reconstruction of the national identity. My contention is that the extent of the activity and the strong involvement of state organizations in the process show that the annexing of the territories to the homeland is not an unpremeditated outcome of the occupation, but a central and significant part of the Israeli state policy in the territories. Another point that deserves consideration in this case is the fact that many young nations have used similar means to attach themselves to their national territory; but they, in contrast, did not activate such means in the territories defined by them as occupied territory, as Israel legally defines the territories.

MECHANISMS OF NATIONAL TERRITORY CONSTRUCTION: PRACTICES OF THE STATE

Acquisition of Land

The acquisition of land for the Jewish nation was a central tool of Zionism, which aspired to connect a nation without a land with a land without a nation. The ideology of "dunam by dunam" also turned the land into a central arena in the conflict between the Zionist movement and the Palestinian nationalist movement. The mainstream approach of the Zionist movement, in contrast to the Jabotinski approach, was not satisfied with attaining sovereignty over the territories. The Zionists also declared the aim of redeeming the land—by acquiring lands, settlement, and agriculture—as a means of redeeming humanity. Accordingly, the Zionist movement continued to aspire to establish a Jewish majority in parts of the land where it was possible to achieve a solid Jewish majority, avoiding settlements in areas heavily populated by Palestinians (Gorny, 1993; Kellerman, 1989). In the years 1947–1967, from the decision of the United Nations to divide the land to the Six Day War, the great majority of the citizens of the Jewish state and its political elite accepted the defined borders of the land. This decision had sparked public debate much earlier, in 1937, in the Zionist view of the Peel Commission, and later in the words of Ben Gurion in the Knesset in 1949, who stated that "Between a Greater Israel or a Jewish State, we have chosen the Jewish State." The policy of occupation after the Six Day War also included seizing lands from the territories, by means of a series of government decisions and initiatives by the settlers, but this deviated from the tradition of preserving the balance between territories intended for occupation and the demographic ability to maintain a Jewish majority in them.

Three periods of seizing control over lands in the territories can be identified. The first, up to 1977, was characterized by control by the Labor Party, which implemented a policy formulated by Yigal Alon in his renowned plan (Admoni, 1999). The second period continued until the Oslo Accords, characterized by cooperation between the Likud government, Gush Emunim, and the Judea and Samaria Council. The third period began with the Oslo Accords and continues to up the present.

During the period of the Labor Party government, between 1967 and 1977, the Alon Plan laid out the map for seizure of lands. To implement the plan, the government declared that it had acquired land from the Jordanian state and subsequently activated the Absentee Property Act, enacted in the early years of the state, which had led in the 1950s to the expropriation of approximately 1 million dunams of land from Israeli Arabs. Of all the lands that the state acquired following the Six Day War, more than a third were attained by means of this law. The total area of expropriated land reached approximately 1.15 million dunams, of which 700,000 dunams belonged to the state and 430,000 dumans were expropriated. The seizure of 43,000 additional dunams for military needs and the declaration of 100,000 dunams as nature reserves completed the picture and enabled the government to annex about one-quarter of the land of the West Bank (Azulai & Ophir, 2008; Benvenisti & Khayat, 1988; Eldar & Zertal, 2004). Close to half of these areas (300,000 dunams) were located in the Jordan Valley and the foothills of Judea and Samaria. These were vast adjoining areas that had served the Jordanian army and had not been populated by Palestinian settlements. The second most important concentration of lands was that in the Jerusalem area—an annexation that enabled the expansion of the city and its construction boom.

The second period, which lasted from the time of the Likud Party government in 1977 until the Oslo Accords, was characterized by the creation of new tools for the seizure of land in the territories. The most prominent example of this is based on the legal opinion of Pelia Elbak, deputy state attorney at the time, who exploited an Ottoman law from 1858, according to which any land that is unregistered (without a land registry certificate), and that is not worked, belongs to the state. The burden of proof of ownership of such land, including the right of possession, is on the claimants to the land, not on the state. Many Palestinians had abandoned agriculture and sought hired work in Israel,, which facilitated the expropriation of lands for the benefit of the state and the settlement enterprise. The land area controlled by the state and private Jewish factors thus increased to include more than half of the lands on the West Bank, which were used by the settlers without considering the Palestinians' right of possession. In addition, the government relaxed the possibilities of trading in land by introducing private factors into the real estate market in the West Bank.

The third period, beginning with the Oslo Accords, brought under direct Israeli control (Area C) about 66% of the West Bank. The increasing waves of Palestinian uprising created the need to develop a major system of bypass roads for the settlers and ensure their security. For security reasons, the Palestinians were forbidden to approach the roads and settlements by more than 1 km in order to work their fields. This decree in fact expropriated additional land from direct Palestinian control; further, if the land was derelict, not registered to any private owner, and not worked, then according to the military government protocol, the state was entitled to seize it. The establishment of legal and illegal settlements on these lands enabled a creeping process of expansion of the security perimeter around the roads and settlements. The establishment by the Judea and Samaria Council of about 100 such illegal settlements along these roads reveals a methodical trend to exploit this system by the settlers with the state's backing. It further reveals that the Oslo Accords created a new system to intensify Israeli control of the area by establishing a model of territorial control based on direct control of the main arteries and splitting up the Palestinian territory into scattered patches separated from each other. These tactics of split and control replaced the former stages of direct control over the lands settled by large Palestinian communities.

In summary, the process of controlling the lands on the West Bank has been consistent and methodical and initiated by the state. It was largely successful, bringing under control more than two-thirds of the lands while leaving compact areas of the Palestinian population under Palestinian direct control but indirect Israeli control. On the fringes of the process is the trend of Jewish factors to purchase Palestinian land. Such purchases are usually carried out in secret, using straw companies, often on the edge of the law, but they are minimal in the overall scheme of things.

SETTLEMENT

The settlement process in the territories can be divided into three periods paralleling the periods of acquiring lands, with both policies tightly linked. During the first period the Labor government inaugurated the settlement plan through the Alon Plan, which had been formally adopted by the Labor party, although already at that time new forces were pushing to expand the settlement process beyond the guidelines of the Alon Plan. The total number of Jewish settlers in the territories during this period was only 3,176. Two-thirds of them settled in the Jordan Valley according to the Alon Plan and an additional quarter in Hebron, Gush Etzion, and the Jerusalem periphery. The remainder were scattered among a number of small settlements. The small number of settlers in the first decade expressed the ambivalent approach of the Labor party regarding settlement. On the one hand, expansive plans for settlement had been made and the government had given in to activist pressure within the Labor party and to external pressure by such groups as Gush Emunim; on the other hand, it did very little to implement these plans.

The Alon Plan recommended the construction of a line of settlements along the Jordan Valley, in the Gaza Strip, and surrounding Jerusalem. The line of settlements along the Jordan Valley was intended for fertile land that was unpopulated; had water sources that flowed freely into the River Jordan and the Dead Sea; and was based on the perception that settlements could, over time, secure sovereignty over areas of strategic importance (Admoni, 1999; Benvenisti & Khayat, 1988). The settlement in the Gaza area was intended to create three buffer regions between concentrations of Palestinian populations to enable control of the area in the face of the uprising that had erupted in the Gaza Strip in the early 1970s. The settlement had a dual role: first, to restrict movement and communication among the Palestinians in parts of the area and, second, to show the Palestinian population that Israel intended to remain in the Gaza Strip and that it would be better for the Palestinians to cooperate with the authorities. The construction of new neighborhoods surrounding Jerusalem stemmed more from national-historical considerations than from security concerns, but also from the need to secure free movement between the center of the country and the Jordan Valley.

The second period, between the rise of the Likud party to power in 1977 and the Oslo Accords in 1993, was characterized by an accelerated settlement that reached its peak in the 1980s, following the appointment of Ariel Sharon as Minister for the Settlements. The period began with an official plan by the Department for Settlement, established by the Likud government in the Jewish Agency. The plan adopted the Gush Emunim plan, expanding it and providing a strategic-security rationale in addition to the religious-messianic rationale of Gush Emunim (Schnell, 2009). Drobless (see Benvenisti & Khayat, 1998), in a plan similar to the Gush Emunim plan, proposed creating two lines of settlements from south to north, one on the eastern slopes and the other on the western slopes of the mountains of Judea and Samaria. These two lines of settlements were intended to protect one another and ensure the settlers' control of the new area. They were also intended to prevent the establishment of a Palestinian state in the future. Emphasis was placed on setting up groups of settlements that would each assist and protect its neighbors, and locating them along the main arteries between Israel and the Jordan Valley (Drobless, 1980, in Benvenishti & Khayat, 1988). The plan proposed founding 86 settlements for approximately 120,000 settlers.

In actuality, up to 1982, about 70 settlements had been founded. Most of them had been set up by Gush Emunim, with groups of supporters establishing a number of settlements, each one in turn by leaving the previous settlement almost empty of inhabitants. Despite the impressive number of new settlements, they included only about 21,000 new residents. In 1982 it seemed that the reserve of volunteers from Gush Emunim was approaching its limit. Secular settlers avoided settling in the distant, isolated settlements that had been planned by Drobless and were located in the vicinity of crowded Palestinian centers. A breakthrough in new settlements came in the 1980s following Arik Sharon's decision to populate the western mountain area of the West Bank with a line of suburban settlements affiliated with the cities of Jerusalem and Tel Aviv. Within ten years, about 100,000 Jews had settled in new settlements there. Some of them were established on the Green Line in order to blur it and erase it from the national memory. Prominent in this respect was the Seven Stars plan, by which settlements were founded on both sides of the Green Line, and a line of satellite towns grew to include over 10,000 inhabitants each (Ariel, Ma'ale Adomim, Beitar Elite, and others).

An additional settlement enterprise from the same period took place in the Gaza Strip. Whereas during the first period only 3 settlements were established there, 2 of them as *Nahal* (semimilitary) outposts, during the second period 14 settlements arose, most of them in Gush Katif, and populated by about 6,000 people. On the eve of the Oslo Accords the number of settlers in the territories had reached approximately 200,000.

The third period was characterized by expansion of the settlements and massive construction, mainly around Jerusalem, as well as the establishment of about 100 illegal settlements, mostly intended to expand and reinforce settlement along the main arterial roads controlling the West Bank. Despite the State of Israel's obligation to seek a solution of peace based on two states for two nations, the pace of settlement increased. In 2005 the number of settlers reached over 250,000, even after evacuation of around 8,000 settlers from the Gaza Strip (and not including a similar number of settlers in the territories of Jerusalem). This enterprise, which intensified over the years, reveals the desire to annex the territories while employing spatial strategies enabling control over all the territories, even though the Jews would be a minority in the area.

MAPS

Maps, as noted, are an accepted method of constructing a national identity. The State of Israel has demonstrated strong sensitivity to the importance of the map in the public discourse and the educational system. The maps printed after founding of the state clearly differentiated between the international borders, which had become permanent and recognized, and the cease-fire lines, whose main significance lay in their temporary nature. In accordance with this principle, the borders with Egypt, Lebanon, and Jordan, excluding the Gaza Strip and the West Bank, were declared as international borders, while the borders with the Gaza Strip and the West Bank were defined as temporary cease-fire lines. This decision is important given the sense of siege and strategic threat that the state felt regarding its neighbors across the border (Leuenberger & Schnell, 2010). Berger (2008) saw in this decision an expression of the state's failure to come to terms with the borders that separate the State of Israel and the biblical homeland, and that leaves the state in an inferior geo-strategic position. The Jewish state's lack of commitment to a clear border expresses the pragmatic view of the Zionist leadership, which, along with the dream of a "Greater Israel," had agreed to a compromise over the limited political borders (Gorny 1993). The map providing the most important expression of the determination to avoid any particular border is the "Blue Box" map of the Jewish National Fund, intended to brand the national territory among the Jewish communities in the Diaspora and mainly among Israel's children (Bar-Gal, 1999; Leuenberger & Schnell, 2010).

In contrast to the earlier declarations by Israel's leaders following the Six Day War that the territories are a peace card, the then Minister of Labor, Yigal Alon, produced an order forbidding the state survey office—the only body that published official maps of the State of Israel—to publish maps that incorporated the 1949 cease-fire lines. In his announcement to the Knesset that same year, the minister compelled the State Department to denote only the new cease-fire lines as temporary borders of the state (Oren & Regev, 2008). Alon thereby acted to obliterate the Green Line from the map delineating the national territory. This act, which accompanied the process of determining

Israel's secure borders along the River Jordan and across the Gaza Strip, is highly significant. It reveals the methodical attempt of the ruling powers to incorporate the new territory within the borders that annex the territories to the State of Israel.

This action by Minister Yigal Alon was not a one-time phenomenon but part of a consistent trend of the entire Israeli government over the years. Moshe Braver, who had published a series of atlases that had long been a central educational tool in geography, confirms that the omission of the Green Line from his atlases did not derive from his academic recognition that this was correct. It was forced upon him by the Housing Department that published the atlas and by the Ministry of Education, which made its authorization for their use in schools conditional upon this step (Leuenberger & Schnell, 2010). This is reinforced by two conflicts that developed between government factors and the editors of the atlases.

The first conflict was between the Minister of Housing, David Levy, and the editor of the *Israel Atlas*, David Amiran (1982), after the latter wrote, in a description of the settlements, that their location was based on political purposes rather than geographical logic. The minister asked him to change the wording and define these settlements like any others in the State of Israel and when Amiran refused, the minister asked other authors to write a corrected appendix to the atlas. When all of Israel's geographers refused to question the integrity of Professor Amiran, the minister had a nongeographic writer provide the appendix page (Leuenberger & Schnell, 2010). The second conflict was between the Minister of Education, Limor Livnat, and Professor Braver. Representatives of the Judea and Samaria Council complained that the index of the *Israel Atlas* referred to Judea and Samaria as areas affiliated with Israel and not as an integral part of the state, even though the borders of the Green Line had been deleted from the map. The minister demanded that Professor Braver remove this reference to Judea and Samaria as a condition for approving the use of the atlas in schools. After Professor Braver was awarded the Israel Prize, however, the minister decided to give up this battle, and the contested affiliation remained on the maps (Leuenberger & Schnell, 2010). These events reveal how the state persisted in devising the maps in a way that would incorporate the occupied territories within the national territory.

PLACE NAMES

Place names as part of a language are a dominant component in the cultural unification of a nation and an identifying link between a people and its territory. Place names as a toponymic system create an inclusive system of signifying space within the national culture. Place names thereby create the sense of an authentic bond between the nation's past, culture and language, and its territory (Even Zohar, 1986) by reifying space (Duncan & Duncan, 1988). The process of name-giving thus reveals the approach of those in power and authority in determining names in order to express the hegemonic ideology (Carter, 1988). This is a dual process: first, place names indicate the significance and identity of a place; second, they are an external expression of the ideological structures that guide the choice of names (Eco, 1972). In the national connection, enlisting history for signifying identity by means of names is an important trend (Billig, 1995; Gillis 1994). Thus, the determination of names that refer to past periods of glory—golden ages—of the nation, and the determination of names of national heroes, is common practice in areas that have come under new authority or been divided up and wish to apply the new national identity to the territory (Azaryahu & Zelinski, 1988; Golan, 2001). The Hebraicization of the map of the settlements and places in Israel was defined as a national enterprise immediately following the founding of the state. A government committee was set up to determine names for the settlements, and it still functions today according to the same principles (Azaryahu & Golan, 2001). The committee has never defined clear criteria for naming settlements, but its coordinator published the principles, which have since informally guided the committee. The committee members, in giving names, emphasize expression of the strong bond between the nation and its land by reviving historical Hebrew names and names from Jewish sources (Bitan, 1992).

Cohen and Kliot (1981) have discerned six categories of names, and Darzia (1993), using these categories, compares the division of names of settlements in the territories and those of settlements within Israel proper. Table 3.1 reveals that, similar to the country in general, more than half of the names are derived from the golden ages of the Bible or the Mishnah, and from the wish to commemorate individuals and events associated with independence, very similar to the processes of name-giving in any young country. The prominent trend in the territories is a proliferation of biblical names (see Table 3.1). This trend derives, on the one hand, from the fact that this land area is at the heart of the land of the Bible and, on the other hand, from the wish to emphasize the return to the homeland rather than control over occupied territories. A comparison between the criteria for name-giving in the Galilee and in the territories reveals that in the Galilee too, many of the names given to settlements in the early years were biblical, and it was only later that Mishnah names became common. This is also the case in the territories, although the multitude of potential names for the area explains the difference. This trend also attests

TABLE 3.1 *DIVISION OF SETTLEMENTS ACCORDING TO TYPE OF NAME (%)*

Category	Israel	West Bank
Biblical names	28	44
Mishna and Talmud names	11	6
Symbolic names	26	21
Commemorative names	14	9
Hebraized names	7	10
Names from nature	14	10
Total	100	100

to the preference for biblical names that characterize the map of settlements in Israel. Settlement in the territories, furthermore, emphasizes the return to the land of the forefathers and the roots of the neo-Zionist movement, which is identified with the settlement as lying at the heart of the renewed national identity.

NATIONAL EDUCATION

Education is perceived as a central mechanism for transmitting the national heritage to the younger generations (Anderson, 1991; Gelner 1994; Sarup 1996). Joseph Azariyahu and Ephraim Auerbuch, who helped to establish the foundations of Hebrew education in Israel, were aware of this and chose the German *Heimatkunde* (home studies) model, which emphasizes love of the homeland as a central aim of the educational system. Consequently, they committed the subjects of Bible studies, nature studies, history, and mainly geography to this principle (Bar-Gal, 1993; Schnell, 2000). This approach remains important in Israeli education to this day. Its most prominent trends can be seen in the state religious schools. The seeds of a spiritual, messianic awakening of the national religious youth, who felt that their parents had been pushed to the margins of Israeli society, had already been sown in the state religious education system, in the Bnei Akiva youth movement, and in the accommodated yeshivas (Orthodox-religious colleges) before the Six Day War (Peleg, 1997). Hoffman (2002) notes that the curriculum for 1961 emphasizes the study of history as part of the "love of homeland" studies. He shows that within the five aims set out by the plan, the first three emphasize the teaching of history to reinforce the bond between student and homeland. General history studies are offered merely as a background for the understanding of Jewish history. History studies begin with the biblical period and lead to the conclusion that Zionism is the only solution to ensuring the existence of Jews.

Moreover, the division between state education and state religious education is widening. While the Zionist solution is presented in state education as the product of a process of rational historical development, in state religious education it is presented as the outcome of the messianic redemption of Israel (Hoffman, 2002). However, despite these important differences in educational vision, the study books used in state education have remained similar to those used in state religious education. Attempts to develop more critical study curricula, emphasizing the importance of studying general history, have not been fully realised, despite the declared intentions of the formal curricula. The same applies to the attempt to create a less ethnocentric historical narrative concerning the national dispute between the people of Israel and the Palestinian people (Firer, 1985; Podeh, 2002). Two examples of the success of right-wing groups in barring such study programs from state education are the textbook *The 20th Century on the Threshold of Tomorrow*, by Eyal Naveh, and the textbook *A World of Exchanges*, edited by Danny Jakobi. Both books attempted to present the dispute between the Palestinian and the Jewish movements from a critical standpoint, but both were recalled by the Ministry of Education due to their critical perspective (Hoffman, 2002). As a result, statements of intent regarding changes in the history program in state education, intended to expose the student to general history and to a critical understanding of the national dispute over land, were never issued. This means that the ethnocentric textbooks of the state religious education system have continued to cast their shadow over the textbooks in the state education system.

While history continues to be taught as a series of events that led to the unavoidable conclusion of the Zionist solution, the teaching of geography focuses on presenting the right of the Jewish people to the land and the area of Judea and Samaria as an integral part of the homeland. The curriculum adopts the *regional geography* approach as its main method, and one that has served national projects around the world (Buttimer, 1993; Hooson, 1994). In the spirit of the German *Heimatkunde,* the students begin to learn about their own immediate neighborhoods in primary school; from there, in increasing circles, they learn about the broader area, the state and the world. Emphasis is placed on direct experience with the landscapes of Israel to reinforce the emotional bond with the homeland (Schnell, 2000). Bar-Gal quotes Jakob Ushpiz, who wrote about education in 1927, that "A system of up-to-date teaching about the homeland will succeed in silencing the wars that are generated in the heart of our new pupil and make him cherish the land" (Bar-Gal, 1993, p. 55). Schnell (2002) quoted from an interview with Professor Dov Nir, one of the senior authors of the geography textbooks, which determined that the curricula continued to be based on the regional method, even though it had lost its importance in the geographic discourse, as there was still a need to reinforce the identification of new immigrants with the homeland.

The right to the land is seen as based on the historical-biblical right to the land, but also to an equal extent by the right of determination, ideological fervor, and willingness to fight tempestuous nature and defeat it, a challenge that the Arabs of the land, who were perceived as part of that nature, could not withstand (Schnell, 1999, 2001). The Jewish superiority in subduing nature in the process of building a homeland is emphasized in the textbooks in three ways. In the book on the coastal plain published by the Educational Television channel, it is noted that the coastal plain, which is controlled by the forces of nature—drifting sands and swamps—had been left bare of human inhabitants. The Zionist landscape, in contrast, which is controlled by humans, is a thriving landscape of settlements and industrial plants, green fields and fish ponds. In descriptions of the Galilee, a proud Arab is quoted as saying that the settlement has transformed the traditional village into a developed and flourishing urban settlement under the rule of the Jewish state. The text makes no mention of the massive expropriation of lands or the processes of glorifying space to which geographers frequently refer in the academic discourse.

The second way in which Jewish superiority is conveyed relates to the way the areas of Judea and Samaria are presented in the textbooks. First, in a book on Israel, these areas are incorporated as legitimate areas, like any other in the country, with no mention of their special status as occupied territory. Furthermore, the description of these areas does not relate to the national dispute and the national aspirations of the Palestinian people, aspirations that were obliterated by the governments of Israel, with the exception of a few mentions in connection with Jerusalem. The Palestinians are presented as members of a traditional society that, in contrast to the Arabs of the Galilee, have not managed to undergo the modernization inspired by the development that the Zionist settlement has brought to these areas.

The third way Jewish superiority is described relates to the Arabs of the Middle East. The book *Geography of the Middle East* by Arnon Sofer presents the efforts at development of the Arab states in the area of the Nile and the Euphrates as a tale of stinging failures in the struggle of humanity against nature. These failures are derived from, on the one hand, and explain, on the other, the backwardness of the Arab states. Such claims are revealed against the background of the success of the Zionist enterprise in subduing tempestuous nature (Schnell, 2002). The conclusion that the student is asked to draw although it is unintentional, is that the State of Israel presents a model for the establishment of an advanced civilization in the hostile environment of the Middle East. This success, in comparison with the failure of the Arabs to develop the country, reinforces the validity of the historical justification for the existence of the State of Israel, for which Judea and Samaria constitute the heart of the homeland.

ARCHAEOLOGY

Archaeology confers a tangible, material meaning on the historical tale, bringing selected periods from the past into the present and conferring on archaeological sites significance as links in the chain of events that construct the national history. Exposing certain sites and not others, removing certain strata, and reconstructing and preserving others are all practices by which archaeologists introduce a chosen historical story into the present and conceal any alternatives stories. The material significance of the archaeological sites creates a refictionalization of the historical national story and confers authenticity upon it. Furthermore, controlling what is to be exposed of the past is an important power in managing the desired national story. Until the 1970s, Israeli archaeology had enlisted in the national mission, but then it began to adopt more critical approaches. Against this background, it is interesting to examine the extent to which archaeology was enlisted in the project of annexing the territories to the national territory.

Archaeological activity began immediately after the Six Day War. A survey carried out by Kochavi (see Greenberg, 2008) was also initiated immediately after the war, and it located 800 archaeological sites. Today the archaeological map denotes 5,400 such sites, of which approximately 900 have been wholly or partially excavated. All the excavations were carried out under the supervision of the district manager while apparently conforming to the regulations pertaining to occupied territory. For example, Israel honored its obligation to prevent removal of found artifacts from excavations in the territories. Nevertheless, Israeli control of archaeological activity was important in serving Israel's national aims. Academic archaeological research served two main declared purposes. The first is exposure of the biblical past and tracing early Christianity (Finkelstein, 1999; Greenberg, 2008). A study of 188 sites in an advanced state of excavation and research, carried out by a team from Tel Aviv University (Greenberg, 2008), reveals that 45% of them were mainly Christian sites, 41% were mainly Jewish sites, and only 24% were Muslim sites. The remaining 2% were Samaritan sites. It can thus be seen that the Muslim-Arab roots have received very little exposure in archaeological research.

The Palestinian complaints about this archaeological research reveal the reasons for this discrimination. Palestinian archaeologists complain mainly about their exclusion from research in the territories and their lack of accessibility to the digs at the sites there. In addition, they state that defining the sites as more than 300 years old is against their interests and prevents the Palestinian building tradition of the last centuries from receiving archaeological exposure. They want every site more than 100 years old be defined as an archaeological site (Greenberg, 2008). In this connection, it should be noted that no claims have been heard from Palestinian archaeologists regarding the removal of strata from the Muslim period at the sites that have been excavated, or of the neglect of such sites. An additional complaint relates to the fact that the artifacts found at the digs are transferred to East Jerusalem, which is perceived as part of the territories by the international community but as part of Israel by the State of Israel. Many artifacts are also lent to museums in Israel without ensuring their safe return to their original owners in the territories. The Israeli archaeologists thereby circumvent the international protocol regarding the archaeological rights of an occupied people.

From the Israeli perspective, the critical viewpoint of the Israel Academy is prominent in studies of the Jewish roots in the homeland. The most salient of these studies is that of Finkelstein and Silberman (2001), who concludes from the excavated Jewish sites that the kingdom of David and Solomon was smaller and less developed than might have been thought based on the stories from the Bible. This research led to a drop in the biblical-based paradigm, which used the Bible as a main source for guiding archaeological studies among the mainstream in Israel's academic community.

Thus far, I have discussed the activities of academic archaeology, but its task was only secondary to archaeological research in the territories. Up to the 1980s very few studies were carried out there, and following a fruitful period lasting for about a decade, the Israeli Academy avoided research in the territories following the Oslo Accords and the outbreak of the *intifada*. Most of the task was left in the hands of the district manager, who ran the archaeological department. His activities had no organized public supervision and received no official report. Despite this, a certain reflection of the archaeological activities can be found in the publications of Ariel College (located in the territories). The college produces an annual publication of academic research in Judea and Samaria, which collates all the research in the territories. A sizable chapter is dedicated to archaeological research. Examination of the publications between 1993 and 2003 reveals that approximately 70% of the articles concerning archaeology are related to the Jewish heritage in the territories. The remaining articles concern the Hellenistic-Roman-Byzantine heritage and methodological subjects. Only three or four studies have dealt with the Arab-Muslim heritage. In other words, the bias in such research on the Jewish heritage is greater than in academic research on the territories.

Beyond this, the archaeological research, as reflected in the Ariel College publications, relies heavily on the biblical tradition of archaeological research, which was undermined by mainstream Israeli archaeology. A good example of this can be found in Shimon Riklin's research on the location of the biblical city of Ai (Riklis, 1995). Following a discussion of the biblical sources and identification of archaeological sites that had not been excavated or at which no relics from the appropriate period had been found, Riklin concluded that the location of Ai was east of Beth El, based on the close mention of the two cities in the Bible. In his summary, he states that "It seems that the historical (biblical) description, with all its limitations, is still in many cases preferable to an analysis of material findings in the field. In this article too, an attempt was made to draw assistance as far as possible from the biblical description, for it is only due to this description that we know the story of Ai and its assumed location" (pp. 29–30). Clearly, under the auspices of the district manager, such enlisted archaeology develops to its fullest extent, while disqualifying any critical approach to the project of annexing the territories to the national territory.

The alternative archaeological research provides a way of disseminating popular knowledge on the territories by means of tourist maps of the heritage sites there, distributed by the Judea and Samaria Council and the local councils subordinate to it, as well as via the field school system that disseminates information with the help of the Ministry of Education. The Judea and Samaria Council distributes a tourist map of the territories that presents a list of Jewish tourist sites reconstructed according to biblical archaeology. Moreover, every local council disseminates tourist maps that incorporate the Jewish settlements in the territories, access roads to the area from the Green Line, and historical Jewish sites. These maps completely erase the Palestinian space and present the territories as part of the continuous territory of Israel, both spatially and temporally.

Only four field schools function in the West Bank, and they have become the distribution agents of alternative archaeological knowledge. The fact that the Ministry of Education sends dozens of classes from the state education and state religious education systems on annual field trips under the instruction of these field schools gives them official government backing. For example, the website of the Kfar Etzion field school notes that approximately 50,000 pupils from 50 schools and approximately 10,000 private visitors passed through the school in 2009. An article by Meir Tori on the website reveals that the school is involved in the excavations and archaeological research focusing on exposing the biblical and *mishnaic* past of the area. The school emphasizes three subjects among its educational activities: revealing the Jewish past in the area as a means of understanding the connection between nation and land; research and teaching about the heritage of the warriors of Gush Etzion; and the lifestyle of the Arabs, exhibited in a museum, as a model of the biblical lifestyle. These subjects, taught under the auspices of the Ministry of Education, serve the purpose of defining the territories as part of the national territory in Israeli public awareness.

MECHANISMS FOR CONSTRUCTING THE NATIONAL TERRITORY

Daily Life of the Settlers

Memmi (1985), in his book on the occupier and the occupied, examines how daily life under an occupying power affects both of these communities. His main contention is that both sides, even basically decent people, are trapped in a reality of oppression and exploitation The mechanism of occupation forces the oppressors, even against their wishes, to devalue the oppressed and ensure their submissive behavior in order to guarantee their control. The use of terror by the oppressed as a means of protest and struggle for independence forces the oppressor to use even harsher means of suppression. These mechanisms become an existential necessity for the conqueror, a mechanism that reconstructs the identity of both occupier and occupied (Tajfel, 1978).

The bloody dispute between the two sides, saturated with bitter incidents of violence and reaction to violence, obscures the actual sources of the dispute in the mutual desire for revenge (Girard, 1977). In this process, the occupier must seek ways to preserve his own positive self-image in the face of the increasing cruelty of the mechanism of occupation. Such a mechanism dehumanizes the occupied, creating an image that is reinforced in public opinion in the face of the violence used by the oppressed in their struggle for independence (Derrida, 2005; Korf, 2006). The occupation creates dimensions that resemble the reality described by Memmi as leading to the establishment of an oppressed/oppressor relationship, characterized by the dehumanizing of each side by the other. The settler constructs a self-image of peace-seeking, of having settled in the territories in order to live in peace with his Palestinian neighbors, for his own well-being as well as for the economic well-being of those neighbors (Bar-Tal, 2007). The settlers frequently claim that they have brought development to the territories and provided work for the Palestinians, with whom they wish to live in peace. Many nostalgically recall the wonderful neighborly connections between themselves and the Palestinians until the outbreak of Palestinian violence, which they consider as having damaged this relationship. They add that they provided employment for the Palestinians that allowed them to live with dignity under the occupation. The settlers thereby ignore their own latent violence as occupiers, settling under the protection of the Israeli army and a support system of control of the territories—perceived by the Palestinians as Palestinian territory—as well as the systematic dispossession of Palestinians from their lands and their sources of existence.

These territorial examples of daily reality under an occupying power demonstrate the establishment of latent violence as a means to ensure the submission of the occupied. The best example is the fact that every settler on the streets in the territories carries a gun for self-defense. This makes any encounter between a settler and a Palestinian unequal and forces the latter to accept the settler's advantage of power. In such a reality there is no need to use the weapon in order to demonstrate the unequal power relationship. This inequality affects the behavior of both sides at every encounter, whether in the market, during a neighbors' quarrel, or following mutual provocation. Despite this, the settlers on more than one occasion either use or threaten to use their weapons against certain Palestinian protest behaviors, such as stone throwing, even when it is doubtful whether the settlers' lives are in immediate danger.

Another example derives from the settlers' behavior on the roads. Their feeling that stopping at an intersection exposes them to potential terrorist activity led in the 1970s to the establishment of a specific driving norm: any vehicle with an Israeli license plate crosses the intersection first, regardless of its direction. The Palestinian vehicles must wait at the intersection until the Israeli vehicles have passed. This norm has led to a practice that reestablishes the settlers' dominion over the conquered people. When it proved insufficient against overt Palestinian violence, thousands of dunams of Palestinian land were expropriated for security purposes in order to build separate roads for the settlers that bypass the Palestinian towns and villages. This expression of latent violence against Palestinian interests is perceived by the occupiers as a means of defense against the savage enemy and not as an act of violence toward that enemy. The reality of daily life under an occupying power abounds with such practices, which lead to shaping a superior/separatist settler who learns to diminish the value of the other.

The dozens of roadblocks on the roads in the territories also emphasize the Palestinian inferiority in comparison with the Jews. Jews pass unchecked through these roadblocks. The Palestinians, in contrast, are required to undergo a lengthy wait in line for a security check, which on occasion involves humiliating practices, and leaves those wishing to pass at the mercy of arbitrary, and sometimes even cruel, decisions a theme that repeats itself in Machsom Watch reports over the years (*Reports from Roadblock Watch*). Another practice is that of emphasizing the Jewish appearance of the place and thereby denoting it as Jewish. The settlers living in areas close to a Palestinian village adorn the roofs of their houses with large national flags. Their homes are surrounded by defensive fences, powerful night lighting, and armed guards. The devices that emphasize the Jewish appearance of the place give the impression that Jewish settlements have gained control over vast areas of the space. Their topographically high location and their security measures give them a dimension of control of the area and a sense of surveillance over the neighboring Palestinian areas. For their own security, the Palestinians need to go around these sites and keep away from them. Moreover, the fact that the settlers frequently encounter Palestinians in their daily lives in the centers of these towns and villages reinforces the settlers' sense of surveillance that the settlements and army posts in Arab neighborhoods impose upon the Palestinians. There is much evidence of the overturning of market stalls, and of cursing and spitting at the Palestinians over minor disputes. At each such event the Palestinian is afraid to react, for he knows that the nearby policeman or soldier will not protect his rights and that the armed settler may endanger his life; therefore, he submissively accepts these provocations. Many murders of Palestinians have never been solved, despite suspicion falling on the settlers, since there was no appropriate follow-up by the police. The settlers frequently attach the Israeli flag to their vehicles in order to let the Palestinians know that these are settlers' cars whose occupants are armed and willing to use their weapons. This practice has more than once been recalled with pride by settlers who announce that "The Palestinians don't dare to mess with us, so the flag on the car enhances our safety on the roads" (interviews by me with several settlers in the territories during the years 1990–1993). Such daily incidents establish the sense of humiliation of the Palestinian and the sense of superiority of the settler. The settler feels that the territories are a wilderness waiting to be conquered, while the Palestinian is seen as simply a part of the savage reality that must be restrained.

These examples indicate the unequal, institutionalised, daily oppression that establishes the position of inferiority of the Palestinians when confronting the settlers and Israeli soldiers. Hundreds of thousands of young Israelis and reserve duty soldiers are partners to this experience during their military service, and they bring back this memory to their civilian life behind the Green Line. These examples, however, are only the tip of the iceberg of a government system that denies Palestinian rights. A Palestinian citizen requires many permits from the military authorities. He is forced to wait in long queues, to deal with arbitrary responses and with a list of restrictions on his movements, his right to ownership, and so on. All these conditions deepen the sense of humiliation that the Palestinian carries with him, in particular the shame that accompanies the humiliation of parents in front of their children and of women in front of their husbands.

It is hard to prove the effect of these institutionalized practices of oppression in the territories on Israeli society as a whole. However, the events of October 2000, in which Arabs/Palestinian citizens of Israel violently demonstrated in support of the Palestinians, and were confronted by even more violent police force that led to the loss of life of seven Arab/Palestinian demonstrators and one Jew, offer an indication of the trickling down into the State of Israel of certain perspectives and patterns of behavior that have become established in the territories (Rosler et al., 2009). Already in the 1990s, a study by Schnell (1994) revealed that while the Arab citizens of Israel perceive themselves as Palestinians, they distinguish between their status as Israeli citizens and that of the Palestinians in the occupied territories. In contrast, interviews with a Jewish control group from settlements near Arab towns revealed that the Jews did not distinguish between Palestinians who were Israeli citizens and Palestinians from the territories; instead, they perceived all of them as a hostile society endangering the state. The demonstrations of October 2000 ended with 13 Arabs being killed after police shot into the crowd of demonstrators, similar to the behavior of the security forces at the demonstrations in the territories, and in contradiction to the norms applied to equally violent demonstrations by ultra-Orthodox Jews.

CONCLUSIONS

Long occupation and conquest of others' lands are common in human history. The historian David Day (2008) suggests some generalization to the dynamic of conquest. He states that any conquest starts with developing a narrative that legitimizes the territorial claim and implants this claim in public awareness by symbolic means like the use of maps and language. However, practical control over the territory is necessary to press the claim. This includes effective use of lands and resources in the claimed territories and, above all, the settlement of the territory by the occupier's population. The occupier also needs to invent a moral justification for the occupation. At the same time, the occupier needs to suppress the occupied population, either expelling them, marginalizing them, or assimilating them. Day argues that this basic model applies to ancient societies as much as to the occupation of Tibet in the 1950s and to the colonial world, from which he draws most of his evidence, in between.

The main stages in Day's model have been further developed by other scholars. Bar-Tal (2000) argues that the need for moral justification is rooted in occupying societies' need to maintain a positive self-image. Anderson (1991) demonstrates how different territorial mechanisms are used to consolidate the national identity. Geographers further developed an understanding of the use of symbolic representations of territories in nation building (Leuenberger & Schnell, 2010; Passi, 1999). Memmi (1985) specifies the mechanisms that lead to the vicious circle of growing violence and suppression of the occupied. Despite the fact that after World War II the international community tended to delegitimize occupations, there are several examples of such occupations, like those of Tibet and Cyprus. It seems that despite the delegitimization of occupation, the international community intervenes only when the occupier loses control over the territory, as in the Palestinian uprisings of the 1990s and 2000s—in contrast to the former period, when Israel effectively controlled the territories, and unlike the Tibetan and Cypriot cases, in which the international community avoided any action against their occupations.

The State of Israel decided to confront the risk of international delegitimization of the occupation of the Palestinian territories by avoiding open annexation of the territories and by declaring its intention to respect the international conventions that define the behavior of occupiers in occupied territories, despite the doubts raised by some Israeli jurists in regard to the international status of the territories. The findings of the present study reveal that this decision was not strategic, but rather purely tactical. It was aimed at enabling the State of Israel to systematically activate practices of de facto annexation without arousing active objections by the international community, while preserving the possibility of maintaining a military government in the territories to suppress any attempt by the Palestinians to rebel against this creeping process of annexation. These mechanisms are not unique to the State of Israel; many other young countries have used them to give the public a sense of national identity connected with a territory perceived as national territory. The uniqueness of the Israeli case lies in the annexation of territory that the state itself has defined as occupied territory and not as part of the homeland. A dual regime has thereby been created: (1) a distinction between the formal status of the occupied territories and the effort to annex these territories to the national territory for reconstruction of the Israeli national identity and (2) a distinction between the military government that rules the Palestinians in the territories, as required by the international conventions regarding the population in occupied territory, and the increasing Jewish population in the territories that enjoys full citizens' rights.

According to Azulai and Ophir (2008) this duality, already long established, has created a regime that constitutes part of the political structure of Israeli society, and not control over foreign territory. Within this regime, part of the population enjoys full citizens' rights, while another part does not, in a way that undermines the democratic foundations of the state, while democracy is preserved both within the Green Line and in the territories in regard to the Jewish population, so that it cannot be claimed that the State of Israel is not a democratic state. Such duality has increased; between 1949 and 1967, part of the Arab population lacked basic rights as subjects of the military government despite having been defined as citizens of the state. The central conclusion of this discussion is that the Israeli political system has found ways to deprive the Palestinian population of their basic rights without undermining the democratic legitimacy of the state, either internally or externally. Although this framework of restricted rights has been altered over the years, Palestinians' deprivation of their basic rights still lies at the foundation of the Israeli political structure.

Most of the practices used to ensure Jewish control over the territories, and to develop territorial awareness among the Jewish people in regard to the new territories, were carried out by the state's official institutions, occasionally while putting pressure on various academics and professional bodies that refused to cooperate. Control of the land, the settlements, map design, education, and so have all been directly controlled by state institutions. The extent of activity of these mechanisms, their systematic activation, and their consistency and multidimensionality reveal that the project of connecting the new national identity with the new territories was a deliberate endeavor and not an indirect consequence of indecision by the government of Israel. It would seem that the activities of groups such as Gush Emunim and the Judea and Samarian Council have become assimilated within the activities of state institutions, which have continued to provide active backing even during times of tension between government groups and the settlers' organizations.

The effect of these processes on Israeli society is reflected in the renewed definition of Israeli identity, which increasingly stresses the Jewish component of the identity as a democratic Jewish state due to the centrality of the new territories in constructing the national identity. This trend is expressed in the transformation of the state's political discourse since its occupation of the territories. The central agent of this trend has been the Gush Emunim movement. This group swept along the national religious movement into taking a stand aimed at leading the Zionist movement toward an emphasis on the Jewish identity of the state, and at converting Judea and Samaria into the moving force driving the political activities in this direction. Over the years since the occupation began, Israeli politics has established two competing coalitions. The right-wing coalition emphasizes the particularistic Jewish identity, while the other coalition, including the left-wing parties, emphasizes the universal, humanist identity. These two viewpoints also relate to the stands taken on Israeli control of the territories. The left-wing coalition aspires to achieve peace with the Arab states, which involves renouncing control of the territories. The right-wing coalition has defined the territories as constituting the heart of the Land of Israel; its control expresses the essence of the identity of the state as a Jewish state.

The sharp focus on the national identity as a religious identity has not been restricted to Gush Emunim and the religious Zionist movement, but has deeply pervaded many other sectors in Jewish society. The tendency to shift between a humanist, universalist stand and a particularistic Jewish one has mainly characterized activist elements in the Labor party and Liberal party. The Six Day War brought to the public stage the Movement for a Greater Israel, composed of members of the Achdut Avoda (workers') party and activists from Mapai (the main branch of the Labor party). These groups joined the right-wing parties that supported annexation of the territories. The Liberal party too joined the right-wing Herut party, which continued to believe in a Greater Israel. This union was derived from other, more complex factors in Israeli politics, but the enthusiasm that had swept along many elements in Israeli society due to the conquest of biblical lands also drew the liberals into adopting right-wing stands. The increasing involvement of the ultra-Orthodox in Israeli politics and the enthusiasm resulting from the return to the land of the forefathers persuaded the ultra-Orthodox too to adopt a right-wing stand, demanding annexation of the territories. Moreover, despite the rabbis' support for compromise in regard to the territories, these same rabbis did not press their followers to accept a solution of territorial compromise for fear of losing the support of those who had adopted a right-wing stand in regard to the territories. The fact that the government had settled many of them in the territories also meant that the continued occupation reflected the personal interest of many of these individuals.

The tension between the desire to annex the territories and the demographic equilibrium established in these territories has created for the first time a dialogue in which the components of the national identity of a democratic and Jewish state are perceived as two conflicting identities. On the one hand, annexation of the territories upsets the demographic equilibrium, which in turn may be translated into political power at the polling booth, a fact that threatens the democratic and Jewish nature of the state. On the other hand, relinquishing the territories, which constitute the cradle of Jewish culture and identity, neutralizes the demographic threat but also amounts to relinquishing the Jewish nature of the state deriving from its bond with and loyalty to its traditions. This would seem to be the main issue that the Israeli public is unable to decide. In the meantime, the demographic tension is encouraging a public discourse that supports restricting the rights of the minority and emphasizes preserving the Jewish nature of the state. Derrida (2005) and Agamben (2005) both note that threats to a democratic nation's identity trigger among the majority "mechanisms of self-immunization," which may lead to public support for denying the democratic rights of minorities that threaten the identity of the majority. Various surveys reveal that many Israelis have been ready in recent decades to restrict the rights of the minority in order to secure the Jewish identity of the state. The High Court of Justice is perceived by these elements, and by the right-wing political elite, as an anti-Jewish factor when it strives to preserve the democratic values of Israeli society. Consequently, the territories as an incubator of Jewish identity, and handed to the public in a series of institutionalized practices, have succeeded in altering the public awareness in Israel in the discourse on identity.

REFERENCES

Agamben, G. (2005). *State of exception* (K. Attel, Trans.) Chicago: University of Chicago Press.

Anderson, B. (1991). *Imagined communities.* Verso: London.

Azaryahu, M., & A. Golan, A. (2001). Renaming the landscape: The formation of the Hebrew map of Israel 1949–1960. *Journal of Historical Geography, 27*(2), 178–195.

Bar-Tal, D. (2000). *Shared beliefs in a society: Social psychological analysis.* Thousand Oaks, CA: Sage.

Benvenisti, M., & Khayat, S. (1988). *The West Bank and Gaza atlas.* The Jerusalem Post: Jerusalem.

Billig, M. (1995). *Banal nationalism.* London: Sage.

Brown, B. B. (1987). Territoriality. In D. Stokols & I. Altman (Eds.), *Handbook of environmental psychology* (pp. 505–529). New York: Wiley.

Buttimer, A. (1976). Grasping the dynamism of the life world. *Annals of the Association of American Geographers, 56*(2), 277–292.

Buttimer, A. (1981). Social space and the planning of residential areas, In A. Buttimer & D. Seamon (Eds.), *The human experience of space and place* (pp. 21–54). New York: St. Martin's Press.

Buttimer, A. (1993). *Geography and the human spirit.* Baltimore: John Hopkins University Press.

Carter, P. (1988). *The road to Botany Bay.* New York: Blackwell.

Chisholm, M., & Smith, D. (1990). *Shared space, divided space.* London and Berkeley, CA: Unwin Hyman.

Cohen, S. B., & Kliot, N. (1981). Israel place names as a reflection of continuity and change in nation building. *Names, 29*(4), 653–680.

De Certeau, M. (1984). *The practice of everyday life*. Los Angeles: University of California Press.
Derrida, J. (2005). *Two essays on reason*. Stanford, CA: Stanford University Press.
Duncan, J., & Duncan, N. (1988). Rereading the landscape. *Environment and Planning D: Society and Space, 6*, 117–126.
Eco, U. (1972). *Einfuhrung in de Semiotik*. Munich.
Even Zohar, I. (1986). Language conflict and national identity: A semiotic approach. In J. Halper (Ed.), *Nationalism and modernity: Mediterranean perspectives* (pp. 126–135). New York: Praeger.
Finkelstein, I., & Silberman, N. A. (2001). *The Bible unearthed: Archeology's new vision of ancient Israel and the origin of its sacred texts*. New York: Free Press.
Gelner, E. (1994). *Conditions of liberty: Civil society and the rivals*. New York: Penguin Press.
Girard, R. (1977). *Violence and the sacred*. Baltimore: John Hopkins University Press.
Giddens, A. (1991). *Modernity and self-identity: Self and society in the late modern age*. Cambridge: Polity Press.
Gillis, J. R. (1994). *Commemoration: The politics of national identity*. Princeton, NJ: Princeton University Press.
Greenberg, R. (2008). *The West Bank and East Jerusalem Archeological Data Base Project*. The S. Daniel Abraham Center for International and Regional Studies. Retrieved May 21, 2010, from http://www.tau.ac.il/humanities/abraham/archiological-database.html
Hooson, D. (1994). *Geography and national identity*. Blackwell: Oxford.
Korf, B. (2006). Who is the Rouge? Discourse, power and spatial politics in postwar Sri Lanka. *Political Geography, 25*, 279–297.
Kellerman, A. (1989). *Time, space and society: Geographical and societal perspective*. Dordrecht: Kluwer.
Knight, D. B. (1982). Identity and territoriality, geographical perspectives on nationalism and regionalism. *Annals of the Association of the American Geographers, 72*, 514–531.
Lefevre, H. (1971). *The production of space*. Oxford: Blackwell.
Newman, D. (2001). From national to post-national territorial identities in Israel-Palestine. *Geojournal, 53*(3), 235–246.
Paasi, A. (1999). Boundaries as social processes: Territoriality in a world of flows. *Geopolitics, 3*(1), 69–88.
Podeh, E. (2002). *The Arab-Israeli conflict in Israeli history textbooks, 1948–2000*. Westport, CT: Bergin & Garvey.
Redfield, M. (2003). *The politics of aesthetics*. Stanford, CA: Stanford University Press.
Rosler, N., Bar-Tal, D., Sharvit, K., Halperin, E., & Raviv, A. (in press). Moral aspects of prolonged occupation: Implications for an occupying society. In S. Scuzzarello, C. Kinnvall, & K. R. Monroe (Eds.), *On behalf of others: The psychology of care in a global world*. New York: Oxford University Press.

Sarup, M. (1996). *Identity, culture and the postmodern world.* Athens: University of Georgia Press.
Schnell, I. (1999). Narratives and styles in regional geography of Israel. In A. Buttimer, S. Bruhn, & U. Wardenga (Eds.), *Text and image: Constructing regional knowledge* (pp. 215–225). Leipzig: Institut fur Landerkunde.
Schnell, I. (2000). *Heimatkunde* in Israeli regional geography. In A. Hoffman, I. Schnell, G. Stephan, G. Brauer, & P. Fenn (Eds.), *Identity and education in Germany and Israel* (pp. 89–120). Hamburg: Verlag Dr. Kovac.
Schnell, I. (2001). Transformation in territorial concepts: From nation building to concession. *Geojournal, 53*(3), 221–234.
Schnell, I. (2004). *Territoriality and identity: Perceptions of Israeli Arabs.* Avebury, Ashgate, UK: Aldershot.
Shilhav, Y. (2001). Religious factors in territorial disputes: An intra-Jewish view. *Geojournal, 53*(3), 247–259.
Soja, E. (1996). *Third space.* Oxford: Basil Blackwell.
Tajfel, H. (1978). Social categorization, social identity and social comparison. In H. Tajfel (Ed.), *Differentiation between social groups* (pp. 61–76). London: Academic Press.
Zelinski, W. (1988). *Nation into state.* Chapel Hill: University of North Carolina Press.

In Hebrew

Admoni, Y. (1999). *Settlement after 1967: Ten years of settlement.* Jerusalem: Masada.
Azulai, A., & Ophir, A. (2008). *This regime that is not one.* Tel Aviv: Rassling: Tel Aviv.
Bar-Gal, Y. (1993). *Homeland and geography: One hundred years of Zionist education.* Tel Aviv: Am Oved.
Bar-Gal, Y. (1999). *Israeli propaganda agency: The Jewish National Fund, 1924–1947.* Haifa: Haifa University Publications.
Bar-Tal, D. (2007). *Living with the dispute.* Jerusalem: Carmel.
Berger, T. (2008). How to do things with a map. In T. Berger (Ed.), *In the gap between world and play* (pp. 47–62). Tel Aviv: Ressling.
Bitan, H. (1992). Government naming committee. *Land of Israel, 23,* 366–371.
Darzia, A. (1993). *Space and names: Names of settlements, national processes and social attitudes.* Ph.D. thesis, Geography Department, Haifa University.
Day, D. (2008). *Conquest: How societies overwhelm others.* Oxford: Oxford University Press.
Eldar, I., & Zertal, I. (2004). *Lords of the land: The settlers in the State of Israel.* Or Akiva: Zmora-Beitan, Kinneret Dvir.
Finkelstein, Y. (1999). The beginnings of the state in Israel and Judea. *Land of Israel, 36,* 132–142.
Firer, R. (1985). *Agents of the Zionist education.* Tel Aviv: HaKibbutz HaMeuchad/ Sifriat HaPoalim.
Gorny, Y. (1993). *Policy and imagination.* Jerusalem: Yad Ben Zvi.

Hoffman, I. (2002). Between national history and general history. In I. Hoffman & Y. Schnell (Eds.), *Values and aims in Israel's study curricula* (pp. 131–162). Tel Aviv: Achs.

Leuenberger, C., & Schnell, I. (2010) The politics of maps: Constructing national territories in Israel. *Social Studies of Science, 40*(6), 803–842.

Memmi, A. (1985). *Portrait of the conquered and portrait of the conqueror.* Jerusalem: Carmel.

Oren, A., & Regev, R. (2008). *A land in khaki.* Haifa: Carmel.

Passi, A. (1999). The changing pedagogies of space: Representationof the other in Finnish school geography textbooks. In A. Buttimer, S. D. Brun, & U. Wardenga (Eds.), *Text and image: Construction of regional knowledge* (pp. 226–237). Leibzig: Institute for Landerkunde.

Peleg, M. (1997). *Disseminating God's wrath.* Tel Aviv: HaKibbutz HaMeuchad.

Ravitzky, A. (1993). *The end revealed and the Jewish state: Messiahs, Zionism and religious radicalism in Israel.* Tel Aviv: Am Oved.

Riklin, S. (1995). Proposal for identifying the Ai adjacent to Maaleh Machmesh. In *Studies of Judea and Samaria* (pp. 27–33). Ariel: Judea and. Samaria Academic College.

Schnell, I. (2002). Geography as an educational challenge. In I. Hoffman & Y. Schnell (Eds.), *Values and aims in Israel's study curricula* (pp. 163–186). Tel Aviv: Reches.

Schnell, I. (2009). The territorial strategy of the occupation. In E. Lavie (Ed.), *Settlement and the formation of the Israeli boundaries.* Tel Aviv: Shteinmetz Center for Peace Studies, Tel Aviv University.

Schnell, I.(2012). The territorial strategy of control in the territories.. In S. Hasson (Ed.), *Design of settlement space in Israel* (pp. 107–123).

Sheleg, Y. (2000). *The new religious.* Jerusalem: Keter.

CHAPTER 4

Psychological Legitimization–Views of the Israeli Occupation by Jews in Israel: Data and Implications

Tamir Magal, Neta Oren, Daniel Bar-Tal, and Eran Halperin

When the 1948 war ended with the signed armistice agreement in 1949, it was hard to predict that eighteen years later there would be another war in which, within six days, Israel would conquer the whole Sinai, the Gaza Strip, the West Bank, and the Golan Heights. It was even harder to imagine that in 2012 Israel would still be occupying the West Bank and the Golan Heights, as well as controlling to a large extent almost all spheres of life in the Gaza Strip, in spite of the unilateral disengagement from this area in 2005. This prolonged occupation not only reflects a military and political situation with strong economic, societal, cultural, and religious implications for the state of Israel, but also necessarily affects the sociopsychological and political repertoire of its Jewish society (Bar-Tal, Halperin, & Oren, 2010). The results of the 1967 war, and especially the conquest of the West Bank and the Gaza Strip, constituted a determinative turning point in the views of the Israeli Jews. Until the 1967 war, most Israeli Jews accepted the Green Line of the armistice set in 1949 as the final borders of the state of Israel and did not aspire to the conquest of additional territories.[1] The conquest of the territories in 1967 dramatically changed these views within a very short time. It also created the idea that these territories, especially the West Bank and the Gaza Strip, are liberated because they are part of the deserved Jewish homeland and/or are needed to secure the existence of the State of Israel.

The purpose of this chapter is to elucidate the various orientations regarding the status of the occupied territories and the views about the Palestinian nation that have prevailed among Israeli Jews from 1967 to the present. It focuses on their reflection in the platforms of the political parties, in the expressed beliefs of the leaders, and in public opinion.

The basic assumption underlying this line of analysis is that the way leaders and members of society view these two issues (i.e., the status of the territories and the image of the Palestinians) has important implications for their readiness to accept various general principles to resolve the Israeli-Palestinian conflict; to accept the specific proposed solutions for the peaceful settlement of this conflict; and to view and treat the Palestinians justly. We suggest that these views have had a profound effect on the readiness to terminate the occupation and on the political acts that followed. First, however, we will comment on the general meaning of occupation.

Meaning of Occupation

Military conquests and foreign rule of one nation by another have been widespread in human history. But today they are rare. In the twenty-first century, prolonged occupation of one nation by another is viewed by the international community as unacceptable, negating international laws and immoral (see Roberts, 1990, for elaboration). Thus, from a psychological perspective, the term "occupation" bears negative connotations: it indicates an inherent conflict of interest between occupier and occupied; it means that the context is characterized by violence; it reflects wrongdoing, injustice and immorality; it involves a large degree of empathy toward the occupied and a negative attitude towards the occupier, and finally, it conveys an expectation that the situation is temporary and will be terminated (Halperin, Bar-Tal, Sharvit, Rosler, & Raviv, 2009). Thus, an occupation has harsh implications for the occupier, not only because of the criticism and sanctions that the occupying society encounters, but also because of the sociopsychological implications of the occupation for this society (Rosler, Bar-Tal, Sharvit, Halperin, & Raviv, in prep.).

We do, however, recognize that not all cases of prolonged occupation have negative implications. In some cases of foreign rule, the "occupied society" might consent to the situation or even support continued foreign rule. Acquiescence might result from lack of national consciousness or from deep feuds and divisions within the occupied society (e.g., Kashmir before 1989 [Puri, 1993]). Support for continued foreign rule might result either from a need for support and/or deterrence against a greater threat (e.g., Cyprus, southern Ossetia [Oberling, 1982, Cornell, 2002]) or from a desire to get the rewards and privileges associated with the occupying of another country (e.g., Gibraltar, Guadeloupe, and Martinique [Hills, 1974]). Acceptance of foreign rule may also be supported because of a cultural and religious affinity between the two societies (e.g., Cyprus, southern Ossetia [Cornell, 2002]). Also, in some cases, long periods of foreign rule have been accepted by the international community, even though they have been resisted by the occupied society. Some instances of prolonged occupation have a long history, predating the colonialist period (e.g., the Basque country, Corsica [Conversi, 2000, Gregory, 1985]). These cases have been legitimated by the international norm of sovereignty.

Therefore, the occupying societies needed to establish conditions that would satisfy the occupied society and reduce resistance.

The noted cases are special instances because the occupied societies accepted the occupation, either from the beginning, seeing it as a beneficial situation, or with time when the satisfactory conditions were achieved. But in other cases of occupation, members of the occupying group often used force and violence, and at times performed acts that contradicted moral norms because, in the great majority of the cases, at least some segments of the occupied society resisted occupation in different nonviolent and violent ways (see the recent examples in Iraq, Afghanistan, and Chechnya). In addition, prominent reference groups in the international community have criticized acts performed by the occupying forces as part of the occupation. Such processes threaten the basic need to maintain the self-esteem of the individual members and the collective, as well as the reputation of the occupying state in the world. That is especially true if the society wishes to adhere to the international norms and be accepted by the enlightened part of the international community. Hence, a central psychological challenge of an occupying society is resolving the discrepancies between the motivation to maintain self-esteem and the negative implications of the state of occupation (see elaboration in Halperin et al., 2009). Obviously, one way to resolve this troubling discrepancy is to end the occupation. Thus, it appears that the willingness of the occupying society to recognize the situation as an occupation may be a necessary (albeit not sufficient) condition for termination of the occupation.

We suggest that for an occupation that is resisted to take place and persist, the occupying society must be driven by significant motives to initiate it and then to maintain it. Thus members of such a society must either construct a convincing rationale for the act of occupation or deny its existence. As we review the different rationales for an occupation, we find various possible reasons. Sometimes members of the occupying society believe that the occupation serves important superordinate goals of many other nations and that it is necessary in order to prevent a higher-level disaster and/or to achieve a highly valued goal (e.g., the occupation of Iraq by Americans). In other cases, members of the occupying society believe that the occupation is necessary to ensure their own imperative goals and interests or even goals of existential nature, without which they believe their society cannot survive (e.g., the occupation of Manchuria by Japan or of Chechnya by Russia). Sometimes members of the occupying society believe that there is a need to punish the other nation for its wrongdoing (e.g., the occupation of Afghanistan by Americans). In still other situations, the occupying society may refuse to accept the definition of the reality as a state of occupation and define it as "liberation" or use another, more acceptable term (e.g., the occupation of certain regions of Georgia by the Russians or of Tibet by China).

We suggest that in the present era, all of the occupying societies that encounter resistance from the occupied societies have to construct a well-developed rationale and justification, first of all for the members of the occupier and then for the international community that tries to impose moral codes of international conduct. Within this framework, we will now examine the case of the Israeli society, with its long-lasting occupation of the Palestinian land, and the resistance of Palestinian society.

The Israeli Case of Occupation

Our analysis of the Israeli occupation begins with a discussion between Chief of Staff Yitzhak Rabin and Minister of Defense Moshe Dayan that took place about six weeks after the end of the 1967 war (for the complete story, see Segev, 2007). The original notes referred to one of the topics on the agenda as "occurrences in the occupied territories." A few days later, an "invisible hand" amended the protocol in handwriting and replaced the term "occupied territories" with the term "liberated territories." The latter term ,of course, has acceptable social-political connotations and therefore was used even at the early stage of the occupation.

The conquest of the territories beyond the Green Line in the 1967 war caused a profound change in the views of many Jews in Israel, who within a very short time changed their fundamental beliefs about the territories. The conquest of the territories dramatically increased the view that these territories—especially the West Bank and the Gaza Strip—should be part of the Jewish state. Thus, a consensus emerged that these territories had been liberated and that the Jews had returned to their homeland. This idea became hegemonic among most segments of Israeli-Jewish society after the 1967 war. It was expressed by almost all the leaders, by the media, by the political parties, by many members of the political and cultural elite, and by the public (Naor, 2001). With this idea also emerged the conviction that Israel cannot withdraw from the occupied territories. This conviction was based on arguments from religious, national, historical, cultural, political, and military domains.

We suggest that from the first moment of the occupation, various views, which can be located on a continuum, emerged in Israel. At one extreme were Jews (the great majority) who viewed the occupation as liberation; at the other extreme were Jews (a very small minority) who objected to the occupation on moral grounds. These polarized views are illustrated in two competing declarations published, incidentally, on the same day shortly after the 1967 war. The first declaration, published by 57 renowned public figures from the political, cultural, and military spheres in Israeli society, stated:

> The Land of Israel is now in the hands of the Jewish people. Just as we are not permitted to relinquish the State of Israel, so we are commanded to maintain what we have received from its hands: the Land of Israel. We are hereby loyally committed to the wholeness of our land, with respect both to the people's past and to its future, and no government in Israel is entitled to relinquish this wholeness. (Bondi, 1967, p. 17)

The second declaration, published by 12 relatively marginal Israeli intellectuals, claimed just the opposite:

> Our right to defend ourselves against destruction does not confer on us the right to oppress others. Conquest brings in its wake foreign rule. Foreign rule brings in its wake resistance. Resistance brings in its wake oppression. Oppression brings in its wake terror and counter-terror. The victims of terror are usually innocent people. Keeping the occupied territories will convert us into a nation of murderers and murder victims. Let us leave the occupied territories immediately. (Haaretz, 1967, p. 10)

Looking back, we suggest that it is possible to differentiate between Israeli Jews' political orientations toward the situation of occupation on the basis of two dimensions: value orientation and nature of the worldview. The "value orientation" dimension pertains to the types of values that underlie the view of the situation. At one end of this dimension are persons who are motivated by particular nationalistic-religious Jewish values, needs, sets of beliefs and goals. Examples include Jewish religious dogmas that focus on God's promises to the Jewish people regarding the land or belief in the exclusive right of the Jews to the territory between the Jordan River and the Mediterranean Sea. At the other end of this dimension are persons who are driven by the universal-moral values of justice, freedom, equality, and especially human rights and collective rights.

The "nature of the worldview" dimension refers to the features characterizing the views of the situation. At one end of this dimension are persons whose views of the situation are completely dominated by ideological consideration; at the other end are those whose views are entirely dependent on the pragmatic evaluation of the situation. These two dimensional distinctions create a 2x2 typology of four basic orientations within Israeli-Jewish society toward the occupied territories (see Table 4.1). Nevertheless, we recognize that these four basic orientations are not mutually exclusive. In fact there is a need, especially within the pragmatic orientation, to see the

TABLE 4.1 *BASIC ORIENTATIONS WITHIN THE ISRAELI-JEWISH SOCIETY TOWARDS THE OCCUPIED TERRITORIES*

	Ideological	Pragmatic
Nationalistic	Nationalistic-ideological	Nationalistic-pragmatic
Universal	Universal-ideological	Universal-pragmatic

nationalistic-universal distinction as being a continuum rather than a dichotomy (see also Rynhold, 2001).

Each of these orientations has well-defined implications, not only for the view of the situation of occupation, but also for the tolerance and acceptances of this situation, the implied beliefs about it, the emotions that accompany it, and the behavioral tendencies that appear to terminate or continue this situation. We will now describe these four major orientations as prototypes. However, as noted, in reality individuals with the two pragmatic orientations can hold complex views with different combinations of nationalistic and universal arguments.

Nationalistic-Ideological Orientation

Members of this category view the territories as part of the Jewish homeland that belongs exclusively to the Jewish people. They base this view on the belief in God's promise of this land to their Jewish forefathers and on the fact that the roots of the Jewish nation are planted in the heartland of the occupied territories, which were part of the Jewish historical homeland, where the culture and heritage of the Jewish people were created and then continued to constitute the foundations for Jewishness throughout all of the generations up to the present time. Therefore, these persons deny the Palestinian claim to the West Bank and the Gaza Strip, viewing them as liberated territories that should be annexed to the Jewish state. These persons face a discrepancy in their views and experience distress when the state raises the possibility of terminating the occupation by withdrawal from the territories. They are proud of Israel's control of these territories and work to prevent any withdrawal from them. To define this orientation operationally, we have used the following criterion in assessing the views of groups and individuals: supporting the *exclusive* right of the Jews to the whole of Eretz Israel; unwillingness to withdraw from the occupied territories, which are viewed as the Jewish homeland; support for the Jewish right to settle in every part of Eretz Israel; and disregard of the Palestinians' national identity and their national right to the country and state.

Nationalistic-Pragmatic Orientation

Members of this category view the territories as belonging exclusively to the Jewish people, but they take into consideration the internal, regional, and international conditions that determine how to handle the issue of the territories and the Palestinians. These persons are usually dominated by fear, which is aroused by perceived threats. This group is further divided on the basis of how its members understand these specific conditions and their implications. This understanding is translated along the dimension of the willingness to withdraw from the territories. At one end of the dimension is the "national nationalistic-pragmatic" suborientation, which focuses on the possible security threats and dangers that may arise as a result of *any withdrawal* and believes that withdrawal from the West Bank and the Gaza Strip may jeopardize the very existence of the State of Israel. At the other end of the dimension, the "practical nationalistic-pragmatic" suborientation focuses mainly on two types of threats to the Jewish and democratic nature of the state as a result of *maintaining control* over the territories. The first type of threats pertains to the loss of Jewish dominance as a result of demographic shifts accompanying the annexation of the large Palestinian population in the territories. The second type of threats refers to the possible loss of the democratic nature of the Jewish state as a result of continuing control of the territories populated by the Palestinians (these are two sides of the same coin). This suborientation may support even a substantial withdrawal, believing that only this act can secure the Jewish and democratic character of the State of Israel. This group may also recognize the right of the Palestinians to statehood. To define this orientation operationally, we used the following criteria for assessing the positions of groups and individuals: viewing the territories as belonging exclusively to the Jewish people; using a combination of nationalistic and threats-oriented arguments to justify either opposition to or support for territorial compromise; recognition of the Palestinian people as having a distinct national identity; and willingness to reach some territorial compromise with the Palestinians in the context of final peace accords.

Universal-Pragmatic Orientation

Members of this category use universal moral values and norms as major arguments for their views, but at the same time they take into considerations the special conditions in which the State of Israel exists. Persons who hold this orientation acknowledge the situation as an occupation, viewing it as an act of defense that was necessary, but they recognize that termination of the occupation is necessary because of moral considerations and Israel's interests. At the same time, they demand that any withdrawal from the territories, either completely or in part, depend on fulfillment of the security needs of the State of Israel.

These persons are usually dominated by fear that is aroused by perceived threats, but they also may experience guilt and shame because of their values. To define this orientation operationally, we used the following criteria when assessing the positions of groups and individuals: recognition of a distinct national existence for the Palestinian people; recognition of the right of the Jews and Palestinians to a national homeland in Eretz Israel; willingness to reach a territorial compromise with the Palestinians in the context of final peace accords; and use of moral arguments and security considerations to support a territorial compromise.

Universal-Ideological Orientation

Members of this category are driven solely by universal moral values and norms. They view occupation as a violation of basic moral codes and therefore demand complete withdrawal from the territories, which they view as being occupied and the occupation as causing unjust transgression. Some of them even engage in various activities to terminate the occupation. These individuals face a discrepancy between the desired moral ought and the reality, and therefore experience guilt and shame. To define this orientation operationally, we used the following criteria for assessing the positions of groups and individuals: use of moral arguments in relation to the Israeli-Palestinian conflict and the desire to resolve it peacefully; recognition of the right of the Palestinians to a national homeland in Eretz Israel; and willingness to divide the land with the Palestinians in the context of final peace accords.

We will now review the prevalence of the four described orientations in Israeli- Jewish society between 1967 and 2009. This will be done by dividing the timeline into four periods distinguished by major political events.[2] For each period, we will try to determine the strength of each of the approaches in Israeli-Jewish society by examining political parties' platforms,[3] leaders' opinions, and public opinion polls.

THE FIRST PERIOD: 1967–1977

Views of the Political System

The 1967 war and the conquests of the West Bank and the Gaza Strip brought about a wave of national sentiments, which swept across the Israeli-Jewish public as well as most of its political leadership:

> Prime Minister at that time Levy Eshkol said: "I see myself as an emissary of the whole Jewish people, as a representative of many generations of our people, who craved for Jerusalem and its holiness.... Blessed is the Lord,

who has kept us alive, and has preserved us, and enabled us to reach this time." (Teveth, 1973, p. 39)

Defense Minister at that time Moshe Dayan said: "we returned to our holiest of sites, and we shall not relinquish them ever again." (Teveth, 1973, p. 36)

The mainstream Israeli political leadership referred to the historical and national rights of the Jewish people to the Land of Israel (whole Eretz Israel). However, each political faction used a different emphasis and drew different conclusions from these historical rights.

The *nationalistic-ideological orientation* was most prominent in religious and nationalist parties like Mafdal[4] and Likud.[5] Mafdal was part of the coalition, and Likud joined it for a brief period in 1967. The leaders of these parties viewed the West Bank and the Gaza Strip as the heartland of the Jewish people, as an indivisible part of Eretz Israel, the Jewish Promised Land. The platforms of both of these parties clearly stated this belief:

> The national right of the Jewish people to the land of Israel is undeniable and is integrated in our people's right and desire for security and peace. We shall refuse any offer which necessitates a renewed division of Western Eretz Israel. (Likud, 1973)

> The Mafdal believes in the eternal connection between the Jewish people, Eretz Israel and the Jewish Gospel; and, based on this connection; it aspires to ground the state of Israel and the life of the Jewish people on Jewish religious principles. (Mafdal, 1977)

Both platforms stressed the need for "Jewish settlement on a large scale" of the "liberated parts of Eretz Israel," and both ignored the existence of the Palestinians, referring to them as "the residents of Eretz Israel."

> The Mafdal view the Arab residents of Eretz Israel as equal citizens bearing rights and duties towards the state. They owe the state their full and active loyalty, together with the maintenance of their distinct cultural-religious heritage. (Mafdal, 1977)

> In the state Israel there will be a complete equality in rights for all its citizens and residents.... Any resident of Eretz Israel, without prejudice of race, nationality or religion, who would seek citizenship of the state and who will swear allegiance to it—will be granted. (Likud, 1973)

For Menachem Begin, leader of the nationalist party Likud, the West Bank was part of the Jewish heritage, as he declared:

These are liberated territories belonging to the Jewish people... there will be no annexation as these are our lands and not the lands of foreigners. (Zertal & Eldar, 2007, p. 84).

For Begin, a withdrawal from these territories was comparable to treason:

This joy of dividing this piece of land of our ancestors, of ourselves, of our sons, is the weirdest phenomenon in Jewish history. For thousands of years we have demanded our full rights to the whole Eretz Israel, and now—divide? (Begin, 1970).

Begin absolutely rejected a distinct Palestinian identity, stating in the Israeli parliament (Knesset) in 1975: "there is no Palestine here and therefore there is no entity, no identity, and no nation that is called Palestinian" (quoted by Auerbach & Ben-Yehuda, 1987, p. 330). He thus used the label "Arabs of Eretz Israel" when he referred to the Palestinians.

On the basis of the above views about the territories and the Palestinians, it is not surprising that the Likud party objected to any type of withdrawal from the occupied territories:

The stated policy of the Labor government, which strives for the renewed division of Western Eretz Israel, poses a threat to the future of the state of Israel, and its very existence. (Likud, 1973)

This orientation emphasized exclusive Jewish national rights over the "liberated" territories while utterly rejecting Palestinian nationality.

The *nationalist-pragmatic orientation* during this period supported the idea that the whole of Eretz Israel (the entire land) belongs to the Jews. Nevertheless, this orientation was divided between two major suborientations, represented by Shelomzion and the Labor party—between political leaders who opposed territorial compromise and those who supported it on the basis of various considerations. The "national nationalistic-pragmatic" suborientation was represented by Ariel Sharon and his party Shelomzion,[6] as well as by some of the more hawkish leaders of the Labor party,[7] like Moshe Dayan. This orientation, while recognizing the existence of the Palestinian people, emphasized nationalistic and security arguments in order to legitimize continued Israeli control over the West Bank and Gaza.

The platform of Shelomzion referred to the right of the Jews to whole of Eretz Israel and therefore supported their settlement in the conquered territories:

> Jews will be allowed to live in every part of Eretz Israel, as it is our undeniable historical right. As Arabs live today in all parts of Eretz Israel so will the Jews. (Shelomzion, 1977)

At the same time, the party recognized the existence of the national identity of the Palestinians, which would necessitate negotiations with them:

> Peace will be achieved in direct negotiations between Israel and the relevant Arab actors, involved directly in the conflict, including the Palestinians. (Shelomzion, 1977)

Ariel Sharon, who headed Shelomzion, recognized the Palestinian identity but regarded Jordan as the Palestinian state in reality (Auerbach & Ben Yehuda, 1993). He was even ready to recognize the Palestine Liberation Organization (PLO) as the genuine representative of the Palestinian people, in contrast to almost all other Israeli leaders, saying in 1977 that "Israel must talk with the PLO representatives if they represent the Palestinians" (quoted by Auerbach & Ben Yehuda, 1993, p. 154).

For Sharon, Jews have historical rights to the liberated territories:

> These places (Judea and Samaria) were so much a part of our heritage.... The basic fact was that these areas were part of the country that had been captured by the invading Arab armies in 1948. Now we had come back to them. (Sharon, 1989, p. 208)

But in addition to the ideological historical-national argument, he presented arguments concerning security, which emphasized the strategic importance of maintaining Israeli control over the West Bank:

> We did not need or want the agricultural lands. But I was just certain that we did need the important road junctions and the high controlling terrain... to protect and give depth to the tiny heartland along the coast, to be able to defend ourselves on the line of the Jordan River, and to secure Jerusalem as the capital of the Jewish people forever. (Sharon, 1989, p. 208)

Defense Minister Moshe Dayan was another leader with a national nationalist-pragmatic orientation. Although a member of the Labor party, Dayan emphasized Jewish historical rights while acknowledging the distinctive Palestinian identity (Auerbach & Ben-Yehuda, 1987):

> We have returned to our holiest of sites. (Cited by Teveth, 1973, p. 39) This territory is part of [the] historic Jewish homeland. (Dayan, 1974, p. 1)

Dayan also acknowledged the role of the PLO in settling the Israeli-Palestinian conflict:

> The PLO isn't just the terrorists or the terrorist organization. It's also the civilian part of it. That is to say, the Palestinian refugees.... No one thinks a final settlement of the conflict in the Middle East can be achieved without a settlement of the refugees. (Dayan, 1979a, p. 14)

Nevertheless, Dayan rejected the Palestinians' connection to Palestine, suggesting that their place is in Jordan (Auerbach & Ben-Yehuda, 1987).While declaring his support for a peace agreement, Dayan put off any notions of territorial compromise so long as there was no full peaceful settlement of the wider Israeli-Arab conflict:

> I support fully the formula set by the government of Israel that, as long as there are no full and fair peace agreements—such as any country has with its neighbors—we should continue our hold over these territories. (Cited by Teveth, 1973, p. 119)

At the same time, Dayan thought that holding territories that provide depth for defense was more important than peace.

A somewhat different suborientation, which we call "practical-nationalistic-pragmatic" was shared by other leaders of the Labor party, which led the government in this period. This suborientation emphasized the salience of maintaining the Jewish and democratic character of the State of Israel over Jewish historical rights. Their perceptions of threats, deriving from the loss of either the Jewish or the democratic nature of the State of Israel, justified the need for territorial compromise.

The Labor party's platform emphasized the Jewish character of the State of Israel and its connection with the Jewish historical homeland:

> The state of Israel was created for the Jewish people, and it is the homeland of every Jew who whishes to return here.... [The state's roles includee] the concentration of the Jewish people in its historical homeland. (Labor, 1969)

> Israel is the homeland for the whole Jewish people. It must continue to nurture its Jewish national character. (Labor, 1977)

Furthermore, Labor's platform emphasized the Jews' right to settle anywhere in Eretz Israel, but it subordinated this right to security considerations:

> The settlement of the whole of Eretz Israel is the highest commandment, from Zionist, security and societal perspectives.... [The government] should continue to expand and strengthen the [Jewish] urban and rural settlements in the Jerusalem area, the Golan, the Jordan valley, the Raffah area, and along the [R]ed [S]ea. These settlements should be established according to government policy of securing defensible borders (Labor, 1977)

However, the Labor party acknowledged the existence of the Palestinian people while negating their claim for an independent state:

> Israel negates the establishment of an independent Arab-Palestinian state west of the river Jordan. The national identity of the Palestinian and Jordanian Arabs will be fulfilled in the neighboring Jordanian-Palestinian state. (Labor, 1977)

While expressing a readiness for territorial compromise, the Labor party used security considerations to negate Israel's withdrawal to the 1967 borderlines:

> Based on past experience of decades of animosity around us, and on the necessity of guaranteeing Israel's future security, Israel will never again return to the ceasefire lines before the Six-Days war. (Labor, 1969)

> While expressing readiness for territorial compromises with each one of the neighboring Arab countries, the Labor negates the policies of return to the 1967 lines, which relinquishes the claim for defensible borders. (Labor, 1977)

However, Labor's platform expressed readiness to grant some form of autonomy to the "local population" in the territories:

> The government of Israel will assist the independent activities of the local population [in the territories] in areas of education, culture, and religion, and in nurturing the principles of democracy and progress in societal, municipal, and public life. (Labor, 1977).

Finance Minister Pinhas Sapir was among the first to clearly state the demographic threat of continued occupation:

> I'm against the addition of one million Arabs to the [already existing] 400 thousands Israeli Arabs, which will then form a 40% minority within the

Israeli population.... It will not be difficult to predict when there will be an Arab Majority within the state of Israel. (Cited by Teveth, 1973, p. 288)

Yitzhak Rabin, who was appointed Prime Minister in 1974, emphasized the Jews' claim to their homeland:

> The right of the Jewish people to live its life in its own state, free, independent and in peace.... To insure the existence of our people in their homeland. (Rabin, 1967, p. 3)

Rabin also stated his support for the right of the Jews to settle anywhere in Eretz Israel:

> I do not agree with the rule that it is OK to settle near Jericho, but it is wrong to settle near Kfar-Saba. I do not understand why it is OK [to settle] in the Jordan Valley and forbidden on the mountains of Samaria. (Cited by Zertal & Eldar, 2007, p. 76)

However, he recognized the existence of moral considerations, which serve to limit these rights: "I acknowledge that it is immoral to settle through the dispossession of Arabs and disregard towards their sentiments" (cited by Zertal & Eldar, 2007, p. 76).

Rabin also recognized the Palestinians as a distinct group, stating in 1977: "We recognize the existence of a 'Palestinian problem'" (Rabin, 1979, p. 431). However, he objected to the establishment of a Palestinian state, claiming that Jordan should become a Jordanian-Palestinian state (Auerbach & Ben Yehuda, 1993). He spelled out his ideas very clearly in his 1974 inauguration speech as Prime Minister:

> Even in the framework of peace accords, we will not withdraw to the 1967 lines, which are untenable, and which encourage aggression against us. We aspire to achieve [a] peace agreement with Jordan which will be based on the existence of two independent states: Israel, with united Jerusalem as its capital, and an Arab state east of Israel. The neighboring Jordanian-Palestinian state will express the political identity of both Palestinians and Jordanian Arabs. Israel totally objects to the establishment of another Arab state between us and Jordan, West of the Jordan River. (Rabin, 1979, p. 424)

Deputy Prime Minister Yigal Alon emphasized his commitment to Jewish national rights:

> The historical right over the fatherland is what makes the fundamental difference between a just return to Zion and a colonial settlement. Our

historical rights over Eretz Israel are the moral basis for the existence of Israel in any borders. (Alon, 1973)

However, Alon also acknowledged the collective rights of the Palestinian people while emphasizing their connection with Jordan:

A deeply rooted Arab population has been living in Eretz Israel for hundreds of years, during which time it has developed its own unique characteristics.... Actually, in the borders of historic Eretz Israel—on both sides of the river Jordan—there already exists, in principle, two national homelands, an Arab and a Jewish. If the name given to the Arab homeland is the Hashemite Kingdom of Jordan, that's their own affair. (Alon, 1973)

Alon emphasized the dangers posed by annexation of the territories to the Jewish character and moral nature of the State of Israel:

The choice before us in this matter is brutally clear: If we annex the densely populated areas [of the West Bank] to Israel, while giving their inhabitants full civil rights—then we will cease to be a Jewish state. If we annex the territories without giving their inhabitants full civil rights—we will cease to be a democratic society.... There is a real danger of a "Rhodesian" process within the Israeli society. (Alon, 1973)

Alon further expressed more universal values, stating in 1977:

Committing justice with another people...I mean the Arab Palestinian nation that resides on the banks of the Jordan, in the historical Land of Israel is also in itself of historical significance. (Ben Yehuda & Auerbach, 1991, p. 530)

Finally, Alon emphasized his explicit support for territorial compromise while negating withdrawal to the 1967 borders:

If I support territorial compromise, it is not in the absence of national historical rights, but in spite of these rights, and for a much higher historical cause—peace.... There can be no peace with full [Israeli] control of the territories, as there can be no security with a total withdrawal [to the 1967 border lines]. (Alon, 1973)

Defense Minister Shimon Peres (1974–1977) also upheld Jewish historical rights:

The validity of the Jewish historical rights over Eretz Israel...was carried by the Jewish people in its heart, its consciousness, and its fate, throughout the centuries of its wandering. (Peres, 1978, p. 94)

However, Peres emphasized the importance of a Jewish majority in securing these historical rights and warned against a pending demographic problem:

> The continuing political and security struggle of the Jewish people must be guided by the ideal definitions of Zionism—the concentration of the majority of the Jewish people in the largest part of Eretz Israel.... If we had 6 million Jews in Israel... it would have been possible to solve the "Palestinian problem" without fear of the "Demographic problem." It would have been possible to maintain the Jewish character of the state of Israel, together with greater flexibility in solving the Palestinian problem within [Israel]. (Peres, 1978, p. 94)

Peres justified the necessity of territorial compromise with the need to maintain the Jewish national character of the State of Israel:

> The territorial compromise, as suggested in our platform, is not a goal in itself, but a price... a necessary guarantee for preserving the Jewish character of the state. (Peres, 1978, p. 35)

However, all three leaders opposed the establishment of an independent Palestinian state, claiming that Palestinian national aspirations should be settled in the context of a Jordanian-Palestinian state (see Agid-Ben Yehuda & Auerbach, 1991).

These leaders, while recognizing Jewish historical rights, placed special emphasis on threats posed to the State of Israel by continued occupation of the territories. Furthermore, they acknowledged the distinct national character of the Palestinian people, and they referred to the demographic threat as well as the threat of losing the democratic nature of the State of Israel, which would lead to the necessity for some kind of compromise. However, they rejected the idea of an independent Palestinian state, giving priority to security as a major consideration in delimiting possible withdrawal from the territories.

The *universal-pragmatic orientation* was expressed by groups and parties on the left in the Israeli political spectrum, which considered themselves Zionist parties. The Zionist left was comprised in this period of such parties as Mapam[8] and Ratz,[9] as well as the "Peace and Security" List.[10] These parties, which represented a small minority (Mapam even entered into an alliance with the Labor party in 1969), while supporting the right of the Jewish people to its historical homeland (but not as being exclusive and without referring to the extended boundaries), espoused recognition of Palestinians' national rights as well and objected to permanent annexation of the "held territories":

Ratz focused on Jewish return to its historical homeland, while Peace and Security emphasized the national rights of both nations:

> Peace will be based on the aspiration to guarantee the existence of the state of Israel as the sovereign state of the Jewish people which has returned to its historical homeland. (Ratz, 1977)

> The movement will fight for strengthening the recognition that ending the Middle Eastern tragedy will not be accomplished by way of coercion and outside intervention...rather, only by way of mutual understanding, moderation, and a respect for the national rights of all the nations in the region...consideration for the justified national rights of the Jewish and the Palestinian people. (Peace and Security, 1968, 1969a)

Both platforms emphasized the temporary nature of Israeli control over the territories:

> The territories, which are under Israeli military rule since the 1967 war, have not been annexed by past Israeli governments, and are held by us as a guarantee only, for achieving peace and security. (Ratz, 1977)

> The Israeli government should clearly state that Israel does not aspire to annex any territories, and that it adopts, as before, the principle of evacuating held territories as a consequence of peace accords. (Peace and Security, 1969a)

Peace and Security further emphasized moral and democratic considerations in support of territorial compromise:

> The domination over another nation, against its will, undermines the moral justification for the very existence of the state of Israel. How can a nation, whose sole justification for sovereign statehood lies on its being a persecuted minority without a homeland, [claim independence] while he himself denies the same right from its neighbors, the Palestinian people, and coerce them, against their will to become an oppressed minority. The domination over the Palestinian people...will ruin the Jewish-Democratic fabric of the state [of Israel], because it is an impossibility to grant the minority full civil rights without jeopardizing the security and national character of the state. It is also an impossibility to deny them these rights without turning Israel into a police-state, which uses its brute force to intimidate a hostile minority. (Peace and Security, 1969b)

However, both platforms still put considerable emphasis on Israel's security and remained vague about the future status of the West Bank and Gaza:

> In exchange for peace agreements with the confrontation states, there is a place to accede to territorial compromises in all sectors, which will guarantee Israel's existence and security requirements. (Ratz, 1977)

> An Israeli peace plan...will be predicated on the following elements: readiness to negotiate a settlement which will establish secure and recognized borders for Israel and its neighbors; readiness to include the Palestinian inhabitants of the "held territories" as an actor in the efforts towards peace.... The most vital of national interests must motivate all of us to object to any annexation plans and to aspire, as soon as possible, to reach peace accords, which will enable us to hand over populated areas [in the West Bank]—to the other nation. (Peace and Security, 1969b)

The *universal-ideological orientation* was represented by the alternative negligible left party of HaOlam HaZeh, later called MERI.[11] This orientation recognized both Israeli and Palestinian national rights and strongly emphasized universal values of self- determination, equal national rights, and peaceful conflict resolution.

> Eretz Israel is the homeland of two peoples: the Jewish people and the Arab-Palestinian people. The state of Israel is the embodiment of the national rights of the Jewish people.... The national rights of the Arab-Palestinian people were not fulfilled. The Palestinian people have the right for self determination, and its fulfillment will be achieved based of coexistence in peace with the state of Israel. (MERI, 1973)

In line with these principles, the party opposed any annexation, called for full Israeli withdrawal to the 1967 borders, and asserted that peace would be the ultimate guarantor of security:

> The border between the State of Israel and the Palestinian Arab state will correspond to the pre-war lines of June 1967. (MERI, 1973)

Views of the Jewish Public

Public opinion polls of the Israeli Jews referred to several topics that are relevant to the present interest: the legitimacy of the Israeli claim for the land in the territories, the illegitimacy of the Palestinian claim, and the willingness to withdraw from the territories. In the polls conducted in later years, we can also find views about the idea of a Palestinian state and whether a Palestinian state is a threat to the state of Israel.

The polls indicate that in line with the nationalistic-ideological orientation, most of the Jews in Israel during this period did not recognize the unique identity of the Palestinians as a nation. For example, in the 1973–1977 period, 70% of Israeli Jews agreed with the statement "'The Palestinian Arab Nation' is an artificial concept that has only emerged in the last years due to developments in our area."

The polls taken at that time did not directly ask the Israeli-Jewish public about their perception of the conquered territories or about the reason for continuing to hold them. It is interesting to note, though, that the wording of questions in polls from this period referred to the territories mostly as the "administered territories" rather than as "liberated territories" or "occupied territories." Some polls used the Hebrew name of these territories (e.g., Judea and Samaria), indicating that they are Israeli territories. Still other polls referred to this area as "the West Bank."

The polls did, however, ask the respondents whether Israel should continue to hold these territories. The data indicate that during the years 1967–1972 most of the respondents (more than 60%) thought that Israel should keep the territories. Since 1973, the Israeli public has been divided on that issue (see Figure 4.1).

Also, most of the respondents perceived a Palestinian state as a threat to the State of Israel (about 90% thought so; see Figure 4.2). Therefore, opposition to the idea of a Palestinian state during the years 1976–1977 was very high (more than 85% opposed this idea; see Figure 4.3).

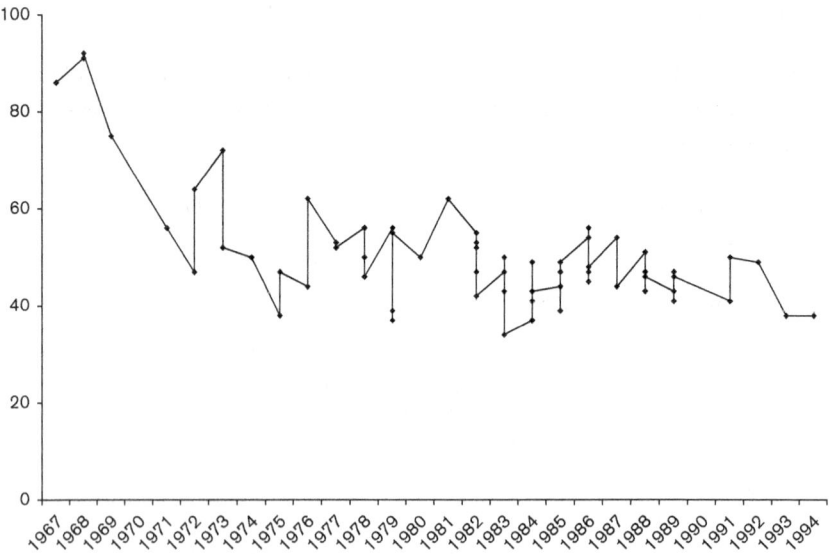

FIGURE 4.1 Percentage of Jews in Israel Not Willing to Return Territories: The West Bank, 1967–1994.
Sources: Israel Institute of Applied Social Research (the Continuing Survey). The Israel Institute of Applied Social Research was closed in 1992. All the data in the figure are taken from its publications.

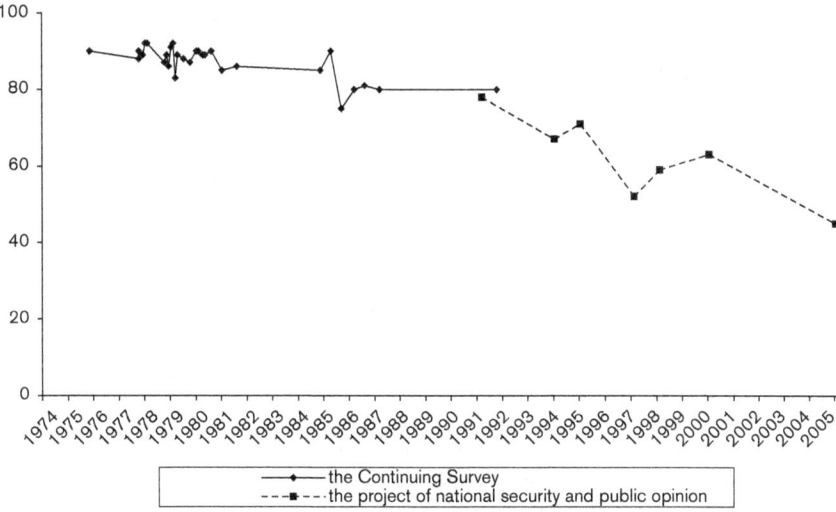

FIGURE 4.2 Percentage of Jews in Israel Who Perceived the Palestinian State as a Threat to Israel, 1974–2005.

Summary

The great majority of the Israeli public, as well as its mainstream political leaders and political parties during 1967–1977, emphasized Jewish exclusive national rights and security considerations as a rationale for continued Israeli control over the territories. At the same time, the majority of the Jews in Israel denied the existence of the Palestinian people and viewed the Palestinian state as a great threat to Israel. The Likud party, which was part of the mainstream, fully adhered to the nationalistic-ideological orientation. The other part of the political mainstream, which constituted a majority at that time (i.e., the Labor party), advocated the nationalistic-pragmatic orientation. This orientation was divided—between the nationalist suborientation, emphasizing security threats and the need to maintain Israeli control of the conquered territories, and the practical suborientation, emphasizing the Jewish and democratic character of the state, which necessitates a territorial compromise and at least a partial withdrawal. Only a very small minority during this period focused on the universal values recognizing the rights of the Palestinian to self-determination and their own state.

THE SECOND PERIOD: 1977–1992

The political upheaval of 1977, which brought to power a nationalistic coalition headed by the Likud party, served as a background for changes in the political

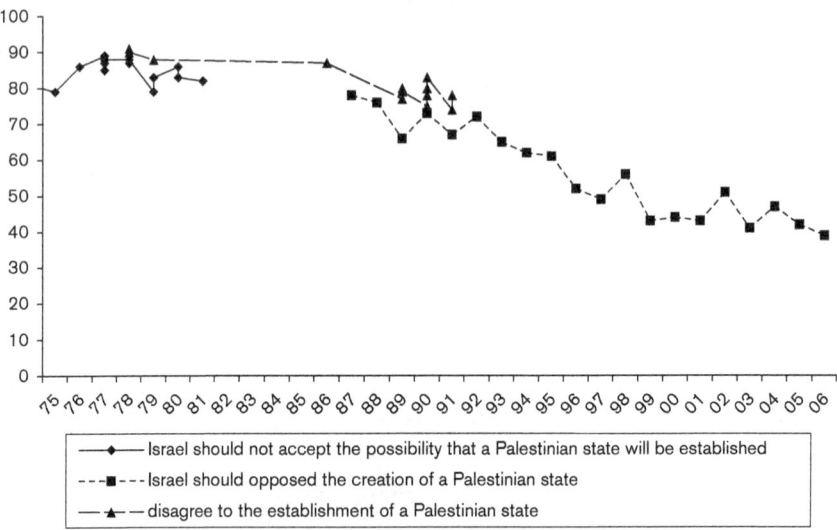

FIGURE 4.3 Percentage of Israeli Jews Opposing Establishment of a Palestinian State Through the Years.
Sources: Israel should not accept a Palestinian state: Israel Institute of Applied Social Research. Israel should oppose a Palestinian state: Jaffee Center for Strategic Studies. Disagree to the establishment of a Palestinian state: Israel Institute of Applied Social Research. The Israel Institute of Applied Social Research was closed in 1992, while the Jaffee Center for Strategic Studies was incorporated into the Institute for National Security Studies in 2006. All the data in the figure are taken from the publications of these institutions or from their Web sites.

orientation on the nationalistic side. Following the Camp David Accords, and Israel's recognition of "the legitimate rights of the Palestinian people" (Camp David Accords, 1978), the Likud party began to veer toward a more nationalistic-pragmatic orientation. This became evident with the entrance into the newly formed government of more pragmatic political figures like Sharon, Weitzman, and Dayan.

Views of the Political System

The *nationalistic-ideological orientation* came to be represented by smaller nationalistic parties like the Mafdal, Tzomet,[12] and Tehiya.[13] However, within the Likud party, there were some leaders and supporters who continued to maintain this orientation. This orientation emphasized the exclusive right Jews to all the territories between the Jordan River and the Mediterranean Sea, continued to ignore the existence of the Palestinians, espoused no form of territorial compromise over "liberated" territories, and advocated Jewish settlements within them.

The Mafdal platform throughout the 1980s stressed Jewish historical rights and values and negated any form of "ceding":

> The movement sees the religious and historical right of the Jewish people over the whole of Eretz Israel, as the foundation of its ideological and educational course of action... Between the sea and the river Jordan there can be only one state, the state of Israel. There can be no ceding of any part of Eretz Israel to foreign rule or foreign sovereignty... and no independent Arab national entity can be established in Eretz Israel. (Mafdal, 1988)

Referring to the Palestinian inhabitants, Mafdal stated:

> There should be held honorable and fair negotiations with the Arab inhabitants of Judea, Samaria and Gaza, on their rights and obligations, in the personal and the municipal levels, towards the state of Israel, and on their citizen rights in the framework of a neighboring Arab state. (Mafdal, 1988, 1992)

Following the outbreak of the Palestinian *intifada*, Rafael Eitan, leader of the Tzomet party, stated:

> I would have declared, right now, [that] Eretz Israel belongs solely to the Jewish people. There will be no compromise on any inch of land. The Arab inhabitants of Judea and Samaria are citizens of Jordan. (Barzel-Miurski, 1988, p. 6)

Yitzhak Shamir,[14] a leader of the Likud party, was a prototypical representative of the nationalistic-ideological orientation. Shamir viewed Jewish national rights and the idea of Greater Israel as superior to any other value (even to democracy):

> The "security" of our ownership of Eretz Israel is beyond all questions of security.... For democracy I will not give up on Eretz Israel. (Cited by Aronoff, 2009, pp. 46, 50)

> Jews are forbidden from relinquishing any part of their historical homelands. (Cited by Naor, 2001, p. 13)

Shamir warned against the existential threat posed by the Palestinians:

> The Intifada... proved to me once more that the conflict was not over territory, but over Israel's right to exist.... The Palestinians threaten our survival, as long as we are here, they won't be satisfied. (Cited by Aronoff, 2009, pp. 51, 54)

The only way to reach an agreement [with the Arabs] is an Iron Wall. (Cited by Aronoff, 2009, p. 48)

The *nationalistic-pragmatic orientation* continued to be divided into two major suborientations, represented by part of the Likud part and the Labor party. These suborientations remained divided on the issue of territorial compromise.

The national nationalistic-pragmatic suborientation became embodied in some parts of the Likud party that, throughout the 1980s, began to use security considerations to legitimize its support for some concessions in the form of the Autonomy plan. Nevertheless, it continued to reiterate its commitment to Jewish exclusive national rights over Eretz Israel, to Jewish settlement of the territories, to negation of the Palestinian identity, and its refusal to any meaningful withdrawal from the territories:

The right of the Jewish people over Eretz Israel is an internal right, which may not be disputed, and is combined with the right for peace and security....Any plan which includes the cessation of parts of Eretz Israel to foreign rule, as offered by the Labor party, undermines our rights over the land....The Autonomy arrangements, agreed upon at Camp David, are the guarantee against the creation, in the western part of Eretz Israel, of a Palestinian state. (Likud, 1981, 1988)

Referring to the Palestinians, the Likud platform referred to "Arab inhabitants" and expressed readiness to grant them some autonomy:

Most of the Jordanian population came originally from the West Bank of the Jordan, and the Arabs of Judea and Samaria are Jordanian citizens. The Likud will continue to negotiate with representatives of the Arab inhabitants of Judea and Samaria, in order to arrive to Autonomy arrangements according to [the] Camp-David accords. (Likud, 1988, 1992)

Menachem Begin, who served as prime minister between 1977 and 1983, referred to the West Bank as "liberated territory," part of the eternal "promised land" of the Jewish people. Following the Camp David Accords, Begin explicated on the nature of the proposed concessions:

The true meaning of the Camp David agreement is this: Autonomy for the Arab inhabitants of Judea, Samaria and the Gaza strip; Jews and Arabs living together in Eretz Israel; and security for Israel and all its citizens. (Begin, 1979)

Moshe Dayan, moving from the Labor party to the Likud government, emphasized Jewish historical rights in the territories and the right to establish settlements:

> The Israeli settlements in Judea, Samaria and the Gaza district are there as of right. It is inconceivable to us that Jews should be prohibited from settling and living in Judea and Samaria which are the heart of our homeland. (Dayan, 1978, p. 4)

As a result, Dayan could not imagine giving up the West Bank:

> I cannot see giving up the West Bank to Jordan as been accepted by any Israeli party or government. (Dayan, 1977)

> The change, which autonomy will bring about, will be in status and not in the way of living of the Arab population and of the Jewish settlers. (Dayan, 1979b)

Ariel Sharon, a leader of the Likud party, used the outbreak of the first Palestinian *intifada* to stress the security rationale for continued Israeli control over the West Bank:

> Realistically speaking, there's only one solution, a Palestinian state in Jordan.... It is unacceptable to take the security responsibility over the West Bank and Gaza away from Israel. (Barzel-Miurski, 1988, p. 6)

While offering some form of autonomy to the "Arab inhabitants" of the territories, even the most pragmatic leaders of the Likud party still opposed any meaningful territorial compromise.

The practical nationalistic-pragmatic suborientation was represented by the Labor party, which in the mid-1980s was in the coalition with the Likud party. This suborientation emphasized the demographic and moral dangers of continued Israeli control over the population of the West Bank and the Gaza Strip.

The Labor platform, while insisting on the Jewish historical rights in Eretz Israel, also emphasized the need to maintain the unique Jewish character of the State of Israel:

> The Labor [party] will enhance the efforts of the people to build an independent Israel, and to realize the goals of Zionism, predicated on the historical right of the Jewish people to establish and maintain a state in its homeland. The state of Israel was always meant to be a Jewish, democratic and independent state, which maintains full equality to all its citizens. (Labor, 1981, 1984)

> Israeli security needs and the maintenance of its unique national character, realization of Zionist goals and the aspiration to establish Israel as a westernized democratic society will guide to policies of the government towards permanent borders. (Labor, 1984)

The Labor party warned against the demographic threat to the Jewish character of the state:

> This policy [of annexation] will lead to Israel turning from a Jewish state to a bi-national state. Even in the context the moral and societal essence of the state of Israel, the Labor [party] rejects the notion of permanent domination over the million and 200 thousands Palestinian-Arabs, the inhabitants of these territories. (Labor, 1981)

Furthermore, the Labor party emphasized the destructive consequences of continued Israeli control over the territories for the democratic character of the Israeli society:

> The domination policies of the Likud government in Judea, Samaria, and Gaza have already caused alarming undermining of the democratic and moral values of the Israeli society in regard to the rule of law, equality before to law, and the treatment of Israeli Arabs. The Labor position is that maintaining a democratic regime in Israel, which is predicated on equal rights to all of its citizens, does not coincide with permanent domination over the Arab Palestinian inhabitants of Judea, Samaria, and [the] Gaza strip. (Labor, 1984)

However, the Labor party also emphasized Israeli security concerns and the need for "defensible borders," objecting to the possibility of a withdrawal to the 1967 lines:

> The state of Israel needs defensible borders which will allow her to effectively defend itself against all imminent attacks. Demilitarization and other security arrangements will be included in future peace accords in addition to, and not instead of defensible borders. Israel will insist of recognized defensible borders...and will not return to the 1967 lines, which posed a temptation for aggression. (Labor, 1984)

Furthermore, Labor's platform emphasized the vital role of "security settlements" as part of these defensible borders:

> The settlements—in the Jordan valley, the North West shores of the Dead Sea, the Ezion Bloc, and the Jerusalem vicinity—are vital for Israel's security...the Israeli government will insist that in time of peace, all these settlement areas will be included under Israeli sovereignty. (Labor, 1984)

While recognizing the existence of a "Palestinian problem" and acknowledging Palestinians' national rights, the Labor party clearly negated the notion of an independent Palestinian state, emphasizing the solution of the Palestinian issue in the context of a Jordanian-Palestinian state:

> Being aware of the existence of the Palestinian problem Israel is willing to assist in solving this problem, in the context of a Jordanian-Palestinian state. The Jordanian-Palestinian state would include the territory of Jordan, [in] which the majority of its citizens are Palestinians, as well as densely populated areas in Judea, Samaria and Gaza, which the IDF will evacuate with the advent of peace. Only in the context of this territorial and political unit can the national identity of the Palestinian Arabs be realized and the question of Palestinian refugees be settled. Israel negates the establishment of an additional Palestinian state on the territories between Jordan and Israel. (Labor, 1981)

The Labor party reiterated its commitment for withdrawal from "densely populated Palestinian areas": "Withdrawal from densely populated Palestinian areas, in the context of peace accords—is a vital contribution to the security of the state of Israel" (Labor, 1981).

Labor leaders used considerations of threat to justify territorial compromise. The party realized that holding the conquered territories might lead to a binational state, which would threaten Jewish dominance. Both Rabin and Peres emphasized the consequences of "continued domination over another nation":

> I do not know of any nation of 3.5 million people which absorbed another nation of 2.3 million against their will, there is no historical precedent for it, not now and not in the past....A Jewish sovereign state does not go along with annexation, with the whole of Eretz Israel. Those who wish for the whole of Eretz Israel...*it's a racial state with Apartheid, there is not other alternative.* (Rabin, 1989; emphasis added)

> The democratic principle of majority rights and majority rule has become well accepted in international relations today. Being a majority is the dominant factor in defining identity and assigning rights. (Peres, 1978, p. 94)

Peres also empathized with the Palestinians and upheld their right to determine their own future. In 1979 he declared: "Our rejection of the PLO is not linked with rejecting the rights of our neighbors, the Palestinian Arabs. We mean them well. We want to bestow good and honor on them, on their identity, their heritage, their children, and their future" (Agid-Ben Yehuda & Auerbach, 1991, p. 530).

However, while recognizing the need for territorial compromise, both Rabin and Peres emphasized security considerations, opposed full Israeli withdrawal, and negated the idea of a Palestinian state:

> I'm against a withdrawal to the 1967 borders, no way. Jerusalem will remain united under Israeli sovereignty, and I'm not prepared, for security considerations, to return to the 1967 border. (Rabin, 1989)

> Negotiating with the PLO means a Palestinian state between us and Jordan, to which I utterly object. It also means the return of Palestinian refugees which today live outside the borders of British Palestine. (Abramovitz, 1989, p. 5)

> The settlements along the Jordan valley are meant, in practice, to fix the Jordan River as Israel's security border. The settlements on the Western slops of the Judea and Samaria ranges are meant to redeem us form the curse of the "slim waists" of the state of Israel. (Peres, 1978, p. 47)

The *universal-pragmatic orientation* was represented by the very small Zionist-left parties Ratz and Mapam (which ended its alliance with the Labor party in 1984), which placed greater emphasis on the discourse of mutual rights:

> Eretz Israel is the joint homeland of the Jewish people, which has returned to its homeland, and the Arab-Palestinian people who live in it. Both peoples have the right to realize their national self determination in their homeland, based on mutual recognition, in the framework of mutual compromise, and in secure and recognized borders. (Mapam, 1988)

> Two nations live in Eretz Israel—the Jewish people and the Arab-Palestinian people, both with historical and natural rights over the land.... Israel should acknowledge the Palestinian right for self determination, and demand from the PLO to acknowledge Israel's right for secure and safe sovereign existence. (Ratz, 1988)

However, the Zionist Left still referred to Israeli security considerations in determining the future status of the West Bank and Gaza:

> In the framework of peace agreement, Israel will be willing to withdraw, gradually and sequentially, from the West Bank and Gaza, which will then be demilitarized in order to avoid security threats to the state of Israel. (Ratz, 1988)

One of the most unlikely representatives of this orientation was Labor's Member of Knesset (MK) Yossi Beilin, who proposed the establishment of a Palestinian state in Gaza:

I do not propose a Palestinian state only in Gaza. Instead of an interim agreement in the West Bank and Gaza, I'm offering a state in Gaza now, and autonomy in the West Bank. The Palestinians in the West Bank would be able to exercise their right for self determination following peace accords with the rest of the Arab world. (Levy, 1991, p. 16)

Ratz leader Shulamit Aloni expressed greater empathy and a humane approach toward the Palestinians in her assessment of the effects of the ongoing occupation on the Israeli society:

We have no inhibitions in our relations with the Arabs, as the Kozaks in Ukraine had no inhibitions towards the Jews. We perform the same kind of de-legitimization that was directed towards us.... So many myths ha[ve] been build around Judea and Samaria, it has become very hard to break them. However, even today, as a matter of fact, although it has been erased again and again, there's no one in Israel which does not know about the Green Line. (Golan, 1991, p. 3)

The *universal-ideological orientation* was represented by the very marginal alternative Left party SHELI.[15] This party emphasized recognition of Palestinian national rights and claimed the fulfillment of these rights to be the ultimate guarantor of peace.

There's only one political solution to the Israeli-Palestinian conflict, in which Israel will acknowledge the right of the Palestinian people for self determination in its own state, alongside the state of Israel, and this in the framework of mutual recognition and peace agreements which will guarantee Israel's security. (SHELI, 1978)

The platform declared the need for a full Israeli withdrawal and the creation of an independent Palestinian state:

[The] Israeli-Palestinian problem...should be resolved in the framework of negotiations with the Palestinians over national independence in the West Bank and Gaza, alongside Israel. (SHELI, 1982)

This marginal party espoused a clear discourse based on universal rights.

Views of the Jewish Public

During the years 1976–1992 fewer Israelis concurred with the nationalistic-ideological perspective, which viewed Palestinian nationality as an artificial concept (50% in 1979 and 1983). Still, a 1985 survey by the PORI Institute indicates that 60% of the respondents thought that the Palestinians did not have the right to a Palestinian state. Most of the Israeli Jews in this period thought that Israel's claim for the territories was just and that it was more established than the Palestinian claim for the land. For example, in a 1986 survey, 70% of the respondents thought that "Jews have the rights to the Land of Israel that are more just and compelling than those of the Arabs" (Zemach, 1987, p. 4).

Furthermore, while referring to the reasons for holding on to the territories, at the beginning of this period the respondents clearly preferred the ideological reasoning. For example, in a continuous time-series survey conducted in 1986, 50% of Israeli Jewish respondents ranked "Israel's right to the Land" higher than the other security-pragmatic reasons.[16] However, the percentage of respondents who held this belief decreased steadily (see Figure 4.4), while the percentage of those who referred to pragmatic reasons for holding on to the territories (such as "to maintain strategic depth for military operations" or "to use it in future negotiation") more than doubled at the end of this period (Arian, 1995). The data, then, indicate a shift during these years from ideological to more pragmatic reasons underlying the discussion about the future of the territories, that is, a shift from the nationalistic-ideological orientation to the national nationalistic-pragmatic one.

This tendency appears in another time-series survey that was done during these years. Respondents were asked to rank four values (democracy, peace, Greater Israel, and a Jewish majority in Israel). During the years 1988–1992 the percentage of respondents ranking Greater Israel (e.g., the ideology of keeping

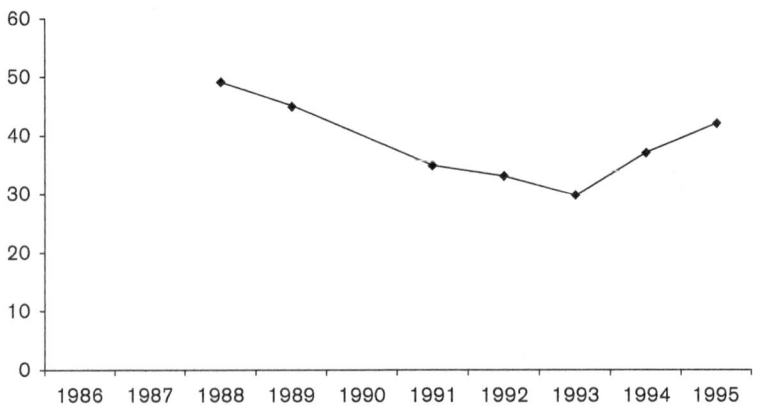

FIGURE 4.4 Percentage of Israeli Jews Who Choose the Right to the Land as the First Reason to Hold the Territories, 1986–1995.
Sources: Institute for National Security Studies (formerly Jaffee Center for Strategic Studies). The Jaffee Center for Strategic Studies was incorporated into the Institute for National Security Studies in 2006. All the data in the figure are taken from the publications of this institution or from its Web site.

the territories) as either first or second in priority decreased from 38% in 1988 to 24% in 1991 (Shamir & Shamir, 2000).

The data show that the Israeli public is still divided on the question of whether to keep the territories (see Figure 4.1). Yet, the opposition to the Palestinian state dropped from 90% during the years 1978–1986 to about 70% during the *intifada* years (1987–1993; see Figure 4.3). The polls further indicate that the percentage of respondents who perceived a Palestinian state as a threat to the State of Israel dropped from about 90% in 1985 to about 80% in 1992 (see Figure 4.2),

Summary

The second period represents two major shifts in the Israeli political discourse. On the one hand, the fault line of the political mainstream—located between Labor and Likud—shifted as the Likud party adopted a more pragmatic orientation. This shift occurred as the issue of Jewish exclusive national rights became less consensual within public opinion and the negation of the Palestinian people became a more contested issue. The nationalistic-pragmatic orientation remained divided between the national suborientation, espousing continued Israeli control of the territories; and the practical suborientation, espousing territorial compromise in order to maintain Israel's Jewish and democratic character. However, the fault lines between the pragmatic mainstream and the ideological perspectives became sharper and more pronounced. Both ends of the political spectrum gained power as they adopted a clearer discourse about the rights to the occupied land.

THE THIRD PERIOD: 1992–2000

The 1992 elections brought a second turnover in Israeli political life, with a Labor government being formed after 15 years of Likud rule (during 1984–1990 in a coalition with the Labor party). This political landmark was soon followed by a historical landmark in the Israeli-Palestinian conflict with the signing of the Oslo Accords in September 1993. The Oslo Accords spelled out, for the first time, mutual recognition of the Israeli and Palestinian national rights.

Views of the Political System

The *nationalistic-ideological orientation* continued to be represented by right-wing parties such as Mafdal, Moledet, Tzomet, and, later, Ihud Lehumi,[17] which increased their electoral power in the 1992 elections.[18] There were also leaders and groups in the Likud party who supported this orientation. However, this orientation faced its greatest challenge following the Oslo Accords. The platforms of these parties continued to emphasize the claim for exclusive Jewish national rights:

> The Mafdal is adamant on the guiding principle of Zionism from its early days—Eretz Israel to the Jewish people, in light of the Jewish gospels. (Mafdal, 1996)

> Eretz Israel is the homeland of the Jewish people, based on its tradition and heritage, home for the return to Zion.... The party would strive to exercise Jewish sovereignty over all parts of Eretz Israel under our control. (Ihud Leumi, 1999)

Palestinians were regarded as "Arab inhabitants" who were entitled to respectful treatment and some form of autonomy:

> The state of Israel should hold honorable and fair negotiations with the Arab inhabitants of Judea and Samaria, regarding their autonomous conduction of municipal, social, and cultural life. (Mafdal, 1996)

However, no meaningful territorial compromise was deemed feasible:

> The party would strive to exercise Jewish sovereignty over all parts of Eretz Israel under our control. Jerusalem, the eternal capital, would remain solely in Israeli sovereignty. The party would strive to enhance and strengthen Jewish settlements in all parts of Eretz Israel. (Ihud Lehumi, 1999)

Any concession in the West Bank and Gaza was deemed a grave risk to Israel's security:

> The Mafdal would object to any autonomy plan which would raise the risk of the creation of a Palestinian state, and would jeopardize Jewish settlement activity in Judea and Samaria. (Mafdal, 1992)

> The Way, Hebron, and Oslo agreements impinge on our [national] rights, and are leading to more bloodshed instead of peace.... The party negates any claims for "right of return" of the Arab population to any parts of Eretz Israel. (Ihud Lehumi, 1999)

The West Bank and the Gaza Strip were deemed "liberated territories," and no reference was made to "domination" or "occupation" of these territories.

The *nationalistic-pragmatic orientation* remained divided between two sub-orientations over the extent of territorial compromise.

The national nationalistic-pragmatic suborientation was represented by the Likud party, which regained the ruling position following the 1996 elections. The party's politics during this period represented a contradiction between ideological and pragmatic orientations. The party maintained its commitment to "Jewish exclusive national rights" while acknowledging later Israel's commitment to the Oslo Accords and recognizing the existence of the Palestinian Authority. This difference reflected two periods: the earlier period, when the Likud party was in opposition, and the later period, when the party was the leading political force in the newly formed government. During the term of the Labor-led government (1992–1996), and especially following the Oslo Agreement, the Likud party followed a nationalistic-ideological orientation supported by security considerations. Its platform clearly expressed exclusive Jewish national rights while denying the unique character of the Palestinian people and their claim for self- determination:

> The state of Israel has a right and a claim for sovereignty over Judea, Samaria, and [the] Gaza [S]trip. These claims will be upheld by the end of the interim agreements, and Israel will act to realize them.... The Arab people had been given ample rights for self determination, by establishing 21 independent Arab states. (Likud, 1992)

Referring to the "Arab inhabitants" of the territories, the Likud platform expressed its commitment to "interim agreements," which negated any form of territorial compromise, or the possibility of a Palestinian state:

> The Likud-led government will continue to negotiate with the representatives of the Arab inhabitants of Judea, Samaria, and [the] Gaza [S]trip, in order to reach interim agreements in the framework of the Camp-David accords. These accords are the guarantee that there will be no more territorial divisions in the Western part of Eretz Israel, and that under no conditions there will be an independent Palestinian state. (Likud, 1992)

Benjamin Netanyahu, who was the leader of the Likud party after 1992 and later served as prime minister (1996–1999), made extensive references to Jewish historical rights while denying the existence of the Palestinian people:

> The areas of Judea and Samaria are the heartland of the Jewish people.... The claim of "Palestinian" Arabs for self determination is false. The inhabitants of Jordan are all Palestinian Arabs.... Most Palestinian Arabs live today on the largest part of Mandatory Palestine—Jordan. (Netanyahu, 1993, p. 150)

Furthermore, Netanyahu justified Israel's continued control over the West Bank based on security considerations:

> The utmost importance should be attributed to the fact that these territories were used by the Arab regimes as staging ground for the attack on Israel in the 1967 war. (Netanyahu, 1993, p. 143)

He also warned against the establishment of an independent Palestinian state:

> We can fathom the grave strategic danger that an independent Palestinian state in Judea and Samaria represents for Israel. (Netanyahu, 1993, p. 276)

However, before the 1996 elections, Likud's platform was amended to accommodate a more pragmatic view of the changes in the political context and in Jewish public opinion. The platform acknowledged the Oslo Accords and the establishment of the Palestinian Authority while emphasizing its threat to Israel's existence. It moved to the practical nationalistic-pragmatic suborientation:

> The Israeli government will honor international agreements…it will acknowledge the existence of facts on the ground, created by previous accords, *and will act to limit the dangers these accords present to Israel's security and future existence*. The Israeli government will negotiate with the Palestinian Authority for the conclusion of final status accords, conditional on Palestinian fulfillment of all their obligations. (Likud, 1996; emphasis added)

The Likud platform further acknowledged the existence of the Palestinians and their right to self-rule. However, it reiterated its opposition to an independent Palestinian state:

> The Israeli government will allow the Palestinians to manage their own affairs freely, in the framework of self rule. However, issues of foreign affairs and security, as well as other issues which demand coordination, will continue to be the sole responsibility of the Israeli government. The government opposes the establishment of an independent Palestinian state. (Likud, 1996)

Furthermore, the platform defined stringent Israeli restrictions on any future territorial compromises:

> Israeli security forces will continue to enjoy, as the need arises, full freedom of action [in the West Bank] in their war on terrorism; vital security areas and Jewish settlements will remain under full Israeli control; Israel

will safeguard vital water resources in Judea and Samaria... the eastern border of the state of Israel, south of the sea of Galilee will be the Jordan River. (Likud, 1996)

Prime Minister Netanyahu also amended his positions, acknowledging the existence of the Palestinian Authority and expressing his willingness for Palestinian self- rule. However, he negated any form of Palestinian sovereignty:

> We need a new model, where a national group could exist under an arrangement less than sovereignty, but that enables that group to control and govern just about every aspect of [its] national life. I don't want to run their lives, I don't want to dominate them, nor do I want them to have those powers that would threaten my country... Palestinian autonomy should incorporate most of the Palestinian population. (Schmemann, 1996, p. 2)

Ariel Sharon, one of the leaders of the Likud party during this period, expressed tentative support for territorial compromise:

> Although I'm not in favor of territorial compromise, if I had to choose between territorial compromise and autonomy, I would prefer territorial compromise. Territorial compromise means a Palestinian state in part of the Territories, whereas Autonomy means a Palestinian state in all of the Territories. (Kadmon, 1994, p. 3)

However, Sharon also placed a series of restrictions on any future compromise:

> The government may gain the support of the opposition if it declares that there will be no independent Palestinian state... the application of Autonomy or Self-rule only in areas which hold a majority of Arab inhabitants; [if it declares] that areas populated by Jews, security areas, and major routes which connect the coastal plain with the Jordan valley, will be left outside the jurisdiction of the Autonomy. (Kadmon, 1994, p. 4)

Avigdor Liberman, head of the newly established Israel Beytenu[19] party, also adopted the practical nationalistic-pragmatic suborientation. While reiterating his commitment to historical Jewish rights, he expressed a readiness to make territorial compromises:

> I believe in the Greater Eretz Israel, not willing to relinquish anything. We have full rights to both banks of River Jordan.... However, on the practical level, I'm willing to accept the situation as it is, de-facto.... Regarding final

status agreements, I'm willing to accept an Alon Plus plan, which enjoys the greatest Zionist consensus, including all vital security areas. 55% of the territories will remain in our control, and the rest is for them. (Caspit, 1998, p. 4)

Regarding the "occupied" status of the territories, Liberman commented:

Before 1967, they [the Arabs] had full control over these territories and no one talked about creating a Palestinian state, about autonomy, about nothing. (Caspit, 1998, p. 5)

However, Liberman also expressed his objection to a fully independent Palestinian state:

Regarding a "Palestinian state," it will be an entity, not exactly a state. We will not be able to relinquish control over the exterior borders...it will not be a state in the full sense of the word; it's a far fledged autonomy. (Caspit, 1998, p. 6)

The Labor party moved somewhat further within the practical nationalistic-pragmatic suborientation to use more saliently arguments taken from the arsenal of universal values. The party, while referring to Jewish national rights, supported territorial compromise on the basis of arguments focusing on threats to the Jewish and democratic nature of the state. At the same time, it emphasized concern over Israel's security needs, which dictated the extent of the withdrawal from the territories. It also began to raise the possibility of establishing the Palestinian state.

The Labor platform clearly stated the connection of the Jewish people to Eretz Israel:

Our essence and identity are linked with the Jewish tradition. A direct pathway leads from the roots of our cultural and religious traditions to the future of the state of Israel....A Jewish state with deep roots and irreversible ties to Eretz Israel. (Labor, 1999)

The platform further emphasized the need for the Jewish and democratic character of the State of Israel and the importance of maintaining a Jewish majority:

We want peace and we need it—in order to maintain a democratic regime, to secure a Jewish majority in the start of Israel, to create a homogeneous society, and to assist with the absorption of emigration. (Labor, 1992)

We are currently preoccupied [with] the construction of the state of Israel as a Jewish, Zionist and democratic state. A state which realizes its commitment to humanistic values, as well as values relating to social justice, equality, liberty, and love for mankind as expressed in the Jewish tradition. (Labor, 1999)

However, the Labor platform also recognized the existence of the Palestinian people and acknowledged their collective and national rights:

Recognition of Palestinian rights, including their national rights, and on the basis of their participation in determining their future. (Labor, 1992)

We acknowledge the Palestinian Authority and recognize its leaders as the representatives of the Palestinian people. (Labor, 1999)

The Labor platform also emphasized its objection to the "domination over another nation" on moral grounds:

Predicated on the belief that a Jewish state should not dominate another nation, the Labor proposes to initiate physical disengagement between the two nations.... Only such disengagement will guarantee personal security to its citizens and will serve the political, security, and moral interests of Israel. (Labor, 1999)

The Labor platform reiterated its commitment to territorial compromise within the framework of peace accords. However, the platform also emphasized the party's commitment to Israel's security needs and security considerations:

Israel will progress in negotiations towards peace accords, predicated on [territorial] compromise, with the Palestinians and Jordan. These accords will be predicated on guaranteeing Israeli security needs. (Labor, 1992)

Under no circumstances shall we return to the 1967 borderlines. We shall not compromise the security of the state of Israel and its citizens. Any accord will be predicated on guaranteeing defensible borders and enabling us to defend the state and its citizens. (Labor, 1999)

The platform further elaborated on the security restrictions with regard to the concept of territorial compromise:

Negotiations with the Palestinians will be based on the Oslo accords, and Israel will insist on the following principles: united Jerusalem the capital of Israel in Israeli sovereignty; Israel will not dominate the Palestinian people; the River Jordan will be the Eastern security border of Israel, and no foreign army will be stationed on its western shores...Israeli sovereignty over the Jordan valley, the north shores of the Dead Sea, Etzion Settlement Bloc, and vital security areas in the West Bank. (Labor, 1996)

Furthermore, the platform emphasized its objection to the establishment of an independent Palestinian state but also raised the possibility of its establishment:

> The creation of a Jordanian-Palestinian confederation is the preferable option, from the Israeli perspective. A Palestinian state shall never be an Israeli objective. However, if a Palestinian state will be the outcome of the permanent agreement, there's need to insure that the political and security restrictions agreed upon correspond to the vital interests of the state of Israel. (Labor, 1999)

Taken at face value, the platforms of both the Likud and Labor parties differed somewhat in the extent of territorial compromises and in the possible final solution. They also presented very different positions regarding the nature and valence of the Oslo Accords. For the Likud party, the Oslo Accords presented a threat that Israel needed to guard against; for the Labor party, they presented an opportunity to realize the vision of a new Middle East.

Prime Minister Yitzhak Rabin emphasized the demographic threat to the Jewish character of the state while stating his personal commitment to Jewish exclusive historical rights over Eretz Israel:

> I believe in the right of the Jewish people to the whole of Eretz Israel, however, what is the current reality? Currently there are over two million Palestinians in the territories. Add to that over a million Israeli-Palestinian citizens. If you realize the Greater Israel you will get 4.4 million Jews with over 3 million Palestinians. Is that a Jewish state? We said in advance: we do not want the whole of Eretz Israel, we want a Jewish state not a binational one. (Ben, 1995, p. 5)

In addition, Rabin emphasized security considerations in determining the future of the territories and limited Palestinian sovereignty:

> However, we will not return to the 1967 lines.... Eventually, the overall solution is in the triangle of Israel and Jordan as sovereign states, and between them, a Palestinian entity in the most parts of the West Bank and Gaza Strip, which is less then a [sovereign] state. (Ben, 1995, p. 5)

Ehud Barak, the Labor leader in the late 1990s, also stated the Jewish historical connection with the West Bank:

> [These are] parts of the homeland from which we had been separated by a hostile border and to which we returned.... A natural expression of our

love for and historic bond with this land, which has been our patrimony and homeland since antiquity. (Barak, 2000)

Barak also acknowledged Palestinian national aspirations, and empathized with the Palestinians' anger:

Both our peoples have aspirations, rights, and legitimate interests, some of which are inimical to each other. Both have dreams and desires, some of which are incompatible.... We have no desire to rule over you or to deprive you of your expression of self-determination. (Barak, 2000)

I imagine that if I were [a Palestinian]... I would at some stage get involved in one of the terror organizations and join the struggle....I don't accept their methods, but what I understand is that the Palestinians feel they have been cornered by the historic circumstances. (Barak, 1998)

Furthermore, Barak emphasized the need for territorial compromise in order to maintain the Jewish national character of Israel:

The gist of our vision is a Zionist, Jewish, and democratic state living in security and peace with its neighbors.... If it wishes to attain peace and preserve its character as a democratic, Jewish state, Israel cannot retain all the territory it captured in 1967 and rule over another people. (Barak, 2000.)

Barak further emphasized the threat to democracy because of continued occupation:

Israel cannot afford and shouldn't try to govern over another people....I think we should separate ourselves from the Palestinians. We do not need here either a kind of apartheid, or a Bosnia. (Batia, 1997, p. 14)

However, Barak also emphasized Israeli security needs as limiting any compromise:

It may be possible to conclude an agreement on the most important issues, in which we disengage from them with actual, physical separation under five major guidelines: United Jerusalem under our sovereignty; No return, under any conditions, to the 1967 borders; No foreign army west of the Jordan River; Most of the settlers, not necessarily most of the settlements, under our sovereignty. (Dankner, 1998, p. 9)

Barak also clearly stated Israel's objection to an independent Palestinian state while acknowledging the possibility of such an outcome:

We should prefer a Palestinian-Jordanian confederation, but we are not in a position to dictate it. (Beck, 1997, p. 12)

It is obvious they will demand an independent state, what will they want, a circus? Ariel Sharon has been saying for some time that they already have a state, de-facto. (Dankner, 1998, p. 9)

Labor leaders continued to emphasize ending "domination over another nation" while limiting the extent of proposed territorial compromise on the basis of security considerations. Of special interest is their use of moral arguments that come to reinforce the need for withdrawal from part of the territories.

The *universal-pragmatic orientation* was represented by a minority Zionist-Left party, Meretz.[20] On the one hand, the Meretz platform for the 1996 election echoed the Right's discourse and emphasized Palestinian national rights and its support for an independent Palestinian state:

Meretz perceives the implementation of the Palestinian national right of self determination as a solid foundation for any future peace accords. The meaning of such declaration is the recognition of their right to establish an independent state alongside Israel, which lives in peace with Israel, on the basis of marinating the security of both sides and the strict implementation of these accords. (Meretz, 1996)

However, the platform also emphasized the importance of security and demographic considerations in determining the future of the territories, echoing the security discourse:

Eventually Israel will have to evacuate most of the territories conquered in the Six-days' War, as will be agreed upon. The salient considerations in determining the borders should be the security and the demographic considerations, so the Israeli security will be enhanced and the continuation of Israeli rule over Palestinian inhabitants of the territories should be avoided as much as possible. (Meretz, 1996)

Beginning with the 1992 elections, the *universal-ideological orientation* ceased to be represented by any Jewish party.[21] However, the universal rights' discourse continued to be propagated by various nongovernmental organizations (NGOs) operating outside of the institutionalized political system.

Views of the Jewish Public

In this period, respondents in polls began increasingly to accept the idea that the Palestinians have the right to establish their own state. For example, in a Gallup poll of March 1997, 50% of the respondents thought that the Palestinians have the right to have their own state (45% thought that they do not have this right; *Maariv*, March 28, 1997, p. 16). A 1996–1999 Peace Index survey indicates that the percentage of respondents who believe in the justness of the Palestinians' demand for their own independent state rose during these years from 45% in June 1996 and September 1998 to 55.6% in March 1999. However, as will be shown below, a minority believed that the fact that the Palestinians also have a right to the land is a reason to give up the territories.

As can be seen in Figure 4.4, in 1992 and January 1993 (before the Oslo Accords) only 30% of the Jews in Israel identified "Israel's right to the land" as the main reason to hold on to the territories. At the same time, the percentage of respondents who referred to pragmatic reasons to hold on to the territories continued to grow and by 1993 was almost equal to the percentage of those who preferred the ideological reasons (Arian, 1995). Furthermore, Arian found that during 1992–1993 among those who cited the ideological "right to the land" reason, the percentage refusing to return the land decreased. In other words, "not only was the 'right to the land' camp in retreat, but in addition there was a softening of commitment to retaining the land among those who remained in the ideological grouping" (p. 31). This indicates again a shift toward the practical nationalistic pragmatic orientation.

The tendency to prefer pragmatic reasons to return the territories appeared in another question that was asked in 1994 and 1995: 39% thought that the main reason for returning the territories was to lower the risk of war and 27% thought that the main reason was that there was no alternative. Only about 17% expressed the universal orientation that the reason to return the territories was that "Palestinians and Israelis both have the right to live here." A similar percentage thought that the reason to return the territories was "to preserve Israel as a Jewish state" (Arian, 1998). Unfortunately, these questions about the reasons to keep or return the territories were not repeated after 1995, so we cannot determine the trend in later years.

We do have, however, data from later years about the percentage of respondents ranking "Greater Israel" and a "Jewish majority" as the most important values. These data indicate a further decrease in those who advocated "Greater Israel": from 14% in 1992 to 7% in 2000.[22] At the same time, the value "Jewish majority" was ranked as the most important value by a higher percentage of respondents (29% in 2000). This trend also appeared in Peace Index surveys: in June 1996, 54% ranked preserving the Jewish majority as more important, while only 25% gave preference to the Greater Israel value.[23]

Overall, this period is also characterized by a significant decrease in opposition to the idea of a Palestinian state (see Figure 4.3). In fact, at the end of this period, most respondents (57%) accepted the idea of a Palestinian state. There was also a decrease in the percentage of respondents who perceived a

Palestinian state as a threat (see Figure 4.4). The combination of Figures 4.3 and 4.4, then, indicates that, with the exception of 1999–2001, the perceived threat of a Palestinian state and levels of support for a Palestinian state were inversely related: as the perception of the threat declined, support for a Palestinian state gradually increased.

After the Oslo Accords, public opinion revealed an increasing gradual trend toward greater willingness to return the occupied territories to the Palestinians (Arian, 1995, 2002). Nevertheless the polls also showed that most respondents thought that Israel should keep the Jordan Valley, Gush Etzion, and East Jerusalem.

Summary

The third period is characterized by decreasing support for the idea of Greater Israel. This decrease was related to growing acceptance of the ideas of territorial compromise and an independent Palestinian state. These trends are mirrored in the political discourse, with blurring of the fault line within the pragmatic mainstream between the Labor and Likud parties. The controversy between security needs and compromises was replaced with the controversy over the extent of the proposed compromise. However, as the pragmatic sphere became blurred, the political power of both the Zionist Left and the Zionist-National Right parties grew substantially. Nevertheless, the universal-ideological orientation ceased to be represented within the Jewish political spectrum.

THE FOURTH PERIOD: 2000–2009

The events of October 2000 and the outbreak of the second *intifada* (al-Aqsa *intifada*) caused an emergence of consensual beliefs in the Israeli political system. The peace camp was decimated, and many of its members moved toward the Center and the Right (Bar-Tal & Sharvit, 2008; Halperin & Bar-Tal, 2007). All the Israeli Zionist parties condemned Palestinian violence and supported an Israeli "war on terrorism."

Views of the Political System

The *nationalist-ideological orientation* was represented in the Knesset by Mafdal and Ihud Leumi. This orientation continued to reiterate the ideology of the Jews' national right to the whole of Eretz Israel and called for the annulment of the Oslo Accords, but even these parties rejected absolute views. They utterly objected to any form of territorial concessions, but tacitly they also acknowledge the reality of the Palestinian Authority and the need for some compromises.

> The Mafdal supports direct negotiations for peace with the Arab countries and the Palestinian Authority based on the following principles: 1) An unrelenting struggle to annihilate terrorism across the country and its borders. 2) Between the River Jordan and the sea there should be only the state of Israel. No Palestinian state should be established. 3) United Jerusalem is the eternal capital of the Jewish people and Israel alone, and will not be divided. (Mafdal, 2003)

> A cantons' program will be implemented for those Arab inhabitants who are not residents of the refugee camps. This program will be based on local and authentic leadership, not imported from Tunisia, and under full Israeli sovereignty and security control. (Ihud Lehumi, 2003)

Furthermore, these parties refused to recognize the collective and national status of the Palestinian people, continuing to refer to them as "Arab inhabitants."

The *nationalist-pragmatic orientation* remained divided between two primary suborientations. The national nationalistic-pragmatic suborientation continued to be represented by the Likud and Israel Beytenu parties. While insisting on the exclusive right of Jews to all of Eretz Israel, these parties began to realize that there was demographic threat to the Jewish character of the state of Israel caused by continued control over the territories:

> The Arab population of Judea and Samaria...constitutes a demographic threat on the Jewish character of the state of Israel. This threat may reach a point of an overall change in the demographic balance in Israel, which will be turned in a short time from a Jewish state into a state with an Arab majority. (Israel Beytenu, 2006)

Thus, these parties came to acknowledge the need for territorial compromise while placing serious limitations on its implementation:

> Only actual disengagement of Israel from the Arab inhabitants of Judea and Samaria, and from the majority of the Muslim Arabs within Israel, will be able to prevent this irreversible process. (Israel Beytenu, 2006)

> The overall purpose of final-status accords with the Palestinians is the ending of conflict between Israel and the Palestinians on the basis of agreed, stable and lasting cooperative relations, including safeguarding Israeli national interests as a secure and prosperous Jewish Zionist state. (Likud, 2003)

The Likud platform continued to object to an independent Palestinian state but in 2006 did not oppose it explicitly:

> Israel will not allow the establishment of a Palestinian Arab state west of the River Jordan. The Palestinians would be able to govern their lives freely, in the framework of self rule and not an independent sovereign state. (Likud, 2003)

However, Israel Beytenu accepted the need for territorial compromise and complete separation from the Palestinians:

> Israel will initiate an act which will set its border with the Palestinians. The new border will guaranty a stable and secure Jewish majority in the state of Israel for years to come. (Israel Beytenu, 2006)

Benjamin Netanyahu, who served as leader of the Likud party in the second half of the 2000s, represents a borderline case between an ideological and a pragmatic nationalist leader. Netanyahu challenged the view of the territories as occupied and repeated his commitment to Jewish national goals:

> This [the territories] is a contested area, not an area of occupation. (Barnea, 2004, p. 2)

> The connection between the Jewish people and the Land of Israel has lasted for more than 3500 years. Judea and Samaria.... This is the land of our forefathers. (Netanyahu, 2009)

However, Netanyahu did acknowledge the existence of a Palestinian people:

> Within this homeland lives a large Palestinian community. We do not want to rule over them; we do not want to govern their lives; we do not want to impose our flag and our culture on them. (Netanyahu, 2009)

Furthermore, Netanyahu expressed his readiness for a Palestinian state:

> In the framework of a permanent agreement I will be willing to seriously consider this idea [of a Palestinian state]. I'm in favor of a Palestinian self-rule, except for certain authorities which may undermine Israel's security. (Blum, 2006, p. 14)

> In my vision of peace, in this small land of ours two peoples will live freely, side-by-side, as good neighbors with mutual respect. Each

will have its own flag, its own anthem, and its own government. (Netanyahu, 2009)

Netanyahu, however, emphasized security considerations, placing strict limits on future Palestinian sovereignty:

> We ask for clear commitments that in a future peace agreement, the territory controlled by the Palestinians will be demilitarized: namely, without an army, without control of its airspace, and with effective security measures to prevent weapons smuggling into the territory—real monitoring, and not what occurs in Gaza today. And obviously, the Palestinians will not be able to forge military pacts.... Israel needs defensible borders, and Jerusalem, the capital of Israel, must remain undivided with continued religious freedom for all faiths. (Netanyahu, 2009)

Avigdor Liberman, leader of Israel Beytenu, and the Foreign Minister emphasized the sinister nature of the Arabs and the threat they posed to Israeli security:

> At the moment when there's a temptation, when it seems possible to destroy us, to annihilate us, then our enemies grow stronger all the time. They do the same between themselves. Once one side is weaker, they immediately take advantage of the situation. This is the nature of any tyranny. (Duek, 2001, p. 3)

Liberman also challenged the concept of causal connection between the occupation and the continuation of the conflict:

> I told Condoleezza Rice that she is mistaken in her assessment that the occupation is the cause of this conflict. It is clear for everyone that even if we were to return to the 1967 border, it will not change anything. (Duek, 2007, p. 19)

However, while formally opposing the concept of 'territories for peace," Liberman later expressed his support for territorial compromise and the concept of a "territorial swap":

> The Israeli Right has not managed to stop the Sinai evacuation, the Oslo process, the Evacuation of Amona and the disengagement.... My conclusion is that we need to adopt a different approach, stop saying always no, and put forward a positive offer. My offer is for territorial swaps: they will relinquish areas in Judea and Samaria, and will receive Wadi Ara. (Duek, 2007, p. 20)

Avigdor Liberman, and his party, Israel Beytenu, represent a borderline position between the national and practical suborientations of the nationalistic-pragmatic orientation.

The practical nationalistic-pragmatic suborientation was represented by the Labor party and the newly formed Kadima[24] party. While reiterating Jewish national rights in the occupied territories, this orientation emphasized demographic (Kadima) threats and the threat of losing the democratic nature of the Jewish state (Labor), which necessitated territorial compromise and the conclusion of peace accords with the Palestinians. However, it also emphasized the security needs of Israel as an important consideration in peacemaking.

Kadima's platform emphasized the demographic threats that necessitated territorial compromise while expressing its commitment to "Jewish historical rights":

> The Jewish people has national historical rights over the Grater Eretz Israel.... The choice between letting every Jew settle anywhere within Eretz Israel, and maintaining the state of Israel as a national Jewish homeland, necessitates relinquishing parts of Eretz Israel. The ceding of parts of Eretz Israel does not constitute relinquishment of this ideology, but the realization of an ideology which seeks to guaranty the existence of a Jewish democratic state in [part of] Eretz Israel. (Kadima, 2006, 2009)

The demographic consideration was also emphasized in Kadima's support for the two-states solution:

> The interest of maintaining a national Jewish state necessitates accepting the principle that ending the conflict will result in the establishment of two nation states, based on the current demographic reality, which will live in peace and security side by side. (Kadima, 2006)

The platform, however, emphasized security and national considerations in its reasoning for opposing full territorial withdrawal:

> The shaping of Israel's borders, in the context of a final peace accords, will be guided by the following principles: 1) The inclusion of areas vital for Israel's security, 2) The inclusion of Jewish holy sites and sites of national symbolic importance, and above all united Jerusalem, the capital of Israel, 3) The inclusion of maximum Jewish settlers, with an emphasis on settlement blocs. (Kadima, 2006, 2009)

Ariel Sharon[25] took a significant step when he recognized the "occupation" of the land of the Palestinian people and in his statement alluded to moral consideration:

> It is impossible to hold 3.5 million Palestinians under occupation...the occupation cannot last indefinitely. (Likud party meeting at the Knesset, May 26, 2003)

Empathizing with the suffering of the Palestinian people, Sharon was willing to consider ideas regarding peacemaking:

> I acknowledge the hardships and suffering of the Palestinian people and I believe we could proceed gradually towards peace, based on an approach of mutual respect and the building of trust and confidence between the two parties. We are willing to review different ideas as to the advancement of peaceful negotiations and the alleviating of the Palestinian suffering. However, this may not be possible under the added pressure of terrorism and violence. (Sharon, 2001)

Nevertheless, Sharon remained very vague about the future of the territories and Palestinian independence, emphasizing again and again his commitment to Israel's security:

> My government will lay the foundations for a different kind of agreement, which is predicated on gradual interim accords, in which the most salient principles will be security for the Israeli citizens, and security for the other side based on reciprocity. (Barnea, 2002, p. 3)

> In my opinion real peace, peace for the next generations, requires concessions, we may have to evacuate some settlements...for the real thing [peace]....I will be willing to make far-reaching concessions. However, I will not make any compromises with regard to the security of Israel and its citizens. (Barnea, 2003, p. 6)

Ehud Olmert, who succeeded Ariel Sharon as head of the newly formed Kadima party as well as the prime minister, clearly expressed his empathy with the settlers and his belief in the Jews' excusive historical right to the land. However, he also acknowledged the existence of the Palestinian people and the demographic threat they represented:

> The existence of [a] Jewish majority in the state of Israel does not coincide with the continued domination over the Palestinian population of Judea, Samaria and Gaza. We insist on the historical right of the Jewish people over the whole of Eretz Israel....However, the choice between the

aspiration to enable every Jew to live anywhere within Eretz Israel, and the existence of the state of Israel as a Jewish state—necessitates relinquishing parts of Eretz Israel. (Olmert, 2006)

Olmert used the demographic threat to justify his support for territorial compromise. However, he still emphasized Israeli security concerns as limiting a future compromise:

> We will make a decisive step towards safeguarding Israel as a Jewish state, with a solid and secure Jewish majority which may not be threatened.... The principle which will guide us in the dialogue [with the Palestinians] is the convergence into the Big Settlement Blocks and the solidification of these settlement blocks.... In any case, our security border will run along the River Jordan. This is due to major strategic considerations, on which we cannot compromise. (Barnea, 2006, p. 3)

Olmert clearly expressed his support for an independent Palestinian state:

> The existence of two nation states, Jewish and Palestinian, is the ultimate solution to the national aspirations of each one of our nations, including the issue of refugees which will be repatriated only in the Palestinian state. (Olmert, 2006)

This orientation emphasized security and demographic considerations in support for a territorial compromise while still proclaiming exclusive Jewish national rights over the territories.

Between 2000 and 2009, the orientation of the Labor party moved toward more nationalistic views, which were blurred with the position of the Kadima party and recently even with that of the Likud party. Like the Kadima platform, the Labor platform recognized the existence of a Palestinian nation and acknowledged the two-states solution while emphasizing peace as a "vital Israeli national interest":

> Political accords are a vital Israeli national interest.... The Labor [party] will strive to renew negotiations with the Palestinian Authority, in order to reach a conclusion which will end the conflict. The principles for the final-status accords [with the Palestinians] are: two states for two peoples, which will live peacefully alongside each other; the border between these two states will be determined in direct negotiations between the two parties. (Labor, 2006, 2009)

However, while acknowledging the principle of "two states for two nations," the Labor platform emphasized the limitations of territorial compromise it was willing to make:

The large settlement blocks will be annexed to Israel, and settlements which are outside these annexed blocks will be evacuated; Jerusalem, including all its Jewish neighborhoods, is the eternal capital of the state of Israel. (Labor, 2006, 2009)

Israeli security considerations were given precedence over mutual agreement:

In the absence of political accords, the government of Israel should strive for a disengagement from the Palestinians and the creation of security borders. The [L]abor [party] will introduce a plan for unilateral disengagement from the Palestinians according to security considerations.... Isolated settlements will be evacuated, especially in Gaza. (Labor, 2003)

The platform also noted the democratic and humanistic values associated with the Jewish character of the state. But they did not appear in relation to the situation of occupation:

We are currently preoccupied [with] the construction of the state of Israel as a Jewish, Zionist and democratic state. A state which realizes its commitment to humanistic values, as well as values relating to social justice, equality, liberty, and love for mankind as expressed in the Jewish tradition. (Labor, 2006, 2009)

Ehud Barak, who returned to lead the Labor party in the second half of the 2000s, acknowledged the Palestinians' right to self-determination:

At Camp David, Begin did not only relinquish the whole of Sinai. He also acknowledged the legitimate rights of the Palestinian people. The whole world understands that "the legitimate rights of the Palestinian people" includes the right for self determination, the right for a state. (Shavit, 2005, p. 18)

However, Barak also specified a series of restrictions on the fulfillment of these rights, emphasizing Israeli security considerations:

Israel should be doing five things: first of all, it should complete the construction of the separation fence over the course of several months. Next, it should evacuate isolated settlements to the east of the fence, in the framework of a total withdrawal plan, and over the course of three years.... Israel should offer the international community the opportunity to take upon itself the mandate of managing the Palestinian territories in order to assist the Palestinian Authority to prepare for the establishment of a Palestinian state. (Shavit, 2005, p. 19)

This orientation presented pragmatic considerations for "ending domination over another people" while maintaining its focus on Jewish character and security considerations.

The *universal-pragmatic orientation* was represented by a small Zionist-Left party, Meretz, which in this period represented a borderline case between the pragmatic and ideological orientations. The Meretz platform emphasized moral values as well as Israel's interest in ending the occupation.

> The Israeli occupation in the territories and Israeli rule over the Palestinian population of the territories constitute a moral, economic, social and political disaster for Israel. The practices of the occupation regime cause daily violations of human rights.... The Israeli interest was, and still remains, in favor of ending the occupation and dividing this land through an agreement in the spirit of the Arab or the Geneva initiatives. (Meretz, 2006, 2009)

Meretz expressed a clear vision regarding the future of the territories:

> Peace agreement will be predicated on the two states for two nations' solution, with the following principles: 1) End of conflict and violence. 2) Permanent borders based on the 1967 lines, with agreed upon territorial swaps. 3) In Jerusalem there will reside two capitals for both states, alongside one another. 4) [A] [m]utually agreed upon solution to the refugee problem. 5) Security arrangements which will enable both nations to live peacefully. (Meretz, 2009)

This orientation echoed the universal rights discourse coupled with security considerations.

Views of the Jewish Public

During this period, most Israelis acknowledged the Palestinian right to self-determination. For example, a recent Peace Index survey showed that a solid majority of Israeli Jews (61%) think that the Palestinians' desire for an independent state is just (Peace Index, November 2008). Furthermore, 62% recognized the existence of a Palestinian people, and the majority of the respondents (53%) supported the idea of a Palestinian state (Peace Index, June 2009). This trend was accompanied by a decrease in a perceived threat from a Palestinian state (see Figure 4.2; Ben-Meir, 2009).

During this period, there was an increase in the percentage of those who thought that a Jewish majority was the most important value: from 29% in 2000 to 42% in 2005, rising to 50% in 2007. At the same time, the percentage of those who thought that Greater Israel was the most important value did not change during the years 2000–2007 (remaining about 9%; Ben-Meir & Shaked,

2007). These findings may indicate the heightened salience of the demographic factor that also appears in the rhetoric of politicians from this period.

However, public opinion polls presented mixed results regarding the perceived status of the territories (occupied or liberated). In August 2004, 51% of the Jewish public regarded the West Bank and the Gaza Strip as occupied territories, while in 2008 55% of the Jewish public regarded the West Bank as liberated territory and 32% considered it as occupied territory (Peace Index, March 2008).

Furthermore, during 2000–2007, there was a decline in support for withdrawal from particular areas in the territories. More specifically, support for returning Gush Etzion declined from 33% to 24%, for returning the Jordan Valley from 32% to 24%, and for returning western Samaria from 51% to 29% (Ben-Meir & Shaked, 2007). The Arab neighborhoods in East Jerusalem are an exception; support for territorial concession in East Jerusalem more than doubled from 2000 (24%) to 2001 (51%). This level of support remained relatively stable until 2006, dropping to 40% in 2009 (Ben-Meir, 2009).

Summary

The fourth period, following the al-Aqsa *intifada*, is characterized by growing public support among Israeli Jews for Palestinian national rights and an independent Palestinian state. It is possible that this trend is a result of growing awareness of the demographic threat posed by the Palestinians if the land is not divided between the two nations. At the same time, a substantial percentage of the Jews in Israel continue to view the territories conquered in the 1967 war as liberated. Nevertheless, public opinion is also characterized by growing fear and skepticism regarding Palestinian sincerity. In the political sphere, the second *intifada* served to further blur the lines within the nationalistic-pragmatic perspective, causing a realignment in the Israeli political Center and the emergence of the Kadima party. However, the growing skepticism and mistrust served to weaken the political power of the Zionist Left espousing the *universal-pragmatic orientation,* while at the same time enhancing the salience and power of the nationalistic-ideological perspective. The mainstream political discourse narrowed down to the specific framing of the political solution, and even those holding the nationalistic-ideological perspective tacitly acknowledged the existence of the Palestinian Authority (see Bar-Tal, Halperin, & Oren, 2010, for further discussion on these points).

IMPLICATIONS

Conquest of the West Bank (including East Jerusalem) and the Gaza Strip in the 1967 war confronted the State of Israel with a determinative question that had not been posed before: what should be done with the conquered territories that were considered crucial by the Palestinian people, the Arab countries, and the international community in the resolution of the Israeli-Palestinian conflict? They all demanded withdrawal from these territories in order to establish there a Palestinian state. In other words, withdrawal from the conquered territories became one of the major preconditions for resolving peacefully the Israeli-Arab conflict. Thus, paradoxically, the 1967 war brought over time the possibility of resolving the conflict peacefully, and with this possibility arose a major dilemma for the Jewish-Israeli leadership and public: whether to withdraw from these territories in exchange for peace.

We assume that the resolution of the dilemma and even its cognitive formulation depend strongly on the perception of the conquest and the related issues in the minds of the Israeli Jews. Viewing the conquest as an occupation; perceiving the Palestinians as a people who deserve self-determination and the establishment of their own state; viewing the land between the Jordan River and the Mediterranean Sea as a homeland of two nations—all these tune the holder of these views to completely different choices of course of action than someone who holds opposing views. The opposing views on these issues consider Jews as having the exclusive right to the land between the Jordan River and the Mediterranean Sea; deny the existence of the Palestinians as a separate nation; and deny their right to self-determination and statehood. Obviously, the views on these issues can be moderated by pragmatic considerations of security conditions, which usually constitute for Jews a major influence in their evaluation of peace agreement proposals, or of the demographic threats to the Jewish nature of the state of Israel which has gained salience in the last decade. Clearly, consideration of other conditions is possible.

This chapter presented the prevailing views in Israeli-Jewish society on the issues about the conquest and the Palestinians since 1967. The analysis indicates that between 1967 and the 1990s, the Israeli political mainstream was dominated by the nationalistic orientation, which was mostly pragmatic with an ideological segment. There was very little consideration of universal values recognizing the conquest as an occupation, acknowledgment of the Palestinians as a nation that requires self-determination, and a perception of the occupation as an immoral situation. The hegemonic orientation viewed the land between the Jordan River and the Mediterranean Sea as belonging exclusively to the Jews. This orientation included almost all Jewish political parties, including the Labor party. The differences among the various major parties pertained to the view of the Palestinians as a nation and pragmatic considerations of security. Nevertheless, since 1992, there has been a clear trend toward adopting pragmatic views by the major political parties.

Since the beginning of the conquest of the West Bank and the Gaza strip in 1967, the Labor party accepted the nationalistic-pragmatic view. The Likud party completely ignored this view until Ariel Sharon, leader of the Likud party and Prime Minister at that time, said that he had reached the conclusion that "it is impossible to hold 3.5 million Palestinians under *occupation*" and that "the *occupation* cannot last indefinitely" (Likud party meeting at the Knesset, May 26, 2003; emphasis added).[26] Nevertheless, in 2008, the majority of Israeli Jews still considered the conquest of the territories as liberation and almost all of the present political and religious leaders consider the land between the Jordan River and the Mediterranean Sea as belonging exclusively to the Jews. From 1967 to the present, orientations based on universal values were marginal and most of the time were negligible.

EMPIRICAL STUDY

Our basic proposition is that the hegemonic views of the Israeli-Jewish leadership and the public about the conquest and the territories have a determinative influence on the way they approach the solution of the Israeli-Palestinian conflict. Based on the conceptual framework presented by Halperin and his colleagues (Halperin et al., 2010), we argue that above and beyond the effect of the ideological beliefs or the political affiliation of an individual, the perception about the accurate definition of the territories (i.e., as occupied versus liberated) will influence his level of support for specific compromises required for peace.

In a recent study by Rosler and his colleagues (Rosler, Bar-Tal, Sharvit, & Halperin, 2009), this assumption was empirically tested using data collected in three nationwide representative samples of the Jewish population in Israel on three different occasions. In all three surveys, the associations between support for specific compromises or proposals for peace and an item capturing subjective perception of the situation of the territories conquered in 1967 were examined while controlling for relevant sociopolitical and other psychological variables.[27]

The first two surveys were based on the Peace Index project and were conducted in August 2004 ($N = 504$) and March 2008 ($N = 496$).[28] Both surveys mirrored the general distribution within Israeli society in terms of political ideology, religious definition, and other relevant sociopolitical factors.

The first survey was conducted in the shadow of the public discourse about the forthcoming disengagement from Israeli settlements in the Gaza Strip and northern Samaria. As a result, we tested the effect of the perceived status of the territories on support for the disengagement plan. In line with our hypothesis, even when we controlled for political ideology and other sociopolitical factors (i.e., religiosity, income, gender, education), the effect of the subjective definition of the situation on support for the plan was significant, positive, and relatively high ($\beta = .29$, $t < .001$).

The second survey was conducted almost four years later during the intensive negotiations between Former Israeli Prime Minister Ehud Olmert and the president of the Palestinian National Authority, Mahmoud Abbas. This time, the question used to capture the subjective perception of the situation of the territories was dichotomous, with 1 representing "occupied territories" and 2 "liberated territories." This method enabled us to compare the level of support for the ongoing negotiations in both groups. As hypothesized, those who defined the territories as occupied were more supportive of continuing the negotiations (M = 2.2, SD = 0.94) as well as making the compromises needed to achieve peace (M = 1.7, SD = 0.46) than those who defined the territories as liberated (support negotiations: M = 1.5, SD = 1.10; support compromises: M = 1.32, SD = 0.47, both t's < .001). Again, these patterns held true even when controlling for all relevant sociopolitical factors.

We (Rosler et al., 2009) conducted the third nationwide survey in order to examine whether the same patterns would hold true when controlling for a series of relevant psychopolitical factors (i.e., political sophistication, support for democratic values, authoritarianism, and perceived threat from Arabs) in addition to the sociopolitical ones that were included in the Peace Index polls.[29] As in the previous surveys, the statistical analysis yielded significant results: those who defined the territories as occupied tended to support compromises ($\beta = .23$, $t < .001$) even when controlling for all above-mentioned factors.

CONCLUSION

It is our major claim that the view of the territories has a determinative influence on the Israeli-Jewish approach to the major issues at the core of the peaceful solution of the Israeli-Palestinian conflict. Viewing the territories as having been liberated because they are part of the Jewish homeland and belong exclusively to the Jews and/or viewing them as being of supreme importance to secure the existence of the State of Israel has imprinting effects on the issue of determining the borders, removal of the settlements, and division of Jerusalem, as well as the establishment of a Palestinian state. It is important to note that this view was relatively marginal before the 1967 war. The conquest of the West Bank and the Gaza Strip in 1967 changed the dominant position of the Israeli-Jewish public.

Having this view, it is not surprising that the Israeli leaders and the public do not easily support withdrawal from these territories and dismantling of the Jewish settlements built in these territories. They have a very clear rationale for continuing the occupation without feeling dissonance, guilt, or shame. According to this rationale, occupation either does not exist and/or is well justified, legitimate, and can continue. Only very utilitarian considerations of threat move the great majority of the Jewish leaders and the public to compromises that accept the idea of dividing the land into two nations and removing at least some of the settlements (for example, the threat of becoming a minority in the land between the Jordan River and the Mediterranean Sea). They do not approach the issue of occupation from moral or human rights perspectives. But even in this position, the strongly dominant view is that Jews will have to make major compromises and sacrifices that are not comparable to those of the Palestinians. They do not share the Palestinian view that considers the emerging peaceful solution as an ultimate compromise—one that gives them only 22% of the deserved land.

In our view, this approach to the occupation is a prominent indicator of the readiness to terminate the occupation not only in Israel but in every place where it occurs. When members of the occupying society view the occupation as liberation, or in other justifying terms, even when the occupied society resists the occupation, it is very difficult to terminate it. Chinese with regard to Tibet, Russians with regard to Chechnya, and even Indians with regard to Kashmir have constructed very powerful justifications for holding the occupied territories. Indeed, in these cases, no signs appear that the occupation may be terminated. It is true, though, that in authoritarian regimes such as China or Russia, holding occupied territories is less costly, as the government can use far- reaching powers and means in putting down resistance in the occupied territories and silencing criticism in their own societies, if it appears. Also, since these countries are superinternational powers, the international community has less will and fewer means to intervene. But Israel claims to be a democracy, observing moral codes of behavior, and therefore is judged differently.

Thus, anyone who tries to understand the Israeli position has to take into account the above description of how Jews in Israel view the occupation. The 1967 war was a major event that changed the perceptions and beliefs of the Jews in Israel and determined their approach to the peaceful resolution of the Israeli-Palestinian conflict. We suggest that one of the conditions for creating support for the emerging solution of this conflict is convincing the Israeli leadership and the public that the West Bank is occupied and has been held for many years in violation of international laws and moral standards to which Israel claims to subscribe, as well as to the views of all the states in the world.

NOTES

1. The idea of challenging the 1949 borders and enlarging the state of Israel was prevalent in some circles, most notably among members of Herut and Ahedut HaAvoda parties (Naor, 2001). However, the majority of Israel's mainstream public distinctly abolished these ideas and accepted the 1949 borders as a matter of *realpolitik*.
2. The major political events mentioned are the electoral upheavals of 1977 and 1992, as well as the outbreak of the Second Intifada in Oct 2000. These events signified major changes in Israeli policies regarding the territories.
3. In our analysis we refer only to parties that are dominated by Jewish members. This is because the orientations of parties in which Arabs constitute a dominant fraction are dictated by different set of considerations and are therefore less susceptible to our proposed conceptual framework.
4. **Mafdal (National Religious Party)** was formed in 1956, and represented the religious Zionist movement. Traditionally Mafdal was a practical centrist party, with a socialist and religious orientation. However, following the 1967 war it began drifting towards the right, and in recent decades it become increasingly associated with Israeli settlers, forming a strong political alliance with the right-wing Ihud Lehumi (National Union). In the 1960s and 1970s its political power constituted of 11–12 seats in the Knesset. However, in the 1980s- 2000s its power diminished towards 5–6 seats. Mafdal participated in every Israeli government, with the exception of 1992–1996.
5. **Likud (The Union)** was formed in 1973, as an alliance of right-wing parties. In 1977 it became the ruling party till 1992. The Likud is a center-to-right party with a nationalistic orientation on issues of the Israeli-Palestinian conflict and conservative orientation on economic and social issues. During the 1970s the Likud gradually increased its political power from 26 to 43 seats in the Knesset, which was maintained during the 1980s. However, in the 1990s its power declined steadily to 32, and later to 19 seats. In the 2000s its power fluctuated sharply between 12 and 38 seats. Likud played a leading role in consecutive governments between 1977 and 1992, and again in 1996 and from 2001.
6. **Shelomzion (Security for Israel)** was founded in 1977 by Ariel Sharon. The party held a nationalistic right-wing ideology, coupled with a conservative economic orientation. Soon after the 1977 elections, where it won 2 seats in the Knesset, it merged into the Likud.
7. **Avoda (Labor)** was formed in 1968 as an alliance of the socialist parties Mapai, Ahdut HaAvoda, and Rafi. The party has a social democratic as well as pragmatic Zionist ideology, coupled with a center-to-left political orientation. During 1969–1984 it was in alliance with Mapam. Throughout the 1970s the party maintained its political power at roughly 50 seats at the Knesset, and during the 1980s at roughly 44 seats. However, during the 1990s its power declined gradually to 28 seats, and during the 2000s towards 19 and even 13

seats. The Party played leading role in all Israeli governments till 1977, when it lost elections to the Likud. It returned again to power in the 1992, and 1999 elections. However, during the 2000s it came to play a minor role in Likud- and Kadima-lead governments.

8. **Mapam (Workers' Union party)** was founded in 1948 as a union of several socialist and workers' parties. The party represented both the agricultural working class' settlements (Kibbutzim) as well as the urban working class. Although being a Zionist party, Mapam espoused Israeli-Palestinian coexistence and later supported the creation of a Palestinian state. On economic issues, Mapam held a strong socialist orientation. Between 1969 and 1984, the party was a part of an alliance with the Labor party, and in 1992 it merged with Shinui and Ratz into Meretz.

9. **Ratz (Runner—Civil Rights and Peace Movement)** was formed in 1973 by MK Shulamit Aloni. The party espoused a secular socialist ideology which protested human rights violations, as well as religious coercion. During the 1980s the party espoused a compromise solution to the Israeli-Palestinian conflict. Ratz political power rose gradually from 1 seat in the Knesset, in the 1970s to 5 seats in the late 1980s. In the 1992 elections, Ratz merged with Shinui and Mapam, to form Meretz.

10. **Peace and Security Movement** was a grass-root organization founded following the 1967 war, which espoused a mutually negotiated solution to the Israeli-Palestinian conflict. The movement was lead by a group of renowned professors from the Hebrew University in Jerusalem. The movement campaigned in the 1969 elections, but failed to win a seat in the Knesset.

11. **HaOlam HaZeh—Koah Hadash (This world—New Force)** was formed in 1965 by the journalist Uri Avnery and held two seats in the Knesset. The party espoused a radical left-wing orientation, supporting the creation of an independent Palestinian state. In 1973 the party changed its name to **MERI** (rebellion), and in 1977 it merged into SHELI. The Party has never participated in any Israeli governing coalition.

12. **Tzomet (Junction)** was founded by General Rafael Eitan in 1983 after his retirement from the position of chief-of-staff in 1982. The party held a secular and right-wing orientation. Tzomet introduced the slogan "peace for peace" instead of "peace for land", and objected to any form of territorial compromise. During the 1980s the party held a modest political power, with 1–2 seats in the Knesset. In 1992 its power increased dramatically to 8 seats. However, in the 1996 elections it lost much of its power, to disappear completely after 1999. The party participated in Likud-led governments in 1990, and again in 1996.

13. **Tehiya (Resurrection)** was formed in 1981 by right-wing public figures who seceded from the Likud party. The party objected to any form of territorial compromise, demanded the annexation of the whole of Eretz Israel, and supported forceful policies towards the Arabs. Its political power during the 1980s was roughly 4 seats in the Knesset. The party ceased to exist by 1992, and was

inherited by Herut, and Moledet. It participated in Likud-led governments in 1981 and 1988.
14. Shamir served as the Prime Minister intermittingly with Shimon Peres (leader of the Labor Party) between 1983 and 1990 and then lead a Nationalistic government between 1990 and 1992.
15. **SHELI (Peace for Israel)** was formed prior to the 1977 elections by the merger of some small radical left-wing movements, including MERI, Moked, and some members of the Black Panthers. SHELI espoused a radical left ideology, supporting an independent Palestinian state. It political power amounted to two seats in the Knesset. The party failed to win reelection in the 1981 election and subsequently disappeared, though many former party members joined the Progressive List for Peace. The Party has never participated in any Israeli governing coalition.
16. Respondents were asked to rank the importance of four contending reasons used by people who want Israel to continue its hold on the territories: "Israel's right to the Land", "to prevent the establishment of a Palestinian state", "to maintain strategic depth for military operations", or "to use in future negotiation". The question was no longer asked after 1995.
17. **Ihud Lehumi (National Union)** was formed in 1999 as a coalition of several small right-wing parties, including Moledet, Herut, and Tequma. The party holds right-wing nationalist-religious ideology with strong support for the settlers' movement, coupled with a conservative orientation on economic and social issues. During the 2000s its political power rose steadily from 4 to 9 seats in the Knesset. The party participated in the Likud-led government between 2001 and 2005.
18. The right wing parties (HaThiya, Mafdal, Moledet, and Tzomet) won 17 seats in the 1992 elections, as opposed to 12 seats at 1988, 11 seats in 1996, and 13 seats in 1999.
19. **Israel Betenu (Israel our home)** was founded in 1999 by Avigdor Liberman, as a secular party which caters for the Russian population. This party holds a nationalistic political ideology, coupled with a conservative economic orientation. However, Israel Betenu supports territorial swaps, in order to maintain a homogenous Jewish state. The Party's political power has grown dramatically during the 2000s from 4 to 15 seats in the Knesset. Israel Betenu has participated in recent Israeli governments since 2001.
20. **Meretz (Vigor)** was founded in 1992, following the union of Mapam, Ratz, and Shinui. Meretz is a social-democratic secular party which espouses a negotiated solution to the Israeli-Palestinian conflict, together with a liberal economic orientation. The party's political power during the 1990s was relatively stable with 10–12 seats in the Knesset. However, in the 2000s, its power gradually declined from 6 to 3 seats. Meretz participated in the Labor-led governments in 1992 and 1999.
21. In our analysis we refer only to parties that are dominated by Jewish members. This is because the orientations of parties, in which Arabs constitute a

dominant fraction, are dictated by different set of considerations and are therefore less susceptible to our proposed conceptual framework.
22. We thank Michal Shamir and Asher Arian for the data.
23. Respondents were asked: "In your opinion, which of these two objectives is more important: preservation of the Greater Israel or of the Jewish majority?".
24. **Kadima (Forward)** was formed in 2005 by then PM Ariel Sharon. The party incorporated leading political figures which seceded from both the Likud and the Avoda parties. The party holds a center political ideology with a strong emphasis on Israeli national interests, coupled with a liberal economic orientation. The party's political power, since its inception, has been steady 28–29 seats in the Knesset. Kadima played a leading role in the government between 2005 and 2009.
25. Sharon served as Prime Minister for the Likud party in the early 2000's and later seceded to form Kadima party.
26. Of interest is the fact that Elyakim Rubinstein, the Attorney General of Israel, objected to the use of the term "occupation" by Ariel Sharon claiming that all the Israeli governments considered the territories as "territories in dispute" and the Prime Minister agreed to change the term he used (Zertal & Eldar, 2007).
27. The exact wording of the "occupation" item was "Some people argue that the Israeli domination over the West Bank constitutes an occupation. To what extent do you agree or disagree (1 = not at all, 6 = very much) with this claim?"
28. The Peace Index polls are monthly polls that have been conducted by the Tami Steinmetz Center for Peace Research at Tel-Aviv University since 1994 (for more information about the Peace Index project see www.tau.ac.il/peace). All Peace Index polls include several fixed questions regarding support for and belief in the peace process between Israel and the Arab world.
29. The sample included 716 respondents representing the adult Jewish population residing within the 1967 borders of Israel, of whom 46.5% were men and 53.5% women. The mean age was 45.9 years (SD = 16.49). Regarding political orientations, 45.8% of the respondents defined themselves as Hawkish, 37.7% as Centrist, and 16.5% as Dovish.

REFERENCES

Abramovitz, A. (1989, February 10). If only the Israeli people will be patient: Interview with Defense Minister Rabin. *Maariv*, p. 5 (in Hebrew)

Agid-Ben Yehuda, H., & Auerbach, Y. (1991). Attitudes to an existence conflict: Allon and Peres on the Palestinian issue, 1967–1987. *Journal of Conflict Resolution*, 35, 519–446.

Alon, Y. (1973, March 6). *A strategy for peace*. Lecture at the Eshkol Institute at Hebrew University, Jerusalem (in Hebrew).

Arian, A. (1995). *Security threatened: Surveying Israeli opinion on peace and war*. Cambridge: Cambridge University Press.

Arian, A. (1998). Opinion shift in Israel: Long-term patterns and the effects of security events. In D. Bar-Tal, D. Jacobson, & A. Klieman (Eds.) *Security concerns: Insights from the Israeli experience* (pp. 267–286). Stanford, CT: JAI Press.

Arian, A. (2002). *Israeli public opinion on national security 2002.* Memorandum No. 61. Tel Aviv: Jaffee Center for Strategic Studies at Tel Aviv University.

Aronoff, Y. S. (2009). When do hawks become peacemakers: A comparison of two Israeli prime ministers. *Israeli Studies Forum, 24*(1), 39–61.

Auerbach, Y., & Ben-Yehuda, H. (1987). Attitudes towards an existence conflict: Begin and Dayan on the Palestinian issue. *International Interactions, 13*, 323–351.

Auerbach, Y., & Ben-Yehuda, H. (1993). Attitudes to an existence conflict: Rabin and Sharon on the Palestinian issue, 1967–1987. In K. S. Larsen (Ed.), *Conflict and social psychology* (pp. 144–167). Oslo: PRIO.

Barak, E. (1998, March 6). Uproar in Israel over Barak's identification with terrorists. *BBC.*

Barak, E. (2000, November 8). *Address by Prime Minister Ehud Barak on the fifth anniversary of the assassination of Yitzhak Rabin.* Retrieved December 1, 2009, from http://www.mfa.gov.il/MFA/Government/Speeches+by+Israeli+leaders/2000/Address+by+PM+Barak+on+the+Fifth+Anniversary+of+th.htm

Barnea, N. (2002, February 1). We are at war: Interview with Ariel Sharon. *Yediot Aharonot,* pp. 2–5 (in Hebrew).

Barnea, N. (2003, April 16). I am not giving free gifts to anyone: Interview with PM Sharon. *Yediot Aharonot,* pp. 6–7 (in Hebrew).

Barnea, N. (2004, October 1). If there will be a catastrophe, Sharon will stop the disengagement: Interview with finance minister Netanyahu. *Yediot Aharonot,* pp. 2–4 (in Hebrew).

Barnea, N. (2006, March 10). These are my borders: Interview with Acting PM Ehud Olmert. *Yediot Aharonot,* pp. 2–5 (in Hebrew).

Bar-Tal, D., Halperin, E., & Oren, N. (2010). Socio-psychological barriers to peace making: The case of the Israeli Jewish society. *Social Issues and Policy Review, 4*, 63–109.

Bar-Tal, D., & Sharvit, K. (2008). The influence of the threatening transitional context on Israeli Jews' reactions to Al Aqsa Intifada. In V. M. Esses & R. A. Vernon (Eds.), *Explaining the breakdown of ethnic relations: Why neighbors kill* (pp. 147–170). Oxford: Blackwell.

Barzel-Miurski, B. (1988, January 15). What is their solution: Shamir, Peres, Rabin, Sharon and Raful. *Yediot Aharonot,* pp. 6–7. (in Hebrew).

Batia, S. (1997, June 4). Barak has power in his sights. *The Guardian,* p. 14.

Beck, E. (1997, January 26). Barak conditionally supports Palestinian state. *Jerusalem Post,* p. 12.

Begin, M. (1970, April 23). *Eretz Israel.* Begin's speech at the annual National Council of Herut party (in Hebrew). Retrieved December 1, 2009, from http://www.betar.org.il/world/ideology/erets.htm

Begin, M. (1979, June 11). *Statement issued by Prime Minister Begin on Israeli settlements*. Retrieved December 1, 2009, from http://www.mfa.gov.il/ MFA/Foreign%20Relations/Israels%20Foreign%20Relations%20since%20 1947/1979–1980/23%20Statement%20issued%20by%20Prime%20Minister%20 Begin%20on%20Isr

Ben, A. (1995, April 14). Separation as a political worldview. *Haaretz*, p. 5 (in Hebrew).

Ben-Meir,Y. (2009). Public opinion and the political arena. In S. Brom & A. Kurz (Eds.), *Strategic survey for Israel, 2009*. Tel Aviv: Institute for National Security Studies.

Ben-Meir, Y., & Shaked, D. (2007). *The people speak: Israeli public opinion on national security 2005–2007*. Memorandum No. 90. Tel Aviv: Institute for National Security Studies.

Blum, G. (2006, October 13). The strengthening plan: Interview with Benjamin Netanyahu. *Yediot Aharonot*, pp.13–15 (in Hebrew).

Bondi, R. (1967, September 15). Everyone and his own Whole Eretz Israel. *Davar*, p. 17 (in Hebrew).

Camp David Accords (September 17, 1978). Retrieved Decmber 1, 2009, from http:// www.mfa.gov.il/MFA/Peace+Process/Guide+to+the+Peace+Process/

Caspit, B. (1998, April 3). Some of the Yesha council leaders . . . : Ivet Liberman talks. *Maariv*, pp. 4–6 (in Hebrew).

Conversi, D. (2000). *The Basques, the Catalans and Spain*. Reno: University of Nevada Press

Cornell, S. E. (2002). *Autonomy and conflict: Ethno-territoriality and separatism in the South Caucasus—case in Georgia*. Report No. 61. Department of Peace and Conflict Research, Uppsala University.

Dankner, A. (1998, April 10). Eating humus, thinking sushi. *Maariv*, pp.5–6 (in Hebrew).

Dayan, M. (1974, March 3). Israeli premier Meir to form a new coalition. *New York Times*, p. 1.

Dayan, M. (1977, June 2). *Interview with Foreign Minister Dayan on ABC Television*. Retrieved December 1, 2009, from http://www.mfa.gov.il/MFA/ Foreign+Relations/

Dayan, M. (1978, October 9). *Address to the United Nations General Assembly by Foreign Minister Dayan*. Retrieved December 1, 2009 from http://www.mfa.gov. il/MFA/Foreign+Relations/

Dayan, M. (1979a, February 14). Dayan states: Israeli cannot deny the PLO *Washington Post*, p. 14.

Dayan, M. (1979b, April 24). *Remarks by Foreign Minister Dayan on the future of settlements in Judea, Samaria, and the Gaza district*. Retrieved December 1, 2009, from http://www.mfa.gov.il/MFA/Foreign+Relations/

Duek, N (2001, December 23). Liberman: Transfer to some of the Israeli Arabs. *Yediot Aharonot*, pp. 2–4 (in Hebrew).

Duek, N (2007, August 17). Damascus first: Interview with Minister Avigdor Liberman. *Yediot Aharonot*, pp. 18–20. (in Hebrew).
Golan, A. (1991, August 16). For the victim everything is allowed: Interview with MK Aloni. *Haaretz*, pp. 3–4 (in Hebrew).
Gregory, D. (1985). *The ungovernable rock: A history of the Anglo-Corsican kingdom and its role in Britain's Mediterranean strategy during the Revolutionary War, 1793–1797*. London: Farleigh Dickinson University Press.
Haaretz. (1967, September 22). Our right to defend ourselves against annihilation does not give us the right to oppress others (in Hebrew). Retrieved December 1, 2009, from http://cafe.themarker.com/media/t/501/07/file_0_big.jpg
Halperin, E., & Bar-Tal, D. (2007). The fall of the peace camp in Israel: The influence of Prime Minister Ehud Barak on Israeli public opinion—July 2000–February 2001. *Conflict & Communication Online*, 6(2), 1–18. Retrieved December1, 2009, from www.cco.regener-online.de/2007_2/pdf/halperin.pdf
Halperin, E., Bar-Tal, D., Sharvit, K., Rosler, N., & Raviv, A. (2010). Social psychological implications for an occupying society: The case of Israel. *Journal of Peace Research, 47*, 59–70.
Hills, G. (1974). *Rock of contention: A history of Gibraltar*. London: Robert Hale Press.
Ihud Lehumi (National Union). *Israeli political parties' platforms*. The Israel Democracy Institute. Retrieved December 1, 2009, from http://www.idi.org.il/elections_and_parties/Pages/parties_ihud_leumi.aspx
Israel Beytenu (Israel our home). *Israeli political parties' platforms*. The Israel Democracy Institute. Retrieved December 1, 2009, from http://www.idi.org.il/elections_and_parties/Pages/parties_israel_beytenu.aspx
Kadima (Forward). *Israeli political parties' platforms*. The Israel Democracy Institute. Retrieved December 1, 2009, from http://www.idi.org.il/elections_and_parties/Pages/parties_kadima.aspx
Kadmon, S. (1994, July 8). Arik Sharon: Interview. *Maariv*, pp. 2–4 (in Hebrew).
Labor (Avoda). *Israeli political parties' platforms*. The Israel Democracy Institute. Retrieved December 1, 2009, from http://www.idi.org.il/elections_and_parties/Pages/parties_Avoda.aspx
Levy, G. (1991, January 4). But the nickname "Pudel" already stuck: Interview with MK Beilin. *Haaretz*, pp. 16–17 (in Hebrew).
Likud (Union). *Israeli political parties' platforms*. The Israel Democracy Institute. Retrieved December 1, 2009, from http://www.idi.org.il/elections_and_parties/Pages/parties_likud.aspx
Mafdal (Zionist Religious party). *Israeli political parties' platforms*. The Israel Decocracy Institute. Retrieved December 1, 2009, from http://www.idi.org.il/elections_and_parties/Pages/parties_mafdal.aspx
Mapam (United Workers' party). *Israeli political parties' platforms*. The Israel Democracy Institute. Retrieved December 1, 2009, from http://www.idi.org.il/elections_and_parties/Pages/parties_mapam.aspx

Meretz (Energy). *Israeli political parties' platforms.* The Israel Democracy Institute. Retrieved December 1, 2009, from http://www.idi.org.il/elections_and_parties/Pages/parties_meretz.aspx

MERI. (1973, May 29). *Proposal for peace articles in MERI platform. U. Avneri and Y. Tzaban* (in Hebrew). Retrieved December 1, 2009, from http://israeli-left-archive.org/cgi-bin/library?site=localhost&a=p&p=about&c=electora&l=en&w=utf-8

Naor, A. (2001). *Greater Israel: Theology and policy.* Haifa: University of Haifa Press (in Hebrew).

Netanyahu, B. (1993). *A place among the nations: Israel and the world.* New York: Bantam Books.

Netanyahu, B. (2009, June 14). *Address by Prime Minister Benjamin Netanyahu, Begin-Sadat Center at Bar-Ilan University* (in Hebrew). Retrieved December 1, 2009, from http://www.pmo.gov.il/PMO/Communication/PMSpeaks/speechbarilan140609.htm

Oberling, P. (1982). *The road to Bellapais: The Turkish Cypriot exodus to northern Cyprus.* New York: Columbia University Press.

Olmert, E. (2006, January 24). *Acting PM Ehud Olmert's speech at the Herzeliya conference* (in Hebrew). Retrieved December 1, 2009, from http://www.herzliyaconference.org/?ArticleID=2106&CategoryID=258

Peace and Security. (1968, March 1). *One year after the Six Day War we are still far from peace and security* (in Hebrew). Retrieved December 1, 2009, from http://israeli-left-archive.org/greenstone/collect/peaceand/index/assoc/HASH0e3b.dir/6803.jpg

Peace and Security. (1969a, January 1). *Newsletter No. 1* (in Hebrew). Tel Aviv: The movement for Peace and Security. Retrieved December 1, 2009, from israeli-left-archive.org/greenstone/collect/peaceand/index/assoc/HASH4696.dir/doc.pdf

Peace and Security. (1969b, September 1). *Position paper on peace* (in Hebrew). Tel Aviv: The movement for Peace and Security. Retrieved December 1, 2009, from israeli-left-archive.org/greenstone/collect/peaceand/index/assoc/HASH0164.dir/doc.pdf

Peace Index (1993–2009). The Tami Steinmetz Center for Peace Research at Tel Aviv University. Retrieved December 1, 2009, from http://www.tau.ac.il/peace/

Peres, S. (1978). *This time tomorrow.* Jerusalem: Keter Press (in Hebrew).

Puri, B. (1993). *Kashmir: Towards Insurgency.* New Delhi: Orient Longman.

Rabin, Y. (1967, June 30). *Address by IDF Chief-of-Staff Lieutenant-General Yitzhak Rabin on acceptance of honorary doctorate from Hebrew University.* Retrieved December 1, 2009, from http://www.mfa.gov.il/MFA/Facts+About+Israel/State/Address+by+IDF+Chief-of-Staff+Lieut-Gen+Yitzhak+Ra.htm

Rabin, Y. (1979). *The Rabin memoirs.* Boston: Little, Brown.

Rabin, Y. (1989, August 8). *Rabin's speech at the annual Labor party national council* (in Hebrew). The Moshe Sharett Israeli Labor Party Archive, 2–023–189–139.

Ratz (Civil Rights and Peace). *Israeli political parties' platforms.* The Israel Democracy Institute. Retrieved December 1, 2009, from http://www.idi.org.il/elections_and_parties/Pages/parties_ratz.aspx

Roberts, A. (1990). Prolonged military occupation: The Israeli-occupied territories since 1967. *The American Journal of International Law, 84,* 44–103.

Rosler, N., Bar-Tal, D., Sharvit, K., & Halperin. (in prep.). On the effect of the perception of occupation on support for compromises for peace: Evidence from the Israeli-Jewish society.

Rosler, N., Bar-Tal, D., Sharvit, K., Halperin, E., & Raviv, A. (2009). Moral aspects of prolonged occupation: Implications for an occupying society. In S. Scuzzarello, C. Kinnvall, & K. R. Monroe (Eds.), *On behalf of others: The psychology of care in a global world* (pp. 211–232). New York: Oxford University Press.

Rynhold, J. (2001). Re-conceptualizing Israeli approaches to "land for peace" and the Palestinian question since 1967. *Israel Studies, 6*(2), 33–52.

Schmemann, S. (1996, July 5). Netanyahu hints at easing barriers against Palestinians: Interview with Prime Minister Netanyahu. *New York Times,* p. 2..

Segev, T. (2007). *1967: Israel, the war, and the year that transformed the Middle East.* New York: Metropolitan Books.

Shamir, J., & Shamir, M. (2000). *The anatomy of public opinion.* Ann Arbor: University of Michigan Press.

Sharon, A. (1989). *Warrior: The autobiography of Ariel Sharon.* New York: Simon & Schuster.

Sharon, A. (2001, March 7). *PM Ariel Sharon inauguration speech. The proceedings of the Knesset* (in Hebrew). Retrieved December 1, 2009, from http://www.knesset.gov.il/Tql//mark01/h0021486.html#TQL

Shavit, A. (2005, May 20). Listen to me: Interview with Ehud Barak. *Haaretz,* pp. 18–20 (in Hebrew).

SHELI. (1978, March 30). *On the crossroad between war and peace. Decisions of the SHELI council* (in Hebrew). Retrieved December 1, 2009, from http://israeli-left-archive.org/greenstone/collect/socialis/index/assoc/HASH8f06.dir/sheli%20780330.jpg

SHELI. (1982, June 20). *SHELI grieves.* Flier (in Hebrew). Retrieved December 1, 2009, from http://israeli-left-archive.org/greenstone/collect/socialis/index/assoc/HASH0167.dir/sheli%20820620.jpg

Shlomzion (The Whole of Zion). *Israeli political parties' platforms.* The Israel Democracy Institute. Retrieved December 1, 2009, from http://www.idi.org.il/elections_and_parties/Pages/parties_shlomtzion.aspx

Teveth, S. (1973). The cursed blessing: The story of Israel's occupation of the West Bank. London: Weidenfeld and Nicolson.

Tzomet (Junction). *Israeli political parties' platforms*. The Israel Democracy Institute. Retrieved December1, 2009, from http://www.idi.org.il/elections_and_parties/Pages/parties_tzomet.aspx

Zemach, M. (1987). *Through Israeli eyes: Attitudes towards Judaism, American Jewry, Zionism and the Arab-Israeli conflict*. New-York: American Jewish Committee, Institute of Human Relations.

Zertal, I., & Eldar, A. (2007). *Lords of the land: The war over Israel's settlements in the occupied territories, 1967–2007*. New York: Nation Books.

II

Political Effects of Occupation

CHAPTER 5

The Occupation and Israeli Democracy

Yaron Ezrahi

A state of occupation may be compatible with a democratic regime only for a short time. In the case of Israel, the occupation following the 1967 war has existed so far for two-thirds of the life of the state, and as of this writing, its end does not seem any closer than in the past. If, despite massive denial, Israel's occupied territories and their Palestinian population are considered an integral part of the current Israeli regime, the question of Israel's democratic character requires a serious reassessment (Azoulay & Ophir, 2008). The most important long-term impact of the occupation on the regime will depend on when and if the massive Jewish settlements in the occupied territories will influence the process of choice whereby what is now the State of Israel will still emerge as a constitutional democracy that managed to negotiate with its neighbors agreed-upon boundaries that ended the occupation; whether Israel will continue instead to be largely a repressive nation-state, an ethnic democracy that discriminates against its non-Jewish Arab population; or finally, whether it will become a binational state ruled by a common Jewish-Arab government in a loose federation of Jewish and Arab territories .

This chapter examines specific consequences of the practices of the Israeli regime in the occupied territory for the part of Israel that most Israelis consider the proper part of the state: the area within the Green Line drawn before the 1967 war. My assumption is that even if the occupation ends today, the impact of decades of occupation will still leave sufficiently deep imprints on the structure and political culture of the Israeli regime to significantly stifle its future democratic character.

Any assessment of the impact of Israel's occupation on aspects of Israeli democracy since the Six Day War, and especially the impact of decades of expanding controversial Jewish settlements in the occupied territories, faces the methodological difficulty of attributing specific regressions in Israeli democracy since 1967 to the causal effects of the occupation. The difficulty resides in the fact that social and political transformations, types of leadership as well as changes in the economy, patterns of migration and immigration, shifts in collective values, and developments in political culture, may have had deleterious effects on Israeli democracy regardless of the occupation. Nevertheless, while I do not intend to discuss hypothetical speculative history, I think that the omnipresence of the occupation in the life of the Israeli democracy provides a wide-ranging basis for substantiating preliminary observations on the impact of the occupation on Israeli politics, legal structure, the military, social perceptions of the limits of legitimate internal and external uses of force, norms and practices of the bureaucracy, the educational system, the formal and informal status of Israeli Arabs, the relations between religion and politics, and the international legitimacy of Israel as a democracy.

Inasmuch as democracy is a system of government based on the rule of law and the legal control of the uses of force, it is no exaggeration to claim that the illegal and violent history and the corrosive effects of the huge settlers' project on the territories occupied in the Six Day War have become the most serious threat to Israeli democracy. Partly due to the concealed yet deliberate acquiescence of the elected politicians of the state, the legal and law enforcement authorities of the state of Israel persistently failed to subordinate the settlers' illegal and often violent actions to the law. One can say therefore that following the Six Day War, the process of self-democratization of the state (marked, for instance, by the earlier disbanding of the pre-state underground quasi-military armed groups by Ben Gurion and the abolition of the military government over Arabs living in Israel in 1965) was seriously hampered, if not reversed.

Many modern democracies were born out of bloody revolutions and conquests using brutal illegal force to kill loyalists of the old regime, destroy or evict native civilian populations, and force migration. Following their bloody birth, some modern states became democratic by drawing a clear line between the arbitrary revolutionary illegal force that established the new order and the postrevolutionary order-preserving force restrained and institutionalized within a formal or informal constitution. Reasonably successful democracies were those that were able to draw such a line between law-creating and law-preserving force, thus redefining force unregulated by the new state as arbitrary and therefore illegitimate (see Dahl, 1990; Huntington, 1991; and *The Federalist* [*c. 1787*], 1937; and on the dilemma of constitutionalization in modern Israel, see Ezrahi & Kremnitzer, 2001).

THE FAILURE TO TAME EXTRALEGAL FORCE

According to the legal and moral norms of the old regime, the violence of the revolutionaries constitutes a breach of the law and an assault on the hegemonic ethos. Therefore, successful revolutionaries or conquerors tend to move quickly to replace the existing legal system with their own alternative system, embedding their force in a novel theory of political justice and its legal structure. In the transition from Palestine to Israel, the state's founder, David Ben Gurion, replaced the Zionist paramilitary organizations and underground units that were engaged in the struggle for independence by a state army, the Israel Defense Forces (IDF), based on formal state law and subordinate to the civilian authority (Shapira, 1992).

My principal claim is that although, following the establishment of the State of Israel on May 14, 1948, the new state has moved along the arduous path from a new order-creating illegal force to an order-preserving regulated force, it has failed to effectively control the former. Although it had moved to establish a regime based on free periodic elections, three distinct branches of government, an army to handle external threats subordinated to civilian authority, a police assigned to keep civil order, an infrastructure for a future formal constitution, and a free press, its progress toward a constitutional democracy has been gradually stifled by the settlers' Gush Emunim movement and its staunch right-wing, and even some key left-wing, political supporters in the Knesset and Israel's cabinets for over four decades (Eldar & Zertal, 2004; Sprinzak, 1999). Furthermore, large parts of Israeli society— consisting of Jewish immigrants from nondemocratic countries in Eastern Europe, North Africa, and the Middle East who were unacquainted with, and ambivalent toward, democratic political institutions based on compromises rather than on hierarchical authority and ideological or religious principles— were inspired and galvanized by the idealistic religious-nationalistic settlement project of the settlers' movement. The cocktail of messianic Jewish elements, aggressive nationalism, and practical settlement projects that appeared to the followers of Gush Emunim to revive the pioneering spirit of the pre-state Yishuv settlements had much greater appeal to these groups than the often ambiguous and contradictory political deals of parliamentary politics and the strictures of the law.

The problem was of, course, that this settlement project was conceived and executed not in the pre-state Yishuv phase, in defiance of a foreign government, but within a framework painstakingly created during almost two decades of Israeli statehood in defiance of Israel's formal law, Israel's Declaration of Independence, and international law, and with the usually silent compliance and illegal cooperation of Israeli law enforcement agencies. It is true that from the beginning of the settlement project the political support for the settlers came from a wide spectrum of political interests, from Left to Right, and that Israeli governments provided the settlers with a great deal of logistical and political support for decades. However, this does not alter the fact that the settlement project created a deepening wedge between the principles and institutions of Israel as a democracy and Israel as an increasingly nationalist enterprise prone to bend its laws and its commitment to democracy to encourage, encompass, and solidify the settlements (see the chapter by Magal, Oren, Bar-Tal, and Halperin in this volume). As a matter of fact, the tacit role of Israeli governments in both enabling and supporting the settlements in the occupied territories probably warrants renaming what is called "the settlements' project" the "informal project of the state" and therefore an integral part of the Israeli regime (this is clearly the position expressed in Azoulay & Ophir, 2008). Predictably, this clash between the commitment to democratic rules and the commitment to a radical right-wing and messianic interpretation of Zionism triggered antagonisms between the settlers and Israeli institutional guardians of laws and human rights like the Supreme Court. These antagonisms were accompanied by both a long history of populist, politically motivated domestic attacks on the Israeli legal and court system and some problematic adaptations by the courts and law enforcement agencies to these mounting pressures. The net result of these domestic tensions damaged the independence and reputation of the judicial branch, Israel's defense forces, and the integrity of law enforcement agencies in the occupied territories. In fact, it contradicted the settlers' aspirations to be regarded as legitimate heirs of the spirit of the original Zionist pioneers of the pre-state period, inscribed in Israel's Declaration of Independence, who dreamed of a Jewish democratic state.

The incompatibilities between the covert and, later, more overt endorsement of a group of armed civilians united by a minority religious-nationalistic faith, protected by the army and right-wing parties, and the self-perception of Israel as a democracy have produced many anomalies. These include the use of legal language and procedures to whitewash the deployment of raw power by the settelers, by the military, and later by the civil authority backed up by the government. Israelis who object to the visible "unenlightened" occupation of the territories taken during the Six Day War have tended to regard the occupation as temporary and therefore compatible with their long-term commitment to peace and democracy. This, however, does not brighten the grim picture that emerges from even an initial analysis of their failures to convert their objections to the occupation into significant political opposition to the accumulated practices of the branches of the state and their consequences in the occupied territories since the 1967 war.

Obviously, the failure of Israel to establish a formal constitution during its first years, and the legacy of the conflation of pre-state resistance to the

British Mandatory regime and local Arabs and the practices of the settlers and their supporters, were congenial for the post- 1967 war return of the culture of "idealistic" ideological illegality and "Zionist" rationalization of the anti-Arab violence of the settlement movement after only about twenty years after independence. Even the rare half-hearted efforts of the state to subordinate the settlers' project to the law were continually undermined by top political leaders who usually collaborated secretly with the settlers, thus unofficially helping to replant in the heart of the new State of Israel the pre-state illegal revolutionary force formerly directed against British authorities and Arab resistance. These developments gradually created the anomaly of a dual system of law and law enforcement practices that adds up to a whole illegal subculture with corrosive effects on Israeli democracy, law, the army, the civil service, the educational system, and the nation's international status as a democracy (see Gordon, 2008; Kretchmer, 2002; and the chapter by Kretchmer in this volume). This illegal culture that continually generated multiple forms of coercion and violence remained protected by Israeli ministers, by the occupying army, by the government administration, and increasingly by ideologically and religiously committed settlers who have not hesitated to ignore or defy Israeli courts and initiate—through their supporters in the Knesset and the government—legislation designed to circumvent Supreme Court rulings. (On the gaps between the law and its enforcement in the occupied territories see the *Karp Report*, 1984, and the *Sasson Report*, 2005). In the *Karp Report* on the settlers' violence, the settlers' refusal to cooperate with civilian police was described as "tantamount to civil rebellion" (ibid., p. 46). The political power of the settlers has progressively increased, for a wide spectrum of Israeli politicians, the political costs of criticizing the settlement movement. Even Labor leaders, like Rabin and Barak, who sought to negotiate an agreement with the Palestinians tried to avoid political trouble by delaying a confrontation with the settlers ostensibly until the decisive moment of the final agreement—which has never arrived. The evasions, delays, and manipulations of state agencies that tried to avoid confronting the settlers and their political supporters—together with the relentless determination of the settlers, many of whom penetrated the security forces and the Civil Administration—have enabled the settlements to grow from a few thousand to about 350,000 by 2012 (or more if one includes the settlers in the periphery of Jerusalem). In the post-1977 period, following the dramatic defeat of the Labor coalition after twenty-nine years of hegemony by the right-wing bloc headed by Menachem Begin, the massive growth of the settlements has become politically more openly supported and facilitated by the acquiescence of the shrinking Labor party and its desperate, and usually unsuccessful, attempts to win potential Labor, religious and centrist-nationalist voters who identified with the settlers' project. The increasing political inefficacy of the Israeli Left except in moments like the second Rabin government or the brief period following Barak electoral victory (1999), the often small difference in the relative numerical strength of the Left and Right political blocs, and the political logic of a multiparty and coalitional governmental system have allowed a small group of radical settlers to control the votes of a sufficient number of politicians to gain disproportional political power to extract concessions from the big parties and decide whether the government will be led by the political bloc of the Right or the Left. In this system the Right has usually had the upper hand, creating a political environment favoring the long-term success of Gush Emunim and their civilian "troops" (on the dynamics of Israeli politics see Arian, 2005).

As a result of the reopening of the question of Israel's territory and borders, and the relapse into the practices and rhetoric of pre-state revolutionary violence, the Israeli society, which moved after decades of struggle to establish itself as a normal formal state, managed by a monumental feat of collective denial to ignore the fact that the occupation and the open-ended settlements' project have been perpetuating Israel's condition as an unfinished state. For decades Israel has slipped back to an earlier stage of its formation (*lemedina baderech*), becoming a state not only without a formal constitution and recognized boundaries, but one whose leaders lack the political resources and will to effectively cope with the challenges of the settlers' project to Israel's governability, security, diplomacy, and moral self-confidence. As Azouly and Ophir (2008) have noted, this state of affairs threatened from the very beginning to redefine what was long perceived as the settlers' project in occupied territories external to the democratic regime of Israel proper as an integral part of a Jewish ethnocracy.

THE DEFENSE ARMY BECOMES AN ARMY OF OCCUPATION

The disruption of the democratic constitutional process that subordinated unofficial force to the law was compounded by the normative and practical adaptation of the Israeli army. The original purpose of the army was to handle external threats. It has now become an occupying army responsible for keeping order in a territory whose native inhabitants have been dispossessed of their political and human rights (see also the chapter by Pedatzur in this volume). In fact, the governments of Israel have deployed its army in a moral and legal no-man's-land where soldiers are charged with keeping civil order while simultaneously but asymmetrically protecting (often armed civilian) Israeli settlers against resisting occupied Arabs. As citizens of Israel, the Jewish settlers were ostensibly entitled to protection by the IDF, and as occupied subjects the Palestinians were entitled to equal protection. But in this complex situation where the army has been in charge of protecting both these antagonistic populations, Israeli soldiers have constantly failed to keep the balance. In addition to the natural ethnic solidarity between the soldiers and the settlers, the army's gradual but relentless adaptation to the needs, friendliness, and demands of the settlers has blurred the line painfully drawn in 1948 between prelegal and legal force and between governing the internal territory of Israel and the occupied territory officially external to it. Furthermore, charging the Israeli "defense army" with keeping civil order by disciplining and protecting both settlers and Palestinians entangled in reciprocal violence and a maze of legal Israeli and Jordanian laws and military decrees has confounded the tasks of military and police forces and blurred the distinctions between their respective codes of conduct (Ezrahi, 1997). The IDF has been converted into an occupying army at the cost of the gradual erosion of the distinction between domestic and external deployments of state power. This has undermined the ethos of the IDF as a people's army, an army of democratic citizen-soldiers defending their country against external enemies. Moreover, an army facing stone-throwing civilians, including women and children, could not continue to nourish the Israeli ethos of military heroism or create the kind of soldiers whose courage and sacrifices could command admiration and serve as a model for Israeli youth (see Ezrahi, 2011). In this situation, the occupation has inevitably damaged earlier perceptions of the IDF in Israeli society as a politically neutral national army, a fighting defense force. Since settling in the occupied territories has become the most politically divisive issue in modern Israel, the IDF's attempt to both take the side of the settlers and maintain its political neutrality was doomed to fail (Eldar & Zertal, 2004, pp. 373–438).

Equally important is the fact that in many respects the IDF, as a carrier of the rights of the sovereign in the occupied territories, has used its administrative powers and physical force to make law, issue edicts, and apply them. Military decrees and violence, by creating situations some of which were legalized by the courts only retroactively (often rationalized by the "absence of sufficient evidence" or ambiguous "security needs"), have turned the army into a de facto unified legislative and enforcing agency that created realities seemingly backed up by the law despite the supposedly superior formal position of the Knesset and the courts (see, for example, Azoulay & Ophir, 2008, pp. 71–77; Kretchmer, 2010). Moreover, by mixing elements of pre-state formative force with state-regulated force, the government of the occupation created ambiguities conducive to the exercise of arbitrary power. This ambiguous state of affairs has naturally increased the incentives of the IDF to expand its authority to define the "requirements of security" far beyond reasonable needs of keeping order in the occupied territories. This process served politicians who were happy to pursue religious, ideological, and territorial aspirations under the umbrella of "professional" military considerations of security.

Perhaps the most extreme application of the authority and powers of the IDF as the sovereign, the actual legislator in the occupied territories, to matters beyond keeping order and security is its decision to found a settlers' university in the West Bank in defiance of the persistent objection of the Israeli Council for Higher Education (this decision was announced in early January 2010). Members of the Council who have continually objected to the establishment of an eighth university in northern Israel or elsewhere due to the structural needs of the Israeli academic system have also expressed grave doubts about the mediocre academic research and educational quality of Ariel College, designated by the general in charge of the occupied West Bank as Israel's eighth university. Ehud Barak, the politically weak Defense Minister, was strongly motivated to instruct the general in charge of the occupied territories to elevate the status of this academically dubious college to that of Israel's eighth university. The negative spillover effects of this decision on Israel's higher education are obvious. It is a bold step toward the politicization of the Israeli academic system, a blow to the authority and efficacy of the delicate system of institutions like the Council for Higher Education and its Subcommittee of Budgeting and Planning, which were created several decades before as a buffer between academia and the state in order to prevent political intervention in the academy, scientific research, and teaching. This decision has also exposed Israeli academics and students within the Green Line to the risk of becoming targets of worldwide sanctions against the occupation.

THE UNCIVIL ADMINISTRATION

Another apparent victim of the occupation has been the relatively neutral professional civil service in the modern State of Israel. Like the dismal record of the Israeli occupying army, the record of the corruption and politicization of the Civil Administration in charge of the occupied territories is often visible to observers but not sufficiently documented. (On glaring examples of corruption in the administration and regulation of the occupied territories and its spillover effects on the conduct of officials and contractors within the Green Line, see, for instance, Eldar & Zertal, 2004, pp. 87–90; Sprinzak, 1986, pp. 116–118.) Still awaiting substantial investigation is the spreading massive collaboration between settlers, soldiers, and civil clerks in applying arbitrary extralegal powers to discriminate between native Arabs and Jewish settlers in the occupied territories and its profound effects on practices of the IDF and the Israeli bureaucracy within the Green Line. Much of this corruption has focused on the economics of the settlements, especially the transactions between construction contractors, regulators, and right-wing politicians (Navot & Kremnitzer, 2008). Here, however, I will highlight only a few aspects of these practices and note their larger consequences for the Israeli political and administrative systems.

There is perhaps no better place to observe how Israeli clerks backed up by the military have daily been crossing the line separating legally and morally constrained decisions and naked arbitrary power than the Israeli Planning Authority, an arm of the Civil Administration in charge of approving demolition and construction in the occupied territories. Formally, the Israeli Civil Administration in the occupied territories has responsibility for the welfare and needs that arise from the "natural growth" of both the Arab and Jewish populations. In fact, the decisions and operations of the Planning Authority reveal a consistent pattern of discrimination against the Arab residents. The Authority has issued thousands of demolition orders for "illegal" construction by Palestinian villagers while systematically approving the expansion of the settlements and their construction projects into lands that were vital to the natural growth of the Palestinian villages. The Civil Administration has canceled the planning committees that, during Jordanian rule, enabled local residents to present their needs of, and objections to, construction on both private and public lands. It has constituted itself as a centralized authority with almost unrestricted powers to carry out a policy severely limiting the living space available to the villagers (Bimkom, 2008). The Civil Administration has justified this systematic discrimination by the use of a wide range of excuses that appear at first sight as professional considerations serving the welfare of the public. Many restrictions on the construction of houses for the expanding Palestinian population were defended by glaringly unwarranted stretching of professional considerations such as protecting the integrity of land designated for agriculture, protecting the environment, preserving archaeological sites, and responding to unspecific "security needs" (ibid). The use of the professional authority of city planners, environmental experts, lawyers, archaeologists, and soldiers to cover up the political-demographic priorities of the occupying regime has been too transparent, of course, to mislead Palestinians, unbiased Israelis, and international observers. The tacit goal of these massive violations of human rights, due processes of law, professional integrity, and administrative rules was to weaken the Palestinian population by territorial fragmentation and ethnic discrimination in the allocation of resources and services. The high population density imposed on the Palestinians, whose living space was systematically restricted, seemed intended to reduce their quality of life in order to encourage migration. The rhetorical and gestural rationales legitimizing such use of arbitrary power were readily adopted by politicians, ministers, economic interests, and public spokespersons who benefited politically, professionally, and financially from supporting the settlers. The picture that emerges from the accumulation of multiple specific local decisions is clear. The Palestinian villagers in the occupied territories, lacking the political, legal, administrative, and military resources available to the settlers, have become the victims of systematic discriminatory rule disguised as "enlightened occupation" supposedly guided by universal professional and legal norms and the public interest.

It is probably too early to claim sufficient evidence for attributing the glaring spread of law violations, disrespect for administrative procedures, and massive corruption in the Israeli Public Service within the Green Line to the practices of the Israeli occupation. Studies have shown that Israeli domestic immigrant social traditions from nondemocratic countries and cultures are the source of many elements of such behavior, which can be traced to factors and conditions having very little to do with the occupation and the settlers' movement. Given these qualifications, to deny that large parts of the Israeli governmental, legal, administrative, and economic systems remain unaffected by massive systematic and ideologically sanctioned violations of democratic, political, legal, and administrative codes of conduct would run against common sense. For over four decades, the government of the occupied territories and the government of Israel within the Green Line have formed two parts of the same system of governing, and despite the official policy of denial they are intimately linked in thousand ways. Therefore, it is not surprising to also find in Israel proper many illegalities, systematic failures to enforce laws, occasional ignoring of Supreme Court rulings, and discriminatory practices against non-Jews, including the Bedouins in the Negev. In many cases, the same ministers, members of the Knesset, administrators, party activists, and contractors who were deeply involved in the illegal and discriminatory practices in the occupied territories were associated with similar violations on the other side of the Green Line, as indicated by several famous indictments (see, for instance, the case of Shmuel Enav in Eldar, 2005). There is a massive record of disregard for the law by law enforcement agencies despite the repeated protests of the state comptroller, the attorney general, and the Supreme Court against arbitrary actions. Combined with a variety of lenient rulings by the local courts (especially between 1977 and 1989 during intensive expansion of the settlements), this situation has created a dangerous gap between law and power, with far-reaching implications for the entire regime (see the *Karp Report* and the *Sasson Report*). The huge volume of law violations by diehard ideological and religious agents, basically acting with impunity for well over four decades, has seriously hampered, and in some cases actually reversed, early efforts to develop a law-abiding and rule-respecting culture on the Israeli side of the Green Line. Evidently, there is an easy transition from justifying "lying for the nation" (lying for the state was publicly justified by Prime Minister Yitzak Shamir when he said that "it is permissible to lie for the Land of Israel," cited by A. Eldar in *Haaretz*, November 24, 2003) to lying for the party or for personal gain. Again, the pre-state culture of illegality, which historically was part of Jewish resistance to the British Mandate and was repressed during the early years of the new state, was revoked and resanctioned on the political-nationalistic-religious grounds of the mission to settle Jews on all, or most, of the lands occupied during the 1967 war. A project that over time has come to block the path to a peace agreement with the Palestinians was able to grow against a background of political instability, ambivalence, and weakness of almost all the parties on the Left and the relentless self-determination of the settlers and their supporters in the governments and administration of the state.

THE OCCUPATION AND ISRAELI ARABS

No speculative utopian history is needed to assume that even a cold peace agreement between Israel and the Palestinian would have led to less discriminatory and more peaceful relations between the Jewish majority and the Palestinian minority within Israel. Also in this context, factors not directly related to the Israeli occupation would have probably made their contributions to the continual strife between Jews and Palestinians within Israel anyway (see, for instance, Benziman, 2006). But the open, bleeding wound of the repressive occupation and the violent confrontations between Jews and Palestinians it propagated apparently made a huge difference. The unresolved conflict provided religious fundamentalists from both sides with a powerful engine for the mobilization of wide support for their goal of spreading religious fundamentalism and ethnocentric nationalism in their respective societies. The temporal conflation of the fundamentalist religious-nationalist movements of Arabs and Jews, respectively, and the Israeli-Palestinian conflict has turned the conflict into an indispensable resource for these movements. The principal goal of these movements, apparently, has not been resolve the conflict but rather to resist secularization and achieve hegemony in their respective societies. Against the background of neo-liberal values and the cult of "economic individualism," the appeal of idealism sanctioned by both religion and nationalism has been proven irresistible to large segments of Israeli youth. It is not a coincidence that the motives to use lethal force, unrestricted by the commitment to protect the lives of innocent civilians on the enemy side, have often seemed more acceptable among fighters motivated by religious ideology. Such religious perspectives tend to encourage the view that the mere fact of belonging to a rival religious group is a sufficient reason to treat an individual as a legitimate target. Both the Arab terrorist mentality and the random killing of civilians are associated with attitudes that intend to punish or frighten groups, not individuals. There is probably a significant difference between Jewish and Islamic traditions of religious violence and the willingness to ignore the humanity of their adversaries. But within each of these societies, Jewish and Moslem fundamentalists, often reinforced by nationalism, have tended to be both less restrained in using lethal violence toward the other side and more inclined to draw continually on the conflict in order to fuel the antagonism between Arabs and Jews within Israel.

These tendencies, combined with the natural solidarity of Arabs living in Israel with Palestinians in the occupied territories, have had increasingly dangerous effects on Israeli democracy. Influenced by the second *intifada*, the October 2000 riots in northern Israel, in which thirteen Arab Israelis were killed by live fire from the police, demonstrated the role of the occupation in increasing tensions between Arabs and Jews within Israel and in importing from the occupied territories techniques of controlling riots like live fire in handling domestic Arab—albeit aggressive—demonstrators. The October riots were not, to be sure, an exception. But as the less violent Aker riots in September 2008 indicated, they demonstrated the links between the natural solidarity of Arabs in Israel and in the occupied territories and the tensions between Arab and Jewish citizens. The Or Commission, which was established to investigate the October riots, noted that against the background of these continuities between Israeli police violence within Israel and in the occupied territories, it is hard to define these riots as just a local disorder (see the *Or Commission Report*, 2003). This observation indicates the difficulties that both Israeli Arabs and Jews have in perceiving the Arabs living in Israel as equal citizens.

THE OCCUPATION AND THE PLACE OF RELIGION IN ISRAELI DEMOCRACY

Occupying territories that were a part of ancient biblical maps of Hebrew kingdoms corresponded with Jewish religious-nationalist visions of the new Israel as a station in a sacred redemptive history. An influential minority of nationalistic Orthodox Israeli Jews have ascribed a religious meaning to the spectacular swift Israeli victory in the 1967 Six Day War. Within a short time after the war, the increasing affinity between the actual territories added to Israel by the occupation and religious conceptions of the Greater Land of Israel reinforced the image of a messianic process. In this process, force and territory provided a palpable material dimension to religious dreams that had lived in the minds of Diaspora Jews for many generations merely as prayers, prophecies, abstract objects of faith, and Jewish religious poetics. Elements of these links existed, of course, in religious Zionism as well as in secularized forms in the labor and nationalist strains of Zionism (see, for instance, Elboim-Dror, 2009). But as is widely recorded in the Israeli press and in public discourse, control of the vast territories occupied in the 1967 war has radically intensified these formerly weak and general links, unprecedented in modern Jewish history, between military force, territory, religion, and politics. This process has deeply affected the place of religion and the limits of democracy in modern Israel. Lending religious meaning to the victory in the 1967 war greatly facilitated not only the settlement movement but also the spread, among many believing Jews, of the idea that there is a mandate from heaven for returning to Greater Israel even in defiance of the political mandate of Israeli governments elected by the people (Sprinzak, 1991). Ultranationalist and nationalist orthodox Jewish rabbis and soldiers were locked into a contradiction between regarding the army as a sacred army and on the other side—when the army was instructed to evacuate Jewish settlements—as the army of illegitimate secular pagan tyranny. Years later, among a significant group of nationalist religious soldiers, this contradiction became a clash between the authority of military commanders and the alternative authority of rabbis demanding that these soldiers (especially settlers) in the occupied territories disobey commands that seemed to contradict their rulings.

Since the 1970s, and particularly following the 1977 elections—when, after twenty-nine years of Labor-led coalitions the national religious party broke its traditional alliance with Labor and joined the right-wing bloc—the issue of settlement in the territories occupied in 1967 has become the most divisive issue in Israeli politics. Leaders of Israel's largest nationalist Zionist party, Likud, and the National Religious Zionist party and their followers quickly discovered that stressing the deep affinities between religious and nationalist visions of Greater Israel served their political interests. The secular nationalists achieved a religious sanction for what became a policy of annexation by settling in the occupied territories, and the religious nationalists inspired their youth by a powerful, intoxicating cocktail of messianic religious vision and a Zionist-like use of pioneering settlements to "liberate" the holy land (on the alliance between Likud and the National Religious Party, later reinforced by the ultra-Orthodox party Shas, see Ezrahi, 2000, pp. 782–789). The political-ideological alliance between religion and right-wing nationalism has progressively distanced secular liberal and social democratic Israelis from religion. It has also contributed to the emergence of profoundly competing conceptions of politics and legitimate power. The goal of advancing the settlements in the occupied territories, within the agenda of the nationalist-religious parties' alliance, has largely controlled the dynamics of Israeli politics ever since while eclipsing the important traditional differences between left- and right-wing parties' domestic social and economic policies. The political marginalization of these differences impoverished the Israeli political discourse and reduced the political resources used to close the gaps between rich and poor in Israel. Consequently, Israel has shifted from one of the most egalitarian countries in the world during its early decades to one of the countries suffering most from social and economic inequalities in the contemporary Western world (see the periodic reports by the Adva Center for Equality and Social Justice in Israel).

The institutional separation between "church" (synagogue) and state was very weak in Israel from the beginning. After 1977, this separation was further undermined by the increasing interpenetration between politics and religion and the strained merger between religious and civil democratic vocabularies. Since ultimately religious and democratic authorities rest on profoundly different foundations, this alliance—and particularly the welding of occupying force and religious political-theological rationales—was bound eventually to trigger two results: corrosive delegitimation of Israeli secular laws and law enforcement authorities and a decline in the spiritual and ethical appeal of Judaism to the vast majority of nonreligious Israelis. Most seriously, however, the unprecedented use of religious justifications for the use of military force in the occupied territories, as well as the tendency of key leaders in the cabinet and the army to regard the settlements as a religious-historic project that legitimates massive informal repressive physical and organizational measures against the local Arabs, have made the force of the IDF less bound to the common norms of democratic armies.[1] Furthermore, as I indicated above, the strategic political influence of narrow Orthodox and ultra-Orthodox nationalist parties on most right- and left-wing government coalitions has both blunted effective political and governmental resistance to the settlers' movement and periodically paralyzed the efforts of Israeli peace coalitions to move toward a settlement based on two-state solution to the conflict. The most dramatic illustration probably is the ultra-Orthodox Rabbi Abraham Verdiger's role in blocking Shimon Peres's attempt to topple the Shamir government in 1990 and replace him as Prime Minister by the last-minute reversal of his crucial vote in the Knesset..

THE OCCUPATION AND THE DETERIORATION OF CIVIC EDUCATION

The generations that lived through the transition from the pre-state revolutionary phase to the postindependence phase were exposed both to the extralegal culture of the revolutionary Zionists, including the brutal violence that creates a new order, and to the postindependence phase when the new state was trying to subordinate all violence to the law of the new order. By contrast, Israeli-born children were expected to grow up exposed only to a democratic nation-state that cultivated a democratic civic culture. The revolutionary generation underwent the difficult process of disciplining the illegal force of the subversive pre-state phase and becoming law-abiding citizens. In the long run, however, a constitutional democracy in Israel cannot be sustainable when generations of citizens are time and again exposed from an early age to irresolvable ambiguities between legal and illegal conduct. Democracies can be established by law-subverting citizens, but they are not sustainable in the long run without law-abiding citizens, educated by proper democratic institutions, who as soldiers are ready to risk their lives in order to defend an already existing free society ruled by law—not a democracy whose policies and actions are hijacked by fanatics who resist law and order in the name of totalistic sectarian ideological or religious visions.

Israelis who were born since 1967 have been exposed to the confusions and ambiguities of a state that both insists on law-abiding behavior and endorses a wholesale violation of the law by settlers, who are often armed civilians, engaged in supposedly informal missionary violence in the occupied territories. Currently, Israel is a state that displays classical democratic virtues like free elections and a free press and, at the same time, sends its armed soldiers and policemen to protect Israeli citizens who grab land and water from Palestinian villagers against the law and the resistance of their Palestinian victims (on these discriminatory practices, see Grossman, 2009, pp. 70–74).

Put differently, the legal-administrative system that emerged after 1967 has created conditions whereby the ethos of constitutional democracy—what official Israel repeatedly calls "the only democracy in the Middle East"—must have appeared to many high school Israeli students attending classes in civic education just before they were inducted into the army as increasingly hollow and hypocritical. The failure of Israel to draw a sharp line between legal and illegal force, between the illegal culture of the pre-state resistance to the British

Mandate and the legal culture following the establishment of the state, and between the preindependence and postindependence phases of state building has severely damaged democratic civic education as an investment in the future of Israeli democracy (Halperin & Bar-Tal, 2006). It is, of course, hard to assess the specific long-term effects of repressive occupation on the oppressors and their youthful witnesses, but it is not difficult to expect that it will lay a heavy burden on the generations to come. For well over four decades, what is widely taken for granted as a democratic system of government has coexisted with an occupied territory in which the state enables a culture of illegality and repressive violence directed often by armed civilian settlers against an occupied, disenfranchised local population. This duality has trained generations of young Israelis to believe in a fantastic notion of democracy, in a concept of democracy that is compatible with occupation and ideological lawlessness that does not set limits on nationalism, radicalized by political messianism. (On the cognitive and moral contradictions to which Israeli youth are exposed as members of an occupying society and their deleterious effects on their education and conceptions of democracy, see Halperin,,Bar-Tal, Sharvit, Rossler, & Raviv, 2010.) To reiterate, for most Israelis born after 1967, the illegal violent settlement project has undermined the credibility of democratic civic education based on stressing the dramatic transition from prerevolutionary to postrevolutionary legally regulated violence. The generation gaps in experiencing the meaning of democratic statehood may partly explain why the number of Israelis available for the Israeli peace movement has dwindled so dramatically in recent decades. Jean Jacques Rousseau insisted long ago that what educates a people are its institutions; good institutions make good citizens. In Israel, the occupation since 1967 and the record of largely informal government-supported repression is a case of bad institutions that produce bad citizens and contribute to the deterioration of democratic civic culture.

THE OCCUPATION AND THE INTERNATIONAL LEGITIMACY OF ISRAEL AS A DEMOCRACY

Besides the visible disruptive effects of the occupation on the status of Israeli democratic institutions, its political discourse, its laws, law enforcement record, party system, the civic ethos of the army, the relations between religion and the state, the civil service, the place of the Arab minority in Israel and Israeli civic education, the occupation, and the settlements have over the years corroded the international perception of Israel as a democracy and its legitimacy in world opinion. Official Israeli attempts to enlist the support of world public opinion have repeatedly failed due to Israel's visible status as the stronger conquering and occupying state that continually uses its superior force to discriminate against and repress a weaker occupied people. The Israel that enjoyed a fair amount of external legitimacy, reinforced by worldwide sympathy for the Jews as victims of the Nazi genocide, has been suffering a growing legitimation deficit the more the victims and their children have been perceived as victimizers. The attempt to legitimate as liberating and religiously redemptive the post-1967 settlement project, which appeared to display all the classical attributes of a colonial enterprise, was doomed to failure in the modern postcolonial era from the beginning. Despite the serious flaws of the Israeli democracy, the fact that most Israelis—including those from nondemocratic societies in Eastern Europe, the Middle East, and Asia—have come to be proud of Israel's image as a democracy has continually helped to rein in internal antidemocratic forces. Nevertheless, there is always a danger that if Israel's partly exaggerated international reputation as a democracy is greatly damaged,, many Israelis may feel it unnecessary to continue to make the "sacrifices" to defend it. This reaction was manifest in Israel's initial official and public responses to the United Nations–sponsored *Goldstone Report* on Israeli military violations during the 2008–2009 Gaza operation. It is, of course, both tragic and ironic that the same Israel that pioneered the development of international jurisdiction by trying in Israel the Nazi Adolf Eichmann for crimes committed in other lands (1961) has come to worry about the freedom of movement of its own soldiers abroad. It is also both tragic and ironic that Israeli defense experts have suggested that Israel will lead an international effort to revise the conventions of war in order to relax restrictions on the use of lethal force in urban confrontations between a regular army and armed guerrilla or terrorist fighters wearing civilian clothes.

In conclusion, it seems obvious that the fragile foundations of democratic institutions and the political culture in contemporary Israel can be greatly strengthened by a peaceful end to the occupation. Currently, although it is hard to be optimistic about the prospect of a peaceful resolution of the conflict that will liberate both Jews and Palestinians from their deadly entanglement, the possibility cannot be ruled out. Be that as it may, democracy as a form of government is always in some respects more a utopia than a historical reality. Closing the gap between this idea and reality may be particularly difficult in the Middle East but not impossible. But because in recent centuries the idea of democracy has globally become the most pervasive idea of legitimate power, the vision of democracy is bound to continue to inspire the criticism of arbitrary power and the attempts to replace it by governments of laws and justice.

NOTE

1. On November 15, 2009 Avichai Rontzki, the Chief Rabbi of the Israel Army (himself an ultra orthodox settler) was quoted in the Israeli daily Haaretz as saying that "troops who show mercy to the enemy will be "dammed". He is quoted also as saying "that religious soldiers are better fighters". During the Gaza operation Cast Lead this Rabbi was severely criticized for lending religious meaning to the use of force against the Palestinians. Despite the corrosive effects of fusing religion and military force or fighting spirit and religious motivation to fight, on the civic solidarity of the soldiers of a democratic state most of whom do not belong to a religious minority, the rabbi was not removed from his post. Another question concerns the long term impact of the international criticism of the norms guiding the operations of the Israeli Army (for example the Goldstone UN Report on the conduct of the IDF in the Gaza operation (2009) on its future practices.

REFERENCES

Arian, A. (2005). *Politics in Israel: The second republic* (2nd ed.). London: Chatham House.

Azoulay, A., & Ophir, A. (2008). *This regime which is not one: Occupation and democracy between the sea and the river (1967–)*. Tel Aviv: Resling (in Hebrew).

Benziman, U. (2006). *Whose land is it? A quest for a Jewish-Arab compact in Israel*. Jerusalem: Israel Democracy Institute (in Hebrew).

Bimkom-Planners for Planning Rights. (2008). *Hatchum Haasur: Israeli planning policy in the Palestinian villages in area C*. Den Haag: Oxfam Novib (in Hebrew).

Dahl, R. A. (1990). *After the revolution: Authority in a good society*. New Haven, CT: Yale University Press.

Elboim-Dror, R. (2009, November 27). God promise of land to Jews has deep pull on secular Israelis. Retrieved October 16, 2010, from http://www.Haaretz.com

Eldar, A., & Zertal, I. (2004). *Lords of the land: The settlers and the state of Israel 1967–2004*. Or Yehuda: Kinneret, Zmora Bitan, and Dvir (in Hebrew).

Ezrahi, Y. (1997). *Rubber bullets: Power and conscience in modern Israel*. New York: Farrar Straus and Giroux.

Ezrahi, Y. (2000). 1977. In E. Barnavi & S. Friedlander (Eds.), *Le Juif et le siecle XXe* (pp. 782–789). Paris: Calmann Levy.

Ezrahi, Y. (2011). Soldiers' violence and the dialectics of citizenship and victimhood in contemporary Israel In Y. Peled et al. (Eds.), *Democratic citizens in war* (pp. 132–143). New York: Rutledge.

Ezrahi, Y., & Kremnitzer, M., with Cohen, M., & Alimi, E. (2001). *Israel towards a constitutional democracy*. Jerusalem: Israeli Democracy Institute (in Hebrew).

Goldstone, R. (2009, September 15). *Report: Human rights in Palestine and other occupied Arab territories*. UN Doc. A/HRC/12/48. New York: UN Human Rights Council, United Nations Fact Finding Mission on the Gaza Conflict.

Gordon, N. (2008). *Israel's occupation: Sovereignty, discipline and control*. Berkeley: University of California Press.

Grossman, L. (2009, October 23) A law violating state: Interview with former Deputy Attorney General Judith Karp. *Kol Ha'ir* no. 1625, 70–74 (in Hebrew).

Halperin, E., & Bar-Tal, D. (2006). Education toward democracy in Israel: Its effect on youth and Israeli democracy. *Democracy and Security*, 2, 169–200.

Halperin, E., Bar-Tal, D., Sharvit, K., Rosler, N., & Raviv, A (2010). Socio-psychological implications for an occupying society: The case of Israel. *Journal of Peace Research*, 47, 59–70.

Hamilton, A., Madison, J., 7 Jay, J. (1937). *The federalist [c. 1787]*. New York: The Modern Library

Huntington, S. P. (1991). *The third wave of democratization in the late 20th century*. Norman: University of Oklahoma Press..

The Karp report: An Israeli government inquiry into settler violence against Palestinians on the West Bank. (1984). Washington, DC: Institute for Palestine Studies.

Kretchmer, D. (2002). *The occupation of justice: The Supreme Court of Israel and the occupied territories*. Albany: State University of New York Press.

Kretchmer, D. (2010, January 10). Deception number 443. *Haaretz Daily*, p. B2.

Navot, D. under the supervision of Kremnitzer, M. (2008). *Political corruption in Israel*. Jerusalem: Israel Democracy Institute (in Hebrew).

Or Commission. (2003). *Report of the State Commission of Inquiry to investigate the clashes between the security forces and Israeli citizens in October 2000*. Jerusalem: Government Printing Press (in Hebrew).

Sasson, T. (2005). *The Sasson report: Illegal outposts*. Jerusalem: Special Report to the Prime Minister's Office (in Hebrew).

Shapira, A. (1992). *Land and power: The Zionist resort to force 1881–1948*. Oxford: Oxford University Press.

Sprinzak, E. (1986). *What was right in his own eyes: Illegalism in Israeli society*. Tel Aviv: Poalim Library (in Hebrew).

Sprinzak, E. (1991). *The ascendance of the Israel's right*. New York and Oxford: Oxford University Press.

Sprinzak, E. (1999). *Brother against brother: Violence and extremism in Israeli politics from Altalena to the Rabin assassination*. New York: Free Press.

State of Israel. (1948). Declaration of independence. Tel Aviv: Published in the *Official Gazette*, May 14, 1948.

CHAPTER 6

The Occupation and Its Effect on the Israel Defense Forces

Reuven Pedatzur

The Six Day War and its results had far-reaching consequences for Israeli society in general and the Israel Defense Forces (IDF) in particular. The occupation of the territories (the Sinai Peninsula, the West Bank, and the Golan Heights) increased the area under Israel's control threefold and created a new geostrategic situation for the region. "The territories," as they were immediately called after the war, quickly became a focus of debate over the renewed approach to Israel's national security. For the first time since the establishment of the State of Israel, there was an urgent need to confront the basic components of the national security policy, which had been consolidated in the 1950s by the then Prime Minister and Minister of Defense, David Ben-Gurion. The occupation confronted the policymakers with the need to accept, within a short period of time, far-reaching decisions in regard to the future of these territories. These decisions were perceived as of strategic importance, whose influence on the future of the State of Israel and its future image would be crucial.

Ministers in the national unity government headed by Levi Eshkol, which came to power at the beginning of June 1967 on the eve of the war, were psychologically unprepared to deal with the issues of the occupied territories and unable to develop an effective decision-making process in regard to the territories' future. They had been surprised by the fruits of victory of the Six Day War. They had not been partners to the planning of the battles, and it had not been they who had delineated the war's objectives. Prior to 1967, the West Bank, the Sinai Peninsula, and the Golan Heights had not been perceived by them as of essential security value. The basic national security policies of all of Israel's governments had never included the need to conquer these territories, or part of them, as an essential component of the security requirements of the state. "The war," noted the then Minister of Defense, Moshe Dayan, three days after it had ended, "developed and moved toward fronts that had not been intended and had not been predetermined by anyone, including me" (Pedatzur, 1996, p. 27).

The somber atmosphere prevailing in Israel during the three weeks preceding the war also affected the policymakers. The source of this atmosphere was the existential threat to the state. Prominent expressions of this anxiety during the waiting period could be seen in the preparation of no fewer than 14,000 hospital beds for the expected wounded, consecration of public parks as cemeteries (as well as thousands of coffins), and a sense of helplessness derived from the inability to protect against the possible use of chemical warfare by the Arab states. Following the immense victory this atmosphere underwent an abrupt change, and the government ministers breathed a huge sigh of relief and experienced a pleasant sense of euphoria. They also experienced a no less pleasant sense in being the leaders who had led their country to victory in its greatest hour of need.

The relief experienced was focused mainly on security. The IDF's victories were perceived as eliminating to a great extent the severe security threat that had occupied the state's policymakers during the period prior to the war. The general feeling of these policymakers, as expressed at every discussion and meeting in which they took part, was that under no circumstances was Israel to return to the previous security conditions that could force it to experience a similar trauma. In order to understand the policy consolidated by the government in the months following the war, it should be noted that from the start its ministers agreed that any policy in regard to the future of the territories, and any plan or proposal transmitted to the enemy, had to first meet the security needs of Israel. The territories were thus perceived as a security guarantee allowing the state finally to be able to solve many of the national security problems and the existential physical distress of the state, whose source lay in the bind in which Israel had found itself in its location within the Green Line, as delineated after the War of Independence in 1948. These territories were, according to the ministers, the most valuable cards that had fallen into Israel's hands in the prolonged "game" of its very existence, which it had played for nineteen years against its neighbors. The victory in the Six Day War, as perceived by Israel's policymakers, changed the rules of the game in the Middle East. Suddenly, almost all the cards were for the first time in Israel's hands, and it had the power to dictate the rules for the state's use.

The consensus now enjoyed by all of the government's ministers, in which the future of the territories had become a security issue, now also constituted the basis for decision making in this area. One of the ramifications of this perception, according to which any agreement with Israel's neighbors would depend on the nature of the security arrangements, was that the formulation of any future agreements would be entrusted to security experts. The significant discussions about the territories, necessarily including security, were therefore to be held in a forum in which senior military personnel, that is, those perceived as security experts, would have a decisive role. The more time that passed, therefore, the greater became the military's involvement in the decision making. Entrusting the territories to the military government, following the decision not to annex them but to leave their status as occupied territory, gave the IDF almost unlimited authority in all matters concerning consolidation of the territorial policy. In the continuing occupation, including direct control over millions of inhabitants who were not citizens of the State of Israel, there were far-reaching implications, mostly negative, regarding the actions and image of the IDF.

The crushing victory by the IDF over six days in June 1967 led to a spiritual weakening among the IDF leaders and to the development of rigid thinking that resulted in the consolidation of a misguided military doctrine, belittling of the enemy, and, finally, the failure that resulted in the Yom Kippur War.

The aim of this chapter is thus to examine the consequences of the Six Day War (the military victory), and particularly the repercussions of controlling the occupied territories on the actions of the IDF, its image, policies, value system, and norms.

THE OCCUPIED TERRITORIES AND THE CONSTRUCTION OF "DEFENSIBLE BORDERS"

The lands conquered in the Six Day War provided Israel with comfortable lines of defense, distanced the main population centers from the borders, shortened the land border, and gave the country greater geographical and strategic depth. For the first time since the establishment of the state, the IDF was given the opportunity to plan and carry out defensive actions comparatively far from civilian centers and to prepare itself for the possibility of conducting mobile defensive battles. Following the Six Day War, Israel, for the first time in its history, possessed a territorial space that could be called "strategic depth" in the Sinai and operational depth in the Golan Heights and the West Bank. Thus, for the first time, there arose the potential to add two new components to Israel's perception of security, from which the military doctrine was derived:

1. The ability to absorb an initial blow, enabled by exploiting the vast area of the Sinai Peninsula as a defensive area.
2. Political flexibility, which enabled the leadership to decided whether to attack or to wait for an attack by the enemy.

These two components were lacking in David Ben-Gurion's perception of security after the War of Independence. In relation to the "narrow waist" of

Israel's 1949 borders, the belief was that the IDF could not afford to adopt a doctrine of defense, but had to carry the war to the enemy's territory. An additional component of the military doctrine prior to the Six Day War was that if it became clear that war was about to break out and could not be prevented, it should be preempted by striking first (Alon, 1959, p. 76; Peres, 1965, pp. 9–15).

The need to take an offensive approach and carry the war to enemy territory, and the necessity to strike first, were derived from the strategic inferiority resulting from the 1949 cease-fire borders. These borders had eliminated any real space between the front line and the essential inhabited areas. Jerusalem, Tel Aviv, and the other towns were all within artillery range from the West Bank, and the airports were within ground-to-ground missile range from the neighboring countries. The Gulf of Eilat, the only outlet to South and East Asia, was constantly in danger of siege and closure by Egypt, Jordan, or Saudi Arabia. Not one single point in Israel was more than two to five minutes' flying time from the closest border. Haifa and Yerucham were effectively the only towns in Israel located more than 40 km from any border. It was clear that the Jordanian and other armoured forces, if they crossed the West Bank and were assisted by the infrastructure planned there for them, would be within a driving distance of only minutes from the Mediterranean Sea. The radar systems installed on top of the Samaria and Judea mountains could impair Israel's ability to provide an early warning, and thus also to surprise the enemy, and the airfields that enabled takeoff and landing from the West Bank increased the chances of a surprise attack against Israel.

Following the Six Day War, the IDF effectively failed to exploit the possibility of making appropriate military use of the Sinai area and the operational depth of the Golan Heights, and stuck to its traditional approach, despite the significant change that had taken place in the geostrategic conditions. The IDF paid the price for this failure in the Yom Kippur War, as discussed below. One of the most serious problems that occurred following the Six Day War was that the IDF senior staff was held captive to the professional-military approach to decisions, or perhaps more accurately the nondecisions, taken by the political echelon. When the politicians began to discuss the future of the territories immediately after the war, the talks stagnated due to the policymakers' inability to reach an agreement (see also the chapter by Magal, Oren, Bar-Tal, and Halperin in this volume). The status quo thus became a policy, and as Minister Yigal Alon put it, "We decided not to decide."

Given the lack of agreement among the policymakers concerning the desired borders and the future of the territories, no binding government policy was developed. This caused the various policymakers to consider independently, from time to time, the issue of defining borders. Their statements on this subject were based mainly on security claims, but in principle only, without a deeper understanding of the security components inherent in the preparation and significance of new borders. They employed broad use of the term "security borders" and later also of the term "defensible borders." The use of such terms was intended to make it clear that the border changes demanded by Israel were essential to its security needs. Such needs were perceived as more legitimate than other supporting, claims, such as the territories being "the land of our fathers" or "the promised borders" or "the land of the Bible."

Prime Minister Levi Eshkol was the first to employ the term "security borders." (Davar, 1972). This is a military concept, not a political one, and the prime minister consequently believed that the security border did not have to become the country's political border. Minister Yigal Alon objected to this perception, contending that every border defined as security must first and foremost be a political border: "A security border that is not identical to the political border—is not a security border," he announced to members of the Labor party. Elsewhere, at a meeting with young members of the Kibbutz Artzi movement in 1969, Alon stated: "A peace accord accompanied by [an] effective security arrangement, which means safe borders, also permits the existence of demilitarized areas with effective supervision, but under no circumstances instead of a secure border that is also a political border" (Pedatzur, 1996, p. 102). The Minister of Defense, Moshe Dayan, also believed that Israel must adhere to the principle of defensible borders. "Israel has publicly announced," he wrote, "that due to its right to secure borders, defensible borders, it will not return to the pre-June 4, 1967 lines" (Dayan, 1982, p. 521).

Shortly after the war, Dayan clearly expressed the feeling among Israel's policymakers in regard to the IDF's military achievements in the war. At a meeting of the senior command staff on June 29, 1967, he announced: "The geographical, military and political achievements of this war have first and foremost provided the optimum line that anyone could ever have dreamed of for Israel's ideal borders" (Nadel, 2006, p. 10). This statement led to a consensus that the cease-fire lines were the best ones possible to ensure Israel's security. Following the stagnation and the "decision not to decide" created by the political echelon, a feedback process began between the politicians and the senior military command. The new term "defensible borders" became a political as well as a security term. It was clear to all that the defensible borders were the cease-fire lines—the Suez Canal, the Golan Heights, and the River Jordan.

The policymakers' approach to the issue of the desired border on the eastern front (the West Bank) served to increase confusion in the military command, which attempted to interpret the political perception and translate it into military doctrine. Prime Minister Eshkol supported from the outset the unequivocal determination of the River Jordan as the security border. Nonetheless, Eshkol did not state this publicly in the early months after the war, confining his remarks within closed circles. It was only much later that the Prime Minister publicly stated his views in regard to the desired border.

At a meeting with members of the Movement for a Greater Israel on November 12, 1967, Eshkol set out his perception of the future of the territories. In regard to the West Bank, he stated: "We have still not said 'no' and not said 'yes' regarding annexation of the West Bank. However, we have said that the Jordan [River] is Israel's secure border." In a newspaper interview on May 31, 1968, he decided to go public, with making his approach the official government position, but without the government's having taken any definite decision, as that (nondecision) was its official stance: "The Jordan River will be the border, for which the Jordanian tanks and military will be permitted to deploy only east of it, and Israeli tanks and forces will guard it from the west." One month after his interview with the daily newspaper *Lamerchav*, the Prime Minister announced in a radio interview that "from our point of view the Jordan [River] is Israel's security border" (Pedatzur, 1996, pp. 103–104).

The senior military staff hurried to adopt Prime Minister Eshkol's position, translating his political approach into military-security language. Thus, following the Prime Minister's announcement, Chief of Staff Yitzhak Rabin stated that in his opinion the Jordan River did indeed constitute the security border. In a discussion at a forum of the general staff on December 27, 1967, Rabin presented his approach in regard to Israel's desired future borders. In reference to the West Bank, he declared the "Jordan as a line of defense."

The problem deepened when the senior military staff began to discuss political issues. This occurred shortly after the end of the war, at a meeting of the general staff on December 27, 1967, devoted to a discussion of the future of the occupied territories. Some members of the senior command warned against this trend, such as General Israel Tal, who contended that "carrying out such a free discussion by the general staff deviates from the standing orders for operations." In contrast, General Matti Peled contended that the general staff should advise the political echelon on strategic matters too. Finally, General Tal's contention was rejected, and the general staff discussed political matters that were not necessarily connected to the issue of security. Most members of the general staff agreed that there was no chance of peace in the near future, that peace was not necessarily security, and that it would be better to forgo it in the coming years. This was argued against by Generals Matti Peled and Haim Bar-Lev, who saw peace as a condition for developing a normal life and a goal to be pursued. Peled proposed to consolidate a plan as a basis for the future arrangement, and Bar-Lev suggested that they define the aims of peace. However, Peled and Bar-Lev were in the minority among the senior military command.

Most of the participants at this meeting objected to any sort of withdrawal from the territories held by Israel after the war and adhered to the position that only full control over all the territories would ensure security, as stated by General Ariel Sharon: "To leave the territory to some sort of arrangement means that we are condemning ourselves to a disaster." Generals Ezer Weizmann, Motti Hod, and Ariel Sharon, while presenting arguments of security, also voiced ideological arguments against returning the land of Israel's forefathers. General Tal expressed his objection to mixing ideological reasoning with military considerations. The only one to support returning part of the West Bank territories was General Matti Peled, who advised against annexation and instead suggested that they develop the notion of a Palestinian state in these territories. He even suggested initiating withdrawal from the "Little Triangle" (a concentration of Israeli-Arab towns and villages adjacent to the Green Line, located in the eastern Sharon Plain) in order to reduce the number of Arabs in Israel and to do so even before arrival of the United Nations envoy, Gunnar Yaring. General Bar-Lev agreed with his statememt that the only solution would be a Palestinian state but expressed concern regarding an additional independent Arab state. The other participants rejected the idea of a Palestinian state (Rosenthal, 2005, p. 562).

Chief of Staff Yitzhak Rabin, summarizing the discussion, did not steer clear of discussing purely political matters, although it is doubtful that a military officer should have dealt with them:

> As a solution I begin with the basic assumption that the State of Israel is ready to reach an arrangement with all of the Arab States and with each one individually, knowing which is important and which is less important, but ready with each one separately to enter into talks with the following guidelines:
>
> The problematic in regard to Jordan [its source], with the following assumptions:
>
> a) In respect to the peace arrangement too, the Jordan [River] is Israel's line of defence.
> b) The State of Israel cannot support the recognition of the West Bank's annexation to Jordan. In other words, even with the agreement with [King] Hussein, the West Bank has a different status. Although I shan't go into technical formulas, I believe that if the State of Israel will

recognize annexation of the West Bank or part of it to Jordan—this will be a mistake, it is inconceivable.

c) I believe that to hand over the Arabs wholesale to civilian or Jordanian or Palestinian government has a two-fold aspect. In any case this seems to be a reasonable border and I suggest that we not go into this or that nuance. I propose three principles:

1) A different status for the West Bank from that of Jordan.
2) Civil government, or a political solution of a Palestinian State or a Jordanian civil government.
3) The Jordan River as the line of defense. (Rosenthal, 2005, p. 564)

In my opinion, we cannot withdraw from Syria. I don't want to discuss whether or not there is a chance of peace with Syria, but although it may be possible to withdraw half a kilometer here and half a kilometer there, fundamentally there should be no withdrawal. Regarding Egypt—I suggest, as a basic assumption for any peace accord, that the minimum line of defense does not necessarily have to be the Suez Canal.

I remind you once again of my point of departure, that no withdrawal should take place unless [it is] within the framework of a permanent arrangement, one of whose components is that of an open border. And I do not want to enter into a discussion of where the line lies. One thing is clear: under no circumstances can we give up the Sharm el Sheikh area "as Israeli territory." We also cannot give up El Arish, more or less. And all the rest, how exactly the territory should be divided, I'm not ready to say at the moment. My point of departure is that I don't believe it possible to seriously propose peace to Egypt while the border remains along the [Suez] Canal (Ibid.)

The Deputy Chief of Staff, General Haim Bar-Lev, told the Chief of Staff: "I haven't understood the matter of the West Bank status." Rabin replied: "I am ready to explain myself. I believe this is not only for political reasons, although I am not ignoring reasons of education and tradition. Even the bad decision of 1947 did not see annexation and a growth in Arab countries. There was a political decision by the UN regarding two States—the Palestinian and the Jewish. If I'm not wrong, I don't know how many of the countries in the world recognized annexation of the West Bank to Jordan. In any case, not everyone accepted this as de facto. Even Arab countries did not formally recognize it. In my opinion regarding the West Bank—the State of Israel does not need to find itself among the countries that recognize the West Bank's full annexation to Jordan."

And there is a need to move toward preserving the special status of the West Bank. A status that will enable unimpeded Israeli movement within the territory, which will provide many things. I don't believe that it is important to enter into minute detail. But when there will be an Israeli-Hussein accord in regard to an arrangement between us and the Jordanians—then is the time to determine a special status for the West Bank that will give civil control to Jordan, and security to Israel. If you don't try, it won't work. (Rosenthal, 2005, p. 565)

The senior military staff, without exception, agreed that the cease-fire lines were optimal from the military point of view. In a closed meeting on December 31, 1967, the chief of the general-staff branch, General Ezer Weizmann, contended that "from a purely military perspective there could be no better borders and any withdrawal from these will only complicate the security situation and in any case push peace further away." The commander of the air force, General Motti Hod, said at a meeting on December 27, 1967, "We are sitting on ideal borders...we have no complaint today about our current borders and nor should there be." The head of the Southern Command, Yishayahu Gavish, stated at the same meeting that "these are borders that provide security." The head of training department, General Ariel Sharon, noted: "In my opinion the borders that we need to retain are the current borders, with no withdrawal and no arrangement that will not ensure our complete military control of the territory." The Deputy Chief of Staff, General Haim Bar-Lev, who one day after this meeting of the General Staff, on December 31, 1967, was about to be appointed Chief of Staff, clarified his viewpoint in respect to the future borders: "The only handover to the Egyptians can be—the [Suez] Canal, open and under our control... militarily, the West Bank cannot be given up...regarding the Syrian [H]eights, we aren't able to move even one millimeter" (Rosenthal, 2005, pp. 96–100).

In other words, the senior military officers of the General Staff had no hesitation in discussing political issues, which without doubt reflected declarations and assertions of clear political significance.

However, it became clear that the senior officers had not been included in the process of policy determination, as the government compartmentalized them and kept them in the dark regarding the strategic decisions over the future of the territories. A situation thus arose in which the General Staff "played solo" and debated over alternative policies, while the government had already decided on its favored policy. The senior command of the IDF was unaware of the government's decisions taken on June 19, 1967, according to which Israel agreed to give up all the occupied territories taken from Egypt and Syria in exchange for a peace agreement with those countries.

Consequently, General Haim Bar-Lev's comment rejecting giving up "even one millimeter" of the Golan Heights and Chief of Staff Yitzhak Rabin's statement on the necessity to remain in Sharm el Sheikh were unconnected to the policy determined by Eshkol's government. Even Rabin was not informed of the June 19 decision, which was passed on to the U.S. government to be presented to the Egyptian and Syrian leaders (Rabin, 1977, p. 227).

In other words, this far-reaching strategic decision by the Israeli government could in no way influence the plans of the IDF senior commanders because it was unknown to them.

The government decision of June 19, 1967, determined, among other things, the following:

Egypt:
Israel proposes the signing of a peace agreement with Egypt based on the international border [dating from the British Mandate] and Israel's security needs.
The peace agreement will obligate:
1. Assured freedom of shipping in the Tiran Straits and the Gulf of Solomon [the Gulf of Aqaba].
2. Assured freedom of shipping in the Suez Canal.
3. Assured freedom of flight above the Tiran Straits and the Gulf of Solomon
4. Demilitarization of the Sinai Peninsula.

Syria:
Israel proposes the signing of a peace agreement based on the international border [see above] and Israel's security needs:
The peace agreement will obligate:
1. Demilitarization of the Syrian heights currently held by the IDF.
2. Complete assurance of undisturbed flow of water from the Jordan River sources to Israel. (Pedatzur, 1996, pp. 55–56)

Because the senior IDF officers were unaware of the government decision regarding the necessity to hand back the entire Sinai Peninsula and the Golan Heights, they needed to translate the term *defensible borders* into a military doctrine. However, instead of taking a clear professional stance, the IDF began to tread carefully, mainly in order to please the political echelon, which had been unable to decide what to do with the occupied territories (the policymakers rescinded the June 19 decision about four months later, after it became clear that the Egyptians and Syrians had rejected the Israeli proposal for peace agreements in return for Israel's withdrawal from Sinai and the Golan Heights). The General Staff understood, without even the need for discussion, that if they were to take a clear public stand regarding Israel's future borders, this would constitute a political decision reflecting a political discussion (Horowitz, 1985).

In a meeting analyzing the future borders, one of the participants, Uzi Narkiss, head of the Central Command, raised the point that "I don't believe that we have ever held such a discussion, and I don't know whether or not it is a good idea to do so" (Nadel, 2006, p. 97).

To avoid the perception that the army generals were considering political matters, the senior command avoided any public discussion of necessary future borders and adopted the obscure term "defensible borders." The translation of this term into practical military language led to the decision that the military's aim in regard to the new cease-fire borders was to prevent, at any cost, any force from crossing the cease-fire lines on the three fronts. With the outbreak of war, the General Staff decided that not even the smallest area was to be retaken by the enemy—not in Sinai, not on the West Bank, and not on the Golan Heights.

A new approach was thus adopted, one that can be termed "not one millimeter." In the IDF this was supposed to be a nonpolitical term, intended to present a professional military approach. In actuality, the senior command was dragged in the direction of a political interpretation for this military term too. In a discussion held on November 21, 1968, on the defense of the Sinai Peninsula, the head of the Southern Command, General Yishayahu Gavish, presented the plan prepared by the command: "The principles upon which the plan is constructed are as follows: We must defend the front line of the canal. The defense must prevent crossing of the canal...we must hold the eastern bank [of the Suez Canal] and not allow penetration of even one meter into the East Bank...of course the significance of the deployment [of the Israeli forces] on the canal is a consequence of two considerations: 1, military; 2, political" (Nadel, 2006, pp. 97, 156).

One of the reasons for seeking a firm defense of the Suez Canal was the recognition that this was what the political echelon wanted. Indeed, Prime Minister Golda Meir (who headed the government in March 1969 after Eshkol's death), as well as ministers Yigal Alon and Israel Galili, assumed that without the solid presence of the IDF along the water line the Egyptians would quickly encroachment on areas under IDF control. They would also be tempted to initiate surprise raids and effectively invite the intervention of the superpowers in order to deprive Israel of the time needed to repel any Egyptian forced landing on the east bank of the canal (Yaniv, 1994, p. 221). The necessity for a firm defense was thus consolidated, meaning that the interception line was also the line of defense as well as the cease-fire line. If the aim was to prevent the Egyptians' invasion of the east bank of the canal, then they had to be stopped at the water line. This was the reason for establishing the Bar-Lev line (Bartov, 1979, pp. 174–176).

There was no other reason for its establishment, as from the military point of view there was no logic to not exploiting the Sinai as a defensive space. There was no logic to attempting to stop an entire army at this line. The Sinai Peninsula, which had no civilian population, urban buildings, or obstructions to hinder the conduct of war, was supposed to be an ideal area for the types of mobile battles with which the IDF was experienced and preferred. Therefore, military logic should have allowed an attack by Egypt to advance and reach deep into the Sinai; and there, where the IDF had a topographic advantage (such as in the area of the Mitla and Gidi passes), it would destroy the attacking Egyptian force. (Fortified posts had to be constructed along the Bar-Lev line in order to protect the soldiers deployed there from artillery fire or attack by the Egyptian army.)

However, as the senior command had not been able to decide that in case of war Israel would be ready to fight in the Sinai, the Bar-Lev line was established. In the discussion held by the General Staff in which it was decided to create the Bar-Lev line, the Chief of Staff clarified the rationale behind this fortification: "Our aim is to stay there at the waterside and prevent the Egyptians from any territorial attainment. Due to the concrete political problems we don't see a possibility of doing this in a way that would be easiest for us militarily—to let them enter and let them have it, so that they can't exploit their artillery or make any of the preparations necessary for a war" (Guy, 1998, p. 178). In other words, the Chief of Staff did not use professional-military considerations, but instead based his decision on political considerations that should not have been the concern of the military high command.

Upon his appointment as Chief of Staff on January 1, 1968, Haim Bar-Lev presented his approach to the IDF's deployment lines following the war and again emphasized the need to continue to hold, among other areas, the Suez Canal: "As the Arabs do not see themselves able to drive Israel back to the previous borders, a real alternative from their point of view is a restricted action possibly focusing on 'opening the Suez Canal'...and so we must hold on to these lines as a deterrent, frustrating any desire on their part to attack. While we occupy the canal, Jordan and the Golan Heights, the odds are in favor of our forces, and the borders are easier to defend" (Guy, 1998, pp. 158–159). It was only a small step from here to justifying establishment of the Bar-Lev line. It was thus unclear whether the Sinai would protect Israel or Israel would now have to defend the Sinai (Ben-Dor, 2009, p. 97).

Other senior officers too considered the Bar-Lev line and the security policy as political issues. General Dan Lanner, summarizing the "Battering Ram" exercise in early August 1972, noted: "Of course it is necessary to stop any Egyptian attempt to cross—immediately. The considerations must be political rather than military." General Ariel Sharon stated: "My opinion is that we should strike immediately" (Gordon, 2008, p. 35).

The so-called War of Attrition, which broke out in March 1969, added another layer to the claims of those advocating the firm defense of the Suez Canal line. For if Israel were to withdraw from the canal under Egyptian fire, it would simply invite similar attacks. In other words, withdrawal from the canal while the Egyptians were shooting would lead to continued and escalated attacks by them. The Suez Canal was also perceived by the IDF's armored corps' experts as the best anti-tank canal in the world, which the Egyptians would not be able to cross with a large force.

In January 1970, following the appointment of Ariel Sharon as head of the Southern Command, a discussion took place regarding the aims of the Bar-Lev line. General David Elazar declared that "In fact it's impossible to imagine a line along which we can be more at ease than the Suez line." Minister of Defense Moshe Dayan added that he had "had never seen an alternative to the water line" (Guy, 1998, p. 191). "The mission was clear," wrote General Israel Tal, "a hard-line defense with the aim of not losing ground" (Tal, 1996, p. 152). The cease-fire line thus had to achieve two military aims simultaneously: defense and interception. In retrospect, it is clear that the decision not to set a line of defense deep inside Sinai was an obvious military error.

There was a similar perception regarding the Golan Heights, although the fortifications there were less massive than those at the Suez Canal (Asher, 2003, pp. 63–78). The early hours of the Yom Kippur War proved that neither the Bar-Lev line nor the one on the Golan Heights was able to achieve these two military aims.

The decision to prepare a hard-line defense at the Suez Canal and the Golan Heights led to constant hostilities between the IDF and the enemy forces, requiring the IDF to maintain a large force along the front lines. This decision also led to a new logistical situation. The IDF was forced to set up immobile maintenance and supply centers in new areas in the north, and mainly in the Sinai.

In adopting the not one millimeter approach in Sinai and in planning to take the fighting to enemy territory (Egypt) in case of future war, the IDF supported the political decision that the Sinai was not occupied territory but rather, in certain respects, part of the homeland. The IDF also supported the policy of giving historical and Jewish names to military sites in Sinai. Sharm el Sheikh, for example, was renamed Ophira, and the air force base there was named Ophir. The military zone at Bir Gafgafa was given its biblical name, Refidim. The not-one-millimeter approach, as noted, was used by the IDF not only in Sinai but also on the Golan Heights. The "Rock" battle command (it was not an "order of the day"; it was a "battle command" that the IDF prepared for a future confrontation), updated before the Yom Kippur War, stated: "The Northern Command will defend its area and prevent enemy intrusion into its space. Defense of the Golan Heights will be based on a hard-line defense along the border" (Gordon, 2008, p. 137). While the officers of the Northern Command were presenting the defense plans to the Chief of Staff, David Elazar, on April 26, 1973, the latter instructed the officers: "The Syrians must be prevented from making any local or temporary advance, and following a brief interception stage, there should be a move to swift attack into enemy territory" (Nadel, 2006, p. 154).

THE MILITARY AND SETTLEMENT IN THE OCCUPIED TERRITORIES

The Six Day War and the ensuing occupation had a decisive effect on military thinking and actions and on the norms of the IDF in regard to activity in the occupied territories. The IDF began to become involved in the settlement process, which was mainly political, because a military government was set up in the territories, making the IDF the sovereign authority there. As time passed, the IDF became an increasingly central player in settlement politics. Many decisions regarding settlement were decisions that the officers in the field had presented to the government and that had given it a pretext to establish settlements under the guise of security settlements, employing the NAHAL (pioneering military youth—a special unit of the Israeli army involving settlements) units to do so. The important role in settlement played by the military was attested to by General Rehavam Zeevi in a discussion held in 1981. "The role and involvement of the IDF in the settlement has been immense. The military has been a supportive, and even initiating, factor in establishing settlements. Merom Golan [the first settlement in the Golan Heights] would not have been founded without the support of Dado [David Elazar, head of the Northern Command]" (Dapei Elazar, 1981, p. 112).

An important example of the IDF's involvement in issues of settlement in the territories soon after the end of the Six Day War was the initiation of settlement on the Golan Heights. On July 30, 1967, two weeks after arriving in the area and long before the subject of settlement was discussed by the government, the first settlers on the Golan Heights were given a written permit by the IDF to occupy the abandoned Syrian army camp in Alieka. The permit was signed by Major Akiva Feinstein, the military governor of the Golan Heights (Pedatzur, 1996, p. 167).

Shortly after the end of the war, the IDF prepared a map of suggested settlements in the territories conquered in 1967. It thereby gave itself a role that was political in essence and without military or security connections (Pedatzur, 1996, p. 190). The IDF had begun to weigh political considerations. Its commanding officers also allowed the government's exploitation of the military for political use, such as founding civilian settlements under the guise of NAHAL outposts. This was a decision by the senior staff to collaborate with the political deception, which was intended to reject any international pressure in regard to settlement in the territories.

The idea was first suggested to the government as "a proposal for action" by the minister Israel Galili on October 1, 1967. Galili considered it possible to moderate international pressure by presenting the settlements in the territories as NAHAL outposts. His idea was based on the assumption that representing such settlements as military outposts would not arouse objections, as they fulfilled legitimate needs in an occupied territory that still faced acute security problems. Nevertheless, it was clear that Galili did not mean to stop at army outposts; these were intended to provide cover for a broad settlement program in which civilian settlements would be established.

The need to find a military cover for civilian settlement intensified after the government ministers had been informed that settlement in the areas, of any sort, contradicted international law. In a government discussion on September 10, 1967, the Minister of Justice, Yaakov Shimshon Shapira, clearly stated the legal position. In considering the various ideas regarding settlement in the territories, Shapira determined that "We can do so, but we have to know that in this regard we are acting not only against the Geneva Convention, but also against the orders of the General Staff" (Pedatzur, 1990, p. B1). Four days later, on September 14, 1967, the Foreign Minister was given a memo prepared by Theodor Miron, the legal adviser to the Foreign Office, which stated that establishing settlements in the territories was against the Geneva Convention: "My conclusion is that civilian settlements in the held territories contravene specific directive article 4 of the Geneva Convention. I suspect that the world is highly sensitive toward any question of Jewish settlement in the held areas and any legal arguments that we may attempt to find will not remove the heavy international pressure that will be put on us even from friendly countries, based on the Geneva Convention, article 4" (Pedatzur, 1996, p. 195).

However, even before the government was able to discuss the proposal to use the NAHAL troops for settlement purposes, its official speakers were forced to try to camouflage the settlement activities, which had taken on a clear civilian character under the guise of military outposts.

After the *New York Times* published Levi Eshkol's declaration regarding the need to establish settlements in the Golan Heights and the West Bank, the Israeli delegation to the UN sent an urgent telegram to the Prime Minister in order to obtain clarification that would enable denial of this information. The UN delegation was unaware of the planned settlement activity and thus also did not know whether the information published by the *New York Times* was true or false. "Please respond urgently," demanded Moshe Raviv, a member of the Israeli delegation to the UN, in a telegram of September 24, 1967, sent to the director of the Prime Minister's office, Adi Yafeh: "What was actually said and what is the content of the announcement. If nothing was said— we wish to issue an immediate denial." In the reply sent the next day, on September 25 (one day following the Banias settlement [in the Golan Heights] and on the same day the Kfar Etzion settlers established the settlement [on the West Bank]), Yafeh wrote: "There is no such announcement, just a government decision to the establishment of outposts. Repeat, military outposts in Gush Etzion, and a plan to establish additional outposts. At Ramat Banias the first outpost was already established yesterday in the Golan." Following this answer, on September 26, the Israeli UN delegation issued a statement that the NAHAL outpost had been established by the IDF as "military units in border areas, combining defense roles with agricultural work. The NAHAL outpost in Gush Etzion is established for military security purposes." The next day, two days following the settlement in Kfar Etzion, Foreign Minister Abba Eban announced in Strasbourg, France, that "the outposts on the Golan Heights and West Bank are an emergency step of military nature, and will not impact the discussion on territorial matters within the framework of the peace negotiations" (Pedatzur, 1996, pp. 196–197).

Moshe Dayan, the Minister of Defense, supported the notion of using Nahal for settlement purposes in the territories. "It's possible that in another month or two the situation will be different. But for the initial, preliminary phases, I suggest we deal with settlement but only within the NAHAL and army camps framework. I suspect that we are making things harder for ourselves, that we [should be] doing the opposite. Why the opposite? Because we are behaving like sheep in wolf's clothing, instead of what we need to do now, which is behave not like a wolf but like half a wolf, and in sheep's clothing" (Admoni, 1992, pp. 32–33).

Minister Israel Galili, at a government meeting on October 1, 1967, formulated a decision on which there could be agreement: "In the near future we shall decide on a general formula for settlement, within the NAHAL framework, or as agricultural military outposts. I'm not sure that the term 'NAHAL outpost' is absolutely temporary. It can be temporary, but does not have to be. In a few months we shall change the formula. For the period ahead of us, in which all sorts of troubles can arise, regarding settlement there is nothing better than the formula of security needs. We can also give it various external indications that will justify this definition" (Pedatzur, 1996, p. 200).

The military thereby became a central player in the settlement project following the government's decision to use the NAHAL outposts for the purpose of establishing civilian settlements. After Minister Galili's proposal had been accepted by the government, the military command acted to put it into practice. General David Elazar, head of the Northern Command, and his chief of staff, Brigadier-General Dan Lanner, pressed the first settlers on the Golan Heights to accept the proposal and agree to turn their settlement into a NAHAL outpost. The two officers explained that due to political constraints, as well as pressure by the Foreign Minister, Abba Eban, they should agree to the proposal in order to avoid international criticism of the settlement. After a stormy discussion, the settlers finally agreed. At the entrance to the settlement they erected a signpost saying "NAHAL Kuneitra," with the Israeli flag on the flagpole, as accepted military practice (Pedatzur, 1996, pp. 194–203).

Senior IDF officers, who understood that the government was ready to turn a blind eye to the groups that were organizing to establish settlements in the territories, cooperated and did not prevent these groups' activities even when their members broke their agreement with the military government. This was the case with Hebron. On the eve of Passover 1968, Rabbi Moshe Levinger and his followers approached Uzi Narkiss, head of the Central Command, with a request to hold the Seder (Passover eve service) in the Jewish Quarter of Hebron. General Narkiss authorized the request while "shrugging his shoulders" and telling them, "I don't care. I don't know anything. Hire a hotel, put up tents, and I don't know" (Eldar & Zartal, 2004, p. 375). Levinger and his people promised that they would leave the town immediately after the Seder night. On April 11, 1968, they set out to celebrate the Seder night in rooms rented in the Park Hotel in Hebron. It swiftly became clear that the request to celebrate the feast in Hebron was a ruse; Levinger's aim was to remain there with his followers and thereby establish the settlement as a fait accompli. The following day, Levinger declared that they "were a group of initial settlers who had come to renew the Jewish settlement in Hebron. A settlement that had been destroyed 39 years earlier" (Pedatzur, 1996, p. 233). When the ruse became clear and it was obvious that Levinger's followers had no intention of leaving the area, the senior officers made no effort to remove them. They understood that the government ministers wanted them there, and they decided to cooperate with the political echelon.

When Minister of Defense Moshe Dayan was informed that Levinger's group was asking to remain in Hebron even after the Seder night, he did not order an action to remove them. In fact, he did the opposite, instructing the IDF to ensure the personal security needs of the settlers in Hebron. A short time later, based on a decision by the ministerial committee for security matters on May 12, 1968, the Minister of Defense decided to relocate the settlers from the Park Hotel to a military government installation on a hill at a slight distance from the town itself. The settlers moved into rooms cleared for them in the west wing of the main building, and the army began to build huts for them inside the fenced area of the installation (Tevet, 1969, p. 237). The army thereby gave its backing to the settlement activity, which contravened military government protocol and had been achieved deceitfully. The Minister of Defense even confirmed in the Knesset that the IDF had provided Levinger's group with weapons and that a lieutenant had given them weapons training in the headquarters of the military government (The Knesset Minutes, 1968, p. 2231). The behavior of the senior command in the "Levinger affair" had a severe impact on the prestige, authority, and image of the IDF.

Following the establishment of Israeli settlements on the Golan Heights and the West Bank, a new security problem arose. The IDF had a new task—to protect these settlements. The strategic advantage of depth in both areas as a result of their occupation no longer existed. One of the previous principles of security thus had to be abandoned: that the Syrian Heights would provide an area in which Israel could fight to protect the Galilee. And so, as expected, during the Yom Kippur War the worst scenario of all happened. Not only did the settlements on the Golan Heights not participate in the defensive struggle by the IDF against the Syrian army, but they also reduced the IDF's fighting resources, as these were needed to evacuate the civilian population immediately before the outbreak of the battle. The mission of protecting the Israeli citizens quickly expanded to the West Bank, the Gaza Strip and Sinai. This was a mission for which the IDF was not intended.

However, there were many in the IDF who not only did not see a problem with this mission but even volunteered to assist settlement in the territories. The head of the Central Command, for instance, General Rehavam Ze'evi, stressed to the settlers in the Jordan Valley: "The army is here to serve you. This is our purpose after 2000 years. Go to this land you have inherited." In his address to the first NAHAL soldiers who were there to complete their military-civilian service and who had decided to found an outpost in the territories, he said: "You will set up a home and the IDF will protect you" (Eldar & Zartal, 2004, p. 380).

The IDF, as noted, immediately following the war prepared a map of settlements incorporating purely civilian settlements, with no intention of establishing them as NAHAL outposts. The IDF proposal to establish civilian settlements in the territories served the policymakers' need to decide upon these same settlements. Prime Minister Levy Eshkol thus exploited this situation during a discussion by the policy committee of the Ma'arach party on

August 18, 1967, that dealt with issues of settling the land at Kfar Etzion. In relation to the pros and cons of authorizing settlement on the land, the Prime Minister noted that "The map prepared by the IDF, including proposals for settlement, incorporates a region of settlements in Gush Etzion" (Pedatzur, 1996, p. 190). On the same map, the army also proposed to establish a settlement in Beit Aharava in the area north of the Dead Sea.

The IDF, however, was not satisfied with just the proposals for settlement, but even determined the settlements' locations and the dates for their establishment. This was the case with the settlement founded in the northern Jordan Valley (Mehola). Following a tour of the area by Minister of Defense Dayan, Colonel Shlomo Gazit produced a document titled "Working Lands in Bardala and the Jordan Valley," dated January 11, 1968. Among other things, it noted that "On January 16 plowing will commence of land in Bardala [a village in the northern part of the Jordan Valley, located 13 km northeast of Tubas and 28 km northeast of Nablus] carried out by the Israel Land Administration, by means of the tractor station of the Upper Galilee farms, in coordination with the Central Command and the Military Government." The document was also related to the locations of the settlements that would be established in the area of Bardala, even though the government had still not decided upon this. "Location of the settlement, following its authorization, will be at elevation point 144, or at any other location determined by the command" (Pedatzur, 1996, p. 214).

In actuality, the IDF provided its services to all the settlements established in the territories, and in later years also to settlements established illegally, those termed the "illegal settlements." These services included, in addition to guarding the settlements, linking them to the national electricity and water grids and paving access roads. The IDF even increased its aid to the establishment of settlements by supplying heavy military vehicles and helicopters that were used in constructing the settlements on the ground, for example at Alon Moreh (High Court of Justice, 1979).

The army also became a key player in the legal field (see the chapter by Kretzmer in this volume). IDF officers appeared at High Court deliberations in cases in which Palestinian residents of the territories had appealed against the expropriation of lands for settlement. In one case, Suleiman Toufik presented two appeals against the Minister of Defense over the expropriation of land in the area of El bira, in the district of Ramallah, near army camp Beth-El, and land in the area of Tubas, in the district of Nablus, not far from the Jordan Valley. The purpose of the expropriation was to establish Jewish settlements, including Beth-El. General Abraham Orli, coordinator of activity in the territories, appeared in the High Court on behalf of the state and declared that "Establishment of the settlement in the area of the Beth-El camp not only does not contradict military need but even serves it, in constituting part of the government's security approach, which bases the security framework, among others, on Jewish settlements. Accordingly, all the Israeli settlements in the territories held by the IDF constitute part of the broader defense framework of the IDF. Moreover, these settlements are given the highest classification within the mentioned broader defense framework, as expressed in the official allocation of manpower and other means. During times of calm these settlements serve as observation posts etc., mainly for purposes of presence and the control of vital territories. The importance of the settlements increases in particular in time of war when the armed forces are generally moved from their bases for operational needs, and the settlements are intended to constitute the main component of security presence and control in the areas in which they are located" (High Court of Justice, 1978, p. 9). There is no doubt that General Orli was aware that the settlements established in the territory would contribute nothing to security, and in fact would even cause a security problem for the IDF due to the need to protect them.

Within a few months, Palestinians appealed against the expropriation of their lands on which the Alon Moreh settlemsnt was going to be established. This time the Chief of Staff, Raphael Eitan, appeared as a witness, declaring that it would be impossible to ensure the security needs in the discussed area without the establishment of a civilian Jewish settlement in this area. Eitan emphasized the importance of establishing the settlement in order to secure the roads and enable free movement of the reserve duty soldiers called up in time of war. It is not necessary to be an expert in military matters to understand the exaggeration of this claim, as indeed the former Chief of Staff, Haim Bar-Lev, had contended; he too had appeared in court and stated that, in his opinion, a settlement located in the heart of the Arab population would not only not contribute to security, but in fact would actually burden it (High Court of Justice, 1979, p. 4).

There were also cases in which IDF officers initiated plans to establish NAHAL outposts and even civilian settlements. Such was the case in which the head of the Southern Command, Ariel Sharon, in the early 1970s cleared thousands of Bedouins from the Rafiah area in order to make the territory available for Jewish settlements. In a High Court hearing dealing with the issue of removing the Bedouins, General Israel Tal, head of the general staff branch General Headquarters, stated that the Rafiah area from which the appellants had been cleared "had served for a long period as a focus for hostile terror actions and a place for the movement of terrorist acts beyond the area, such as mining roads and passes, shooting at passing Israeli vehicles and the murder of local inhabitants, as well as sabotaging buildings and installations in the Rafiah area, the Sinai, Gaza Strip and in Israel, as a place to stockpile and transfer weapons and ammunition for the terrorists who operated in the Gaza Strip and Israel, and as a way station, shelter and hiding place for Egyptian intelligence agents sent to carry out missions in the Sinai, Gaza Strip and Israel, as well as for terrorists" (High Court of Justice, 1972, pp. 2–3). General Tal knew that the Bedouins had not been removed for security purposes but in order to clear the area for the establishment of settlements. Nevertheless, he was prepared to testify to the importance of this activity for security.

The most negative action performed by the IDF, however, was expressed in the affair of the illegal settlements. The IDF functioned as an emissary in the settlement enterprise, consciously assisting the lawbreakers and contravening government decisions. The military effectively became an active partner in the illegal settlements. Its actions in this respect were exposed in a report submitted in March 2005 at the request of Prime Minister Ariel Sharon by the attorney Talia Sasson, who had previously served as director of the department for special tasks in the Attorney General's office. Sasson analyzed, among others, the role played by the IDF in the process of establishing the illegal settlements:

> [There had existed] the security concept in which in every place in the territories where anybody decides to establish a settlement—protection would be provided. Accordingly, any place that anyone decided to set up an outpost—IDF soldiers would arrive to guard them. The result was that the IDF, even when unwilling, was dragged into rubber-stamping the illegal settlements simply by being present and guarding the settlers there; in fact its presence and protection there of those same lawbreakers determined the facts in the field, along with the lawbreakers themselves. Instead of removing them—it protected them.... It would seem that breaking the law had become institutionalized and institutional. We do not make deals with criminals or criminal groups who act against the law. The picture revealed to the observing eye is one of crude lawbreaking by certain State authorities, public authorities, local councils in Judea and Samaria and settlers, all while deceptively suggesting an institutionalized and institutional system acting according to the law.... This situation sends a message to the IDF, to its soldiers, its officers. To Israel's police force and its officers. To the settler public in particular and the broader public in general. The message that the settlement activities in the unauthorised settlements, despite their illegality, are Zionist acts, and thus should be ignored, winked at, is an ambiguous one. The effect of this message is serious, both for the IDF and Israel's police force. (Sasson, 2005, p. 44)

EFFECT OF RECIPROCAL LINKS BETWEEN THE IDF AND THE SETTLERS

The establishment of Jewish settlements in the occupied territories under military control necessarily created a problematic relationship between the IDF officers and the settlers. The latter remained Israeli citizens but managed their lives in an area in which the military, rather than the government, ruled. Basically, a problematic situation arose in which citizens of the state, bound by its laws, inhabited an area not belonging to the state and governed by military rule. The problem increased with the growing friction between the Jewish settlers and their Palestinian neighbors. IDF officers were often forced to intervene. The more time passed, the stronger became the reciprocal links between the IDF and the Jewish settlers in the territories, to the point where the army in many cases carried out settlers' activities. Amos Harel noted that

> the basic origin of the army-settler relationship did not allow separation between the sides. In every army office in the territories, divisional or company, the military aim was formulated: protect the lives of the Israeli civilians. The settlers are not just passive "service recipients," but active partners in the effort—as regular or as reserve soldiers, as GSS [General Security Services] coordinators and border police officers, and as civilians, functioning in emergency squads in the settlements or as security officers of the local councils.... [T]errorist acts against the settlers have increased the soldiers' identification with them. The decision to transfer IDF posts to inside the settlements, in order to protect against the threat of Palestinian infiltration, has blurred even more the differences between soldiers and civilians [w]hile the severity of the threat has obliged the commanding officers to maintain continuous daily contact not only with the security officers but also with the heads of their local councils. (Harel, 2003, p. 12)

One of the negative outcomes of this relationship that developed between the IDF and the settlers was expressed in the decisions by many officers serving in the territories that were influenced by political considerations. Army officers supporting the settlement enterprise and the settlers themselves became the settlement advocates in dealing with the political echelon and the military's commanding officers. "Army officers stressed the closeness of the settlers to the politicians' ears, and their power to influence promotion within the military and beyond it. They came to learn that sticking to the law and to orders from the General Staff was not necessarily the key to a successful career. The politicization of the territories sucked into it the commanders in the territory, who began to speak and act politically. The senior echelon in the IDF appointed officers according to the required qualities" (Eldar & Zartal, 2004, p. 384).

The officers serving in the territories knew that the accessibility of the settlers to the policymakers and the media, and the settlers' increasing willingness to confront the security branches, including the IDF, was a potential threat to their own careers if they could not avoid any confrontation with them (Hofnung, 1991, p. 269).

Army officers are still concerned today about being drawn into conflict with the settlers and their supporters, and the possibility of being stuck with the label "leftist." Service in key roles in the territories during the period of the two *intifadas* became a necessary way station on the route to the General Staff, but for many officers the wish to be on the battlefront was also accompanied by a concern over complications. Many officers knew that stubbornness on the questions of law and legality would classify them as Arab sympathizers. This happened not only to reserve officers but also, for example, to Amram Mitzna, head of the Central Command, in the months preceding the first *intifada*. Furthermore, Lieutenant General (then Brigadier-General) Benny Gantz, commander of the IDF forces in the West Bank at the beginning of the second *intifada*, was smeared simply because the settlers thought that he had not displayed enough initiative in removing hikers who were attacked on Mount Ebal. As brigade commander in the Ramallah area, Colonel (now Brigadier General) Yossi Heiman, who belonged to a religious family, many members of which live in the settlements, dared to stand against the settlers' attitude to the law. The result was a poisonous article against him printed in *Ma'ariv* accusing him of responsibility for the movement of suicide bombers from Ramallah toJerusalem (Harel, 2003). This was also the case of Brigadier General (now Major General) Nitzan Alon, who was the commander of the Judea and Samaria division. The settlers attacked him as a leftist who was against them and who was supporting the Palestinians (Buchbut, 2011). The diplomatic, political, and manipulative skills of the army officers serving in the territories became more important than their ability to command the army units in battle. Indeed, as Eldar and Zartal wrote, "Military service in the territories plunged the uniform-wearers all at once into the endless abyss that separates between occupation and democracy" (2004, p. 375).

The interference of citizen-settlers in military operations is another source of unceasing tension and constant threat to the apolitical status of the army. The destructive ramifications of the daily interaction were described in the *Karp Report* (composed in 1982 by Deputy Attorney General Yehudit Karp on law enforcement in Judea and Samaria), which described cases of the military authorities turning a blind eye to provocations and violent acts of which settlers were suspected (Hofnung, 1991, p. 269). There were even cases in which military government officers gave assistance to settlers acting violently against the Palestinians. The most prominent case was one in which two officers, Captain Shlomo Leviathan and Major Roni Gilo, were convicted of assisting members of the "Jewish underground" to attempt to kill the mayors of towns in the West Bank.(*Haaretz*, April 15, 1986).

With his appointment as Chief of Staff, Raphael Eitan decided to transfer many of the reserve duty soldiers living in the settlements from their reserve units and to deploy them in a defense framework throughout the territories. They received weapons, which they kept at home, and used the IDF installations in the territories. Since then these settlers have become active soldiers, the darlings of the political establishment of the Likud government. The more time that passed, the more the settlers' security demands grew. They demanded that the IDF act according to the policy that they themselves had consolidated, calling, for example, for the deployment of roadblocks in places of their choosing. "The result was that a local armed militia came into being in the territories. A complex relationship was thus created between the settlers and the army. The settlers are dependent on the army to supply weaponry, pay wages and train the local militias, while the army is dependent on the militias as entities whose good will determines how things are managed, whether in accordance with military instructions or in opposition to it" (Levy, 2003, p. 343).

The situation became complicated when the settlers established in 1980 a "security committee" that confronted the army with their security problems. This body won the blessing of the Minister of Defense, Ariel Sharon, who invited its members to participate in military operational discussions of the senior command in the territories. The Western Wall tunnel incident, in September 1996, described below, led to the decision to set up select units from among the settlers. The direct command of these units was given to officers resident in the settlements (Schiff, 1999).

The Hasmonean Tunnel is an extended part of the Western Wall Tunnel and is 20 meters in length, running along the outside of the Temple Mount. During the process of excavation, the Israeli government allowed the opening of a new exit to the tunnel in the area; previously, visitors could walk back from the tunnel only by retracing their steps, and it sparked the Kotel Tunnel Incident.

The Tunnel was opened on the night of September 23, 1996. Palestinians were infuriated when they learned what had happened and were particularly outraged on discovering the proximity of the Temple Mount and the Al-Aqsa Mosque with the new exit. What began as public protests turned into full-fledged armed battles between Palestinians and Israeli forces. The fighting, which started on September 24, lasted until September 28; it was then quelled to some extent before dying down completely. The causalities of this fighting are said to be 100 Palestinians and 15 Israeli soldiers.

In the report she prepared for Prime Minister Sharon, Talia Sasson referred to the IDF's law enforcement in the territories and the willingness of army officers to ignore the settlers' illegal activities:

> IDF soldiers are supposed to deal with security in the territories as their primary mission. The role of Israel's police force is to enforce the law. However, the work of law enforcement frequently falls to the IDF. Legally, it is the commander in the area who has sovereign authority in the territories. It is his consequent and comprehensive responsibility to maintain order and security in the territories. Israel's police force in the district is subordinate to him.... The inclusive responsibility of the IDF pertains not only to formal matters. It is the IDF soldiers who are in the territories—in contrast to the small police force in the district; the IDF is first on the scene when Israelis transgress the law, the police often arrive only later; sometimes, due to security conditions, the police are not even able to reach the scene. Thus, every security event in which IDF soldiers are involved has the potential to turn into a criminal event, and vice versa..... The IDF soldiers have the authority to enforce the law as police, derived from the protocol of law enforcement in the territories incorporated in military orders. In practice, however, the IDF soldiers do not enforce the law, are not familiar with the protocol and are not interested in the least in functioning as policemen. The "spirit of the commander," as described to me, requires that the soldiers will not examine through the eyes of the law the acts of the settlers, who perform a Zionist deed in establishing the settlements, despite the fact that is illegal. This "spirit of the commander" is nourished, among others, by the involvement of State and public authorities in establishing unauthorized settlements. The approach to the settler law-breakers is generally one of tolerance. The outcome of this tolerance is the intensification of such illegal acts. (Sasson, 2005, p. 45)

The result was that IDF offices often preferred to ignore the acts of violence by the settlers. This was also found by the Betzelem investigators:

> In many cases in which soldiers are present during acts of violence by the settlers against Palestinians, they do not attempt to stop or prevent these acts or at least to take the perpetrators' personal details and report to the police. The attempts by the IDF to prevent illegal acts by the settlers against the Palestinian inhabitants or to arrest those who participate in them, if they occur at all, are few and feeble. There are cases in which not only do the soldiers not attempt to stop the violent actions of the settlers, but they themselves are partner to such acts. (Betzelem, 1994, p. 19)

In many cases of violent activity by the settlers the IDF impose movement restrictions, including curfew, on the Palestinian inhabitants, but do not do so on the Jewish inhabitants. This is done to protect the Palestinians from the settlers, but leads to an absurd situation, when restrictions are imposed on the attacked and not on the attacker.... In contradiction to its obligation, the IDF reveals a continuing lack of ability in its dealings with violence by the settlers against Palestinian inhabitants. This inability is not coincidental, but the consequence of the firm connection between the IDF and the settlers. According to the official standpoint, the security forces are the sole responsible body for maintaining order and enforcing the law in the territories. Together with the other branches of the government, the IDF perceives in the settlers a population that contributes greatly to the security and maintenance of public order in the territories, and even cooperates with it officially in its activities.... With the repeated failure of the IDF to react to the settlers' violent acts, despite various and repeated warnings by politicians, journalists and human rights organizations, it can be concluded that these failures are not exceptional, but indicate a comprehensive policy by the IDF. Against the background of this special connection between the IDF and the Jewish inhabitants of the territories, a suspicion arises that this policy is the consequence of a situation in which each of the sides is aware of the contribution of the other to reinforcing the mechanism of Jewish control in the area.... The IDF has continuously failed to impose law upon the settlers in the territories and to protect the lives, the bodies and the properties of the Palestinian inhabitants from various and repeated attacks by Jewish inhabitants. The approach of the IDF toward these displays of violence wavers between 'deliberate non-intervention' and more active forms of cooperation. As long as the IDF adheres to this tolerant and compromising policy, and even active cooperation with those who demonstrate violence, it is actively contributing to the continuation of violent acts. (Betzelem, 1994, p. 19)

On the IDF's turning a blind eye to the settlers' activities, Tali Sasson wrote further:

The IDF soldiers, and even their commanders, see themselves as primarily responsible for ensuring security in the area...the role of law enforcer for the settlers is not perceived as an integral part of the IDF's task...the result is that the soldiers and even their commanders frequently do everything in order to disrobe themselves of the policeman's uniform in which, according to them, they have been artificially clothed. It thus appears that the soldiers are not interested in passing information to the police about the criminal acts that have apparently been carried out in front of them.

They are not interested in reporting the uprooting of 600 olive trees near Yitzhar, carried out over three days adjacent to the IDF unit stationed nearby; and when an IDF officer was commanded to send soldiers in this area to report to the police, he demanded that the Israeli police inform him in advance as to what questions it intended to ask the soldiers, as a precondition for agreeing to their interrogation.... When two caravans arrive at an illegal settlement, an IDF officer arrives at the place and confronts the settlers, ordering that the caravans return to their place of origin. In the end the yarmulke on his head is snatched off and thrown aside; he is beaten up; he refuses to make a complaint but his commander insists that he does. Finally, the settler is brought to court and receives a trifling punishment. When a senior IDF officer receives a slap in the face from a known female settler—he refuses to make a complaint. Such examples are numerous. (Sasson, 2005, p. 258)

As a rule, the IDF soldiers are not interested in being policemen, and even less interested in being part of the conflict between the settlers and the Palestinians over lands and control of the territories; and from the moment that the Palestinian terror activity began—the picture has become even more complex. As I was informed by a senior IDF officer who is very close to the subject—from the nature of things, first they deal with terror and only afterwards (if at all) they deal with settlers' law-breaking.... An additional difficulty lies in transmitting too gentle a message, sometimes transferred by the IDF soldiers regarding the settlers' transgressions, in regard to the soldiers themselves. If in the process of removing the caravans a settler damages the tires of a vehicle belonging to an officer present in the area and who doesn't make a fuss about it—then a message is conveyed to the settlers objecting to the removal, a message that can lead to more serious transgressions the next time that a caravan is removed. If the IDF soldiers allow a caravan to reach its forbidden target, due to their not wishing to confront the settlers—then a message of turning a blind eye is conveyed. When the soldiers arrive to remove the caravans with hammers in their hands and not with tractors—the norm in Israel when destroying illegal structures—a message is conveyed. The result of this tolerant approach to law-breakers is an increase in number of illegal acts, shamelessly, determined, without hesitation. (Sasson, 2005, p. 259)

The most serious aspect in the entire affair of the relations that developed between the IDF and the settlers is that the senior military commanders, including the Chief of Staff, take no firm stand on the matter. They also prefer to ignore those cases in which soldiers and officers are harmed, and do not demand forceful and uncompromising treatment of the settlers who harm them.

THE MILITARY GOVERNMENT AND THE OCCUPIED TERRITORIES

During the more than sixty years of existence of the State of Israel, there has been less than one year in which there was no military government of any sort. Until 1966 there was a military government within the Green Line; for four months there was a military government in Gaza and Sinai, in 1956–1957, following the victory in the Sinai Campaign; and from 1967 a military government has ruled in the territories conquered in the Six Day War. Since the war the IDF has maintained sovereignty in the territories. The commanding officers have become in effect functionaries of a colonial regime. The problem is that some of the senior officers also take pleasure in this role. It is sufficient to recall the photographs of senior officers surrounded by dignitaries from the territories making a pilgrimage to them. This would seem to have conveyed a very pleasant sensation.

Having no other choice, the IDF began to deal with civilian matters. It was the authority in the territory and thus had to deal with all areas of life of the civilian population. The military government dealt with sewage, agriculture, archaeology, and education. Because of the absolute control of the IDF in the territories and the blind belief in the IDF by the political echelon, the government did not always know about everything that the military was doing there. In many cases the army acted in the territories, and still does, in contradiction to what the government had decided.

Having no previous experience in controlling a large non-Israeli civilian population (except for the short episode in Sinai in 1956–1957), the IDF needed to quickly organize a control system in the territories of a clearly civilian nature. In the first weeks after the Six Day War, the division of responsibility between the political echelon and the military was still not completely clear in matters relating to control of the territories' inhabitants.

The statement by the Chief of Staff, Itzhak Rabin, at a meeting of the general staff on June 19, 1967, exemplifies the confusion among the senior command in this regard:

> The organization is very complicated. There are army commanders with full command responsibility for the matter, to establish order, control, etc. There is another matter, a ministerial committee, with an accompanying directorial committee...it constitutes the channel to determine civilian matters such as whether or not to supply flour. It works via army officers, via regional security. In other words, [with] currency exchange value, banks and other matters that we have no experience of dealing with. Now there's a third matter. A political adviser to the Minister of Defense, this

will be General Herzog. A team whose task will be to establish contact with the mayors of towns on the West Bank. It will have a representative from the Foreign Ministry and the Interior Ministry. It will propose political solutions... I don't yet know what they are. They have no authority to give directives. We need to give them authority to engage should any proposal be made and presented to the Prime Minister or anyone. If a directive is given it is to be given as a command via the command channel. (Rosenthal, 2005, p. 518)

The General Staff of the IDF, in the years immediately following the war, saw the task of establishing and activating the military government in the territories as a marginal issue of no particular importance. The IDF also dealt with other new tasks related to military deployment in the occupied territories, and military government was not perceived as a true military task. The result was the deployment of low-quality officers and low-standard army manpower to fulfill the tasks of the civilian government. Shlomo Gazit, the first coordinator of activities in the territories, wrote: "Following the Six Day War the load on the IDF officers and the General Staff increased. The [military] government was lowest on the list of preferences and the General Staff accordingly did its best not to appoint the best officers to the system. The officers themselves were concerned that their appointment to such roles might, in time, harm their promotion within the military." The result was, as expected, that the military government functioned at a low level of efficiency, leading more than once to problematic relations developing between the conquering army and the inhabitants in the territories.

Despite initial attempts to fill important positions in the military government with senior civil servants (e.g., the head of the economics branch and the head of the administrative and services branch), senior functionaries in the government ministries refused to cooperate, and the IDF was forced to give its officers these roles, which were clearly of a civilian nature. What contributed further to the military takeover of the civilian posts was the fact that the Minister of Defense, Moshe Dayan, reduced his direct involvement in appointing key people to important posts in the military government. For senior members of the General Staff this was a good solution. "It was convenient for them to work with army people, particularly in anything relating to discipline and establishing authority. From lack of alternative they were forced to appoint mediocre personnel to these posts" (Gazit, 1985, pp. 75–76).

Military personnel thus became representatives of the civilian government in the territories. Their direct responsibility was, of course, to the General Staff and the Chief of Staff, not to the relevant government ministry. The policy decided upon by Minister of Defense Dayan shortly after the war—a policy according to which the IDF would be responsible for the security aspect of actions in the territories but not for the content or nature of activity by the government ministries, each in its own area—was thus doomed to failure. In effect, it was the IDF that consolidated policy in the territories regarding civilian matters, with government ministries maintaining minimal involvement. The unavoidable consequence was the creation of a policy in the territories based on military considerations, even when the issues at stake were civilian.

Nor did IDF officers hesitate to exploit military resources in order to finance the settlers' needs. For example, the head of the Central Command, Rehavam Ze'evi, budgeted money from the Head of Command Fund in order to finance the wedding celebration of a NAHAL member, Israeli Nadivi (Eladar & Zartal, 2004, p. 380).

The head of Central Command was actively responsible not only for managing the lives of the inhabitants of the West Bank but also for the settlement there. The commanders had complete freedom of action in regard to the settlements and made major decisions without involving the government. For example, the declaration by the head of the Karnei Shomron council in July 1999 appeared perfectly normal: according to him, Moshe Ya'alon, as the commander of Central Command, had authorized the addition of 2000 dunams of land to the settlement (Shelah, 2003, p. 100).

THE EFFECT OF ACTIVITY IN THE TERRITORIES AND THE FIGHT AGAINST TERROR ON THE PREPARATION FOR WAR

As a result of the Six Day War, an additional effect on military thinking and on the actions of the senior command was the need to fight terror or guerrilla warfare in the territories. The intensification of military actions in the territories in routine security matters, particularly following the outbreak of the second *intifada,* at the close of 2000, led to the neglect of preparations for an all-out war. The senior command decided that preparing the army for such a war was less pressing, and that "nothing was urgent" and military matters could be dealt with in the future. The IDF therefore neglected training and the maintenance of stocks of the necessary equipment for a major war. In parallel, arrogance raised its head once more. This time the derided rival was the Hizbullah. The second *intifada* forced the IDF to allocate regular divisions and even to call up reservists to protect the settlements in the territories. An IDF report revealed that about 600 soldiers were engaged in guarding the settlers and thereby precluded from any other military activity.

In 2005 the army, following a prolonged internal discussion, consolidated a new approach (military doctrine). This approach gave precedence to the threat of terror over that of conventional war and stressed the component of firepower over that of maneuvers and occupying a territory. Moreover, extensive organizational changes took place in the structure of the army (Golan, 2008). The Vinograd Committee, which investigated the Second Lebanon War, pointed out the implications of this new approach:

> The IDF's new doctrine was supposed to provide a suitable answer also to a state of all-out war, to its traditional components, as well as to a restricted conflict in the framework of what was called low-intensity fighting against armed sub-State factors. Due to the circumstances, first the reduced concrete threat of war against the Arab States and then the intensified armed confrontation with the Palestinians (the *intifada* within the territories), the main emphasis was placed on developing and applying a new approach to this asymmetrical, restricted fighting, while attempting to find answers through a buildup of forces and their activation.
>
> We are certain that this new approach created problems in the IDF in the period prior to the War in Lebanon. The idea that a final victory could be achieved by finding indirect and effective levers as a substitute for the classic method of conquering and controlling and destroying... the concept of the new approach assumed that the use of accurate firepower combined with maneuverability would be activated at every level of the battle. (Vinograd Commission, 2007, p. 49)

This statement expresses part of the army's stagnation. Many officers who participated in the war did not understand what it was about, but they kept quiet. For how could they not understand what these "levers" were? Indeed, many orders and speeches were not understood by the commanders or the ordinary troops in the battlefield.

The control of the territories and the need to combat terror led to failed thinking among the senior commanders, who devoted most of their professional attention to events in the territories and to terrorist activities (i.e., at the tactical level) and ignored the need to consolidate an approach to war at the strategic level too.

The result, as noted, was expressed in the IDF's failure in the Second Lebanon War. The IDF was an army whose thinking had frozen. "[M]oreover," wrote two investigators who analyzed the failures in this war,

> as proven by the Israeli air force's destruction of the long-range rocket system in the first two days of the war, the IDF had in its possession detailed

information on the *Hizbullah's* military deployment. Nonetheless, despite the details being known, its significance does not seem to have been internalized. And if it was internalized, it was not acted upon. In the years 2000 to 2006, the IDF was mired in fighting terror in Judea and Samaria, new approaches were developed to deal with this threat, and an entire operational culture was developed to respond to the unique conditions in the territories. The Lebanon arena and the constant threat from the *Hizbullah* were, from the IDF viewpoint, of second priority. The War in Lebanon served from this viewpoint as a significant watershed for the IDF in comprehending the nature of the threat, its force, significance and the operational response that needed to be developed in order to deal with it. (Siboni & Kulik, 2009, p. 58)

The flaws in perception, the stagnation of thinking, and the effect of activity in the territories were also attested to by the then Deputy Chief of Staff during the period of the Second War in Lebanon, General Moshe Kaplinsky:

Following the increasing terror the understanding has gradually crept into our awareness that if we don't start dealing with the wave of suicide terrorists, this may well prove to be an existential threat to Israel. The IDF in these years has done what was required to contain this phenomenon... among others it was decided to redeploy all the regular forces to the continuing fight against terror, as well as to divert resources to this fight, both at the expense of long-term reinforcements and the neglect of war-reserve-stores unit... we thus stressed the operational issue and surgical actions at the expense of large-scale actions with the participation of a large number of troops... as part of this operational culture we also demanded of our divisional commanders that they operate from the rear. Perhaps it was there that we created what was later termed by the public "the plasma commanders"... as unlike in the past, when fighting the suicide terrorists, the army effectively ceased to train... the combination of these two factors, fighting terror and repeated and changing security budget cutbacks, and their effect on the army's training program, led to the IDF arriving in Lebanon unprepared for its task. The squad commanders had not received centralized training. Officers who since their enlistment had dealt only with fighting terrorism in the territories found themselves in Lebanon for the first time leading a full complement of troops without having undergone training with their troops. Regimental commanders who had never led a tank regiment were sent to Lebanon; and there were reserve units that for six years had never performed a live exercise... our first error or failure as commanders was in the lack of our overall success... to change the approach or the public opinion, but mainly within the army. We failed to clarify, and perhaps did not ourselves understand to various extents, that the conflict with *Hizbullah* was not a direct continuation of the routine actions that we had carried out in Judea and Samaria during the six years prior to the war, but that it itself was war. (Kaplinsky, 2009, pp. 19–23)

Clearly, the operational readiness of an armored corps that dealt with roadblocks diminished their declared military role, and an infantry brigade that did not carry out brigade exercises for two or three years, due to its dealings with the territories, hindered its functioning when called to engage in war. The Second Lebanon War witnessed arrogance in confronting Hizbullah, a lack of equipment, neglect of the home front, confusion and turmoil among the senior command, and hesitation in deploying the forces. All of these factors are largely connected to the negative effects of the victory in the Six Day War.

SUMMARY

Paradoxically, the IDF's impressive military victory in the Six Day War and the prolonged occupation that followed it sowed the seeds of the evil that followed, and their negative effect continues to the present time. The victory in war was a pyrrhic victory, leading the army from bad to worse. As Avner Yaniv wrote:

> Large armies and complex bureaucratic bodies [do] not generally tend to[ward] innovation; they sanctify by their very structure stagnation and deter their subordinates from unorthodox thinking. It is thus also predictable when there are no great achievements by the system in which to boast, and even more so when there are even greater achievements, such as those by the IDF before it had even celebrated its 20th anniversary. From this aspect one of the worst things that can happen to an army—to any army, including the IDF—is a crushing and seemingly effortless victory. (Yaniv, 1994, pp. 214–215).

Indeed, this "worst thing" was what happened to the IDF. It won an incontestably crushing victory. The consequence was stagnated thinking among the senior command and a focus on the tactical level while neglecting strategic thinking. Between the Six Day War and the Yom Kippur War the IDF employed a very successful military tactic with its forces, but this only encouraged the tendency to ignore the need to consolidate a strategic approach. Military thinking thus became "schematic, stagnated, full of contradictions and the assumption that it was equally valid for other times and under other hostile conditions, territories and arenas" (Yaniv, 1994, p. 241).

The schematic military thinking was expressed in the fact that although Israel's borders had expanded sufficiently to provide strategic depth, the decision makers in the IDF continued to think in terms of a small country under siege that could not allow itself an operational or even tactical retreat. Instead of exploiting the Sinai area to plan a mobile defense strategy, employing the new strategic depth, the IDF established an Israeli "Maginot line" along the banks of the Suez Canal. The extent of this stagnated thinking is attested to in a statement by General Avraham Adan, one of the architects of the Bar-Lev line, who stated at a meeting of the General Staff that "I planned the fortifications according to the compact model of Nirim [the small settlement in the Negev that had been attacked by the Egyptians on May 15, 1948]" (Golani, 2002, p. 213).

These negative implications for the IDF were increased by the fact that it had been abruptly transformed from a fighting army into an army also sovereign over a conquered territory populated by 1 million inhabitants deprived of citizenship. As soon as the occupation began, the IDF was forced to swiftly consolidate, without prior preparation, a system of military government with all of its civilian components. Generals became governors and were forced to deal with problems they were not trained to solve.

The daily work of enacting laws in the territories was also carried out by the IDF. This was done by directives issued by the local military commanders who, according to international law, were authorized to enact laws. The longer the Israeli occupation of the territories went on, the greater was the spread of laws enacted by military commanders, including those in areas affecting the inhabitants' way of life. This enactment of laws by the military created a situation in which the basic values of legislation, such as equality before the law and constancy of law, did not exist. There was no equality between Jews and Palestinians in the territories. The IDF also became a patron of the Jewish settlers in the territories, and in many cases collaborated—whether openly or by turning a blind eye—with the violent actions of these settlers against the Palestinians.

The control over another people who were in search of a national identity quickly led to conflict between the IDF and the Palestinians, which began with mob disorder and developed into terrorist actions. The army was thus forced to allocate many resources to police duties: enforcing order in the territories and battling against terror in the territories and against their occupants, who had also begun to carry out actions within Israel itself. The terror intensified with the outbreak of the first *intifada* in December 1987, increasing with the *Al Aksa intifada* in September 2000. The friction between the IDF troops in the territories and the Palestinians, consisting mainly of the IDF actions against the

Palestinians during the two *intifadas*, led to the engagement of an increasing number of soldiers in irregular actions, including beating up civilians, abusing prisoners, destroying property, looting the houses that they were searching, and so on (Betzelem, 2001, 2002, 2007).

To all this should be added the negative effect on the behavior of the soldiers at the roadblocks set up throughout the West Bank and the negative implications of implementing curfews or closures on the behavior of the troops in the territories. The unavoidable consequence was the development of obtuseness, iniquity, and corruption.

The allocation of so many resources to activities in the territories came at the expense of preparation for war. Training was neglected, new theories of combat were not developed, and the senior command was once again characterized by stagnant thinking. The flawed functioning of the army in the Second Lebanon War was a prominent expression of all these failures.

Furthermore, the IDF became a key player in the process of settlement in the territories. In this area the army began to engage in political thinking while providing support and legitimization, including testimony in court, to the political echelon, whose decisions regarding the settlement were not based on security considerations. Senior officers became major settlers in the territories, and later also supported the flouting of the law by the settlers who set up the illegal settlements.

As time passed, the IDF developed the doctrine that settlement in the occupied territories answered a security need even beyond that of its military importance in supplying strategic depth. The continued control of the territories became an aim in itself, as each evacuation from the territory, even of a solitary outpost, could be perceived by the Palestinians as Israeli weakness. When the Chief of Staff announced that the evacuation of an isolated settlement, such as Netzarim (in the Gaza Strip), signaled a weakness that could strengthen the Palestinian enemy, this led to an ever tighter link between the ideological perception of the settlement in the territories and security. The evacuation of any such occupied area was considered the equivalent of an IDF declaration of defeat; it was interpreted, along with relinquishing occupied territory (however small), as "putting wind in the sails of terror" (Shelah, 2003, p. 106). The senior command therefore also objected to the peace agreement with Egypt, which included returning the Sinai; to the Oslo Accords, which meant giving up most of the West Bank; and to the separation plan, which included giving up settlement in the Gaza Strip.

The Six Day War was a continuation of the path of force chosen by Israel, which had peaked sometime between 1967 and 1973. Israel had celebrated the victory of force, whose faithful servant was the IDF. The uniqueness of the 1967 war lay in its considering Israel's path of force, which had been the established approach since 1956, as something to be proud of. A catchphrase coined by the Chief of Staff, Haim Bar-Lev, that "[we will win] fast, strong, and elegantly" offered a sharp, clear description of the reality perceived by most Israelis (Golani, 2002, pp. 205–206). Ironically, it was precisely Bar-Lev's term as Chief of Staff that witnessed the decline in the IDF toward an army that was "slow, very forceful and inelegant." The negative influence of the IDF's 1967 victory in war, with the consequent occupation of the territories, has continued to exact a high price to this day.

THE ISRAELI OCCUPATION AND OTHER OCCUPATIONS–COMPARATIVE VIEW

The effects of the lasting occupation of the Palestinian territories on the Israeli society and army are not unique. Studies show that similar effects and impacts, on societies and armies, occur in other cases of colonial occupation.

The most widely researched case, with similarities to the Israeli situation, is the lasting occupation of Algeria by France. Observers, researchers, participants, and intellectuals find significant parallels between the two cases, emphasizing the impacts of the occupation on the morality, ethics, and integrity of the French and Israeli societies and armies.

On May 9, 2002, Tony Judt, professor of history at New York University, began an essay on Palestinian resistance to Israeli occupation with a quote from Raymond Aron's book on the 1954–1962 Algerian War of Independence from French colonial rule (Aron, 1958). France, Aron argued, could not impose its administration on the Algerians indefinitely, nor was it willing to integrate them into French society. Until they left Algeria, Aron argued, the French were harming themselves more than the Algerians (Gallagher, 2002, p. 44).

Aron's observation of the French case can be applied fully to the Israeli case. Like France, Israel cannot impose its administration on the Palestinians indefinitely, nor is it willing to integrate them into Israeli society. Paraphrasing Aron's conclusion, we can state that as long as Israel remains an occupier, "the Israelis are harming themselves more than the Palestinians."

Referring to the similarity between the Israeli and French cases, Judt concludes his essay with a rhetoric question: "De Gaulle pulled France out of Algeria. Why can't the Israelis realize the inevitable and do the same?" According to Judt, the lesson is clear. An occupation has negative effects on a democratic society—any democratic society. These negative effects will lead eventually to an inevitable decision to end the occupation and leave the occupied territories.

Andrew Mack, the director of the Human Security Centre at the University of British Columbia, also compares the Palestinian and Algerian struggles. Mack reveals that Israeli Prime Minister Ariel Sharon "was reading Alistair Horne's magisterial account of the Algerian conflagration, 'A Savage War of Peace.'" Mack asks if Israel might not have reached the same point as France, when the political, social, and economic price of continuing its colonial project became too high to justify. He sadly concludes, "Israel's tragedy is that Ariel Sharon is no Charles de Gaulle" (Mack, 2002, p. C3).

Mack is right, of course. Sharon is no de Gaulle. But it seems that Sharon, like other Israeli politicians, recognized the similarity between France's and Israel's experience as occupiers.

There is another observation, which allows us to generalize on the effects of a lasting occupation on the armies of the colonial states. It seems that the process by which the army becomes a political player is inevitable. It happened in Israel and it happened in France. The armies that rule the occupied territories design their own policies, based on what their commanders see as the army's interests, in many cases ignoring the orders and directives of the political echelon.

"The army of France broke a long tradition of political abstention and overtly intervened in French political life in May 1958," concludes Menard in an article dealing with the relations between the army and the state (Menard, 1964, p. 123).

The French army in Algeria, argue Sutton and Lawless, ignored the directives of civilian authorities (Sutton & Lawless, 1978, pp. 331–350).

At the end of the 1950s, the French army devised its own policy regarding the future of Algeria. Contrary to the official policy of the de Gaulle's administration, which planned the evacuation of Algeria, "To the army the 'most French solution' meant only one thing: the defeat of the FLN followed by a policy of 'integration' whereby, in fact as well as in constitutional language, Algeria would become a part of France, 'a province like Alsace or Britanny'" (Kelly, 1964, p. 335).

The same pattern, of generals who devise their own policy regarding the future of the occupied territories, can be detected in the Israeli case, as expressed in the meeting of the general staff on December 27, 1967 (as indicated above).

The next development in the relationship between the government and the army in France was the political echelon's growing skepticism about the loyalty of the army. "By 1958, and even well before the coming of the de Gaulle regime," observes Kelly, "the French Army, long trained to submit to civilian command and operate discreetly within a penumbra of silence, had not only discovered language but the gift of speaking with many tongues. The *grande muette* of former times had become an incorrigible *grande bavarde*, spewing its pent-up feelings about politics, doctrine, and, above all, Algeria at an insouciant public, a scandalized regime, and a restricted but fascinated international audience. This served to confuse the problem of loyalty and discipline still further and to confirm frustrated elements of the service in the political vocation they had chosen... For the army, on the other hand, not only was de Gaulle's mixed entourage distasteful, but there was something fundamental, nothing empirical or negotiable, about Algeria" (Kelly, 1964, p. 337).

There was a good reason for the politicians to be skeptical about the loyalty of the senior army officers. The French officers (like their counterparts in Israel) interpreted the official policy from their own point of view, which was not necessarily compatible with that of the politicians. Paillat describes the way the senior officers of the French army interpreted de Gaulle's policy. "When General de Gaulle posed the three alternatives of 'independence,' 'francization,' and 'association' in his famous self-determination speech of September 19, 1959, with a scarcely disguised preference for the last, no implementing directives followed the declaration. Colonel Gardes, Chief of Psychological Action, launched an immediate campaign for 'integration' (the more usual word for the second option) with the conditional approval of General Challe. Before a month had passed he was abruptly called to order by M. Paul Delouvrier, the Minister-Delegate. Hints had been received from Paris: don't go too strong on the second solution. But hints were all: a succession of critical events passed, and still the equivocation was never entirely dissolved" (Paillat, 1961, p. 298).

But the army went even further in its attempts to determine the France's policy in Algeria, as Menard explains. "The army of the Fifth Republic attempted to use its newly found political power to influence elections in its Algerian fief, and as de Gaulle's liberal policy towards Algeria evolved, the army endeavored to veto that policy" (Menard, 1964, 123).

When an army controls the occupied territory (like the French army in Algeria and the Israeli army in the West Bank) its commanders can conceal information from the decision makers, who depend entirely on this information. By doing so, the army can lead the government to make decisions furthering the army's interests. "It seems also that the government lacked, at critical moments," concludes Kelly, "the precise information it needed to deal with the bewildering complexity of the Algerian affair. At the outbreak of the barricades insurrection M. Debré [Michel Jean-Pierre Debré, Prime Minister of the Fifth Republic. He served under President Charles de Gaulle from 1959 to 1962] was forced to make a hurried and emotional night journey to Algiers to form an on-the-spot impression of the balance of forces despite the fact that numerous military and political consultations had been held in Paris prior to his departure" (Kelly, 1964, p. 342).

It seems that the impact of a lasting occupation on the army is the inclination to intervene in the government's policy and to become a political player. Menard finds this phenomenon, which we can trace in France of the 1950s and in Israel in the last four decades (both are "advanced states") very interesting. "The noteworthy factor in the political activity of the French army is in finding a political army in an advanced state. Such armies are generally associated with politically underdeveloped nations where the differentiation of political roles is poorly marked. Under these conditions, the crossing of institutional borders by an army to enter the political pastures occasions less surprise than in the state where the military and political bournes are clearly established and respected. However, France, an advanced state [like Israel] with a long tradition of military abstention from political involvement, found itself confronted with eager praetorians" (Menard, 1964, p. 124).

We can also detect the impact of the armies' activities (of France, Israel, and also Great Britain) in the occupied territory on the political and legal systems, and, of course, on the armies themselves. These armies had to wage war against terrorists (in Algeria, in the West Bank and Gaza, and in Ireland, respectively). It became evident that in this war the army was not refraining from using torture. Using of torture became an open secret, and the legal systems ignored these illegal acts. "French justice in Algeria had become the corrupt handmaiden of an army whose political power had grown to ominous proportions," concludes one researcher (Vidal-Naquet, 1963, p. 142).

It seems that using torture is the common denominator of armies that rule over an occupied population that uses terrorist acts to resist the occupation. A detailed description of the French army's behavior in Algeria and its policy of torture can be found in many sources (Campbell, 2005; Gallagher, 2002; Horne, 2006; Obuchowski, 1968; Servan-Schreiber, 1977; Sutton, 1999)

Even the British military, which "has remained under the firm control of civilian authorities" (Campbell, 2005, p. 2), used torture in its war against the Irish Republican Army activists. "Clearly, even a cursory examination of the British record in Northern Ireland since 1969," says Campbell, "reveals instances of illegality, brutality, and coverup" (ibid., p. 4).

Also worth mentioning is the price that colonial democracies pay for their armies' illegal activities, which become the standard operating procedure. "But at what price?" asked Campbell when he analyzed the impact of the torture in Algeria on French society and its political system. "Although torture and murder occurred throughout the war, following the operations in Algiers, such actions became systematic and even institutionalized. From then on, with the tacit approval of the government, the French Army consistently relied on these methods in all its dealings with the FLN" (Campbell, 2005, p. 4).

Horne describes the negative effects of the torture policy on the French army and on French society. This negative influence, he writes, "lasted many years after the Algerian war ended" (Horne, 1989, p. 215.) Probably the most appropriate observation of the negative effects of the illegal acts of occupying armies belongs to Vidal-Naquet, who defines torture by the army as the "Cancer of Democracy" (Vidal-Naquet, 1963).

REFERENCES

Admoni, Y. (1992). *A decade of reasoning*. Tel Aviv: Hakibbutz Hameuchad (in Hebrew).
Alon, Y. (1959). *A curtain of sand*. Tel Aviv: Hakibbutz Hameuchad (in Hebrew).
Aron, R. (1958). *Algérie et la République*. Paris: Plon.
Asher, D. (2003). *Breaking the concept*. Tel Aviv: Maarachot (in Hebrew).
Bartov, H. (1979). *Daddo—48 years and 20 more days*. Tel Aviv: Maariv (in Hebrew).
Ben-Dor, G. (2009). The degeneration of the Israeli security concept thinking following the Six Day War. In E. Lavi (Ed.), *40 years of ruling the territories* (pp. 93–103). Tel Aviv: Tel Aviv University (in Hebrew).
Betzelem. (1994). Law enforcement upon Israeli civilians. *Jerusalem*: R. Rosen (Author; in Hebrew). Retrived May 15, 2012, from www.btselem.org/hebrew/publications/.../199403_law_Enforcement
Betzelem. (2001, May). *Routing actions—Beatings and abuse of Palestinians by armed forces during the al-Aqsa Intifda*. Jerusalem: Y. Stein (in Hebrew). Retrieved May 15, 2012, from:www.btselem.org/download/200105_standard_routine_heb.doc
Betzelem. (2002, December 3). *Abusing Palestinians in Hebron* (in Hebrew). Retrieved May 15, 2012, from http://www.btselem.org/Download/200212_Hebron_Barbershop_Abuse_Heb.pdf
Betzelem. (2007, December). *Human rights situation in the occupied territories: 2007 annual report* (in Hebrew). Retrieved May 15, 2012, from http://www.btselem.org/Download/200712_Annual_Report_Heb.pdf
Buchbut, A. (2011, December 15). Brigadier General Alon will be the head of the Central Command. *Walla*. Retrieved May 15, 2012, from http://news.walla.co.il/?w=/2689/1885783
Campbell, J. D. (2005, March–April). French Algeria and British Northern Ireland: Legitimacy and the rule of law in low-intensity conflict. *Military Review, 85*, 2–5.
Dapei Elazar. (1982). Tel Aviv: Amikam (in Hebrew).
Dayan, M. (1982). *Milestones*. Jerusalem: Idanim (in Hebrew).
Eldar, A., & Zartal, I. (2004). *Lords of the land*. Tel-Aviv: Dvir (in Hebrew).

Gallagher, N. (2002, Winter). Learning lessons from the Algerian war of independence. *Middle East Report, 225,* 44–49.
Gazit, S. (1985). *The stick and the carrot.* Tel Aviv: Zmora Bitan (in Hebrew).
Golan, E. (2008, March 9). The failure of the army. The responsibility of the politicians. *New Horizons, 42,* 76–79 (in Hebrew).
Golani, M. (2002). *Wars don't just happen.* Tel Aviv: Modan (in Hebrew).
Gordon, S. (2008). *Thirty hours in October.* Tel Aviv: Maariv (in Hebrew).
Guy, C. (1998). *Bar-Lev.* Tel Aviv: Am Oved (in Hebrew).
Harel, A. (2003, September 26). The IDF in the service of the settlers. *Haaretz,* p.17 (in Hebrew).
High Court of Justice. (1972). 302/72. Sheich Suleiman Hussein Uda Against the Government of Israel (in Hebrew).
High Court of Justice. (1978). 606/78. Sulieman Tawafiq and Others Against the Minister of Defense and others (in Hebrew).
High Court of Justice. (1979). 390/79. Izat Muhamad Mustafa Daweikat and 16 Others Against the Government of Israel, the Minister of Defense, and Others (in Hebrew).
Hofnung, M. (1991). *Israel – Security needs vs. the rule of law.* Jerusalem: Nevo (in Hebrew).
Horne, A. (1989) *A savage war of peace.* Tel Aviv: Maarachot (in Hebrew).
Horowitz, D. (1985). The permanent and the dynamic in Israel's security doctrine. In A. Yariv (Ed.), *War by choice* (pp. 57–115). Tel Aviv: Hakibbutz Hameuchad (in Hebrew).
Kaplinsky, M. (2009, October). The IDF in the years before the war. *Military and Strategy, 1*(2), 19–23 (in Hebrew).
Kelly, G. A. (1964, September). Algeria, the army, and the Fifth Republic (1959–1961): A scenario of civil-military conflict. *Political Science Quarterly, 79*(3), 335–359.
The Knesset Minutes. (1968, June 12). Vol. 52 (in Hebrew).
Levy, Y. (2003). *The other army of Israel.* Tel Aviv: Yediot Acharonot (in Hebrew).
Mack, A. (2002, May 7). Sharon's Algerian shadow. *Globe and Mail.* Retrieved May 15, 2012, from http://www.theglobeandmail.com/news/opinions/sharona-algerian-shadow/article460243
Menard, O. (1964, Autumn). The French army above the state. *Military Affairs, 28*(3), 123–129.
Nadel, C. (2006). *Between the two wars.* Tel Aviv: Maarachot (in Hebrew).
Obuchowski, C. W. (1968). Algeria: The tortured conscience. *The French Review, 42*(1), 90–103.
Pedatzur, R. (1990, March 16). Young goats that became he-goats. *Haaretz,* p. B1 (in Hebrew).
Pedatzur, R. (1996). *The triumph of embarrassment.* Tel Aviv: Bitan (in Hebrew).
Peres, S. (1965). *The next step.* Tel Aviv: Am Hasefer (in Hebrew).
Paillat, C. (1961). *Le dossier secret de l'Algerie.* Paris: Presses de la cite (in French).

Rabin, Y. (1977). *Service notebook*. Tel Aviv: Maariv (in Hebrew).
Rosenthal, Y. (Ed.). (2005). *Yitzhak Rabin, prime minister of Israel, 1974–1977 and 1992–1995*. Jerusalem: State Archives (in Hebrew).
Sasson, T. (2005, March). *Opinion on unauthorized settlement, submitted to Prime Minister Sharon* (in Hebrew). Retrieved September 26, 2009, from http://www.pmo.gov.il/NR/rdonlyres/0A0FBE3C-C741-46A6-8CB5-F6CDC042465D/0/sason2.pdf
Schiff, Z. (1999, August 9). Fear of a political army. *Haaretz*, p. B1 (in Hebrew).
Servan-Schreiber, J.-J. (1977) *Lieutenant in Algeria*. Wesport, CT: Greenwood Press.
Shelah, O. (2003). *The Israeli: A radical proposal*. Tel Aviv: Kineret, Zmora-Bitan (in Hebrew).
Siboni, G., & Kulik, A. (2009). Summary—The second Lebanon War as a watershed. *Military and Strategy*, 1(2), 55–60 (in Hebrew).
Sutton, K. (1999, November). Army administration tensions over Algeria's Centres de Regroupement, 1954–1962. *British Journal of Middle Eastern Studies*, 26(2), 243–270.
Sutton, K., & Lawless, R. I. (1978). Population regrouping in Algeria: Traumatic change and the rural settlement pattern. *Transactions* (Institute of British Geographers), 3, 331–350
Tal, I. (1996). *National security—Few against the many*. Tel Aviv: Dvir (in Hebrew).
Tevet, S. (1969). *The curse of the blessing*. Tel Aviv: Schoken (in Hebrew).
Vidal-Naquet, P. (1963). *Torture: Cancer of democracy. France and Algeria 1954–62*. Harmondsworth: Penguin Books.
Vinograd Commission. (2007, April). *The commission of inquiry into the events of military engagement in Lebanon 2006, preliminary report* Jerusalem: Government Printing Office (in Hebrew).
Yaniv, A. (1994). *Politics and strategy in Israel*. Tel Aviv: Sifriat Poalim (in Hebrew).

CHAPTER 7

Intradomestic Bargaining Over the Lands and the Future: Israel's Policy Toward the 1967 Occupied Territories

Gideon Doron and Maoz Rosenthal[1,2]

INTRODUCTION

Following the 1967 war, Israel has settled a large proportion of the Jewish population in areas formerly occupied by Egypt, Syria, and Jordan. From Egypt, Israel had captured the desert known as the Sinai Peninsula and the densely populated Gaza Strip; from Syria, the eastern shore of the Sea of Galilee and the mountain ridge surrounding it (i.e., the Golan Heights); and from Jordan, the area between the Jordan River and the so-called Green Line (i.e., the armistice line agreed to by Israel and Jordan in 1949). This last area is known in Israel as "Judea and Samaria" or the "occupied territories" and elsewhere as the "West Bank." Within the West Bank there were, in 2007, over 2 million Palestinian-Arab residents next to about 300,000 Jews living in separate settlements.[3]

The settlement project in these territories presents myriad policy paradoxes. It is not formally supported by Israeli government policies but its interests are represented in the Israeli parliament (the Knesset) and in the government by parties known as the "radical Right." Since the early 1980s these parties have featured on the political map, showing a volatile tendency to unite, break up, and re-form parties. Their main and often only issue is the settling of Jews in the West Bank. However, when governments become resolute about conducting talks with the Palestinians and about withdrawals from these territories, such moves take place with little if any consideration of the settlers' interests. Hence, in the Israeli context, radical Right parties have become partisan veto players (Tsebelis, 2002) in right-wing governments. As such, they can bargain for budgets for their favored policy goals (the settlement project). When these governments are reshuffled and center-left parties enter, however, and policymakers become less resolute in supporting the settlements or, even, support their evacuation, then they lose this position of power as well as access to government budgets. This phenomenon reflects the bargaining perspective of public policymaking in democracies (Doron & Sened, 2001). It assumes that the cohesiveness and resoluteness of policy processes depend on the institutional and partisan veto players involved in these processes as part of the ruling coalition. Obviously, such players will either veto an undesired policy process or alter it to coincide with their wishes; or else they will veto either its design as a policy or its implementation (Cox & McCubbins, 2001; Tsebelis, 2002). The stability of the ruling coalition and the gains for its members depend on the ability of those members to obtain payoffs through the bargaining process. Such a process may appear in different forms and contexts, but its outcomes depend on conflict and strategy as much as on the structural rules of the game (Doron & Sened, 2001).

This account shows how Israeli Prime Ministers, acting in the context of a parliamentary multiparty system, must function to sustain their coalition and decrease the likelihood of conflict and friction with the United States over policy issues. The United States has usually encouraged Israel, using varying levels of pressure, to withdraw from the territories, including evacuating the settlements. Because the United States is considered to be Israel's main strategic ally, this small Middle Eastern country has been sensitive to signals coming from the United Stated regarding the settlement policy (Bar-Siman-Tov, 1998). As long as the pressure is not too strong, Israeli prime ministers who are considered to have a right-wing orientation include the radical Right in their governments and give them the position of a partisan veto player. In such situations, state funding to the settlements increases.

However, when international pressure is too strong to resist, then all the prime ministers concede to U.S. demands. Either because of their long-term ideological perspective or because of their sensitivity to their voters, the radical-right parties, however, must maintain their campaign promises or else they will not be reelected. Hence, they will need to quit the government. Thus, although radical right-wing parties are able to transfer budgets to the settlements when they are in power, they cannot acquire a permanent veto position over settlement evacuation. This, unintentionally, creates a different veto dilemma for them: that of who will implement the evacuation—the Israeli political Right or the Israeli political Left?

Hence, the settlement project is sustained by a combination of macrostructures and microinterests. As in many other complex political ventures, the praxis of analysis is to understand the combination of these two: the analysis of macrostructures as creating a set of incentives and principal-agent relations at the micro level that can sustain the general framework (Bates, Grief, Levi, Rosenthal, & Weingast,1998). In the following discussion we contextualize the research problem; present the developments, changes, and outcomes of the Israeli radical Right since 1967; and conclude with a summary of our arguments.

CONTEXTUALIZING THE PROBLEM: THE SALIENCE OF THE SETTLEMENT PROJECT ISSUE IN THE ISRAELI POLICY SPACE

The source of political issues that characterize political systems and the discourse that emanates from within them is not always clear (Riker, 1980). Once political issues become relevant, however, they coincide with clear political position that divide the political players and reveal their location between the two poles of Right and Left. Such divisions allow political players to become distinct, attract voters, and allocate budgets to specific causes as they interact within the institutions to which they have been elected (Austen-Smith & Banks, 1988). In the Israeli case, it was an exogenous event that changed the political space by introducing a new issue: the 1967 war, in which Israel occupied several territories won from Arab countries, territories that included a Palestinian civilian population. Almost immediately after the war, the policy issue arose concerning whether Jewish civilians should be settled in these territories (see also the chapter by Pedatzur in this volume). As we show below, this issue interacted with the most salient political positions in the Israeli policy space, which had defined Israel's political friends and foes from the pre-state era until the 1967 war.

As a consequence of this new issue, political players started defining themselves with respect to it. As is often the case with new issues in political systems, its entry led to the emergence of new political loyalties, gradually creating the policy space that defines the Israeli polity to this day (Arian & Shamir, 2008). Such shifts in loyalties were, for instance, reflected in traditional supporters of the Labor movement who started to support civilian settlements in these territories. In general, these players had supported statist socialism in a line that should have located them in a left-wing position on the socioeconomic sphere, along with leftist groups that had originally opposed the occupation from its outset and now support the settlement project (Doron, 2005). Their new loyalties, however, defined them as members of the same political camp as the traditional spokesmen of Israel's Right (Naor, 2005a). The Jewish Orthodox, who perceived Israel as the beginning of the redemption of the Jewish people, realized through sovereignty, occupation, and the settlements, were supposed to be strong supporters of civilian settlement in the occupied territories. However, some of them strongly objected to both the occupation and the settlements, fearing that they would create an antidemocratic state that would destroy the vision of a Jewish-democratic state (Leibowitz & Egan, 1986). Moreover, it seems that even within the more solid political blocs, the way political parties related to this topic was tentative and contextual, mainly seeking political leverage within the possibilities at that time afforded by the political set of opportunities (Doron, 2005).

During the 1970s and 1980s this issue interacted with two major divisions. The secular-religious division relates to the interaction between state and society. This is essentially reflected by one side claiming that the state should be based on religion, while the other side claims that the state should not interfere in religious issues. Traditionally, the Jewish Orthodox have supported retaining the territories and settling them as part of their religious commitment (Arian & Shamir, ibid). The other division with which the settlement issue interacts is that of the ideology relating to the Arab-Israeli conflict and defining Right and Left in terms of debating the level of conciliation that should be used with respect to the Arabs as a whole and the Palestinians in particular. Traditionally, the Left has supported conciliation with the Arabs as the general strategy that will maintain Israel's existence as a Jewish state in an environment that can at least tolerate its existence (Naor, 2005a). The Right has been associated with a more nonconciliatory stance toward the Arabs within the array of solutions to the Arab-Israeli conflict, striving for a land that will include all of the historical borders of the Land of Israel until (if ever) the Arabs accept Israel's existence as a sovereign power that legitimately controls the land between the River Jordan and the Mediterranean Sea (Naor, 2005b). Hence, the issue of the settlement project's legitimacy has influenced the Israeli domestic arena and in many ways has probably defined the very nature of this issue of space (Peled, 2008; Smooha, 2002; Yiftachel, 2006). Since our assumption is that the play of these issues is both contextual and dynamic, and that the emergence of such issues and the political maneuvers of politicians in order to gain increased political capital (Doron, 2005) are at the heart of our analysis, we attempt here to study the way the political game has been affected by the settlement project and, no less important, to what extent this project has been affected by the Israeli political game.

THE RADICAL RIGHT AND ISRAELI COALITION POLITICS

In this section we first provide an historical account of the ideological and popular roots of the radical political Right in Israel. We then trace the reasons for the shift by the radical Right from operating through an extraparliamentary movement to advancing their cause via the parliamentary arena. Finally, we analyze the way the radical Right obtains power in parliament within the limitations imposed by the Israeli political system.

The Formation of Israel's Political Radical Right: From the Hills to the Parliament

The territories that Israel conquered during the 1967 war reinforced and increased the saliency of an existing ideological divide in the Israeli political system [see also the chapter by Magal, Oren, Bar-Tal, and Halperin in this volume]. This divide juxtaposed two competing views on the role and context of the Israeli State and society (Shamir & Arian, 1999). One view, associated with Israel's political right, perceives Israel as a society based on a continuation of the ancient biblical Jewish kingdom. Consequently, one of its main imperatives is to occupy all the lands that are part of the ancient Land of Israel (*Eretz Israel*), which were previously settled by people from those ancient kingdoms whose center was the contemporary West Bank area. Thus, as a part of the implementation of that perspective, no existing Israeli secular polity has the legitimacy to withdraw from these territories. The second viewpoint, associated with Israel's center and moderate left, is of a Zionist State that is intended to solve the modern "Jewish problem" (i.e., being in an exilic condition—a people/nation without a land) within a territory that has a link to the Jewish people's historical cradle. Accordingly, if transferring authority over these territories to Arab States will reduce the regional level of conflict, then this is the right step to take (Dowty, 1998, pp. 226–229).

Politically, until 1977 the initiatives for increasing the number of settlements being established in the occupied territories came from two main sources. One was the advocates of a Greater Israel, located within the political center, notably the Maarach (Alignment) government ministers; the other source of support was the veteran yet newly resurgent right-wing party Likud (Unity). This party had encouraged the civilian settlement efforts from the opposition benches. In 1973, the prominent leaders of the settlement movement joined the Likud and ran together in the election. From 1977, when the Likud became the ruling party, it supported the settlements from the Prime Minister's office and from other government ministries (Sprinzak, 1991, pp. 61–69).

Another source promoting the settlements came from outside the government: a civilian nongovernmental organization called Gush Emunim (Bloc of Believers), which was replaced during the 1980s by the Yesha (an acronym for Judea, Samaria, and the Gaza Strip) council. The Gush Emunim organization was comprised of young religious and nationalist activists who made it their purpose to settle the entire Greater Israel area and believed that it was a *mitzva* (sacred command) to inhabit the territories occupied in 1967. Their activities were based on challenging the military and the ruling governments. Until 1981, the Gush was included in a party that served as its natural representative, Mafdal (National Religious Party or NRP).

The NRP was led by the traditional national-religious sector leadership. They allied with Labour (then called the Alignment) and have participated in all of Israel's governments, maintaining an ongoing documented compromise called the Status Quo Agreement of 1947 (Doron, 2006, pp. 54, 155): This agreement, signed by the representatives of the religious and secular communities, confirmed the preservation of Israel as representing the practicing principles of Judaism (*Halacha*) without turning it into a religious state. The spirit of compromise, however, did not coincide with the religious command to inhabit the Greater Israel area. Eventually, the NRP left the government. In 1976, when the Labor government violated the Sabbath Law,[4] with a consequent vote of no confidence in parliament, the NRP chose to leave the coalition and the government fell (Rabin & Goldstein, 1979, pp. 538–540). When the Likud came to power in 1977, the NRP rejoined the government.

The first serious threat to the concept of a Greater Israel came from President Anwar Sadat of Egypt. In November 1977 he came to Israel to advance the peace process between the two nations. This initiative led, in 1982, to the withdrawal of Israeli forces and the evacuation of civilian settlements from the Sinai Peninsula. The evacuation of Yamit, a newly constructed town on the Mediterranean shore, was violent. All in all, however, the right-wing government was not dramatically challenged because the Sinai desert had never been considered to be a part of the Land of Israel. Negotiations over the peace treaty led the Israelis and Egyptians to talks regarding the future of the West Bank and the Gaza Strip. These talks were led by the NRP leader Yossef Burg. Moreover, in 1979, Israel's Supreme Court determined that the establishment of new settlements should be subject to the law. Despite the resentment of the Gush and its Likud supporters, Menachem Begin, the Likud Prime Minister, did not contest this decision. Hence, even under the Likud, the settlements were not immune from evacuation (Zertal & Eldar, 2007, pp. 355–361). The split between the Gush leadership and the veteran leadership was imminent: the old guard failed to serve its true purpose (ibid).

The Establishment of the Israeli Radical Right's Electoral Market

After the Israeli-Egyptian peace agreement was signed in 1978, and in an effort to halt the withdrawal from the Sinai desert, prominent Gush members joined former Likud members of the Knesset to form a new party. This party, Hatechia (Revival), was the first post-1967 radical Right party and constituted the political support of the active grassroots resistance to evacuation of any of the 1967 territories. That is, it became the political formal manifestation of the Greater Israel ideal (Sprinzak, 1991).

Hatechia participated in the 1981 elections and won three seats.[5] These seats were probably gained at the expense of the NRP, which lost six seats.[6]

Hatechia was not able to stop the withdrawal from Sinai. During the 1980s, it joined the Likud coalitions because the latter were not at the time promoting a peace process with an Arab partner. Hatechia also joined forces in the Knesset with Tzomet (Crossroad), formed during the 1980s by an ex-general, Raphael Eitan. Tzomet's rationale for its uncompromising support of Israel's continued control of the territories was based on a geopolitical analysis rather than a religious-historical perception of the Israeli state and society. Tzomet also differed from Hatechia in its secular and antireligious stance. Because of the tensions that erupted in 1988 over the issue of state and religion, in addition to personal issues, Hatechia broke up and Eitan and Tzomet ran separately in the general elections.

Two other radical right-wing parties were formed during the 1980s: Moledet (Motherland) and Kach (This Way). Moledet received two seats in the Knesset. Like Hatechia, it supported the perception of Greater Israel while invoking geopolitical and religious justifications to support this position and to claim wide public legitimacy. Unlike Hatechia, however, Moledet called for the transfer of Arabs from both Israel and the occupied territories. Kach, led by Rabbi Meir Kahane, also supported the policy of transfer and was eventually banned from political activity in 1988 because of this party's racist position toward the Arabs (Sprinzak, 2000). Hatechia, Moledet, and Tzomet were considered viable coalition members when the Likud was the coalition framer and was not involved in a conciliation process with an Arab partner. Throughout this period, the NRP held no more than an average of five seats in the Knesset and continued to participate in all the governments in power during the 1980s (Doron & Rosenthal, 2008).

However, in parliamentary regimes that are established under the method of proportional representation, due to the Prime Minister's need to form a coalition, even small parties that control less than 5% of the parliamentary seats can be very influential in affecting public policy while not needing to deviate from the preference profiles of their supporters (Sened, 1996). Thus, throughout the 1980s, Israeli radical right-wing parties positioned themselves within a part of the policy space that rejected territorial compromise at its more moderate pole and supported transferring all Arabs out of Israel and the territories at its more radical pole. This diversification within the radical Right also occurred with respect to other issues. That is, while Tzomet held a secular view of the state and religious issues, Hatechia and Moledet held mixed views and Kach an ultra-Orthodox view (Sprinzak, 1991, 2000; Doron & Rosenthal, 2009).

During the 1980s, a balance of votes and powers was created between the two political blocs. On the one hand, the Likud led the right-wing and religious parties, with Labor heading the left-wing and Arab parties. While members of the left wing sometimes leaned on the Arab parties to block the formation of a right-wing religious parties' coalition, they seldom considered adding them to their own coalitions (Doron, 2005). They preferred to have an ultra-Orthodox party in such coalitions. Because of the political stalemate in 1984, the two leaders of Likud and Labor decided to form a joint coalition. Following the 1988 elections this coalition was repeated, and it continued until 1990. For the Likud, the multitude of new parties representing the radical Right was used as a credible threat against Labor in case their cooperation turned sour. Labor did not have that advantage, since the left-wing parties did not hold enough seats to form a minority ruling coalition and the Arab parties were unwilling (and uninvited) to participate in a Zionist coalition. In 1990 the Likud-Labor partnership collapsed, resulting in a right-wing cabinet formed by the Likud, based on the radical right-wing and religious parties (Doron, 1993).

The Creation of a Limited Partisan Veto Player

Between 1990 and 1992, Prime Minister Itzhak Shamir successfully led a right-wing- based minority ruling coalition in the Knesset. During its first year, it seemed that Shamir had the potential to retain power and win the following elections (Doron, 1993). However, intraparty rivalry arose within the Likud. Moreover, when in 1991 the Americans pressed Shamir to promote peace with the Arabs (which would include, of course, the evacuation of settlements), Shamir had to maneuver in order not to frustrate either the radical Right parties or the Americans.[7] Hence, he accepted the American invitation to the multilateral Madrid Talks in 1991, and later also in Washington, while stalling and avoiding any real breakthroughs in these negotiations. When, as part of that strategy, the Israeli delegation to the Washington talks offered a bogus proposal for Palestinian self-rule in the territories occupied by Israel in the 1967 war, the five members of the two radical right-wing parties Tsomet and Tehiyah—crucial partners in Shamir's sixty-five-member coalition—defected (Rosenthal & Doron, 2009).

These parties' move to the opposition paved the way for new elections (Shlaim, 1994). The Right lost the elections despite winning almost as many votes as the Left. While the reasons for the Left's victory were numerous (Doron, 1993), in our context two issues are critical. First, the radical Right's uncompromising ideological position forced Shamir to move from the center and lose the median voter to Rabin, Labor's leader. Second, the diversification within the radical Right led to splits in existing parties, thereby leading radical right-wing voters to cast votes for parties that failed to pass the 1.5% electoral threshold (Rosenthal & Doron, 2009).

Throughout the 1990s, a pattern emerged in the interaction between radical right- wing parties and government coalitions. Because of its decision not to negotiate peace, the radical Right brought down governments that leaned on the radical Right for survival and started negotiating peace. In turn, the radical Right and its supporters received a government that made more radical concessions. The strategic reason is clear: when no viable peace process existed, these parties could join the Likud whenever it is the framer of the coalition. This is because, on most policy issues, the radical right-wing parties were able to accept compromises, obtain government portfolios, and allocate resources to the settlements. Yet the limitations were clear; whenever a government started talking seriously about peace in exchange for territory, the damage to its political survival could be fateful. Consequently, instead of becoming a veto player that could at least influence evacuation processes, the radical Right could only become a veto player in regard to which political coalition would lead the settlement evacuations, a right-wing-based coalition or a left-wing-based coalition.

The leader of the left bloc, Itzhak Rabin, who became Prime Minister for the second time in 1992, firmly led a peace process with the Palestinians. He was willing to make more concessions than any Prime Minister before him had made. Within this framework he led the military redeployment in the Gaza Strip and the West Bank. Yet, throughout this process, not one civilian settlement was evacuated. Certainly, from 1994 to 1996, no new settlement was built. Nevertheless, existing settlements were allowed to expand "naturally." In November 1995, Rabin was assassinated by a radical right-wing supporter..

In May 1996, general elections took place under a new and unique electoral method: the voters chose their candidates using two tickets. One ticket was used to vote for the candidate for Prime Minister; the other ticket was for a party list already determined by the parties' leadership and members using various primary election methods (Doron, 2002). Both votes were cast on the same day and, along with a low threshold, the Israeli voters now had an incentive to "mix their votes"—to vote strategically and sincerely: that is, to vote first for a candidate for Prime Minister from the Labor or Likud and second for a party closer to their political ideals. This resulted in the election of a Prime Minister who needed to contend with a diversified Knesset and a coalition comprised of many players and interests. Thus, the new electoral method turned them into potential partisan veto players with no incentive to compromise (Nachmias & Sened, 2001). This made Likud leader Benjamin Netanyahu's 1996–1999 term hectic and crisis prone (Doron, 2002). Netanyahu's sixty-six-member coalition was comprised of the Knesset's right-wing elements, from the center-right's Haderech Hashlishit (The Third Way) to the extreme radical right's Moledet (Arian, 2005, pp. 145–146; Diskin, 1997).

In 1997, under strong American pressure, Netanyahu's government started negotiating with the Palestinian Authority, with only Likud ministers voting for this policy (Diskin, 1997). In February 1997 Netanyahu ordered the Israel Defense Forces (IDF) to withdraw from certain parts of the city of Hebron, leading to the resignation of Benny Begin, a Likud minister whose ideological position was the closest to the radical Right. Throughout 1997, Netanyahu found himself maneuvering between right-wing ministers, Likud leadership challengers, a cohesive Labor-Meretz opposition and U.S. President Bill Clinton's pressure to make progress on the peace process. Toward the end of 1997, Netanyahu's coalition started crumbling in the face of the annual budget deliberations (Diskin, 1998).

In October 1998, Netanyahu capitulated to President Clinton's pressure and signed the Wye Plantation Agreement, in which he committed himself to further redeployment of the IDF in the West Bank. This created an obvious reaction: the radical Right ceased to support the government. The agreement was nonetheless approved by the Knesset due to the opposition's support and its promise to give Netanyahu a "safety net" as long as he promoted the agreement. The cooperation was not maintained for long, however, and in January 1999 the Knesset scheduled new elections for May (Diskin, 1999). Hence, again, as in Shamir's cabinet, due to exogenous pressure, the Prime Minister had to promote the peace process. Subsequently, the radical Right ceased to support the government and new elections were called.

Netanyahu was defeated by Ehud Barak, the Labor leader.[8] The parliament Barak was facing was even more fragmented than it had been during Netanyahu's rule. Barak's coalition included left-wing parties (Labor and Meretz) and ultra-Orthodox parties (Shas and Yahadut Hatora), as well as center parties and right-wing parties (NRP and Israel B'Aliyah (Israel on the Rise). As expected, this coalition began crumbling bit by bit, first with the loss of Yahadut HaTorah, followed by that of the radical Right and then Shas.

In July 2000, Barak flew to the United States to negotiate peace at Camp David with Palestinian Authority (PA) Chairman Yasser Arafat, but with no effective coalition to back him. The failure at Camp David, a controversial visit to the Temple Mount in September by the Likud leader Ariel Sharon, and the frustration of the Palestinians all yielded a violent eruption in the West

Bank and the Gaza Strip in October 2000—the first *intifada*. Facing a crumbling coalition and the threat of Netanyahu's reentering the political system, Barak called for early new special elections, only for the office of Prime Minister (Diskin, 2001). In these special elections, held in February 2001, Sharon defeated Barak.

Faced with the continued Palestinian violence and low prospects for peace negotiations, there was no political obstacle to forming a new unity government, which included the radical right-wing parties: Haichud Haleumni (National Unity), headed by Rechavam Zeevi (nicknamed Gandhi), the leader of Moledet, which combined forces with Israel Beitenu (Israel Is Our Home), headed by Avigdor Lieberman,[9] as well as Israel Baaliya. Barak temporarily withdrew from politics, and it was now Prime Minister Sharon who was facing the security crisis. Following a series of drive-by shootings and suicide attacks against Israeli civilians, Sharon turned to the use of military power against the Palestinians, with little if any internal resistance and few external pressures. During 2002 the ongoing battles with the Palestinians escalated, with deadly attacks on the civilian Israeli population. In March 2002, the radical right-wing ministers resigned because of what they perceived to be the government's weak reaction to the Palestinian violence. In June 2002, President George Bush presented his vision for a solution to the Israeli-Palestinian conflict. Earlier, in May 2002, due to budgetary disputes, Sharon had fired the Shas ministers, and afterward the Labor leadership resigned. Eventually, Sharon called for new elections to be held in January 2003 (Diskin, 2003).

The 2003 elections saw a return to the former one-ticket parliamentary electoral method with a small increase in the threshold percentage and the introduction of a constructive no-confidence vote in the Israeli parliament.[10] Sharon's Likud won 38 seats out of 120 and absorbed Israel Baaliya, giving it 2 more seats. The Likud's strength and its location at the center of the policy space effectively turned it into what Schofield (1995) referred to as a "structure-stable-core party" that could form a coalition with either side of the political spectrum and decisively lead the country toward the chosen policy.

At first, Sharon formed a right-wing coalition and maintained a firm stance against the Palestinians, increasing targeted killings of Palestinian leaders, continuing to build a security barrier wall separating the West Bank from Israel, and destroying the Palestinians' military infrastructure. In April 2003, the United States and the European Union announced a "roadmap for peace," which followed President Bush's 2002 vision. In July 2003, Sharon signed an agreement with the PA leadership to promote the plan. However, no real progress was made during most of 2003. In December 2003, due to both increasing international pressure and presumably his continual mistrust of Arafat's ability to deliver peace, Sharon decided to initiate a unilateral withdrawal from the Gaza Strip and the northern West Bank, including Jewish civilian settlements.

This plan was not rejected by the United States, and Sharon decided to implement it. In June 2004, before the government voted on the plan, Sharon fired the ministers of HaIchud HaLeumi-Israel Beitenu, who had tried to influence the process from within the government rather than as part of the opposition. The NRP split during the process due to the desire of its leader, Eitam, to leave the government; another leader, Orlev, insisted on staying in the government to influence the process from within. Consequently, Sharon had fifty-nine members in his coalition. Destabilizing the situation even more were the seventeen members of the Likud (Sharon's party) who were actively working against Sharon's plan in the Knesset. In November, following the legislative processes establishing the grounds for the disengagement plan, the remainder of the NRP left the government. Following budgetary disagreements, Shinui (Change), a centrist party, also left the government. Using his core position, Sharon summoned Labor to join his coalition in January 2005 (Diskin, 2005; Doron, 2006, pp. 273–274, 289). This coalition led to the disengagement plan, which involved evacuating both Israeli military camps and civilian settlements from the Gaza Strip.

Thus, for Israel's radical right-wing parties, the pattern is clear: enter a right-wing-oriented government, wait until the peace process advances, and then leave the government, even if this means new elections, which may bring about a more leftist government or wider and deeper territorial concessions. However, did these entrances of radical right-wing parties into the government help their constituency? In order to present a systematic answer to this question, we will now study these effects quantitatively.

Radical Right-Wing Political Parties' Effects on Governments' Settlements Policies

We shall examine this question using a simple analysis of variance. The dependent variables we test are two:

1. The number of new settlements built
2. The number of new buildings in settlements

Data on the settlements and new buildings are official and are provided by Israel's Central Bureau of Statistics. The independent variables for this analysis are two:

1. Whether the radical right-wing parties are in the coalition
2. How many ministerial portfolios radical right-wing political parties have

3. Whether the Likud is the coalition's framer

We assumed that if the radical Right is in the coalition and has many portfolios, and the Likud is the framer, that would imply a significant variance in the number of new settlements and/or the number of new buildings in the settlements. We also assumed that the effects of governance take time. This means that budgets allocated in a given year (t) will have an effect on the ground at least on $t +$ one year. Thus, we are checking here whether a pro-right coalitional setting on a given year has a significant effect on settlements' policies in the following year. Table 7.1 presents the results of the analysis of variance.

In general, when the radical Right is in the government, the Likud frames the coalition, the number of portfolios allocated to the radical Right increases, then both the number of new settlements and the expansion of existing settlements increases. These differences are statistically significant in two instances: new settlements when the Likud is the coalition framer and the number of expansions when the number of radical-right portfolios surpasses four.

TABLE 7.1 *IMPACT OF RADICAL RIGHT-WING PARTIES—ANOVA*

	Radical Right in Coalition	Radical Right not in Coalition	Df	F
Number of new settlements	7.2 (6.66)	4.8 (7.529)	24	.495
Number of settlements' expansion	2697.14 (383.59)	1935.5 (557.78)	26	1.068
	Likud the coalition framer	*Likud not the coalition framer*		
Number of new settlements	9.538 (7.113)	3.667 (4.960)	24	5.637*
Number of settlements' expansions	2994.466 (1809.447)	1944.666 (1082.112)	26	3.128
	0–3 portfolios in the previous year	*4–7 portfolios in the previous year*		
Number of new settlements	5.833 (6.317)	9.00 (7.788)	24	1.115
Number of settlements' expansion	1987.526 (900.194)	3811.25 (2163.16)	26	9.888**

S.D. in parentheses.*$p <$; **$p < .01$.

Hence, the mere presence of the radical Right in government is not sufficient to make a significant change on the ground. Yet, if the Likud frames the coalition, it significantly forms new settlements. This increases the number of new settlements, which is considered a major change in settlements' policy. When the right- wing parties increase their number of government portfolios (usually under the Likud's leadership), they can create changes on the ground in exiting settlements. These maintain their constituency and are not considered strategic changes. For these they need the Likud. Yet, the likelihood of catering their existing efforts increases as their influence in the government increases.

The intriguing fact is that these differences are, however, insignificant in all other instances. This means that activity on the ground continues even when the radical Right is not in the government and even when the Likud is not the coalition framer. This demands further analysis of this aspect of the policy process that focuses on the activities of the Israeli bureaucracy in the territories (see also Doron & Rosenthal, 2008). We will now show how these lessons are applicable to other cases of political settlements in disputed areas.

GENERAL LESSONS AND A BASIS FOR A COMPARATIVE ANALYSIS

We have been describing a set of events that appears to be particularly relevant to the Israeli case. However, settlement projects also characterize policies used by other territory-seeking countries aiming at increasing the payoffs of their population (defined by a dominant ethnic origin or by a shared perception of their country's joint purpose), even if this includes resettling their own population and evacuating other populations (Jansen, 2010). Our analysis (see also Spruyt, 2005, pp. 234–263) claims that when such countries have elected elites competing with each other for power and influence, then—as in any political competition (Doron & Sened, 2001)—coalitional bargaining will determine the way the occupied territories are handled.

To illustrate the relevance of our claims to a comparative context, we need to theoretically clarify the main variables we use in our analysis as a basis for the choice in a comparative case. That is, we need to choose a case that also shows variance in the main dependent and independent variables. Yet, we also need to choose a case on the basis of variance in control variables that propose alternative hypotheses to our main hypothesis (King, Kehoane, & Verba, 1994, pp. 91–99). The main assumption we have used here is that interested players enter a political decision-making setting characterized by a given set of policy dimensions and a given structure of preferences' aggregation schemes. They then make decisions regarding support for coalitions that would yield the best outcome for them (Austen-Smith & Banks, 2005, pp. xv–xvii). Since we have emphasized coalitional bargaining based on the use of the structure of policy dimensions by political entrepreneurs to make and break coalitions (Doron Sened, 2001, pp. 99–101) as the main influence on the dependent variable (settlements' expansion), then the main control here would be the structure of the political rules that aggregate preferences (Shepsle, 2006). That is, in line with our analysis of the Israeli case, we need to find a case in which a multitude of policy dimensions are politically associated with the settlements' project and influence the coalitional structure. However, to control for the effect of this independent variable, we create variance in the structure variable. Thus, we need to find a case in which the political system is not based on a proportional representation, low-threshold, multiparty parliamentary system like the one used in Israel.

A case that fulfills these two criteria is that of the settlements' project after the Balkan war by Croatia in the Krajina region.[11] As we show below, this area has been at the heart of the controversy regarding the settling of Croats in territories occupied during the Balkan war, territories that were formerly populated by Serbs (Leutloff-Grandits, 2008). Moreover, this area has been symbolically attached to the emergence of Croatian nationalism during the nineteenth century (Bax, 2000). Furthermore, the settlements in that area after the war were supported by subsidies from the Croatian government as part of its policy to increase the number of Croatian settlements in the area. Additionally, these settlements were the source of external economic and political pressures on Croatia by the European Union (EU). Also, the decisions regarding the fate of that region, such as the return of deported Serbs and the relocation of Croats who settled in Krajina, were a matter of internal political controversy that affected the way national political coalitions were formed in Croatia since 2000 (Leutloff-Grandits, 2008). It should be noted that the main policy dimensions in the political system of postwar Croatia are the territorial extent of Croatia's ethnic sovereignty, the position of the Catholic Church in Croatia, and the socioeconomic divides within Croatian society (Vukovic, 2010). The Krajina issue was relevant to all of these policy dimensions: it was an area of dispute for cultural-nationalist reasons, the Catholic Church was an active political player in these debates, and the inhabitants in the area (a periphery in economic terms) are economically marginalized and deprived in comparison to the rest of Croatian society (Leutloff-Grandits, 2008). Consequently, the Krajina issue and the settlers there are a matter of political contention affecting the making and breaking of coalitions that takes place in that multidimensional setting.

As for the electoral method, after the collapse of the Socialist Federalist Republic of Yugoslavia (SFRY), Croatia adopted the semipresidential system. Effectively during the 1990s the president's powers were continuously expanded until the government was almost a presidential regime (Soberg, 2007, p. 55). However, in 2000, after Franjo Tudjman, an authoritarian figure who established modern Croatia out of the ruins of the SFRY, passed away, his successor as president, Stjepan Mesić, led a series of reforms that weakened and limited the powers of the president, turning over most of the executive power to the parliament (ibid., p. 50). Yet, the president is still directly elected, is deeply involved in foreign affairs, and takes an active part in ameliorating tensions in the Croatian political system (ibid.). Hence, even if it moved toward the parliamentary system, the way the Croatian presidency functions makes its government system different than the Israeli one (in which the president is merely a symbolic figure).

Croatia's parliament has gone through a series of reforms that increased representation and—to some extent—political rights (Deets, 2006;Kasapović, 2000). That is, due to a compromise between the leading parties, it moved from a bicameral to a unicameral structure. The elections for seats in parliament were changed from a majoritarian single-member district method to a multimember open-list district method similar to that of the German Bundestag (Soberg, 2007). Again, however, even if these changes have moved closer to the Israeli parliamentary method, Croatia's electoral method is still very different than the proportional representation, 2% threshold, closed-list method in which the whole country is considered one electoral district—that is, the Israeli electoral method.

Thus, despite the variance in the ideological and historical reasons for the emergence of the Croatian and Jewish modern national movements,[12] we see the post–Balkan war situation in Croatia as fit for comparison with the Israeli case and a validation for our claims outside the Israeli context: it relates to a settlements' project as an outcome of elected governments' decisions taken in a multidimensional political context within a structural setting different from the Israeli case. Let us turn to the analysis of the Croatian case on the basis of these lessons.

THE POST–BALKAN WAR CROATIAN SETTLEMENTS' PROJECT: THE CASE OF KRAJINA

The Krajina region has been one of the sources of ethnic disputes between Croats and Serbs since the nineteenth century. For the Croats this area includes important sites of Marian Catholicism and apparitions of the Virgin

Mary—namely, Sinj—two issues closely linked to Croatian nationalism (Bax, 2000). The Krajina area was included within the Croatian part of the SFRY. Yet, within it resided a population of Serbs that maintained a Serbian identity, and opposed the Croatian attempts to succeed the SFRY at the beginning of the 1990s (Blitz, 2008). Moreover, when hostilities began, this population took an active part in the Serbian anti-Croatian political and then violent attacks (Caspersen, 2003).

At the beginning of the interethnic violence in the Balkans in the 1990s, the Serbs in Krajina declared self-autonomy in the territory of Krajina, naming it the Republic of Serb Krajina. By the summer of 1991, this self-proclaimed state was supported by the Serbian-Yugoslav army in a full-scale war against the newly formed state of Croatia (Blitz, 2008). During the period 1991–1995, this territory saw first the ethnic cleansing of Croats by Serbs and then, in 1995, the ethnic cleansing of Serbs by Croats. This second act of deportation of Serbs was accompanied by the settling in Krajina of Croats who had previously resided in that area alongside new Croat settlers. Both groups were encouraged by the Croatian government to settle in this area on the basis of nationalist claims and by the promise of economic benefits that they could not have received in other places in Croatia (Capo-Zmegac, 2005; Leutloff-Grandits, 2008).

As in our claims regarding the Israeli case, coalition politics also plays a critical part here. The post-SFRY party system in Croatia was based on ethnic identities, with Croat nationalists identifying themselves with the nationalist Croatian Democratic Union party (the HDZ) and the Serbs identifying themselves mainly with the ex-Communist party, the Social Democratic Party of Croatia (the SDP). Soon the political system was dominated by the HDZ and, within it, by the radical Right faction, which demanded more territories for Croats, including Krajina and western Herzegovina (Pickering & Baskin, 2008). For several years the settling of Croats and the denunciation of the settlers' rights by Serbs continued in reaction to external pressures and support of the HDZ and its far-right allies (Leutloff-Grandits, 2008).

During the war years, the nationalist HDZ president, Franjo Tudjman, was the sole leader of Croatia, sustaining the party's position in a semiauthoritarian system concerned with the "battle for the homeland" (Pickering & Baskin, 2008). However, from 1998 on, when the level of interethnic hostilities decreased, international pressure was placed on Croatia to allow the return of Serbs to the territories and houses from which they had been transferred from (Blitz, 2008; Leutloff-Grandits, 2008). Moreover, in 1997 a new Serbian party was formed—the Democratic Serbian Party (SDSS)—in order to sustain the rights of Serbs who remained in Croatia. Among other things, the SDSS encouraged the return of Serbs to Croatia as a whole and to the area of Krajina in particular (Pickering & Baskin, 2008).

Croatia passed laws sustaining these efforts. It also created government agencies to implement the policy demanded by international law. Yet, the nationalist President Franjo Tudjman was far from enthusiastic about that policy. Tudjman and officials at various levels of the Croatian government, along with the Catholic Church, tried to block the implementation of laws supporting the Serbs' return and the evacuation of Croatians from Krajina (Blitz, 2008Leutloff-Grandits, 2008). Consequently, Tudjman's nationalist anti-Serb policy led to an increase in Croatia's international isolation and to an economic crisis (Leutloff-Grandits, 2008).

In 2000, following Tudjman's death, and due to corruption within the HDZ as well as the desire of many Croats to become part of the EU, the SDP was able to form a coalition in parliament and then to take over the presidency. The SDP has promoted many reforms, including speeding up the resettling of Serbs in Krajina (Pickering & Baskin, 2008). Yet, like Barak's 1999–2001 coalition in Israel, the SDP's broad coalition crumbled bit by bit with every left-leaning policy step it took. By 2003, it collapsed and new elections were called. Thus, like other policy issues, the Krajina settlers' matter was not solved (ibid). In the 2003 national elections the nationalist HDZ returned to power, led this time by Ivo Sanader as Prime Minister.

Utilizing the EU policy dimension, Sanader formed a surprise coalition with pro-Serb opposition parties. He campaigned as a centrist (median) leader against both the SDP and the rightist faction in his own party and won. As Prime Minister, Sanader advanced a *European*-oriented rather than a *Balkan*-oriented policy (Pickering & Baskin, 2008). This implies that a Balkan-oriented policy is less progressive, drawing away from modern Europe, which represents Croatia's supposed national potential (Obad, 2010). Moving in that policy direction, Sanader promoted local arrangements needed to advance the return of Serbs to the Croatian territories in Krajina (Leutloff-Grandits, 2008). Yet, he failed to achieve other reforms he sought (Pickering & Baskin, 2008).

Thus, despite the variance in institutional structures (electoral method), the main outcome in Croatia is similar to the Israeli case: different coalitions within a multidimensional setting yield different support patterns for settlements in disputed territory that are held by one of the various ethnic groups. Hence, it is the transfer of intentions to the ruling coalition's political structure that sustains (or destroys) the political support for disputed settlement projects and the actual policy related to them. As long as the radical Right is able to influence the coalition's leadership, the evacuation of settlements will not happen. Yet, when the Center-Right decides to evacuate these settlements, the radical Right does not have any influence on processes and disputed settlement projects are brought to a halt. Therefore, this analysis of the Croatian case reveals that the political dynamic we described in Israel also exists in other countries facing the same issues.

CONCLUSION

The question we have tried to answer here is: what are the factors that allow the settlement project in the territories occupied by Israel in 1967 to continue, despite the ongoing controversy related to this issue in the Israeli political system? Here we have emphasized the radical Right's political behavior within the Israeli government as a factor sustaining this noncohesive policy. To support this claim, we surveyed the events that led to the success of this project and those leading to its demise. We showed that the coalitional interests of the radical Right allow the radical right-wing parties to take part in governments without alienating their voters. This complicated situation, of course, collapses when the political center decides that it is in its interest to withdraw from these territories, even if this means the evacuation of civilian settlements. In such instances, the veto powers of radical right-wing parties are reduced to determining who will lead the evacuation process rather than influencing it. Hence, unlike other accounts of Israel's policy regarding the 1967 territories, we have shown here that in order to fully explain the policy, it is necessary to relate to the strategic aspects of the Israeli polity rather than adhere to general structuralist claims about it. As a prologue to an analysis of the validity of these claims outside the Israeli political system, we described the Croatian settlements' project, with its similarity to (and difference from) the Israeli settlements' project. This description has shown a very similar pattern to the Israeli case despite the fact that the Croatian political structure is different from the one in Israeli.. The Croatian governments evacuated their own settlers and allowed the return of Serb inhabitants only because the Center-Right leaders were able to maneuver between policy dimensions and form a coalition with the political Left and Center-Left. Thus, coalition politics is necessary to sustain disputed settlements' projects or end them.

NOTES

1. Gideon Doron passed away in December 2011 before the book was published. This chapter is dedicated to his memory.
2. The authors wish to thank the Open University of Israel, the Interdisciplinary Center (IDC) Herzliya, Tel-Aviv University and the Betty and Whitney McMillan Center at Yale University for supporting parts of this paper. We

also thank Carolin Leutloff-Grandits, Orlanda Obad and Michaella Schwell for supplying us useful information and good advice about the Croatian case. We also thank Moshe Alexenberg and Ronit Berger for research assistance, and Barbara Grant for editing parts of this paper. Responsibility for faults and errors is all ours.
3. See Israeli Centre Bureau of Statistics, 2007 Population Summary Reports http://www.cbs.gov.il/shnaton59/st02_09x.pdf
4. The government flew combat planes from the USA to Israel on a Friday evening.
5. Most Israeli election data and government compositions are taken from the Israeli Parliament's (Knesset) website: http://www.knesset.gov.il.
6. The other three seats went to the newly-formed religious Oriental Jews' party Tami (Movement for Israel's tradition).
7. It should be noted that Shamir's attempts to forestall advances in the peace process yielded one of the most serious crises in the history of Israel-US relationships (Hadar, 1992).
8. In 1999 Labour consisted of three parties: Labour. Gesher and Mimad, which competed in the election under the unifying banner "One Israel."
9. Gandhi, a minister in Sharon's government, was assassinated in Jerusalem by a Palestinian terrorist on October 10, 2001.
10. A vote of no confidence is when the opposition attempts to gain a majority in order to bring down the government and call for elections. In a constructive non-confidence vote the opposition must show that it can form an alternative government to the one that rules
11. It should be noted that we are not doing an analysis as detailed in terms of data as we did in the Israeli case. The point here is illustrative and therefore we relate to the main concepts that were developed in the analysis of the Israeli case.
12. In this comparison we keep in mind the hostilities and terrible memories from the way Croatian nationalism has been manifested during the Holocaust and the *Ustasha* rule which cooperated with the Nazis in the mass murder of Jews. Yet, Croatian formal post-war nationalism has distanced itself from these elements, and is a legitimate national movement which does not negate the right of other ethnic groups to unite and peacefully determine their future. Thus, we believe that this comparison is not controversial.

REFERENCES

Arian, A. (2005). *Politics in Israel: The Second Republic*. Washington, DC: CQ Press.
Arian, A., & Shamir, M. (2008). A decade later, the world had changed, the cleavage structure remained Israel 1996–2006. *Party Politics, 14*(6), 685–705.
Austen-Smith, D., & Banks, J. S. (1988). Elections, coalitions and legislative outcomes. *American Political Science Review, 82*(2), 405–422.

Austen-Smith, D., & Banks, J. S. (2005). *Positive political theory II: Strategy and structure*. Ann Arbor: University of Michigan Press.

Bar-Siman-Tov, Y. (1998). The United States and Israel since 1948: A special relationship?" *Diplomatic History*, 22(2), 231–262.

Bates, R. H., Grief, A., Levi, M., Rosenthal, J. L., & Weingast, B. (1998). *Analytic narratives*. Princeton, NJ: Princeton University Press.

Bax, M. (2000). Warlords, priests and the politics of ethnic cleansing: A case study from rural Bosnia-Herzegovina. *Ethnic and Racial Studies*, 23, 16–36.

Blitz, B. K. (2008). Democratic developments, judicial reform and the Serbian question in Croatia. *Human Rights Review*, 9, 123–135.

Capo-Zmegac, J. (2005). Ethnically privileged migrants in their new homeland. *Journal of Refugee Studies*, 18(2), 199–215.

Caspersen, N. (2003). Thorny issue of ethnic autonomy in Croatia: Serb leaders and proposals for autonomy. *Journal on Ethnopolitics and Minority Issues in Europe*, 4(3), 1617–5247.

Cox, G. W., & McCubbins, M. D. (2001). The institutional determinants of economic policy outcomes. In S. H. McCubbin (Ed.), *Presidents, parliaments, and policy* (pp. 21–63). Cambridge: Cambridge University Press.

Dawish, K., & Deets, S. (2006). Political learning in post-communist elections. *East European Politics & Societies*, 20(4), 691–728.

Diskin, A. (1997). Israel. *European Journal of Political Research*, 32, 405–416.

Diskin, A. (1998). Israel. *European Journal of Political Research*, 34, 441–445.

Diskin, A. (1999).Israel. *European Journal of Political Research*, 36, 429–435.

Diskin, A. (2001). Israel. *European Journal of Political Research*, 40, 335–339.

Diskin, A. (2003). Israel. *European Journal of Political Research*. 42:986–989.

Diskin, A. (2005). Israel. *European Journal of Political Research*, 44, 1056–1062.

Doron, G. (1993). Labor's return to power in Israel. *Current History*, 92(570), 27–31.

Doron, G. (1996). *Strategy of election* Rechovot: Kivunim (in Hebrew).

Doron, G. (2002). A recipe for failure. In D. Korn (Ed.), *Public policy in Israel* (pp. 95–107). London: Lexington.

Doron, G. (2005). Right as opposed to wrong as opposed to left: The spatial location of "right parties" on the Israeli political map. *Israel Studies*, 10(3), 29–53

Doron, G. (2006). *A presidential regime for Israel*. Jerusalem: Carmel.

Doron, G., & Sened, I. (2001). *Political bargaining*. London: Sage.

Doron, G., & Rosenthal, M. (2008). Trapped in strategy: Israeli radical right-wing parties and the peace process. *Issues in Israeli Society*, 6, 44–67 (in Hebrew).

Doron, G., & Rosenthal, M. (2009). Two-way barriers: The "occupied territories" and Israel's domestic politics. In E. Lavi (Ed.), *40 years of occupation: Influences on the State of Israel* (pp. 63–78) Tel Aviv: The Tami Steinmentz Center for Peace Studies (in Hebrew).

Dowty, A. (1998). *The Jewish state: A century later*. Berkeley: University of California Press.

Hadar, L. T. (1992). The last days of Likud: The American-Israeli big chill. *Journal of Palestine Studies*, 21(4), 80–94.

Jansen, S. (2010). *Refuchess*: Locating Bosniac repatriates after the war in Bosnia-Herzegovina. *Population, Space and Place, 17*(1), 140–152,

Kasapović, M. (2000). Electoral politics in Croatia 1990–2000. *Politika Misao, 5,* 3–20.

King, G., Keohane, R. & Verba, S. (1994). *Designing social inquiry: Scientific inference in qualitative research* (pp. 3–28). Princeton, NJ: Princeton University Press.

Leibowitz, Y., & Egan, J. P. (1986). Yeshayahu Leibowitz: Liberating Israel from the occupied territories. *Journal of Palestine Studies, 15*(2), 102–108.

Leutloff-Grandits, C. (2008). Contested citizenship: Between national and social rights in post-war Knin, Croatia. *Sociologija, 1*(4), 371–379.

Nachmias, D., & Sened, I. (2001). Governance and public policy. *Israel Affairs, 7*(4), 3–20.

Naor, A. (2005a). Behold, Rachel, behold: The Six Day War as a biblical experience and its impact on Israel's political mentality. *The Journal of Israeli History, 24*(2), 229–250.

Naor, A. (2005b). Hawks' beaks, doves' feathers: Likud prime ministers between ideology and reality. *Israel Studies, 10*(3), 154–191.

Obad, O. (2010). *The importance of being Central European: Traces of imperial border(s) in Croatian accession to the EU.* Presented at the Workshop Time: Pasts and Futures. Herzliya: Interdisciplinary Center (IDC).

Peled, Y. (2008). The evolution of Israeli citizenship: An overview. *Citizenship Studies, 12*(3), 335–345.

Pickering, P. M., & Baskin, M. (2008). What is to be done? Succession from the League of Communists of Croatia. *Communist and Post-Communist Studies, 41*(4), 521–540.

Rabin, I., & Goldstein, D. (1979). *Pinkas Sherut*. Tel Aviv: Maariv Library (Hebrew edition).

Riker, W. H. (1980). Implications from the disequilibrium of majority rule to the study of institutions. *American Political Science Review, 74,* 432–446.

Rosenthal, M., & Doron, G. (2009). Israel's 1993 decision to make peace with the PLO or how political losers (this time) became winners. *International Negotiation: A Journal of Theory and Practice, 14*(3), 449–474.

Schofield, N. (1995). Coalition politics: A formal model and empirical analysis. *Journal of Theoretical Politics, 7*(3), 245–281

Sened, I. (1996). A model of coalition formation: Theory and evidence. *Journal of Politics, 58*(2), 350–372.

Shamir, M., & Arian, A. (1999). Collective identity and electoral competition in Israel.

American Political Science Review, 93(2), 265–277.

Shepsle, K. A. (2006). Rational choice institutionalism. In R. A. W. Rhodes, S. A. Binder, & B. A. Rockman (Eds.), *The Oxford handbook of political institutions* (pp. 23–38). Oxford: Oxford University Press.

Shlaim, A. (1994). Prelude to the accord: Likud, Labor, and the Palestinians. *Journal of Palestine Studies, 23*(2), 5–19.

Smooha, S. (2002). The model of ethnic democracy: Israel as a Jewish and democratic state. *Nations and Nationalism, 8*(4), 475–503

Soberg, M. (2007). Croatia since 1989: The HDZ and the politics of transition. In: S. P. Ramet & D. Matic (Eds.), *Democratic transition in Croatia* (pp. 31–62). College Station: Texas A&M University Press.

Sprinzak, E. (1991). *The ascendance of Israel's radical right*. New York: Oxford University Press.

Sprinzak, E. (2000). Extremism and violence in Israeli democracy. *Terrorism and Political Violence, 12*(3&4), 209–236.

Spruyt, H. (2005). *Ending empire: Contested sovereignty and territorial partition*. Ithaca, NY: Cornell University Press.

Tsebelis, G. (2002). *Veto players*. Princeton, NJ: Russell Sage.

Vukovic, M. (2010). *Leader based voting in Croatia in longitudinal perspective: 1990–2007*. MA thesis, Central European University.

Yiftahel, O. (2006). *Ethnocracy*. Philadelphia: Pennsylvania University Press.

Zertal, I., & Eldar, A. (2007). *Lords of the land*. New York: Nation Books.

CHAPTER 8

The Impact of the Occupation of the West Bank and the Gaza Strip on the Political Discourse of the Palestinians in Israel

Muhammad Amara and Mohanad Mostafa

INTRODUCTION

The war in June 1967, resulting in the Israeli occupation of the West Bank and Gaza Strip, is the second major event (the first was *Al-nakba*, described below) that has greatly influenced, both directly and indirectly, the Palestinian minority in Israel. Various studies have focused mainly on the influence of the occupation on the identity issue. Most of these reveal that the occupation has strengthened the Palestinian identity of Palestinians living in Israel as opposed to their Israeli civilian identity. These processes have been called by some researchers "Palestinization." and "Israelization," respectively.

However, the impact of the Israeli occupation has not been confined to the identity issue; but is also reflected in many other domains. Here we summarize the influence of the 1967 war and the following occupation on Palestinians in Israel in the following domains:

1. **Identity and affiliation, as examined in various studies** (e.g., Al-Haj, 1993, ; Amara & Kabaha, 1996; Ghanem, 1996; Riter, 1995; Rouhana, 1993; Smooha, 1990, 2002). Many researchers have focused on the social identity of the Palestinians, and the nature of the relationship between the civil and national components in different periods of the development of Palestinian society in Israel (e.g., Amara & Schnell, 2004; Hofman & Rouhana 1976; Nakhleh, 1979; Peres & Davis, 1969; Rouhana, 1993; Smooha, 1992; Suleiman, 1999). The studies reveal that the Palestinian national identity became salient among Palestinians in Israel following the 1967 war. The religious component also started to appear in the identity of Palestinians in Israel after the war, due in part to their renewed contact with the Palestinians in the occupied territories (Rekhess, 2007).

2. **The effect of the Israeli occupation on the political organization of Palestinians in Israel.** Two movements emerged that were influenced by the consequences of the Israeli occupation: *"abnaa" al-balad* (the Sons of the Village) and the Islamic movement. They were a result of the encounter with the nationalist and Islamic streams in the Palestinian occupied territories in the West Bank and Gaza Strip.
3. **The effect of the Israeli occupation on the socioeconomic situation of Palestinians in Israel.** Before the 1967 war, the Palestinians in Israel were at the bottom of the Israeli economic ladder. After the war they moved up, due in part to the entrance of unskilled, cheap Palestinian laborers from the occupied territories into the Israeli labor market. The improvement in their economic situation led to the emergence of a Palestinian middle class in Israel and an increased number of those with a higher education (Haider, 1990).
4. **The influence of the occupation on the political discourse.** The 1967 war led Palestinians in Israel to decide on the issue of their citizenship. Terms such as "equality" and "peace" started to dominate their political discourse, and became the two major demands that formed the essence of the discourse. It is on this discourse that this chapter will focus.

This chapter concentrates on the impact of the Israeli occupation on the political discourse of the Palestinian citizens of Israel. It examines the nature of the relationship between nationalist and civil dimensions. It engages with the changes in the characteristics of the political discourse compared with that prevailing before the occupation. We also investigate the ramifications of this discourse in regard to the political organization of Palestinians in Israel and their relationship with the state.

We identify three periods in the development of this political discourse. The first period lasted from the establishment of the State of Israel until 1967. Due to the isolation of the Arabs in Israel from their brethren in the neighboring states, the lack of an independent Palestinian liberation movement, and the shock of the defeat of the Arab states in the 1967 war, identity and political debates were extensively characterized by the civil component. This component was not connected to the nationalist one during the second period, which lasted from 1967 to the beginning of the 1990s. During this period, the political discourse closely linked the two components, civil and nationalist. The third period, starting in the mid-1990s (specifically after the Oslo Accords), was influenced by the renewed encounters with Palestinians in the occupied territories and the resistance of the Palestine Liberation Organization (PLO). As a consequence, a new political discourse emerged, linking the civil status of Palestinians, on the one hand, with the essential nature—the essence—of the country and its character, on the other. This discourse, unlike that of the second period, did not link the Palestinians' civil status with a solution to the Palestinian question

This chapter contends that the 1967 war, the occupation, and the Palestinian struggle transformed the civil discourse that had dominated the political discourse before 1967 into a national discourse that entered the Palestinian political debate in Israel forcefully after 1967, albeit still dependent upon and not separated from the civil issue. Rather, the two interacted, with mutual influence.

THE POLITICAL REALITY OF THE PALESTINIANS IN ISRAEL BEFORE THE 1967 WAR

Two major regional events played a crucial role in the lives of the Palestinian minority in Israel, influencing it politically, socially, and economically. The first event was the 1948 war, known in the Arab and Palestinian literature and political discourse as *Al-nakba* (the catastrophe).[1] The 1948 war led to the displacement of vast numbers of Palestinians, the destruction of their cities and their countryside, and the disappearance of the social and political leadership that had flourished during the decades preceding the war, leaving behind in the newly established State of Israel a feeble Palestinian society (Kimmerling & Migdal, 2003). The Palestinian settlements remaining in the state were mainly rural, characterized by a peasant economy.

Many researchers contend that the political reality that emerged after *Al-nakba* prevented the Palestinian minority from reorganizing and rebuilding itself politically, despite the fact that the Palestinian society was an indigenous one. It was, however, a defeated society, with few material and cultural resources and lacking national, social, and political elites (e.g., Ghanem & Rouhana, 2001; Lustick, 1980; Zureik, 1976). Although the above-mentioned researchers based their studies on the same facts of the political reality that emerged after 1948, they employed different tools: Zureik employed the model of "internal colonialism," examining the relations between the society of settlers and the indigenous society; Lustick studied the situation from the perspective of power relations between the State of Israel and the Palestinian society, and the attempts of the former to dominate and control politically the development of the latter, and Ghanem and Rouhana considered the development of the Palestinian society as unnatural, affecting its political organization and political behavior. Generally speaking, the above-mentioned characteristics of the Palestinian society that remained in Israel hindered the development of its political organizations and political discourse during the first period. In addition, Kimmerling and Migdal (1993, p. 163) suggest that the shock of *Al-nakba* was twofold in the case of the Palestinian minority due to the absence of an effective national political leadership, which enabled the local traditional leadership to fill the vacuum.

With the establishment of the State of Israel and the signing of cease-fire agreements between Israel and the Arab countries, Israel imposed military rule upon the Palestinians who remained within its territory. The period of military rule is considered one of the most important periods in influencing the political development of Palestinians in Israel. It imposed a complete system of obstacles and constraints on Palestinians' freedom of movement between their settlements (Jiris, 1967). The system of permits was subject to security considerations and local interventions in which the military government exploited the heads of *Hamulas* (extended families) and traditional leaders as channels for granting government privileges in various domains, including education, jobs, and movement from one place to another (Jiris, 1967; Lustick, 1980). The military rule aimed at gaining control and surveillance over the Palestinian community remaining in the newly established State of Israel (Boymel, 2002; Lustick, 1980; Ozacki-Lazar, 2002).

The Palestinians who remained in Israel formed a marginal group in all aspects of political and daily life (Ghanem, 2001, 2005). They were not only marginal in Israeli society but had also constituted a marginal part of Palestinian society before 1948: "Their contribution to the national Palestinian movement is summarized in their participation in the 1936–1939 Revolt,[2] and they did not have a prominent role in the Palestinian cultural movement that developed in the urban centers" (Bishara, 1998, p. 22). This marginal group in the newly established state lacked political and cultural elites as well as a middle class. The process of proletarianization, shifting from an agrarian society to a proletarian one, is considered the most important socioeconomic transformation to have occurred in Palestinian society during the military rule (Zureik, 1979). Due to the absence of both a Palestinian national economy and a middle class, the laborers moved to work from the Palestinian towns and villages to the labor market in the Jewish urban centers.

Two different systems were established in Israel during this period: a democratic system that ruled the Jewish sector, expressed culturally, politically, and even religiously through the definition of the country as the State of the Jews and as a Jewish state, and a nondemocratic system that governed the Palestinians through military rule with its various branches. Though the state granted the Palestinians some political rights, such as the right to vote, after they had been granted Israeli citizenship, it reduced to a large extent other political rights normatively given in democratic systems and with citizenship, such as the freedom to organize politically and the right to free movement and gatherings. The military government also administrated a separate judicial system for the Palestinians (Saban, 2000), who were subject to military courts, whereas the Jews were subject to civil courts (Ozacki-Lazar, 2002). The separation between Palestinians and Jews underscored the Jews' collective and national rights, while the Palestinians enjoyed only unequal individual rights (Peled, 1993).

During this period of military rule, various political organizations and parties appeared. Each political system focused on specific political and ideological questions in which the Israeli Communist party and the Arab Lists[3] connected with the Zionist parties played the major role. While the Communist party concentrated on racial discrimination, the Arab Lists mediated between the Palestinian population in Israel and the military government and succeeded in obtaining the majority of Palestinian votes. Generally speaking, these two political groups focused on civil issues. While the Communist party demanded the abolition of military rule in order to promote Israeli citizenship, the Arab Lists were interested in the issues of daily life, such as providing permits for work and movement from one place to another, achieving some of the people's basic needs. The nationalist issue during this period was at the margins of the Palestinian political discourse.

In addition to these two groups, which employed different political means but sought change from within the Jewish state, other political organizations also appeared on the scene, with different political assumptions based on national identity and on belonging to the Palestinian nation. These included *Harakat al-arad* (the Land Movement) and *Al-jabha al-sha'biya* (the Democratic Front).[4] Military rule and the Israeli establishment dominated the development of Palestinian politics in Israel through their official mechanisms, by which the Palestinians were excluded from the social, administrative, and political systems in order to effectively impose political control upon them. Tom Segev (1986) summed up the political goals of military rule in its first years as follows:

> The government's policy sought to divide the Arab population into ethnic groups and regions. Granting the Arab villages councils [local government] on the one hand, and creating an atmosphere of competition in the elections of local councils on the other, deepened the division within the villages, and these two matters, the ethnic politics and the familial disputes in the villages, impeded forming the Arab population in one unit. (Segev, 1986, p. 78)

Military rule, it seems, thus enhanced the dominance of the local and ethnic organizations, and the traditional leadership became the central leadership in Palestinian society in Israel.

The Arab Lists were given different names on the eve of each Knesset election, and the choice of their members and funding was made by Mapai,, the ruling party from 1948 to 1977, or Mapam, the left-wing party (Cohen, 1989; Landau, 1993; Rekhess, 1993). The names of these lists often changed from one Knesset election to another, aimed at recruiting the greatest number of votes. In each election, various lists were established, according to regional, ethnic, and familial divisions, which the Israeli establishment and the military rulers wanted to maintain in Palestinian society. The names given to these lists defined the incentives and the role that they played in forming local identities and agendas, emphasizing the needs of daily life rather than the national identity or political agendas.[5] These lists used daily life not as part of a political program, struggling against discrimination, but in order to link loyalty to the state with the acquisition of some civil privileges. This was in addition to their role in capturing Palestinian votes during Knesset elections.

The emphasis of the Arab Lists on local, ethnic, and familial identities was an attempt to weaken any political organization on nationalist grounds. This approach characterizes settlement societies in their relationships with the natives, in determining the latter's national identity and political behavior, achieved through "establishing an ideology among the natives justifying reality, especially their situation and the policy taken toward them" (Haider, 1996, p. 36). The traditional local leadership played a similar role in the same direction, in which it dominated the affairs of the local government in Palestinian society. The local councils coordinated with the military government to stifle any political protest or political activity, serving as tools of the military rulers in order to control the Palestinian population (Al-Haj & Rosenfeld, 1990).

The Arab Lists obtained the majority of Palestinian votes in the various elections during the period of military rule, though they witnessed, over the years, a continuous decline in the percentage of voting among the Palestinians for the Zionist parties, as well as, to a lesser extent, for the Communist Party (see Table 8.1).

It seems that the further the Palestinians got from the shock of *Al-nakba*, the more they started exploring and crystallizing their political choices anew.[6] The heads of the Arab Lists, representing the traditional leadership, did not progress to regional or national leadership. They based their legitimacy on the traditional framework, which had undergone little or no modernization. This stagnation had helped them to maintain their dominance in Palestinian society for two decades. Military rule also directly strengthened the status of this

TABLE 8.1 *DISTRIBUTION OF PALESTINIAN VOTES DURING THE PERIOD OF MILITARY RULE*

Year	Voting Percentage	The Arab Lists (%)	The Communist Party (%)	MAPAI Party (%)	Other Parties
1949	79	51	22	10	17
1951	86	55	16	11	18
1955	91	48	15	14	23
1955	85	42	11	10	37
1961	83	40	22	10	28
1966	82	38	23	13	26

Source: Neuberger (1998), p. 123.

leadership by giving it special privileges for personal benefit. The role of this leadership was confined to mediating between the Palestinian population and the officials in the state, and it was not possible for an ordinary Palestinian citizen to reach the authorities without the support of the traditional local leadership ('Ibilini, 2006, p. 61).

In conclusion, the Palestinian political discourse that had crystallized during the period of military rule aimed at overcoming the reality of defeat and maintaining the status quo among Palestinians who had remained in their homeland after the 1948 war. This was achieved by the excessive presence of a civil discourse,[7] based on entering the establishment in order to obtain a few rights and freedoms for the Palestinian citizens, in order to provide the minimum level of secure living and existence for the defeated and weakened Palestinian society after *Al-nakba*. During this period, a national discourse emphasizing the question of the Palestinian nationality and its connection with the reality of the Palestinians in Israel was extremely limited, if not absent. The military rule severed the Palestinians in Israel from their Arab-Palestinian surroundings, and their political struggle reached its peak in seeking to abolish this rule without connecting it to the nationalist question. In short, the discourse in this period was mainly civil, detached from the political national discourse that considers the Palestinians in Israel as part of the Palestinian question.

THE PALESTINIANS IN ISRAEL AFTER THE 1967 WAR: BASIC TRANSFORMATIONS

The 1967 war had important consequences for the social, economic, and political life of the Palestinians in Israel. The deepening of their national consciousness led to their establishment of national institutions. The beginning of the 1970s saw the emergence of a class of highly educated people and the expansion of the Palestinian middle class. National institutions for organizing Palestinian society in Israel began to be established, such as the National Committee for the Heads of the Arab Local Authorities in Israel (1972), the National Union for Palestinian University Students (1974), the National Union for Palestinian High School Students (1975), The Defense Committee on Palestinian Lands (1975), and the Higher Follow-up Committee for the Arab Population (1982). These institutions marked the serious beginnings in the reorganization and building of Palestinian society in Israel after many years of fragmentation following *Al-nakba* (Bishara, 1998; Ghanem, 2001; Landau, 1993; Rekhess, 1993).

The rapid process of collective reorganization of the Palestinians in Israel started after the 1967 war and the occupation of Arab lands. Mar'i (1984) concludes that the reunification with the Palestinian nation led to a state of extensive and comprehensive public politicization among Palestinians in Israel. Mar'i explains in another study (1988) that the Palestinian Arabs have succeeded not only in preserving their identity in Israel, but also in contributing directly to enriching the Palestinian identity in spoken and written words, in prose and poetry, and in real practice, in the political and social struggle to keep pace with the flow of Palestinian consciousness and elevate it to an expression harmonious with the requirements of each stage in the development of the Palestinian question (Mar'i, 1988, p. 35).

The 1967 war and the reunion of the Palestinians in Israel with their Palestinian brethren in the occupied territories increased their sense of a shared fate, strengthening their feeling that the Palestinians in Israel are also part of the Palestinian question. In his book *Contained Relationships*, Portugali (2006) describes the impact of the occupation and the 1967 war on both the Israelis and Palestinians. He believes that the contact between the two groups that was enabled after the war was actually a contact with the history and geography of the past, creating a cognitive map (in addition to the physical one) in the awareness of both Jews and Palestinians, with the past becoming the center of the present.

The increasing participation of Palestinians citizens of Israel in the armed struggle that the Palestinian movement launched against Israel is one indicator of this change. From the end of the war in June 1967 to June 1970, the Israeli courts convicted 120 Palestinian citizens of Israel on security grounds and 27 people were held under administrative arrest (Qahwagi, 1972). According to Rekhess (1993), in October 1968, 48 Palestinians were investigated in security operations. One year later the number had risen to 115 Palestinian security prisoners, and between 1967 and 1973, 320 were arrested and convicted on security charges (ibid., p. 114). This did not mean that Palestinians gave up their Israeli citizenship; on the contrary, the majority struggled to continue within the framework of Israeli citizenship. The 1970s witnessed vigorous political activities due to the Palestinians' enhanced perception of their identity as Arab citizens of Israel. Many political activities against the Israeli occupation increased in the Arab street and among Arab students in the Israeli universities. The demonstrations against land confiscation increased, reaching their peak on the first Land Day, March 30, 1976. The National Committee for the Heads of the Arab Local Authorities in Israel was established in 1972, expressing the beginning of social organization and demanding Arab budgetary rights and the equality of Arab local authorities with the Jewish ones (Ghanem & Mostafa, 2009)

The 1970s witnessed the emergence of a strong emphasis on higher education and academic credentials due to the increasing number of university students. In the academic year 1970–1971 there were 607 Palestinian students in Israel, a threefold increase in comparison with 1965. In 1975 the number rose to 1,281; toward the end of the 1970s it was 1,634, and in 1985 it was 4,097 (Al-Haj, 1995). The number of Palestinian students continued to rise in the 1990s, reaching 5,400 in 1995 (5.6% of the total number of students in Israel); by 2005 it had risen to 10,000 students, constituting 8% of the student population of Israel (Mostafa, 2006, p. 81)

The increase in the number of university students led to an increased awareness of the importance of education in general, and higher education in particular, among the younger generation, which perceived it as an important tool for social mobility. As a result of this awareness, Palestinian students started to integrate their personal goals of education (as one of the most important tools for socioeconomic mobility) with the collective goals of Palestinian society as a means of development. In a study carried out by Benyamin and Peleg (1977) among Palestinian students at Haifa University, it was clear that those who complete their academic studies gain personal resources, increase their opportunities for integrating into the wider society, and have the potential to bridge the gap between their society and the wider society through bidirectional contact: receiving scientific and other education and transmitting these back to their society. They are also better able to represent their society, and to assist it in formulating its requests and achieving them, in order to integrate economically, politically, and culturally.

It was evident that the contact between the Arab students from Israeli universities and Palestinian students from the West Bank (especially between students from Hebrew University and the University of Bir Zeit, and with students from colleges of Islamic law in Hebron) had an impact on the awareness of the Arab students in Israel. They observed their brethren in the West Bank universities taking a leading role in the nationalist movement outside the universities and struggling against the Israeli occupation. Those who studied at Islamic law colleges in the West Bank (such as Sheikh Raid Salah) returned to Israel and established the Islamic movement there, inspired by the Islamic activists in the West Bank (Ali, 2004).

Along with the local leadership, the Palestinian national political leadership has developed greatly in the last few decades, in its performance, types, and characteristics, influenced by the Israeli context and reality (Jamal, 2006). In the first years following establishment of the State of Israel, this leadership was a remnant of the Palestinian leadership that had once been part of the Palestinian Communist party and the National Liberation League (*u'sbat al_tahreer al-wtani*), which continued its political activities after establishment of the state through the Israeli Communist Party. The Palestinian leadership of the Communist party offered a political alternative to the local leadership that the military rulers encouraged to run Palestinian daily life.

The 1970s was a crucial decade in the history of the Palestinians in Israel, witnessing an accelerated process of building local and national institutions. This peaked with the establishment of the Higher Follow-Up Committee for the Palestinians at the beginning of the 1980s. A new young leadership came to the fore, originating from university graduates, emphasizing the Palestinian nationalist affiliation. The new leadership introduced a different agenda from that of the Israeli Communist party.

The young Palestinian leadership was also concerned with the national issue as well as the civil one. This leadership challenged the traditional leadership politically and publicly. The victory of Tawfiq Ziad, who represents the new leadership in Nazareth, the largest Palestinian city, over the candidate of the traditional leadership, Seef Al-Din Zoubi, indicated the beginning of the emergence of a political leadership that has been named the "national leadership," demonstrating that it seeks not only to achieve the necessities of daily life, but also to support the Palestinian people in achieving their national rights.

The national issue distinguishes between the local leadership and the new national leadership; the latter brought to the fore the national political discourse so decisively that it began to dominate the civil discourse. The universities were the arena in which the debates on the national issue began. The new political leadership that had experienced the shock of the 1967 war and appeared in the 1970s was the main force that crystallized the new national political discourse, linking the national dimension with the civil one.

The 1970s also witnessed the appearance of the Palestinian student movements through the organization of university student committees.[8] They introduced a national political discourse that emphasizes the national Palestinian affiliation. In the agendas of university student movements, this discourse came to dominate the civil discourse. The Arab Committee at Hebrew University was a pioneer in the protest against the Israeli occupation. This may be attributed to its closeness to the suffering of the Palestinians in the occupied territories. The meeting of Palestinian students from Hebrew University with students from Bir Zeit University in the West Bank led to mutual cooperation; the news from Bir Zeit University was reported in the newsletters of the students' committee at Hebrew University. This interaction brought about the establishment of a solidarity committee with Bir Zeit University, reflecting the consciousness and the progressive political discourse that the student movement had achieved during that period.

THE PALESTINIAN POLITICAL-IDEOLOGICAL DISCOURSE IN ISRAEL AFTER THE 1967 WAR

Various studies (e.g., Cohen, 1990; Landau, 1971, 1984, 1993; Peres &Yoval-Davis, 1968; Rekhess, 1989) reveal that the Palestinian minority in Israel has undergone rapid modernization, reflected in the rise in their level of education and standard of living, which in turn has led to a rise in their level of expectations. Palestinian society evaluates its status through various civil criteria that it compares with those in Jewish society. These criteria and other factors have led to frustration and attempts at betterment among Palestinians in Israel and have caused them to adopt radical attitudes and radical political behavior. This started mainly after the 1967 war. Until then, and because of their dissociation from the Arab world and the strict control imposed on them by the military government, a moderate balance between the various levels of affiliation was preserved.

The modernization theory was adopted by several Israeli researchers (e.g., Cohen, 1990; Landau 1981). Rekhess (1989) contends that the contact that occurred between the Palestinians in Israel, on the one side, and the Palestinians in the West Bank and Gaza, on the other side, following the 1967 war was one of the most important factors influencing the Palestinians in Israel and enhancing their struggle. Rekhess (1989) suggests that this contact revealed the inferiority of the Palestinians in Israel compared with their brethren in the West Bank, whether in education or political organization, and increased their alienation from the State of Israel, intensifying their radical attitudes. Rekhess believes that in light of the orientation of Palestinians in Israel, they saw the PLO as a national liberation movement and wished to join it and carry out military operations on its behalf. This did not happen, however, due to the deterrence of the Israeli security forces and the Palestinians' fear of losing their sources of income and material interests. However, in his analysis, Rekhess ignores the fact that the Palestinian citizens of Israel had determined that their struggle would be carried out mainly through their rights as Israeli citizens. Landau (1984) divides the history of the Palestinians in Israel into two periods. The first period, up to 1967, was characterized by an integrative orientation. The second period, after the 1967 war, was characterized by radicalism and alienation. The evidence he uses to support this claim is the rise in the average number of votes for parties opposing Zionism, especially the Communist Party, and the rise and quality of the protest on issues related to Palestinian equality within the state and against the continuing occupation of the West Bank and the Gaza Strip.

Cohen (1989) sees in the 1967 war and its consequences, including the renewed contact between the two Palestinian groups, important proof of the radicalization process among Palestinians in Israel. He contends that until the war they had preserved a "moderate balance in their complex affiliations," belonging to both the Arab and Israel worlds. However, the war "shuffled all the cards," so that their membership in the Arab-Palestinian nation dominated their membership in the State of Israel. Cohen also believes that "after the first shock of the rapid war and its immediate results came the shock of the collapse of the Green Line." He suggests that the Palestinians in Israel adopted strategies and techniques similar to those adopted by the Palestinians in the occupied territories, in which they struggled for liberation from Israeli control and the right to self-determination.

The decade and a half that followed the 1967 war saw the beginning of the crystallization of Palestinian political parties in Israel. In the period that preceded the war, the Arab Lists connected with the Zionist parties had played an important role in Palestinian society. Also alongside the Israeli Communist party was a Jewish-Palestinian party, whose leadership was mainly Jewish (Rekhess, 1993). The crystallization period of political party organization brought with it a new political discourse that came to dominate Palestinian politics in Israel for many years.

During these years, four political-ideological movements were established. What characterizes them is their connection of the civil issue with the national one and their definitions of the Palestinian identity in Israel. In other words, the new political organizations that were established after the 1967 war produced a new political discourse inspired by the new political reality. The four movements, in chronological order, are as follows: *Abna' al-balad* (the Sons of the Village), established in 1972, considered itself part of the national Palestinian movement and the status of the Palestinians in Israel as part of the solution of the Palestinian question (Haider, 1996). It considered any talk of equality without a solution to the national question as a distortion of the status of the Palestinians and their identity.

The second movement, *Al-jabha Al-demokratiya lilsalm wa-almusawa* (the Democratic Front for Peace and Equality), as indicated by its name, linked Palestinian equality in Israel with the Palestinian question. More than any other movement, it linked the civil question with the Palestinian question, contending that the Palestinian struggle should be fought on two fronts: to achieve both equality and a solution to the problem of nationality (Rekhess, 1993). This movement pioneered the political discourse linking civil and national issues among Palestinians in Israel (Rekhess, 1993). It considered peace as a central issue, the achievement of which would lead to greater equality.[9]

The third movement, the Islamic movement, established in the late 1970s, introduced the religious and political discourse. It focused on improving the status of the Palestinians by building a network of social, economic, and educational institutions, as well as by emphasizing a solution to the Palestinian question (Mayer, 1988).

Al-Haraka Al-taqadumiyya Lilsalam (the Progressive List for Peace), the fourth movement, focused on the Palestinian identity component, linking the status of Palestinians in Israel with a solution to the national issue (Ghanem, 2001). Its political platform emphasized the achievement of full equality for Palestinians in Israel, underscoring their nationalist Palestinian affiliation. It also called for the state to recognize the PLO as the sole representative of the Palestinian people, as well as supporting the establishment of a Palestinian state alongside the State of Israel.

Since 1967, the Palestinians in Israel, for various reasons, began increasingly to see themselves as Palestinians. This was due especially to their renewed contact with the Palestinians in the occupied territories and the improved international status of the PLO. This process was accelerated during the 1980s, especially after establishment of the Progressive List for Peace (PLP; Rouhana, 1989), which emphasized the Palestinian roots of the Arabs in Israel. In contrast to the other movements and parties, the PLP made strong efforts to focus on the Palestinian question, largely at the expense of its interest in the issues of daily life occupying the Palestinians in Israel. Even those issues raised by the PLP in regard to the Palestinian citizens and their status in the state, such as granting them autonomy within Israel, were ambiguous.

These four movements and parties, all of which were directly or indirectly influenced by the 1967 war and its consequences, belong to three main political-ideological streams, which still dominate the Palestinian political and ideological discourse today: the nationalist stream, the Islamic stream, and the Communist Palestinian leftist stream. These four streams, whose political orientations crystallized after the war, maintained their validity until the signing of the Oslo Accords.[10]

None of them could possibly have emerged with this ideological wealth before 1967 due to the political disconnection existing at that time between the Palestinian people and the rest of the Arab world. The war led to the emergence of new political organizations among the Palestinians in Israel, whose agendas reflected a new political discourse differing from that before the war.

In the 1970s, while there was an emphasis on political and ideological differences, what characterized this period was the emphasis on the importance of the civil discourse, focusing on daily life concerns and demands along with the sharp ideological debate among the different parties. The civil issue was linked, for the first time in the history of the Palestinian political discourse, to the Palestinian problem and its solution. The differences among the various parties and streams were reflected in an emphasis on the ideological discourse in some and the civil discourse in others; still other parties and streams found a balance between the two.

The 1967 war and the occupation of the Palestinian territories impacted the Palestinian political parties and streams in Israel in two ways: in presenting themselves as an integral part of the Palestinian question and in searching for a new vision for Palestinians' status in Israel. They demanded to be included in any solution to the Palestinian problem, which would influence positively, they believed, their status in Israel. *Abna'a al-balad* went even further, believing that the problem of the Palestinians' status in Israel could be solved by establishing one single secular and democratic state in Mandatory Palestine comprising both Palestinians and Jews.

This stream of thought culminated in the Document of June 6, 1980, which is considered the first political text to express collectively the new Palestinian political discourse in Israel. The link between the national and civil issues is evident. Thousands of people signed the document, which declares: "We are the natives of this country. We do not have a homeland but this homeland.... We cannot deny even, if we face death itself, our deep-rooted origin.... We are a living, conscious and robust part of the Arab-Palestinian people. We have not and we cannot waive the right of this people to self-determination and to its freedom and independence on its homeland soil."

The Document linked the difficult situation of Palestinians in the occupied territories with the deterioration in the situation of Palestinians in Israel. It described how "the continuing deterioration [in the Palestinian occupied territories] directly impacts the life and the future of the Palestinian citizens in Israel, who are victims of national oppression and racial discrimination. Under the current government, especially in the last few months [from March to May 1980], the racial and bloody incitement on the Palestinians has become open and accepted in Israel, starting with the declarations of the Prime Minister and the Minister of Agriculture and ending with the mass media, heads of local councils, and the newsletters of racists in the Israeli universities. We also observe that the racial and bloody atmosphere dominates the arms of the executive body, especially the police, the military and, the border police." The Document, considered the first collective document for the Palestinians in Israel, confirms the features of the political discourse that emerged after the 1967 war, perceiving the relationship between the national and civil dimensions as one of that could not be separated (see Table 8.2).

The political discourse that followed the 1967 war continued to dominate the political arena until the beginning of the 1990s. At that point, the struggle for civil equality was perceived as a failure and was replaced by a new discourse emphasizing the national and/or Islamic aspect of the Palestinian struggle.

The Oslo Accords of 1993 were one the main incentives for a change in the discourse. The new political discourse linked the status of Palestinians in Israel with the essence of the Jewish state. The Palestinians realized that the establishment of a Palestinian state would not guarantee an improvement in their political and civil status in the Jewish state. Following the Oslo Accords, they found themselves marginalized on both sides, by the Israelis and by the Palestinian national movement. At the negotiation table, neither

TABLE 8.2 *DIFFERENCES BETWEEN THE COMPONENTS OF THE PALESTINIAN POLITICAL DISCOURSE BEFORE AND AFTER THE 1967 WAR*

	The Political Discourse Before the 1967 War	The Political Discourse After the 1967 War
Definition	Arabs in Israel	Palestinians in Israel
The essence of the political discourse	Civil, emphasizing survival	Civil-national
The essence of the Palestinian problem in Israel	Military rule, discrimination	Part of the Palestinian question
Solution	Civil equality	Solution to the nationalist question
Agents of political discourse	Traditional leadership	Nationalist and educated leadership

side raised the crucial issues related to the Arab Palestinians within Israel. In response, the Palestinians focused their political struggle on changing the character of the ethnic state, seeking to establish a new political structure. Some adopted the concept of one state for all of its citizens, Jewish and Palestinian; others proposed establishing a binational state within Israel or even a Mandatory Palestine; and still others talked about greater equality for the Arabs/Palestinian citizens of Israel within the Jewish state (Ghanem & Mostafa 2009).

Jamal (2008) describes the characteristics of the political discourse that has developed in recent years, pointing to its major transformations, of which he mentions five:

1. Politicizing indigenousness, emphasizing the indigenous nature of Palestinian society in Israel and its impact on individual and collective rights.
2. Constituting substantial civic and national equality, developing the concept of equality as a constitutional value in Israel, including the right to participate in determining the distribution of the state's budgets and resources and the right to share authority, not merely to demand nondiscriminatory practices.
3. Integrating the politics of resource distribution with the politics of recognition. The Palestinians' approach connects the absence of equality with the essence of an ethnic state (Ghanem, 2001), perceiving discrimination not as a bureaucratic practice but as structurally rooted in the ethnic structure of the state. They claim that a just distribution of resources is impossible without recognizing the Arab society as a national minority.
4. Unification of individual and collective rights, shifting from a policy of individual integration to a policy of recognizing the collective rights of the Palestinians in Israel. This became an integral component of the Palestinians' legal discourse in Israel (Jabareen, 2006; Jamal, 2007).
5. The right to autonomy, involving the right to self-determination, including autonomy within the State of Israel (Smooha, 2002).

This political discourse peaked in the publication in 2006 and 2007 of four documents describing of what have become known as "future visions,"[11] exploring the ethnicity of the state's political regime and the lack of democracy. These documents also reveal the ethnic obstacles that the political regime imposes on both individual and collective equality of the Palestinians in Israel (e.g., Ghanem, 2001, Yiftachel & Ghanem, 2004).

The Palestinians in Israel came to realize that their civil status was not connected to the Palestinian question and its solution but rather was related to their relationship with the state. This political realization led to the formulation of a Palestinian political discourse that underscored citizenship and its potential in the context of the state and its Jewish identity. The most prominent of the four documents was the "The Future Vision of the Palestinians in Israel" issued by the National Heads of the Arab Local Authorities in Israel. It was a collective work drawing its strength from the forty contributors (academics and activists in civil society) drawn from various political and ideological backgrounds. The "Future Vision" posited a symbolic challenge to the hegemony of the majority and presented a political alternative to the existing crisis between the minority and the majority. In addition to describing the symbolic politics characterizing future visions, the "Future Vision" included the historical narrative of the Palestinians in Israel, with a challenge to the historical narrative of the Jewish majority. The most important idea in the "Future Vision" is the realization of the close relationship between the civil status of the Palestinians in Israel and the essence of the Jewish state. This is what distinguishes this discourse from that prevailing after the 1967 war.

CONCLUSION

The nature of the political regime is a key factor in determining the relations between minorities and occupying countries. In the case of ethno-national occupying countries (which are not politically and culturally neutral), which grant privileges to some national group, minorities develop policies and political discourses challenging the occupying state's hegemony. Examples of this situation include Israelis dealing with Palestinians, Turks dealing with Kurds, and Iraqis dealing with Kurds during the rule of the late President Saddam Hussein. The minorities within these occupying countries expressed solidarity with the occupied regions, contributing to the development of the politics of identity, and political regimes became an essential part of the political debate. Improvement of the minorities' status is linked to solving the occupation problem (Gurr, 1993).

However, in culturally neutral occupying countries, which are not identified with a specific national, ethnic, or religious group, the discourse of identities takes a different course, as is the case in India and its occupation of Kashmir. In the Indian case, the political discourse of the Moslem minority remains essentially a civil discourse, because India considers itself a secular and neutral country and does not give an advantage to a specific group. Thus, the political discourse of the minority in dealing with the occupation is from a civic perspective and no politics of identity is developed against the state; instead, basically, the politics of rights prevails (Harel-Shalev, 2010).

The geographical spread of minorities in the occupying country is another important factor. If the minorities are clustered in one district within the occupying country, this assists them in developing struggle and protest instruments, doing collective work, and forming a collective identity focused on the occupation question, as is the case of the Arab-Palestinian citizens of Israel and the Kurds in Turkey. However, if members of the minority are scattered throughout the occupying country, they will be less organized, as is the case of the Greek minority in Turkey in dealing with the Turkish presence in southern Cypress, which they consider an occupation. However, the Greeks do not play a significant role (due to their tiny number) in protesting against the Turkish presence on the island (Yiftachel & Ghanem, 2004).

In the Israeli case, an ethnic country is occupying a territory of a nation while a national minority living within Israel belongs to the occupied nation. This occupying country does not grant expression of the identity and memory of this minority in its symbols, and policies.

In this Chapter, we have shown that the ideological and political transformations that followed the 1967 war, and the occupation, point to crucial changes in both the civil and national political discourse of the Palestinians in Israel. Generally speaking, they adopted attitudes toward a solution to the national question similar to those presented by the mainstream in the national Palestinian movement. Since the 1970s, and because of the dominance of the civil political discourse among Palestinians in Israel, as well as the dynamics of the slogans of equality and partnership, a collective attitude was crystallized, seeking civil equality together with a solution to the national question. The Palestinians in Israel believed that such a solution would improve their civil status, which was linked to the national question as an integral part of the Palestinian identity. This link between political attitude and civil status led to an enhancement of the Israeli component of their identity at the level of consciousness and behavior, as reflected in their practices and political thinking concerning the citizenship issue. In other words, the political discourse of the Palestinians in Israel linked the civil and national dimensions for the first time since 1967; the status of the first issue was connected to the solution of the second.

Most important, the Palestinian political discourse highlights the relationship between the civil and national questions, in spite of the marginality of the Palestinians in regard to both Jews in Israel and Palestinians in the Palestinian territories. Studies examining the relationship between the Palestinians in Israel and the PLO have revealed that the former are doubly marginalized. They are marginal both as citizens of Israel and in terms of the Palestinian national movement (e.g., Al-Haj, 1993; Ghanem, 1996; Suleiman,

1999). The latter does not consider them part of the Palestinian question, they are not part of the national program or the Palestinian political project, and their questions are not part of the negotiations with Israel. This political discourse reveals and emphasizes the problems of the Palestinians in Israel as an integral part of the Palestinian question in the broader sense, and not just as an Israeli problem.

NOTES

1. As to the second major regional event, see for details the next section "The Palestinians in Israel after the 1967 War: Basic Transformations."
2. The 1936 revolt lasted three years, from 1936 to 1939. The main incentive for the revolt was a protest against the Jewish immigration to Palestine and the Zionist enterprise in Palestine, which was considered by the Palestinians as a real danger to their existence. They perceived the British Mandate in Palestine as supporting the Zionist enterprise. The British suppressed the revolt, which came to an end in 1939.
3. Also called "Satellite Lists," considered statist-oriented groups, and part of the moderate camp. They stood for the Knesset elections separately, but fully identified with the ruling party.
4. Two Arab movements appeared at the end of the 1950s. They are considered, especially H*arakat al-arad*, as movements with Arab national characteristics, and were influenced by the Arab nationalist stream in the Arab world, as represented by Jamal Abd Anaser, the President of Egypt from 1954 to 1970. H*arkat al-arad* was outlawed when it wanted to run for the Knesset elections in 1964. For details, see Ghanem 2001.
5. Seen, for instance, the names of the Arab lists that succeeded in the Knesset elections such as: *The Nazareth Democratic List*, *The List of Agriculture and Development*, *The List of Cooperation and Fraternity*.
6. The Arab Lists disappeared from the Israeli Palestinian political scene in 1981, when it failed to acquire the minimum percentage. It seems that when the right-wing parties came to power and with the appearance of new Palestinian political organizations, there was no longer a political need for them among the left-wing Zionist parties.
7. The political discourse that prevailed in those years compared to the that which crystallized in the 1990s, and which is characterized by Arab awareness of the essence of citizenship and rights, preserving their cultural and national uniqueness (See Peled and Shefer 2005).
8. In Tel-Aviv University, the committee was established in 1968; in Haifa University in 1973; in the Technion in 1973; in Bar-Ilan in 1974; in Ben-Gurion University in 1975. (Mar'i 1978; Mostafa 2002)
9. www.aljabha.org/q/index.asp

10. After the Oslo Accords, the Arab political discourse began to emphasize the link between the Arab civil status in Israel and the essence of the country and its Jewish character. The discourse that had been prevalent after the 1967 War, emphasizing the relationship between the civil status and the national issue, entered a continuous decline.
11. The first document, "The Future Vision of the Palestinians in Israel," was published on behalf of "the National Heads of the Arab Local Authorities in Israel" (2006). The second document, "An Equal Constitution for All: On a Constitution and the Collective Rights of Arab citizens," published by Mosaaawa Center, and written by Yousif Jabareen (2006). The third document, "The Democratic Constitution, was publish by Adalah, the Legal Center for Arab Minority rights in Israel (2007). The fourth document, "The Haifa Declaration," was published by Mada al-Carmel Center (2007).

REFERENCES

Al-Haj, M. (1993). The impact of the intifada on the orientation of the Arabs in Israel: The case of double periphery. In A. Cohen & G. Wolsfeld (Eds.), *Framing the intifada: Media and people* (pp. 64–75). Norwood, NJ: Ablex.

Al-Haj, M. (1995). *Education, empowerment and control: The case of the Arabs in Israel*. Albany: State University of New York Press.

Al-Haj, M., & Rosenfeld, H. (1990). *Arab local government in Israel*. Boulder, CO: Westview Press.

Ali, N. (2004). Political Islam in an ethnic Jewish state: Its historical evolution, contemporary challenges, and future prospects. *Holy Land Studies, 3*(1), 69–92.

Amara, M., & Kabaha, S. (1996). *Identity split: Political division and social reflexes in a divided village*. Giv' at Haviva: Institute for Peace Studies (in Hebrew).

Amara, M., & Schnell, I. (2004). Identity repertoire among Arabs in Israel. *Journal of Ethnic and Migration Studies, 30*(1), 175–193.

Benyamin, A., & Peleg, R. (1977). *The higher education and the Arabs in Israel*. Tel Aviv: Am Oved (in Hebrew).

Bishara, A. (1998). *The amputee political discourse and other studies*. Ramallha: Muwatin—The Palestinian Institute for the Study of Democracy (in Arabic).

Boymel, Y. (2002). The military rule and the process of its abolishment—1958–1968. *Hamizrah Hahadash* 43: 133–156 (in Hebrew).

Cohen, R. (1989). *The complexity of loyalty: Society and politics in the Arab sector*. Tel Aviv: Am Oved (in Hebrew).

Document. (1980, June 6). Retrieved from http://www.baqoon.com/w10/6.htm

Ghanem, A. (1996). The Palestinians in Israel as part of the problem, but not part of the solution: Their status in an era of peace. *Medina, Memshal, and Yechsim Benleomiyim, 41–42*, 132–156 (in Hebrew).

Ghanem, A. (2001). *The Palestinian Arab minority in Israel: A political study*. Albany: State University of New York University Press.

Ghanem, A. (2005). The *marginalized in Israel: Challenging the Ashkanazi hegemony*. Ramallaha: Madar—The Israeli Center for Israeli Studies (in Arabic).
Ghanem, A., & Mostafa, M. (2009). *The Palestinians in Israel: The policies of the indigenous minority in the ethnic state*. Ramallah: Madar Center (in Arabic).
Ghanem, A., & Rouhana, N. (2001). Citizenship and the parliamentary politics of minorities in ethnic state: The Palestinian citizens in Israel. *Nationalism and Ethnic Politics, 7*(4), 135–152.
Gurr, T. R. (1993). *Minorities at risk: A global view of ethno-political conflict*. Washington, DC: Institute of Peace Press.
Haidar, A. (1990). *The Arab population in Israeli economy*. Tel Aviv: International Center for Peace in the Middle East.
Haidar, A. (1996). The role of cultural resistance in formulating the collective identity: Studies in the collective identity of the Arabs in Israel. *Al-Mustaqbal Al-Arabi, 205*, 25–48 (in Arabic).
Harel-Shalev, A. (2010). *The challenge of sustaining democracy in deeply divided societies: Citizenship, rights, and ethnic conflicts in India and Israel*. Lexington: Rowman & Littlefield.
Hofman, J., & Rouhana, N. (1976). Young Arabs in Israel: Some aspects of a conflicted social identity. *Journal of Social Psychology, 99*, 75–86.
'Ibilini, M. (2006). Dominance and the things we see. *Mada Akhar, 2*, 57–71 (in Arabic).
Jabareen, Y. (2006). Law, minorities, and transformation: A critique and rethinking civil rights doctrines. *Santa Clara Law Review, 46*(3), 513–565.
Jamal, A. (2006). Arab leadership in Israel: Ascendance and fragmentation. *Journal of Palestine Studies, 35*(2), 1–17.
Jamal, A. (2007). Strategies of minority struggle of equality in ethnic states: Arab politics of Israel. *Citizenship Studies, 11*(3), 263–282.
Jamal, A. (2008). The political ethos of Palestinian citizens of Israel: Critical reading in the future vision documents. *Israel Studies Forum, 23*(2), 3–28.
Jiris, S. (1967). *The Arabs in Israel*. Cairo: Arab League (in Arabic).
Kimmerling, B., & Migdal, J. S. (1993). *Palestinians: The making of a people*. Cambridge, MA: Harvard University Press.
Kimmerling, B., & Migdal, J. S. (2003). *The Palestinian people: A history*. Cambridge, MA: Harvard University Press.
Landau, J. (1971). *Arabs in Israel: Political readings*. Tel Aviv: Ma'rakhot, Ministry of Defense (in Hebrew).
Landau, J. (1981). The Arab vote. In D. Caspi, A. Diskin, & E. Gutmann (Eds.), *The roots of Begin's success* (pp. 169–189). London: Croom Helm (in Hebrew).
Landau, J. (1993). *The Arab minority in Israel, 1967–1991: Political aspects*. Tel Aviv: Am Oved (in Hebrew).
Lustick, I. (1980). *Arabs in the Jewish state: Israel's control of a national minority*. Austin: University of Texas Press.
Mar'i, S. (1978). *Arab education in Israel*. Syracuse, NY: Syracuse University Press.
Mar'i, S. (1984). Education, culture, and identity. *Al-Mawakib, 2*, 5–22.

Mar'i, S. (1988). *Identity, co-existence and the contents of education*. Haifa: Follow-up Committee on Arab Education (in Arabic).

Mayer, T. (1988). *The awakening of Muslims in Israel*. Giv'at Haviva: Institute for Arabic Studies (in Hebrew).

Mostafa, M. (2002). *The Arab-Palestinian movement: A theoretical and historical study on the connection between the university and politics*. Umm Al-Fahm: Center for Contemporary Studies (in Arabic).

Mostafa, M. (2006). *Higher education among the Palestinian minority in Israel: Challenging marginality*. Um-el-Fahem: Arab Association for Education Support in the Arab Society (in Arabic).

Nakhleh, K. (1979). *Palestinian dilemma: National consciousness and university education in Israel*. Belmont, MA: Association of Arab-American University Graduates.

Neuberger, B. (1998). *The Arab minority in Israel: Between alienation and integration*. Tel Aviv: Open University Press.

Ozacki-Lazar, S. (2002). The military rule as a control mechanism on the Arabs in Israel: The first decade, 1948–1958. *Hamizrah Hahadas, 43*, 103–131 (in Hebrew).

Peled, Y. (1993). Aliens in utopia: The civil status of the Palestinians in Israel. *Teorya Ubekoret, 3*, 21–53 (in Hebrew).

Peled, Y., & Shafir, G. (2005). *Who the Israeli is: The dynamics of complex citizenship*. Tel Aviv: Tel Aviv University Press (in Hebrew).

Peres, Y., & Youval Davis, N. (1968). Some observation on the national identity of the Israeli Arabs. *Human Relations, 22*, 219–233.

Portugali, Y. (2006). *Contained relationships: Society and space in the Israel-Palestinian conflict*. Tel Aviv: Hakibutz Hameuchad (in Hebrew).

Qahwagi, H. (1972). *The complete story of the land movement*. Jerusalem: Manshurat Al-Arabi (in Arabic).

Rekhess, E. (1989). The Arabs in Israel and the Arabs in the occupied territories: Political link and national solidarity. *Hamizrah Hahadas, 22*, 165–191 (in Hebrew).

Rekhess, E. (1993). *The Arab minority in Israel between communism and Arab nationalism*. Tel Aviv: Tel Aviv University Press (in Hebrew).

Rekhess, E. (2007). The evolvement of an Arab-Palestinian national minority in Israel. *Israel Studies, 12*(3), 1–28.

Riter, Y. (1995). Between a Jewish state and a state of all its inhabitants: The status of the Arabs in Israel in an era of peace. *Hamizrah Hahadash, 27*, 45–60 (in Hebrew).

Rouhana, N. (1989).The political transformation of the Palestinians in Israel: A psycho-political approach. *Journal of Palestinian Studies, 18*, 38–59.

Rouhana, N. (1993). Accentuated identities in protracted conflict: The collective identity of the Palestinian citizens in Israel. *Asian and African Studies, 27*, 97–127.

Saban, I. (2000). *The legal status of minorities in split democratic states: The Arab minority in Israel and the French-speaking minority in Canada*. Jerusalem: Hebrew University Press (in Hebrew).

Segev, T. (1986). *The First Israelis—1949*. Beirut: Institute of Palestinian Studies (in Arabic).

Smooha, S. (1989). A typology of Jewish orientations toward the Arab minority in Israel. *Asian and African Studies, 13*(2–3), 155–182.

Smooha, S. (1990). Minority status in an ethnic democracy: The status of the Arab minority in Israel. *Ethnic and Recial Studies, 13*(3), 389–413.

Smooha, S. (1992). *Arabs and Jews in Israel*, Vol. 2. Boulder, CO, and London: Westview Press.

Smooha, S. (2002). The model of ethnic democracy: Israel as a Jewish and democratic state. *Nation and Nationalism, 8*(4), 475–503.

Suleiman, R. (1999). On the collective identity of the Palestinians in Israel. *Iyunim Bechinuch, 4*(1), 171–186 (in Hebrew).

Yiftachel, O., & Ghanem, A. (2004). Understanding "ethnocratic" regimes: The politics of seizing contested territories. *Political Geography, 23*(6), 647–676.

Zureik, E. T. (1979). *The Palestinian in Israel: A study in internal colonialism*. London: Routledge and Kegan Paul.

III

Societal Effects of Occupation

CHAPTER 9

The Wallkeepers: Monitoring the Israeli-Arab Conflict

Dan Caspi with Danny Rubinstein

> We can scarcely hate anyone that we know ...
> —William Hazlitt, Twenty-two essays of
> William Hazlitt, 1918, p. 107

During the extended Israel-Arab conflict, the construction of a physical wall between Israel and the Palestinian Authority areas (PAA) was preceded by concerted efforts to build another wall, an Information Wall (IW) to separate the two societies and block the flow of current information, particularly concerning the Palestinians, and thereby influencing conflict management. Paradoxically, the shorter the physical distance between adversaries, the higher the walls of reciprocal ignorance between them.[1] Partial and/or biased information lays the groundwork for mistaken impressions, stereotypes, misunderstandings, and even continuation of the conflict.

In keeping with their traditional functions and their role as a major source of information for Israel's citizens, the Israeli media have always buttressed this IW. The armed confrontation strategy applying to the extended Israel-Arab conflict may well be summed up by the following principle: the less the knowledge about and acquaintance with the adversary, its language, and/or its culture, the more convenient it is to harbor hostile sentiments and the motivation for conflict with that adversary.

By virtue of their status and function, the media are supposed to be involved in social processes, whether as mediators among different sectors of the public or as poll takers and documenters of events in society. The ability to mediate accords the media considerable power; in the case of the Israel-Arab conflict, such power is largely due to an entire range of functions, including supplying information about the adversary, documenting rule in the territories and managing public discussion thereof, and so on.

The primary purpose of this study is to identify an existing phenomenon without expressing any value judgment and to propose a theory for subsequent research of the topic. For many decades, the conflict between Israel and the Arab states was waged on a front teeming with words and information about the respective adversaries. This observation, too, requires a preliminary comment: apparently, all conflicts between communities, nations, or states, especially the extended ones, demand construction of an IW. Perhaps the most famous IW is the one that supported the Iron Curtain during the post–World War II Cold War. In this respect, the IW that separates Israel and the Arab states and differentiates between two communities—Jews and Palestinians—is by no means unique. The needs of the conflict demand control over the flow of information, and the wall is intended to provide it. The essentiality of the IW becomes evident at the end of the conflict, when there is no longer any need for it. At times, toppling the IW is a condition of conflict termination, engendering changes in information flow content and quality. The IW between the rival camps in the Middle East demands particular attention, if only because of its implications for management of the regional conflict: Does the information flowing between adversaries alleviate or intensify the conflict between them? Does information circulated in the media promote understanding among neighbors or nurture fears and suspicions of the enemy? This chapter begins by indicating several major effects that Israel's occupation of the territories has had on the media map and on media functions adopting an institutional approach. The mass media are presented as a social institution interacting continuously with its environment.[2]

DIFFERENTIAL EFFECTS ON THE MEDIA

It was to be expected that control of the territories would yield new media needs and the attendant media organizations to fulfill them. As in other systems, new media institutions and functions were created. Within the present framework, three principal media institutions will be considered, all of which were established as a result of and under the influence of Israeli control of the territories—the inception of television; an alternative settlement media system, and media monitoring bodies—as well as a new media role, the territories correspondent.

The Introduction of Television

Israel Television began broadcasting almost immediately after the 1967 war, as the need increased for an effective means of reaching the population in the occupied territories. After long years of stubborn opposition by Prime Minister David Ben-Gurion, it appeared that the war had compelled the Israeli government to introduce a major policy change and adopt television, if only because it could serve as a bridge to the population of the newly acquired territories. Hence the Israeli government allocated generous resources for commencement of broadcasting. From the outset, it was decided that broadcasts would be in two languages, Hebrew and Arabic; due to a lack of frequencies, they would share airtime on the same television channel (Caspi, 2008). The inception of general television reverberated throughout the media map in Israel, ultimately changing the relationship between the different media. Radio lost its birthright and mainly its dominant status in favor of the small screen, which adopted the role of the "tribal campfire."

Above all, the political and defense establishment's control over all Arabic media, especially radio, proved itself during the six days of fighting: Israel Radio's Arabic broadcasts had a significant role in lowering Arab soldiers' morale and motivation. Consequently, it was to be expected that television would be recruited to a similar objective, this time to intensify the legitimacy of Israeli rule among Palestinians on both sides of the Green Line. Within a few months after the end of the war in 1967, television broadcasts were operating within the framework of the Israel Broadcasting Authority (IBA; Caspi, 2005), with a marked preference for Arabic-language programming—three hours a day in Arabic and only one in Hebrew. In time, the ratio shifted in favor of Hebrew, while Arabic broadcasting became negligible.

With the proliferation of satellite channels in Arabic, which have flooded the airwaves in the last two decades, it was suspected that the Israeli narrative would lose its hegemonic status, but it soon became clear that this was not the case. Deregulation of broadcasting ostensibly exposed the Israeli public to foreign news channels, but most viewers remained loyal to Israeli sources, if only because of the language barrier. Loss of the IBA's monopoly in supplying visual information with the establishment of two additional television channels—Channel 2 in 1993 and Channel 10 in 2000—did not change the situation substantively, if only for one reason: once again, it became clear that a multiplicity of channels and additional news programs are no guarantee of pluralism and a variety of views. Apparently, economic control was no less effective than political control over the Israeli narrative: "In choosing between what the people need to know and what they want, the media today tend toward what the people want" (Bar-Zohar & Georgi, 2009).

Moreover, the national narrative is too well rooted in Israeli public consciousness to allow exposure to or at least reconciliation with any competing narrative. On the contrary, control of the territories and contact between the two nations only intensified and exacerbated the profound contrasts between their respective national ambitions. As the national narrative has a central status in formulating national ambitions, recruitment of the media was essential, if only to disseminate and inculcate the components of the national narrative among the Israeli public.

Alternative Media

Thus, even as Gush Emunim (officially established in 1974) took its first steps as a leading movement of the religious right wing, which called for Jewish settlement in the territories, its activists realized that their chief problem was the media struggle. Not only the Israeli Left (which they nicknamed "Peace NoWay") came out against them but also Menachem Begin, who clashed with them several times during his first term as Prime Minister (1977–1981) and once even called them "arrogant people beset by a Messiah complex" when they broke into Beit Hadassah in Hebron (Rubinstein, 1982, p. 123). The media struggle was reflected in the words of Gush Emunim leader Rabbi Yoel Bin-Nun: "We have not succeeded in settling in their hearts." This statement of frustration with the settlement enterprise was particularly strongly expressed considering the dramatic visit to Israel of Egyptian President Anwar Sadat, who instilled hope for peace, leading to a decline in Gush Emunim's political power and also inspiring energetic activity on the media front.

Ostensibly, this is not the first time that a sector or community in Israel has developed media according to its own unique needs. This time, however, the sector involved has a political consciousness that ascribes clear political goals to the media. The alternative media system includes the monthly *Nekuda*,[3] the Internet radio station *Arutz 7*,[4] and other Web sites, among which the most significant may well be the news site of the Council of Settlements in Judea, Samaria, and Gaza (Gabel, 2006).[5]

Media Monitors

In parallel to the alternative media for dissemination of supportive information, the settlers set up a body to monitor the general media, especially the broadcast media. Its name, Israel's Media Watch, should not mislead anyone.[6] The organization's leaders conduct consistent, well-covered campaigns, sometimes involving scare tactics, primarily aimed at broadcasters suspected of political bias contradicting the settlers' nationalistic values. Its vigorous activity inspired the campaign in the 1990s under the effective slogan "The People Oppose Hostile Media," that is, journalists and media that did not internalize national values and do not support the policy of settlement in the territories.

Monitoring as a means of control of the media immediately crossed the Green Line and the political spectrum. The Keshev Association—The Center for Protection of Democracy in Israel, founded at about the same time as the settler monitoring organizations—monitors Israeli media as well,[7] publishing frequent critical reports about right-wing bias in media coverage of the Israel-Palestine conflict.

At least three additional monitoring organizations were set up over the years, perhaps reflecting the success of this endeavor, covering worldwide Arabic-language media and international human rights organizations that criticize Israel: NGO Monitor, PMW (Palestinian Media Watch), and MEMRI (the Middle East Media Research Institute). Although each of the three has a different monitoring policy,[8] all provide decision makers and senior media staff with biased and selective material.[9]

New Media Role

Coverage of the new realities in the territories upgraded the professional status of Arab affairs reporters/commentators and created a new job—territories correspondent.

At first glance, improving the status of Arab affairs reporters and commentators did not entail any special effort. They were already involved in the Israel-Arab conflict and had developed a tradition of cooperation with the security authorities. All that remained was to assign them another task—coverage of and commentary on affairs in the newly acquired territories. By contrast, the need for a new journalistic role of territories correspondent arose as the wave of settlement in the territories grew and the controversy intensified. A division of labor between the two roles was mandated by the respective job titles: the first dealt with the Palestinians in the territories, while the second reviewed activities of the Jews, covering the transfer of Jews to the occupied territories, that is, settlement.

The fate of the new role, territories correspondent, was and remains closely tied to settlement policy. During the 1970s and 1980s, the status of these correspondents increased as the pace of settlement accelerated and public debate sharpened. Territories reporters accompanied convoys of settlers who set up outposts under cover of night, most of which were controversial and had not been explicitly sanctioned by the authorities. They covered and documented the tense confrontations with the security forces that were sent to evacuate the settlers and remained with them until the crises ended, usually by leaving the outposts untouched. Despite the confrontations and disputes, regular media coverage was capable of accustoming the Israeli public to the new realities of constant settlement in the territories and even to structure reconciliation with this situation.

The more that the Israeli presence beyond the Green Line became an established fact and settlement became part of routine government policy, thus depriving it of news value, the more superfluous the job of territories correspondent became. As such, coverage of events in the territories was assigned to other correspondents—military, Arab affairs, or police affairs, depending on the nature of the event. Moreover, the media's elimination of the territories correspondent was a kind of de facto admission that the territories had been annexed to the State of Israel.

Effects

The settlers' extensive media activity also exerted a considerable effect on the general media map, especially on the function of journalists and of the media in general, as in all other systems beyond the Green Line (Newman, 1985). First, the settlers' alternative media served as a kind of media school and hothouse for an entire generation of journalists with declared right-wing inclinations who later integrated into mainstream media and the public arena. Such people continue to fulfill expectations of "influencing from the inside."[10] Thanks to them, the settlers' national narrative has crossed the Green Line into Israeli society and reinforced nationalist sentiments in mainstream media. Second, thanks to the new journalists, the ratio between the two camps, Left and Right, has balanced out in public discourse, with an increase in the voices of settlers and those who support them, thus creating an overall right-oriented public climate, as expressed primarily in the op-ed sections of newspapers and readers' responses on Web sites. Third, the vigorous activity of bodies monitoring bias in the media—Israel's Media Watch and Keshev—apparently fosters prudent and critical exposure to the media. Frequent criticism of journalists and the media seeks to damage their overall credibility and accelerate delegitimation of free and independent journalism. After long years of hard work internalizing the rules of the game of adversarial journalism in a democracy, the monitoring organizations' critical attitudes and strenuous efforts have returned the public to the previous climate of ideological and partisan journalism, even if most media are privately owned, on one side or the other of the political spectrum. Finally, the new media organizations have managed to supply the public, decision makers, and especially Arab affairs commentators on television with partial and biased information on events in Arab countries and in Palestinian society. Total recruitment to the Israel-Arab war of words was intended to maintain the heat of conflict and to entrench the national narrative, backing the traditional Israeli claim that there is no partner for peace and no purpose to a peace process.

In retrospect, control of the territories only intensified the need for entrenchment of the Israeli narrative—what Israelis tell themselves—and rejection of the alternative narrative, that is, what the adversaries tell themselves in the conflict with Arab states. The media are ideal for this purpose, as they are capable of dealing differentially with the two adversary narratives and thus reinforcing the IW between Israel and its neighbors, as discussed below.

Building the Wall

In this case, as in others, building the wall may not have been possible without cooperation, however incidental, between the two communities. As clarified below, the Arabs' role in building the wall is due in no small part to their inefficient and unsophisticated use of propaganda tactics unsuited to the Israeli public, such as impassioned rhetoric, a blatant war of words laden with stridently hostile expressions and verbal violence, as well as threats and intimidation against the State of Israel and its Jewish citizens. As fresh Holocaust memories were part of the baggage that immigrants to Israel brought with them from Europe, they preferred inuring themselves to the existential threats of Arab spokespersons, if only as a new manifestation of a tried-and-true survival tactic. Under such circumstances, the IW was a mega-strategy for dealing with hostile Arab states and subsequently with the Palestinians as well.

The fiery rhetoric of some Arab spokespersons only encouraged IW builders on the Israeli side, who sought to shield themselves effectively against the outspoken messages of incited speakers. To ensure durability, the wall required two distinct layers: physical and cognitive.

The Physical Layer

Physical blocking was and remains an instinctive, immediate, and simple reaction, but it is not easy to block a broadcast medium capable of crossing geographic borders. The few attempts made reflect various tactics employed in building the IW's physical layer, such as blocking sources and channels, counterpropaganda broadcasts, relentless verbal wars, and stigmatic, functional instruction in the enemy's language—Arabic in this case.

Blocking Sources and Channels

External sources in a state of conflict constitute a substantive threat to the official version. Consequently, the aspiration to preserve hegemony while avoiding competition with alternative sources of information is to be expected, along with attendant operative measures such as restriction or prohibition of interpersonal contacts, control of foreign newspapers in Arabic, disruption of broadcasts from Arab countries and blocking of broadcasting channels in Arabic.

In the overall Cold War climate and in the shadow of recent experience in World War II, the fledgling state's authorities sought an immediate and effective solution on the broadcast propaganda front as well. Israel Broadcasting House (IBH), established in the 1950s as a branch of the Prime Minister's Office, was intended to broadcast in Arabic to the region's population and also to Arabic speakers in the State of Israel (Caspi, 2005, pp. 94–104). For this purpose, powerful transmitters were acquired, originally designed to jam Arab radio broadcasts, in the finest Cold War spirit. Immediately upon their acquisition, however, the authorities realized that they were powerful enough to cover the entire Middle East, enabling a vigorous and effective war of words to be waged against Arab radio stations.

What had been impossible to accomplish in the 1950s became feasible half a century later. Despite the open skies and the plethora of stations offered by cable and satellite TV, the Israeli public is only exposed to a few of the television channels in Arabic. Essentially, each of the two service providers, HOT (cable) and YES (satellite), offers only a few channels in Arabic—those that are not considered overly hostile: Al-Jazeera, MBC, LBC, and stations from Jordan and Morocco. By contrast, only the Wallkeepers have convenient access to the Arabic-language broadcasts of the Palestinian Authority, Hamas in Gaza or channels originating in Syria and Lebanon, which are not included in the channel menu offered the Israeli public.

Restricting or Prohibiting Interpersonal Contacts

It is widely known that interpersonal communication may complement the mass media and even prove effective in fostering dialogue. The post–Six-Day War period was marked by increased potential for routine interpersonal contacts and their attendant benefits, but the existing pattern of practical, functional relations with the Arab minority in the country, mostly restricted to the workplace and law enforcement, also delimited relations with the Palestinians in the new territories.

The conflict has always been conducted simultaneously on two fronts—on the battlefield and in the media. It is only natural that the second front was given less attention. By contrast, the war of words was also waged between battles, in compliance with all conventional rules of propaganda warfare. The numerical advantage of the Arab states accorded them a convenient starting position: like the hundreds of satellite channels today, dozens of radio stations filled the airwaves during the 1950s, bombarding Israel's population with a broad array of messages, mostly directed at Arabic speakers and nearly all of them hostile (Boyd, 1993).

The more central to the conflict the Palestinians became, the greater the apprehension that the consequent reduction of physical distance would weaken the IW, necessitating additional arrangements to tighten information flow control. After the Yom Kippur War, the political status of the Palestine Liberation Organization (PLO) became consolidated (Arafat's speech at the UN) and the international community's recognition of the Palestinian national movement became more extensive. In Israel, many people perceived these developments as an existential threat. The greater its intensity—in the late 1970s and early 1980s the number of PLO embassies in world capitals exceeded that of Israeli embassies—the stronger Israel's demand for consolidation of the IW, primarily between Israel and burgeoning Palestinian nationalism. The matter became critical after the electoral upheaval that brought the Likud to power, particularly during the 1980s. State media were then prohibited from interviewing personalities identified with or supportive of the PLO (on the grounds that it was forbidden to offer a platform to the enemy).

Subsequently, the Knesset passed a law prohibiting Israeli citizens from meeting with PLO representatives (Abie Nathan, who operated a pirate radio station in international waters, was jailed for violating this law). Although the law was repealed when the Rabin government was elected in 1992, Israel's society and media persisted in harboring an overall feeling that the country had to defend itself against the Arab-Palestinian enemy by blocking information.

Fluency in Arabic

Knowledge of a language has always served as a multipurpose window to that language's culture, including the fostering of empathy for its speakers and their views. In this respect, it is only natural that Israelis would learn the dominant language of the region. Conversely, ignorance of the other's language separates nations. During the first few years of mass immigration to Israel, many of the newcomers from Islamic countries were indeed fluent in Arabic and were thus susceptible to the influence of foreign Arabic-language sources of information. In this case, IBH broadcasts in Arabic constituted an effective solution, compromising between the requirement to satisfy the essential cultural needs of Arabic speakers and the requirement to block hostile propaganda. Moreover, the Israeli broadcasts in Arabic served as an agent of socialization for Arabic-speaking Jews, imparting the official views of the State of Israel to many of them. Subsequently, however, whether because of normal sociodemographic processes or ascription of the Arabic language to the enemy, the number of Jewish Arabic speakers decreased steadily. Although Arabic is an official language of the State of Israel, the stigma it acquired deterred youngsters from choosing Arabic as an elective subject at school. By contrast, the defense system invests considerable resources in teaching Arabic to meet its intelligence needs, thereby reinforcing the perception of Arabic as an enemy language studied only by the Wallkeepers.

Post facto, those who understood Arabic were kept from exposure to Arab sources, whether for technical or cognitive reasons, while those who did not were offered "tastes" by Israeli sources, as clarified below, with the assistance of an entire range of Arabic-speaking mediators (Cohen, 2006). Biological processes favored the IW as well, as the number of Arabic-speaking Jewish immigrants who respected the Arabic language and culture began to dwindle and the succeeding generation was educated in a system that was none too favorable toward Arabic language teaching, probably because the language was identified with the enemy. Although Arabic was nominally a compulsory part of the state curriculum, most schools found ways of avoiding its introduction, especially State Religious schools, virtually none of which teach Arabic.[11] Because of its stigma, Arabic language instruction remains controlled and purpose-oriented, as explained below, while the number of Arabic speakers continues to decline.

The Cognitive Layer

Despite all efforts at erecting a physical barrier, it soon became clear that advanced, distance-devouring communications technologies were overcoming physical obstacles and would eventually render foreign and hostile sources of information accessible to the Israeli public. As such, the need for an a priori cognitive layer became even more urgent in the open skies era of foreign satellite channels.

All propagandists address the cognitive systems of their target audiences. Hence, the cognitive layer required is a selective reception screen that protects against unwanted propaganda and persuasive messages. Its height varies according to circumstances and cultural and psychological climate, as skilled propagandists try to lower it and introduce their messages.

One effective method of raising and reinforcing the reception screen was to label radio broadcasts from Arab countries—and later also satellite television channels—as hostile and dangerous propaganda, largely enabled thanks to a mental climate teeming with threats from Arab states (Bar-Tal & Jacobson, 1998; Jacobson & Bar-Tal, 1995). The more recent satellite channels, which adopted Western reporting standards, headed by Al-Jazeera (Miles, 2005), appeared capable of casting off their traditional label, gaining the viewers' trust, and threatening the entire wall. Lapses from professional standards, as in coverage of the Warm Winter campaign of late February 2008[12] and Al-Jazeera's coverage[13] of the release of Samir Kuntar, who was serving a life sentence,[14] were well exploited for delegitimation of the Arab satellite channels and intensified labeling of their content as propaganda.[15]

Credibility has always been a core asset for propagandists. In this respect, the Israeli side had a marked advantage, even among Arabic speakers. Essentially, the Arabic sources and spokespersons contributed markedly to the successful and rapid construction of the IW by employing fiery rhetoric and adopting a transparently propagandist tone.

Disruptions may detract from a message transmitter's credibility and intentions. Indeed, broadcasts in ludicrous Hebrew from Arab countries, first transmitted during wartime and later also between battles, helped imprint a negative label on Arab sources, creating a rejection threshold among the Israeli public. Several Arab radio and television stations—in Egypt, Jordan, Syria, and other countries—attempted Hebrew broadcasting regularly but found it difficult to attain a reasonable rate of exposure each time. Some not only failed to reach the IW, such as Nile TV broadcasts from Egypt, but also generated negative attention as they became the object of ridicule, a regular topic for impressions and jokes in Israeli entertainment.

Directors of Israeli programming in Arabic, together with their colleagues in Israel's information agencies, set up a propaganda system for Arabic speakers as early as the pre-state period, applying a combination of strategies (e.g., sociological and political). Alongside commentary and political speechmaking, the Israeli broadcasters often expressed authentic respect for the Arabic cultural assets and language and for Islam (Cohen, 2008). Many displayed an obvious nostalgia for the cultural roots they had abandoned in Iraq or Egypt (Caspi, 2005; Cohen, 2006).

Credibility of broadcasts, or a reasonable facsimile thereof, yielded ample interest in June 1967, the inception of the Six Day War era, which is also inscribed in historical memory as the heyday of Arabic-language radio. The media in the Arab states, including the popular *Sawt al-Arab* (Voice of Arabia) that transmitted nationalistic broadcasts from Cairo to the entire Arab world, in the spirit of Egyptian President Gamal Abdel Nasser's policies, suffered an even more ignominious defeat than the troops on the battlefield. Even before fighting began, the Arab media conducted enthusiastic propaganda campaigns, describing dramatic victories of the Arab armies as they trampled the Israeli army on all fronts.[16]

Mistrust of broadcasts from Arab countries apparently contributed to the boost in exposure experienced by Israeli media. At that time, an Israeli Arabic daily called *Al-Anba* (*The News*), published under the auspices of the Office of the Advisor for Arab Affairs, a division of the Prime Minister's Office (Kabha & Caspi, 2001), was welcomed among residents of the West Bank and the Gaza Strip. Although this newspaper was considered a propaganda tool of the Israeli government, it was still perceived as more reliable than many Arab papers. *Al-Anba* succeeded in recruiting respected veteran nationalistic Arab journalists to its ranks, such as Muhammad Abu-Shalabiya of East Jerusalem, while Israel Television engaged Arab presenters and journalists, such as Abed al-Wahab Zahdeh of Hebron. The Palestinian public considered the work of these journalists in Israeli state broadcasting to be legitimate, thereby increasing the Israeli version's credibility.

Absolute or near-absolute impermeability to broadcasts from Arab states was intended to block the Israeli public from exposure to alternative sources and other versions, granting hegemony to the Israeli narrative. Labeling broadcasts from Arab countries as hostile and unreliable was essential in dealing with the Arabic speakers among immigrants from Islamic countries. Many of them maintained loyalty to their linguistic and cultural heritage and could thus be exposed to hostile messages from Arabic countries with relative ease. To a great extent, labeling the broadcasts as propagandist helped promote selective exposure patterns: free exposure to music and various types of entertainment and controlled exposure to verbal broadcasts.

Maintaining the Wall

Every wall has its keepers. Generally, those who initiate and build the wall are also concerned with keeping it. The IW required keepers to supervise and control the flow and especially the quality of information available to the Israeli public about the adversary. The roles and functions of officials in charge of media wallkeeping will be examined below.

Institutionalization of a Dual Role System

Management of the extended conflict necessitated an efficient system that relied on duplication of functions, on the maintenance of two coordinated systems—security and civilian. The same applies to keeping the IW. Prima facie, the defense system, especially the Israel Defense Forces (IDF), has a decisive role in managing the conflict, having allocated various economic and human resources for the fulfillment of various communications roles, following a clear division of labor and differentiation among home front, battlefront, and adversary-related functions: gathering information about the adversary, distributing information to the public, preparing the fighters and the public for armed confrontation, or managing psychological warfare. Besides its system of spokespersons, the IDF equipped itself with sophisticated means of intelligence by which to monitor processes and events in enemy countries. Tens of thousands of soldiers were taught the basic skills required for tracking and observing developments in Arab states. Within these units and elsewhere, intelligence goals eliminated the negative label attached to Arabic language learning. In the IDF and other security agencies, a system of unprecedented scope was set up to translate, listen to, and monitor Arab communications.

The monitoring mission, together with maintenance of the defense system's information barriers, would not have been possible without vital input from the civilian sphere. Moreover, a parallel civilian backup system was necessary to ensure civilian careers for security personnel and to achieve constant refreshment of the military system. The duplicate systems coordinated marvelously, with the basic strategic conception calling for pluralism, or at least an impression of multiple views, while preventing "group thinking" and all its implications.

It is also true that the military system depends on and is enriched by civilian input in other professional fields. In each such instance, the formation of reciprocal relations appears to be inevitable. Veterans of military units are often welcomed in civilian sectors, constituting a reserve that has not been worn down by military service but actually improved by it. The military system frequently serves as a training unit for various types of professional reserves. *Galei Zahal* (IDF Radio) may well be the most outstanding example of such training in the media profession. Israel's military radio station has consistently served the country as its key media training school, as it promotes and meticulously selects skilled, capable young people to fill positions in various media organizations (Caspi, 2002): Professional mobility from *Galei Zahal* to a job at a newspaper or broadcasting station is widespread. Station veterans fill tens of thousands of positions in media organizations that are eager to employ young people with extensive journalistic experience. Many of these reporters and journalists perform their reserve duty at the army radio studios. By contrast, the civilian system's contribution to the IDF and its radio station is less transparent and direct. Perhaps it is no coincidence that *Galei Zahal* enjoys public admiration, high ratings, a positive image, and a vital resource—extensive support for its existence and activity. Changes in the broadcasting map, especially the multiplicity of radio stations, occasionally raise questions regarding the need to maintain the station. Each time, however, the questions are stricken from the agenda due in no small part to the determined support of station veterans dispersed throughout the various media systems.

The case of *Galei Zahal* may well underscore the existence of less well known civil information communities that maintain strong reciprocal ties with army units. Even in the pre-state period the community of Arab affairs experts, the orientalists, always served as an intelligence source for the IDF (Eyal, 2005). Over the years, relations between the IDF and the academic world took shape along two major, essential academic tracks: research and teaching.

Prima facie, academic research is likely to enrich general and practical knowledge, including that of defense system heads. Often, however, researchers require military sources in order to study issues and topics to which there is no direct access and no alternative material is available. Unlike their overseas colleagues and experts in other fields, Israeli orientalists find it difficult or even prohibited to visit Arab countries or gather information. Israeli researchers and journalists rarely avail themselves of the opportunities emerging over the past few years to visit and remain in certain Arab countries for extended periods of time, such as Egypt, Jordan, the Gulf States, and several North African countries. Out of habit or convenience, many prefer to rely on military sources, the default for academic research, the lesser of two evils. Some academic experts "wear two hats": besides their activities on campus, they perform their reserve duty by training intelligence cadets to work methodically in response to research needs (Ring, 2008).

Moreover, the defense system commonly develops ties with existing research units and establishes such units on campuses according to predetermined needs—defense strategy, terror, and so on. University research institutes and centers often serve as employment sources for reserve senior officers. Intelligence reports and studies rich in familiar military conceptions are repackaged and are granted the academic seal of approval within these civilian institutes.[17] Furthermore, reserve officers join such institutes after demobilization and apply for strategic and defense research grants.

Reciprocal ties between the two systems are equally close in the instructional sphere. Selected units and corps are accorded preferred treatment and study programs tailored to suit the IDF's specifications. Young soldiers study and teach at university campuses under military boarding school conditions. The study programs raise issues of academic freedom and the concern that preference for special classes reduces the likelihood of young people's free exposure to the full range of views in their age group. On the other hand, refusal to cooperate with the defense authorities is liable to yield various sanctions, including negative publicity in the media (Oren, 2008).[18]

The intensive reciprocal relations model is also reproduced in ties with the media and journalists, even if they are more covert and delicate than those observed in the case of *Galei Zahal*. The model may have affected Arabic broadcasts most of all, first on radio and later on television as well. Defense officials were active partners both in charting IBH policy and in recruiting professional personnel according to security criteria. Representatives of the defense authorities participated regularly in the steering committee alongside Arabic broadcasting executives and Prime Minister's Office and Foreign Ministry officials. The steering committee generally met weekly to consider publicity guidelines and essentially planned the war of words against broadcasting stations in Arab countries (Danin 1987, p. 375). In retrospect, the steering committee, known by its in-house and ironic nickname, the "Arab Higher Committee"[19] (Caspi, 2005, p. 95), shaped future Israeli Arabic broadcasting policy that later applied to multichannel television as well.

The steering committee effectively succeeded in leaving its mark on Israeli Arabic broadcasting policy long after it had been disbanded, having been deemed superfluous. Subsequently, elimination of the long-term objection to television broadcasts and the decision to establish Israel Television were supported by security considerations. After the Six Day War, television was perceived as a "bridge between nations" extending to the populations of the new territories (Kabha & Caspi, 2011). For this purpose, Arabic speakers were recruited from among ISA (then known as the GSS—General Security Service) personnel, who were trained as television broadcasters. Furthermore, the program schedule was divided from the outset into three hours daily of Arabic and one of Hebrew. Even when commercial channels were established (Channel 2 and later Channel 10), the same orientation was maintained: programs for Arabic speakers in Israel were scheduled for nonprime daytime hours and generally did not address controversial political issues.

Routine Operation

The dual (military/security and civilian) Wallkeeper system includes a variety of agencies that specialize in information gathering, sorting, screening, decoding, and distribution according to target audiences and goals. In general, officials and experts maintain a division of labor according to geographic area (there are experts on Syria and on Iran, for example) or field of concentration (terror organizations, weapons development monitoring, etc.). Civilian research and monitoring institutes work alongside military intelligence units. Both rely primarily on open sources, generally the media in Arab countries and the PAA, which tend to supply mostly partial and biased information. The abundant information so generously provided is likely to fill a media gap and compensate for the absence of free and unmediated information flow. Post facto, the intelligence system gains from the extended conflict and therefore is also likely to display an immanent interest in preserving it and in reinforcing the IW in particular.

From the outset, the intelligence system and all its subsidiaries adopted the working assumption of "know thine enemy" rather than "get to know your neighbor." As such, they aim at gathering relevant information with an eye toward confrontation. By contrast, every bit of information that differs from or defies the confrontation climate is liable to embarrass and at times to disrupt traditional working assumptions. Consequently, the working assumption largely dictates selective gathering of information about the adversary. The dominant conflict orientation requires many agencies engaged in regulating information, if only to construct a pluralistic picture: several sources prophesying with the same voice and providing similar or identical messages retroactively validate the basic patterns and buttress the negative image of all Arabs (Meital, 2006).

Academic research institutes and civilian monitoring organizations benefit from generous grants for participation, whether direct or indirect, in training IW keepers (Eyal, 2005). The various media—newspapers and broadcasting stations—contribute their part to the intelligence system and participate in routine IW keeping. Nearly all news organizations have institutionalized positions specializing in covering the conflict. Those who fill these positions, such as Arab affairs reporters/commentators, military correspondents, and territories/PAA correspondents, enjoy a respected status. Their presence is not a guarantee of the quality of the information published; perhaps the contrary is true. At times, military correspondents cannot free themselves from past orientations and even continue to function as IDF spokespersons (Yaron, 2001). Functionaries, both individually and collectively, effectively participate in regulating information from and about the adversary beyond the wall and thus also guard the IW.

Effectively, none of the media is equipped with the resources and tools required to cover all aspects of the conflict. Hence, the various functionaries require input from the relevant branches of the military intelligence system. As indicated, the Israeli media avoid sending correspondents to Arab countries, if only for practical reasons. Many of the Arab affairs correspondents are known to have close contacts with the defense system that are liable to endanger them by marking them as desired intelligence targets in those countries. Under such circumstances, intelligence agencies enthusiastically feed journalists information that accumulates in huge quantities in reports and internal and classified position papers, as their publication in the media not only distributes the information to the public at large but also may yield public relations benefits for these agencies and their activities.

Several of the new systems institutionalized a division of labor among Arab affairs experts, especially between correspondents and commentators, with a clear hierarchy prevailing: the former focus on covering and reporting incidents, while the latter specialize in giving them interpretation and meaning. For various reasons, the experts are generally introduced as commentators rather than correspondents. One reason may be rooted in the objective difficulty of observing and covering events directly and then cross-referencing sources—de rigueur in journalistic practice. This applies particularly to Arab affairs correspondents, who, like their academic colleagues, have to rely on secondary sources, usually those of the military intelligence system.

Moreover, Arab affairs is the most complex and complicated area of specialization in the news department, as its experts must be familiar with the entire Arab/Islamic world, from East Asia to West Africa, from Indonesia and Afghanistan to Algeria and Sudan, not to mention having the ability to interpret developments in the PAA and at times also among Palestinians in Israel. In such cases, commentators may create additional sources of information for themselves within the PAA, visit them frequently, and perhaps also provide unmediated coverage of events. With one exception, Israeli Arab affairs experts do not actually remain in the PAA and cannot experience the pulse beat of life there firsthand. Reports of the one correspondent who did remain in the PAA were read with some hostility, if only because they threatened "selective knowledge" in the shadow of the IW (Hass, 2008). At the end of the day, experts return to their homes in Israel, generally laden with anthropological impressions and observations. Traditionally, Arab affairs experts embrace a monolithic conception of the enemy that may well entrench the dichotomous perception of "them" versus "us."

Because of the coverage burden, Arab affairs experts rely on several "listeners"/monitors who function as sensors, reviewing the Arab printed press and broadcasts from various Arab stations, covering hundreds of satellite channels and countless radio stations, daily newspapers, and other publications originating in Arab countries (Ayish, 2002; Kraidy, 2002; Miles, 2005). Despite the logistic assistance, which is not available in every organization, Arab affairs experts have considerable difficulty keeping up-to-date on highly significant developments in the Arabic world, if only because they are dependent on intelligence personnel. As many journalists were themselves educated in various intelligence branches, they maintain social contacts that also help keep up routine work ties, thanks to the mutual trust obtaining between them and their former and present colleagues. This marvelous symbiosis between Arab affairs experts and intelligence personnel influences the media agenda, public discourse, and presentation of the enemy in the Israeli media (Meital, 2002).

Conclusion: A Comparative Perspective

What human beings use to tell things to themselves seems to be more crucial and vital than any fact or reality. Narratives may strongly frame the interpretation of actuality. Thus, the cultivation of efficient narratives is a basic need in managing the perpetual Israel-Arab conflict.

Numerous studies address the flow of information between nations and states—especially in the era of globalization—and its contribution to the development of relations across physical borders (Mohammadi, 1997; Mowlana, 1997). By contrast, little attention has been paid to the circumstances under which parties in conflict initiate and build barriers to the free flow of information. The conflict in the Middle East may serve as a test case of controlled information flow disruption.

Information walls appear to be present in numerous many conflicts. The fiercer and more extended the conflict, the more evident is its blockage of information flow concerning events taking place in the enemy camp. Information walls are often constructed in external conflicts, between countries and blocs, such as the one set up during the Cold War between the two blocs on either side of what was to be termed the Iron Curtain (Gaddis, 2006). Each bloc/side thus entrenched itself behind a barrier that halted the flow of information and effectively protected against its exposure to the other side (Jenks, 2006; Schwoch, 2009).

Apparently, there is nothing like occupation to lay the groundwork for an IW, especially one constructed by the occupier, such as the French in their violent and extended battle in Algeria (Servan-Schreiber, 1957) or the Chinese in Tibet today (Lee, 2009). Prima facie, the wall facilitates matters for the occupier and the occupation, but only in the immediate period. As time passes, ignorance of what is happening on the other side of the wall is liable to yield some unpleasant surprises, including uprising and termination of the occupation.

One outstanding example of such consequences may be found in the history of the French occupation of Algeria, which ended in the 1954–1962 war and invites comparison with the armed and political conflicts between Israel and the Palestinians after the former's occupation of the West Bank and the Gaza Strip in the 1967 Six Day War (Kies, 1975; Lustick, 1993). The two situations differ in some aspects but resemble one another in others, including the cognitive IW that is supposed to provide the occupiers with immediate-range protection from what is happening among the occupied. The most salient difference, of course, is the physical distance between the European colonizer and the North African colony, occupied by the French army in 1830, as contrasted with the geographic proximity of the Jewish and Arab-Palestinian communities that live in one country, alongside one another and within each other's territories. Naturally, the two conflicts also differ in political and social circumstances, including Jewish religious and historic attachment to the occupied territories.

Another reason for comparing the two situations is the Palestinians' attempt, especially during the early years of occupation, to derive legitimacy for their national struggle and emulate the popular revolt model applied by Algerian nationalists, who ultimately triumphed over France and won political independence. For example a Palestinian poster from September 1967 stated that "the legendary stand of Algeria, that sacrificed more than a million victims, will serve as a lamp unto our feet. It is incumbent upon us to know that the occupation is the inception of a revolutionary war of liberation"

(Yaari, 1970). Palestinian newspapers, such as *Falastin al Sawra*, frequently cited passages from a highly influential book by Franz Fanon (1925–1961), a Martinique-born French psychiatrist, who was among the outstanding proponents of Third World anticolonialism (Fanon, 1961).

Despite all the differences, in Algeria, as in the territories, an extended military occupation regime persisted, under whose auspices the *pieds noirs* (French and other European colonists) settled there.[20] The early European settlers included numerous demobilized veterans of the French army who had served in Algeria, as well as people fleeing the political upheavals in Europe between 1845 and 1870, among them many refugees of the 1870 war in Alsace-Lorraine. Most of the foreign settlers in Algeria may not have been of French origin but rather Spanish and Italian, along with a community of Maltese origin (Abitbol & Zisenwine 2005, p. 37). During the war years (1954–1962), the *pieds noirs* numbered about 1,300,000 persons, nearly all of them Roman Catholics. Since the inception of European settlement in French Algeria at the end of the nineteenth century, the settlers constituted a kind of social, cultural, and political enclave that was totally separate from the indigenous population, numbering some 15 million persons after the Second World War, about 75% of whom were Arabs and Bedouins and the remaining 25% Berbers, all of them Muslims (Abitbol & Zisenwine, 2005, p. 47).

Like the Israeli settlers, the *pieds noirs* enjoyed full citizenship in the occupying country and controlled a significant share of the occupied land's resources, including the most fertile soil, water, and civil service positions. In 1954, shortly before war broke out in Algeria, the European settlers, who accounted for 11% of the population, held 42% of the jobs in industry, whereas only 19% of employees in economic enterprises were Muslims. The French authorities ostensibly allowed Muslims to obtain French citizenship as well and to be partners in the institutions of local government, but in practice the path was almost entirely blocked to them, as candidates had to be French army veterans or possess French primary education, conditions that very few Muslims could fulfill. On the eve of the Second World War, 81% of Muslim men and 95% of Muslim women were illiterate. Economic, industrial, and commercial activity was concentrated almost entirely in the hands of *pied noir* European settlers, who were invariably entitled to full French citizenship and had developed a sense of superiority to the Muslims, perceiving themselves as representatives of European culture who were carrying out the French government's *mission civilisatrice* (Abitbol & Zisenwine, 2005, p. 47). The *pieds noirs*, who were totally alienated from the Muslims, developed their own identifying features, songs, and even a kind of national anthem. They had social, educational, cultural, and communications systems of their own that guaranteed separation from and hegemony over the Muslims. Several elements of their behavior that are reminiscent of those of the Jewish settlers in the West Bank and the Gaza Strip (before the evacuation of Israelis from the latter), such as demanding that the army clamp down on the Muslim population, forcefully repressing signs of hostility and attempted rebellion, withholding concessions from Muslims, and blocking any attempts at improving conditions for them. In Algeria, as in Israel, the settlers gained the support of the nationalist right and were constantly censured in left-wing circles. In Algeria, as in the West Bank, the settlers were viewed as a spearhead, as brutal representatives of a conquering, repressive regime. Hence, it was considered permissible and even obligatory to strike at them with harsh acts of terrorism. Conversely, the French always considered the Algerian nationalist fighters to be terrorist miscreants who carried out horrendous acts of murder and torture (Horne, 1977) and did not allow the media to interview spokespersons and leaders of the National Liberation Front (FLN), just as the Israeli media were enjoined not to interview those of the PLO.

There are certain similarities in rhetorical behavior as well, especially regarding the development of whitewashed terminology. For years, the French would not use the term "war" to describe the revolt and the violent conflicts in Algeria, referring to them as "incidents perpetrated by a few terror gangs." Subsequently, they referred to the situation, perhaps sarcastically, as *la guerre sans nom*. In Israel and elsewhere, the situation was referred to by the Arabic term *intifada*, apparently to avoid such constraining terms as "revolt," "uprising," or "murderous riots."

Media realities in France largely resembled those that prevailed during the first two decades of Israel's rule in the territories; in both cases, they facilitated IW maintenance. In France, as in Israel, there was one monopolistic television channel, RTF, as well as public radio under government control that enjoyed a near monopoly except in border locations where Radio Luxembourg and Europe n° 1 (now called Europe 1) could be picked up. The printed press, too, was largely conformist and responsive to the censor's demands (Harrison, 1964). Furthermore, the French censor succeeded in delaying the screening of noted director Jean-Luc Godard's film *Le Petit Soldat* (1960), claiming that the torture portrayed did not reflect historical reality. A similar ban was imposed on Gillo Pontecorvo's film *La Bataille d'Alger* (1966), with censors claiming that it could cause trauma among the *pieds noirs* then living in France.[21]

By controlling the media, the French government succeeded in popularizing its own preferred version of the security situation in the occupied territories in North Africa, depicting a revolt perpetrated by a handful of terrorists and the potential achievement of peace that did not require political negotiations with the Algerian nationalists. Reports of the events of October 17, 1961, may well represent the most outstanding manifestation of the French IW regarding the war in Algeria. In this case, the issue was not censorship or concealment of information about remote events but rather false and incomplete reports about the massacre of Algerian demonstrators by the French police, commanded by Maurice Papon.[22] The incident took place in the heart of Paris during dispersal of a demonstration by about 30,000 people of Algerian and other North African origin, during which anywhere from several dozen to nearly 200 demonstrators were apparently slaughtered (these figures, too, are subject to debate). The particulars of the incident were hushed up by the Paris police, with government encouragement, only to be revealed gradually, years later, in a series of publications, primarily by historian Jean-Luc Einaudi,[23] as well as in reports in the French press.[24]

The fierce extended conflict between Israel and the Arab world intensified the need to rally the Jewish public around the flag. For this purpose, an IW was erected to separate the two populations, with viewing apertures available only to a select few: namely, the Wallkeepers. To guard the Israeli narrative, the existing media and a few new alternative media were efficiently mobilized in reinforcing the traditional frames of the conflict. Thanks to the IW, an atmosphere of confrontation continued to prevail between Israel and its adversaries. The Wallkeepers' efficiency made it possible to control the flow of information between the two communities, supervise content and citizens' knowledge, reinforce the climate of conflict, preserve a strong motivation for armed confrontation, conduct an effective war of words, construct negative images of adversaries, render the adversary detestable to the point of demonization, easily rally the masses to the extended conflict, and more.

The IW proved its effectiveness in the coverage of Operation Cast Lead in Gaza, which began toward the end of December 2008, primarily with the story of the physician Dr. Abu Al-Ayash of the Jebaliya refugee camp, whose three daughters were killed. The various Wallkeepers, military correspondents, commentators, and columnists in all mainstream media cooperated with the IDF spokesperson in a long list of confusing announcements intended to show that it was not the IDF that had killed the girls. In the shadow of the efficient IW, the general public—and particularly the woman who admonished Dr. Abu Al-Ayash in the hospital corridor—had difficulty absorbing the fact that an Israeli shell had indeed hit the young women, thus undermining the IW. Some even tried to blame the doctor.[25] Once the truth was revealed, the media downplayed the incident.

The IW grew higher as the physical distance between the rival populations decreased, remaining stable and effective after the occupation of the territories.

Despite the unmediated encounter between Israelis and Palestinians, information about the adversary continued to rest chiefly on an aggregate of stereotypes and images rather than facts and data (First, 1998). However, routine encounters and interpersonal contacts between the two communities could topple the wall and weaken the tension required to maintain the conflict (Maoz, 2006: Maoz & Ellis, 2008). With the requisite measure of caution, one may assume that the possibility of such encounters impelled the Wallkeepers to increase the IW's height and intensify the control of information flow about and from Palestinian society. The dual intelligence system rallied once again to raise the IW and preserve the public consensus regarding conflict with the enemy, especially with the Palestinians.

As anticipated, the Wallkeepers are still developing immanent interests in perpetuating the IW, which is apparently far more difficult to topple than a physical wall. Superfluous cracks or dismantling of the IW could endanger their status. Today, as always, the Wallkeepers may be contributing more to maintaining the conflict between Israel and its adversaries than to its resolution and termination. A cognitive wall is more durable but also more difficult to remove than a physical one, a feature that simultaneously constitutes its greatest advantage and its most serious drawback.

Even if media and technological realities are different and more complex today than they were in the 1950s and 1960s, largely thanks to the multiplicity of media—satellite and Internet communication—that ostensibly guarantees free flow of information, an IW can still be erected and situations of conflict and occupation sealed behind it. A comparative study of IWs, especially in situations of occupation, may contribute to the understanding and resolution of conflicts. In Algeria, in Tibet, or in the case of the Israeli-Palestinian conflict, the following question arises repeatedly: to what extent did the IW contribute to the violent national conflict and would the historical process have been different had an IW not been erected between occupier and occupied?

NOTES

1. This article was written in one of the northern neighborhoods of Jerusalem at a distance of about 5 km from Ramallah and with virtually total dependence on Israeli media regarding what is happening "around the corner."
2. The media as a whole are thus perceived as one institution comprising several organizations, each of which has functionaries fulfilling roles guided by values and norms. Like all institutions, the media institution maintains reciprocal relations with other institutions in society and manifests a variety of orientations that create the moral climate affecting such relations (Caspi 2006, 241–281).

3. This periodical commenced publication in 1980 at the settlement of Ofra in the Binyamin District, edited by Israel Harel on behalf of the Council of Settlements in Judea, Samaria and Gaza, with a right-wing, nationalist orientation. At first, the monthly was financed by municipal taxes at settlements that included subscriptions for residents. After many of them cancelled their subscriptions, whether for ideological or financial reasons, the publication's leaders had to find alternative sources of income and began selling it at newsstands on both sides of the Green Line. In 2004, *Nekuda* was acquired by Shlomo Ben-Zvi and a right-wing media conglomerate. For further details (in Hebrew), see http://he.wikipedia.org/wiki/%D7%A0%D7%A7%D7%95%D7%93%D7%94_(%D7%9B%D7%AA%D7%91_%D7%A2%D7%AA). All Internet references in this article were retrieved on April 17, 2009.
4. Hebrew: http://www.inn.co.il; English: http://www/israelnationalnews.com; *Besheva* weekly (Hebrew): http://www.inn.co.il/Besheva and radio and television transmissions: http://www.inn.co.il/TV. See also: http://he.wikipedia.org/wiki/%D7%A2%D7%A8%D7%95%D7%A5_7.
5. http://yeshanews.com/archive/20090410123.
6. Israel's Media Watch (http://www.imw.org.il/english) was established in 1995. Its goals include "conducting systematic criticism and monitoring of the media and exposing political and cultural media bias" and left-wing bias in the broadcast media. Heads of the organization are especially active in submitting complaints against broadcasters who do not agree with the right wing's stand on policy and security. In early April 2009, for example, the organization's Director-General and a colleague sent a letter to the IDF Chief of Staff, complaining of *Galei Zahal*'s intention to hire a broadcaster who declared she had evaded army service (http://filesdot.imw.org.il/scans/glz-galili.pdf).
7. *Keshev*'s supporting bodies include the European Union, the Ford Foundation, the New Israel Fund, the United States Institute of Peace, the Friedrich Ebert Stiftung and the Foundation for Middle East Peace. See http://www.keshev.org.il/Site/FullNews.asp?CategoryID=6.
8. In general, there is a kind of division of labor among the three monitoring bodies: PMW (http://www.pmw.org.il), as its name implies, focuses on Palestinian media and topics; NGO Monitor (see http://en.wikipedia.org/wiki/NGO_Monitor) monitors civil rights organizations and identifies bias toward the Palestinian side in their publications and reports and MEMRI (see http://en.wikipedia.org/wiki/Middle_East_Media_Research_Institute), the most balanced and systematic of the three, attempts to provide a daily report on events in the Arab world and the Palestinian Authority Areas in particular, according to Arabic-language media.
9. On April 5, 2009, PMW distributed its film on the Hezbollah spectacle at the Islamic University in Gaza. Several hours thereafter, noted Israeli Arab affairs correspondent Ehud Yaari screened the film, including the PMW identifying title, during Channel 2's top-rated main news program.

10. This group of journalists includes Israel Harel, Hagai Segal, Hayuta Deutsch, Uri Elizur, Elyashiv Reichner, Shai Cherka and (now MK) Uri Orbach.
11. See critical comment on this issue by Prof. Yuli Tamir, Minister of Education. http://news.walla.co.il/?w=/90/1214505.
12. See http://en.wikipedia.org/wiki/Operation_Warm_Winterhttp://www.aqsa.org.uk/Portals/0/Newspapers/NL_32.pdf.
13. See http://www.haaretz.com/hasen/spages/1009172.html.
14. See http://en.wikipedia.org/wiki/Samir_Kuntar.
15. See http://www.ynet.co.il/articles/0,7340,L-3513634,00.htm.
16. In Nablus, for example, as in other places in the West Bank, enthusiastic residents left their homes and cheered the Israeli tanks entering the city, thinking they were Iraqi tanks, as they had been told in the Arab victory broadcasts.
17. Lt.-Gen. (ret.) Moshe Yaalon, former IDF Chief of Staff, a distinguished fellow at the Shalem Centre's Adelson Institute for Strategic Studies, is among the best-known examples (Yaalon 2008).
18. After the Rector of the Hebrew University of Jerusalem, Prof. Haim D. Rabinowitch, opposed a special program for Israel Security Agency (ISA) recruits that offered an undergraduate degree in political science in 16 months, the front page of *Haaretz* featured a letter of complaint by ISA Chief Yuval Diskin to the Prime Minister and Minister of Education (who is also Chair of the Israel Council for Higher Education). Diskin's reasoning speaks for itself: "Rabinowitch's attitude toward ISA personnel, whose job includes prevention of attacks against the university, is patronizing and dismissive" (*Haaretz*, August 4, 2008).
19. The Arab Higher Committee was the central and permanent executive organ of the Arab community during the British Mandate, established in 1936 and presided over by Amīn al-Husaynī (2008).
20. The origin of the nickname *pieds noirs* (black feet) is not clear, but the label clearly identified the settlers as a separate and different community, distinct not only from the Arabs and Berbers in Algeria but also from the settlers' communities of origin in the mother country—France—and elsewhere in Europe.
21. Vehement differences of opinion also emerged in 2010 concerning a new film by Rachid Bouchareb, *Hors la Loi*, based on eyewitness accounts of the massacre in the Algerian city of Sétif in May 1945, just as World War II had come to an end. The massacre, of unknown dimensions (versions range from several hundred to ten thousand fatalities), carried out by French soldiers in Sétif, is considered the first violent and horrendous incident in Algeria's struggle for independence (Ben-Simon, 2007).
22. Later, it emerged that Papon was a Nazi collaborator responsible for sending Jews to the death camps.
23. In a well known *Le Monde* article dated May 20, 1998, Einaudi disclosed: "En octobre 1961, il y eut à Paris un massacre perpétré par des forces de police agissant sous les ordres de Maurice Papon."

24. See, for example, *Le Monde*'s summary on the anniversary of the massacre (October 17, 2001), including the placing of a plaque on the Saint Michel Bridge, from which police cast wounded demonstrators into the Seine).
25. See video footage—http://www.youtube.com/watch?v=bpaIlC3FI88&feature =related: http://www.youtube.com/watch?v=mh_F0p8Jcrc&feature=related

REFERENCES

Abitbol, M., & and Zisenwine, D. (2005). *From colonialism to nationalism: Tunisia, Algeria, Morocco*. Raanana: The Open University Press (in Hebrew).

Ayish, M. I. (2002). Political communication on Arab world television: Evolving patterns. *Political Communication, 19*(2), 137–154.

Bar-Tal, D., & Jacobson, D. (1998). A psychological perspective on security. *Applied Psychology, 47*(1), 59–71.

Bar-Zohar, O., & Georgi, A. (2009). Not Friday observant. *The Marker* (financial supplement), week of April 8; see also http://www.themarker.com/tmc/article.jhtml?ElementId=skira20090408_1077263&from=haaretz (in Hebrew). Retrieved on April 17, 2009.

Ben-Simon, D. (2007, June 12). Still waiting for pardon. *Haaretz*, p. b1 (in Hebrew).

Boyd, D. A. (1993). *Broadcasting in the Arab world*. Ames: Iowa State University Press.

Caspi, D. (2002). *Galei Zahal*—Speaking to the field. In R. Mann & Z. Gon-Gross (Eds.), *Galei Zahal—Speaking from the field* (pp. 96–97). Tel Aviv: *Galei Zahal* and Miskal (in Hebrew).

Caspi, D. (2005). *Due to technical difficulties: The fall of the Israeli Broadcasting Authority*. Mevaseret Zion (Israel): Tzivonim (in Hebrew). http://www.tzivonim.com/xcart/product.php?productid=67&cat=0&page=1. Retrieved on April 17, 2009.

Caspi, D. (2006). The unending institutionalization of the mass media in Israel. In U. Cohen, E. Ben-Refael, A. Bareli, & E. Yaar (Eds.), *Israel and modernity: Moshe Lissak Jubilee Volume* (pp. 241–281). Beersheba, Israel: Ben-Gurion Institute for the Study of Israel, Zionism and the Ben-Gurion Heritage, Ben-Gurion University of the Negev and Yad Itzhak Ben-Zvi. http://www.ybz.org.il/?ArticleID=1586 (in Hebrew). Retrieved on April 17, 2009.

Caspi, D. (2008). Israel: From monopoly to open skies. In D. Ward (Ed.), *Television and public policy: Change and continuity in an era of liberalization* (pp. 305–320). New York: Erlbaum.

Cohen, H. (2006). *Good Arabs: Israeli intelligence and the Arabs in Israel*. Jerusalem: Keter (in Hebrew).

Cohen, H. (2008). Between a rock and hard place: Palestinian pro-Zionist propagandists: Between Zionist institutions and Arab nationalists, 1930–1931. *Israel Affairs, 14*(1), 49–69.

Danin, E. (1987). *An unconditional Zionist—A*. Jerusalem: Kidum (in Hebrew).

Eyal, G. (2005). *Removing the magic from the Middle East: A history of orientalism in the age of Sephardic awareness*. Jerusalem: Van Leer (in Hebrew). http://www.vanleer.org.il/heb/publications.asp?id=64. Retrieved on April 17, 2009.

Fanon, F. (2006). *Damnés de la terre* (with a preface by Jean-Paul Sartre (O. Rosen, Hebrew Trans.).Tel Aviv: Babel.

First, A. (1998). Who is the enemy? The portrayal of Arabs in Israeli television news. *Gazette, 60*(3), 239–251.

Gabel, I. (2006). The national-religious public and the media: A love-hate relationship. Tel Aviv: Herzog Institute, Tel Aviv University. http://www.tau.ac.il/institutes/herzog/relig_pressjul06.pdf (in Hebrew). Retrieved on April 17, 2009.

Gaddis, J. L. (2006). *Cold war: A new history*. New York: Penguin Books.

Harrison, M. (1964). Government and press in France during the Algerian war. *American Political Science Review, 58*(2), 273–285.

Hass, A. (2008, March 4). Selective knowledge. *Haaretz*, p. 16A (in Hebrew). http://www.haaretz.co.il/hasite/pages/ShArt.jhtml?more=1&itemNo=961157&contrassID=2&subContrassID=13&sbSubContrassID=0. Retrieved on April 17, 2009.

Horne, A. (1977) *A savage war of peace*. New York: Viking Press.

al-Husayni, A. (2008). In *Encyclopædia Britannica*. Encyclopædia Britannica Online. http://www.britannica.com/EBchecked/topic/277483/Amin-al-Husayni. Retrieved on April 17, 2009.

Jacobson, D., & Bar-Tal, D. (1995). Structure of security beliefs among Israeli students. *Political Psychology, 16*(3), 567–590.

Kabha, M., & Caspi, D. (2001). From holy Jerusalem to the wellspring: Competing trends in Israel's Arabic press. *Panim, 16*, 44–56 (in Hebrew). http://www.itu.org.il/Index.asp?ArticleID=1205&CategoryID=502&Page=1. Retrieved on April 17, 2009.

Kabha, M., & Caspi, D. (2011). *The Arab in/outsiders: Media and conflict in Israel*. London: Valentine Mitchell.

Kies, N. (1975). The impact of public policy on public opinion. *State, Government and International Relations, 8*, 36–81 (in Hebrew).

Kraidy, M. M. (2002). Arab satellite television: Between regionalization and globalization. *Global Media Journal, 1*(1).

http://lass.calumet.purdue.edu/cca/gmj/OldSiteBackup/SubmittedDocuments/archivedpapers/fall2002/kraidy.htm. Retrieved on April 17, 2009.

Jenks, J. (2006). *British propaganda and news media in the cold war*. Edinburgh: University Press.

Lee, A. W.-M. (2009). Tibet and the media: Perspectives from Beijing. *Marquette Law Review, 93*(1), 209–230.

Lustick, I. S. (1993). *Unsettled states, disputed lands: Britain and Ireland, France and Algeria, Israel and the West Bank-Gaza*. Ithaca, NY: Cornell University Press.

Maoz, I. (2006). Moving between conflict and coexistence: Encounters between Jews and Arabs in Israel. In E. Podeh & A. Kaufman (Eds.), *From war to peace: The Israeli-Palestinian peace process* (pp. 319–341). Sussex, United Kingdom: Academic Press.

Maoz, I., & Ellis, D. G. (2008). Intergroup communication as a predictor of Jewish-Israeli agreement with integrative solutions to the Israeli-Palestinian conflict: The mediating effects of out-group trust and guilt. *Journal of Communication*, *58*(3), 490–507.

Meital, Y. (2002). The Lighthouse. *Haayin Hashviit*, p. 41 (in Hebrew). http://www.the7eye.org.il/dailycolumn/pages/article4116.aspx. Retrieved on April 17, 2009.

Meital, Y. (2006). *Peace in tatters: Israel, Palestine, and the Middle East*. Boulder, CO: Lynne Rienner.

Miles, H. (2005). *Al-Jazeera: How Arab TV news challenged the world*. London: Abacus.

Mohammadi, A. (Ed.). (1997). *International communication and globalization: A critical introduction*. London: Sage.

Mowlana, H. (1997). *Global information and world communication: New frontiers in international relations*. London: Sage.

Newman, D. (Ed.). (1985). *The impact of Gush Emunim*. London: Croom Helm.

Oren, A. (2008, August 29). Shin Bet chief: "Hebrew Univ. Rector slandered my agency." *Haaretz*, p. 1 (in Hebrew). http://www.haaretz.com/hasen/spages/1016066 (in Hebrew); http://www.haaretz.com/hasen/spages/1016179.html (in English). Retrieved on April 17, 2009.

Ring, I. (2008, March 7). Our commander...oops...Our commentator is here with us. *Haaretz* supplement, p. 10 (in Hebrew). http://www.haaretz.co.il/hasite/pages/ShArt.jhtml?more=1&itemNo=961157&contrassID=2&subContrassID=13&sbSubContrassID=0. Retrieved on April 17, 2009.

Rubinstein, D. (1982). *On the Lord's side, let him come unto me—Gush Emunim*. Tel Aviv: Hakibbutz Hameuhad (in Hebrew).

Schwoch, J. (2009). *Global TV: New media and cold war 1946–69*. Urbana and Champaign: University of Illinois Press. http://books.google.com/books?id=bFCbAn5j6gIC&printsec=frontcover&hl=iw&cd=1&source=gbs_ViewAPI#v=onepage&q&f=false. Retrieved on April 17, 2009.

Servan-Schreiber, J.-J. (1957). *Lieutenant in Algeria* (R. Matthews, Trans). New York: Knopf. Translated into Hebrew by Uri Dromi. Published Jerusalem: Keter, 2002.

Yaalon, M. (2008, September 2). A new strategy for the Israeli-Palestinian conflict. *Jerusalem Issue Brief*, *8*(10),

Yaari, E. (1970). *Strike terror: The story of Fatah*. New York. Sabra Books.

Yaron, N. (2001). *Channel 2: The new statism*. Tel Aviv: Resling (in Hebrew).

CHAPTER 10

Economic Cost of the Occupation to Israel

Shir Hever[1.]

The forty-three years of Israeli occupation in the West Bank (including East Jerusalem) and the Gaza Strip have had a transformative effect on the Israeli economy. Unlike the Israeli occupation of the Golan Heights, and the past occupations of southern Lebanon and the Sinai Peninsula, the occupation of the Palestinian territories (hereafter referred to as the "territories") has been defined by means of the large civilian population that has come under Israeli control. Though Israeli economists have tried to dismiss the importance of the occupation in the overall analysis of the Israeli economy, one can trace the pervasive impact of the Israeli policies in the territories on Israeli society itself, in which the economic sphere was not the least affected.

The question addressed in this chapter is that of the cost of the occupation to Israel. Before delving into the economic calculations, however, some clarifications are in order. First, the goal here is to focus on the cost of the occupation to Israel, not to the Palestinians. The term "cost" is relevant when discussing an expenditure for something optional, and one can safely say that the Israeli government, backed by popular support, has elected to maintain its control over the territories despite opportunities to end the occupation. The Palestinians, however, did not choose to be occupied. The occupation is not a product that they purchased, and therefore a more appropriate term would be the "damage" of the occupation rather than the cost. A detailed and up-to-date study of the damage of the occupation to the Palestinians has unfortunately yet to be compiled.

The term "Israel" too should be clarified. Israel is a state and, as such, it is comprised of institutions. These institutions are charged with public funds, which are spent on various projects. This study focuses on the costs incurred by institutions that are part of the state apparatus of Israel. It does not focus on the costs for individual Israelis. For example, many Israelis own firearms that they purchase because they believe that they need them for their security should they be attacked by Palestinians (usually inside the territories). The cost of purchasing these firearms is not included in the calculations presented here.

Furthermore, all the costs presented in the following calculations are only for expenses above the normal public expenditure per average Israeli citizen. The underlying hypothesis is that even if Israel had withdrawn from the territories, it would still have been required to fund public services for its citizens living within its legitimate borders rather than in the illegal settlements. Thus, all the calculations focus on the extra subsidies that settlers enjoy and that ordinary Israelis do not receive.

The costs that will be calculated are only economic costs, loss of assets whose value can be assessed in monetary terms. Loss of life, injury, and psychological damage incurred as a result of the occupation and the resistance to it are not discussed here, but not because such losses are seen as less important. Compensation from the Israeli National Insurance Institute (NII) to victims of Palestinian resistance, however, is included. This obviously leaves much of the cost of the occupation in the dark, because the Israeli economy has clearly lost a great deal as a result of personal hardship, pain, and suffering caused by the Palestinian resistance to the occupation, as well as the deterioration of Israel's rule of law and of transparent government practices, as a result of the clandestine funding of the settlements for decades.

Finally, when one discusses costs, it is also important to talk about profits. Israeli authorities and companies have implemented various mechanisms to exploit the Palestinian economy, as will be described below. When calculating costs, it is necessary to deduct from them the income that Israel has generated from the occupation. The argument here that the occupation has overall been a burden on the Israeli economy rather than an asset is not a trivial one and requires proof, which will be presented.

HISTORICAL OVERVIEW

The Israeli expenditure on the occupation, and the income generated from it, are not constant. Analyzing the occupation over three periods of time reveals the main developments in Israel's economic relations with the territories:

1. Early occupation: 1967 to 1986.
2. Late occupation (years of resistance): 1987 to 2001.
3. Privatized occupation: 2002 to the present.

During the first period, from 1967 to the mid-1980s, Israel's control over the territories was achieved with minimal efforts by the Israeli military. The few troops stationed there were enough to control the civilian population with relatively few instances of fighting (compared to other military occupations around the world; Gordon, 2008). The costs of maintaining the occupation were low. The Israeli economy also profited from the occupation for the following reasons:

1. The taxes collected by the Israeli government from the Palestinians exceeded the expenditures of the Israeli institutions in the territories (Swirski, 2005).
2. The Palestinians were a captive market for Israeli goods, especially low-quality goods unfit for sale in the Israeli market (Strassler, 2005).
3. Israeli employers hired Palestinians at very low wages, thus boosting their profits (Swirski, 2005).
4. Israeli illegal settlements in the territories expropriated land and water resources from the Palestinians (B'tselem, 2002).
5. Israeli construction companies set up quarries in the West Bank and Gaza Strip; over the decades of occupation, they have depleted a significant proportion of the Palestinian natural resources (Rinat, 2008).

Though the early period of the occupation was profitable for Israel, this situation gradually changed during the 1980s. The settlement expansion became a growing drain on the Israeli public budget, and Palestinian resistance to the occupation took on new proportions with the first *intifada*. Israel had to deploy more troops and equipment to fortify the settlements, checkpoints, and military installations. Exports to the territories were cut almost in half (mostly as a result of a Palestinian boycott of Israeli goods), and tourism to Israel dropped (Gordon, 2008). The occupation ceased to be profitable in the 1980s when the costs of maintaining it became greater than the income it generated. The negative impact on the Israeli economy reached a peak during the second *intifada*, when Israel fell into a deep recession. The income generated by controlling the territories did little to offset the mounting costs of the occupation.

The third period of the occupation overlaps the second and continues to do so. After the second *intifada*, the Israeli military and political leadership tried to adapt to the U.S.-led approach to "war on terror."[2] This adaptation included changes to Israel's military structure, as well as massive privatization of many of the military's roles, including maintenance of the checkpoints (Buhbut, 2008) and settlements defense (Cohen, 2008). In addition, there was a withdrawal of Israeli settlers from the Gaza Strip, and construction of the separation wall began.

The new structure did not reduce the costs of occupation for the Israeli government, but it did create numerous business opportunities for private security companies. These companies—some previously government-owned and later privatized, others set up by retired Israeli army officers—are well positioned to land contracts with the Israeli government, selling their wares to the Israeli army. Later, they can use the fact that they already supply their products to the Israeli army as a selling point when negotiating with potential buyers around the world. Their expertise in equipment, services, and techniques, which have already been used to "fight terrorism," helps them convince buyers to pay high prices for their products (Klein, 2007a).

Since the mid-1990s, international aid efforts to the territories have also created another source of income for the Israeli economy. Since Israel controls all the points of access into the territories, aid agencies must use Israel's seaports, airports, and land transportation, and often buy goods intended for distribution from Israeli companies, because those products are exempt from customs. Furthermore, international aid creates a foreign currency inflow into Israel, because aid funds must be converted into Israeli currency before they can be used locally. The percentage of aid money that ends up in the Israeli economy has not yet been estimated. Palestinians do not have a separate currency, making it very difficult to trace the distribution of aid money between Israel and the territories (Hever, 2008).

ECONOMIC DISCOURSE ON THE COST OF OCCUPATION

Israeli economists have expressed differing opinions regarding the economic aspects of the occupation. In each of the periods described above, a different discourse was prevalent.

During the first period, Israeli mainstream economists rarely dealt with the effects of the occupation on the Israeli economy, focusing more on its effects on the Palestinian economy. At the time, there were many indications that the occupation was beneficial to the latter, and was a point of pride for Israeli economists who used economic argumentation to justify the morality of the occupation (e.g., Bergman, 1974). The occupation's effects on the Israeli economy were a topic addressed mostly by Marxist economists (e.g., Khouri, 1980), who applied theories of imperialism to argue that it was a source of profit.

During the second period following the first *intifada*, it became increasingly difficult to ignore the mounting cost of the occupation to the Israeli economy, as well as the devastation of the Palestinian economy. Furthermore, Israel's heavy hand in quelling the Palestinian resistance, while simultaneously pushing forward with illegal settlement expansion, has meant a high level of government intervention in the economy. Such intervention has become increasingly unpopular in the eyes of neoliberal economists. After the Oslo peace negotiations in the early 1990s, neoliberal economists began to argue with increasing vehemence that the occupation was a burden on the Israeli economy and that peace could lead to improved economic conditions in Israel (Hever, 2006). These arguments were strengthened by the outbreak of the second *intifada* in October 2000, which led to one of Israel's deepest recessions.

The third period has added a layer of complexity to the discussion. Although government spending on the settlements and military operations in the territories has not diminished, several private businessmen have found ways to exploit the situation to their advantage. They began to develop a new business sector of "homeland security," focusing less on developing traditional weapons, munitions, vehicles, and other tools for military use and more on surveillance, sophisticated armaments, perimeter security, specialized training of security personnel, and other such activities aimed at private companies and nonmilitary institutions, such as civilian airports. These new companies (or existing companies with new homeland security products) found the Israeli Ministry of Defense to be a willing customer and soon also began to export their products worldwide,[3] contributing to Israeli exports and to rising stock prices in the Tel Aviv stock market. Moreover, while its neoliberal policies (including tax cuts and slack regulation) have lured international companies into increasing their investments in Israel, the Israeli government has used the "security emergency" argument to push through rapid neoliberal reforms with minimal social resistance (see below). All of these factors have contributed to a period of high growth in the Israeli economy.

In light of this high growth rate, economists have found it easy to ignore the significance of the occupation to the Israeli economy. Despite a standstill in the peace negotiations, they have begun to argue that peace is not a requirement for prosperity (Landau, 2008).

GROWING AWARENESS OF THE COST

Most of the writings dealing with the cost of the occupation appeared between the beginning of the Oslo negotiations and the end of the second *intifada*. One of the most comprehensive works was written by Israeli sociologist Shlomo Swirski (2005), who attempted to summarize various estimates and sources of the cost of occupation.

Swirsky's book is a culmination of Israeli writings on the adverse effects of the occupation and the high cost of the settlements. Rubinstein (2005), Arnon, Luski, Spivak, and Weinblatt (1997), Ben-David (2005), and Berglas (1989) are among the noted Israeli economists who began stressing the economic burden of the occupation to the Israeli economy even before the second *intifada*. Most of these economists lean toward a right-wing economic perspective. Due to their objection to the occupation, however, they associate themselves with the Israeli Left. All of them have warned that the occupation is an expensive project that is dragging down the Israeli economy.

The surge of research on the economic costs of the occupation includes a study by Tsaban (2003), an extensive research project conducted by the newspaper *Ha'aretz* (2003), a paper by Gamliel (2005), and two studies by the Adva Center (Swirski, 2008a; Swirski, Konor-Atias, & Etkin, 2002). These studies suggest that the costs of the occupation apply to Israeli society as a whole, as a form of foregone utility from lost venues of investment, and that many aspects of the Israeli economy have been strained as a result of resources being spent on maintaining Israeli control over the territories.

Swirski argues that the Israeli decision to prevent the development of the Palestinian economy has contributed to the Palestinians' commitment to resisting the occupation, and it is due to this resistance that Israeli companies have lost their opportunities to continue to profit from the captive Palestinian market. The violent conflict has dissuaded Israelis from hiring Palestinians, and Palestinians have tried to boycott Israeli goods. Swirski also acknowledges that the occupation's impact on the Palestinians has been far more severe than its effect on Israelis (Swirski, 2005).

BREAKING DOWN THE COSTS

It is impossible to separate the cost of the settlements from the cost of the occupation itself. Military outposts and forts established to defend the settlements also become sources of oppression and subjugation of the local Palestinian population. It is easier for settlers to expropriate lands for expanding settlements in areas where the Israeli army exercises more control. These new settlements expand rapidly, and settlers quickly cry for more protection from the Israeli army, which readily obliges by expanding its presence. The engine of expenditure is thus almost self-propelling: civilian expenses lead to military expenses and vice versa (B'tselem, 2002; Sasson, 2005).

An inherent flaw in research of this type is that the necessary data from the Israeli army and the Ministry of Defense are unavailable. These data, which are essential for a comprehensive analysis, remain withheld under the guise of national security, making it impossible to conduct an accurate calculation of how much money Israel actually pays for the occupation (Lan, 2005).

The only recourse is therefore to make do with the available data, itemize the bill, and draw up a list of expenses versus income. The cost of the occupation is made up of numerous fragments, pieces of a puzzle that must be brought together. Trying to aggregate these numbers is risky. It requires an extrapolation of data that are available only for selected years. Therefore, estimates should only be considered as an approximation of the true cost. Nevertheless, it is important to make the attempt and offer a figure that can serve as a rough estimate and basis for future debates. The estimate offered by Swirski in 2005 was about NIS 100 billion (about US $23 billion), but that did not take into account price changes and accumulated interest. Furthermore, it was based on a rough impression, garnered from the figures and reports that Swirski put together, and not on a methodical tally (ibid.). Swirski's calculation also omitted the costs of increased security procedures inside the Green Line because of the occupation, increased police expenditure, and the construction of more prisons and police stations (both inside Israel and in the territories), which together form the biggest item of expenditure on the occupation.

THE HIDDEN FACTS

The difficulty in obtaining the relevant data does not stem from any lack of effort by the various researchers who have looked into the cost of the occupation and published their findings, but rather from the Israeli government's deliberate policy of keeping the facts obscured. Data on the occupation are systematically concealed by the Israeli government (Blau, 2009). One example of this clandestine spending is that of the municipal subsidies to settlements. Following the Oslo Accords, Israel began to secretly funnel millions of shekels to the settlements every year through the Ministry of the Interior. These transfers came to as much as NIS 66 million annually. In 2004, the sum transferred to the settlements by the Ministry was identical to the total sum allocated to the impoverished municipalities within the Green Line (Strassler, 2004).

A defiant minister leaked the details of this process to the press. Half of the sum was labeled "Oslo grants" and the other half "*intifada* grants." The names indicate that the justification given for these grants was to compensate settlers for enduring the Oslo process, in which Israel had discussed the possibility of evacuating settlements (the grants were used as a sort of bribe to keep the settlers from protesting against the negotiations, although as such they were not effective and the settlers did, in fact, protest), and for the hardships of living in a Palestinian area where the population is in rebellion against the Israeli occupation (Gamliel ,2005; Strassler, 2004).

Ironically, even government ministers are unable to access the actual data regarding the cost of the occupation, as is evident from the experience of several who tried but failed (Gamliel, 2005; Strassler, 2004). Even simple pieces of information such as the municipal boundaries and jurisdictions of settlements were withheld by the Israeli government until 2005, when they were disclosed following a petition by the Association for Civil Rights in Israel (ACRI, 2005).

There are two reasons for the clandestine manner in which fund transfers are made. One is to avoid public outrage inside Israel at the favoritism that the settlers enjoy. The second is to avoid international outrage at Israel's violations of international law. The special subsidies given to the settlements encourage people to move to them, thus violating the Fourth Geneva Convention, which forbids the transfer of civilian populations to an occupied territory. To hide the extent of the incentives that the government creates for would-be settlers, the subsidies are distributed into countless special budgets, one-time grants, ad-hoc funds, and so on, creating a financial maze that can only be navigated with great difficulty.

CAREFUL CALCULATION

Calculating the actual costs of the occupation to Israel requires a great deal of extrapolation. Often, data for only a few years are available, at the prices that were current during that period. Thus, the first step of the present calculation is to present the sums in terms of December 2007 prices. The next step is to estimate the accumulated cost for the entire period of the occupation. If data are available for only a limited number of years, the figures must be multiplied, based on the assumption that Israel has been subsidizing the settlements during the entire period 1970–2008. It is assumed here that costs between 1967 and 1969 were relatively negligible.

Simple multiplication won't do, however, because subsidies are proportional to the size of the population that is being supported by the government. The annual cost is adjusted to fit the changes in the settlement populations.[4] As there are no accurate figures for these populations between 1970 and 1975, the calculation will factor an estimated average population of 1,600 settlers, half the number listed for 1976. It is assumed that the settler population grows steadily and that there were no settlers prior to the occupation—ignoring, for the sake of simplicity, the surges and lulls in the rate of growth of the settlements.[5] Figure 10.1 shows the number of settlers for each year (Jerusalem Center for Israel Studies 2003, 2006; Peace Now, 2007). For example, the extra cost of education services to settlers in 2003 was estimated at NIS 118 million (already adjusted for 2007 prices; see below). In order to apply that cost to the entire period 1970–2008, the amount must be divided by the number of settlers for 2003, namely, 407,000. This means that the government paid about an extra NIS 290 per settler, on average, every year. By adding up the total education subsidies paid every year between 1970 and 2008, based on the number

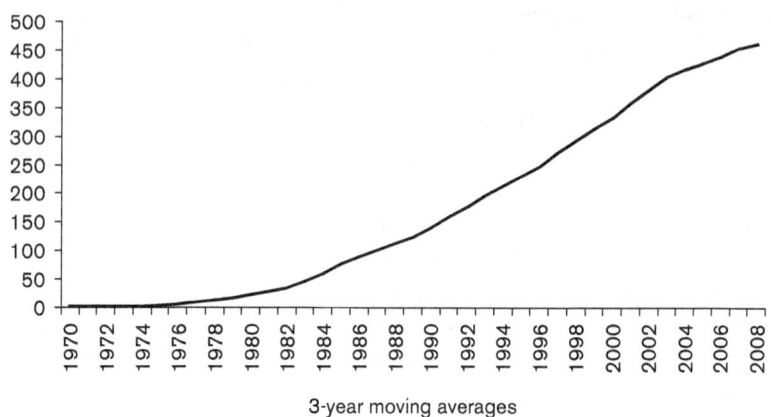

FIGURE 10.1 Settler population (thousands).

of settlers who lived in the territories each year, and adding interest (for the hypothetical investments that this money could have been used for if it hadn't been used for settlement subsidies), one can calculate an estimate of education subsidies of NIS 5.8 billion for the entire period.

This kind of extrapolation has been made wherever appropriate. When it was not appropriate (for costs or forms of income that only existed during certain years), I note for which years I have extrapolated.

THE CALCULATION

Interest

When discussing the concept of the "cost of the occupation," the hypothesis is that had there been no military occupation of the territories, the Israeli government could have allocated its funds in different ways and developed the Israeli economy instead. The cost is therefore measured not only in simple nominal terms, but also as foregone utility to the Israeli economy.

One could argue that economic investment in the settlements also has its own returns. This is indeed true, and the rapid expansion of the settlements is a telltale sign that the investment has borne fruit. Yet the question here is what could have been saved, in resources, if Israel had relinquished the territories. In order to answer this question, we must assume that the saved funds would not simply have been laid aside unused, but would have been incorporated into Israel's government budget and used for public services, for paying off debt, and for national projects.

Moreover, in the event of an Israeli withdrawal from the territories, the investment in the occupation would be largely lost to Israel, in which case it would indeed become a straightforward loss to the Israeli economy. For that reason, it is important to add interest to the calculation. There is no accurate way to determine what would have been the return on investing moneys in civilian projects in Israel instead of funding the occupation. In this calculation, the Bank of Israel interest rate is used as an approximation of that rate of return (since this is an approximation of the average interest rate available to Israeli investors; Israeli Central Bureau of Statistics [ICBS], various years). Interest has been added only to estimates that do not already include an interest value. After adjusting for interest, all the figures are given in 2007 prices.

Income

The costs to Israel's government of maintaining the occupation must be compared to the income it generates in order to obtain an idea of whether the bottom line is positive or negative. For the purposes of this calculation, only costs paid directly by the Israeli government have been tallied, although on the income side estimates were also made for income to other nongovernment authorities in Israel. This is because it is difficult to determine what percentage of the income of private companies and institutions from the occupation is later appropriated by the government through direct and indirect taxation. Since what actually concerns us is the cost paid by the Israeli public, it can be assumed that some of the income generated by nongovernment Israeli authorities reaches a part of the Israeli public.

The income generated to the Israeli economy from the occupation can be divided into several categories:

- *Social Security*: Prior to the Paris Accords, the Israeli government levied taxes on Palestinian workers who worked in Israel and in the settlements; social security payments between 1968 and 1993 were estimated at NIS 1.327 billion. The services normally awarded in return for this tax were not provided to the Palestinian workers. This figure was calculated by economists Stanley Fischer and Thomas Shelling (Swirski, 2005).
- *Wage Additions*: Kav Laoved, an Israeli workers' rights organization, found that NIS 953.65 million was confiscated in various other forms of wage additions between 1984 and 1992. For example, Palestinian workers in Israel had to pay a "security tax" for the costs of monitoring them in the workplace (Swirski, 2005).
- *Union Fees*: Palestinian workers were forced to pay union fees to the Israeli Histadrut (the Federation of Labor Unions in Israel), even though

the Histadrut offered them no protection or assistance. These fees were estimated at NIS 567.96 million (Swirski, 2005).
- *Economic Exploitation*: Income was also generated through the exploitation of Palestinian cheap labor, the captive market, and water and land resources. Economists Bichler and Nitzan (2001) estimated that this exploitation accumulated to 10% of Israel's GDP in 2001, or NIS 58.99 billion.[6]
- *Transfers to the Palestinian Authority*: In order to keep the calculations as accurate as possible, it is important to account for the fact that since 1994 Israel has been obligated to transfer funds to the Palestinian Authority (PA), collected on its behalf. The sums include customs, tariffs, value-added tax (VAT), and taxation of Palestinian workers (Swirski, 2005). These transfers aren't really a cost of the occupation, since they are simply sources of PA income that are collected by Israel. Israel levies administrative fees and commissions before transferring the funds to the PA, and even allows Israeli companies to collect debts for services rendered to the PA or to Palestinian municipalities directly from these funds before they are transferred to the PA, without an arbitration process (Swirski, 2008b). In order to keep the calculation as accurate as possible, transfers to the PA should be subtracted from the income that Israel gains from controlling the Palestinian market. They are, in effect, a partial refund of the profit that Israel makes from the occupation. For 1996–2006, the sum of payments was NIS 29.34 billion. It is not extrapolated backward, because Israel only began to make these payments in 1996 (Israeli Revenue Authority, 2007).

SETTLEMENT SUBSIDIES

Transferring civilian populations to live in an occupied territory is a violation of the Fourth Geneva Convention, to which Israel is a signatory. Although the Israeli government doesn't force Israeli citizens to live in the settlements, the many economic incentives offered to settlers and to settlement municipalities are part of the reason for the rapid migration of Israelis to the territories.

The subsidies are divided into several categories:

- *Agriculture*: The World Zionist Organization (WZO), ostensibly working for the benefit of the Jewish people, has been used systematically as a primary apparatus for investments in the settlements. Funded heavily by the Israeli government, the WZO spends money developing agricultural projects in the settlements that are owned by Jews. Swirski (2005) estimated that between 2000 and 2002 alone, NIS 454.13 million were spent by the WZO on such projects.

- *Education*: The Israeli government invests more in schools in the settlements than in average schools inside Israel. Incentives to teachers, transportation for children, and fewer pupils per classroom all contribute to this excess expenditure as opposed to the expenditure on average Israeli pupils. Saar (2003) has estimated that the extra funds came to NIS 118 million for 2003 alone.
- *Health Care*: The settlements enjoy an extensive overinvestment in health care. Isolated settlements have a clinic for every 50–100 residents, far higher than the ratio of clinics to population inside Israel. Furthermore, the medical staff receives benefits for operating in the settlements, and extra costs are incurred by special security measures, armored vehicles, guards, and so on. Swirski (2005) quotes the *Ha'aretz* estimate of NIS 2.07 billion for the extra healthcare costs in the settlements until the year 2002.
- *Housing*: These costs include government subsidies for housing in the settlements and subsidized loans and grants to settlers to buy their houses. Swirski (2005) estimates this cost at NIS 3.39 billion between 1990 and 1999.
- *Industry*: Industrial zones built inside the settlements for the benefit of the settlers were bolstered by extra subsidies of NIS 280 million, accumulated between 1997 and 2001, according to an estimate by Tsaban (2003). This refers only to government expenditures, not private investments.
- *Municipalities*: In recent years, the Israeli government has implemented cuts in the budgets of local municipalities in Israel, except for the settlement municipalities, which have continued to receive funding above the Israeli average. Some of the budgets were used by the settlers to fund demonstrations and campaigns against evacuation (Strassler, 2004; Yoaz, 2005a). Swirski (2005) estimates that a total of NIS 2.7 billion was provided in the 1990s as extra funding to the municipalities of the settlements. This means that settlements received more than double the equivalent per capita funding for municipalities within the Green Line.
- *Roads*: A special network of bypass roads, for the exclusive use of settlers, allows access to every isolated settlement while dividing the Palestinians into isolated and blockaded enclaves. Road construction in and to the territories settlements far exceeds the rate of construction inside Israel. The journalist Ze'ev Sheef estimated that between 1993 and 2002, a total of NIS 1.47 billion was spent on road construction for the settlements, but the true costs remain hidden because the budget for

bypass roads was transferred to the Ministry of Defense in order to conceal it (Gamliel, 2005; Swirski, 2005).
- *Tax Benefits*: Settlers also receive tax breaks simply for having their permanent address in a settlement. Their biggest tax break is in income tax. A report by *Ha'aretz* estimated that settlers received discounts worth a total of NIS 1.69 billion up to 2003, although other reports (such as Gamliel, 2005) estimated that tax breaks were almost double that amount (*Ha'aretz*, 2003). The more conservative estimates are used here.
- *Water*: Israel has invested a great deal in creating a water infrastructure for the settlers, based mostly on exploiting the mountain aquifer in the West Bank and preventing the Palestinians from using it. It is important to note that Palestinian water consumption per capita is one-third that of Israeli water consumption (Lein, 2000). The expenditure on water infrastructure beyond the average water costs for the Israeli population within the Green Line was NIS 562 million in the decade up to 2003 (*Ha'aretz*, 2003).

SECURITY COSTS

The settlement subsidies still attract Israelis to move to them, but Palestinian resistance to the Israeli occupation has created additional costs for the Israeli government in maintaining control over the territories. The Palestinian resistance, violent or nonviolent, has been met with the use of overwhelming force by Israeli authorities, and though the damage inflicted upon Palestinians during the conflict certainly has been greater than that suffered by Israelis, the economic cost to Israel should not be underestimated.

Since 1967, in order to secure Israeli control over the territories and to safeguard Israeli citizens from the violent aspects of the Palestinian resistance, Israeli authorities have pursued policies of spatial control through surveillance, patrols, fences, walls, checkpoints, and permits. This complex system has become the largest component of Israeli expenditure in the territories (Gordon, 2008). The investment of money, equipment, manpower, and effort, as well as the use of force by the Israeli authorities, has not been confined to maintaining the security of Israelis. It is also an effort to perpetuate the hierarchical relations in the territories in order to keep Israel in complete control of movement, knowledge, and economic activities in the area (Azoulay & Ophir, 2008). Furthermore, a great deal of effort is spent on trying to keep the Israeli and Palestinian populations separated—not only to prevent Palestinians from entering Israel and interacting with Israelis, but also to prevent Israelis from entering Palestinian communities and interacting with Palestinians.[7] The

Israeli authorities also strive to project the image that Palestinian violence is under control and can be contained by the use of force. Although in this chapter the loss of human lives as a result of Palestinian resistance to the occupation will not be discussed, it is important to calculate the compensation paid by the Israeli NII to those injured by Palestinian resistance or to the families of those killed by Palestinian violence.

Security costs are particularly difficult to estimate because the expenditure is distributed among many budgets, some of which are confidential. For example, the budget for settlement roads mentioned above used to include a clause for "security," comprising 19% of the overall allocation; but when road construction for the settlements was transferred from the Ministry of Transportation to the Ministry of Defense, the budget became confidential, and as a result the security component is now hidden (Gamliel, 2005).

Security costs are calculated here only for activities such as guarding the settlements, or for actions taken in the territories with the intention of maintaining control over the area and the people, and of preventing or defeating Palestinian violence against the settlements or against Israel. Since the Israeli authorities do not publish these figures, an estimate is used. The components of this estimate are:

- *Special Additions to the Defense Budget*: The special budgets for military actions in the territories have exceeded NIS 30.6 billion since 1989, in addition to the regular defense budget, part of which covers actions in the territories anyway (Swirski, 2008a). There is also the budget of the Unit of Government Activities in the Territories (COGAT), which since 1994 has been in charge of coordinating military activities there. This unit's budget was NIS 3.42 billion for the years 1994–2008, based on the budget reports of the Ministry of Finance.
- *Compensation to Civilians injured by Palestinian Violence*: Between 1980 and 2003, compensation to those directly injured or killed in Palestinian attacks totaled NIS 2.776 billion. According to Swirski (2005), before 1980 there were very few injured and dead on the Israeli side, so there is no point in extrapolating this sum backward.
- *Police and Internal Security*: By far the biggest security expenditure of the Israeli government on the occupation is for police and internal security because of the massive efforts required to contain the resistance to the occupation and to retain control over the territories and over dissenting voices within Israel. The Israeli internal security forces are charged with fighting terrorism; fighting crime is only their second priority (Swirski, 2005). The average rate of annual increase in the various government

budgets dedicated to internal security (the police force, the border police, the prison authority, and other forces) has more than doubled since 1968. By creating a hypothetical extrapolation of these budgets for the years 1968–2008 based on their annual growth rate before 1968, and comparing it with the actual budgets approved by the Israeli governments for these years, a wide discrepancy is revealed.

In the years 1968–2008, the Israeli government invested a total of 17.3% more on these budgets than it would have been expected to spend without the increased burden incurred by the occupation. After applying interest (see below), this becomes the largest portion of the cost of the occupation and is divided as follows: 4.2% for construction of extra jails and police stations, 7.4% for extra expenses for the border police, 14.9% for extra expenses for the prison authority, and 73.5% for other security-related expenses (based on Israel's budget accounts in various years). Such expenses include purchasing armored vehicles, arming and training settler militias (which organize patrols in the settlements where they live), surveillance gear, fences and walls, and a plethora of weapons and ammunition for uses ranging from suppressing demonstrations to targeted killings and house demolitions (Swirski, 2005).

The Separation Wall

Although the wall's main purpose is not security but separation, it certainly falls under the category of "security costs." It is a military project, patrolled by soldiers or private security companies. Surveillance equipment and remote-controlled armaments are installed upon it. The wall is not a permanent fixture and is constantly being contested by Palestinian, Israeli, and international activists, who argue that its route has been declared illegal by the International Court in the Hague.[8] The wall's route is also contested by settlers and military officers, who are attempting to incorporate as many settlements and strategic assets as possible on the wall's western side (Azoulay & Ophir, 2008). As a result, the course of the wall is constantly being changed, and sections of it have been destroyed and rebuilt, turning it into a very expensive project. Furthermore, its path snakes around settlements and cuts deep into the West Bank, creating a longer route at a higher cost. The wall in 2004 was already double the length of the Green Line (which is the international border between Israel and the West Bank; *Ynet*, 2004).

The wall's total cost is therefore estimated at about NIS 13 billion (Swirski, 2008b). This calculation does not take into account the compensation that Israel has paid to Palestinians whose lands were confiscated for the purpose of building the wall. This is because the vast majority of Palestinians have chosen not to apply for compensation (because requesting it could be interpreted as accepting the confiscation as legal) and because those few who did apply have received compensation mostly in the form of state lands in the occupied West Bank (Yoaz, 2005b).

Redeployment in Gaza

Although the Disengagement Plan, which was implemented by Israel in September 2005, has evacuated Israeli settlers from the Gaza Strip, this did not end Israeli control over the Gaza Strip. Once the settlers were removed, the Israeli army was able to use massive shelling against the civilian population there and to block all movement into or out of it, allowing only the entry of essential humanitarian supplies, without endangering Israeli settlers. Shelling began in late 2005, immediately after withdrawal of the settlers. The withdrawal from Gaza cost Israel over NIS 11.25 billion, based on a study conducted by the Alternative Information Center (Hever, 2005). Of this sum, about one-third represents the cost of relocating military installations and two-thirds is compensation to the settlers. As the number of settlers evacuated from the Gaza Strip amounted to about 3% of the total settler population, the hypothetical cost of compensating the remaining settlers in the West Bank, based on the Gaza withdrawal precedent, would be prohibitive, as discussed below in greater detail.

SUMMING THE COST

The various costs described above do not constitute an exhaustive list, but they can serve as a basis for an estimate of the overall burden that the occupation poses to the Israeli economy. Adding interest to the above figures, the costs total as follows:

- Income from the occupation: NIS 39.64 billion[9]
- Settler subsidies: NIS 104.46 billion
- Security costs: NIS 316.21 billion
- Total (net) cost: NIS 381.02 billion

These totals include the extrapolation for the entire period 1970–2008 and adjustments for price changes and for interest (Figures 10.2 and 10.3). The totals do not, however, include the benefits to the Israeli economy from international aid to the territories, or from the U.S. aid to Israel, which has largely corresponded to the years of the occupation.

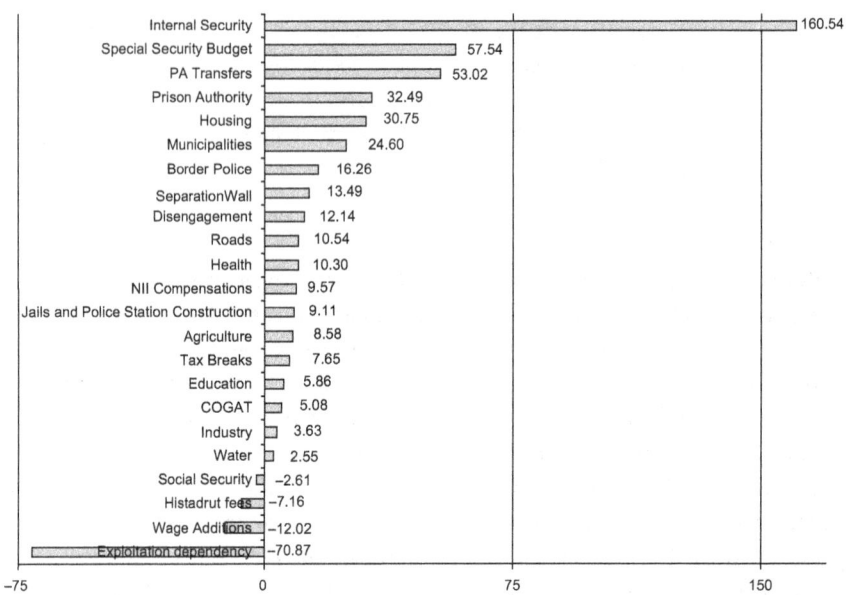

FIGURE 10.2 Costs of the occupation (billions of NIS, 2007 prices).

SECURITY IMPLICATIONS

The security costs are nearly triple those of the settler subsidies. The fact that security costs far outweigh all the other civilian costs means that the main reason for the occupation's costliness is Palestinian resistance. The Palestinians are the true force that is driving Israel out of the territories, making every move by Israel there difficult and expensive and turning the occupation into an increasing burden.

This point cannot be overstated. The fact that the armed resistance to Israel's occupation by the Palestinians is an effective means of eroding Israel's economic strength may not be, in itself, a justification for violence. It does, however, indicate that the effectiveness of armed struggle is not limited to the battlefield (where Palestinians almost always lose) but is also relevant in the economic sphere. In that sphere, the struggle is not about who can inflict the most damage on the other side but who can endure longest.

The Palestinians certainly suffer greater economic hardship than Israelis as a result of the occupation. However, the only economic requirement they have in order to keep the struggle going is the ability to stay alive, which is assisted by international aid. Israel, on the other hand, needs a much more elaborate system of technological and military superiority, social cohesion, and popular

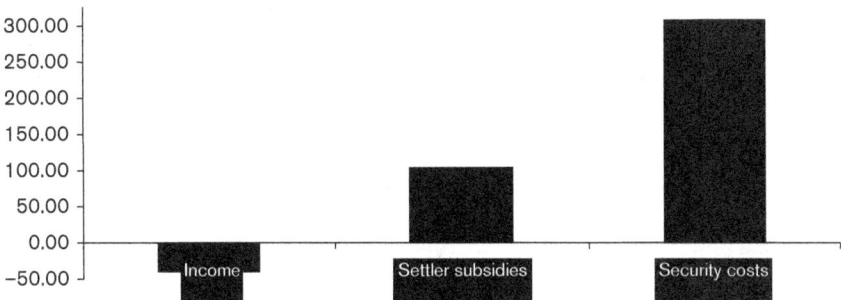

FIGURE 10.3 Total cost of the occupation (billions of NIS, 2007 prices).

support in order to keep the trappings of the occupation in place, and these requirements depend on Israel's continued economic growth.

COMPARISONS OF TOTALS

Different studies of the cost of the occupation to Israel have provided different estimates of the total cost of the occupation based on different assumptions about the right way to perform the calculation. At the lower end of these estimates is the one published by *Ha'aretz*, which is limited to the years 1970–2003 and does not include the security costs and accumulated interest on the sums involved. The total estimate is NIS 50.62 billion (in December 2007 prices). At the upper limit, estimates of the cost reach as high as NIS 600 billion, but without figuring in the income generated by the occupation for Israel.

If we proceed with the above calculations, we find that the first forty-one years of occupation have cost the Israeli government over NIS 381 billion as of 2008. This is not a static cost but rather a constantly growing expenditure. Thus, a more useful number is US $6.84 billion (NIS 26.3 billion), which is the annual cost of the occupation as of 2008.

The direct expenses incurred by the occupation currently comprise 8.72% of Israel's budget. According to this calculation, the government spends an average of NIS 40.89 thousand on the average Israeli citizen but more than double that amount—NIS 93.1 thousand—on the average settler (135.03% more). In the years 2003–2008, the Israeli budget grew by an average of 2.3% annually, while the number of settlers has risen by an average of 7.13% annually since 1991. This trend is unlikely to continue, since if it does, by 2038 more than 50% of the Israeli budget will be spent on maintaining the occupation of the territories.

Such a long-term projection is bound to be inaccurate, however, and extremely unlikely to come true. No developed country can sustain a budget burden of 50% to fund the occupation of a foreign territory. Therefore, it is not very useful to ask, "What will happen if the cost of the occupation becomes 50% of the Israeli budget?" A more useful question is: "What might happen between now and 2050 that could stop the rate of increase in the cost of the occupation?"

As the occupation becomes increasingly expensive, the political pressure for change will likely grow stronger. Whether it will eventually convince Israel to withdraw, prompt Israel to reform its mechanisms of control and find ways to cut costs, incite Israel to perform genocide, or bring about the collapse of the State of Israel only time will tell.

COMPENSATION

When Israel evacuated the Jewish settlements in the Gaza Strip in September 2005, the government implemented a complex system of compensation to the evacuated settlers. They were compensated for the value of the real estate they left behind, for the jobs they had, for businesses that used to operate in the settlements, and for the discomfort of relocation. Although settlers are considered criminals under international law, and although it was their choice to live in the Gaza Strip, the Israeli government couldn't deny that it had encouraged Israelis to settle in the territories and had to take responsibility.

Fewer than 8,000 settlers were evacuated, but the cost of compensating them was immense. Supporters of the withdrawal in the Israeli parliament pushed for high compensation in order to help the evacuation go smoothly (effectively bribing the settlers to leave without a struggle). Those opposed to the withdrawal pushed for even higher compensation, once they realized that they could not stop the evacuation, in order to set a precedent of unaffordable compensation and thus prevent future evacuations. Eventually, the average settler received more than NIS 1 million, equivalent to about 200,000 euros (Hever, 2005).

The implication of this precedent is that should Israel decide to evacuate the illegal settlements in the West Bank, where 471,000 settlers dwelt in 2008, it will have to deal with their demands for compensation. The settlers could use the precedent of the Gaza withdrawal and demand that the same formula be applied to them, which would mean that compensation could reach NIS 471 billion, certainly more than the Israeli government can afford to pay and more than 1.5 times its annual budget.

On the other hand, if the settlers are not evacuated and the cost of occupation continues to grow, Israel could end up paying even more. When the above calculations of the cost of the occupation are considered, the Israeli government would be making a sound economic decision if it chose to borrow enough money to fund compensation for the settlers, and then paid interest on the loan instead of paying for the settlement subsidies and settlement security. Such a decision would save money for the Israeli government at interest rates of over 5%, even disregarding the fact that evacuated settlers would probably spend their compensation money in the Israeli economy and generate tax revenues for the government.

The current political situation in Israel is hardly congenial to such calculations. The cost of the occupation isn't acknowledged by the government, nor is it often discussed in the Israeli media. The leadership of the settlers has become increasingly militant and is willing to use force even against Israeli authorities to prevent evacuations (thus making them even costlier), and the very idea of evacuating the settlements and returning to the 1967 borders is still unacceptable to most Israelis, as can be inferred from statements by elected Israeli politicians. The results of the February 2009 elections in Israel further demonstrate this point, with the far Right having increased its strength and newly elected Prime Minister Binyamin Netanyahu arguing that he is opposed to the idea of a two-state solution.

PROFITS OF THE OCCUPATION

The profits of the occupation are too widespread and diffuse to be fully discussed here, but it is important to understand them when analyzing why the occupation continues. The occupation has not only caused significant economic damage, but actually involved a substantial redistribution of income. Whenever the government has spent extra money on funding the occupation, someone has taken their own cut of this money. The redistribution is very difficult to follow, since Israeli companies systematically hide their operations in the territories. Government tenders for construction in the settlements are intentionally obscured, and the names of the companies that win the tenders are often not published (as opposed to tenders for construction projects within Israel).

The above listing of settlement subsidies may have given the impression that settlers benefit from the occupation, and that they enjoy better living conditions than the average Israeli citizen. In some settlements this is indeed true, but the subsidies to settlements are not distributed equally among all of them. Most of the illegal settlements in East Jerusalem, for instance, fall within the municipal boundaries of Jerusalem and thus do not receive special benefits, other than cheaper housing. Also, settlements that are in more isolated and dangerous parts of the West Bank, or those that are relatively far from Israeli urban centers, confront settlers with daily difficulties for which the subsidies cannot fully compensate.

Some of the biggest profiteers from the occupation, however, are Israeli military companies and homeland security industries, mentioned above. Military exports from Israel exceeded US $4 billion in 2004, not counting homeland security exports (Klein, 2007a; Zuriel-Harari, 2005).

However, the profits from the occupation are certainly not limited to Israelis (individuals or companies). There are many international companies and governments that have a vested interest in the continuation of the occupation. In addition to companies that provide Israel with weapons, construction equipment, and the services needed to maintain the occupation, the most notable profiteers from the occupation are international oil companies and arms manufacturers. As long as the occupation continues, the level of violence in the Middle East will remain high. The Palestinians serve as a symbol for many political groups in the Middle East (including terrorist groups), and Palestinian refugees in Arab states in the Middle East continue to constitute an important pool of candidates for recruitment to these organizations.

Israel's aggression, and the aggression toward Israel, has only served to increase the level of violence and uncertainty in the Middle East. Each cycle of violence raises the price of weapons and generates uncertainty regarding future oil production in the Middle East, raising the price of oil as well. Studies conducted by Nitzan and Bichler (2002, 2006) have shown that wars in the Middle East (to most of which Israel has been a party) have dramatically increased the relative profits of weapons and oil companies.

Although the Palestinians in the territories are neither oil producers nor large-scale weapons importers, the Palestinian refugees scattered across Arab countries support an end to the Israeli occupation. This is the basis for the long-standing hostility between Israel and Lebanon, with repeated Israeli attacks against Lebanon from 1978 to 2006.

IMPACT OF THE OCCUPATION ON ISRAELI SOCIETY

Not all the costs of the occupation to Israeli society are paid in cash. The socioeconomic implications of the occupation reach far beyond the sums of money involved, and it can be useful to give a few examples on how the occupation has left its mark on various aspects of Israeli society.

The heavy military burden on the Israeli economy creates profits for the military industry but impedes the growth of the economy in the long run. Security needs created by the ever-escalating conflict make many economic transactions in Israel more expensive than in other places in the world, starting with the simplest act of shopping. Israelis who spend money thus receive less in return than Europeans and Americans, as they are also paying for the salaries of the security guards in the shopping venues.

At first glance, the Israeli economy appears to be strong and prosperous (Levy, 2008), but a closer look reveals that decades of keeping social goals and public services at a low priority compared to security and territorial expansion have expanded social gaps, eroded the resilience of Israel's public institutions, and left the Israeli economy in a fragile state. Indicators of flight safety, corruption, environmental standards, and freedom of the press reveal that Israel has deteriorated to the level of developing countries. International comparisons show not only that Israel is lagging far behind most developed countries, but that its relative position is in decline too, indicating that Israel is not only nor catching up but is actually falling behind (Detal, 2009).

The argument that decades of occupation have eroded the foundations of Israel's economic well-being, and threaten the quality of human capital of Israelis and the long-term growth prospects of the Israeli economy, has been articulated in two recent reports. These reports, published by *The Economist* (2008) and by the Adva Center (Swirski, 2008a), both shed light on the magnitude of the impact of the occupation on Israel's economy and show that the data often invoked to demonstrate Israel's prosperity are a poor indication of future trends.

The Israeli economy appears strong due to several macroeconomic indicators, which give only a partial picture of the state of Israel's economy. The country's state of continual conflict and outbursts of escalating violence along its borders could be a contributing factor in the short term to its growth rate, although this state of affairs certainly does not contribute to the well-being of Israel's citizens or to the long-term growth of the Israeli economy (Abu-Bader & Abu-Qarn, 2003).

Israel's average annual GDP growth rate in the years 2003–2007, for instance, was 4.66% (CBI, 2012), but this rate continues to be lower than the average growth rate of other Middle Eastern countries during these years: 6.02% (World Bank, 2008). Israel has in fact never regained the growth rate prior to the 1967 occupation, which was 5.7%, and would have brought Israel to the per capita GDP of the United States by 1990 if it had continued (Ben-David, 2003). A few years into the occupation, Israel's GDP growth began gradually to slow down, to an average level of 1.81% for the years 1973–2005, below the average of Organization for Economic Cooperation and Development (OECD) countries (Ben-David, 2003).

Before the 1967 occupation, Israel's labor market was split between better-paying jobs with extensive benefits and high job security, held primarily by Ashkenazi Jews, and low-paying jobs with minimal benefits and low job security, held mostly by Mizrachi Jews of and Arab Palestinian citizens of Israel. The occupation of the West Bank and Gaza Strip in 1967 created a third tier of completely unprotected workers, who received even lower wages and fewer benefits. This tertiary labor market had a profound impact on the Israeli economy, bringing rapid profits to large companies and select individuals who benefited from the exploitation of Palestinian labor, at the expense of widespread unemployment (Dagan-Buzaglo, 2009).

Israeli businesses have become accustomed to using cheap labor rather than updating their capital investment, technology, and worker productivity (Bartram, 1998), a trend that persists to this day. The problem has been compounded by the importing of foreign labor immigrants to replace the Palestinian workers who have been denied entry into Israel since the closure policy of the 1990s began.

Competition over the low-paying jobs drove Israel's official unemployment up to 7.8% in the first quarter of 2009. This is more than double the 3.6% unemployment rate that Israel had prior to the occupation, in 1961–1965 (ICBS, 1966). The official unemployment rate gives only a partial picture of Israel's labor market. Policy reforms have eroded the rights of unemployed persons, and have stricken many from the unemployment lists by making the criteria for qualifying for unemployment benefits increasingly difficult (Fraenkel, 2001). The official rate also does not measure the growing phenomenon of underemployment, which, if included, would indicate no less than 13.65% unemployment (Ben-Shakhar, Schuldineger, & Toker-Maimon, 2006). In 2003–2006, for example, even as the official unemployment rate declined, the actual amount of work performed by Israeli workers (in terms of number of hours) fell by 1%, while the population grew by nearly 5% (ICBS, 2008).

Israel today has become more unequal than ever in its history, and while a small percentage of the population continues to prosper, the majority are left behind. Israel's poverty rate has increased sharply over the past three decades, especially among children. In 1979, 23.8% of the population and 23.1% of children lived below the poverty line. In 2007, the numbers increased to 32.5% and 39.9%, respectively.[10] Poverty is more pervasive in Israel than in any OECD country except Mexico (*The Economist*, 2008; NII, 2008).

The result of the immense spending on the occupation, on settlements, and on security has left fewer available resources for public spending. Resources include not only funds, but also skilled workers who work in the military instead of in the public service, or talented people who leave the country in search of a safer or less morally ambiguous life.

Public services such as health, transportation, and welfare have all suffered, but the main public service that has suffered and continues to suffer is education. Education, which fuels Israel's high-tech industry, which in 2006 comprised 46% of Israel's exports (ICBS, 2008), is an essential resource for the Israeli economy. The rapid deterioration in the education levels in Israel include growing inequality (Resnik, 1999; Spiegel, 2001); erosion in public investment in schoolchildren and university students (ICBS, 2007), who have fallen behind in international exams; and the rapid emigration of academic scholars (Ben-David, 2002, 2008). Such a decline could hurt Israel's most important export—high technology—and devastate the economy (*The Economist*, 2008).

Israel's foreign trade is also threatened by international pressure because of the occupation. Following a widespread call by Palestinian civilian organizations for a boycott of Israel (PACBI, 2005), the worldwide BDS (boycott, divestment, and sanctions) campaigns against Israel have multiplied. Legal struggles were launched against international and Israeli companies that operate in the settlements. Several companies have already pulled out, while others suffer from consumer boycotts (Handmaker, 2009).

The magazine *Al Majdal* surveyed a sample of boycott campaigns that took place in seventeen different countries in 2008 (Badil, 2008). Following the Israeli attack on Gaza in December 2008–January 2009, the European Union (EU), Israel's biggest trading partner, decided to freeze its upgrade of trade relations with Israel (DPA, 2009).

INTERNATIONAL COMPARISON

In many ways, the challenges faced by Israel's economy as a result of the occupation of the Palestinian territories are unique. Almost no other contemporary modern economy is engaged in direct colonial practices. Here I will only compare the Israeli-Palestinian case to other cases involving capitalist economies, for occupations by planned-economy states (such as the Soviet occupation of Afghanistan) create very different economic situations. The dramatic changes in the economic practices in the capitalist system since the previous wave of decolonization have greatly impacted the economic significance of Israel's policies. Direct exploitation of occupied natural resources, cheap labor, and captive markets are no longer widespread colonial practices in the world today. They have been replaced by indirect and more sophisticated methods of exploitation relying on imbalanced trade agreements, debt structures, financial speculations, and international corporations (Nkrumah, 1965).

The previous wave of decolonization in the world, beginning with the end of the Second World War (Strang, 1992), occurred in an economic environment that stressed Keynesian policies of massive government investments, protectionist trade policies (especially in the developing world; Klein, 2007b), and the beginning of the Cold War.

During that time, "military Keynesianism" provided a wide venue for military expenditure for Western powers (Nitzan & Bichler, 2006), and the complex apparatuses needed to control subjugated peoples contrasted with the North Atlantic Treaty Organization (NATO) focus against the Soviet Union (Markusen, 1992). In 1955, the average military expenditure in the OECD as a percentage of GDP was 4.2%, which declined gradually to 3.1% by 1985 and dropped sharply to 1.4% by 2009. Israel, by comparison, spent 8% of its GDP on its military in 2009, according to very conservative estimates that do not take into account nonmonetary allocations of resources by the Israeli government to the military (OECD, 2010; Wolfson, 2009).

This is an indication that the Israeli market is suffering from a serious handicap compared to almost any other economy in the world. This is a direct result of carrying the ball-and-chain of its military expenditures, a large portion of them to maintain the occupation of the Palestinian territories.

The Israeli government has responded by attempting to turn the occupation itself into a commodity. Israel's rapidly expanding arms manufacturing sector, and its leading role in the "homeland security" industry, is largely based on the ability of Israeli companies to test their products in the occupied territories and to employ staff with actual experience in conflict situations (Gordon, 2009; Klein, 2007a). Thus, Israel is able to turn its repressive policies into a form of exportable "technology" and a source of income for certain aspects of the Israeli business sector. Nevertheless, total Israeli arms exports are estimated at US $6.75 billion in 2009 (Israel World Trade Center, 2011), comprising merely 3.3% of Israel's GDP for that year, a far cry from paying for the economic burden of military spending, which is over 8% of the GDP.

As a globalized economy, the burden of occupation serves as a deterrent for international investors from investing in Israel (Baron, 2006), and as a reason for mass emigration of educated and skilled people who seek to improve their standard of living (Ben-David, 2008).

Another important way in which contemporary developments differentiate the Israeli case from other military occupations is the changed role of the global media and the unprecedented access to information available in the age of the Internet. During the subjugation of the Algerian rebellion, the French government could successfully limit the press coverage of the fighting, torture, killing of unarmed civilians, and so on (Harrison, 1964). Israel does not have this privilege, as anyone with Internet access and the desire to do so can access reports, photos, and videos on the occupation within hours after the events take place.

The economic significance of the occupation's visibility is that the information flowing to the international community moves civil society organizations, grassroots organizations, labor unions, and individuals to support the Palestinian struggle by boycotting Israel. The BDS movement's rapid expansion can be attributed to this fact.

This brings me to the final comparison that can shed light on the cost of the occupation to Israel, which is apartheid South Africa. Despite the many differences between the two historic cases, in both of them the repressed population chose to call for international support to be expressed in the form of boycott.

Much controversy exists regarding the boycott's impact on apartheid South Africa. South Africa's wealth in natural resources, and the fact that decades of boycott occurred before the age of globalization made South Africa as dependant on international trade as it is today, convinced some scholars that the boycott had not been the decisive factor in toppling apartheid (Crawford & Klotz, 1999). Israel, however, is a fully globalized economy that relies heavily on exports, imports, and cross-country investments. Furthermore, Israel is not rich in natural resources, and in 2009, 67% of its imports were raw materials (including energy products; ICBS, 2010). These factors make Israel far more vulnerable to a boycott campaign than apartheid South Africa ever was, and perhaps the impact of the boycott, which has not yet been properly studied, should be added to the cost that Israel pays for the occupation.

Thus, despite the many similarities between Israel's occupation of the Palestinian territories and various military occupations in history, the Israeli occupation is unique in its global visibility and in its existence within an economic framework of global capitalism.

CONCLUSION

In monetary terms, funding its occupation of the territories has been the most expensive project undertaken by Israel since 1967. The reason for this is that Israel has chosen to suppress the economy, welfare, culture, human rights, and dignity of the Palestinians. The Palestinians have not sat idly by, however, as Israel exploited and suppressed them, and their efforts to break free from Israel's control have forced Israel to constantly increase the spending on security, and in consequence to assume all the trappings of a militarized state, constantly on guard against the resistance of the oppressed Palestinians.

The occupation continues because Israel still has the means to perpetuate it and defeat Palestinian resistance. Although the Israeli economy is showing the strain, U.S. funds continue to reach Israel and allow it to maintain its military superiority and violent control of the territories. The ongoing efforts by Israeli authorities to suppress the Palestinian resistance, however, are costing Israel precious resources, and the burden of the occupation has taken its toll on Israeli society too.

The Israeli economy is definitely less stable and prosperous than the mainstream macroeconomic indicators would appear to suggest. Moreover, Israel lacks the mechanisms to correct these problems. Social solidarity is very weak in a country where national and ethnic identity determines socioeconomic policies more than class divisions.

A major reason for the paralysis in Israeli institutions is that security issues always override the need for social change. Officials maintain that the Israeli economy is a success story because that argument justifies their own past policies and because wealth continues to accumulate in the hands of a few powerful financiers. Economic elites in Israel have an incentive to keep the existing system in place.

The general Israeli public prefers not to inform itself about the minutiae of the occupation. Israelis spend their time concerned with other things, and they rarely see the impact of the occupation on their daily lives. They do not realize how ever-present the occupation is in the lives of Palestinians, and the Israeli authorities and mainstream media help the public to stay willfully ignorant by releasing only sporadic and incomplete information about the territories (Azoulay & Ophir, 2008).

Furthermore, there are those who profit from the current state of affairs. Large companies extract high profits with minimal regulation and taxes. Those who profit from the occupation have no incentive to help resolve it. The occupation, the conflict, and the war on terror have all helped to obfuscate the redistribution of wealth that has been picking up pace, leading to a less equal society; and have also helped to disarm the social resistance to this redistribution.

Due to backing from the United States and certain European countries, Israel's international standing has allowed it to pursue policies that would not be legitimate if implemented by other countries, including targeted killings, collective punishment, intentional pauperization and the near starvation of large civilian populations, and many other actions that violate international law. However, international support for Israel is not a bottomless pit, and if Israel's international standing gradually weakens, this could affect its place in the global economy (Swirski, 2008a).

Israel's economic prospects increasingly hinge on its distinctive feature as a relatively secure country, despite the fact that it is in a constant state of conflict. As Israelis' motivation to risk life and limb in military service drops,[11] as social solidarity crumbles, as more Israelis hope to leave the country, and as Israel's chief ally (the United States) begins to change its position regarding its unconditional support for Israeli policies, the prospects for Israel to successfully suppress Palestinian resistance over time seem slim. The emphasis on short-term security solutions, says *The Economist* (2008), is hurting the security of Israelis in the long run.

NOTES

1. This chapter has been adapted from two chapters in my book, with the permission of Pluto Press: *The Political Economy of Israel's Occupation: Repression Beyond Exploitation*, Pluto Press 2010.
2. Following the events of September 11, 2001, Israeli politicians began to market Israel as a country at the forefront of the war on terror, and argued that the Palestinian movement for national liberation from Israeli occupation is, in fact, a part of the "world Islamist terror movement." Binyamin Netanyahu, who was Israel's Prime Minister in 1996–1999 and again in 2009, commented that the 9/11 attacks were good for Israel, because they helped sway international public opinion in Israel's favour (*Ha'aretz* and *Reuters*, 2008).
3. Due to the clandestine nature of this industry, information on the extent of such exports is limited to what the companies are willing to reveal for commercial purposes. However, over 45 such companies hawked their wares at a trade show in Tel-Aviv for "counterterrorism" technology (Mitnick, 2004).
4. The decision to fix the costs for the estimated settler population in the territories yields a higher emphasis on more recent costs. In the *Ha'aretz* estimate, for example, it was estimated that the costs in the first decade were half that of in the second decade of the occupation (Ha'aretz 2003). My own estimate is that since the settler population has increased by a factor of ten, so have the costs. The reason for fixing the costs for the population is that many of the subsidies are granted on a per-family or per-individual basis.

    As regards spending that could be more cost-effective in large cities than in isolated outposts, it should be noted that settlement growth usually follows irregular patterns, thus burdening the military with more complex areas to secure and utility companies with complex infrastructure requirements. This erratic growth prevents central planning of settlement growth, and causes waste in the distribution of resources and infrastructure (Sasson 2005).
5. The data on the settler population in the territories refer to the West Bank (including East Jerusalem) and Gaza Strip only, as this discussion does not encompass the Golan Heights. Unfortunately, Peace Now, an Israeli NGO that surveys the size of the settlements, does not count those settlers who are

illegally living in East Jerusalem (Peace Now 2007). This is because Peace Now has adopted the Israeli perspective, according to which annexed land is no longer occupied, which of course is not the case according to international law. In order to complete the statistics, information on the settler population in East Jerusalem has been added (based on the Jerusalem Centre for Israel Studies, 2003 and 2006).

6. Since this estimate applies to economic growth and development that has been funnelled from the Palestinian economy into the Israeli economy, interest calculations will not be applied to this figure, since the alternative uses for the resources are already encompassed in the calculation.
7. Brigadier General Yair Golan, who was at the time the commander of the Israeli forces in the West Bank, gave a lecture on the Israeli mechanisms of control and separation at the Van Leer institute on April 20, 2007. He noted that separation and not security is the main reason for building the separation wall, and that security could have been achieved more effectively and more cheaply by other means.
8. See the International Court's press release, July 2004, at http://www.icj-cij.org/icjwww/ipresscom/ipress2004/ipresscom2004-28_mwp_20040709.htm.
9. After deducting transfers to the PA between 1996 and 2008.
10. Poverty in Israel is measured as living below half the median income, adjusted for standard number of people in the household. The figures here are before taxes and transfer payments.
11. Though later conscription rates became confidential, there are many indications that they continue to fall. The August 2007 draft was called the smallest draft "in many years" (Shenfeld 2007). In 2009, the commander of the Israeli army department of manpower revealed that only 74.2% of Jewish men and 56% of Jewish women enlist every year. If that figure is adjusted for the entire population of Israeli (not only Jewish) citizens, it means that less than 49% of Israelis enlist. With a majority of Israelis no longer enlisting in the Israeli army, the willingness and motivation of other young Israelis who come of age to enlist is also falling (Pfeffer 2009).

REFERENCES

Abu-Bader, S., &Abu-Qarn Aamer, S. (2003). Government expenditures, military spending and economic growth: Causality evidence from Egypt, Israel and Syria. *Journal of Policy Modeling*, 25(6–7), 567–583.

ACRI (Association for Civil Rights in Israel). (2005). *Authorities must provide information on jurisdiction areas and settlement outline*. Retrieved [September 9, 2012] from http://www.acri.org.il/he/?p=1076.

Arnon, A., Luski, I., Spivak, A., & and Weinblatt, J. (1997). *The Palestinian economy, between imposed integration and voluntary separation*. New York, Leiden and Koln: Brill.

Azoulay, A.,& Ophir, A. (2008). *This regime which is not one: Occupation and democracy between the sea and the river (1967-)*. Tel Aviv: Resling.

PACBI (Palestinians for the Academic and Cultural Boyoctt of Israel). (2005). *Palestinian Call for Boycott, Divestment, and Sanctions (BDS)*. Retrieved [September 9, 2012] from http://www.pacbi.org/etemplate.php?id=66.

Badil. (2008, Summer). *Al Majdal*, vol. 38, Bethlehem, entire magazine.

Baron, O. (2006, October 16). Foreign investments in Israel reached an all-time high in 2005. *NRG*...

Bartram, D. V. (1998, Summer). Foreign workers in Israel: History and theory. *International Migration Review, 32*(2), 303–325.

Ben-David, D. (2002, July). *The central socio-economic problems and central policy foci*. Working Paper, Department for Public Policy, Tel Aviv University.

Ben-David, D. (2003, March). Inequality and growth in Israel. *Economic Quarterly, 50*(1), 27–104.

Ben-David, D. (2005, June 9). The values of the settlers. *Haaretz..*

Ben-David, D. (2008, January). *Brain drained*. Working Paper, Department of Public Policy, Tel Aviv University.

Ben-Shakhar, A., Schuldineger, Z., & Toker-Maimon, O. (2006). *Unemployment report 2006*. Jerusalem: Commitment to Peace and Social Justice.

Berglas, E. (1989). The Israeli economy and the held territories: War and peace. *Economic Quarterly [Rivon Lecalcala], 139*, 599–600.

Bergman, A. (1974). *Economic growth in the administered areas 1968–1973*. Jerusalem: Research Department, Bank of Israel.

Bichler, S., & and Nitzan, J. (2001). *From war profits to peace dividend: The global political economy of Israel*. Jerusalem: Carmel.

Blau, U. (2009, February 1). Secret Israeli database reveals full extent of illegal settlement. *Haaretz,*

B'tselem. (2002, May). *Land grab: Israel's settlement policy in the West Bank*. Retrieved from http://www.btselem.org/download/200205_land_grab_Eng.pdf.

Buhbut, A. (2008, March 18). The big crossings are released from the IDF. *NRG*.

Central Bank of Israel (CBI). (2012). *Table B1: Gross domestic product and its components. Main indicators on the Israeli market*. Retrieved May 8, 2012, from http://www.bankisrael.gov.il/deptdata/mehkar/indic/heb_b01.htm

Cohen, S. (2008, April 30). Security of settlements goes to private hands. *Arutz 7,*

Crawford, N. C., & Klotz, A. (Eds.). (1999). *How sanctions work: Lessons from South Africa*. New York: St. Martin's Press.

Dagan-Buzaglo, N. (2009, March). The cellars of the labour market: The crisis and the secondary labour market. In S. Swirski & D. Filk (Eds.), *Israel and the world crisis: Another way is possible* (pp. 19–23). Tel Aviv: Adva Center.

Department of Political Affairs (DPA). (2009, April 23). EU commissioner: Time "not right" for EU-Israel upgrade. *EarthTimes*.

Detal, L. (2009, May 15). More corruption than Qatar and less equality than Uzbekistan, Israel is deteriorating. *The Marker*.

The Economist. (2008, April 5). The next generation. *The Economist, 387*(8574).

Fraenkel, A. (2001, February). *Unemployment benefits in Israel: Trends and legislation changes: 1985–2000*. Tel Aviv: Adva Center.

Gamliel, N. (2005). *The cost of the settlements: How much do we pay?* Unpublished.

Gordon, N. (2008). *Israel's occupation.* Berkeley, Los Angeles, London: University of California Press.

Gordon, N. (2009, April 28). *The political economy of Israel's homeland security/surveillance industry.* Working Paper III. Kingston: The New Transparency.

Haaretz. (2003, September 26). The price of the settlements. New Year's Supplement, *Haaretz.*

Handmaker, J. (2009, February 20). Global boycott movement marks its successes. *The Electronic Intifada.* Retrieved May 8, 2012, from http://electronicintifada.net/content/global-boycott-movement-marks-its-successes/8075

Harrison, M. (1964, June). Government and press in France during the Algerian war. *The American Political Science Review, 58*(2), 273–285.

Hever, S. (2005, October–November). The Gaza withdrawal—winners and losers, *Economy of the occupation,* Part 4–5. Jerusalem: Alternative Information Center.

Hever, S. (2006, June 6). The occupation through the eyes of Israeli economists, *Economy of the occupation,* Part 9. Jerusalem: Alternative Information Center.

Hever, S. (2008, November). Political economy of aid to Palestinians under occupation, *Economy of the occupation,* Part 17–18. Jerusalem: Alternative Information Center.

ICBS (Israeli Central Bureau of Statistics). (1966). *Annual statistics reader 1965.* Jerusalem: Author.

ICBS (Israeli Central Bureau of Statistics). (2007, July 30). *National spending on education 2003–2006. Press release.* Retrieved from http://www1.cbs.gov.il/reader/newhodaot/hodaa_template.html?hodaa=200708138.

ICBS (Israeli Central Bureau of Statistics). (2008). *Statistical yearbook 2007.* Jerusalem: Author.

ICBS (Israeli Central Bureau of Statistics). (2010, December). Foreign Trade, Table 8/2: Foreign trade balance. *Israel Monthly Statistical Digest*

Israeli Revenue Authority. (2007). *Annual report 2006, No. 55.* Jerusalem: Israeli Ministry of Finance.

Israel World Trade Center. (2011). *Security exports.* Retrieved January 2011 from http://www.israelwtc.co.il/%D7%99%D7%A6%D7%95%D7%90_%D7%91%D7%99%D7%98%D7%97%D7%95%D7%A0%D7%99. from

Jerusalem Center for Israel Studies. (2003). *On your stats, Jerusalem, 2002–2003: Current situation and trends of change.* Jerusalem: Author.

Jerusalem Center for Israel Studies. (2006). *Statistical digest of Jerusalem, 2005–2006,* No. 22. Jerusalem: Author.

Khouri, R. G. (1980, Winter). Israel's imperial economics. *Journal of Palestine Studies, 9*(2), 71–78.

Klein, N. (2007a, July 14). *Laboratory for a fortress world.* Retrieved May 8, 2012, from http://www.naomiklein.org/articles/2007/06/laboratory-fortressed-world

Klein, N. (2007b). *The shock doctrine: The rise of disaster capitalism.* New York: Metropolitan Books.

Lan, S. (2005, May 2–3). Check, please!," *Globes*.
Landau, P. (2008, January–February). Dealing with the wealth. *Eretz Aheret*, 43, 42–46.
Lein, Y. (2000, July). *Thirsty for a solution: The water crisis in the occupied territories and its resolution in the final-status agreement*. Jerusalem: B'tselem.
Levy, T. (2008, November 3). Optimism at the Central Bank: The global crisis finds the Israeli market at its best since the foundation of the state. *The Marker*.
Markusen, A. (1992, Summer). Dismantling the cold war economy. *World Policy Journal*, 9(3), 389–399.
Mitnick, J. (2004, March 26). Israel selling its warfare expertise. *Jewish Week*.
NII (National Insurance Institute). (2008, February). *Poverty rate and income gaps 2006/7, main findings*. Jerusalem: National Insurance Institute, Department of Research and Planning.
Nitzan, J., & and Bichler, S. (2002). *The global political economy of Israel*. London: Pluto Press.
Nitzan, J., & Bichler, S. (2006, July). Cheap wars. *The economy of the occupation*, No. 10. Jerusalem: Alternative Information Center.
Nkrumah, K. (1965). *Neo-colonialism, the last stage of imperialism*. London: Thomas Nelson.
OECD (Organization for Economic Cooperation and Development). (2010, January). *OECD reviews of labour market and social policies*. OECD Publishing.
Peace Now. (2007, May–October). *Settlement construction continues—periodical report, summer 2007*. Tel Aviv: Peace Now—Settlement Watch Team.
Pfeffer, A. (2009, March 1). Head of the IDF's manpower department, Major General Zvi Zamir: The number of non-enlisted has grown, obligatory service will not be shortened. *Haaretz*.
Resnik, J. (1999, Winter). Particularistic vs. universalistic content in the Israeli education system. *Curriculum Inquiry*, 29(4), 485–511.
Rinat, T. (2008, December 15). "Yesh din": Israel uses occupied land's natural treasures for its own purposes. *Haaretz*.
Rubinstein, A. (2005, May 15). The command of the market. *Haaretz*.
Saar, R. (2003, September 26). Summer vacation starts in August. *Haaretz*.
Sasson, T. (2005, February). *Illegal outposts*. Special Report to the Prime Minister's Office.
Shenfeld, Y. (2007, July 17). 25% of 18-year-olds don't conscript to the IDF. *MSN*.
Spiegel, U. (2001, June). *Youth motivation for service in the IDF*. Jerusalem: Israeli Knesset: Research and Information Center.
Strang, D. (1992). The inner incompatibility of empire and nation: Popular sovereignty and decolonization. *Sociological Perspectives*, 1(2), 367–384.
Strassler, N. (2004, November 18). The domino theory. *Haaretz*.
Strassler, N. (2005, August 18). Sharon's speech. needs reading too. *Haaretz*.
Swirski, S. (2005). *The price of occupation*. Tel Aviv: Adva Center, MAPA Publishers.
Swirski, S. (2008a, June). *The cost of occupation: The burden of the Israeli-Palestinian conflict, 2008 report*. Tel Aviv: Adva Center.

Swirski, S. (2008b, August). *Is there an Israeli business peace disincentive?* Tel Aviv: Adva Center.

Swirski, S., Konor-Atias, E., & Etkin, A. (2002). *Government funding of the Israeli settlement in Judea and Sumeria and in the Golan Heights in the 90s: Municipalities, housing construction and paving roads.* Tel Aviv: Adva Center.

Tsaban, D. (2003, November). *Partial estimate of government budgets directed to the settlements in the West Bank and the Gaza Strip and of the over-funding in 2001.* Tel-Aviv: Peace Now.

Wolfson, T. (2009, December). *The security burden and the Israeli economy: A second look at the official statistics, 2009.* Unpublished paper.

World Bank (2008, April). *World economic and financial surveys*. Retrieved from http://www.imf.org/external/pubs/ft/weo/2008/01/weodata/index.aspx

Ynet. (2004, February 3). The cost of the separation fence is double than a fence on the 1967 lines. *Ynet.*

Yoaz, Y. (2005a, April 19). Cleaning house in the West Bank Municipalities Council. *Haaretz.*

Yoaz, Y. (2005b, May 6). Palestinians that were hurt by the wall will be compensated with state lands. *Walla.*

Zuriel-Harari, K. (2005, May 18–19). Mofaz: My help? Uniting all of Israel's military industries into one big company. *Globes.*

CHAPTER 11

Gendering the Discourse on Occupation: A Sociological Perspective

Hanna Herzog

On October 31, 2000, the United Nations Security Council adopted Resolution 1325, which calls for embracing a gender perspective in dealing with armed conflicts, security, peace, and reconciliation. (http://www.un.org/events/res_1325e.pdf). The resolution calls on all actors in a conflict to increase the participation of women in peace negotiations and in building a sustainable peace. The call for the inclusion of women, apart from being embedded in the equal rights perspective, assumes that a woman's viewpoint can reveal the gendered social arrangements that are taken for granted and that tolerate direct or indirect violence against women. The woman's standpoint extends our understanding of marginal and excluded groups in general and of women in particular (Harding & Hintikka, 2003). While much of the literature discussing Resolution1325 deals with legislation and strategies of implementation, I argue that a prerequisite for such analysis is to understand the social and cultural mechanisms that allow the gender aspect of any armed conflict to be ignored and disregard the fact that civilians, particularly women and children, are the vast majority of those adversely affected by war. Life in Israel under a protracted conflict with the Arab states, and particularly with the Palestinians, enables me to suggest an analysis of general cultural mechanisms as well as ones more specific to the Israeli case.

The social discourse in Israel, like the dominant academic discourse, treats the State of Israel as though it were an entity that is separate and distinct from the occupied territories. The relations between these two social entities are framed in terms of armed conflict between two separate national units. Hence, many of the issues in the fields of economy, security, culture, and society are referred to in terms of "there" and "here."

This dichotomy is misleading because it ignores the depth of the connection between "there" and "here." From the outset, the conquest of the territories had a great impact on Israeli society in general and on the status and condition of women in Israel in particular, but this aspect of society has been shunted to the sidelines of the public discourse and also marginalized in academic research. Studying the question of whether and how the protracted occupation reproduces the gendered structure of society still encounters opposition and is not perceived as a legitimate research question or as a question central to the understanding of the Israeli society. This chapter suggests a gendered approach to the occupation that not only changes the understanding of the different effects of the occupation on men and women, but also proposes a new perspective for understanding the sociology of the occupation and the analysis of society in general.

SOME REMARKS ON THE SOCIOLOGY OF THE OCCUPATION

What marks the institutionalization of a new field of knowledge? First and foremost, a growing number of studies belong to this field. Second, there is an acknowledgment that this field has a separate identity, and there are publications devoted exclusively to this field, such as booklets on the subject, journals, books, and so on. Third, it becomes a subject that is taught. Fourth, conferences are held, professional associations are formed, and sessions in general conferences are devoted to this subject. Last is the existence of consumers who need the accumulated knowledge of this field. These include not only students, but also professionals and consultants who require this knowledge as part of a process of planning and decision making. It is true that there are only a few studies whose point of departure for analyzing Israeli society is the occupation (Shenhav, 2008) but there is no doubt that a growing number of studies are looking at this issue indirectly even without declaring their approach. By these criteria, the occupation is an emerging distinct and explicit field for examining Israeli society, and this book is another stage in establishing this as a field of knowledge.[1]

The sociology of knowledge, as an academic field, examines scientific knowledge as part of social praxis requiring analysis like any other domain of social action (Bourdieu, 1993). Such analysis is beyond the scope of this short chapter. But I wish to focus attention on one parameter that may explain the expansion of the occupation paradigm in Israel—the generational dimension. Drawing upon the work of Mannheim (1952), a generational analysis is composed of three basic elements: the generational site, the generational interpretation, and generation as actuality (see also Corsten, 1999). The generational site is the structure of opportunities in which individuals are located, and is influenced by sociohistorical conditions that define the social experience and the range of existing opportunities or, to put it another way, the existential experiences that shape generations. The generational interpretation refers to the way the generational experience is interpreted, experienced, and creates generational semantics. Generation as actuality refers to the existence of groups that develop ways of responding to generational problems as generational units. Unlike various scholars who have adopted or emphasized only one of these elements, I believe that the contribution of the concept lies in the intersection between the three components.

I claim that the sociology of the occupation is a paradigmatic change conveyed by a generational unit of scholars who were born and raised in Israel and who came to political and professional adulthood after the 1967 Six Day War under conditions of the normalization processes of control of the occupied territories. In comparison to the preceding generations of native-born Israelis for whom the experience of wars were constitutive experiences, the generations that attained maturity after 1967 were transformed from combatants to soldiers who maintained the occupation. The normalization of the *war* became the formative experience of generations of Israelis (Lomsky-Feder, 1997) and led many researchers to question how the army and militarism have shaped society and culture in Israel (for example, Ben-Eliezer, 1995; Kimmerling, 1993a; Lomsky-Feder & Ben-Ari, 1999).[2] However, as the war gave place to the routine of the occupation, the question of how the *occupation* and its normalization have shaped Israeli society has arisen more and more frequently. In this sense, I claim that the scientific changes need to be understood in the context of society (see the discussion in Herzog, 2007; Ram, 2006, pp. 127–151). The protracted occupation has produced generational units that are left-wing and right-wing. The left wing produced conscientious objectors like the members of the Yesh Gvul (Hebrew for "there is a limit") movement, who refused to serve in the war in Lebanon and in the occupied territories; the New Profile movement; and the Breaking the Silence movement; and all of this took place alongside the protest activity of women who proposed alternative collective definitions as a basis for citizenship and for defining the boundaries of the collective as well as the territorial boundaries (Helman, 1999; Helman & Rapoport, 1997). In tandem with the left-wing generational units, right-wing generational units emerged on the backdrop of the same events. But they had different generational interpretations leading to opposing political activities (Feige, 2002; Herzog, 2009). It is no surprise that sociologists belonging to those same generational units were drawn to examine these phenomena, as they had been raised in a society in which the occupation had become a formative experience and an existential question.

The sociology of the occupation as the basis for an examination of society in Israel is in its early stages. As noted, some of the studies have not explicitly defined themselves as being part of this new paradigm, but they throw light on generational semantics and literature that challenge the accepted sociology that adopted the Green Line (the 1949 armistice lines between Israel and its neighbors after the 1948 Arab-Israeli war) as the boundary unit of sociological analysis. The sociology of occupation does not only include the territories and the activities taking place in them as another field of research, but also attempts to explain deep-seated processes in society in terms of this paradigm (Bar-Tal, Halperin, Sharvit, Rosler, & Raviv, 2008; Gutwein, 2004; Herzog,1999b; Sachs, Sa'ar, & Aharoni, 2005; Shenhav, 2010).

THE OCCUPATION AS A CRITICAL TURNING POINT FOR ISRAELI FEMINISM

During the 1960s, when the Western world was in the throes of an in-depth discussion of the issues of equality that had come to the fore due to the student uprisings, the movements for civil liberties, the peace movements, the movements for civil rights, and the second wave of feminism, Israel entered into a euphoria of power following the Six Day War. The question of territorial boundaries and national security was at the center of the public discourse and political activism, resulting in a shutdown of feminist discourse in society.

The upheaval of the Yom Kippur War in 1973 opened large cracks in the policy of the exclusion and silencing of women. The three weeks of hostilities until the cease-fire, together with the subsequent months of stepped-up mobilization of reservists, revealed the full intensity of the gendered structure of the public sphere and women's marginality within it. The massive and swift mobilization of the country's males when the war erupted almost brought civilian life to a complete standstill, especially in the three weeks of full hostilities before the cease-fire took effect. Factories, businesses, offices, and schools shut down. Without men, the national economy virtually ground to a halt. Public transportation was sparse: there were no female bus drivers. For the first time, it was disclosed that the two bus cooperatives that monopolize public transportation in Israel (Egged and Dan) neither allowed women to become members nor employed women as drivers on a contract basis.

Feminist voices, few in number though they were, began to make themselves heard. Marsha Freedman, who was elected to the eighth Knesset in 1973 on the Ratz list was the first member in the history of the Knesset to raise the issue of domestic violence against women, and she encountered derogatory and insulting responses. One of the silencing statements hurled at her was that "there is and never has been violence in Jewish families."

In 1975, Yitzhak Rabin, serving his first term as Prime Minister, appointed a commission to examine the status of women. This was done not because he subscribed to a feminist outlook, but as a response to the UN condemnation of Zionism as racism and because Zionism had been cited alongside colonialism, foreign conquest, racism, ethnic discrimination, apartheid, and infringement of women's rights at the International Women's Year Conference in Mexico City in 1975. The report of this commission was submitted to Prime Minister Menahem Begin in 1978. Since then, of the 241 sections in the report that revealed deep-seated problems related to the issue of women's status in Israeli society and that required action to correct them, fewer than half have been acted upon; nor does this necessarily mean that the problems were resolved in those that were acted upon. The recommendation to establish an authority for the advancement of the status of women was eventually put into effect some twenty years later, and even then it lacked authority and was given a minuscule budget (Herzog, 2008). It is worth noting that since the 1970s, though suffering ups and downs, there has been widespread and determined feminist activity in Israel that has attained more than a few admirable achievements (see, for example, Herzog, 1999b; Kamir, 2007). Nevertheless, cultural and structural obstacles have perpetuated social inequalities. The potential that existed in the increase in women's education, in their accelerated entry into the labor market, and in their willingness to integrate into politics was never utilized to the fullest degree. There is no doubt that gender inequality, chauvinistic positions, arrangements, and perceptions that discriminate against women existed before the occupation too. But the protracted occupation gave added force to the inequality and prevented the introduction of many changes, even causing harm to women and making them more vulnerable.

Until the early 1990s, research on women tended to focus mainly on Jewish women, largely from the dominant groups, and ignored almost completely the issue of the occupation and the part it played in shaping the status of women in Israel.[3] The outbreak of the first *intifada* (December 1987) can be viewed as a generational turning point both for the Palestinians in the West Bank and Gaza and for Jewish and Palestinian citizens of Israel. This was a generation that knew not the Six Day War and had grown up in the shadow of the protracted occupation (Bucaille, 2004; Rabinowitz & Abu Baker, 2005).

The first *intifada* began as a grassroots uprising with the participation of young activists in the field, children, and women. It was a strong protest against the establishment of settlements, arrests, demolition of houses, oppression, and all aspects of the twenty-year control over the territories. This rebellion destabilized the dominant occupying force as well as the social order of the Palestinians through, for example, women's entry into the public arena.

For many Israelis, it served as a catalyst for a discussion about the occupation and for research studies that began to question the effect of the occupation on society. A notable aspect of the discourse that developed during this period was that it gave prominence to women, both Palestinian and Jewish, as political actors in civil society and as researchers challenging the dominant discourse.

While most of the books written immediately after the *intifada* dealt with its causes and characteristics, and placed heavy emphasis on its military and political aspects (Shalev, 1991), women questioned the effect of the *intifada* on everyday life in general and on women in particular. In 1994 the first collection of articles edited by Tamar Mayer (1994) was published. It analyzed various aspects of the effect of the Israeli occupation on women. This was an anthology of articles written by male and female researchers, and by Jewish and Palestinian activists from the occupied territories, as well as by Israeli citizens, and was the first to turn its attention to the price paid by both the occupiers and the occupied at one and the same time, despite the asymmetrical division of power between them. It challenged the national categories by which the Palestinian-Israeli conflict was constructed, and was the first to raise women's objection to the myth of security and the precedence accorded to a national agenda that served as an instrument for marginalizing women, both Jewish and Palestinian. One of the justifications expressed over and over again for the continued control over the occupied territories is that it ensures the continued existence of Israel and provides security for its population. The concept of security, emphasized by the sense of existential anxiety of the Jewish people in general and of those living in Israel in particular, became the main building block in the construction of the political, economic, cultural, and social reality in Israel (Bar-Tal, Jacobson, & Klieman, 1998).

My claim is threefold. The first is that the perception of national security in its dominant sense is a narrow one. It assumes a distinction between "there" (Palestinians in the occupied territories) and "here" (Israeli society, mainly the Jews) and views the external danger to which Israel is exposed as the chief security threat, thereby bolstering the centrality of the army and militarism as the main pattern of thought. This perception takes for granted a distinction between the public/male world and the domestic-private/female world, thus reproducing gendered inequality.

My second claim is that the narrow perception of security conceals personal-social insecurity. The dominant perception of the security threat creates a deviant awareness in the collective Israeli consciousness that the most frightening thing for all Israelis is an attack from outside. In other words, the security threat in its narrow traditional interpretation is built on the politics of fear of an enemy or, in Huysmans's (2002) terms, the "politics of insecurity." But, contrary to the firm impression created by the aura of national security, the personal insecurity of the majority of the population in the State of Israel lies elsewhere: lack of economic and social security due to the collapse of the welfare state; an increase in economic, gender, and national inequality; poverty and unemployment; nonviolent crime, murder, and physical violence; an increase in traffic accidents; and the deterioration of the environment (e.g., Jacobson & Bar-Tal, 1995). All of these are immediate factors affecting the lack of security in everyday life for most of the population. In other words, the dominant meaning of national security as it has been framed in the State of Israel does not allow for the introduction of competing perceptions based on alternative logics such as that of a welfare regime and/or of human security promoted by a global feminist discourse.

My third claim, which links the other two, is that the protracted occupation has become a reproductive and silencing mechanism that has facilitated the exclusion of and control over weakened populations, including women. This is a mechanism that erodes basic perceptions about social and civil equality in the social discourse in general and particularly that of women. Women constitute one of the most vulnerable populations in this situation. The narrow perception of national security does not take into account the importance of personal-social security that encompasses the gendered world and the marginalization of women. On the contrary, it facilitates the protracted occupation, which is justified in terms of national security. Thus, it becomes a major mechanism for the reproduction of gender inequality, and even intensifies the weakening and vulnerability of women and the harm caused to them.

NATIONAL SECURITY AS A GENDERING MECHANISM

The concept of security in the Israeli discourse in the sense of an existential threat is a subject of mythic stature. It relates to basic perceptions of law and order, protection of the individual from external harm, and the concrete danger of violence and war. In the deeper sense, national security is perceived as the ability to maintain a sovereign Jewish state. In short, the concept covers a broad range of personal and collective existence and survival approaches (Gamson & Herzog, 1999; Herzog & Shamir, 1994). Because it has a broad and deep-seated resonance for Israeli culture, the concept of security can be enlisted to justify social reality, decisions, or lack of decision making about policy (Al-Haj & Ben-Eliezer, 2003). Time after time, the public tends to support government positions when a situation is defined as a security event, regardless of the party the person belongs to. The first reaction, which is taken for granted, is for all to converge in the face of the threat. Only later does a public-political discourse begin on the extent of the threat and the legitimacy of military retaliation (Arian, 1995, pp. 54–90). The majority of the research on security approaches the issue from the Jewish point of view; however, Smooha (1992) suggests that the agreement about the principle of security forms the basis for the social negotiation between Palestinian and Jewish citizens of Israel. Security and the security discourse are the main formative factors that shape identity, and political positions and policy, for both the Jewish and Palestinian citizens of Israel. This constitutes the basis for social and political disagreements, but no one disputes one basic assumption—that this subject is important. Paradoxically, security, in the narrow sense, is both the basis for the conflict and the strong adhesive that unites the various sectors of Israeli society. This convergence around the subject and/or the disagreement about it has revealed no differences between men and women (Arian, 1995, pp. 114–119).

The centrality of the perception of security in its dominant sense—as a defense against an external threat—is a factor that reproduces a gendered perception of the world. The inequality between the genders that exists in Israeli society does not stem from the security threat in which the Israeli-Palestinian conflict is immersed, nor is it grounded in the protracted occupation, although these do constitute supporting factors in perpetuating inequality and even serve to legitimize its continuance. Gender inequality in modern Western society in general, and in Israel in particular, arose from the cultural and structural separation between two spheres of life—the private-domestic and the public—priority and prestige being the province of the public domain (Pateman, 1989). This worldview depicts the public world as the world most suited to men, whereas the domestic domain is considered more suited to women. In national societies, women are perceived as representative of and preservers of the collective, as expressed in the common phrase "mothers of the nation." They are viewed as having responsibility for the continuity of the nation, both in their role as childbearers and educators of the younger generation and as those who transmit culture from one generation to the next. They represent the honor of the nation, and as such they define the symbolic boundaries of the collective (Yuval-Davis, 1997). This cultural perception not only reproduces the restriction of women to the private sphere but even reinforces it. This reinforcement is bolstered by a strong sense of belonging and contributing to the collective that obscures the discriminatory and subjugating dimension concealed within the gendered division of roles (Berkovitch, 1997). Moreover, the public-domestic dichotomy incorporates a presumption about the hierarchy between the two spheres, whereby the former is more highly regarded and considered to lie at the heart of social action, and the qualities it requires are considered more suited for filling contemporary social roles. Therefore, the link between masculine or feminine qualities and compatibility with the various spheres also contains within it the existing hierarchy between female and male qualities and domains or, to put it simply, between women and men.

The introduction of women into the public domain without repudiation of the cultural outlook differentiating between the masculine and the feminine worlds produces a situation in which women are considered by society, and often by themselves, as invaders of a domain to which they do not belong and for which they do not possess the correct attitudes and the appropriate resources for effective functioning. Despite the entry of women into economic and political activity, they are still expected to continue to be responsible for homemaking and children. It is presumed that they have a preference, first and foremost, for their family roles, and that in the event of a conflict between the needs of the family and the requirements of public office, they will always give precedence to the family. In the spirit of these conventions, the images of the roles of the two genders in society, and to a large extent their sexual identities, are being shaped. These perceptions do not only determine the preferences of men and women, but also intrude upon women's chances for promotion in the workplace or in politics and interfere with their ability to negotiate in the labor market and in politics (Herzog, 1999a; Izraeli et al., 1999).

In all Western societies there is a gendered division of roles and precedence given to the public domain over the private-domestic one, but in Israel this prioritization enjoys an additional justification: security considerations. These engender patterns of thought in which an assumed precedence is given to military personnel and to listening to their opinions in civil and political society. The emphasis on security and militarism has become a central peg in Israeli political culture (Al Haj & Ben-Eliezer, 2003). The army is not only the organization in which there is the most explicitly gendered division of labor, but it has also produced a masculine culture that has spread beyond the boundaries of that organization (Enloe, 1988; Sasson-Levy, 2003). Prolonged control over the territories provides a hothouse for the continued militarization of the state and society in Israel, which is expressed in deep involvement of the army in political life (Peri, 2006). This is not all: the most significant aspect is in shaping patterns of thought based upon military thinking that permeate all social locations and become an integral part of the social stratification in Israel (Kimmerling, 1993b).

The dominance of security thinking reinforces more than just masculine thinking; it also strengthens the patriarchal structure of the state. It is bound up with reproducing the traditional division of roles: the army and militarism define the masculine roles and the masculine identity of the Jewish male, and also give legitimacy to the preferential status of men, whereas the home and domesticity are the province of women. This perception locates women as marginal to the labor market and to politics. Moreover, in Israel there is a trend taking place that is the reverse of what is happening in the Western world: while in most of the Western countries the importance of family is diminishing, the family in Israeli society (Jewish and Arab) still holds a very important place (Fogiel-Bijaoui, 2002). Israeli society places cultural emphasis on the family and family values. Israeli families, even the secular ones, tend to be larger than the average American family, the divorce rate is lower, the network of kinship interconnections is broader, and many of the cultural and legal arrangements view the family as something to be taken for granted. On the one hand, the centrality of the family has accorded women in Israel many achievements that feminists in other Western countries are still battling to attain, such as paid maternity leave and a birth grant, the legal prohibition on dismissing a woman who has given birth, and the assurance that her position at work will remain available to her upon her return from maternity leave.[4] On the other hand, these are the very achievements that have become obstacles for women, particularly in the present labor market, which has become increasingly privatized, because employers prefer not to hire women of childbearing age. Today, more than ever before, women are expected to enter the labor market, but they find themselves faced with a conflict of roles and must make tireless efforts to bridge the gap between the expectation that they will share in the burden of breadwinning as well as fulfilling their family-domestic roles.

The gendered perception that draws a distinction between the roles of men and women becomes heightened in the light of the security threat. A woman is expected to provide support to a man serving in the army while she fulfills her domestic roles; and this is so whether the man is her husband doing reserve duty or her son doing his compulsory military service or reserve duty. Mothering roles last longer, particularly in families with an average of three children.[5] Moreover, in Israel, great social pressure is exerted in relation to female fertility. Fertility has been recruited to the demographic discourse to maintain the Jewishness of the state with a Jewish demographic majority (Portugese, 1998). In the early 1950s, the high fertility rate of Arabs was already perceived as a demographic threat to the Jewish majority of the nation (Melamed, 2002). However, the demographic threat became an obsession among Israeli leaders after Israel's occupation of the West Bank and Gaza Strip, which increased the number of Palestinians under Israeli control (Masalha, 2000; Sofer, 2002; Zureik, 2008).[6] Women have become the social carriers of the national task to fight the demographic threat. This effect is especially noticeable among the national-religious public in the West Bank settlements, where an increasing proportion of educated women have six or more children. This is a case of the convergence of religious and ideological stances, and in this these women differ from the national-religious women within the Green Line (Herzog, 2006, pp. 253–254). Israel, with its national health service, is the country that allocates the greatest investment to fertility technology; there is almost no limit on the number of fertility treatments a woman can undergo, nor is there any age limit or a requirement that she should be in a normative family (Goldin, 2008).[7] Having a large number of children increases the woman's dependence on the man, reinforces the traditional division of roles in which the mother is perceived as responsible for raising the children, and creates an additional burden on women who work outside the home. Despite the heavy investment in promoting fertility, the state provides very little institutional assistance to facilitate child rearing in families in which both parents work outside the home, such as day-care centers, an extended school day, or tax rebates for families employing child minders.

PERSONAL AND HUMAN SECURITY—A RENEWED DEFINITION OF THE SECURITY PARADIGM

In contrast to the paradigm of national security as protection of the state boundaries, an alternative paradigm is being developed that places human beings at the heart of the discourse. This security paradigm shifts the spotlight to personal and social insecurity, poverty and unemployment; crime; environmental conditions; economic, gender, and national inequality; the lack of rights of noncitizens; and more (Hamber et al., 2006). All of these constitute the immediate factors contributing to the extreme lack of security experienced by sections of the population, the most vulnerable of which are women. Differentiation exists between the social and the political lacking humaneness—the human face behind the conflict—and there is attrition in the consciousness of the role of the general population and its social responsibility toward weakened groups.

The right to live safe from wars and terrorist acts is a basic human right, but the fear of these dangers has been exploited by Israeli governments and the army to bring the issue of security to the forefront and to silence public debate about whether the occupation and control of the territories is moral, legitimate, and worthwhile. The economic and social price Israeli citizens pay for maintaining the security apparatus is enormous, and despite this, there has been a gradual reduction in the personal security of citizens within the Green Line.

The protracted occupation necessitates the allocation of vast economic resources. It is true that the ups and downs of the Israeli economy do not result only from the Israeli-Palestinian conflict, but it is undoubtedly affected by the security upheavals and the investment in construction in the settlements (or in evacuating them afterward), in building access roads to these settlements, in building the separation fence, and in maintaining the checkpoints and control of the occupied areas (Hever, 2005). Swirski (2008) has proposed measuring the economic security burden and comparing it to the long- and short-term social costs—for example, in comparison to the investment in education, health, social security, and prevention of inequality. The erosion in social investment has a dual impact: it damages existential security and reduces the quality of life of individuals as well as decreasing social solidarity.

The parliamentary commission of inquiry on the social gaps in Israel that studied the increase in the gaps from 1982 to 2002[8] found that there was a rise in inequality in most of the indicators and an increase in the number of poor people by a factor of 2.5–2.7. This was confirmed in the annual report on poverty and income gaps in 2006, published by the National Insurance Institute, which showed a continued increase in the rate of child poverty and a growing gap between the average income of families above and below the poverty line (Endblad & Cohen, 2006). At the same time, studies indicate the feminization of poverty (Stier & Lewin 2002), which means that women pay the highest price in the growth of inequality. Gutwein (2004) associates the erosion in all aspects of the welfare state with the occupation. He posits that privatization and the occupation are complementary components of right-wing policy. Most of the Israeli governments in the past decades have advanced the privatization of the welfare state. The universal welfare state that has been dismantled in Israel continues to exist in the territories on a sectoral basis. The excessive benefits for housing, education, health, taxation, and infrastructure beyond the Green Line have become a mechanism to compensate the lower classes residing there for the harm caused by the privatization of social services in Israel, and it was this that prompted the migration to the territories and the perpetuation of the occupation. In the meantime, the retreat of the welfare state within the Green Line has worsened the lot of the weakened population and has negatively affected women the most.

The protracted conflict has had a tangible effect upon the sense of personal security, especially in the light of terrorist attacks and actions. In 1998, Natal, the Israel Trauma Center for Victims of Terror and War, was established on a national level in order to provide assistance to those hurt in Israel's wars and in terrorist actions, as well as other stressful and traumatic events arising from the Israeli-Arab conflict. Somer (2005) reports that more than half a million Israelis suffer from post-traumatic stress syndrome, which results in mental distress and deficient functioning. It is apparent from these findings that it is not necessary for a person to be directly involved in a terror incident in order to suffer from post-traumatic stress. Traumatic injury exerts a personal price as well as a collective price asserts Bleich, chairman of the Natal steering committee: "Being caught up in a psychological siege position (the 'Massada syndrome') and in the perception that one is a threatened victim, fixes our consciousness in a stereotypical mode and makes it difficult for us to display the flexibility necessary for initiating, locating and taking advantage of opportunities for a different approach in our region. Awareness of these processes is essential for establishing a dialog in Israeli society for navigating through the stormy seas of the existential wars forced upon us."[9] I would like to note that Bleich draws a connection between personal security and collective security. Somer and Bleich (2005) show that a sense of vulnerability to trauma has increased among immigrants from Russia, among Arab Israelis, and among the less educated population. They conclude that the explanation for this stems from the limited resources weakened and subordinated groups have at their disposal for combating threats against their person in comparison with the resources allocated to coping in other areas. This is to say that the gap between the strong and the weakened groups is not limited to gaps in income, but is manifested in their distress and emotional resilience. Furthermore, these researchers state that the proportion of women among those suffering from post-traumatic stress disorder is greater than that of men.

THE EFFECT OF THE PROTRACTED CONFLICT ON WOMEN

Violent conflicts affect the lives of people of both genders but have a more notable impact on women. The women's movements at the Fourth World Conference on Women in Beijing (1995) placed the negative effect of violent conflicts on the lives of women on the agenda: Resolution 1325 adopted this statement and extended it to a demand for women's inclusion in peace negotiations and conflict settlements. In recent years, more and more women's movements in Israel have been moving toward gendering the discourse on the Israeli-Palestinian conflict and have been calling the public's attention to the effect of the armed conflict on groups of women from different classes and on various ethnic and national groups. One of the organizations at the forefront of this attempt to show the connection between national security and personal security is Isha L'Isha (Woman to Woman), a feminist center in Haifa in which Jewish and Arab (Palestinian citizens of Israel) women take action together. Among its activities are several studies that have been undertaken and that included Palestinian women in Israel and in the territories (Sachs, Sa'ar, & Aharoni, 2005).

Studies all over the world have shown that women's condition worsens particularly during periods of increasing political violence. Under these circumstances, the economic situation in general deteriorates and that of women particularly so, and this goes hand in hand with an increase in the rate of sexual violence. Sachs and colleagues (2005) pursue this gendered perspective on the occupation in their paper entitled "Silent Witness." In their study, undertaken between 2004 and 2005 among 552 female citizens of Israel, both Jewish and Palestinian (including a small group of women from the West Bank settlements), they investigated the exposure to political violence (during the period of the terrorist attacks and the retaliation for them) and its effect on women, looking at the relationship between women's exposure to political violence and to violence of a gendered nature, as well as the impact of the conflict on women's economic situation, their health and welfare, and their requests for assistance and support. Their study focuses on peak periods of violence, but the findings serve as a magnifying glass of the relationship between exposure to violence and the status of women and their vulnerability.

Studies show that during an economic recession women suffer the most hardship. Economic recessions affect women more than men for several reasons: women constitute the majority of the poor in Israel (Stier & Lewin, 1999, 2002); their income is lower; their level of unemployment is higher; and their child-care duties make it harder for them to integrate into the labor market. Women head most of the single-parent families and more often need welfare services and National Insurance stipends. Their economic weakness increases their dependence on men and/or on institutions. Cutbacks in the benefits from the National Insurance Institute due to security exigencies harm women more than other weakened groups.

Poverty increases exposure to political violence. The poor are less able to purchase security. For example, they don't own private cars; thus, during a period of attacks on public transportation they are more exposed. They live in poor housing conditions and thus have less access to secure spaces during missile attacks. Also, they are more exposed to bereavement because men from marginal groups are overrepresented among casualties and fatalities. Poverty-beset areas like Sderot and Kiryat Shmone suffer more from terror than established areas (Sachs et al., 2005, pp. 13–14).

In correlation with the reduction in personal security arising directly from the Israeli-Palestinian conflict, there has been an increase in reports of domestic violence. As people move from military service to civilian life, there is a danger of replicating violence on the women at home (Sachs et al., 2005, p. 16).

Between 2000 and 2003 there was a 57% increase in the number of applications for restraining orders connected to domestic violence. In 2003 the number of cases filed against men suspected of attacking their domestic partners increased by a factor of 2.3 compared to 1999. This increase correlates with the peak period of the second *intifada*.

It is impossible to separate life in the shadow of the protracted conflict from gender-related and sexual violence. During the years of the second *intifada*, there was an increase in the number of people requesting information, emotional support, and legal advice from the authorities in connection with sexual and emotional exploitation (Sachs et al., 2005, p. 19).

From the outbreak of the second *intifada* in September 2000 to 2004, thirty-eight women were murdered by their partners with light weapons; in eighteen of these cases the perpetrators had a license for the weapons, and these included police or military weapons or weapons in the possession of partners or family members employed as security guards! At the end of 2003, there were 340,000 licensed weapons in the hands of security firm members. The number of requests filed for weapons licenses doubled between 2001 and 2002. Some 75% of the security guards come from weakened social strata and they are employed under bad working conditions; this contributes to violent behavior. Enhancement of the sense of security in the public space (efficient control of the territories) increases the feeling of insecurity in the private space. The weakening of security in the private space is linked to military reserve duty, which carries an economic and personal price in that it moves the established violence from the territories into the home (most of the murdered women were killed by men holding licensed weapons). Paradoxically, securing the public space erodes citizens' private security (light fingers on the trigger in civilian disputes), but the harm mostly affects women (Sachs et al., 2005, pp. 20–21). The above data make it clear that the concept of national security cannot be separated from personal security because there is a link between political and social violence.

CONCLUSION: GENDERING THE OCCUPATION DISCOURSE–A NEW LOOK AT SOCIETY

The occupation and its consequences are not gender neutral. The Israeli case demonstrates how a prolonged conflict replicates the gendered division of roles and the gendered hierarchy. It allocates men and resources to carry on the occupation and emphasizes women's domestic roles. The traditional preference of the public sphere as men's sphere is reproduced, thereby elevating men's status and prestige as protectors of the family and the nation and strengthening the masculine discourse and values. It is true that men in Israel are more exposed to military conflict and terror, but women pay a particularly high price due to their social roles: concern and responsibility for the everyday functioning of the family, whereas men—sons and husbands—do compulsory service in the army and do reserve duty. It falls to the women to care for children and aging parents; this includes coping with emotions in the course of providing support in everyday life and for trauma victims. The findings show that the stresses on men affect and cause harm to women in the form of domestic violence, which is liable to end in murder. The damage caused to women is not uniform: women from weakened groups (poor women, peripheral women, and Arab women) are more likely to be negatively affected than those from more established strata. Thus, the prolonged occupation becomes a social mechanism that increases gender differentiation and discrimination.

The analysis shows how the dominance of the security discourse obscures the lack of gender security. "Resilience and security for whom?" asks a position paper prepared by the Isha L'Isha organization and the Women's Coalition for Peace (Nagar, 2006). It explains that "violence based upon gender is violence against women merely because they are women (including violence that does not have a sexual dimension). In practice, the right to gender protection is not recognized and is not grounded in social norms nor in the law" (ibid., p. 7). Traditionally, men are expected to be responsible for women's safety and general well-being. But this narrow definition both reproduces the dependency of women on men and prevents the formulation of a general policy for ensuring gender security for women as women. The existence of prostitution, pornography, and trafficking in women are some additional forms of women's insecurity that are not being dealt with. Though these kinds of sexual violence are not necessarily the outcome of the occupation, ignoring them stems from the dominant perception that frames national security as being confined to protection against outside threats and displaces personal security and its gender aspects from the agenda. Such a narrow definition of security, in effect, means that the state withdraws from its responsibility for the security of women in various groups and thereby denies the basic rights of women to enjoy personal/human security. It would be incorrect to attribute this situation to women alone. The absence of appropriate legislation and the lack of enforcement of existing laws related to the security of citizens in general and of women in particular together constitute a blow to democracy. Analyzing security issues in terms of an outside threat ignores the effect of the occupation on society. Moreover, the dominance of this security discourse tends to silence the discourse about the connection between the occupation and personal insecurity. The gender analysis breaks this silence and challenges the silencing mechanisms. It suggests the need for a reconceptualization of human security. It also makes it possible to turn attention to civil society, including women's organizations working to change this worldview and to propose a normative social agenda that advances peace; works to overcome infringements of human rights, including women's rights; and promotes action for peace, coexistence, and mutual recognition.

NOTES

1. See, for example, Theory and Criticism 31 (2007); Israeli Sociology Vol 9:2 (2008). These journal issues are devoted to an analysis of the occupation as an integral part of economic, political, cultural and social processes that shape Israeli society.
2. The examples cited are largely drawn from the field of sociology which is where my expertise lies, but this development also occurs in other disciplines of the humanities and social sciences.
3. On the development of research on and about women in Israel see Herzog, 2000; Motzafi-Haller, 2000;2001.
4. Despite the existence of this law, its enforcement is incomplete. Furthermore, there is an increasing number of cases in which women are not hired for jobs for fear that they might become pregnant and take maternity leave.
5. The average number of children per family in Israel has remained at three over a long period, with slight increases and decreases. See Patterns of Fertility in Israel in 2006, Central Bureau of Statistics, which states that the fertility rate is 2.9 (http://www.cbs.gov.il/www/hodaot2007n/01_07_215b.doc).
6. It should be noted that the discourse of demographic threat is directed to other issues such as the Jewish ethnic dimension (Melamed, 2002) and the democratic dimension. The latter relates to the demographic growth of both Palestinians and ultra-Orthodox Jews. However, the woman's womb is involved in each of the venues that is driven by the discourse.
7. Single women, single-sex couples, and unmarried couples are entitled to receive fertility treatment.
8. See the report of the commission at http://knesset.gov.il/mmm/doc.asp?doc=m00416&type=pdf accessed July 20, 2008.
9. http://www.natal.org.il/?CategoryID=392 accessed September 10, 2008.

REFERENCES

Al-Haj, M., & Ben-Eliezer, U. (Eds.). (2003). *In the name of security: The sociology of peace and war in Israel in changing times*. Haifa: Haifa University Press and Pardes Publishing House (in Hebrew).

Arian, A. (1995). *Security threatened: Surveying Israeli opinion on peace and war*. Tel Aviv and Cambridge: Jaffee Center for Strategic Studies, Tel Aviv University and Cambridge University Press.

Bar-Tal, D., Halperin, E., Sharvit, K., Rosler, N., & Raviv, A. 2008. Prolonged occupation: Socio-psychological implication for the occupying society. *Israeli Sociology, 9*, 357–386 (in Hebrew).

Bar-Tal, D., Jacobson, D., & Klieman, A. (Eds.). (1998). *Security concerns: Insights from the Israeli experience*. Stamford, CT: JAI Press.

Ben-Eliezer, U. (1995). A nation-in-arms: State, nation, and militarism in Israel's first years. *Comparative Studies in Society and History, 32*, 264–285.

Berkovitch, N. (1997). Motherhood as a national mission: The construction of womanhood in the legal discourse in Israel. *Women's Studies International Forum, 20*, 605–619.

Bourdieu, P. (1993). *Sociology in question*. London and Thousand Oaks, CA; Sage.

Bucaille, L. (2004). *Growing up Palestinian: Israeli occupation and the intifada generation*. Princeton, NJ: Princeton University Press.

Corsten, M. (1999). The time of generation. *Time & Society, 8*, 249–272.

Endblad, M., & Elul Cohen, R. (2006). *Poverty dimensions and income gap 2006—main findings*, edited by National Social Security. Retrieved May 7, 2012, from http://www.btl.gov.il/SiteCollectionDocuments/btl/Publications/DochHaOni/oni-2006.pdf

Enloe, C. (1988). *Does khaki become you? The militarization of women's lives*. London: Pandora/HarperCollins.

Feige, M. (2002). *One space, two places: Gush Emunim, Peace Now and the construction of Israeli space*. Jerusalem: Hebrew University Magnes Press.

Fogiel-Bijaoui, S. (2002). Familism, postmodernity and the state: The case of Israel. *The Journal of Israeli History, 21*, 38–62.

Gamson, W. A., & Herzog, H. (1999). Living with contradictions: The taken-for-granted in Israeli political discourse. *Political Psychology, 20*, 247–266.

Goldin, S. (2008). Technologies of happiness. In Y. Yonah & A. Kemp (Eds.), *Citizenship gaps—Migration, fertility and identity in Israel* (pp. 167–206). Tel Aviv: Van Leer Jerusalem Institute/Hakibbutz Hameuchad Publishing House (in Hebrew).

Gutwein, D. (2004). Class aspects of occupation: Some remarks. *Theory and Criticism: An Israeli Forum, 24*, 203–211 (in Hebrew).

Hamber, B., Hillyard, P., Maguire, A., McWilliams, M., Robinson, G., Russell, D., & Ward, M. S. (2006). Discourses in transition: Re-imagining women's security. *International Relations, 20*, 487–502.

Harding, S. G., & Hintikka, M. B. 2003. *Discovering reality: Feminist perspectives on epistemology, metaphysics, methodology, and philosophy of science*. Dordrecht and Boston: Kluwer.

Helman, S. (1999). Redefining obligations, creating rights: Conscientious objection and redefinition of citizenship in Israel. *Citizenship Studies, 3*, 45–70.

Helman, S., & Rapoport, T. (1997). Women in black: Challenging Israel's gender and socio-political orders. *British Journal of Sociology, 48,* 682–700.
Herzog, H. (1999a). *Gendering politics—Women in Israel.* Ann Arbor: University of Michigan Press.
Herzog, H. (1999b). Women's status in the shadow of security. In D. Bar-Tal, D. Jacobson, & A. Klieman (Eds,), *Security concerns: Insights from the Israeli experience* (pp. 329–346), Stamford, CT, and London: JAI Press.
Herzog, H. (2005). From gender to genders: Feminists read women's locations in Israeli society. *Israel Studies Forum: An Interdisciplinary Journal, 20,* 64–94.
Herzog, H. (2006). Trisection of forces: Gender, religion and the state: The case of state-run religious schools in Israel. *British Journal of Sociology, 57,* 241–262.
Herzog, H. (2007). Mixed cities as a place of choice: The Palestinian women's perspective. In D. Monterescu & D. Rabinowitz (Eds.), *Mixed towns, trapped communities: Historical narratives, spatial dynamics, gender relations and cultural encounters in ethnically mixed towns in Israel/Palestine* (pp. 243–257). Hampshire, England, and Burlington, VT: Ashgate.
Herzog, H. (2008, June). Re/visioning the women's movement in Israel. *Citizenship Studies, 12,* 265–282.
Herzog, H. (2009). Imagined communities: State, religion and gender in Jewish settelments. In H. Herzog & A. Braude (Eds.), *Gendering religion and politics: Untangling modernities* (pp. 51–73). New York: Palgrave Macmillan.
Herzog, H., & Shamir, R. (1994). Negotiated society? Media discourse on Israeli Jewish/Arab relations. *Israel Social Science Research, 9,* 55–88.
Hever, S. (2005). *The settlements—Economic cost to Israel.* Alternative Information Center. Retrieved May 7, 2012, from http://www.alternativenews.org/images/stories/downloads/socioeconomic_bulletin_02.pdf
Huysmans, J. (2002). Defining social constructivism in security studies: The normative dilemma of writing security. *Alternatives, 27,* 41–62.
Izraeli, D., Friedman, A., Dahan-Kalev, H., Fogiel-Bijoui, S., Herzog, H., Hasan, M., & Naveh, H. 1999. *Sex gender politics—women in Israel.* Tel Aviv: Hakibbutz Hameuchad (in Hebrew).
Jacobson, D., & Bar-Tal, D. (1995). Structure of security beliefs among Israeli students. *Political Psychology, 16,* 567–590.
Kamir, O. (2007). *Israel's dignity-based feminism in law and society.* Jerusalem: Carmel.
Kimmerling, B. (1993a). Militarism in Israeli society. *Theory and Criticism: An Israeli Forum, 4,* 123–140 (in Hebrew).
Kimmerling, B. (1993b). Patterns of militarism in Israel. *Archives of European Sociology, 34,* 196–223.
Lomsky-Feder, E. (1997). Life stories of war veterans: The interplay between personal memory and the collective memory of war. *Theory and Criticism—An Israeli Forum, 11,* 59–79 (in Hebrew).
Lomsky-Feder, E., & Eyal Ben-Ari, E. (Eds.). (1999). *The military and militarism in Israeli society.* Albany: State University of New York Press.

Mannheim, K. (1952). The problem of generations. In P. Kecskemeti (Ed.), *Essays on the sociology of knowledge* (pp. 276–320). London: Routledge & Kegan Paul.

Masalha, N. (2000). *Imperial Israel and the Palestinians: The politics of expansion.* Sterling, VA: Pluto Press.

Mayer, T. (Ed.). (1994). *Women and the Israeli occupation—The politics of change.* London and New York: Routledge.

Melamed, S. (2002). *The Janus face of the "demographic threat": Gender, ethnicity, nationalism and the politics of fertility in Israel in the 1950s.* Tel Aviv: Department of Sociology and Anthropology, Tel Aviv University (in Hebrew).

Motzafi-Haller, P. (2000). Reading Arab feminist discourses: A postcolonial challenge to Israeli feminism. *Hagar: International Social Science Review, 1,* 63–89.

Motzafi-Haller, P.. (2001). Scholarship, identity, and power: Mizrahi women in Israel. *Signs: Journal of Women in Culture and Society, 26,* 697–734.

Nagar, N. (2006). *Resilience and security for whom?* Haifa and Jerusalem: Women's Coalition for Peace and Isha L'Isha (in Hebrew).

Pateman, C. (1989). *The disorder of women: Democracy, feminism and political theory* (pp. 118–140). Cambridge: Polity Press.

Peri, Y. (2006). *Generals in the cabinet room: How the military shapes Israeli policy.* Washington, DC: United States Institute of Peace Press.

Portugese, J. (1998). *Fertility policy in Israel: The politics of religion, gender, and nation.* Westport, CT, and London: Praeger.

Rabinowitz, D., & Abu-Baker, K. 2005. *Coffins on our shoulders: The experience of the Palestinian citizens of Israel.* Berkeley: University of California Press.

Ram, U. (2006). *The time of the "post": Nationalism and the politics of knowledge in Israel.* Tel Aviv: Resling (in Hebrew).

Sachs, D., Sa'ar, A., & Aharoni, S. (2005). *Silent witness: The influence of the armed Israeli-Palestinian conflict on women in Israel.* Haifa Isha L'Isha (in Hebrew).

Sasson-Levy, O. (2003). Feminism and military gender practices: Israeli women soldiers in "masculine" roles." *The Sociological Inquiry, 73,* 440–465.

Shalev, A. (1991). *The intifada: Causes and effects.* Jerusalem and Boulder, CO: Westview Press.

Shenhav, Y. (2008). Sociologists and the Israeli occupation of Palestinian territories. *Israeli Sociology, 9,* 263–270 (in Hebrew).

Shenhav, Y. (2010) *The time of the Green Line: A Jewish political essay.* Tel Aviv: Am Oved (in Hebrew).

Smooha, S. (1992). *Arabs and Jews in Israel: Conflicting and shared attitudes in divided society.* Boulder, CO: Westview Press.

Sofer, A. (2002, March). *Demographics in the Israeli-Palestinian dispute.* Special Policy Forum, Report No. 370. Washington, DC: Washington Institute for Near East Policy.

Somer, E., & Bleich, A. (2005). *Mental health in terror's shadow: The Israeli experience.* Tel Aviv: Ramot–Tel Aviv University (in Hebrew).

Stier, H., & Lewin, A. C. (1999). *Poverty among women in Israel*. Tel Aviv: Israel's Women's Network (in Hebrew).

Stier, H., & Lewin, A. (2002). Does women's employment reduce poverty? Evidence from Israel. *Work, Employment and Society, 16,* 211–230.

Swirski, S. (2008). *The price of occupation*. Tel Aviv: Adva Center (in Hebrew).

Yuval-Davis, N. (1997). *Gender & nation*. London, Thousand Oaks, CA, and New Delhi: Sage.

Zureik, E. (2008). Comments on the demographic discourse in Israel. In Y. Yonah & A. Kemp (Eds.), *Citizenship gaps—Migration, fertility and identity in Israel* (pp. 39–55). Tel Aviv: Van Leer Jerusalem Institute/Hakkibutz Hameuchad (in Hebrew).

CHAPTER 12

The Psychological and Moral Consequences for Israeli Society of the Occupation of Palestinian Land

Charles W. Greenbaum and Yoel Elizur

INTRODUCTION AND OVERVIEW

This chapter will attempt to analyze the effects of the occupation by Israel of Palestinian lands on the thinking, feeling and behavior of Israelis. We will first discuss the conceptual and methodological difficulties in drawing conclusions from studies of occupation. We will then discuss psychological research in the context of the occupation on moral thinking and violence in Israeli society with these difficulties in mind. Our main conclusion will be will be that while events surrounding the occupation have exposed Israelis of all ages to trauma, leading to a variety of stress reactions, the most direct and far-reaching effect of the occupation may be increasing violent behavior both within Israeli society and by the development of violent behavior by Israeli soldiers and settlers in the occupied territories toward Palestinians.

These processes have affected the major ethnic groups in Israeli society: Jews, who comprise 75.5% of the population of 7.59 million people (as of 2009); Arab-Palestinian citizens (the majority of whom are Moslems, with a minority of Christians), who comprise 20.4%; and other smaller groups (4.1%), largely Druze and Circassian peoples (Eglash, 2010, reporting data from the Israel Central Bureau of Statistics). The research we review on the Israeli military studied Jewish soldiers almost exclusively, while the research on the civilian population related to both the Jewish and Arab-Palestinian groups. Both the military and civilian studies did not distinguish between Jews and Arab-Palestinian citizens of Israel. Therefore, since most of the population in both sets of studies is Jewish, the conclusions in this chapter apply primarily to this group. The implications of the occupation for the Arab-Palestinian population are profound and are beyond the scope of this chapter.

We will suggest two major processes underlying the development of violent behavior in Israeli society: the development of norms in small groups and the development of defense mechanisms, particularly rationalization of the violent behavior. Each of these major processes involves subprocesses that we will describe. There is also evidence for mental distress in Israeli perpetrators and in witnesses to nonnormative violent behavior; for altruistic behavior on the part of some Israelis in opposing the occupation; and for the development of norms objecting to violence in some parts of Israeli society. We will draw tentative conclusions and formulate policy implications of psychological processes underlying the influence of the occupation on the occupiers.

DEFINING AND MEASURING EFFECTS OF OCCUPATION: CONCEPTUAL AND METHODOLOGICAL PROBLEMS

An analysis of the effects of the occupation is fraught with conceptual and methodological problems, which seriously qualify any conclusion made about the occupation. We will briefly describe some of these problems.

A conceptual problem concerns the use of the term "occupation" in the context of the Israel-Palestinian conflict. This term is controversial in Israel, and the use of it for the titles of this book and this chapter reveals a political orientation that favors ending the situation called occupation of land belonging to another people. For right-wing theorists, Israel is not occupying the West Bank and the Golan Heights but is in these places by right for two reasons. First, the land is historically that of the Jewish people who lived there 2000 years ago, and Israeli Jews from right-wing and national religious groups have seen themselves as the successors of those people (for a review of right-wing Israeli ideology, see Sprinzak, 1991). In addition, all Palestinian or Syrian land that is not occupied for historical reasons is needed for security reasons. This argument is also part of the right-wing ideology regarding the West Bank. Indeed, about 300,000 Israeli Jews now live in territories that the Palestinians consider their own, and the number is growing consistently (for an account of the development of these views, see Gorenberg, 2006).

For left-wing political groups in Israel and for the Israeli peace movement, the occupation is illegal and immoral and must be ended quickly, even if historical and security claims exist for the land. The argument from the peace movement point of view is that making claims to the land should be secondary to having a democratic state with a Jewish majority, since it will be impossible for Jews as a minority to rule a Palestinian people that will be the majority in the land (see Bar-On, 1996, for a comprehensive history for the Israeli peace movement up to 1995).

It is important to clarify these different views since writers and researchers with different political orientations will have different starting points for their analyses. The fact that the present book uses the term "occupation" thus implies a political-moral orientation aimed at ending the occupation. The authors of this chapter share this orientation. Psychological research on the effects of the occupation that assumes that the occupation is in Israel's best interests and that perceives Palestinians as implacable enemies may come to conclusions different from those indicated below (e.g., Milgram, 2008).

The controversy between Right and Left affects basic issues, such as the name used for the territories outside of Israel's 1967 borders in which Israel has a presence. For the right wing, the territory is called Judea and Samaria (e.g., see Segal, 1987, and the chapter by Tsur in this volume), emphasizing the identification of the territories with the presence there of the ancient tribes of Israel. This is also the official name used by the Israel Defense Forces (IDF). Most Israelis call the Palestinian homelands the "territories" or refer specifically to the two separated areas constituting the homelands as the "West Bank" and "the Gaza Strip." The United Nations and many countries in the world refer to the Occupied Palestinian Territories (OPT); this is the term that will be used in the present chapter.

Finally, there have been historical changes over forty-five years in the characteristics and effects of the occupation (for histories of the occupation see Oren, 2007; Zertal & Eldar, 2007). Concerning the occupation of Palestinian territory, we note a process that began with Israel experiencing a euphoric victory in the Six Day War of 1967, when the occupation of the West Bank, Gaza, and the Syrian Golan Heights started; it then focused on the day-to-day problems of administering a conquered territory and people through a military government; and eventually moved to an agreement on partial autonomy for the Palestinian territories within the Israeli military context after the Oslo Accords of 1993. The psychological effects of the occupation on Israeli society are also difficult to define and characterize; they have included euphoria in taking on the aggressive role of policing an occupied people, witnessing and partaking in settlement activity in the occupied lands, and coping with the stress and trauma of the Palestinian attacks (Gorenberg, 2006; Zertal & Eldar, 2007).

For some Israeli Jews, the prolonged occupation also evoked guilt and a sense of wrongdoing by Israel, leading to attempts to help the Palestinian people and to work for peace and human rights in groups associated with the Israeli peace movement (e.g., Avnery, 1968; Shulman, 2007). In the absence of empirical research, we will not be able to deal systematically with these effects. Finally, since other political, military, social, and economic events were (and are) taking place at the same time as the occupation, it will be difficult to determine whether the occupation or other events were responsible for or contributed to any effects on Israeli society. This conclusion is consonant with methodological analyses of the effects of traumatic political and economic events on group and individual behavior (Landau, 1998a). Attributing effects to the occupation is thus risky, and any conclusions about the occupation's effects, including those described in this chapter, must be viewed with caution. However, such conclusions, which are in the form of hypotheses for further research, may serve as warning signs for the development of moral problems in a society that engages in occupation.

While Israel has been involved in the past in other occupations (in Egypt and Lebanon) and has annexed the Syrian Golan Heights, this chapter will concentrate on the effects of occupying Palestinian land since that has been the most long-standing occupation and the one with the greatest friction with the occupied population (Oren, 2007).

Aggression in Israeli Society as a Result of the Occupation

This chapter will focus on the possible effects of the occupation on the moral behavior and self-perceptions of Israelis in two contexts. One context is military: here we willl review studies of Israelis, primarily Jewish soldiers who participated in the occupation. The other context is civilian: here we will review the possible effects of the occupation on criminal behavior in Israeli civilian society. The research in these areas has made the best case, in our opinion, for identifying specific effects that are attributable to the occupation rather than to any other cause.

We will not deal in detail with the important question of the effects of the occupation on the occupied peoples; these phenomena, including particularly the effects of trauma, have been reported elsewhere (see Giacaman, Shannon, Saab, Arya, & Boyce, 2007; Qouta & El Sarraj, 2006; Solomon & Lavi, 2006; Thabet, Abdulla, Elhelou, & Vostanis, 2006).

SOCIAL-PSYCHOLOGICAL EFFECTS OF THE OCCUPATION

Theoretical views on aggression relate it to social learning, particularly imitation, through others' behavior (Bandura, 1973). Social learning theory conceives aggression as a learned reaction to stress, including frustration (Bandura, 1973), or as a protective mechanism against real or imagined threats attributed to another person or group (Bailey & Ostrov, 2009; Dodge, Bates, &

Pettit, 1990). Stress is likely to increase the appearance of learned aggression in social situations, especially those involving stress. When such processes occur in groups, norms permitting aggression may be established (Zimbardo, 2007); these norms will also increase the chances for aggressive behavior. Stress, learning of aggressive responses, and social norms thus are likely to lead to aggressive behavior, including physical violence. The aggressive behavior may appear not only in situations of immediate self-defense, but also in contexts in which the aggressor was not threatened (Dodge, et al.; 1990; Owens & Straus, 1975). While models of interpersonal violence such as those developed in the studies just cited may be instructive for the study of inter-nation violence, the experience of interpersonal violence may not affect individuals' attitudes regarding resolution of conflicts with other nations (Owens & Straus, 1975).

In understanding the phenomena presented here, we suggest that two processes are involved: deviant norm-setting and the rationalization process. Groups of people that feel isolated from, or exploited by, the larger society may motivate their members to develop norms of behavior that are unacceptable to the larger society. A lack of solidarity in the society as a whole may trigger the development of deviant norms, including aggressive behavior that violates the larger society's norms (Landau, 1997). Particular groups in the society, including groups in large organizations such as an army, may adopt norms that are different from the generally accepted societal or army-wide norms, as exemplified by such statements as "In this unit everyone does that." In situations in which the individual identifies with the group, he or she may perceive the group norm as applying to the self. In addition, he or she may rely on his or her own small group for support. The process is strengthened by the group's ability to enforce its own norms with attendant rewards and punishments (Zimbardo, 2007). Deviant norm-setting processes may occur in civilian (Landau, 1994) or military organizations (Elizur & Yishay-Krien, 2009).

The second process, taking place at an individual level, is suggested by psychoanalytic theory. According to the theory explicated by Anna Freud, individuals employ ego defenses when their perceptions of themselves are threatened by information inconsistent with those views (Freud, 1937/1966). Different types of ego defenses may be employed, but regarding possibly immoral behavior a dominant defense mechanism is rationalization. In Bowins' (2004) view of the ego defense of rationalization the individual justifies his or her behavior in one of two ways or through a combination of both. One is *dissociation* from the behavior ("It wasn't really me who did this"). We suggest that the dissociation process is similar to the process of moral disengagement described by Bandura (2004). A second mode of ego defense takes place through *justification* of the behavior. In this case, the individual actively searches for and finds reasons to justify the behavior. Bandura and his colleagues as well as Festinger (1957), in describing a similar process called "dissonance reduction," present a number of ways in which such rationalization could be performed, including denigration or delegitimizing of the victim (Bar-Tal, 1989) and diffusion of responsibility for the behavior (e.g., "Everyone is doing it").

Individuals who do not successfully disengage from the behavior, or who are unable to rationalize it, may suffer mental distress, since illicit violent behavior is dissonant with their self-image as normative persons (Kimhi & Sagy, 2008). Witnessing illicit violent behavior as a bystander may also cause mental distress to the witness if he or she is unable to employ ego defense mechanisms to justify the behavior (Zimbardo, 2007). The above description of the processes of rationalization is consonant with those of Bar-Tal (1989) and Halperin, Bar-Tal, Sharvit, Rosler, and Raviv (2010) in their theoretical analysis of the effects of the occupation on Israeli society.

We suggest that processes of developing norms of aggression and subsequent rationalization are heightened in times of stress, as indicated above: members of an army unit under threat of attack, or having suffered losses, will be likely to engage in violent behavior toward perceived enemies, even when not under attack. The members of the group will disengage from the behavior, will rationalize it (e.g., "Those people deserved it"; "We needed to do this to educate them"; "We're following orders"), or will engage in both dissociation and rationalization.

STRESS, DEVIANT NORM-SETTING, AND RATIONALIZATION IN ISRAELI SOCIETY

There is little doubt that Israeli society has been subjected to high degrees of stress since its inception. According to Ministry of Defense data (reported by Hason, 2010), since the establishment of the State of Israel in 1948 Israeli society has suffered the loss of 22,684 soldiers, most of them in combat-related activities, and 3,971 civilians have died as a result of hostile activities emanating from neighboring countries; the majority of these civilian deaths have been at the hands of Palestinian armed individuals or groups, often called "terrorists" in Israel, who have invaded or bombarded Israel (Hason, 2010).

Research on effects of exposure to political violence in Israel and in the OPT cited earlier, as well as research performed in other countries experiencing political violence, such as Northern Ireland (Cairns, 1996), has reached a clear conclusion: exposure to violence, including injury and loss of life, increases the appearance of symptoms associated with stress. These symptoms include feelings of anxiety and fear, lessened ability to function in everyday life, disturbances in personality, and aggression (Cairns, 1996).

The persistence of such symptoms, or the appearance of such symptoms at a later time, is often called "posttraumatic stress disorder" (PTSD; Solomon & Lavi, 2006). Exposure to political violence is thus clearly stressful for all people, but the effects of stress may vary with the age, gender, ethnic group, and social situation of the individual, as well as with the specific response studied (Cairns, 1996).

The variables of gender, social class, and response mode have shown inconsistent effects. In addition, the long-term effects of stress in the Israeli-Palestinian conflict are not yet known, and there is evidence on both sides of the conflict that some individuals and groups may show resilience in the face of the stress involved in exposure to violence, while others report suffering from the trauma for years (Cairns, 1996; Giacaman et al., 2007; Solomon & Lavi, 2006).

Much Israeli research on political aggression has been performed within the context of two uprisings (called *intifadas* in Arabic) directed against the occupation: the *intifadas* were characterized by an upsurge in Palestinian violence against the occupation in comparison to other time periods. The first *intifada* took place between late 1987 and 1993 and was characterized by Palestinian demonstrations involving stone throwing, tire burnings, and work stoppages as well as shootings. Approximately 1,100 Palestinians were killed during the first *intifada* by Israeli security forces (army and police) and by Israeli civilians; some of the killing of Palestinians by Israeli soldiers and civilians occurred when the Israelis were under attack, but many Palestinians were killed in offensive or reprisal actions (B'Tselem, 2008).

The second *intifada*, also known as the Al-Aksa *intifada* since the uprising is thought to have begun at the Al-Aksa Mosque in Jerusalem at the beginning of the hostilities, took place between 2000 and 2006 and was more violent than the first *intifada* on both sides. B'Tselem (2008) reports over 4,900 Palestinian deaths at the hands of Israeli security forces during the second *intifada*; 45% of those killed were not participants in the hostilities. During the same period, 1,062 Israelis were killed (including security personnel) by the Palestinians. These statistics leave no doubt about the stress and loss experienced by both sides. The Palestinians suffered many more losses than the Israelis, and both sides suffered considerable stress (Solomon & Lavi, 2006).

In the following section, we present some studies on the effects on Israelis who experienced these stressful situations.

EFFECTS OF THE OCCUPATION ON SOLDIERS OPERATING IN THE OPT: RESEARCH ON VIOLENCE DURING THE FIRST AND SECOND INTIFADAS

The reaction of the Israeli authorities to the First Intifada was to chase and physically beat the demonstrators. Yitzhak Rabin, then the Minister of Defense, allegedly passed on the word, in referring to Palestinian demonstrators, to "break their bones." In a number of instances, live fire was used against the demonstrators. In spite of denials by Rabin that he issued orders to that effect, the spirit of the order pervaded units of the IDF serving in the OPT (Zertal & Eldar, 2007). Studies of soldiers' thinking and behavior include studies by the IDF on the behavior of its soldiers toward civilians in the OPT; reports by human rights organizations such as B'Tselem on fatalities and injuries to civilians in the same population (B'Tselem, 2008); small-scale narrative studies on soldiers after their release from the IDF; and effects of soldiers' participation in the occupation on their behavior toward Palestinians (Bar & Ben-Ari, 2005; Kimhi & Sagy, 2008; Linn, 1997), which provide a glimpse into the nature of the events and their consequences. Other sources are trials and hearings of soldiers accused of offenses against the Palestinian population; to our knowledge, there has been no psychological study based on these trials and hearings.

The study of soldiers operating in the OPT should show the effects of the occupation most clearly, since these soldiers are the ones who carry out the policy of the occupation and have the most face-to-face contact with the civilian population and the militants of the Palestinian society. Yet, this type of research on soldiers is largely restricted to classified studies carried out by the IDF, which are inaccessible to the general public.

We will report here three studies conducted on IDF soldiers and officers during the occupation. The first study was performed by Bar-On and Greenbaum and is reported in an interview (Matalon, 1988). It was performed at the beginning of the First Intifada in 1988. The second study (Elizur & Yishay-Krien, 2009) was performed during the Second Intifada. These two studies were chosen because they are the only publicly available systematic research known to us that investigated the behavior of soldiers directly during their army service and are not based on recollections from soldiers who were released. The third study (Kimhi & Sagy, 2008), is based on soldiers' recollections after their release; it is a systematic and quantitative study of the effects of service in the occupation on moral thinking and behavior.

Bar-On and Greenbaum carried out an IDF-sponsored study of violence in the First Intifada as part of their army reserve service. The full report has not been released for publication by the IDF; some of the major conclusions from the study are described in an interview of the authors by Ronit Matalon, a correspondent for the Israeli newspaper *Ha'aretz* (Matalon, 1988), and portions of the report of the study were quoted by Pedhazur (1988) in a later newspaper account. The study itself, based on a large sample of IDF soldiers serving in the OPT, used questionnaires, interviews, and observations.

The results of the study showed that a majority of soldiers engaged in or witnessed physical violence against the civilian Palestinian population. The soldiers stated that much of the violence was not carried out in direct fighting with militants but as a reprisal or as "education" of the population to "motivate" them to cooperate with the Israeli authorities. The soldiers reported that a social norm was established that allowed violence against civilians that was officially outlawed by the IDF but carried out within the context of the group. Much of the violence, according to observations of the authors, occurred in units that were not monitored closely by the higher command.

The recommendations of the report included specific education of soldiers for their roles in coping with civilians, tighter supervision by commanders at different levels of command of soldiers' behavior, and a less confrontational strategy in coping with Palestinian violence.

Open-ended interviews in the study by Bar-On and Greenbaum revealed a small number of soldiers who were disturbed by the violence; some of them found it unbearable and told the investigators that they wanted to leave their units. Some of these soldiers who were disturbed by what they were doing and what they had witnessed included officers. One officer reported in an interview that in order to adhere to the informal but accepted norms of acting aggressively toward Palestinians, he had to order his soldiers to engage in violent behavior and even set an example for them. This situation created enormous dissonance and distress for him. At the same time, the large majority of soldiers and officers continued with their tasks undisturbed and successfully rationalized their behavior.

Publication of an account of the research based on the interview with the authors (Matalon, 1988) resulted in the removal of Bar-On and Greenbaum from their functions in the IDF reserve force as military organizational psychologists. After the report was issued, after the receipt of complaints from Palestinians about illegitimate use of force, and after the demand of the Legal Adviser to the government of Israel to restrict the IDF in opening fire and violent behavior by soldiers, the Chief of Staff of the IDF, General Dan Shomron, issued an order calling for such restrictions (Ittim, 1988). This in itself was a major change in IDF policy and may have saved some lives and injuries to Palestinians and soldiers. The initial reluctance of the IDF to act on the implications of the report was thus overcome: the IDF made an attempt to reduce the violence of soldiers after parts of the report became known to the public.

However, it is our impression that there were few long-term effects over the years. The recommendations were not heeded in the long term and the violence against Palestinians continued, with greater intensity and frequency in the second *intifada* and in Operation "Cast Lead" in Gaza in 2008 (B'Tselem, 2008).

Elizur and Yishay-Krien (2009) provide a detailed understanding of the processes that may lead soldiers to participate in aggressive and even brutal acts. They report on a study of twenty-one soldiers from various parts of Israeli society who served in two combat infantry units in the Golani Brigade of the IDF in Gaza during the second *intifada*. One of the authors, Nufar Yishay-Krien, a female conscript in the IDF, served as a paraprofessional army social worker helping soldiers with their problems with army service. Yishay-Krien gained the confidence of the soldiers, and they described their experiences in their contacts with the local population. She also interviewed the soldiers after their release from compulsory service.

Elizur and Yishay-Krien (2009) found a culture of violence toward the civilian Palestinian population among the majority of the soldiers in the unit studied, but not all of the soldiers adhered to this norm. The authors suggested five subgroups characterized by different motivations for participating or not participating in violence: callous/impulsive, ideologically violent, followers, restrained, and incorruptible.

Participation in violence, as indicated by belonging to one of these groups, was a function of the inner-directedness and moral standards of the individual soldier. Finally, the investigators described a surprising development over time: the norms of the unit changed as a result of a later clash between the soldiers who had a culture of violence and normative soldiers in a neighboring unit who adhered to the army's professed and formal ethics of not being violent except in battle or self-defense. Eventually, one of the officers was convicted of abusing teenage prisoners, and Yishay-Krien observed that that the soldiers in the initially violent unit became much less violent (Elizur & Yishay-Krien, 2009).

The violent behavior of the soldiers developed in a "cultural island" without monitoring by higher levels of command. The low monitoring by the higher command of the actions of small units was also found by Bar-On and Greenbaum (see Matalon, 1988). Independently, both studies concluded that their data have implications for the IDF command structure. The implication for military policy of both studies is that the behavior of soldiers at all levels of command has to be closely monitored to prevent the development of norms permitting and encouraging violence against the civilian population by isolated groups.

The findings of Bar-On and Greenbaum (Matalon, 1988) and Elizur and Yishay-Krein (2009) are in line with those of qualitative studies on moral behavior of soldiers that present accounts from soldiers who engaged or witnessed nonnormative violence perpetrated against Palestinian civilians (Bar & Ben-Ari, 2005; Dar & Kimhi, 2000; Linn, 1997). Some of these soldiers found rationales for their behavior, some disengaged, and some justified it.

In a quantitative study of the effects of the *intifadas* on soldiers based on recollection after release, Kimhi and Sagy (2008) reported on 170 soldiers who had served at army roadblocks inside the West Bank for a month or more during their compulsory military service from the ages of eighteen to twenty-one. These roadblocks were not border posts but were placed inside the OPT territory to discourage potential armed Palestinians and to force them to travel longer distances and thus increase the chances of their being apprehended. Such service involved danger, stress, and fear (Bar & Ben-Ari, 2005), and there have been reports of humiliation of Palestinian civilians at roadblocks (Dowty, 2008; Rubinstein, 1991). On the basis of Bandura's self-disengagement theory (Bandura, 2004), the authors hypothesized and found that the greater the moral justification that soldiers had for the use of the roadblocks, the more the soldiers felt that they were well adjusted to their situation. In accordance with a hypothesis derivable from dissonance theory, there was a low but significant correlation between the amount of time served and the degree of justification of the soldier's duty. Wainstein (1991), in a study of soldiers serving in the first *intifada*, found that the longer the soldiers served in the OPT, the more moderate their political attitudes became. Future studies on the effects of serving in the OPT on political attitudes, justification of the duty, and adjustment would contribute to understanding how political attitudes develop during long-term military service facing a civilian population.

The results confirm the conceptualizations derived from the psychoanalytic, dissonance, and moral disengagement theories and the findings of the previous studies just cited: justification for behavior that may be seen as nonnormative in civilian life will be less likely to affect adjustment (and presumably less likely to lead to mental distress) if there is a moral justification for the nonnormative behavior. Taken together, the studies show that there are two stages in the development of violent behavior during the occupation: first, the development of social norms for aggression in situations that evoke fear in the soldiers, and, second, post hoc coping with the dissonant nonnormative acts by means of dissociation and/or rationalization of the behavior. These studies span two decades and do not indicate a weakening of the norms or of the use of self-defense mechanisms for justification of the behavior.

EFFECTS OF AGGRESSION ON THE AGGRESSOR: CASE REPORT

We will extend the concepts developed in the previous section to the understanding of the effects of aggression against occupied people by examining an instance of occupation-related violence toward civilians.

A Twelve-Year-Old Killed on Her Way to School

We suggest that the processes described above are evident in an account of the killing of a twelve-year old girl, Iman al-Shams, in Rafah, Gaza, in October 2004 (Harel, 2005). One element in the development of violent behavior against innocent civilians in an occupation is the fear of soldiers constantly on their guard while serving in hostile territory. According to the account in the investigation of Captain R., commander of the unit that was responsible for killing the girl (Harel, 2005), Iman al-Shams was walking to school close to an Israeli outpost but in a direction away from it such that the outpost was in back of her. She was walking away from the outpost but in territory forbidden to the local population. In doing so, she was shot and killed by the soldiers in the outpost.

According to testimony at the trial of Captain R. (Harel, 2005), a reason for this tragic occurrence was that the girl was considered to be a decoy for Palestinian adults near the outpost who were suspected of attacking the soldiers, reasoning that shows the fear of the soldiers in the face of this seemingly innocent behavior. A second element evident in the communication among the soldiers was the use of social influence on the soldiers by the commander of the unit.

This influence is evident in an account of the incident that was presented on an investigative television program hosted by journalist Ilana Dayan (Zarchin, 2012). After the soldiers discussed what the age of the girl could be, a voice on the intercom insisted that she had to be shot, no matter what her age (Harel, 2005). The voice was later identified by Dayan as that of Captain R., the commander of the outpost (Zarchin, 2012). Dayan also presented a recording of Captain R. reporting to his superiors that he had killed the girl. It is evident from this account that a group norm was quickly established that countermanded all previous norms known to the group: suddenly, it was permissible to shoot a child, even if she was walking away from the post.

An additional element evident in the soldiers' testimony is self-justification or dissonance reduction after deciding to act. The act was seen by the soldiers as necessary to protect themselves, even though the evidence for this justification was very weak. Dissonance reduction is often used by soldiers in such situations (Greenbaum, 2006), as we have seen in the previous research accounts.

The incident was investigated, and Captain R. was brought to trial and acquitted No one has been convicted of the killing. Ilana Dayan, who reported on the case, was at first found by the district court to have libeled Captain R. for claiming that he killed the girl, but on appeal to the Israeli Supreme Court she was exonerated (Zarchin, 2012) All of these events are indications that the situation was highly disturbing to the Israeli public and revived long-standing controversies concerning the behavior of soldiers in the occupation. Yet, the fact that there were no convictions in a case in which soldiers killed a twelve-year-old girl on her way to school raises questions about the readiness of Israeli society to face the consequences of its illegal actions toward an occupied people.

We suggest that the studies and the testimony summarized above indicate that Israeli soldiers, like soldiers everywhere, are beset by a number of processes that increase the likelihood of brutal behavior toward civilians, including children: feelings of threat to self, the quick evolution of group standards of "preventive" violence against members of the enemy population, and lack of clear orders and supervision by higher levels of command. In addition, the probability of arrest for any crime committed against the Palestinian population while on military duty is low, and the chances of conviction are even lower (Yesh Din, 2008). In none of the situations described in the two research studies described above, and not even in the killing of Iman al-Shams, has anyone been convicted.

At the same time, the case example shows that not all soldiers are violent, that some soldiers are disturbed by the violence, and that the culture of violence may change over time. We lack information on the effects of these experiences on soldiers after their return to civilian life.

THE DEVELOPMENT OF SOLDERS' AGGRESSION TOWARD CIVILIANS

We suggest that there are seven elements, representing social and psychological processes common to the studies just presented, that influence and maintain soldiers' aggression against the civilian population in an occupation situation. One is the fear reported by soldiers in their confrontation with the civilian population, which is seen as a constant physical threat. A second is the power felt by the soldiers in defending themselves against the threat: all soldiers were constantly armed and used weapons, giving them a feeling of power and ability to cope with threat. This feeling of power carries over into situations in which contact with the Palestinians poses no threat, such as the detention of prisoners. The need to demonstrate power, sometimes by humiliating others, is thus always present, and it becomes threatening to lose power in the presence of Palestinians.

A third element is the perception of the Palestinian civilian, including the Palestinian child, as the "other" who does not belong to the soldiers' group and also threatens the group. The fourth element is the freedom from supervision and the likelihood that unauthorized acts against Palestinians may be carried out with impunity: this situation negates the professed IDF norm of reward for good behavior and punishment for bad behavior.

The fifth element is group solidarity, found in the observations of soldiers in both studies: the group demands that nonnormative behavior not be reported to outsiders and punishes those who do not obey this rule. A sixth element is diversity: in both studies cited above, there are descriptions of soldiers who did not act violently and of some who opposed the violence. These conscience-driven soldiers feel mental distress and endure social isolation.

A seventh element was described in detail by Halperin et al. (2010):.the soldiers in these units who use violence to justify their acts through a number of defense mechanisms, including dissonance reduction, rationalization, and repression (Bowins, 2004). As a result of these processes, the self of the perpetrator is preserved but the damage to the other has been done.

Not all of these processes work on all soldiers, and some are able to resist them at various stages. The studies presented suggest that these processes may be present whenever soldiers operate among occupied peoples.

EFFECTS OF THE OCCUPATION ON CIVILIAN CRIME IN ISRAEL

The strongest quantitative evidence for the influence of the occupation on the moral behavior of Israelis is provided by studies on the relation between level of hostility between Israel and the population of the OPT and recorded criminal behavior in Israeli society. In a series of studies, Simha Landau and his colleagues investigated the relationship between social stressors and social support mechanisms and the rates of severe crimes, particularly homicide and robbery. A major stressor that was investigated was the frequency of hostilities taking place between Israel and its neighbors, particularly those hostilities with a specific focus on the first *intifada*. Among the findings are the following:

Crimes of violence in Israeli society are positively related to stressors associated with the economic, security, or political situation and negatively related to indicators of national solidarity (Landau, 1997). As indicated above, a major factor in the security situation has been the level of hostilities in the OPT.

Homicide and robbery in Israel increased after the Six Day War in 1967, when the occupation of Palestinian lands began. Except for short, temporary periods, these levels of crime never returned to their prewar levels (Landau, 1998a).

While economic stress indicators had the strongest effects on violent crime, security indicators, while rising and falling with events, also have a significant effect (Landau, 1997, 1998a).More specifically, the number of casualties that Israel experienced during hostilities, including those associated with clashes in the OPT, had a marginal but significant effect on homicide rates (Landau & Pfefferman, 1988).

There was an increase in violence due to domestic conflict during the First Intifada in December 1987 (Landau, 1998b).

In a study of the second *intifada* and its effects, Sela-Shayovitz (2005) found that violent crime rates, specifically assault, robbery, and murder among adolescent males, were higher during the Second Intifada than during the years before this event. These effects were not found for females. In addition, male violence rates were related specifically to the number of terrorist attacks on Israeli society.

When seen as a whole, the findings support the habituation-depreciation hypothesis formulated by Archer and Gartner (1984): human life takes on less value during war as individuals become habituated to the killing that goes on in wartime and generalize the permission to kill and injure others to their own society. This hypothesis is based on the authors' conclusions from a crossnational study involving 110 nations (Archer & Gartner, 1976) that showed a general increase in violence in nations following the cessation of hostilities in which the nation was involved.

We suggest that the processes postulated by Archer and Gartner are special cases of the dissociation and moral disengagement theories described previously. Habituation to news of violence or to the witnessing of nonnormative violent behavior and depreciation of human life may be means of dissociation or disengaging from an event threatening to a person's ego identity. Such habituation may lead to a delegitimization of the other (Bar-Tal, 1989). At the same time, the norms allowing nonnormative violence are internalized.

In addition to the effects of occupation-related hostilities on crime rates, a recent study found a relationship between exposure of children to political violence and their aggressive behavior. In this study, Landau and colleagues (2010) interviewed 450 dyads of Jewish and Israeli-Arab parents and children about exposure to various kinds of violence and aggressive behavior. They found that the greater the exposure of Israeli schoolchildren to political violence, particularly attacks by Palestinians, the greater the children's aggressive activity. In both ethnic groups, exposure to political violence and to violence in the other ecological contexts had a strong effect on aggression. The study thus demonstrates the detrimental impact of exposure to political conflict and violence on both Arab and Jewish Israeli children's aggression.

The studies reviewed here indicate an additional and specific validation of the situation-depreciation hypothesis: not only do the processes of habituation and depreciation of human life occur after the cessation of hostilities. The research on civilian violence during the *intifadas* indicates that this violence may mirror the level of hostility to which Israeli society is exposed as a result of the occupation.

The reported increase in crime with increased hostility between Israel and the Palestinians, we suggest, leads to the following conclusion: if the occupation is "quiet" and without hostilities, the normative structure of Israeli society is relatively unaffected, and the crime levels of Israeli society are similar to those in peacetime. It appears that moral and normative behavior in Israeli society is affected primarily when the occupation encounters violent opposition, while the occupation in itself has little effect on crime or childhood aggression. These results may reflect the effects of the occupation on Israeli life in general: when all is quiet, there is little regard to what is happening to people in the OPT, and life continues as normal.

The violence of the right wing and of religious extremists, often triggered by suicide bombings or other attacks by Palestinians or by a motivation to block actions of the peace movement and left-wing political groups, has resulted in deaths and injuries of Palestinians and Israelis, including the assassination of Prime Minister Yitzchak Rabin in November 1995 and the killing of Palestinians (B'Tselem, 2008). It is unclear whether any aspects of the occupation are responsible for this increase in political killings and injuries, yet the possibility of such influence exists..Aspects of the occupation that could affect political killings could include fear of losing the settlements in the OPT due to Israeli action, revenge for Palestinian killings of Israelis, the desire to make salient a political cause that would continue Israeli rule over the OPT, or the need to follow the real or imagined instructions of rabbis who openly permit such violent actions in an atmosphere of accusations (see Segal, 1987). It is highly likely that these violent acts are associated with the occupation, since they were extremely rare in the years before 1967, when the occupation began (B'Tselem, 2008).

In sum, the occupation is associated with an increase in violent civilian behavior unrelated to the occupation when the level of hostility related to the occupation is high. The level of political violence has also increased since the occupation began and has had profound effects on Israeli society. We have yet to understand the details of the psychological processes involved in the relations between the occupation as a long-term state of affairs and individual motivation to commit a violent act, whether political or nonpolitical. In the following section, we present a model of psychological processes involved in aggression by soldiers in an occupation army and the possible generalization of this violence to the society of the occupier.

PSYCHOLOGICAL PROCESSES UNDERLYING THE EFFECTS OF OCCUPATION OF ANOTHER PEOPLE

We suggest that the psychological processes related to the occupation operating on society involve the following elements: Occupation leads to violence by the occupied, resulting in repression by the occupier. The occupiers cope with the stress of the occupation and their fear reaction by behaving aggressively, not only to the occupied people but also to their compatriots. New norms of behavior are established in the occupier society that allow higher levels of aggression in the civilian society as well as in the military than those that are usually tolerated. The occupiers use defense mechanisms such as justification, rationalization, and dissonance reduction to justify their behavior.

We suggest that this state of affairs leads to a cyclical situation: the greater the repression by the occupier, the greater the violence by the occupied peoples, leading to more repression, intrasociety violence, and increased use of psychological defense mechanisms. We suggest that these processes are the basis for the cycles of violence that have been described by observers of the Israeli-Palestinian conflict (Zertal & Eldar, 2007).

Other processes, leading to resistance to the violence, may exist for some sections of society, though they have not been systematically studied. As indicated earlier, the Bar-On and Greenbaum research sample included soldiers and officers who concluded that the violence against Palestinians was unjustified. Elizur and Yishay-Krien (2009) found similar opposition to violence among some of the soldiers they studied: these soldiers were called "incorruptible." Indeed, in the unit that they described in which excesses took place, the soldiers were very much affected, and their norms changed under the influence of individuals in another unit that had a norm of adherence to army rules of not harming civilians.

However, individuals who opposed violence in the unit that engaged in aggressive action found it difficult to employ psychological defense mechanisms to avoid the violence that they witnessed. Some soldiers and officers in the Bar-On and Greenbaum study who engaged in violence reported a great deal of mental anguish and social isolation. Persons opposed to violence depend on social support, since isolation and group punishments for a nonconformer to the group norm can be distressing. More research is needed to determine how prosocial processes evolve under environmental stress and how the mental stress associated with such processes can be reduced.

We suggest that processes similar to those characterizing the behavior of the soldiers in the studies reviewed may be taking place in Israeli civilian society as well. A majority appears to be indifferent to the violence committed against an outgroup, justifying it in various ways. Some of these same people may be engaging in violence against their compatriots in response to new norms permitting such action (Landau, 1998; Sela-Shayovitz, 2005). A second group opposes violence and works to prevent or reduce it. It will be important to understand the underlying psychological processes involved in establishing the different paths taken by the different groups in both military and civilian settings.

The prevalence of stress in the face of exposure to political violence in the Israeli and Palestinian societies has been studied (Solomon & Lavi, 2006), but the means of preventing and reducing stress are not well understood. It is important to investigate further the prevalence and durability of stress in exposure to conflict, the social factors that could mitigate or exacerbate the stress, and the kinds of individuals who are prone to it. We suggest that it is more important to study the development of approaches to the protection of children and families from physical danger and stress (Greenbaum, 2006).

While the emotional distress level of Israelis does not appear to be affected by the occupation except as a result of their own losses, we suggest that there is cause for concern when violence toward an occupied population rises and there is little public opposition or mental distress. This may indicate apathy born of dissociation and justification on the part of society toward the suffering of others.

It is necessary to know more about individuals who manage on their own to overcome the cycle of threat and stress leading to aggression or acceptance of aggression toward occupied peoples and justification of the aggression as described above. While the soldiers in the military samples cited who opposed violence were under a great deal of mental stress, others, who also had military backgrounds, managed to oppose violence. In the civilian area as well, individuals and groups have opposed nonnormative violence by political means and by publication of their views (Avnery, 1968; Shulman, 2007). We need to know more about the ways in which the stress of exposure to illicit violence can be transformed into constructive opposition to it.

POLICY IMPLICATIONS

The processes that we have described have implications for policy. The peaceful management of conflict, and respect for the viewpoints and rights of others, need to be taught widely in Israeli and Palestinian societies. Adwan and Bar-On (2001) have suggested one approach to this problem: teaching people on one side of a conflict the narrative history of the conflict according to the other side. However, their approach has not been widely adopted. It is time to intensify efforts to teach basic human ethics, international law, and nonviolence toward both children and adults on both sides of a conflict, particularly for Palestinians and Israelis. Since such efforts are directed to the long term, efforts must be intensified to protect civilian populations from violence in conflict when it occurs (Greenbaum, 2006).

The training of soldiers in behavior toward the civilian population needs to be developed in the IDF and in all armies that have contact with civilian populations (Greenbaum, 2006). The IDF, according to the personal testimony of IDF officers to the authors, has instituted such training in some units, mostly from a legal-procedural standpoint. The studies reviewed here indicate that armywide training that includes intensive role playing in specific situations, and that takes place under the supervision of psychologists or other professionals well schooled in the social sciences, could be effective in changing the behavior of soldiers without endangering them. The effects of such training should be assessed.

In the specific case of Israel and the Palestinians, the solution for ending the occupation appears remote at this writing (see Zertal & Eldar, 2007). Part of the reason for this state of affairs may be psychological barriers to mutual concessions leading to reconciliation that have not yet been overcome by both sides in the Israeli- Palestinian conflict (Bar-Tal & Bennink, 2004; Kelman, 2008). As long as the psychological cost to the occupying power is perceived to be low, so are the the chances of ending the occupation. We suggest that when Israeli society becomes aware of the continuing psychological and moral cost of the occupation, efforts to attain a peaceful solution for the Israel-Palestinian dispute will increase. The means for moderating and solving the conflict are available, but these involve concessions that both sides are not yet ready to make (Oren, 2007; Zertal & Eldar, 2007). Reducing or eliminating violence toward the Palestinians in the OPT may be a good way to encourage a solution to the conflict, and this step could serve as a model for the management and solution of other conflicts involving an occupied people and an occupier. The research reviewed here suggests that such a reduction in violence would have a salutary effect on the occupier, in this case the Israeli society, as well as on the occupied Palestinian society.

IMPLICATIONS FOR THE WORLDWIDE STUDY OF MILITARY OCCUPATION

In considering the wider implications of the results reported here, we must first emphasize again the methodological limitations of drawing conclusions about the effects of occupying another country on the occupying power. There are three limitations, or threats, to the validity of the results presented. As we indicated previously, one threat to the validity of any of the effects discussed here is that of *confounding factors* (Cook & Campbell, 1979). Confounding factors are those that occur previously to or contemporaneously with the event investigated (in this case, occupation) that could cause the results even in the absence of the event. A second limitation of the results presented here relates to the dependent variables involved, that is, the *nature of the effects* themselves. A third limitation is the *lack of comparability* of different occupations that have taken place in different parts of the world. We will suggest that each occupation has a unique profile that makes comparisons among them difficult. Let us briefly consider each of these limitations in turn. In doing so, we will suggest possible directions for future research on the effects of occupation.

Confounding Factors

We suggest that there are two sets of confounding factors in assessing the effects of occupation. One set consists of *societal events* that occur contemporaneously with the occupation, including those that occurred for a limited time before the occupation began. A second set of confounding factors consists of *ideological elements* in society that are associated with occupations but may also exist without an occupation. These include the existence of armed forces with or without military conscription; training of soldiers regarding the human rights of the peoples opposing them, including children and civilians; the reputation of the armed forces in society; the frequency and intensity of battles in which the armed forces participate; and statements by military leaders concerning human rights.

Both sets of factors, societal events and ideological elements, may affect the thinking of a society even in the absence of occupation. One hypothesis is that once extraneous factors and militaristic ideological elements in a society have been considered, we will find that the occupation itself may have no effect or only a limited effect on the thinking and behavior of a society. The opposing hypothesis is that the occupation has an effect even when all of the other elements are considered. The strong form of this hypothesis states that the occupation has the dominant effect.

Nature of the Effects Studied

Any research is limited to the effects or dependent variables that the researcher chooses to study. The choice of other effects may lead to different results. This chapter reports on the possible effects of the occupation on crime rates in Israeli society and on the behavior and thinking of soldiers exposed to the occupation. We chose these variables because we concluded that they represent processes that reflect important effects of the occupation. We also hypothesized that these variables were the most likely both to reflect important processes associated with the occupation and to avoid the confounding effects just indicated.

However, there are many other possible effects that should be studied. Among these are attitudes toward human rights, attitudes toward the ethnic groups represented by the occupied people, belief in the efficacy of occupation, self-image as a just society, and belief in the success of negotiation with the occupied peoples. Such research could be carried out on both the occupier and occupied peoples.

A very important area of study is the growth of movements of resistance to the occupation and of organizations that attempt to mitigate the effects of occupation in the occupier society. Such movements have grown in Israeli society in the past thirty years, yet the dynamics of that growth and the specific circumstances in the occupation that led to it are unclear (Avnery, 1968; Shulman, 2007).

Israeli and Palestinian researchers have carried out parallel studies on some of these issues in both societies (e.g., Landau et al., 2010). However, because of the factors we have indicated, it is difficult to attribute the results on either side to the effects of occupation per se.

Lack of Comparability of Occupations

With regard to international implications, the most important threat to any generalization is the fact that no occupation is a replication of any other: each has unique features. One set of such features consists of contextual factors: those involving the social, geographical, and historical background to the occupation in the past and in the present These factors affect thinking about the occupation at every level. The editors and authors of this volume are concerned that Israel has been occupying and annexing the territory of another people with a different ethnic and political identification and, in so doing, has often violated international law. The occupied people, the Palestinians, live in close proximity, and the occupation has continued for forty-five years. Thus, duration of occupation, historical time of occupation, legitimacy of acts performed during the occupation, and geographical proximity of the occupied land are critical aspects in assessing the occupation and its effects.

Other aspects of occupation that should be considered are the circumstances of the capture of the occupied territory: was the occupier or the occupied the aggressor? Does the occupier have a historical claim on the territory of the occupied? To what extent does the occupier allow access to information about the economic and social circumstances of the occupied people? Do the occupier and occupied carry on negotiations? Is the occupied territory a formerly independent state, a potential state in the making, or a portion of an existing state? Is the regime of the occupier democratic or autocratic? How similar are the language and culture of the occupier and occupied peoples? To what extent have there been uprisings in the occupied territories? To what degree do the occupier and occupied operate in accordance with international law? Is the occupied territory unified or does it have geographically separated entities? Do acts interpreted by the occupied and occupier as hostile continue? These contextual factors concerning the occupation may be critical in assessing the effects of the occupation. These factors are only some of the possible influences on thinking about occupation.

The Israeli occupation of Palestinian land has a clear and unique profile. It is an occupation of a neighboring land, consisting of two geographically separate entities, populated by a people with a different language, ethnicity, and culture for over four decades after a war initiated by nations allied with the occupied people. The occupier is represented by a democratic government that makes a historic claim on the land of the occupied. The occupied people have engaged in several uprisings with varying degrees of intensity. The occupier and occupied have carried out intermittent negotiations for over twenty years. The occupied people claim to be an independent nation and have been granted limited autonomy, including a democratically elected body for administering regional and municipal affairs. International law has been sporadically observed by the occupier and occupied, but there have been many violations by both sides. Hostile acts on both sides continue, particularly land confiscation and targeted killings by the Israelis and firing on civilian targets by the Palestinians (Gorenberg, 2006; Oren, 2007).

All of these factors have powerful psychological implications for the thinking and behavior of the occupying and occupied peoples, making any generalization difficult. For example, an entrenched claim of historical (and religious) rights over the occupied territories by large portions of the Israeli public, and by all of the settlers in occupied territories, dominates the consideration of human rights for the occupied. For those truly committed to historical and religious claims of territory in any occupation, there is no cognitive dissonance related to any competing consideration. Therefore, guarantees of human rights for the occupied are not legitimate, and attempts at persuasion on this issue therefore have little chance of success (Gorenberg, 2006).

Given this unique profile, it is difficult to make generalizations to other occupations. For example, some other occupations of the twentieth century have been shorter, particularly the occupation by the Allied countries of Germany, Japan, and Italy during and after World War II, since the Allies had as a goal the return of these countries to full independence (Wolfe, 1984). The Soviet occupation of the neighboring Baltic states lasted for fifty years, similarly to the Israeli occupation of the Palestinians. Unlike the Israeli-Palestinian case, the Soviet occupation was carried out by an extremely powerful autocratic government that had no regard for human rights and carried out the annexation of the occupied states (Walker, 2003).

A Brief Case Comparison

In spite of these problems, it may be instructive to compare the Israeli case with that of other occupations that may be similar, though far from identical in some potentially important aspects. The discovery of psychological effects of the occupation across different occupations may strengthen the claims for effects of the occupation.

A conflict that had some elements in common with the Israeli occupation is the occupation by the United States of Haiti between 1915 and 1934, with continuing external control until 1940. Renda (2001) reported a study of this occupation that we follow here. U.S. marines occupied Haiti, in 1915 in response to atrocities carried out there, and the occupation continued for nineteen years. Unlike the Israeli-Palestinian case, Haiti never threatened the United States militarily, neither side laid claim to the territory of the other, and at least some of the motivation for occupation was economic. Similar to the Israeli-Palestinian case, the lands of the occupier and the occupied people were close geographically and the occupation was long-lasting.

In both cases, the occupying power paid some attention to the development of infrastructure in the occupied territory and allowed the local population a degree of autonomy. However, in both cases attention to the human rights of the occupied people was inconsistent at best. Also, as in the Israeli case, resistance to the occupation of Haiti continued during its entire period, with casualties on both sides. After an incident in which U.S. marines killed twelve people in putting down a disturbance, public opinion in the United States turned sharply against the occupation, which then ended abruptly.

This case shows the difficulty of making comparisons among occupations, as we suggested above. However, some of the dynamics are similar: events in the occupied territory affect behavior and public opinion in the occupier society. In the U.S.-Haiti case this led to the end of the occupation. This has not yet happened in the Israeli-Palestinian case; the trigger for ending the occupation has not yet developed.

Goldstein (2010) presents a comparison of three occupations: Germany's occupation of France in 1940, the Allies' occupation of Germany in 1945, and the U.S. occupation of Iraq that began in 2003. Goldstein suggests that the occupations of France and Germany were "successful" in that they were based on knowledge of the local culture and on coopting the elites of both populations. According to her thesis, the failure of the U.S. occupation in Iraq was attributable to lack of knowledge of Iraqi culture and failure to win the cooperation of Iraqi elites. The Israeli case shows some similarity to the American one in Iraq: misreading of the culture and intentions of the Palestinian people led to faulty, and in many cases unethical, attempts at control. This situation, in turn, led to each side participating in the chain of hostile acts and reprisals described earlier (Zertal & Eldar, 2007).

CONCLUSION

We conclude that the existence of an occupation depends not only on the power differentials between occupier and occupied but ultimately on the values and opinions of people on both sides. In particular, we suggest that the occupation will wither away when the occupier people overcome the need to reduce dissonance and to justify their actions. As a result, the occupiers may learn to understand the effects of those actions and to respect the culture, the human rights, and the legitimate goals of the occupied people. This is a difficult psychological task for the occupier.

There is little research on the psychological processes of occupier peoples, particularly those processes that lead to attitude change toward an occupation. In spite of methodological threats and pitfalls, we suggest that it is important to study the psychological dynamics of different occupations, particularly among the occupiers, in order to understand how occupations may be ended without endangering either side.

ACKNOWLEDGMENTS

The authors wish to thank the editors of this volume for many valuable suggestions and Judith Neipris Greenbaum for conscientious editorial assistance.

REFERENCES

Adwan, S., & Bar-On, D. (2001). *Victimhood and beyond.* Beit Jala, Palestinian National Authority: PRIME.

Archer, D., & Gartner, R. A. (1976). Violent acts and violent times: A comparative approach to postwar homicide rates. *American Sociological Review, 41,* 937–963.

Archer, D., & Gartner, R. A. (1984). *Violence and crime in cross-national perspective.* New Haven, CT: Yale University Press.

Avnery, U. (1968). *Israel without Zionists: A plea for peace in the Middle East.* New York: Macmillan.

Bailey, C. A., & Ostrov, J. M. (2009). Differentiating forms and functions of aggression in emerging adults: Associations with hostile attribution biases and normative beliefs. *Journal of Youth and Adolescence, 37,* 713–722.

Bandura, A. (1973). *Aggression: A social learning analysis.* Oxford: Prentice-Hall

Bandura, A. (2004). The role of selective moral disengagement in terrorism and counterterrorism. In F. M. Mogahaddam & A. Marsella (Eds.), *Understanding terrorism: Psychosocial roots, consequences and interventions* (pp. 121–150). Washington, DC: American Psychological Association.

Bar, N., & Ben-Ari, E. (2005). Israeli snipers in the Al-Aksa intifada: Killing, humanity and lived experience. *Third World Quarterly, 26,* 137–156.

Bar-On, M. (1996). *In pursuit of peace: A history of the Israeli peace movement.* Washington, DC: U.S. Institute of Peace.

Bar-Tal, D. (1989). Delegitimization: The extreme case of stereotyping and prejudice. In D. Bar-Tal, C. Grauman, A. W. Kruglanski, & W. Stroebe (Eds.), *Stereotypes and prejudice: Changing conceptions* (pp. 169–188). New York: Springer.

Bar-Tal, D., & Bennink, G. H. (2004). The nature of reconciliation as an outcome and as a process. In Y. Bar Siman-Tov (Ed.), *From conflict resolution to reconciliation* (pp. 11–38). Oxford: Oxford University Press.

Bowins, B. (2004). Psychological defense mechanisms: A new perspective. *American Journal of Psychoanalysis, 64,* 1–26.

B'Tselem. (2008). *Statistics on fatalities, 2000–2008. Bt'selem, the Israel Center for Human Rights in the Occupied Territories.* Retrieved May 1, 2010, from www.btselem.org/statistics

Cairns, E. (1996). *Children and political violence.* New York: Blackwell.

Cook, T. D., & Campbell, D. T. (1979). *Quasi-experimentation: Design and analysis issues for field settings.* Chicago: Rand-McNally.

Dar, Y., & Kimhi, S. (2000). The imprint of the intifada: Response of kibbutz-born soldiers to military service in the West Bank and Gaza. *Armed Forces & Society, 26*, 285–311.

Dodge, K. E., Bates, J. E., & Pettit, G. S. (1990). Mechanisms in the cycle of violence. *Science, 250*, 1678–1683.

Dowty, A. (2008). *Israel/Palestine* (2nd ed.). Cambridge: Polity Press.

Eglash, R. (2010). Israel population hits 7.4 million. *Jerusalem Post*, April 18, 2010. Retrieved May 15, 2010, from http://www.jpost.com/Israel/Article.aspx?id=173452

Elizur, Y., & Yishay-Krien, N. (2009). Participation in atrocities among Israeli soldiers during the first intifada: A qualitative analysis. *Journal of Peace Research, 46*, 251–267.

Festinger, L. (1957). *A theory of cognitive dissonance*. Evanston, IL: Row, Peterson.

Freud, A. (1937/1966). *The ego and the mechanisms of defense*. New York: International Universities Press.

Giacaman, R., Shannon, H. S., Saab, H., Arya, N., & Boyce, W. (2007). Individual and collective exposure to political violence: Palestinian adolescents coping with conflict. *European Journal of Public Health, 17*, 361–368.

Goldstein, C. S. (2010). 2003 Iraq, 1945 Germany and 1940 France: Success and failure in military occupations. *Military Review, 90*, 43–50.

Gorenberg, G. (2006). *The accidental empire: Israel and the birth of the settlements, 1967–1977*. New York: Henry Holt.

Greenbaum, C. W. (2006). Prevention of violence to children in the Israeli-Palestinian conflict: A perspective from ecological systems theory. In C. W. Greenbaum, P. Veerman, & N. Bacon-Shnoor (Eds.), *Protection of children during armed political conflict: A multidisciplinary perspective* (pp. 433–455). Antwerp and Oxford: Intersentia.

Halperin, E., Bar-Tal, D., Sharvit, K., Rosler, N., & Raviv, A. (2010). Socio-psychological implications for an occupying society: The case of Israel. *Journal of Peace Research, 47*, 59–70.

Harel, A. (2005, March 6). Footage said to show Gaza girl could have caused threat. *Haaretz*, p. 1.

Hason, C. (2010, April 19). President Peres: The Iranians shouldn't be contemptuous of our ability. *Haaretz*, p. 1.

Ittim News Agency. (1988, February 24). Chief of staff message to commanders: Avoid humiliation and contemptuous behavior. Reported in *Haaretz*, pp. 1–2 (in Hebrew).

Kelman, H. (2008). Evaluating the contributions of interactive problem solving to the resolution of ethnonational conflicts. *Peace and Conflict: Journal of Peace Psychology, 14*, 29–60.

Kimhi, S., & Sagy, S. (2008, July). *Moral justification and feelings of adjustment in military law-enforcement situations: The case of Israeli soldiers serving at army roadblocks*. Presented at the International Society for Political Psychology conference, July 8–12, 2008, Paris.

Landau, S. F. (1997). Homicide in Israel: Its relation to subjective stress and support indicators on the macro level. *Homicide Studies, 1,* 377–400.

Landau, S. F. (1998a). Crimes of violence in Israel: Theoretical and empirical perspectives. In R. Friedman (Ed.), *Crime and criminal justice in Israel: Assessing the knowledge base toward the 21st century* (pp. 97–121). Albany: State University of New York Press.

Landau, S. F. (1998b). Crime, subjective social stress and support indicators and ethnic origin: The Israeli experience. *Justice Quarterly, 15,* 243–272.

Landau, S. F., Dvir-Gvirsman, S., Dubow, E. F., Huesmann, L. R., Boxer, P., Ginges, J., & Shikaki, K. (2010, June). *The effects of exposure to political conflict and violence on aggressive behavior: The case of Arab and Jewish children in Israel.* Presented at the Conference on Protection of Children During Armed Political Conflict, Jerusalem.

Landau, S. F., & Pfefferman, D. (1988). A time-series analysis of violent crime and its relation to prolonged states of warfare: The Israeli case. *Criminology, 26,* 489–504.

Linn, R. (1997). Soldiers' narratives of selective moral resistance: A separate position of the connected self? In A. Lieblich & R. Josselson (Eds.), *The narrative study of lives* (pp. 94–112). Thousand Oaks, CA: Sage.

Matalon, R. (1988, February 19). Without norms. *Haaretz* supplement, pp. 5–9 (in Hebrew).

Milgram, N. (2008). Ideology and the behavior of perpetrators and victims of violence. In N. Ronel, K. Jaishankar, & M. Bensimon (Eds.), *Trends and issues in victimology* (pp. 12–31). Newcastle upon Tyne, England: Cambridge Scholars Publishing.

Oren, M. (2007). *Six days of war: June 1967 and the making of the modern Middle East.* New York: Presidio Press.

Owens, D. J., & Straus, M. (1975). The social structure of violence in childhood and approval of violence as an adult. *Aggressive Behavior, 1,* 193–211.

Pedhazur, R. (1988, February 24). The policy of beatings harms the best of soldiers and commanders—an alternative must be found. *Haaretz,* p. 1.

Qouta, S., & El Sarraj, E. (2006). Palestinian children and dangerous life: Adjustment during violent and less violent times. In C. W. Greenbaum, P. Veerman, & N. Bacon-Shnoor (Eds.), *Protection of children during armed political conflict: A multidisciplinary perspective* (pp. 111–122). Antwerp and Oxford: Intersentia.

Renda, M. A. (2001). *Taking Haiti: Military occupation and the culture of U.S. imperialism, 1915–1940.* Chapel Hill: University of North Carolina Press.

Rubinstein, D. (1991). *The people of nowhere: The Palestinian vision of home.* New York: Times Books

Segal, H. (1987). *Dear brothers.* Jerusalem: Keter (in Hebrew).

Sela-Shayovitz, R. (2005). The effects of the Second Intifada, terrorist acts, and economic changes in adolescent crime rates in Israel. *Journal of Experimental Criminology, 1,* 477–493.

Shulman, D. (2007). *Dark hope: Working for peace in Israel and Palestine.* Chicago: University of Chicago Press.

Solomon, Z., & Lavi, T. (2006). The psychological toll of the intifada: PTSD, distress and future orientation of Israeli and Palestinian youth. In C. W. Greenbaum, P. Veerman, and N. Bacon-Shnoor (Eds.), *Protection of children during armed political conflict: A multidisciplinary perspective* (pp. 155–168). Antwerp and Oxford: Intersentia.

Sprinzak, E. (1991). *The ascendance of Israel's radical right.* New York: Oxford University Press.

Thabet, A. A. M., Abdulla, T., Elhelou, M. W. A., & Vostanis, P. (2006). Effect of trauma on Palestinian children's mental health in the Gaza Strip and West Bank. In C. W. Greenbaum, P. Veerman, & N. Bacon-Shnoor (Eds.), *Protection of children during armed political conflict: A multidisciplinary perspective* (pp. 123–142). Antwerp- and Oxford: Intersentia.

Wainstein, B. (1991). *Political socialization: The effects of the military service in the occupied territories on attitudes and concepts of soldiers and similarity with their fathers.* Unpublished M.A. thesis, Tel Aviv University.

Walker, E. W. (2003). *Dissolution: Sovereignty and the breakup of the Soviet Union.* Lanham, MD.: Rowman and Littlefield.

Wolfe, R. (Ed.). (1984). *Americans as proconsuls: United States military government in Germany and Japan, 1944–1952.* Carbondale: University of Southern Illinois Press.

Yesh Din. (2008). *Exceptions: Prosecution of IDF soldiers during and after the second Intifada, 2000–2007.* Tel Aviv: Yesh Din, Volunteers for Human Rights.

Zarchin, T. (2012, February 8). Israel High Court accepts journalist Ilana Dayan's appeal against libel verdict. *Haaretz.* Retrieved May 16, 2012, from www.haaretz.com/news/national/israel-high-court-accepts-journalist-ilana-dayan-s-appeal-against-libel-verdict-1.411704

Zertal, I., & Eldar, A. (2007). Lords of the land: The war over Israel's settlements in the occupied territories, 1967–2007. New York: Nation Books.

Zimbardo, P. (2007). *The Lucifer effect: Understanding how good people turn evil.* New York: Random House.

# IV

Cultural Effects of Occupation

CHAPTER 13

Appealing to Enlightened Self-Interest: The Impact of Occupation on Human Rights within Israel

Edward (Edy) Kaufman

INTRODUCTION

This chapter analyzes the impact of the occupation of the West Bank, officially denominated "Judea and Samaria,"[1] on societal attitudes and policies toward human rights (hereinafter HR), in terms of both protection and its absence, in Israel and eventually on the creation of political culture in this regard. At issue is a fundamental question: to what extent do dominant governments' practices in areas outside their formal borders have an impact on the rights of their own people in the metropolis and popular attachment to the rule of law? In the case of Israel, many academics long ago pointed to an ostensible reduction of Israelis' allegiance to the nation's legal precepts, a development that was also underlined in an earlier joint effort (Kaufman, Abed, & Rothstein, 1993). Many Israelis, regularly stressing their unusual situation—a small nation, geographically isolated and surrounded by nations with which they have periodically been at war, with a domestic population that includes a minority overtly at odds with the majority Jewish population—argue that their collective behavior should not be measured by universal standards or at least should be granted some leeway. But this is not a realistic proposition. To all intents and purposes, identity-driven domestic conflicts in most of the cases involve nations and groups that have been at least formally granted equal citizens' rights, albeit often in the context of objective and subjective grievances that were accompanied by strong feelings of threat and sometimes violence. While these minorities often have a shared nationality, regularly recognized in the family of nations, their efforts to achieve collective self-expression may approach self-determination and, in the most extreme cases, secession or a reduction of autonomy within the existing state. This, however, is not the case of the Palestinians in the West Bank and the limited situation in Gaza. They are not citizens of Israel, nor are they allowed the full exercise of rights that representative democracies regularly provide.

Focusing on the West Bank requires highlighting the distinct nature of this occupation and the violation of HR. The situation of the annexed (formerly Syrian) Golan Heights can be at best categorized as a border dispute rather than the locus of vitiated HR. Boundaries have often been altered after military conflagration—for example, following the 1949 world-legitimated armistice agreements resulting in the increase of Israel's size from 55% to 78% of the total area of the British Mandate. The conquest of the Golan Heights also has become the venue for Jewish settlements, but the remaining native population (mostly a mere 20,000 Druze) has been offered citizenship equal to that of any other group within Israel. Hence, the international community has not been highlighting any significant complaints. As for Gaza, Israel's unilateral total withdrawal—settlements included—in 2005 changed the territorial priority of the occupation The critical issues today are mostly limited to the proportionality of noncombatant casualties and physical destruction—often called the "collateral damage" typical of asymmetric warfare. Also at issue are the scope and indiscriminate nature of sanctions amounting to collective punishment, leading to questioning the humanity of its restrictive definition, rather than a less controversial targeting of "smart sanctions" to the Hamas ruling elites.

The prolonged military occupation in the West Bank reveals a pattern of government perhaps best described as permanent "colonial domination" or "occupation." The prevailing power imbalance has encouraged Jewish citizens to establish separate settlements within the occupied territories (hereinafter designated OT) and govern under a policy that amounts to a double standard in the enjoyment of individual HR between Arab and Jew. A corollary of this policy is Israel's retention of practical authority to determine specific delegation of municipal government responsibilities to Palestinian authorities in such areas as infrastructure development and provision of those services associated with the state's police powers (e.g., health care, education, public safety). Regarding East Jerusalem, Israel has unilaterally declared its annexation. However, and differently, it has not granted to most of its quarter of a million Arab inhabitants full citizenship rights, limiting them to a more precarious limited resident status with no voting rights in national elections.

The principal objective of this chapter is to analyze how the effects of occupation, with their gross violation of Palestinians HR, are percolating through Israel itself. As a background to this major theme, the chapter will describe briefly the situation of rights in the Jewish state before 1967, dwell on the development of HR concerns in the international community, and provide a glimpse into the violation of HR in the occupied territories.

BEFORE THE 1967 SIX DAY WAR: SHAPING THE VALUES OF A NEW STATE

The universal aspect of HR—its application to all people, irrespective their ethnic or religious differences—has often received transitory political interest in Israel; on occasion, it has even been ignored. The equal rights paradigm was initially subordinated to raison d'etat or security. In the name of security, Israel selectively violated the rights of the Arab minority during the first eighteen years of the state's existence, conducting expulsions, enacting various restrictive ordinances, and generally using discriminatory treatment. But the occupation of the West Bank and Gaza as a result of the 1967 Six Day War was a major "game-changing" event. Over two-thirds of Israel's history now includes control over the OT, effectively making that political arrangement more the rule than the exception. Sad to say, Israel has been violating the HR of Palestinians there and failing to socialize new generations of Israelis into its appreciation of universal values.

The birth of Zionism in the second half of the nineteenth century embodied the goal of self-emancipation for the Jewish people in the land of their ancestors and promised an exemplary Jewish society. While the state's democratic infrastructure was already developed before independence, it was built for its Jewish settlers. From this perspective, Zionism as the national liberation movement of the Jewish people was not different from the movements of other groups seeking self-determination in a nation-state within recognized borders. By and large, however, it postponed or set aside the "Arab question" (see Gorny, 1987; Shapira, 1992). When the State of Israel was established, the 1948 Declaration of Independence proclaimed a Jewish state granting "complete equality of social and political rights for all its citizens." The inherent tension in this formulation has been ever a source of domestic strife. Many Jews in Israel identify the Arabs' rejection of the "democratic and Jewish" formula with an unwillingness to recognize the majority's legitimate self-interest in this part of the Middle East. However, many within Israel's Arab community resent the formulation as being incompatible with the notion of equal individual rights—a "state of all its citizens"—thereby perpetuating group discrimination, with a concomitant negation of individual autonomy.

The Arab population exodus incidental to the establishment of the Israeli state remains an issue of collective memory to all Palestinians. Irrespective of the hotly disputed causes of this removal—they have been debated ad nauseam—the Universal Declaration of Human Rights (UDHR) affirms that "everyone has the right to leave any country, including their own, and to return to his country" (Article 13, par 2). Thus the question naturally arises: If Jews have the right to return to their homeland after 2000 years, should not the same right be extended to those who were keen to exert their right to return after a war in which the Arabs were defeated sixty-two years ago? For Israelis that matter is not so much principled; rather, it is existential. The first, and overriding, Israeli priority is survival as a homeland for the Jewish people. To the extent that deference to HR raises the prospect of their submergence into an enlarged Arab population, HR loses both its luster and its moral priority. The events of 1948 provide only one example of the problematic standing of HR principles in the State of Israel. There are many other that will be presented later. But a major premise that is advanced in this chapter suggests that this clash comes in the setting of a growing emphasis on HR in the international community.

Paradoxically, it was the Holocaust that triggered the first international HR convention to focus on genocide, even preceding the UDHR. The message was that the international community should not remain idle when innocent people are repressed by their own regime or one from elsewhere. But the lesson of the Holocaust was interpreted differently in Israel and by many of the Diaspora Jews. "Never again" was translated into particular values and considerations. These considerations were encapsulated in the words of numerous Israeli political figures from the entire Zionist spectrum. Prime Minister Benjamin Netanyahu was quite clear. "We must not allow those who want to commit mass murder, those who want to destroy the Jews, to emerge unscathed. That is our lesson from the Holocaust." He went on to say that two important lessons were learned from the Holocaust: Jews must be able to defend themselves, and barbarians must be prevented from acquiring arms (*Haaretz*, August 28, 2009). Years before, former Labor Prime Minister Golda Meir pointed out that after what was done to the Jews in the Holocaust, "we can do what is needed and nobody has the right to criticize us and tell us what to do" (*Haaretz*, August 14, 2009). In fact, there has never been a real difference among the leading figures and major political parties on this matter.

PROGRESS REGARDING HR IN WORLD POLITICS

The 1948 UDHR was the first international document legitimating the protection of individual rights as entitlements. What was earlier considered to be the exclusive domestic jurisdiction of the state was gradually changing; while territorial sovereignty continues to be respected, concern over the way the population under their control is treated does not stop at national borders. Human rights as a distinct international regime (Donnelly, 2002) has developed with a vast set of universal norms, as well as a range of governmental and nongovernmental operational tools—from declaratory statements, through fact-finding, investigation missions, condemnation of gross violations, and cultural, diplomatic, economic, and military sanctions. The old concept of sovereignty is being challenged by humanitarian intervention and the responsibility to protect HR. Current criticism concerns the will and ability of the international community to stop its violations across the globe. Often acts are "too little too late," and double standards prevail for weak and strong states and blocs (Kaufman, 2001).

The initial post–World War II UN impetus for promoting HR came to a halt with the emergence of the Cold War and the new fear of a "nuclear holocaust." The global agenda then moved from the bottom-up defense of the individual to the reduction of the arms race, with a resulting paralysis of governmental action against HR violators. With the advent of détente between the superpowers, in the early 1970s only three countries received condemnation: South Africa for apartheid, Israel in the OT, and Chile under Pinochet's dictatorship; two of these situations ended with regime change. Toward the rest of the violators worldwide was what Amnesty International called then "a conspiracy of silence." Nongovernmental organizations led the HR field into action, successfully lobbying Western governments to widen and endorse their criticism, targeting other powerful countries such as the Soviet Union and China. Furthermore, with the demise of the Soviet Union, a new consensus led the international community to move HR to the forefront of concerns, encompassing their practices everywhere. While still highly politicized, the UN developed mechanisms that were more effective in enforcing its declared policies, with more systematic monitoring, lifting the impunity of violators and increasing endorsement of humanitarian interventions, confronting armed state and nonstate actors. There is no better example of transition than the UN's failure to condemn the genocide of 100,000 Kurds by Sadam Hussein's regime and the 1991 post–Gulf War, and the approval of a "safe haven" in northern Iraq, with an international military presence. Gross HR violations became categorized as war crimes; therefore, perpetrators can be brought to justice by the now functioning International Criminal Court.

September 11, 2001, was a setback in HR advancement. The declaration of the global war on terror by the United States put Israel in the same coalition with many Western democracies and indirectly even with Arab countries that have been victims of such attacks. At different levels, many states restricted the rights not only of their external enemies (i.e., combatants) but also, to a more limited extent, those of their own citizens. But there is a big difference in the comparison, since other democracies fighting wars in Iraq or Afghanistan are not doing it for territorial expansion. At this time in history, the case of Israel is a unique case of colonial occupation. In fact, the State of Israel, for various reasons, did not internalize the changes that were taking place in the international community. Hence, the trend toward progress in the international system (Adler & Crawford, 1990) has been facing a regression in HR by Israel. Israel has been dismissing its increasing isolation as reflecting a biased approach of the UN and the usually hostile world, which is "always against us" (Bar-Tal, 2007).

HR PRACTICES IN THE OCCUPIED PALESTINIAN TERRITORIES

In order to grasp fully the attitudes and practices related to the HR in the OT since 1967, it is necessary to look at the practices that developed in the State of Israel since 1948. For the first eighteen years following independence there were serious HR violations in many domains, especially toward the Arab minority but also toward Jews (Hofnung, 1991). The Arab minority in Israel lived under a military-regulated regime, one that greatly restricted their freedom of movement, residence, correspondence, expression, and privacy. However, with the abolition of the military government in 1965, their situation as well as the general situation in Israel showed signs of improvement. But whatever hopes Israel's Arabs may have nurtured, they were dashed with the outbreak of the 1967 Six Day War. This conflagration diminished the status of the former Jordanians now identified as Palestinians, a situation that eventually would have repercussions for the Arab minority resident in Israel.

Since the focus of this chapter is on HR in Israel, in order to better appreciate the context and understand the specific workings of cause and effect, it is worthwhile to sum up the record in the West Bank since Israel's occupation began in 1967 in order to better comprehend the impact of the government's behavior in that region on Israeli's HR perceptions.[2] An extended review appears in the introductory chapter of this volume. Here, it will be only noted that HR violations have included sins of both commission (e.g., setting a double standard to benefit the Jewish settlers in housing, separate roads, no checkpoints, and access to water) and omission (e.g., failing to stop abuses perpetrated by settlers against the resident Arab population). The impact of Israeli policy is reflected in the very different outcomes in the annexed and occupied areas. The U.S. Department of State's 2009 report identified ongoing respect for basic rights in the annexed Golan Heights territory compared with what can only be described as a disregard for those rights in the OT. For example, and quoting from the report, "The IDF [Israel Defense Force] conducted numerous incursions into Palestinian areas to carry out arrest operations and kill suspected terrorists.... Israeli law prohibits arbitrary arrest and detention, but the security services did not always observe these prohibitions." Conversely, within Israel itself and in the annexed areas, matters were otherwise. Again, quoting from the State Department report, "The government or its agents did not commit politically motivated killings within its territory.... The law prohibits arbitrary arrest and detention [a constraint that was] generally observed.... Arab Israelis are subject to the same laws as all citizens.... Non-Israeli residents of the Israeli-occupied Golan Heights were subject to the same laws as Israeli citizens."

I will now turn to the major part of the chapter and discuss the impact of occupation on HR within the State of Israel.

THE IMPACT OF OCCUPATION ON HR IN ISRAEL

Before beginning this analysis, a few caveats are in order. It would be simplistic to attribute to "colonial domination" the total deterioration of HR norms and values among Israelis. Such factors as, for example, the transition of leadership from the founding fathers to the third generation, wealth generation and economic growth, demographic changes brought about through recent immigration, religious and ethnic-specific birth rates, modernization and development (Goldscheider, 2002), and international processes resulting from consumerism and globalization, as well as fragmentation within Israeli society, have likely all played a part. Over the six decades of its existence Israel has changed, for both better and worse. But we would like to emphasize that in terms of costs and benefits, the occupation has had a mostly negative impact. For Palestinians, in both the OT and Israel proper, the conditions of life have declined relative to the majority population. First, while there has been no direct correlation between each violation in the OT with similar rights of Israeli Jews, certain restrictions are becoming visible for Arab-Israeli citizens (approximately 20% of the total population), members of the Palestinian nation who have maintained solidarity with their brethren in the OT. Simply stated, this population is viewed by the Jewish majority as an internal security threat. One outcome of the poor treatment of Arab citizens is their increased self-awareness of their subordinated status, their increasing marginalization, and the growing polarization of Israeli society (Kretzmer, 1990).

Second, the impact of occupation on societal attitudes, while closely related to a slower process of erosion of moral precepts formally underlying state institutions, must be distinguished from the latter. Reinforcement is not only bottom-up but also top-down, evidenced by the nearly total absence of any mention of HR as universal in the elite discourse.[3] The fight against current anti-Semitism or, for that matter, memorializing of the Holocaust has not occurred in the context of racial discrimination or genocide. Indeed, some of the actions promoted by pro-settler organizations have the backing of right-wing personalities both in government and in the opposition, individuals with no affection for their Arab fellow citizens and no concern for their rights. This, in turn, leads to another consideration: the deterioration of values in specific sectors of society that perpetuated hostile acts toward Arab foreign workers and specific Jewish targeted groups (Kaufman, 1993; Negbi, 2004).

In sum, HR violations by Israeli authorities, in general, originate in the practices of those Jewish settlers—Israeli citizens in the West Bank benefiting from a privileged set of laws and practices—who are disregarding Palestinians' rights. This situation differs markedly from a military occupation when all groups are treated much the same way—equally good or bad—as individuals. Conversely, in the OT, there is a clear discriminatory policy and even worse societal abuses. The settlers also act within Israel and its institutions to ensure their privileges, while the government largely overlooks their unlawful acts (U.S. Department of State, 2009). Jewish settlers burning orchards, uprooting olive trees, and vandalizing Palestinian mosques as retaliatory acts against official Israeli efforts to curb unauthorized outpost settlements demonstrate to the native population that it cannot look to the resident military force for protection of either persons or property (*Haaretz*, April 23, 2010).

We will now briefly discuss the impact of occupation on HR in Israel. Our focus will be on the Arab minority, whose members are formally full citizens in the State of Israel.

THE ARAB MINORITY

As mentioned above, discriminatory practices directed at the Arab minority existed during the first two decades of Israel's independence, albeit slowly subsiding. However, after the 1967 war and in the increasingly common clashes with Palestine Liberation Organization (PLO) military units, Israeli security responses, which invariably snared Arab noncombatants, heightened Israeli Arabs' objective and subjective sense of being treated as second-class citizens (Rouhana, 2010; Sikkuy, 2009). At the popular level this usually took the form of casual bigotry. The use of such insulting expressions as "dirty Arabush"—a minister adding this derogatory suffix to an otherwise ethnic descriptor—did not differ much from comparable social practices in the OT (*Haaretz*, June 19, 2009).

Disturbing as such behavior might be, the ensuing violence was considerably more ominous. Verbally expressed disrespect can lead to violent confrontation. One such example was the shooting with live ammunition of twelve Arabs in Israel in October 2000 in response to stone-throwing demonstrations documented in a wider context in 2003 by the official commission of inquiry led by Judge Theodor Or. Similar violent ultra-Orthodox anti-Zionist Shabbat riots in West Jerusalem have been met with tear gas or water cannons, often at the price of more wounded policemen than demonstrators. Israeli Jews regularly call the OT "liberated areas." This, compounded with the existential threat of the "demographic bomb" (the upsurge in the Arab proportion of the overall population due to the higher Arab birth rate), has generated what amounts to moral dissonance, with ostensibly law-abiding members of society tacitly endorsing (1) the prevention of non-Jewish population growth in Judea and Samaria and perhaps gerrymandering to exclude a large number of Arabs from Israel; (2) such severe restriction of the Arab minority's rights as citizens will frustrate any expectation of participating in a society where "one person, one vote" is no longer acceptable (*Haaretz*, May 11, 2008).

As domestic Arab resistance turned to riots during the second *intifada* in October 2000, Jewish support for universally applicable HR withered as support for limitations on the rights of Israel's resident Arabs increased (Shamir & Sagiv-Schifter, 2006). Sixty-two percent of Israelis considered that the government should encourage its Arab citizens to emigrate from Israel. Twenty-nine percent of Israelis think that crucial decisions concerning Israel's future should be decided by a Jewish majority without counting Arab Knesset members. Nearly 50% of Israeli Jews don't want to live near Arabs, while 56% of Israeli Arabs strongly support living in the same neighborhood as Jews. Thirty-five percent of the Jews and 7% of the Arabs prefer not to see Arab pupils in Jewish high schools, and some 23% of both groups are not in favor of meetings between Jews and Arabs.

Successive governments did little to reduce institutional, legal, and societal discrimination against the country's Arab citizens. For instance, in addition to mandating a curriculum that does not take into account the Arab narrative, Arab schools are overcrowded, understaffed, poorly constructed, more distant from Arab neighborhoods than their Jewish counterparts, or simply unavailable (Human Rights Watch, 2004). Former Prime Minister Ehud Olmert decried the "deliberate and insufferable" gap between the proportion of Arab citizens in Israel and their inclusion in the state's civil service positions (*Jerusalem Post*, July 13, 2008). Figures on socioeconomic gaps show that 50% of Arab families live below the poverty line, a rate three times higher than that of Jewish Israelis. On average, Arabs also earn 30% less than Jews. Certain government agencies won't employ them, with "security" being regularly cited as justification for discrimination. In the words of As'ad Ghanem, "Aside from participating in elections, an extremely limited form of participation for a minority, Palestinians in Israel do not enjoy basic protections or basic rights that ought to be assured by the fact of citizenship" (The Jerusalem Fund, 2008).

PALESTINIANS IN EAST JERUSALEM

East Jerusalem was occupied by Israeli military forces during the 1967 war and was annexed to Israel shortly thereafter. Upon annexation, resident Palestinians were granted the right to request Israeli citizenship, although the majority chose the permanent resident alternative. Requesting Israeli citizenship carried with it the risk of retaliation by PLO operatives. In any event, the Israeli government rarely approved such citizenship applications. However, permanent residency remains a precarious status. Under the 1952 Law of Permanent Residency, such residents risk loss of status if their ties with Jerusalem lapse, even if they were born there and were counted in the post-1967 census. Residency restrictions affected family reunification. Palestinians who were abroad during the 1967 war, or who subsequently lost their residence permits, were not permitted to reside permanently with their families in the OT. Foreign-born spouses and children of Palestinian residents experienced difficulty in obtaining residency compared with the automatic approval for Jews in the same city. Palestinians also reported extensive delays in registering newborn children with Israeli authorities. Municipal services are inferior to those available in other parts of the city (ACRI, 2009).

SOCIETAL TRENDS

Popular Jewish perceptions of Arabs are not conducive to the fostering of a peaceful society (Bar-Tal & Teichman, 2005). However, as the dominant political and social sector of Israeli society, much of the responsibility for bringing popular perceptions into alignment with HR falls to the nation's Jews. Much of this is arguably attributable to a profound change in the popular perception of security (Bar-Tal, Magal, & Halperin, 2009). During the early decades of Israel's existence, the existential threat was national—foreign uniformed enemies. In recent decades—after the experience of *intifada*, suicide bombing, and the like—the threat has become identified with the "enemy from within." As the perception of threat and its attendant dehumanization of Palestinians grow among Israeli Jews, support for objective violations of HR has grown.

Security considerations have an inverse relationship with HR; the principle itself is often perceived as a weapon in the hands of Israel's enemies. This perception was already in place during the Oslo peace process but gained strength during the subsequent Al Aqsa *intifada*.

Public Opinion

In a democracy public opinion ultimately affects official policy, and vice versa. Today Israel is increasingly encouraging a disregard for the rule of law and the establishment of populist, demagogic, and shortsighted policies. A recent survey revealed the lowest support in the last twenty years for the assertion that democracy is the best form of governance: only 77% of the respondents supported this premise compared to 90% in 1999. Israel is also one of only four countries of the thirty-two listed in the study in which most of the public believes that "strong leaders can do more for the country than debates or legislation" (Israel Democracy Institute, 2009).

The fusion of the effects of occupation, wars, and national and personal security concerns has contributed mightily to this ethnocentric trend (Maoz & McCauley, 2008). This was clearly revealed by from the findings of a recent poll of Jewish citizens concerning violation of a general principle found in the UDHR—the fundamental right to life— and, thereafter, its application to the Palestinian minority. In this poll, general support for violation of the fundamental right to life was only 4.5%, but in reference to the Palestinian minority it rose to 20.3%. Support for restricting freedom of movement in general was 17.1% but doubled in relation to the Palestinians to 34.5%; and violation of the right to property in principle was supported by only 7.6% but for the Palestinians by 29.9%.

These discriminatory attitudes become even more plangent in light of answers to questions relating solely to security-related restrictions on Palestinians. Support included the following: torture, 34%; use of live ammunition in curfew enforcement, 36%; house demolition as a response to suspected subversive activity, 47%; prolonged administrative detention without trial, 46%; curfew, encirclements, and enclosures, 50%; and delays at checkpoints, 55%. In sum, an average of 45% of respondents supported flagrant violations of HR precepts. Nonetheless, the survey also indicated that 89% of Israelis strongly support HR, the protections they afford, and the necessity to foster them (Ilani, 2008).

Violent Acts and Threats

The settlement movement was invigorated by zealots with a messianic streak, a small minority of Israel's Jews whose apocalyptic thinking has now permeated all sectors of Jewish society. It has fomented violence, besmirched Israel's good name, brought humiliation to another people, and led some Jews to promote "murder in the name of God," both within Israel's borders and without. And not only Arabs are affected. Those Jews vigorously opposed to the settlement policy have been called "Jewish traitors," and their harm is justified. Threats to peace-oriented leaders and activists have largely originated in organized (and arguably subversive) groups in society rather than from within governmental security forces. Although such cases are isolated—the 1983 murder of Emil Grunzweig while marching in a Peace Now gathering in Jerusalem being a case in point—the most salient act was the assassination twelve years later of Prime Minister Yitzhak Rabin by a young religious zealot when leaving another large peace demonstration in Tel Aviv.

One of the later incidents involved Professor (and peace activist) Zeev Sternhell, who was injured when a pipe bomb, rigged to detonate when his front door was opened, exploded. An extremist group has offered a prize of 1.1 million shekels to anyone who kills a member of Peace Now. Another case involved the distinguished violinist Daniel Barenboim; threats against him required the use of security escorts during his concert season in Jerusalem. While such acts remain the province of small Jewish terrorist undergrounds (or individual fanatics)—and are routinely condemned by the nation's leadership and citizenry alike—they nonetheless dramatize the growing schism in Israeli society.

Civil Disorder

The opposition of settlers and their supporters to government decisions regarding removal of officially or unofficially sanctioned legal settlements or illegal outposts has become a permanent feature of OT public life. Civil disorder has extended to the cutting of roads within Israel, to provocative actions, and to appeals to disobey military orders; all of these activities reduce citizens' adherence to the rule of law as a governing precept (Sprinzak, 1991). The IDF has harshly criticized extremist West Bank settlers, especially those who have attacked Palestinians and soldiers and who regularly engage in sedition by fomenting dissent within the armed forces (Harel, 2008). Furthermore, settler rabbis have urged IDF soldiers to refuse evacuation orders (*Haaretz*, July 11, 2009),[4] and a few have even condoned the killing of innocent non-Jewish civilians (Estrin, 2010).[5] Roi Sharon (*Ma'ariv*, November 9, 2009) observed that "What makes it worse is that the permission to kill is now expanded to all human beings potentially liable to endanger the Jewish people."

The Erosion of Tolerance

Nongovernment organization HR monitors are now routinely condemned as anti-Semitic or even as national enemies when they point to shortcomings in Israeli policy and practice. Societal rejection of the traditional HR monitor's role—a relatively recent development in the Israeli polity—reflects what is now a likely majority opinion among the nation's Jews. As a practical matter, most Israelis believe that these organizations are hostile toward Israel and tarnish its international image. A major anti-HR campaign, instigated by a nongovernment organization (NGO) monitor—whose sole purpose is to criticize HR organizations' work in or about Israel—and the Im Tirzu movement—themselves funded by the "Christian Zionists," among others—have taken to denouncing local Israeli HR organizations as fifth columnists in the pay of the U.S. and European governments. The Im Tirzu added a sentence to a prayer of long standing recited in remembrance of the fallen, stressing those ostensible enemies from within who have condemned the behavior of Israeli soldiers. Labeling individual Jews as "self-hating Israeli traitors,"[6] many of them with distinguished careers in the Zionist movement, the diplomatic corps, law enforcement agencies, and the military is an expression of the lack of prevailing tolerance. In a survey commissioned by Tel Aviv University's Tel Aviv Research Center, a plurality of those polled (including 76% of right-wing respondents) said that HR groups should not have the right to freely publicize immoral or illegal conduct on Israel's part (*Haaretz*, April 28, 2010).

VULNERABLE SEGMENTS OF SOCIETY

The Jewish Orthodox

If many religious Israelis are given over to chauvinism and xenophobia, others retain their attachment to the nation's founding liberal ideals. These exceptions include Meimad (a small political party), NGOs such as Pathways of Peace, Rabbis for HR, several of the founding reserve soldiers in Breaking the Silence, and the founder of the Bereaved Families Forum, as well as distinguished academics, intellectuals, and journalists. Not all of their opponents shrink from violence. For example, Yaakov Teitel, described in the media as a "Jewish terrorist," targeted for attack left-wing Jewish professors, homosexuals, and Christian groups. Adopting what amounts to a regime of vigilante justice, one extending considerably further than legitimating the killing of Arabs,[7] led to the assassination in 1995 of Prime Minister Rabin by Yigal Amir, a law student at Bar Ilan, a religious Orthodox-based university (Zertal & Eldar, 2007).

Israel's Youth

Israel's youth, both Jewish and Arab, manifest far more intolerance than their elders. More of them are both the victims of violence and its perpetrators. A poll of Jewish high school students showed that 49.5% believed that Arab citizens should not be granted equal rights, rising to 82% among religious students. Over 80% of religious students said that Arabs should not be eligible to run for elections to the Knesset, compared to 47% of secular students (*Haaretz*, April 28, 2010).

Such negative attitudes toward the rule of law also extended to the OT. Nearly half of the students stated that they would refuse to order an evacuation of outposts or settlements in the Palestinian territories (*Haaretz*, March 11, 2009). Comparing young soldiers' concerns with humane behavior toward an armed Arab enemy after the 1967 war (The Seventh Day, 1970) and after the 2009 Gaza War, in dealings with unarmed civilians, points to a fundamental erosion of basic values. Some IDF soldiers have adopted unit insignia featuring revolting imagery—dead babies, mothers weeping on their children's graves, a gun aimed at a child or a bombed-out mosque. At least some of this must be attributable to the dearth of military training in required humanitarian treatment of civilians and, on a larger scale, to a comparable absence of education in HR requirements during periods of schooling and superficially during military basic training.

New Immigrants from the Former Soviet Union

Perhaps because they originated in an authoritarian state—one in which HR considerations were theoretical at best—Israel's influx of Russian Jews increased the number of Jews ill disposed toward Arabs' rights. A poll determined that 77% of Russian immigrants support promoting Arab emigration from Israel, as opposed to 47% of native Jews. Thirty-three percent of native Jews accept the presence of Arab political parties within the Knesset, while only 23% of the immigrants do so. Twenty-seven percent of Israelis opposed the statement that "a Jewish majority is necessary for fateful decisions for the country," in contrast to 38% of Russian Jewish immigrants who opposed the same statement in 2003. (Polak, 2009, p. 23).

The University Community

In years past, the university community was a stout supporter of individual rights, even to the extent of alienating the average Jew. While that attitude remains significantly intact, Jewish intellectuals—the core of the university community—no longer retain the almost unquestioned support and respect that they enjoyed only a few decades ago. Lately, the monitoring of critical views of government policies toward the Palestinians has resulted in the sense that government intrusion—Big Brother is watching you—extends even to the classroom. Such watchdog groups as IsraCampus and Israel Academia Monitor are believed to be stepping up their campaigns after the publication in *the Los Angeles Times* (August 10, 2009) of an op-ed article by Prof. Neve Gordon of Ben Gurion University calling for a boycott of Israel. Targeting principally Ben Gurion, Haifa, and Tel Aviv Universities, both groups have been alerting the universities' external donors, mostly American Jews, to what they describe as the questionable behavior and utterances of "subversive" professors as a means of bringing pressure to bear on school administrations to sanction faculty staff critical of Israeli policies. In response, concerned faculty has been split on the issue of internationally boycotting Israel at large and its universities in particular. While a large majority opposes such boycotts, the attempt to limit the freedom of expression of minority views has been called a campaign of McCarthyism.

THE INSTITUTIONAL IMPACT

The above-described deterioration in Israel's attachment to certain ethical values cannot be considered per se an HR transgression. Nonetheless, a democratic society has a moral responsibility to ensure that popular ideas at odds with the nation's generally accepted core beliefs are not allowed to be translated into antisocial behavior. To a limited extent, this has already occurred. Earlier paragraphs have alluded to public discourse in which "might" has been privileged over "right" at the expense of equality and the failure of government agencies to spell out explicitly the merits and obligations of equal treatment. As mentioned by Heiman (2010), Israeli public relations stems entirely from the Zionist Israeli narrative, without any genuine attempt being made to learn the language of HR, which is dominant in international public discourse. Furthermore, it is rightly pointed out that Israelis at large must also be taught the language of rights in order to better understand that the world is not willing to accept the continual undermining of inalienable entitlements for reasons of security, (Heiman, 2010).

In sum, this combination of popular brutishness and government inertia has led to the growth of a democracy deficit (Bovard, 2006), an ongoing corruption of Israel's democracy in which the precept of respect for minority rights has been gravely compromised. Compared to the decades preceding the 1967 war, Israel has experienced decreasing transparency; abuse of power resulting in traduced legal and moral standards; limited accountability that includes withholding evidence in judicial proceedings; restricting or disregarding the functions and findings of commissions of inquiry; a growing gap between poor and rich; the withering of checks and balances within the state's institutions; increased difficulty in securing citizenship; and increased restrictions on freedom of the press, expression of opinion, and the right of association of NGOs.

Unlike other public institutions, Israel's Supreme Court of Justice has enjoyed widespread prestige and has been perceived as a bulwark in the defense of HR requirements, irrespective of religion or ethnicity. But even this highest judicial body appears to be wavering, retreating from past rigor, and deferring to the executive when ostensible security considerations are raised (see the chapter by Kretzmer in this volume).

The Legislative Branch

Israel's Knesset is treading a slippery slope with respect to universal HR, with a tendency toward barring extreme but nonviolent dissident voices. A case in point is monitoring of loyalty to the state. Coalition party Israel Beiteinu's motto, "Without loyalty there's no citizenship," was very effective in the 2009 Knesset elections. The plenary gave initial approval to a bill making it a crime to publicly deny Israel's right to exist as a Jewish state, punishable by a sentence of up to a year in prison. It would outlaw the publication of any "call to negate Israel's existence as a Jewish [polity] and causing an act of hatred, disdain or disloyalty" to Israel. Foreign Minister Avigdor Liberman introduced to the cabinet a bill that would require Israeli citizens to take a loyalty oath to the Jewish state before they could be issued a national identity card (Shragai, 2009). While this legislation is directed against Israel's Arabs, it might well be challenged by anti-Zionist ultra-Orthodox Jewish groups, Naturei Karta being the extreme case. Much—perhaps all—of this is intimately related to difficulties flowing from what amounts to dictatorial occupation. On May 9, 2009, the government's Ministerial Committee for Legislation adopted the proposed *Nakkbah* ("catastrophe" in Arabic] Law, which would prohibit commemorating the exodus in 1947–1949 of three-quarters of the Palestinian people from their land, after replacing an originally drafted criminal penalty with an extreme economic measure whereby the state would cut off funding for organizations and institutions that commemorate *Nakba* Day. In addition, another proposed bill expands the definition of a terrorist organization in order to impede legitimate political activity, specifically that of the Islamic Movement and Balad, both important Arab political parties, thereby enabling the state to ban them. Under the present statute, a terrorist organization is a group of persons who use acts of violence that might cause death or injury to a person or threaten to use acts of violence. MK Michael Ben Ari proposed to add to the definition "movements or parties that encourage a terrorist organization, or support armed struggle against the State of Israel, or seek to impair Jewish sovereignty over the Temple Mount."[8]

Restricting Arabs' freedom of expression and assembly has now been extended to foreign visitors of Muslim or Arab origin, as well as to Jewish and non-Jewish young people who come peacefully to work either for Palestinian universities or NGOs. The list of undesirables has been arbitrarily extended, and its membership is ever-changing. Visitors often discover their listing only upon arrival at Ben Gurion Airport (*Haaretz*, April 4, 2010). Norman Finkelstein and Noam Chomsky, the latter an academic critic of Zionism, has been barred from entering Israel, a decision raising the prospect that Israelis holding similar views may not be allowed to reenter their homeland. In the wake of the Gaza War, a multiparty Knesset effort was launched to limit NGOs' sources of funding following allegations of "unpatriotic" testimony made available to the UN HR Council Report relating to specifics of the IDF winter 2008–2009 Cast Lead operation in Gaza.

Israeli Courts: Fair Trials and Declining Deference to HR

For both Israel's Arabs and dissident Jewish citizens, the nation's judiciary has served as a protective barrier against heavy-handed state activity (Kretzmer, 2002). As a practical matter, the efficacy of judicial holdings has traditionally been the deference that most Israelis have paid to the courts as upholders of the constitution. In recent years, as noted above, the courts have shown signs of retreating from their traditionally independent status. The moral dilemma posed by official (or tacitly approved) use of "moderate physical pressure" in the early years of the occupation—reduction of the suspect's integrity versus the state's responsibility to secure the lives and property of citizens—has in recent years become considerably more acute. It now involves interrogation techniques indistinguishable from those described as torture in documents prepared by the UN Committee Against Torture conducted in the context of "ticking bomb" scenarios (B'tselem, 2007; Kaufman &Tsur, 1989). The hardening of civilian attitudes now extends to noncrisis situations. For example, the High Court of Justice's 1979 decision in the *Elon Moreh* case, which ruled that seizing private lands by executive fiat is illegal, enraged many Israelis and encouraged xenophobic groups to attack the institution.

Like it or not, there is no guarantee that Israel's appellate courts will continue to adhere to universal standards, even in a reduced capacity.[9] Indeed, some of the courts' decisions (e.g., ones relating to removal of illegal outposts or redrafting the course of the separation barrier in the West Bank) were never implemented,[10] an executive response diminishing the courts' image as upholders of the rule of law. Furthermore, Shinar (2009) concurs that "security" arguments have had the same effect on the Supreme Court's judicial opinions that beliefs regarding security have had on the thinking of Israeli Jews at large. "This observation is supported by the findings of a major poll conducted in the early 1990s, according to which the more the Supreme Court was involved in imposing supervision over the security authorities in the OT, the more that popular support for the Court has diminished" (Barzilai, Yuchtman-Yaar, & Segal, 1994, p. 17). Decisions of lower courts have regularly curtailed citizens' rights, although such holdings were regularly overturned on appeal. This state of affairs has become increasingly serious. In sum, the increasing identification of court decisions with evolving and less democratic societal values gives substance to Kimmerling's "incriminating verdict."

Law Enforcement Agencies

Israel's law enforcement agencies fall under the jurisdiction of the Executive Branch and include the IDF—the title itself selected to highlight the limited nature of the use of force in self-defense. And the emphasis was rightly on self-defense. Before the occupation and even during the 1973 Yom Kippur War, the overwhelming majority of Israeli citizens and, for that matter, most Western governments felt that the Jewish state indeed had this inherent right. Furthermore, the wars conducted against national armies, and even the acts of violence against armed and unarmed Arab citizens, were carefully scrutinized. The goal of "purity of arms" (*tohar haneshek* in Hebrew), constrained by limits imposed by humanitarian law, was the official ethical standard of behavior and, in practice, soldiers themselves often agonized about any departures from accepted behavior.

In the face of mounting popular criticism over the large number of Israeli deaths attributable to the second Lebanon War—a public appraisal of the actual state of affairs that many observers considered disproportionate to the outcry—IDF planners were determined that the upcoming Operation Cast Lead in Gaza would have as its highest priority the limitation of Israeli casualties. This, in turn, mandated a moral retreat from the former high standards of behavior in combat (Kasher, 2010). And, as a corollary, the moral integrity of "enemy" civilians was implicated. This shift in thinking has generated a number of unfavorable outcomes. It appears that high-ranking IDF officers are no longer inculcated with the values of HR. The failure of the Israeli government to thoroughly investigate and prosecute IDF members accused of HR offenses raises the possibility that such offenders may be at risk of arrest should they venture outside Israel. And, at a deeper and more profound cultural level, it appears that there has been an intrusion of fanaticism into the ranks, one that the army leadership has only lately addressed. During the Gaza War, a few army rabbis described the effort in virtually messianic terms, calling on troops to banish non-Jews from the biblical land of Israel (Boudreaux, 2009). "This rabbi comes to us and says the fight is between the children of light and the children of darkness," a reserve sergeant said, recalling a training camp encounter. "His message was clear: 'This is a war against an entire people, not against specific terrorists.' The whole thing has turned into something very religious and messianic" (Boudreaux, 2009, p. 7)

While the Security Services (Shin Bet) was rightly the subject of severe criticism for extracting coerced confessions from Arab prisoners, at least there was the possibility (perhaps even, in some instances, the probability) that the victim was actually guilty of the offense in question. However, the Shin Bet, likely for reasons lying deep in organizational culture, underestimated the threat—or even dismissed the possibility—of Jews killing Jews for political reasons, at least until the assassination of Prime Minister Rabin. In response to that outrage, the security service now appears to be spending much of its efforts in monitoring those who struggle peacefully for equal HR, peace, and disarmament. Indeed, Israel has held since December, based on allegations that during her military service she leaked classified documents suggesting that the Israeli army violated laws dealing with targeted killings (Kampeas, 2010). And as for the Arabs in Israel, Yuval Diskin, former head of the Security Services, believed that it is within Shin Bet's charter to carry out surveillance operations, such as phone taps, on individuals deemed to be "conducting subversive activity against the Jewish identity of the state," even if their actions are not in violation of the law.[11]

The Border Police (the organization that monitors and regulates movement between Israel and the OT) and, to a lesser extent, the nation's police forces have been severely criticized for grievous mistreatment of nonviolent peace demonstrators. Even stone-throwing demonstrations by Jewish ultra-Orthodox groups in Jerusalem have resulted in limited police reactions compared to the excessive use of force in confrontations with demonstrators against the Judaizing of Arab neighborhoods.[12] Likewise, violent public protests and civil commotions by settlement supporters have triggered only a modest official response compared to the brutal punishment of opponents of

Israel's military operations or construction of the fence/wall in the West Bank (*Haaretz*, September 22, 2009).[13] Such treatment is now officially extended to women. The Israeli police acted just before the nation's 2009 Memorial Day against New Profile, a dissent movement founded by university women.[14]

Absence of Accountability

Many innocent Palestinians have been victimized, the perpetrators acting with virtual impunity. Accountability has taken a back seat to ethnic and religious considerations, either by turning a blind eye or by imposing absurdly light sentences. Such practices, openly condoned or tacitly tolerated by the authorities, have led to official coverups and have possibly resulted in official disregard of commissions of inquiry that have looked into such matters (Btselem, 2009).[15] As a recent example, an official state document, the *Sassoon Report*,[16] supported the conclusion that all Israeli governmental departments and ministries have engaged in the illicit funding of "illegal settlements" or outposts, violating public law and misdirecting appropriated funds. Most of the facts have been known for a long time, but this was the first time they had been admitted in an official report; the findings, sad to say, were never addressed (Decision to postpone the demolition order of illegal outposts of Hayiovel and Harasha, *Haaretz*, March 21, 2010).[17]

Education and Its Implications

Efforts to socialize Israeli youth into acceptance of HR and the necessity to observe them in order to assure the survival of a vibrant democracy have withered in recent decades, almost to the vanishing point. The attitudes of high school students apparently have been influenced by earlier socialization involving symbols and narratives emphasizing nationalism and exclusive rights. Exceptionally, a few moderate governments sought to introduce into the teaching of civics instruction in pluralistic democracy, as well as school and extracurricular activities focused on peace and coexistence during the Oslo peace process. However, during the past decade, matters have regressed. In 2011a well-orchestrated attack appeared on the limited civic education that presenting it as being controlled by "leftist forces," and it is totally excluded from the curriculum of ultra-Orthodox state-funded schools.

In light of the occupation of Palestinian territories, this trend is extremely worrisome given the growing support among youth for denying to Arabs in Israel the same rights enjoyed by Jews (49.5%) and even the right to participate in elections (56%).

CONCLUSION

In retrospect, what has been the impact of occupation on HR in governance and societal values within Israel? The short answer is somewhere between extensive and substantial. A precise answer will likely never be attained, if only because the unvarnished truth lies buried in the critic's values. In this case of setting the alarm, I may have pointed to the worst possible scenarios rather than focusing on the good news. Nonetheless, given the evidence presented, some reasonable conclusions may be drawn.

First, the social ethos that developed during the pre-1967 period was insufficiently committed to universalized democratic ideals to maintain unstinting support for HR in the later time of stress, when those ideals became increasingly questioned.

Second, the State of Israel came into being so that Jews might have a refuge from discrimination as a minority group as well as denial of fundamental rights and inherent human dignity. Yet, within this same polity today—irony of ironies—overt support for HR has taken on the coloration of an adversary's weapon. What was once and even today so bitterly defended by Diaspora Jews in Israel is now casually ignored.

Third, the settlement enterprise has put Israel collectively on a very slippery slope. Sternhell has described the phenomenon as "colonial Zionism," an odd polity whose "leaders and spokespersons show disdain for both the weak politicians and the basic tenets of democracy itself. They know how to exploit democratic institutions, but they ignore its basic entitlements and recognize only rights for the Jews" (*Haaretz*, October 17, 2008). Yet, within the Green Line, it is not the "apartheid state" whose existence is so casually bruited about by Israel's opponents. And yet, the apartheid type of rule in the OT is penetrating into this state.

Fourth, it is a cruel reality that most of the political elites of both nations and large segments of the public have not been socialized into the language and use of HR as universal principles (Kaufman & Abu-Nimer, 2006, p. 294). To make matters worse, democratic governments often face domestic constituencies that perceive the implementation of specific international HR decisions as a source of weakness, concessions granted solely due to pressure from biased world organizations and powers and antithetical to national interests. Could these popular perceptions be overcome, even under conditions in which national elites favor HR implementation? The jury is still out, but the prospects are not promising.

Fifth, and finally, we are ever reminded of the words in Deuteronomy: "Justice, justice you shall pursue" (Deut. 16:20). The deliberate repetition of the word *justice* is by no means simply a religious requirement for scrupulous Jews. When half of the Jewish people are still living as minority groups throughout the world, it is a reminder of profound wisdom and common sense, a reflection of enlightened self-interest,. And all too often, failure to observe the strictures suggested by our long-standing teachings has led to ruin. Applying that thought to Israel's OT policies, Rabbi Haim Siedler-Feller concluded, "Occupation is the greatest catastrophe to befall the Jewish people in the aftermath of the Holocaust. The settlers and the compliant Israeli government that have supported them have succeeded in overturning two thousand years of a tradition of justice for the 'other' and in transforming the Jewish people into an oppressive occupier" (Seidler-Feller, 2007, p. 18).

ACKNOWLEDGMENTS

I would like to express my gratitude to Daniel Bar-Tal for his significant contribution to the preparations of this chapter as well as to my former student Arjun Sethi for his editorial assistance.

NOTES

1. Interestingly, the capture of Sinai and Gaza from Egypt and southern Lebanon, and the Golan Heights from Syria did not result in the renaming of these territories, as has been the West Bank of Jordan, officially called by the biblical names "Judea and Samaria."
2. In the interest of transparency, it should be noted that the author was a founder, and later chair, of B'tselem (the Israeli Information Center for Human Rights in the Occupied Territories), as well as board member of the International Executive Committee of Amnesty International, and currently serves on the Advisory Board of Human Rights Watch/Middle East.
3. References to HR in the majority of documents relating to the Oslo peace process are both scarce and vague. A content analysis of all speeches by then Prime Minister Ariel Sharon could not identify any mention of HR. Likewise, President Yasser Arafat's references to rights were almost entirely restricted to Palestinians (Kaufman & Abu Nimer, 2006).
4. Settler rabbis—some on the government payroll—said that it is inconceivable that the IDF or police would participate in the "immoral" razing of settlement outposts. Rabbi Zalman Melamed, who is from the West Bank settlement of Beit El, said: "It is completely and absolutely forbidden for any person in Israel to evacuate Jewish outposts in the land of Israel, and just as a person is obliged to refuse an order that desecrates the Sabbath, he must also refuse an order to evacuate an outpost, even if he will be punished as a result" (Haaretz, October 22, 2002).

5. Describing and commenting on Rabbis Shapira and Elitzur's Torat ha-Melekh [The King's Teachings], a vade mecum for ostensibly divinely approved slaying of Gentiles.
6. A list of about 7,000 Israelis could be found on the Internet when querying the letters "S H I T" (Self Hating Israeli Traitors), likely an Internet initiative of Kahana Chai, a small, extremist anti-Arab chauvinist group (http://www.masada2000.org/list).
7. "The prohibition 'Thou Shalt Not Murder'" applies only "to a Jew who kills a Jew," write Rabbis Yitzhak Shapira and Yosef Elitzur of the West Bank settlement of Yitzhar. Non-Jews are "uncompassionate by nature" and attacks on them "curb their evil inclination," while the babies and children of Israel's enemies may be killed since "it is clear that they will grow to harm us" (Estrin, 2010, p. 45). These are the sentiments of a very small minority of Israeli Jews. But the fact that they exist at all is disconcerting, to say the least.
8. Under the proposed ordinance, leaders of such organizations are liable for a penalty of up to ten years' imprisonment, and officials charged with maintaining the rule of law in Israel will receive tools to combat persons who cause incitement and insurrection against the State of Israel and to combat those who seek to impair the sovereignty of the state.
9. Spirited advocacy of HR appears to weaken public support for the principle. In the 2008 Democracy Survey, as in past years, participants were asked for their perspectives on the country's institutions. Public trust in the Supreme Court showed a decline of 12 percentage points; 49% trusted the Court that year compared to 61% the previous year (Israel Democracy Institute annual report, 2009).
10. For example, the September 2007 order of the High Court of Justice directing the defense establishment to consider "within a reasonable amount of time" a fairer route for the separation fence, which sits on land taken from the village of Bil'in, for the benefit of the settlement of Modi'in Ilit drew an inadequate response. At the end of 2008, Supreme Court President Dorit Beinisch declared the chosen alternative noncompliant with the court ruling and ordered the state to dismantle the fence "without further delay." In December 2009, the IDF spokesman declared, "It is the intention of the defense establishment to begin erecting the amended route of the fence right at the beginning of 2010" (Haaretz, December 9, 2009).
11. Oron, Assaf, "Israeli government criminalizes its Arab citizens leaders in Israel: The only democracy in the Middle East," quoting from a letter sent on Sunday to the Adalah Arab rights group and written at the behest of Attorney General Menachem Mazuz, by SBC head Yuval Diskin (May 14, 2010).
12. Uneven treatment of demonstrators in East Jerusalem included the arrest of civil rights activist Hagai El Had, Director of the Association of Civil Rights in Israel (equivalent to the U.S. American Civil Liberties Union) and required the intervention of the Supreme Court to allow the demonstrations in the predominantly Arab neighborhood of Sheikh Jarrah.

13. The Haaretz report provides insight into both the thinking and the mindset of Israeli officials at the time. "This is a time of war, and every [negative] incident harms the people's morale. This was not a sentence in a right-wing journal, but rather a statement by an Israel Police representative during Operation Cast Lead seeking to persuade the Tel Aviv District Court to block anti-war protesters from the city. On the other hand, President Shimon Peres accepted the recommendation by former justice minister Daniel Friedmann to pardon 59 citizens who committed criminal offenses during protests against the Gaza disengagement in August 2005. The president stated that the pardons were being granted out of an understanding for the young people's protests, and awareness that this was an 'unusual, historic event.'"
14. The suspects were charged and later released on bail on condition that they not talk to other women in the movement for an entire month (Reich, 2009).
15. "Discrimination between Israelis and Palestinians is pervasive in all Israeli policies, be it the criminal justice system or the allocation of land and water. There is little accountability, whether on the individual or the collective level; from the soldier standing at the checkpoint to the highest levels of the army and government it is extremely rare for anyone to be accountable for harming Palestinians" (Btselem, 2009, p. 1).
16. The report's 300 pages reveal a steady official channeling of services and maintenance funds to these outposts, even in the absence of government building permission. Prime Minister Sharon vowed to dismantle the outposts. At a cabinet meeting a ministerial committee was appointed to study the report, but at the time of this writing, no significant action has been taken to evacuate settlements. (For a summary of the report see http://www.mideastweb.org/sassonreport.htm.)
17. Issued by the High Court of Justice in 2005. The state responded that it was determining its priorities for the demolition of the outpost. A new reminder was given in 2009 ordering the Defense Ministry to respond by May 1, 2010, when it intended to raze the houses. The homes at Hayovel were built on private Palestinian land, near the settlement of Eli. Among the structures were the houses of two soldiers killed in the second Lebanon and Gaza wars.

REFERENCES

Adler, E., & Crawford, B. (Eds.). (1990). *Progress in post-war international relations*. New York: Columbia University Press.

Amnesty International (UK). (2008). *We are all born free*. Tel Aviv: Kinneret, Zmora-Bitan Dvir (in Hebrew).

Association of Civil Rights in Israel. (2009, May). *The state of human rights in East Jerusalem—Facts and figures*. Jerusalem: Author.

Bar-Tal, D. (2007). *Living with the conflict: Socio-psychological analysis of the Israeli-Jewish society*. Jerusalem: Carmel (in Hebrew).

Bar-Tal, D., Magal, T., & Halperin, E. (2009). The paradox of security views in Israel: Socio-psychological explanation. In G. Scheffer & O. Barak (Eds.), *Existential threats and civil security relations* (pp. 219–247). Lanham, MD: Lexington Books.

Bar-Tal, D., & Teichman, Y. (2005). *Stereotypes and prejudice in conflict: Representations of Arabs in Israeli Jewish society.* Cambridge: Cambridge University Press.

Barzilai, G., Yuchtman-Yaar, E., & Segal, Z. (1994). *The Israeli Supreme Court and public opinion.* Tel Aviv: Papyrus, Tel Aviv University Press.

Boudreaux, R. (2009, March 25). Israeli army rabbis criticized for stance on Gaza assault: Some Israeli soldiers say military rabbis cast the offensive against Hamas rockets as a fight to expel non-Jews. *Los Angeles Times*, p. 7.

Bovard, J. (2006). *Attention deficit democracy.* New York: Palgrave Macmillan.

B'tselem, The Israeli Information Center for Human Rights in the Occupied Territories. (2007, May). *ABSOLUTE PROHIBITION—The torture and ill-treatment of Palestinian detainees.* Jerusalem: Author.

Btselem, The Israeli Information Center for Human Rights in the Occupied Territories. (2009). *Human rights in the occupied territories: 2008 annual report.* Jerusalem: Author.

Donnelly, J. (2002). *Universal human rights in theory and practice.* Ithaca, NY: Cornell University Press.

Estrin, D. (2010, January 20). Rabbinic text or call to terror? *Jewish Daily Forward.*

Goldscheider, C. (2002). *Israel's changing society: Population, ethnicity and development.* Boulder, CO: Westview Press.

Gorny, Y. (1987). *Zionism and the Arabs 1882–1948: A study of ideology.* Oxford: Clarendon Press.

Haaretz. (2003, September 2). The official summation of the Or Commission Report. On-Line English Language Edition. The article can be found in its original Hebrew edition on the *Haaretz* Web site by publication date.

Halperin, E., & Bar-Tal, D. (2006). Education toward democracy in Israel: Its effect on youth and Israeli democracy. *Democracy and Security, 2,* 169–200.

Harel, A. (2009, November 1). Settler admits to murder, several bomb attacks. *Haaretz.* The article can be found in its original Hebrew edition on the *Haaretz* Web site by publication date.

Heiman, G. (2010, February 18). Israel must learn the international language of human rights. *Haaretz.* The article can be found in its original Hebrew edition on the *Haaretz* Web site by publication date.

Hever, S. (2005). *The settlements: Economic cost to Israel.* Bethlehem, West Bank: Alternative Information Center.

Hofnung, M. (1991). *Israel—security of the state and the rule of law 1948–1991.* Jerusalem: Nevo (in Hebrew).

Human Rights Watch. (2004). *Human Rights Watch world report 2003.* New York: Author.

Ilani, O. (2008, December 9). Poll: Most Israelis think human rights groups hostile to their country. *Haaretz.* The article can be found in its original Hebrew edition on the *Haaretz* Web site by publication date.

The Israel Democracy Institute. (2009). *The democracy index, 2008*. Jerusalem: Author.
Israel: The only democracy in the Middle East. (2010). Retrieved from http://theonlydemocracy.org
The Jerusalem Fund. (2008, September). Israel's Palestinian citizens (interview with Dr. As'ad Ghanem). *Jerusalem Fund Report*, p. 2.
Kampeas, R. (2010, March 29). Israel gags news of soldier turned journalist under arrest. *Jewish Telegraph Agency*, p. 1.
Kasher, A. (2010). A moral evaluation of the Gaza War: Operation Cast Lead. *Jerusalem Center for Public Affairs, 9*(18), 4.
Kaufman, E. (1993). War, occupation and effects on Israeli society. In E. Kaufman, S. Abed, & R. Rothstein (Eds.), *Democracy, peace and the Israeli/Palestinian conflict* (pp. 85–134). Boulder, CO: Lynne Rienner.
Kaufman, E. (2001). *Human rights in world politics*. Tel Aviv: Defense Ministry Publishing House (in Hebrew).
Kaufman, E., Abed, S., & Rothstein, R. (Eds.). (1993). *Democracy, peace and the Israeli/Palestinian conflict*. Boulder, CO: Lynne Rienner.
Kaufman, E., & Abu-Nimer, M. (2006). Bridging conflict transformation and human rights: Lessons from the Israeli-Palestinian peace process. In J. A. Mertus & J.W. Helsing (Eds.), *Human rights and conflict: Exploring the links between rights, law, and peacebuilding* (pp. 277–308). Washington, DC: United States Institute for Peace.
Kaufman, E., & Tsur, N. (1989, September–October). Torture in Israel? Walking a tightrope. *Present Tense*, 1989, 39–44.
Kretzmer, D. (1990). *The legal status of the Arabs in Israel*. Boulder, CO: Westview Press.
Kretzmer, D. (2002). *The occupation of justice: The Supreme Court of Israel and the occupied territories*. Albany: State University of New York Press.
Maoz, I., & McCauley, C. (2008). Threat, dehumanization, and support for retaliatory aggressive policies in asymmetric conflict. *Journal of Conflict Resolution, 52*(1), 93–116.
Negbi, M. (2004). *Coming apart—The unraveling of democracy in Israel*. Keter, Jerusalem: Keter (in Hebrew).
PM [Prime Minister Ehud Olmert]. (2008, December 10). Israeli Arabs have suffered discrimination. *The Jerusalem Post*. The article can be found in its original Hebrew edition on the *Jerusalem Post* Web site by publication date.
Polak, D. W. (2009, August 3). The Israeli Democracy Institute on its annual Democracy Index, 2009. *Haaretz*. The article can be found in its original Hebrew edition on the *Haaretz* Web site by publication date.
Print, M., Ugarte, C., Naval, C., & M, A. (2008). Moral and human rights education: The contribution of the United Nations. *Journal of Moral Education, 37*(1), 115–132.
Reich, D. (2009, May 3). No talking, dammit!: The Israeli police crackdown on the new profile women. *Counterpunch*. The article can be found in its original Hebrew edition on the *Haaretz* Web site by publication date.

Rosler, N., Bar-Tal, D., Sharvit, K., Halperin, E., & Raviv, A. (2009). 'Moral aspects of prolonged occupation: Implications for an occupying society. In S. Scuzzarello, C. Kinnvall, & K. Monroe (Eds.), *On behalf of others: The psychology of care in a global world* (pp. 211–232). New York: Oxford University Press.

Rouhana, N. (2010, June 5). A state for all its citizens. *Foreign Policy.*

Seidler-Feller, H. (2007). The withering of the Zionist dream. In *A rabbinic guide to 40 years of occupation* (p. 14). New York: Brit Tzedek v'Shalom [Alliance for Justice and Peace].

Shamir, M. (1990). Kach and the limits of political tolerance in Israel. In D. J. Elazar & S. Sandler (Eds.), *Israel's odd couple: The 1984 Knesset elections and the national unity government.* Detroit: Wayne State University Press.

Shamir, M., & Sagiv-Schifter, T. (2006). Conflict, identity, and tolerance: Israel in the Al-Aqsa intifada. *Political Psychology, 27*(4), 569–595.

Shapira, A. (1992). *Land and power: The Zionist resort to force, 1881–1948.* Oxford: Oxford University Press.

Sharon, R. (2009, November). The complete guide to killing non-Jews. *Ma'ariv.*

Shinar, O. (2010, submitted). *The ethos of the Israeli-Palestinian conflict as reflected by the judgments of the Israel Supreme Court 1948–2006.* PhD research proposal, Faculty of Social Sciences, Hebrew University of Jerusalem.

Shragai, N. (2009, May 27). Knesset okays initial bill to outlaw denial of "Jewish state." *Haaretz.* The article can be found in its original Hebrew edition on the *Haaretz* Web site by publication date.

Siach, I. (1970). *The seventh day: Soldiers talk about the Six Day War.* London: Deutsch.

Sikkuy, the Association for the Advancement of Civil Equality in Israel. *Human rights annual report 2009.* Retrieved from http://www.sikkuy.org.il/

Smooha, S. (1989). A typology of Jewish orientations toward the Arab minority in Israel. *Asian and African Studies, 13*(2–3), 155–182.

Smooha, S. (1990). Minority status in an ethnic democracy: The status of the Arab minority in Israel. *Ethnic and Racial Studies, 13*(3), 389–413.

Sprinzak, E. (1991). *The ascendance of Israel's radical right.* New York: Oxford University Press.

Sprinzak, E. (1999). *Brother against brother: Violence and extremism in Israeli politics from Altalena to the Rabin assassination.* New York: Free Press.

Sternhell, Z. (2008, October 13). Colonial Zionism. *Haaretz.* The article can be found in its original Hebrew edition on the *Haaretz* Web site by publication date.

U.S. Department of State. (2009, February 25). 2008 HR Report: Israel and the occupied territories. In *2008 Country reports on HR practices.* Washington, DC: Author.

Zertal, J., & Eldar, A. (2007). *Lord of the lands: The war over Israel's settlements in the occupied territories, 1967–2007.* New York: Nation Books.

CHAPTER 14

The Occupation as Represented in the Arts in Israel

Dan Urian

In 1970 the Haifa Municipal Theatre staged *Co-existence,* the first play by an Arab writer to be staged in a Hebrew theater. Written by Muhammed Watad and directed by Nola Chilton, it was received to great acclaim by its audiences. *Co-existence* was a dramatic adaptation of an Arab-Israeli dialogue featuring five characters, all played by Jewish actors. The play's title attests to Watad and Chilton's intent of conciliation—"co-existence" was the Israeli government's policy toward Israeli Arabs in seeking to reduce the sense of alienation felt by the Arab minority in the country. The Arab in *Co-existence* is portrayed as a nonthreatening, damaged figure. The dispossession from the land and the refugee problem are only hinted at—the Arab refugee's story in the play ends in his return to his home: a happy end not achieved by more than a million refugees. The play avoids engaging with "the Arabs in the territories" or with the moral, social, and political significance of the occupation. "Then we still didn't know," wrote the poet Dalia Pelach, "that the occupation would be permanent" (Nitzan, 2005, p. 162). The occupation would arrive at Chilton's theater in 2004, in *Winter in Kalandia,* when Chilton directed a work documenting the Kalandia checkpoint (a crossing point between 'e-Raam and Jerusalem, and Ramallah) as a play about the strife between the conquerors and their subjects—dramatizing the impossible situation in which the soldiers find themselves as representatives of the conquerors and the humiliation and suffering of the Palestinians as subjects of the occupation (Figure 14.1).

Co-existence and *Winter in Kalandia* represent two stages in the repertoire of the arts in Israel—a repertoire that began by ignoring the occupation, by relating to the occupied territories as a deposit for a future political arrangement, and even as a model of an "enlightened occupation," and leading to the recognition, from the 1980s, of the harsh and harmful reality, which has particularly intensified since the beginning of the new millennium. This chapter describes the intermediate stages between the two productions as a journey

FIGURE 14.1 Nola Chilton, based on Lia Nirgad's *Winter in Kalandia*. Director: Chilton, School of Theatre Arts, Kibbutz Seminary, 2004. From right to left: David Bilanka, Yafit Assulin, Ayal Salameh, Sharon Burstein, Philip Domarov, Naama Dotan.
Photo: Ayal Landsman

of awakening to an awareness of the occupation by the Israeli arts and their audiences (Urian, 1995, 1997).

The various ways of representing a conflict in the arts reveal certain similarities. This is particularly discernible in the social characteristics of the artists, their audiences, and the approach taken in the choice of genre. Israeli artists (writers, playwrights, script writers, creators in the plastic arts, and musicians), according to Lucien Goldmann's perception of artists, are *transindividuels*—representing the opinions of a particular group in Israeli society. Their world vision (*vision du monde*) and that of their group serves as a "collective consciousness" that mediates between the social reality and its representation in the arts (Goldmann, 1966, pp. 151–165). Just as it is possible to learn from Charles Dickens's novels about solutions to the problems of poverty in Victorian England, as proposed by certain enlightened members of the British bourgeoisie in the nineteenth century (Evans, 1981, pp. 42, 49), so too can Israeli artistic texts inform us about the approach of a secular and hegemonic social group toward various other groups. Moreover, the engaged artist not only has the role of "public emissary" (Eliraz, 1974, p. 15), but also that of an intellectual who evaluates and criticizes his own group (Bourdieu, 1992, pp. 461–472), and is able by artistic means to reveal the motives and interests behind its collective norms. Israeli artists are thus not only representatives of their group but also have the role of critics, whose works of art can illuminate the motives behind the collective agreement, and the exploitative and patronizing hegemonic group's attitude toward the "others," who are generally those groups that do not read literature and do not attend the theater, museum, or concert hall. Nonetheless, the criticism of the majority of artists is directed at acquiring and ensuring the reception readiness of their audiences, whose cooperation is vital.

The majority of the audiences of canonical culture in Israel are of Western descent and have an academic education (Katz & Gurevitch, 1973, pp. 102, 117, 120; Rahav & Weitz, 1985). A 1990 study found that the main characteristics of the theatergoers (Jewish only) relate to education, origin, and extent of religious belief. "The most active individuals from the point of frequency of theater-going are educated, traditional and secular native-born Israelis of western origin", while the group "with the highest level of non-attendance at the theater are Orthodox religious, less-educated and of eastern origin" (Katz et al., 2000, p. 239). There are no significant differences between theater audiences and those who attend "art" films, museums, and concerts: "The higher the level of education, the higher the consumption of cinema, theater, concerts, museums and participation in lectures" (Katz et al., 2000, p. 425). Similar conclusions were reached in a 1998 survey (*Bracha Report*), which determined that "The canonical activities considered to be western, such as classical music concerts, opera and theater, draw more audiences of western origin" (Hass, 1999, p. 112). Israelis relate to literature, theater, cinema, and museums as important platforms (ibid., p. 114) upon which to discuss social and political problems (Katz et al., 2000, p. 270), and the artistic texts are interpreted by these audiences as "a reflection" of the social and political reality (Shaked, 1991).

Both the artists of canonical culture and their audiences in other Western countries (e.g., France; Gourdon, 1982; Guy & Mironer, 1988) share characteristics similar to those found among Israeli artists and their audiences. There is also a similarity among the different cultures in regard to the "disillusionment" of the repertoire in representing a political problem. The beginning of this process lay in disregarding the situation. It continued via the "back door" of comic genres and sometimes also in topical adaptations of classic works. At a later stage works of a documentary nature appeared, offering a study of various problems and their "objective" representation, followed by realistic representations in which the audiences encountered political problems as a reality, direct and unmediated, frequently in combination with artistic and documentary photographs. In the Israeli theater, for example, playwrights and other practitioners chose at first to present the rift between Jews and Arabs through the "back door" of satire and then by means of documentary theatre. Only in the 1990s did they begin to employ realistic presentational means in melodrama, realistic plays, films and television drama.

The battle for Algeria, for example, which divided French society in the mid-twentieth century, was presented in 1961, one year before Algeria's declaration of independence, through the staging of Euripides's play *The Trojan Women*. As Jean Paul Sartre noted: "*Les Troyennes* by Euripides was performed during the Algerian war.... I was greatly struck by its success with an audience that was in favor of negotiation with the FLN" (Sartre, 1976, p. 313). *La Battaglia di Algeri* (*The Battle for Algeria*, 1966) directed by Gillo Pontecorvo, constitutes an additional stage in the process of exposing the dispute. The film is mainly (but not entirely) based on facts, a sort of "docudrama" of Algeria's war of independence. Its screening was banned in both France and Israel. It is possible that the Israeli censor was influenced by the fear of an analogy with the 1967 occupation. Several of the scenes in the film indeed correspond in the Israeli viewer's mind to scenes from the Israeli-Palestinian dispute. In 1972 the film *La Guerre d'Algerie* reached the movie theaters. It is a French documentary of what seem to be mostly old news films with additional commentary and music. Created by Yves Courriere and Philippe Monnier, with a commentary in English, the film is a balanced account of brutality, intensified by a blaring background of patriotic songs and frenzied chanting.

This process of disillusionment has been mostly accompanied by changes and "cracks" in the ideology of the artistic creators and their audiences. In Israel the artists and their audiences, particularly those of the high culture, are influenced by the secular Zionist ideology. The ideological component has a central place in the Hebrew artistic repertoire and finds its way into the majority of texts, leaving the artists themselves often unaware of the fact that they are activated by the Zionist discourse. Since the early 1980s, Israeli artists have introduced into their works the problem of the conflict with the Arabs, and the need for critical examination of the ideology that created the State of Israel, but they have also enabled the policy of occupation. Those issues that Nurit Gertz relates to writers and cinema artists also characterize artists in other fields "[who] obliged Israeli society to examine its Zionist narrative, to point out the contradictions that exist among themselves, between themselves and reality, and between the utopian pretensions of Zionism as a national doctrine based on universal humanistic moral foundations" (Gertz, 1995, pp. 11–12).

LONG SHOT (1967-1982)

From 1967 until the beginning of the 1980s, the occupation was a repressed subject in the arts. Many artists were still filled with the sense of achievement of the war. Among them were those who illustrated the military publications during the battles and afterward; the many victory albums that were published following the war featured artists such as Moshe Kastel, who created "montage" photographs of soldiers at the Western Wall with portraits of Yitzhak Rabin and Moshe Dayan (Sela, 2007, p. 16). One almost unique exception was Ruth Schloss, "who had reacted already in June 1967 with a series of ink drawings, representing the Palestinian refugees crossing Allenby Bridge" (Ofrat, 2007, p. 1). However, in 1967, and for many years afterward, the motif of the occupation in the arts was a "vanished question" (a term coined in 1907 by Yitzhak Epstein, an educator and researcher of the Hebrew language, to characterize the conflict with the Arabs; Epstein, 1907, pp. 193–206), and only a few on the fringes of the cultural system engaged with it.

Among the early works expressing opposition to the occupation, the play *Queen of Bathtub* (1970) by Hanoch Levin is prominent. It was actually staged for the mainstream by the Cameri Theatre. The play is "a satirical review in two parts about comrades in the shadow of the guns," and opens with a interview in which a group of Israeli youths give their "regional views on our relations with the Arabs" in which their replies lack content and are merely a string of conjunctions and conditionals (Levin, 1987, pp. 61–64). The avoidance of the "Arab question" and its repression in Israeli culture of the 1950s and 1960s, as attested to by the empty linguistic patterns of the youngsters, expanded to include the territories following the occupation. In this sense, the sketch "Samatocha" in the review was a change that influenced other playwrights and presented a prototype of the Arab image in Israeli playwriting. Samatocha works in a café in which he serves the Jews. He is the humiliated, exploited Arab, similar images of whom had appeared many times before, but mainly on the stage and the cinema screen. The sketch also deals with the security threat that arose following the Six Day War, with the increase in Palestinian terrorist activities. The Jews know that Samatocha did not plant bombs and is not a terrorist, and flatter themselves that they are not primitive folk who cannot distinguish between an Arab who plants bombs and one who does not, and in the end they let him go, for Samatocha needs to get back to the kitchen to wash the dishes. Already in this early sketch the economic exploitation of the Arab is interwoven with the fear of his violent reaction.

The sketch, like many other artistic texts, was derived from the failure of the public debate on the occupation. The critics and artists, including playwrights and scriptwriters, condemn the disgraceful exploitation of the Arab work force from the occupied territories. The need for a solution to the human problem predated (and prevented) recognition of the national character of the dispute. Research revealing that the national factors—the dispute over land and the situation of the refugee camps—constituted the more important reasons for the Palestinian uprising did not alter the representation of the problem in the arts (Shalev, 1990). The Israeli playwrights, film-makers, writers, and other artists encountered Palestinians in cafes, in restaurants, and at building sites. These artists, however, chose to engage with the "aesthetic" injustice that bothered them and their Jewish target audience, rather than with the national conflict, despite the research and theatrical works such as *The Ninth Wave* (1990) by the Arab playwright Riad Massarweh, a play in which the manual workers who can be found daily in "Slave Square" in Haifa are indeed depicted as exploited, derided, and restricted to manual labor, but whose main focus is on the Palestinian desire for a national identity.

Queen of Bathtub aroused criticism and even controversy, which apparently expressed the fear of a divide in the Jewish-Zionist consensus regarding the Arab question, articulated in public, in a "holy" place in terms of Israeli culture—the public theater. Among the critics was Moshe Dayan, then Minister of Defense, who was convinced that the play reflected the disconnection of its creators from reality, encouraged negative processes, and depicted the State of Israel as "one big stinking cesspool in which they are attempting to suppress the Arabs" (Dayan, 1970, p. 12). Dayan's reaction contributed to the closing of the play.

Public debate in the Israeli theater until the beginning of the 1990s was limited by censorship laws and is restricted even today, in the twenty-first century, by the institutional censors (e.g., governmental public bodies, local authorities or those responsible for performance venues, prize-awarding committees, repertoire committees, etc.), and particularly by censorship activity among the audiences for these plays. Plays such as *Queen of Bathtub* were taken off the stage following pressure by the audiences, writers, and journalists. Yona Hadari-Rammage emphasizes that "whoever 'took off' these plays were in the majority. Not the minority. All attempts to question the Zionist vision, to express reservations and disappointment with it were doomed [then] to failure" (Hadari-Rammage, 2002, p. 270). Nonetheless, the discourse on oppositional plays was particularly lively and received widespread publicity in the newspapers of the time, raising the question in the public sphere and possibly helping to create a fissure in the monolithic perspective.

From the beginning of the 1970s, and particularly in the 1980s and 1990s, the dispute between Jews and Arabs over the occupied territories expanded.

The Arab side—inhabitants of the territories, Arabs in the State of Israel, and the Palestinian diaspora—sees in the Jewish settlements a continuation of a policy that had started at the beginning of the Jewish settlement and whose purpose was to gain control over the entire Land of Israel (Mishal & Aharoni, 1989, p. 68). The discussion in the arts about the dispute over land had been restricted at first to the area of the Green Line (Israel's border prior to June 1967), involving individuals such as the group of artists who spent four months in 1972 in the valley that lies between Kibbutz Metzer and the Arab village Kafr Misr. These artists were influenced by their surroundings, the Arab village and the adjacent kibbutz, and expressed the feelings of the inhabitants of both, as well as initiating encounters and discussion between them. Micha Ullman, an Israeli sculptor, created within this framework the "Land Exchange"—two holes dug in the center of the kibbutz and of the Arab village, with the earth extracted from them being exchanged between the two places. This "co-existence" work was a symbolic alliance between these two neighbors, but it did not relate to the expropriation of lands that had begun in the occupied territories.

The territory conquered in the Six Day War and the establishment of the settlements appear for the first time in *The Governor of Jericho* (1975) by Yosef Mundi. This play brought together on stage the conquerors and the conquered and harshly condemned the degree of logic and justice obtaining in the occupation. More than anyone, the "new immigrant" Mundi (born in 1935 in Rumania, he immigrated to Israel at the age of sixteen) sensed the threat and danger inherent in the oppression and exploitation of the Arabs. The play is strewn with contentions by Israeli Jews such as "We are sitting on their land and claim that historically it is ours!" And the "dominant-separatist" ideologists' (Gorny, 1985, pp. 55–56) reply is, "So what, it's a wasteland here, the land belongs to whoever works it, makes it flourish; he who properly manages it is the lawful owner" (Mundi, 1975, p. 52). The play also gives expression to the Israeli fear of the Palestinian: "They hate us…and they have patience, those bastards" (ibid., p. 18). "I know what awaits me if I fall into their hands," says the governor of Jericho. "They will destroy us all. It will be a massacre, a horrendous massacre" (ibid., p. 25). The "uprooted" Jew, who feels himself a stranger in the new land (and who represents the playwright), encounters an Arab who promises him that he will send him back to where he had come from. "This land is part of me," says the nationalist Arab, "we don't want you here…it will take another year, two years, even five years. But I know that you will leave here…you are all strangers here, all of you!" (ibid., p. 51). Mundi was the first to present on stage a connection that was frequently to appear in the theater later on: that between Samatocha, the exploited and humiliated

Arab, and the terrorist Arab. A "transparent" Arab is employed as a cleaner in the headquarters of the governor of Jericho and also polishes the shoes of the officers. When a terrorist suspect is brought in for interrogation, the cleaner exits; both roles are played by the same actor, who also plays the role of an Arab who stabs a Jew. Samatocha, who had begun in Hanoch Levin's play as a servile and submissive dishwasher, becomes in Mundi's plays the terrorist lying in wait for the Jews at every corner. This duality of the Arab—exploited and threatening—was to be used from then on by other playwrights in creating the Arab image and would return in Hanoch Levin's *Murder* (1997).

There were very few discussions of the occupation in the arts prior to the first war in Lebanon, and most of these were indirect. *Eating* (1979) by Yaakov Shabtai, a modern adaptation of a biblical play, is outwardly a version of the story of the theft from Naboth's vineyard by Jezebel and Ahab. Many of the lines directed the audience to their contemporary reality. For example, Queen Jezebel says, "We can do whatever we want—as long as it's legal. And it will be legal...the law is the law as long as it suits us." The writer Aharon Megged, who saw the play, related its moral to the Jewish settlement in the territories, which he perceived as a chapter in the "forced dispossession, by the ruling powers, against the law, against the 'social conventions' accepted by the civilized world...a case of expropriation of lands that belong to the Arabs...in order to settle Jews upon them; this is a paraphrase, almost complete, of Naboth's vineyard'" (Megged, 1979, p. 8).

The refugee issue, the most difficult issue of all, which began in the War of Independence and intensified with the Six Day War, has been dealt with by very few artists, writers, and theater people. Few of them have engaged with the problem of the dispossessed dispossessing others of their land, of the homeless making others inhabitants of refugee camps, and of the Palestinian refugees creating one of the largest groups of refugees in the world. One exception is S. Yizhar [Yizhar Smilansky]. Yizhar revealed in the story "Khirbet Kizha" (1949) how "we have made them exiles" (Yizhar, 1989, p. 75), and he described the systematic expulsion of the Arab villagers from their homes and their unfeeling dispatch, like a herd of cattle, across the border. Several of the lines in his story continued to find an echo in Hebrew literature and Israeli culture for many years afterward. Yizhar's agonizing is mainly derived from the fact that it was the refugees themselves who caused the dispossession of others: "What has actually happened here today? We Jews have cast others into exile" (ibid.). Yizhar would return to the same subject in 1992 in connection with the expropriation of land in the occupied territories. In a biblical prophetic style he agonized over "every pulling out of the land from beneath the feet of those that inhabit it—here come the days" (Yizhar, 1992a, p. 24), and concerning the refugees who constituted the "determining question" he would say, "They were not blotted out into the night. The expulsion solved nothing" (Yizhar, 1992b, p. 25). A television version of *Khirbet Kizha* (1978), directed by Ram Levy, was the first Israeli drama to introduce to the Israeli public the problem of the Arab refugees and their expulsion. The adaptation for television of the story by Yizhar brought the spectator closer to the Arabs, who until then had, in cinema, been distanced and slain en masse. The Hebrew fighters in the film encounter Arabs, first as long-distance targets for their guns, and then they draw closer to the inhabitants of an Arab village that they conquer. Toward the end, before the expulsion of those who will become refugees, the spectator sees close-up shots of faces or legs struggling in puddles, climbing with difficulty onto the truck that will take them away. The television version aroused angry reactions. These attested to the sensitivity of the establishment and of some sectors of the Jewish society to the public exposure of the Jewish expulsion of the Arabs in 1948, which was repeated in the Six Day War.

MEDIUM SHOT (1982-1995)

The war in Lebanon, initially termed a "war of choice" and later a "cheating war," was a military operation that aroused immense controversy in Israel. The war divided the national consensus and created an opposition movement during years that saw both Israeli soldiers and many Palestinians fall victim. This opposition intensified after the massacre carried out by the Christian phalanges forces in the Sabra and Shatilla refugee camps, which was revealed by the committee investigating the incident. Following these events, some sectors of the Jewish public became increasingly aware that there could be no solution to the dispute, except through an accord with the Palestinians, and opinions on the cost of this solution were greatly divided. The war in Lebanon and the *intifada*, as well as the entry of the Kach far-right political party into the Knesset, led to a strong and consolidated artistic opposition to the right-wing policy. Theater, cinema, literature, art, music, rock music, and folk culture, like soldiers' anti-war songs, in the 1980s and 1990s protested the policy of force and demanded a compromise with the Palestinians.

The Palestinians became part of the daily reality of violent conflict and talk of peace, which brought them ever closer to the world of the Israelis. The Arab question, which was becoming the "Palestinian question," also created among the Israeli Jews a sense of frustration and ethnocentric reactions. The Palestinian was perceived not only as someone who had been victimized by both national and economic injustice, but also sometimes as someone who had coerced young Israelis into missions that contradicted their conscience and their humanistic education. The increase in hostile activities between Israelis and Palestinians strengthened in a large part of the Jewish population the feeling that had existed earlier, a combination of hostility, hatred, and fear of the Palestinians. Benyamini's (1990) study of the Arab image among Jewish-Israeli youth reveals the changes that had taken place following the first *intifada*. Benyamini compared the image of the Israeli Arab and that of the Palestinian Arab between 1984 and 1990. In 1984 those questioned saw almost no important differences between them, while after three years of the *intifada*, "The negative viewpoint perceives the Palestinian Arabs more intensively as a threat." Regarding the image of the Arab inhabitants of the territories, the study found an increase in the perception of such characteristics as treachery, extremism, and brutality. Toward the Israeli Arabs too "the 'negative' attitude is increasing and they have been perceived since the *intifada* as people who cannot be trusted to show loyalty, albeit with a more positive image than that of the Palestinian and seemingly also less frightening" (Benyamini, 1990, p. 7).

Three waves of protest nourished many works by Israeli artists in the 1980s: protest against the war in Lebanon; protest against a wave of racism by Jewish citizens of Israel, and in particular against Meir Kahane and his party, Kach; and protest against the continued occupation that was intensified with the *intifada*. The war in Lebanon was the subject of many works of art, all of which objected to it and demanded its end. David Riv, consistent in his criticism of Israel's policy toward the Palestinians, presented a collaborative exhibition with Gaby Klezmer featuring the colors of the Israeli and Palestinian flags, which elicited a scandalized reaction. The desire for protest and for dialogue with the Arabs led several Jewish artists to mount a collaborative exhibition with Palestinian artists, two of which were held under the titles "Israel and Palestinian Artists against the Occupation" and "Stop the Occupation." The integration of several Palestinian artists into the mainstream culture led to an ironic tension between the differences in the viewpoints of the two cultures regarding the same symbols and icons. Asim Abu Shakra, who painted pictures of "a *tsabar* in a flowerpot," led Tali Tamir to ask: "Can an Arab be a *tsabar*?" (Manor, 1997, pp. 26–27). (A *tsabar* is a cactus plant, whose fruit is used to refer to a native-born Israeli as being prickly on the outside and sweet inside.) In regard to the Palestinian, the *tsabar* bush is used by the farmer to mark the borders of his plot; *tsabar* in Arabic [*sabach*] means "thicket," which also sounds like "patience" and "perseverance." These are meanings that relate to another Arabic word that has earned a central place in the Jewish-Israeli–Palestinian conflict: *tsumud*, meaning "to endure" or "to hold fast"—that is, to stay close to the land and prevent its expropriation.

The *intifada* was perceived by Israeli artists as a particularly severe political and moral problem, causing existential fear. Arnon Ben-David, who combined in one of his works the words "Israel," "P.L.O.," and "God," and below these the name of God inscribed three times, while identifying with the Palestinian struggle, also feared for his fate as a Jew: "The *intifada* has greatly affected me, because I have begun to fear for my physical wholeness, for my ability to exist in this environment" (Riv, 1990, p. 14). Several artists' works deal with the weakening of the Zionist ethos by the policy of force toward the Arabs. These included the *kefiyot* of Tsibi Geva, whose adoption of this Arab headwear by a Jewish-Israeli artist, according to Sarit Shapira, changed him from being a representative of the cultural majority to that of the cultural minority and reinforced the approach to it as a nation possessing its own identity (Shapira, 1993, p. 59). Similarly, the composer Arik Shapira protested the injustice done to the Palestinians, and the war forced upon him, and played the song "Play, Play on the Dreams," by Shaul Tchernikovsky, translated into Arabic and sung by an Arab female singer who sang it in Arabic style, with oriental trills (Shapira, 1988, p. 21).

Like the other arts, the literature and poetry of the 1980s expressed protest against the war in Lebanon, against Kahanaism, and against the *intifada*. Several of the writers who recognized the Palestinians as possessing a national identity also chose them as a subject for their works. The Israeli-Arab and the Palestinian from the territories were no longer secondary characters but equal in their development to the Jewish characters, and also were main characters in several of the novels written during this period. *Good Arab* (1984) by Yoram Kaniuk (written under the pseudonym Yosef Sherara) is the story told in the first person of an Arab who lives in two worlds, the Israeli and the Palestinian, and fails to settle in either. *Martyr* (1989) by Avi Valentine and *Intifada Legends* (1989) by Dror Green chose Palestinian storytellers against the background of the *intifada*. Ittamar Levy (1991) told of the uprising in *Letters of the Sun and Letters of the Moon*, as narrated by a Palestinian boy.

Three of David Grossman's books are about the trend toward change regarding the Arabs, in particular against the occupation. They are *Smile of the Lamb* (1983), *The Yellow Time* (1987), and *Present Absentees* (1992). Only *Smile of the Lamb* is fiction; the other two are a journalist's reports. The relationship between fiction and real materials seems to indicate the desire to release the Arab from his instrumental role in Hebrew culture, characterized by Mordechai Shalev as a "literary solution" to the distress of the Jewish writer (Shalev, 1970, pp. 50–51), and to enable him to represent his problems by himself. Initially, Grossman attempted to reach a dialogue with the Palestinian in the territories through fiction, by means of the character of Khilmi in *Smile of the Lamb*—a character who is an exception to Palestinian society, who lives outside its area and only thus is able to have contact with the Israeli occupiers. *The Yellow Time* offers a collection of reports written during Grossman's wanderings in the West Bank (Grossman speaks Arabic). This document aspires to convince the reader of his need, as a Jew, to give up the Israeli occupation, and to this end it describes in detail the harm done to both the conquerors and the Palestinians. It is the first text in Hebrew to focus on the subject of the Palestinian national identity—not an exceptional Palestinian character from fiction with whom the Israelis can make contact, but a variety of characters who represent an entire society under foreign domination.

Ella Alterman's dramatization of Grossman's book in 1987 encountered public objections, and the senior education officer banned its performance in the military. This adaptation for the theater, more than anything, emphasized for Israelis the impossibility of escaping from the problem presented by the refugees' dreams—the longing of a child in the Dehaishe refugee camp for Jaffa, which he has never seen, the story of a teenage girl from the same camp about "the beauty of Lod," and the threat-promise of an old Arab refugee woman: "We shall always remain. Like a curse." The play deals with the occupation and its effects: the humiliation, dependency, exploitation, and fear that turn the Palestinians into "living dead" but also give them an identity: "We have an identity, and we didn't have one before; and we are learning many things from you." The Israeli is presented in a political allegory about a great king "who sits in his palace with many guards around him and he doesn't sleep at night, for he knows that at any moment someone will come to seize his crown." "What was taken by force will be returned by force," preaches the nursemaid to the children in her care. The intellectual Arab predicts: "If you leave here there will immediately be great slaughter...first they will kill those who had links with Israel...and those suspected of collaboration...and afterward half the population will be killed, they will start to kill one another in a struggle for control." In *Present Absentees* Grossman returned to the borders of the Green Line, to the Israeli Arabs whose process of Palestinization and objection to the occupation were in permanent conflict with their identity as citizens of the State of Israel.

The Israeli cinema of the 1980s turned the dispute with the Palestinians into a central theme and the Arab or Palestinian into a legitimate and even preferred figure, replacing a distant and derided enemy from the cinema of earlier decades with a freedom fighter. Ella Shohat described this process, as a chapter title in her book, as a "Palestinian wave in the new Israeli cinema" (Shohat, 1991, pp. 237–270). Most of the films belonging to the "Palestinian wave" deal with the war in Lebanon and the *intifada*. Several of them examine the dispute with the Palestinians from the viewpoint of the damage done to the occupiers by the occupation—in particular Uri Barabash's film *One of Ours* (1989). In contrast, other films adopt the Arab or Palestinian perspective. In *Fictitious Marriage* (1988) by Haim Buzaglo, a Jew encounters the Israeli reality as one of a group of Palestinian building workers, and the magic that Khilmi works on the Israelis in *The Smile of the Lamb* (1986), by Shimon Dotan, relocates the focus of the film to the Palestinian. In many films of the 1980s the Palestinian appears as an idealist, exuding vitality (including sexual vitality), surpassing in virtue the Jewish protagonist with whom he is contrasted or to whom he is compared. The tendency of several filmmakers to humanize the Arab and to side with his rights, and even to legitimize the struggles of such organizations as the Palestine Liberation Organization (PLO), led them at times to a degree of idealization, described by Yehuda (Judd) Ne'eman ironically as "A good Arab is an Arab in a movie" (Ne'eman, 1991, p. 8).

On the contradiction between the desire for conciliation and the understanding of the extra-cinematic reality as rejecting any possibility of a "positive" solution, one can learn from the endings of the films, which are in the main pessimistic, as are the endings of most of the novels and all of the theater productions. Stories of love between a man and a woman from the two different nations always end in separation or in distancing, voluntary, exile (in *A Very Narrow Bridge* [1985] by Nissim Dayan). Friendships between Arabs and Jews are possible in prison, in *Behind the Bars* (1984) by Uri Barabash, but these too have no chance to last. A friendship established in *Cup Final* (1991), by Eran Riklis, between captors, this time Palestinians, and their prisoners—an Israeli officer and a soldier—ends in the killing of the Palestinians. Even films that feature some degree of closeness between the two nations, such as *The Smile of the Lamb*, "solve" the problem with death as the end. Several of the films borrow an image from the writer Sami Michael: "You've certainly seen more than once two dogs trapped in copulation in the street, writhing and howling and unable to break away from one another's agony, and pulling in opposite directions. These are the Jews and the Arabs caught in their shitty trap" (Michael, 1977, p. 237). In *Night Movie* (1986) by Gur Heller, a reserve duty soldier and a Palestinian youth are handcuffed together against their will, illustrating this coercive bond. When they succeed in ridding themselves of the handcuffs, and—even more significantly—also of their mutual distrust, the youth is shot to death by mistake and this film too ends in tragedy.

The Israeli theater of the 1980s and 1990s focuses on the Palestinian question. More than 100 theatrical texts, directly or indirectly engaging with this subject, were staged during these years. One innovation was that some of them, including *The Palestinian Girl* (1985) and *The Jerusalem Syndrome* (1987), both by Yehoshua Sobol, were staged by the mainstream theaters.

Theaters occasionally stage "key" plays that accelerate the changes that occur in the social consensus and political thinking, among them *The Palestinian Girl* (1985) presented at the Haifa Municipal Theatre, and which was among the first plays to express, following the war in Lebanon, Israeli-Jews' recognition of the Palestinian national identity. The play's title itself—*The Palestinian Girl*—was an innovation in the very mention of the name of the "other"— "Palestinian"—which at that time was still forbidden by law. *The Palestinian Girl* presented for the first time a love story between a Jewish man and an Arab woman on a mainstream stage. Yehoshua Sobol, the playwright, used an indirect strategy of softening the play's "radical" position by organizing the narrative as a play-within-a-play. The play depicts the work of a camera team filming a personal story for television. The script is written by a Palestinian woman called Samira, and in the course of the work a love story develops between her and the Jewish actor. The film being shot in the play is based on the story of an Arab female student called Magda, and she too is in love with a Jewish man. In the very choice of her name, which is a Europeanized form of the Arabic name Majda, Sobol characterized the figure and legitimized her romance with a Jew. The playwright still engaged cautiously with the issue of dispossession. The play opens with a play by Arab students from the university's theater department, who stage the fable of the sheep and the wolf at an Independence Day party. The Arab is the sheep and the Jew is the wolf that plots against him and draws him away from the spring from which his forefathers had drunk. The wolf threatens to punish the sheep and devour him, and the "audience of students," mainly Jewish, cannot bear the provocation and react by frenziedly hitting the "actors." The reception of such "key" plays, and particularly the accompanying arguments in the newspapers, usually turned into a public debate. *The Palestinian Girl* aroused great interest and heated discussion. Most of the critics showed interest in the structure of the play and its ideological message. Roni Pisker was critical of it and offered an explanation for the play's success with the audiences, interpreting it as serving and firmly establishing the beliefs and opinions of the Jewish-Israeli bourgeois audience:

> Sobol is a very successful playwright, because he is a faithful representative of the generation for which he writes...he has a need to be both conqueror and moral at the same time...and the audience of the repertory theatre is right when it hurries to see *The Palestinian Girl*...he enjoys seeing himself as the subject of an important and "cultural" event, without needing to...draw any conclusions. (Pisker, 1987, p. 38)

However, those same subscribers to the Haifa Municipal Theatre later rejected another play by Yehoshua Sobol, *The Jerusalem Syndrome* (1987). They had difficulty recognizing the historical background and understanding its aesthetic characteristics. The main problem was that they were not yet willing to confront its ideological messages.

In *The Jerusalem Syndrome* the analogies between past, present, and near future are explicit: Jerusalem is a city under siege, surrounded by an exhausted and hungry contemporary army. The soldiers encounter a group of mentally ill eccentrics, who are staging a play about the Great Rebellion and the destruction of the Second Temple under the guidance of a professor who is their mad leader. The playwright threatens the audience with additional destruction, while outside the theater the Palestinian uprising is triggered with the first *intifada*.

The Jerusalem Syndrome was a dystopic vision in content and also in its theatrical realization. Sobol chose to write a postmodern work featuring rapid transitions between different levels of reality: scenes from the professor's play from the time of the Second Temple, contrasting near-future scenes from the mad world of the insane and the "sane" world of other figures. The links between the scenes in the play are associative "clips," and the play is composed of fifty-three "transformations" rather than of acts and scenes. The scenes change in unceasing transformation like transitions in a dream, like associations arising from the subconscious. In the play staged by the Haifa Municipal Theatre, for each transformation the actors erupted from below stage, from the trapdoors, onto the stage floor before the spectators' eyes. The stage itself, designed by Adrian Wax, was a raked area, resembling a mirror, which served as a system of mirrors for the actors and audience. By means of the stage design, the play was doubled and reflected in constantly changing reflections of illusion and reality. For the actors, the stage floor was a precarious surface, and the spectators found themselves confronting a theatrical legitimacy that constantly shattered and was rebuilt. This situation of destruction and devastation was also expressed in the costumes—the gray-greenish clothes of the insane were covered in dust. The lighting design too expressed these transitions, as it moved from the destruction of the Second Temple, emphasizing the colorful background featuring the word *Jerusalem*, to the illusionary scenes, seen behind semitransparent screens, and to scenes of the near-future destruction, lit in clear, cold light, sweeping and revealing. Although *The Jerusalem Syndrome* was a failure with audiences, the play did have a discernible influence. It aroused immense controversy that reached as far as the Israeli Knesset and led to a government debate. The performances were accompanied by demonstrations by right-wing groups. Although the objectors had not read the play, which had been printed prior to its opening night, and although most of them had not seen the play, they understood the dystopian vision that the playwright was presenting.

Most of the plays opposing the occupation continue to be staged on the fringes, on small stages or at the Acre Festival for Alternative Theatre. Young artists who had served in the army during the war in Lebanon gave expression to their memories in their plays. Some of them continued to deal with the Palestinian question following the *intifada*. Increasing involvement of Israeli-Arab actors and directors as well as Israeli-Arab playwrights characterizes this period as part of the process in which the Israeli Arab and the Palestinian from the territories speak out on the Israeli stage, either in their own language or in the language of the majority, and present their problems. The uprising has infiltrated into children's theater too—in George Ibrahim's version of *The Emperor's New Clothes* (1993), adapted and directed by Salim Dao, staged in Hebrew and Arabic. This is a political play directed also at the children's parents (Jews and Arabs). The uprising by citizens of the naked emperor's kingdom is represented as an *intifada*. In order to remove all doubt, the writers added the occupied territories to the borders of the kingdom of that same foolish, capricious, and tyrannical emperor. The Israeli-Arab actors present in Hebrew to a Jewish audience a Palestinian fable for children and adults on the uprising of the oppressed against a stupid oppressor, while representatives of the actual oppressed are on the stage and those of the oppressors are in the auditorium. The play ends in an addition by the director that offers a sort of prophetic reference by the Israeli Arab to the Palestinian in the territories and the *intifada*. Dao is not optimistic and fears for the future of the Palestinians, who cannot agree among themselves when they finally achieve independence. Thus, at the end of the play, after the emperor is deposed, pandemonium ensues, and everyone proposes himself as the next ruler, they quarrel, hit each other and fall over on the stage. A policeman enters, shoots into the air and stands aside. The Minister of Communications enters, followed by the emperor, who tramples over everyone, raises his scepter, and announces: "A New Decree!!!"

The plays that in earlier periods had portrayed the Israeli Arab or the Palestinian satirically, in collages or comedy, from the 1980s on also began to portray Arab characters in a style tending toward realism. This may be because the problems were less suppressed and, at least in the theater, were presented as a reality that must be confronted. The approach to design, too, changed. In many plays of the 1970s that feature an Arab character, his place was in a closed, private space. Any connection with the Arab was concealed and restricted to an indoor setting and was not exposed in public places. The plays of the 1980s and 1990s, in contrast, brought together Jews and Arabs on stages featuring public places, including a hospital, television studio, café, holiday resort, and even the Holocaust Museum. In those plays in which the characters were Palestinian they still continued, however, to be concealed in an indoor setting or in rooms within a building. The occupation also reached the stage indirectly, as in *Les Troyennes* by Euripides, in its adaptation by Jean Paul Sartre (1983), in which the analogy was visual, achieved through the stage design by Angelica Edingen, who created a set that evoked associations of a concentration camp with a Palestinian refugee camp and incorporated a glass cell in which slumbered Athena, the goddess of wisdom and war. The designer reminded the Israeli spectator of Adolf Eichmann's glass cell during his trial in Jerusalem and hinted at what awaits a nation that oppresses another nation.

Prophecies and warnings by playwrights of outbreaks of violence were staged from the mid-1980s on. Their understanding of the dangers of the occupation was more accurate than that of the politicians and the experts in Arab affairs. Sobol presented in *The Palestinian Girl* two extremist characters that embodied an Israeli nightmare: a Jew and a Muslim, both of whom have become religious extremists and terrorists. Kobi Niv brought together in *Crembo in Enemy Territory* (1986) two religious extremists, a Jew and a Shi'ite. Niv's comic-strip comedy attached tails to them with a fuse that, if lit, would turn them both into living bombs. Hillel Mittelpunkt turned to a young audience to whom he uncompromisingly presented the dispute with the Palestinians via two rock operas: *Mammy* (1986), which predicts the *intifada*, and *Samara* (1992), in which the *intifada* is already an Israeli nightmare. The Palestinian, who in his earlier plays was only mentioned as an object of fear or was heard responding on tape to interrogation under torture, in *Mammy* becomes a chorus of eight rapists. In *Samara*, the ghost of a Palestinian woman killed in the *intifada* enters as a "dybbuk" into an Israeli reserve soldier, a Palestinian dybbuk intended to provide an interesting ironic tension to those spectators who recalled *The Dybbuk* by S. An-Sky (1922), which gave birth to the Hebrew theater.

Mammy was an immense popular success and its songs were played frequently, becoming part of the popular culture (it was reprised in 2002 during the second *intifada*). The rock opera presented the distress and desire for revenge of the Palestinians as an essential factor in the uprising. Mammy is raped by "seven oppressed/seven Palestinians," to the accompaniment of string instruments and the gentle rock music of Yossi Mar-Haim and Ehud Banai, as a counterpoint to the cruelty of the scene that helps to intensify it: "Twenty years of occupation/we won't wait any longer/with an erection and semen we shall save Palestine." This is violence that cannot be stopped—not by Mammy's pleading, not by the kinship of brotherhood between Ishmael and Isaac, and not by the brotherhood of the "screwed" that exists between the Palestinian camp and the Mizrachi Jews of the development town from which she comes; nothing can help. The Palestinians are fixed in their determination to redeem their honor: "You expelled our children/in the name of democracy/stole our fields/in the name of geography/closed the schools/in the name of pedagogy/called us 'Nazis' and 'cockroaches'/from demagoguery/we shall fuck you ya Mammy, ya Mammy/from ideology."

Three of the plays staged several months before the outbreak of the first *intifada* (December 1987) predict it: *The Yellow Time*, adapted from David Grossman's book (August 1987), *Hamdu and Son* by Yitzhak Buton (July 1987), and *Gazans* by Motti Baharav (October 1987). The three no longer employ indirect techniques but are direct, fairly realistic depictions of the dangerous reality. Two of the plays end in the Arab joining the uprising against the Israeli regime. In *Hamdu and Son*, three cleaners working in a suburb of a Hebrew city are exploited and humiliated by anyone in uniform—"Write down that they squashed your father like a worm." Buton predicted the rebellion by the young Palestinians, children of the occupation, against the norms and values of their parents. The father in the play attempts to satisfy the Israeli ruling powers and requests a permit to return to his home, which has been sealed up, while his son wants "to destroy them." In *Gazans*, staged two months before the outbreak of the first *intifada*, Baharav warns of a great explosion. Gazan society, as Baharav depicts it, is primitive and violent, and the custom of obligatory blood vengeance is widespread. The characters in the play are Gazans who live in Tel Aviv and scrape a living from kitchen and cleaning work. They are exploited and even subjected to humiliating violence. In one scene the border police arrest several of them, beat them, and force them to drop their pants. It was this violence and distress, according to Baharav, that would lead to an uprising. "We shall slaughter you...one by one," one of the Gazans promises the border police. At the end of the play, several of them sing to a recording by the Egyptian singer Um Kultuum and swear not to forget the "holy land"; and, while preparing a bomb, they blow up. Plays by Arab playwrights too accompanied the first *intifada*. *Jabbar's Head* by Sa'ad Allah Vanus was adapted by Adnan Trabshe and Fuad Awad and directed by Awad (1989). The play won first prize at the Acre Festival for Alternative Theatre in 1989. It is doubtful whether those who awarded the prize understood all the topical allusions of the adaptation, allusions that demanded action in the face of the political situation. The play offered its audiences complete identification with the uprising. The final song appealed to the "sleeping" Israeli Arabs not to ignore the bitter fate of others, despite their own good life.

The *intifada* altered viewpoints and images and created hopes and fears. The failure to suppress the uprising, its damage to Israel as a democratic state, and the fears for the education of young Israelis reinforced the standpoint of those who supported conciliation. Zeev Schiff and Ehud Ya'ari are convinced that the *intifada* undermined the self-confidence of Israeli society, and "fears repressed for years were re-awoken" (Schiff & Ya'ari, 1990, p. 325). These fears intensified when the dispute reached the stage that Baruch Kimmerling characterized as "individual but also total conflict," in which "each individual member of the two communities potentially carries the dispute with him wherever he goes, whether as the injurer or the injured" (Kimmerling, 1993, p. 11). Among the Israeli playwrights too, despite the desire for conciliation, the image of the Palestinian in the *intifada* includes threatening components.

Several of the plays staged from 1988 on engaged with the danger of distortion of the moral image of the young Israeli as a soldier in the occupied territories: *One of Ours* (1988) by Benny Barabash, *Ephraim Returns to the Army* (1989) by Yitzhak Laor, and especially *Deception* (1990) by Yitzhak Ben-Ner. Of the three, only the adaptation for the stage of the novel by Ben-Ner is an *"intifada text."* Barabash's and Laor's texts are "occupation texts" written before the *intifada* and staged after its outbreak. *One of Ours* is the story of an investigation into the circumstances of the death of an Arab prisoner suspected of the murder of a paratroop officer. The interrogator, who had previously served in the interrogated unit, is "one of ours," and his comrades expect him to acquit them, despite their having beaten up the prisoner in order to force him to confess, and then killed him. The Arab figure is not seen in the play; he is only heard on the tape that documented his final moments, for he is merely a catalyst for presenting a dilemma among the Jews regarding the cohesive power of comrades-in-arms. The staging of *Ephraim Returns to the Army* was banned in 1985 by the Council for Films and Plays, whose justifications are informative:

> The play distorts the truth...the soldiers in the play...do not hesitate to shoot at a demonstration by youths, women and children, and to kill a youth marching at the head of the demonstration...the interrogation of the Arabs is accompanied by beatings and torture...the events in the territories are represented as a national freedom movement. (The Council for Films and Plays, September 2, 1985, p. 2)

Staging of the play was finally permitted only in 1989, when the extratheatrical reality validated several of its harsh scenes. *Deception* (1990) was the first play in the Israeli theater to deal with the confrontation of the Israeli soldier with the *intifada*. Holly is a soldier hospitalized because of the stench that his body emanates. He has been sick since the outbreak of the uprising. He recounts his life on the platform of a sort of research institution while "flicking through" on a slide projector a "photo album" tracing the typical path of an Israeli child to adulthod: home, kindergarten, Chanuka, Purim, youth movement, army. The opening of the play with the album helps to create a connection with the audience, the majority of whom have similar pictures in their own albums. Ben-Ner aims at the recognition that Holly suffers from a stench syndrome that is not only his personal plight, but also a consequence of the actions and failures of the spectators present in the auditorium. It was the death of a Palestinian boy who had joined them, and mediated between the soldiers and the hostile Palestinian world, that had intensified the Israeli soldier's agony and led Holly to produce the stench: "Well, what, he was only a child and we too were only children. What?!" A main component of the text is fear. Fear lurks at every corner for the soldiers, fear of those inciting riot, their *keffiyot* hiding their faces, fear of stones and bottles being thrown, accompanied by the promises of the Palestinians: "We shall slaughter you. Not a single Jew will remain in Palestine!" Such words arouse violent reactions by the soldiers toward the Palestinians, who "shit on all the country."

Plays that were staged against the background of daily reports of the *intifada* were influenced by its intensification, and their reception was linked to the increasingly threatening image of Palestinian society. The knife as a theatrical prop frequently represented the violent side of that society. In *Masked* (1990) by Ilan Hatzor, set in a butcher's shop with a dirty wall stained with blood, an *intifada* activist stabs to death his brother, who had collaborated with the Israeli authorities. The connection between knife and Palestinian also appeared in Israeli satire. In *Hey Rimona* (1992) by Ilan Hatzor and Ilan Sheinfeld, the Palestinian voice is heard offstage: "To cut or not to cut? That is the question." After this statement he says to the Jewish prostitute: "Come in here beneath the knife...I must have a piece of Jew. For the *intifada* admissions committee." Plays written by women include descriptions of the humiliating and violent attitude toward women in Palestinian society, and they too contribute to the negative image of the Palestinian. These include *Abir* (1991) by Hagit Yaari, who attempts to trace the fate of Palestinian women since the outbreak of the *intifada*. At the beginning of the play the woman has an independent position in society due to her participation in the uprising, but toward the end she is returned to the old patriarchal order, to her inferior status (Kutab 1992, pp. 125–140). The Palestinians in the play force upon their women humiliation, a harsh economic reality, and also sexual inferiority. Abir is forced to have her hymen surgically restored in a scene in which bloodstained sheets serve as a backdrop. In the first part of the play Abir establishes a cooperative of women who earn a living from a bakery, and she carries out various orders given by the uprising committees, such as distributing pamphlets in loaves of bread. In the world of the play there are no men; only the voices of the Israeli soldiers are heard as they knock on the doors of houses in their search for suspects. The voice of the muezzin signifies the increasing influence of religion in the Palestinian camp and announces the return of the woman to her "true" place in conservative Muslim society. Toward the end of the play, the husband who returns from prison is responsible for the reversal: "No Muslim man will let his wife manage his life in his place." He beats Abir, locks her up, and then throws her out without her children.

The occupation becomes a subject dealt with by the educational system, particularly in regard to those youth about to be conscripted. The play *Clouds Over Samaria* (1994) by David Steinberg was originally a high school theater production. A theater producer then took it over and enabled its performance at the Acre Festival for Alternative Theatre. *Clouds Over Samaria* is a play about the human significances of the conciliatory agreements with the Palestinians, the Oslo Accords. The world of the play is populated with representatives of most of the groups involved in the political processes: religious settlers in the occupied territories, local Palestinians, Palestinians from the Diaspora, and Israelis from the Green Line area who object to the occupation and the settlements. Steinberg also presents the voice of an Arab-hating female settler:

> When I was a little girl, I would see pictures of the Land of Israel in books...a small house, two windows and a door, a red tiled roof, garden and tree. Such purity, such cleanliness...the Arabs were there too. We didn't think they had desires or feelings...and we built our settlements. Settlements like those in that book. Red roofs, white houses. And here the dream ended. A fence around the settlement...and the Arab village at the bottom of the road. Noisy, full of dust and anger...this land is hostile... I hate them. The smells and the customs, the sound of their music and language, I hate them!...I know that it's ugly. It's evil. It even goes against every Jewish value. We are all born in the image of God. I know. But I hate them! I loved the fence around the settlement. It protected us from them. From their knives. From their hatred. And now they want to infiltrate and cut the fence.

Clouds Over Samaria has a tragic ending that foretells the continuation of the dispute, despite the fact that several times during the play the impression is formed that even the extremist hawks—Jewish settlers and Palestinian rebels—might reach conciliation by reason of mutual economic interests. The ending confirms the consensus of the society of spectators, who both want conciliation and fear it. The play ends in the murder by other Palestinians, who object to conciliation, of the rebellious Palestinian, who has laid down his weapon. This murder puts an end, at least on stage, to any chance of peace.

CLOSE-UP (1995–)

Beginning in the mid-1990s, the debate in the arts broadened in regard to the policy of occupation and settlement. Yitzhak Laor introduced the Palestinian dream of return in *And with My Spirit, My Corpse* (1998); and in another novel, *Ecce Homo* (2002), the widow of an army general arranges the return of Palestinian refugees to the village from which they had been expelled during the War of Independence. Songs of protest proliferated. Meir Wieseltier wrote about the brutality of the occupation: "*Y'allahruchu min hon* (get out of here [in Arabic])/or we'll fuck you" (Nitzan, 2005, p. 13); and Rami Ditzani admonished his people with "Cry the beloved country": "I cry for my people who have no heart to cry: /I have seen you in your ugliness in your arrogance.../if there is no love for mankind.../and the land, you will inherit all the land?" (ibid., p. 14). David Riv presented the painting "Israel Wants War" (2001). Meir Gal created the series "Bet Hanina/Pisgat Zeev" (1995–1996), in which he photographed street names in the settlement Pisgat Zeev that erased its Arabic identity of Bet Hanina by means of street names such as "Golani Patrol," "The Infantryman," and "Dukifat [hoopoe] Patrol" (Sela, 2007, p. 37). "Irreversible Damage," a painting by David Tartakover (2002), is a critical collage that adapts a well-known photograph by David Rubinger—"Paratroopers at the Wailing/Western Wall" (1967)—as a poster headlined "1967 Irreversible Damage 2002," "35 Years of Occupation," at the center of which are photographs taken at the Wailing/Western Wall, which bears the colors of the PLO flag (ibid., p. 25). The protest was joined by central representatives of the popular culture, prominent among whom was the singer Chava Alberstein, who during the first *intifada* had sung songs against the occupation and whose song "Had Gadiya" describes the bloody cycle as a version of the traditional Passover song from the Seder, in which she asks defiantly: "Until when will this cycle of horror continue?"

The new millennium has seen an increase in the number of films on the occupation. The majority are short and personal documentary in style. Their subjects are varied and introduce material that brings the audience closer to daily life in the occupied territories. They include films on closures, on barriers, on a pregnant Palestinian mother who lost her baby when delayed at a roadblock, on the Jewish settlers in Hebron, soldiers' testimonies on the occupation, on Palestinian day laborers, on Palestinian collaborators, on the children's theater in the Jenin refugee camp, and on the struggles against expropriation of lands. One of them, a scene in the film *Map* (2003) by Amit Goren, is constructed around a poem by Hanoch Levin, "The Classic Recipe for Independence" ("The classic recipe for independence/take people and send them to die/then squash the nation next to you, oppress it to dust/...let the gravedigger win"; Levin 1987, p. 121). The film moves between an actor reading the poem and archive materials that document, among other things, the flight of the refugees during the Six Day War across the Jordan River, which he "infiltrates back" by screening them on billboards, interspersed with views of the comfortable life of Tel Aviv.

Two plays dramatized the damage done by the occupation to the occupiers and their subjects: *Deconstruction* (1999) by Roni Pinkovsky (Urian, 2002a) and *Murder* (1997) by Hanoch Levin (Urian, 2002b). Both raise subjects presented in earlier decades, but the extent differs, the closeness increases, and they are accompanied by a sense of despair and anger.

Deconstruction shows the damage done to the occupiers by the occupation. Gadi Taub, quoted in the play's program notes, had a strong influence on the writing of the play:

> The secular humanist value system embodied in every democratic regime, cannot bear for long a regime of occupation over another people.... A reserve soldier breaking into the houses of Palestinians at night, sees fathers humiliated in front of their sons, finds himself doing what he fears will happen to him and his family. He needs justification for doing these things in order to maintain the very separations between his family and the family whose domain he has breached, and he finds the justification, if he is not religious, in the political realm.... The need for political justification becomes a psychic necessity.... With the passage of time, the political [sphere] absorbs too much of this poison. And it itself becomes polluted with the oppression and the violence. (Taub 1997, p. 14)

In *Deconstruction* the representatives of two generations confront one another—that of the 1930s and that of the 1960s. Three young people, army buddies, share a secret. They have taken revenge on a young Arab boy who had killed their friend, and beaten the boy to death. One of the three, Nado, is the driving force behind the plot. He wants to cure his serious illness by means of purification, by exposing their "shameful deed" that he has committed. Set against the three young men are three veterans who represent the Zionist settlement values, all of them in shabby clothing and speaking a language that has atrophied and become out of touch with modern reality. In one of the violent scenes, which develops into a fist fight between a young man and a veteran, Yitzhak, an adult member of the rural community, turns to Shmulik, a young man who has quit the community to live in the city and is participating in the election campaign as a publicist, and defies him: "We conquered this country with blood. Our blood too was spilt here. So don't cry to me about the blood of Arabs... don't lecture us on morality."

Like *Hamlet*, *Deconstruction* is a play that exposes a central motif—disease, the fatal abscess that contaminates the entire kingdom, and at its heart too are three young men. Its beginning and end feature a monologue by Nado, who is hospitalized because of his serious illness. He seeks a cure in confession. Nado sets out from the hospital on a journey. He meets Shmulik and Momo and takes them back to the past, to the murder. All three are haunted by guilt—Momo has lost his sanity. He is hospitalized and released back to his parents' home. Shmulik, despite having a family and having become a successful publicist, continues to agonize. The political violence creeps into the private events of the play: Shmulik discovers that his wife beats their son. In one scene he hits his wife, and she decides to leave him. The play reaches the rural community too, where Shmulik encounters Yitzhak in a violent scene in which he forces him to the ground and takes Momo back home with him. There Momo encounters Nado and, suspecting that the latter had leaked their mutual secret to a journalist, he strikes him.

The narrative in *Deconstruction* is "rounded": a story with a beginning—Nado in the hospital announces his intention of setting out on a journey of purification that will heal his illness—and an ending—Nado returns to the hospital after having completed his mission. Most of the scenes in both the text and the theater production are clearly interlinked by the plot. The structure is outwardly tight, but the actions are not in a "necessary" sequence, and the breaks between scenes disrupt the narrative. Television or cinematic-type "transitions" occur between the scenes, on a darkened stage to the sound of musical phrases, which deliberately disrupt the arrangement and the sense of realism. There is a clear tension between the narrative that directs the characters and the frustrating reality in which they live. This contradiction is also manifested by the contrast between the acting style, costumes, and dialogue, which are realistic, and the scenery, which is imagistic—scratches on a blue backcloth that becomes a dramatic symbol charged with conflict and a concrete expression of the playwright's contention: "This generation is asked to straddle a spiritual, personal and psychological divide greater than its ability to do so... it confronts something legitimate: a nation's war of independence" (Pinkovitch, 2001). *Deconstruction* does not deal with the Arab, who is missing from the list of characters. The focus is on the young Israeli Jew, whom the remnants of the Zionist narrative continue to activate. In *Murder*, Hanoch Levin brings to the stage Palestinian representatives of the dispute and expands the theatrical debate.

Murder is both similar to and different from other plays engaging with the Arab dispute and staged previously by the Hebrew theater. The resemblance lies in the pessimism found in most of the texts and performances. Almost all of the characters who represent the occupation express a desire for a peaceful solution, but the majority do not find such a solution possible and their endings move between the open and blocked to the pessimistic. Beginning in the late 1970s and particularly in the 1980s, playwrights suggested a solution of compromise over land and recognition of the Palestinian national identity. Although casting doubt on the ability of the Jewish-Israeli leadership to move in a conciliatory direction, and fearing the "murderous" nature of the Arabs, the majority of them nonetheless remained hopeful. Even a dystopic play such as *The Jerusalem Syndrome* ends in a direct appeal by the playwright to the audience, whom he begs to draw the right conclusions about the future. The innovation in *Murder* is the exposure of the pessimistic perception of the conflict from the play's outset, gradually intensifying to the end.

Several of the critiques of *Murder* (both the play's text and its theatrical performance) expressed discontent with the play's disharmony, imbalance (in the representation of Israelis/Jews vs. Palestinians), stereotyping, erratic structure, and superfluous characters. It seems that Levin, who had accustomed his audiences, critics, and researchers to patterns that ascend, explode, and signify within his texts and performances, failed to fulfill the "aesthetic" expectations in *Murder*. This was an understandable disappointment, for after all, the secret of a playwright's success lies, among other things, in raising questions whose solutions arise in the course of their presentation; whereas *Murder* is a play devoid of harmony, fragmented, almost careless, sometimes blocked. *Murder* is a play in which *discrepancy* is the central concern. Nonetheless, there is order in the disorder and logic in the illogic. There is a logic beyond the plot structure, character design, dialogue, or genre; it is the murderous logic of the dispute with the Palestinians. Levin relinquishes artistic devices and stage inventions, and instead creates an apparently improvised play, whose seams are rough and whose means are exposed, in order to represent the damage caused by the occupation. "In *Murder*," wrote Guy Cohen, "[Levin] draws a portrait of the local bloodshed in vivid colors and sharp, clear and precise lines" (Cohen, 1997, p. 6).

The title of the play and its murderous opening eliminate any expectation of mitigation, relief, and conciliation. A coherent dramatic structure does not suit the representation of a chaotic history. The structure of *Murder* is loose, and with the exception of the Palestinian father and the soldier who returns in Act 3, the other characters appear and disappear, and some of them are murdered. From the very beginning to its closing scene, *Murder* is a series of violent acts. Although it echoes Levin's perception of the public debate in the 1970s and the 1980s over the wrongdoings of army generals, settlers, the right wing, the media, and other groups, it deals mainly with the reality of the 1990s, with the terror of and by individuals. Its beginning is the *intifada,* when Israeli soldiers abuse and kill a Palestinian youth. Its continuation is revenge, when the father of the murdered boy kills one of the men who might have been his son's killer. The Arab then rapes the victim's bride and murders her too. This series of killings climaxes when a Jewish mob murders a poor Arab worker, Samatocha, who is both economically and nationally frustrated. *Murder* ends when the "pale soldier," who has gone blind, mistakenly identifies an old man as the bereaved Palestinian father. This mistake, against the background of the assassination of Yitzhak Rabin, can be identified as a metonym for the disappearance of the father figure and of any firm authority (see Figure 14.2).

FIGURE 14.2 *Murder* by Hanoch Levin. Director: Omri Nitzan, Cameri Theatre, 1997. Makroum Khouri and Norman Issa (lying down).
Photo: Gadi Dagon.

Many spectators left *Murder* confused, silent, and overwhelmed (Mashat, 1997, p. 22). Some of them had come of age along with Levin and realized that, since *Queen of Bathtub*, the reasons for the bereavement, the grief, and, mainly the dispute were not only due to the injustice of the politicians, the army generals, or the settlers, but also lay in the stupidity of the enemy, as well as in the blindness to the harm caused by the occupation. It would seem that in *Murder* Levin himself and his audiences understand that it is not enough to protest, to watch plays, and to demonstrate, while at the same time collaborating with the occupation—both directly, through service in the occupying army; and indirectly, through the economic exploitation of the Arabs that contributes to the financial growth and well-being of that same group seated in the auditorium.

The "close-ups" in *Deconstruction* and *Murder* reveal the acute change, but their focus is on the effect of the occupation on the occupiers. *Act of State 1967–2007* (2007), an exhibition by Ariella Azoulay, like the play *Winter in Kalandia*, is a close-up documentation of the reality, including the reality of those subjected to the occupation. The play and the exhibition peel back the artistic coverings and link the spectators and the critics with the occupation.

Winter in Kalandia (2004) is based on the book by Lia Nirgad, an activist in Watch (Women against the Occupation and for Human Rights), and documents visits by the author to the Kalandia checkpoint. Nirgad presents stark pictures of soldiers abusing Palestinians, delaying them unnecessarily, and speaking to them crudely, while the soldiers themselves are the victims of a cruel and dangerous mission and of an arbitrary bureaucracy (Nirgad, 2004). The director, Nola Chilton, adapted Nirgad's reports to the stage and directed them in the framework of the Kibbutz Seminary's School of Theatre Arts. *Winter in Kalandia* directs the audience to a political problem. All means are enlisted to this end, including the exhibition "Breaking the Silence—Fighters Talk about Hebron," which was presented in the two rooms adjacent to the auditorium. The play was presented as a series of documentary reports moving from event to event, including music clips. This set of events created a "thick description" of a disputed junction.

Winter in Kalandia aroused interest and emotional involvement among many spectators and won encouraging critical reviews, apparently due to its ability to express what Raymond Williams terms "structure of feeling." This concept relates to the values shared by a particular group, class, or society. It is a combination of the cultural collective subconscious and ideology, expressed in different forms, such as through song, fiction, theater, architecture, fashion, and other means. The critic Avi Shilon shared with his readers a feeling that had accompanied other spectators: "True sadness" and anger over "a terrible situation, that is going on at 'a distance of an hour and a half from Tel Aviv'" (Shilon, 2004, p. 1).

Ariella Azoulay did not restrict herself to roadblocks. She crossed the border and documented the occupied territories in a selection of 600 photographs, mostly by photographers working with the media, who photographed the inhabitants of the territories. These are documents (and not artistic works) that summarize the distress and injustice of the Palestinians, attesting to such actions as the destruction of houses and eradication of housing areas, mass arrests, prevention of information to or about those arrested, violent suppression of protest demonstrations and strikes, disregard for the Palestinian existence and invasion of their private lives, public bodily searches, physical injury, blindfolding and handcuffing, preventing medical treatment, disruption and damage to the infrastructure, endless delays, expropriation of lands and property, expulsion, withdrawal of status as East-Jerusalem citizens, and actual deportation. "[I]f these acts shown in the photographs presented at the exhibition had not been the actions of a State, any one of the pictures could have served as evidence in the trials of those who had carried out the documented acts" (Azoulay, 2007).

The photographs reveal "the occupation [that] became the central national project of the State of Israel in the last forty years" (ibid.), and they serve as a protest against the brutal state action that tramples over millions of people.

THE OCCUPATION IN THE ARTS (1967-2008)

From the end of the 1960s to the first war in Lebanon the occupation was not a central issue in the arts. The 1970s saw a change in the approach of theater and cinema to Arab figures. Although the artists and their audiences—educated, traditional and secular, native Israelis of Western origin—had now "discovered" the Israeli Arab, the occupation was not on their agenda, and with the exception of a number of disturbing works that identified the political time bomb but failed to alarm their audiences, this was a repressed subject. The intensification of settlement did not encounter broad public objection, nor was such an attitude reflected in any artistic works. The change that began in the 1980s was influenced by the Israeli soldiers coming into closer contact with the Palestinians, first in the war in Lebanon and then in the first *intifada*. Opposition to the occupation began to coalesce in those years. It was no longer a concern only of the fringe organizations but also of the broader public, whose objection to the war with the Palestinians and the occupation was also fed by artistic works. Several of the works gained exposure to a large audience (such as "Halalim" by Itzhak Shmueli, who positioned cardboard human figures as

500 targets representing the dead of the war in Lebanon, deployed in a field between Kibbutz Gaash and the coastal road, so that no one stuck in traffic on the road to Tel Aviv could miss them), and others were revealed to audiences through prose, poetry, theater, cinema, and museums. Many soldiers found themselves, as members of an army of occupation, behaving in direct contradiction to their humanist education. Fear intensified revenge by the oppressed, who have nothing to lose, and enhanced their perceived image as cruel and aggressive; as did the reconstitution of the stereotype of the Arab as a miserable and exploited figure, on the one hand, and violent and dangerous, on the other. Their perception of occupation as a means of financial exploitation still enabled some artists in the 1980s to ignore the desire of the Palestinians for independence. The first and second *intifadas* exposed the nationalist roots of the dispute and reinforced among the artists and their audiences, as seen in many works, an awareness of the harm done by the occupation—to both the Israeli Jews and the Palestinians.

FIGURE 14.3 Concrete Roadblocks.
Photo: Guy Raz, Roadblock (detail), Ongoing Project, 1992.

Critics and artists doubt that art works have the power to influence the viewpoints of their audiences. Nonetheless, readers and audiences of the arts know from personal experience the influence of stories, novels, plays, films, or television series on their own lives and perceptions of the world. Many films and plays from the Israeli repertoire have presented their audiences with dilemmas that led them to ponder on their own lives in Israeli society. One can find in the arts in general, and in the Israeli theatrical repertoire in particular, examples of ideological influence on the spectators, including plays in which the audience participated as if at an important ritual. There were also plays against which the spectators publicly protested, such as *Queen of Bathtub* (1970) by Hanoch Levin and *The Jerusalem Syndrome* (1987) by Yehoshua Sobol. Protest demonstrations and hundreds of angry or supportive reactions in the press also accompanied the premiere of *Hebron* (2007), a play by Tamir Greenberg on the occupation.

The repertoire of novels, films, and plays also has a cumulative effect on its target audiences. The history of the Israeli artistic repertoire has, since the founding of the State, seen a constant rise in the number of works dealing with social and political conflicts. The artistic debate in the main begins with a political problem presented in one or two pioneering plays (e.g., *Co-existence* or *Queen of Bathtub*) that pave the way and create a precedent. With time, and influenced by political events, interest in the problem intensifies among the

FIGURE 14.4 Kalkiliya, 2002.
Photo: Pavel Wolberg and Dvir Gallery, Tel Aviv.

artists and their audiences, and the number of works engaging with the subject increases accordingly—in museums, the cinema, and the theater. Those who persist encounter each new work with the accumulating memories of the works that preceded it. This process of "repertorial accumulation" has many examples in the Israeli arts, particularly on the subject of the dispute with the Palestinians, in which plays such as *Winter in Kalandia* and exhibitions such as *Act of State 1967–2007* provide a bleak exposure of the occupation that no longer allows it to be disregarded, but demands a solution (see Figures 14.3 and 14.4).

REFERENCES

* Some of the quotes from the plays are taken from the theater's work copies and, therefore, have no bibliographical source.

Azulay, A. (2007). *Act of state 1967–2007*. Etgar.electronic version. Retrieved June 24, 2010, from http://etgar.info/he/article 169

Benyamini, K. (1990). *Political and civil standpoints of Israeli-Jewish youth*. Unpublished research report. Jerusalem: Faculty of Humanities, Psychology Department, Hebrew University.

Bourdieu, P. (1992). *Les règles de l'art*. Paris: Seuil.

Cohen, G. (1997, October 8). Obligation. *Ha'Ir*, p. 6.

Council for Films and Plays (the Censor). (1985, September 2). Protocol of the plenary session (unpublished).

Dayan, M. (1970, May 17). Dayan on *Queen of Bathtub*. *Ma'ariv*, p. 12.

Eliraz, I. (1974, January 18). The Israeli playwright as a public emissary. *Davar*, p. 15.

Epstein, Y. (1907). A vanishing question. *Hashiloach*, 17, 193–206

Evans, M. (1981). *Lucien Goldmann*. Sussex, Brighton, England: Harvester.

Gertz, N. (1995). *Captive of a dream: National myths in Israeli culture*. Tel Aviv: Am Oved.

Goldmann, L. (1966) Structuralisme génétique et création littéraire. In L. Goldmann, *Sciences humaines et philosophie* (pp. 151–165). Paris: Gonthier.

Gorny, Y. (1985). *The Arab question and the Jewish problem*. Tel Aviv: Am Oved.

Gourdon, A.-M. (1982). *Théâtre, public, perception*. Paris: Éditions du CNRS.

Guy, J.-M., & Mironer, L. (1988). *Les publics du théâtre*. Paris: La Documentation Française.

Hadari-Rammage, Y. (2002). *Messiah on a tank: The public thinking in Israel between the Sinai campaign and the Yom Kippur War: 1955–1975*. Jerusalem: Shalom Harman Institute, Tzivion Centre, Bar Ilan University.

Hass, H. (1999). Leisure culture in Israel 1998. *Panim*, 10, 107–139.

Katz, A., & Gurevitch, M. (1973). *Leisure culture in Israel: Types of entertainment and cultural need*. Tel Aviv: Am Oved.

Katz, A., Hass, H., Weitz, S., Adoni, H., Gurevitch, M., & Schiff, M. (2000). *Leisure patterns in Israel: Changes in cultural activity 1970–1999*. Tel Aviv: The Open University.

Kimmerling, B. (1993, April 2). Less political, more primitive. *Haaretz*, p. 11.

Kutab, A. (1992). Participation of the Palestinian woman in the intifada—an essential component of the Movement for National Independence. In S. Swirsky & I. Peppe (Eds.), *The intifada—A look from within* (pp. 125–140). Tel Aviv: Mifras.

Levin, H. (1987). *What does the bird care*. Tel Aviv: Siman Kriah, Ha Kibbutz Ha Meuchad.

Manor, D. (1990). Asim Abu Shakra, *tsabar* in a flowerpot. *Studio, 11*, 26–27.

Mashat, L. (1997, August 4). We all murder. We are all victims. *Yediot Aharonot*, p. 22.

Megged, A. (1979, June 15). A very expensive settlement. *Davar*, p. 8.

Michael, S. (1977). *Refuge*, Tel Aviv: Am Oved.

Mishal, S., & Aharoni, R. (1989). *Stones aren't everything—The intifada and the leaflet weapon*. Tel Aviv: Ha Kibbutz Ha Meuchad.

Mundi, Y. (1975). *The governor of Jericho*. Tel Aviv: Achshav.

Ne'eman, Y. (1991, September 8). A good Arab is an Arab in a movie. "Ticket," *Ma'ariv* supplement, pp. 8–9.

Nirgad, L. (2004). *Winter in Kalandia*. Tel Aviv: Hargol.

Nitzan, T. (Ed.). (2005). *With an iron pen. Hebrew songs of protest 1984–2004*. Tel Aviv: Hargol.

Ofrat, G. (2007). *1967: Was there art?* [Internet version]. *Panim* 39. Retrieved June 24, 2010, from http://www.itu.org.il/(Index.asp?ArticleID=9134&CategoryID=1166&Page=1)

Pinkovitch, R. (2001, January 27). Author's interview with Roni Pinkovich.

Pisker, R. (1987). Berl's confusion and Sobol's cover-up. *Proza, 99*, 36–38.

Rahav, G., & Weitz, S. (1985). *Survey of Habima subscribers* (unpublished).

Riv, D. (1990). Israeli artists in the intifada era. *Studio, 11*, 14–15.

Sartre, J.-P. (1976). *Sartre on theater*. New York: Random House.

Schiff, Z., & Ya'ari, A. (1990). *Intifada*. Jerusalem and Tel Aviv: Schocken.

Sela, R. (2007). *Six days and forty years more*. Petach Tikva: Petach Tikva Museum of Art.

Shaked, G. (1991). Light and shadow, unification and plurality. *Alpayim, 4*, 113–140.

Shalev, A. (1990). *The intifada: Causes and effects*. Tel Aviv: Papyrus.

Shalev, M. (1970, September 30). The Arabs as a literary solution. *Haaretz*, pp. 50–51.

Shapira, A. (1988). Yes. I'm an enlisted composer. *Musica, 13*, 18–21.

Shapira, S. (1993). The textile industry. *Studio, 41*, 37–41.

Shilon, I. (2004, December 14). "Winter in Kalandia." *Walla*, p. 1

Shoat, E. (1991). *The Israeli cinema: History and ideology*. Tel Aviv: Breirot.

Taub, G. (1997). The assassination of Rabin and apolitical culture: *A dispirited rebellion*. Tel Aviv: Ha Kibbutz Ha Meuchad.

Urian, D. (Ed.). (1995). *Palestinians and Israelis in the theatre. Contemporary Theatre Review* (Vol. 3, Part 2). London and New York: Routledge, Harwood Academic Publishers

Urian, D. (1997). *The Arab in Israeli drama and theatre.* London and New York: Routledge and Harwood, 1997.

Urian, D. (2002a). Between Zionism and post-Zionism in Israeli theatre ("Deconstruction," 1999). *Kesher, 31,* 37–46.

Urian, D. (2002b). The Arab in the plays of Hanoch Levin—From "Queen of the Bath" through "Murder." *Hebrew Studies, 153,* 217–232.

Yizhar, S. (1989). *The story of Khirbet Khiza and three other tales of war.* Tel Aviv: Zmora-Bitan.

Yizhar, S. (1992a, July 24). Alas all those who pull the ground from beneath the feet. *Yediot Aharonot,* p. 24.

Yizhar, S. (1992b, May 6). Independence, '48–'92. *Hadashot,* p. 25.

CHAPTER 15

Vocabulary and the Discourse on the 1967 Territories

Nadir Tsur

The American poet James Whitcomb Riley, whose works from the 1870s to the second decade of the twentieth century were much enjoyed by the citizens of his home state of Indiana, including children and lovers of nature and humor, is credited with the following saying: "When I see a bird that walks like a duck, swims like a duck and quacks like a duck, I call that bird—a duck."[1] In Israel, on the other hand, it seems that even after more than forty years, what is treated as an occupied territory, what appears to be an occupied territory, and from within which arise voices identified with an occupied territory is not always called such; and for ideological, political, security, social, or religious purposes, it has been given names and labels that have stripped it of its significance over the years.[2]

On May 25, 2003, the government of Israel, led by Prime Minister Ariel Sharon, authorized the Road Map[3] but imposed limitations on it with the adoption of annotations, amendments, and reservations that it passed on to the American government and that appeared in an announcement on May 23, 2003. One day later, during an open media debate by the Likud party, the Prime Minister used for the first time in public the word "occupation" when speaking of the territories that many of his followers were still calling "liberated," "held," or various other terms that also expressed their historical affiliation with the land of the Bible, with the Jewish people, or their perception of that territory as vital to the security of the state and its Jewish inhabitants. Left-wing factions, leaning on the slogan "What can be seen from here cannot be seen from there," tended at the time to believe that Sharon's term as Prime Minister had led the "father of the settlements" to the same conclusion reached by generations before him; other factions, from the right, contended that use of the term "occupation" was destroying the Zionist enterprise.

Sharon's unflinching use of the term "occupation," in addition to his declaration of readiness to march along the route of the Road Map, as well as being daring and heard for the first time, was also sufficiently obscure to continue to leave in Israel's hands for the unforeseeable future the territories conquered in 1967.[4] These included the majority of the settlements, with the exception of the Gush Katif area that was transferred to the Palestinians and the four settlements in northern Samaria whose residents were evacuated. This left a clear impression about Sharon's new political aspirations on both the international scene and the domestic one while creating a jolt that further inflamed the dispute over the Land of Israel and its borders.

WORLD BORDERS ARE VERBAL BORDERS:[5] A GENERAL INTRODUCTION

In providing food for thought, awareness, and an understanding of reality, as well as a method for communication, including during influential processes (Wittgenstein, 1995, p. 172), language is not only a means of expressing concepts, beliefs, hopes, or needs, but also a social or political key and an entrance ticket to the arena of social struggles. Efforts to reach a common interpretation of reality, in its various appearances, depend to a great extent on linguistic choices and preferences. Words, terms, and phrases dictate the boundaries of reality. Therefore, the constant human endeavor, by logical or emotional linguistic means, to fit one's personal or group systems into the construction of reality and to suit it to the mechanisms of hearing, absorbing, understanding, and agreeing with others is only natural.

The wide variety of memories that people carry with them, and whose dimensions increase over time—both individually and within the individual's immediate and more distant circles—turns almost every word and every sentence into a personal enterprise of linguistic decoding. Combining such individual enterprises into a public enterprise results in a mixture of intentions and multidirectional attempts at mutual influence that lead each individual into a labyrinth of thought and consciousness. Within this consciousness act forces that draw individuals and groups toward the core of meanings, while other forces concomitantly thrust them away from the center to the margins of a common understanding.

The messages that flow in the social and political communications networks compete with each other for the attention of the majority, enlist it, and impel it to prefer certain standpoints and opinions over others and to follow those who voice them. These opinion makers nurture the relations between the various elite groups—the decision makers, the creators of public opinion, the economists and media representatives—and, of course, the broad public. In the unceasing competition among social and political agents to fashion reality, to define it and to confer meaning on its various components, language has a central place. It is colored by bold hues and a brightness that capture the senses and the hearts of the broad public. The people, sometimes unaware of language's effect but nonetheless captivated by it, are seduced into supporting a story, a standpoint or a worldview, particularly during times of conflict.

In his essay on rhetoric, Aristotle (322–384 bce) noted that some speakers deliberately choose to obscure their words and offer ambiguity: "Such people are apt to put that sort of thing into verse. Empedocles, for instance, by his long circumlocutions imposes on his hearers; these are affected in the same way as most people are when they listen to diviners, whose ambiguous utterances are received with nods of acquiescence" (Aristotle, 2002, p. 159). In our own era too, this avoidance of plain speaking is familiar and sometimes seems to be spreading. In an appendix to the book *Nineteen Eighty-Four* by George Orwell (1949) the term "Newspeak" appears, referring to a language that is steadily dwindling, following knowledge that is steadily dwindling. At the same time, Newspeak creates new words devoid of their old meaning and reduces the use of words whose meanings are familiar and consensual. Since Orwell's book was written, and particularly with the flourishing of postmodernist notions, language has become enriched with words and concepts, some new, that express reality through a convoluted syntax.

"LAUNDERING WORDS" IN THE ISRAELI POLITICAL DISCOURSE

The notion of "word laundering" in Israeli political talk is introduced in the book *The Yellow Time* (1987) by David Grossman: "There is developing here a new breed of treacherous, enlisted words, words that have lost their original significance, words that do not depict reality, but attempt to hide it" (ibid., p. 44). In this connection, Raphael Nir (1998) contended that in Israel there exists a sociolinguistic situation that is "relatively politically correct," as perceived from several perspectives. Unlike what is acceptable in the United States, where the term "relatively correct" is unacceptable, in Israel its use depends on the person to whom the words are directed and in what political connection they are spoken: "The political divide in Israeli society is well reflected in the choice of vocabulary used by the various political factions. Each branch of Israeli society has adopted a list of its own terms in accordance with the ideology to which it subscribes. The Right, the Left, the secular and the Orthodox all have different criteria by which to determine the political validity of the use of language" (ibid., p. 22). Israeli politicians today employ various methods of deflecting attention by selecting words that obscure any unpleasant reality or that blur controversial political acts and make it easier to achieve a broad consensus.

The Israeli-Arab, Zionist-Palestinian, and Jewish-Muslim dispute has served as a broad platform for various narratives, some contrasting and immediately discernible, others less easy to distinguish. A cluster of symbols, myths, terms, and words has arisen throughout the years in Israel, in times of normalcy and in times of stress, and these reflect the deep dilemmas that can be found in the heart of every Israeli Jew concerning the dispute and its military/security, political, territorial, legal, and other expressions. The mistake is to believe that there are only two different sides, each of which is one-dimensional: a hawkish side and a dovish side or a nationalist camp and a peace camp. Different and complex perceptions, with fine nuances, have gained a grip on the public space in everything connected to the determination of Israel's future borders and, within this issue, the future of the 1967 territories.

No clear political decision has ever been made concerning the fate of the territories conquered in the Six Day War. This fact and the continued occupation of these territories by Israel for more than a generation, justified on religious, historical, security, or other grounds, has verbally enriched the public discourse over the years through the coining of new words, phrases, and concepts. These reflect an unsolved internal conflict that from time to time intensifies but finds no solution.

In almost every decade since 1967, following each of the wars or major political or security events, the country was stirred. The political discourse intensified over these issues, as expressed in the public debates involving persons who differed in identity and ideology; whose supporters often held completely opposite views regarding security, beliefs, law, and morality; and who became mutually alienated. In contrast to a life of mutual cooperation, such individuals are unwilling to compromise and often have no shared and valid system of values, desires, or common interests. In this respect, Israeli society lacks the notion of a social network for exchange of information and viewpoints, as defined by the German philosopher Jurgen Habermas (1998, pp. 360–361) in regard to social cooperation. The unsolved conflicts that continue to intensify with time and exhaust the divided public turn into linguistic battles. These verbal battles sometimes include attempts at deception and Newspeak, or vocabulary laundering, to deliberately create a political appearance that differs from its true meaning. Thus, the leadership has not only used a behavior that the sociologist Eric Hoffer (1951) calls "inflaming conflicts," involving the use of manipulative language that drives the public into taking uncompromising and forceful stands, but has also deliberately created distortion in labeling events. This results in a shallow political discourse and one-dimensional debate about core issues while creating patterns of purely token significance,[6] dull and incomprehensible.

This chapter is based on the assumption that there exists a link between major events resulting from the uncontrolled dispute[7] and the language that characterizes the various speakers who refer to the 1967 territories. A further assumption is that the more time that passes since the Six Day War, the further the language connected to the territories is stretched in structure, in accordance with security, state, international, internal political, socioeconomic, and, of course, ideological-religious circumstances. Moreover, as demonstrated below, there is some coordination between the main social "earthquakes" throughout the years and the political discourse associated with the territories and national security issues. These factors can be divided into four main periods that, coincidentally, closely overlap the division of forty years into decades. The changes reflect various stages in the social and political confrontations in Israel with holding the 1967 territories for such a prolonged period without determining their permanent status. Linguistically,these stages reveal a progression from the religious belief discourse to a discourse of national rights. From this arises the security discourse, whose origin lies in the language of conciliation and peace. And finally, from there, the discourse moves to the language of separation and disengagement, a dull, obscure language that introduces peace and security as two factors that demand a separate confrontation integrating a legal and moral discourse.

THE FREE-HELD TERRITORIES[8]

During the Six Day War, Israel's territories were unilaterally increased in size, but internationally recognized fixed borders were left unclear. Menachem Begin was the first to determine an agreed-upon peaceful border between Israel and Egypt, thereby partially realizing his desire as he stated: "I would like to be remembered as the one who determined the border of the Land of Israel for the generations to come" (Perlmutter, 1987, p. 7). Steeped in a belief in the ethos of the "Greater Israel," Begin proffered an outline for fixed borders. In his book *The Revolt* (1978) he wrote: "He who does not acknowledge our right to the entire homeland also does not acknowledge our right to part of its parts" (ibid., p. 509) The then Minister of Defense, Moshe Dayan, immediately following the Six Day War, stated his far-reaching opinion that "By the right of the great victory Israel can determine as it wishes the borders with its neighbors as well as the future of the Palestinian Arabs under our rule" (Pedatzur, 1996, p. 70), while Minister Israel Galili stated at a government meeting on June 19, 1967, dedicated to the fate of the territories: "I think that we need to prepare ourselves to hold long term the territories that were conquered by the IDF [Israel Defense Forces], from the assumption that there will be no response from the Arab states in regard to a peace negotiation" (ibid., p. 48).

While holding a Bible, shortly after Mordechai Gur, the commander of the paratroop brigade during the Six Day War, had declared that "the Temple Mount is in our hands," the military's Chief Rabbi, General Shlomo Goren, faced the Western (Wailing) Wall and announced: "To Zion and to the ruins of our Holy Temple we proclaim—our sons have returned to their border." This quote, taken from the Book of Jeremiah (chap. 31, verse16), was not incidental. Using symbolic language, Rabbi Goren proclaimed: "The Temple Mount and the Western Wall—symbol of the messianic redemption of the nation—[has been] redeemed today by you, heroes of the Israel Defense Forces" (army radio station, June 7, 1967). These early words were later to be reinforced by clear statements by the military rabbi, who had previously been the Chief Rabbi of Israel.[9] Standing alongside Yitzhak Rabin, the Chief of Staff, and Uzi Narkiss, commander of the Central Command, Moshe Dayan, the Minister of Defense, spoke words that do not necessarily sit well together: "We have returned to our holiest of places, we have returned in order never again to be separated from it. To our Arab neighbors we extend, at this time too, and indeed with greater validity at this time, the hand of peace" (*Yediot Aharonot*, June 8, 1967, p. 5). Two years later, at a press meeting, Dayan stated: "Only in another ten years shall we know whether the territories are conquered or liberated" (*Ma'ariv*, June 6, 1969, p. 3).

The Minister of Defense's words were equivocal for a reason. For then as now, Israel had not achieved a consensus on the future of the 1967 territories, and the different public sectors expressed their various longings, beliefs, and knowledge. The territories that Israel had conquered, mainly from Jordan, thus acquired seven different labels: (1) "occupied territories" or "the occupied territories," (2) "held territories," (3) "disputed territories," (4) "territories" or "the territories," (5) "the West Bank," (6) "Judea and Samaria," and (7) "the liberated territories."

"Occupied Territories" or "The Occupied Territories"[10]

The term "occupied territories" or "the occupied territories" is accepted by those who reject annexation of the territories and control over their Arab citizens. The Palestinians also clearly express their own belonging to their territories in the term "the occupied Palestinian territories."[11] During a debate in the Knesset at the beginning of the fourth season of archaeological excavations at the Citadel, MK Tawfik Toubi of the Democratic Front for Peace and Equality made frequent use of the term "occupied territories": "The excavations carried out and being carried out in East Jerusalem have a political significance, for it is not the advance of science that is the main target, but the concealing of the Arab nature of the conquered territories, reinforcement of the policy of occupation and annexation to Israel and inflating nationalist leanings and emotions against the rights of the Palestinian Arab people in East Jerusalem and in the rest of the homeland in the West Bank and Gaza Strip" (Knesset protocol, August 26, 1981).

"Held Territories"

The term "held territories" is accepted by those neutral factions that observe an existing fact, by legal advocates (Tsur 1973, pp. 154–174), and by those who emphasize the temporary nature of holding the territories and believe in determining their future within the framework of a peace agreement. It was introduced into the vocabulary describing the 1967 territories at the suggestion of the then military attorney-general, Meir Shamgar (Gazit, 1999, p. 251). A semantic parallel term, less often used, was "the enlightened occupation" (*Davar*, June 21, 1991), although the word "occupation" in itself minimized the use of this term, which was in any case somewhat incoherent. An additional term connected to "held territories" is "territories held under belligerent occupation," and this has been accepted in High Court rulings.[12] This concept, it would seem, has become timeless and accompanied the territories from its first use in writing to the present time.

"Disputed Territories"

The term "disputed territories" may seem to indicate an avoidance of taking a stand in regard to the 1967 territories. More important than having no identity value, it ignores a whole list of political, ideological, and legal meanings, particularly those connected with acquisition of the territories through war, in contradiction to what is stated in the introduction to Resolution 242 of the United Nations Security Council.[13] In a parliamentary debate on the International Court of Justice's discussion in the Hague concerning the separation fence, MK Jamal Zakhalka of the Bal'ad party rejected the term "disputed territories" and demanded instead the use of "occupied territories," as expressing their status as he perceived it: "The court will decide about the fence. A positive decision against the fence and a ruling that the territories in relation to the 1967 borders are occupied territories—and not, as claimed by the government, disputed territories—this is a very important contribution to peace" (Knesset protocol, February 25, 2004).

"Territories" or "The Territories"

The term "territories" or "the territories" is accepted by those factions that reject any political labeling in reference to the disputed future. In a question posed by MK Elazar Granot of Mapam to the Minister of Education and Culture in January 1985, following the broadcasting management committee's decision to replace the usual term "territories" with "areas," the speaker complained about the decision—which, in his view, had political motives. Granot explained: "They who came and proposed this change are neither innocent nor pure. What is 'territory' according to the dictionary, for our purposes?— 'an occupied territory that is conquered by a foreign country, a territory held by the occupying forces.' And in contrast, 'area' is 'a territory, part of a country, a district or a city.' Well, when we say 'territories,' we have included a settled territory, an occupied territory, a held territory, everything—according to one's individual preference.... This constituted a deliberate intent to change the proposal, and was deliberately intended to pave the way for what those who propose it are demanding—to annex that same territory. And as they haven't succeeded in their demand, and the territory is still not annexed, they now demand to annex it in the Hebrew language." The then Minister of Education and Culture, Itzhak Navon, who was also the minister responsible for broadcasting, responded: "If journalism routinely refers to the 'territories,' the term 'territories' will not be ruled out. However, I don't know what the decision of the management committee will be. They will decide and give me their decision." Navon added that over the years, the term "territories" had acquired a different meaning from "areas." "It was not this, however, that would determine the political-linguistic dispute being carried on within the institutions of the broadcasting authority and the press," stated Navon (Knesset protocol, January 21, 1985).

In *Lexicon—The Channel 7 Dictionary of Spoken Hebrew*, the term "territories" is a left-wing derogatory term for the areas in Israel that were liberated in the Six Day War. It continues: "Never mention it on our channel" (Segal, 2001, p. 18).

"The West Bank"

The term "West Bank" is accepted by those factions that note the geographical location of the territories but avoid attributing any political significance to holding them; the term is also accepted by those who seek to create a link with the Kingdom of Jordan. For example, Moshe Dayan, two years after the Six Day War, said, "When Jordan joined in [the war], we conquered the 'West Bank' and liberated Jerusalem" (Dayan, 1969, p. 191).

In a meeting of the tenth Knesset plenum, an argument arose between MK Yitzhak Rabin of the Ma'arach party, then a member of the opposition, and Prime Minister Menachem Begin. Rabin claimed that the overall plan for a true peace should have three components: (1) the State of Israel as a Jewish state, with its destiny and values; (2) state security; and (3) a reasonable solution to the Palestinian problem. These factors had already led him to conclude that there was no avoiding the division of the country and the establishment of a Palestinian state to the east of Israel. Rabin stated: "There are no more 'two banks to the Jordan, this is ours and that is too.' We have given up one bank. Therefore, the principle of dividing the Land of Israel is not disputed and the question is now one of how much." Prime Minister Begin responded by turning to the Ma'arach benches in the Knesset and quoting a question posed by an international statesman, one combining a moral claim, national values, and security values: "How can you think at all about leaving 'the West Bank'? The day will come when other nations will recognize this and other governments will argue over it. Your proposal is paradoxical. It does not contain peace. Dividing the Land of Israel means the permanent spilling of blood" (Knesset protocol, October 19, 1982).

"Judea and Samaria"

The term "Judea and Samaria" is accepted by official factions, mainly since the rise to power of the Likud party in 1977, as well as by those seeking to emphasize the historical link between Israel and the territories whose source lies in the Bible. MK Yehoshua Matza of the Likud party asked the Foreign Minister, Shimon Peres, why in an official communication to the Egyptian Foreign Minister, Peres had employed the term "West Bank" instead of the usual term in official documents: "Judea and Samaria." Minister Peres replied: "The protocol regarding correspondence signed by me—both as Prime Minister and as acting Prime Minister—was and remains to relate to the held territories in the accepted terms, whether 'Judea and Samaria' or 'The West Bank.' The policy of the Foreign Office in this respect has not changed, with the exception of the directive to add the terms 'West Bank' and 'held territories' to correspondence in the English language." Matza's opinion was as uncompromising as the directive from the Prime Minister's Office to the Foreign Office. Matza declared that "The right of the acting Prime Minister to say 'No' is subordinate to the Prime Minister's Office. In my opinion he has thereby removed himself from the government. He who changes these concepts is destroying the ground beneath our feet, in both senses, from beneath our settlement in the Land of Israel." The acting Prime Minister and Foreign Minister responded: "I do not accept the bombastic interpretation of MK Matza, as if words change anything. For decades we have said 'the West Bank'—and nothing happened. I am also familiar with the movement raised on the song 'Two Banks to the Jordan.' When there are two banks to the Jordan, one is the West and one is the East" (Knesset protocol, February 17, 1988).

One term that never caught on was coined by the writer Haim Hazaz, one of the supporters of a Greater Israel, who in a speech at the inaugural meeting of the Movement for a Greater Israel defined the territories conquered from Jordan as "Judea and Ephraim," named for the biblical tribe that had settled there[14] (*Davar*, November 10, 1967).

"The Liberated Territories"

The term "liberated territories" is accepted by nationalist and religious factions for whom the territories are part of the Promised Land of Israel. The accompanying ethos is "Wholeness of the Land," pertaining to its religious dimensions. Rabbi Yaakov Halevi Filver, among the founders of the Jerusalem Yeshiva for Youth and a pupil of Rabbi Zvi Yehuda HaCohen Kook, noted in this respect: "The wholeness of the Land of Israel takes precedence over any decision-making by the Israeli government" (Filver, 1975, pp. 232–233). A more nationalist statement was made by Menachem Begin shortly after the war at a meeting of the Likud party in Jerusalem: "The Land of Israel is not annexed. It is being liberated, returned to its legal owner, which is the Jewish nation" (*Today*, June 28, 1967).

During a debate by the Knesset plenum on a vote of no confidence, against the background of a crisis with the U.S. government as a result of enacting the Golan Law, and applying Israeli sovereignty to the Golan Heights, MK Haim Druckman (National Religious Front) quoted from a dialogue in the Book of the Maccabees between a representative of Antiochus VII and Shimon the Hasmonean, in which the representative accepted the Maccabees' stronghold in the "occupied territories" that were not theirs. Shimon replied accordingly: "We did not take a strange land and did not prevail over strangers, but the land of our fathers, which was unjustly occupied by our enemies in times past. And we, when we came into our strength, returned to the land of our fathers" (Knesset protocol, December 23, 1981).

The term "liberated territories" is connected to the slogan "A liberated territory will not be returned!" (*Ma'ariv*, January 30, 1975, p. 3), which was a bumper sticker on the settlers' cars. It expressed an idea stated by Prime Minister Itzhak Shamir: "The Jews are forbidden to give up, under any circumstances, any part of their historical homeland, and the Jewish settlements were not established in order to be uprooted" (Shamir, 1994, p. 176) Use of the term "liberated territories" was criticized by the writer Yizhar Smilansky in an essay entitled *Poets of the Annexation*, written immediately after the Six Day War. The writer, author of the story "Khirbet Khizeh" (1949), rejected the term, stating that the territories are not empty and their inhabitants do not perceive themselves as liberated by the IDF (Yizhar, 2006, pp. 8–12).

FROM "LAND OF OUR FATHERS" TO "PAINFUL COMPROMISES"–LINGUISTIC EXCHANGES OVER FOUR DECADES

In his book *Essay on Language* (1975), Bronovsky stated that language offers the most reliable definition of a nation (ibid., p. 60) and that language documents social processes (ibid., p. 65). Changes that have taken place in Israel since the Six Day War are well reflected in the public discourse on the 1967 territories. During this prolonged period, currently entering its fifth decade, internal struggles have more than once erupted over basic issues of identity and culture. Since 1967, Israel has been engaged in wars and is still dealing with the waves of terrorism and security issues that the dispute in the Middle East so readily supplies. Concomitantly, efforts have been made to settle the dispute or to manage it. However, apart from the two peace agreements with Egypt and Jordan, none of these efforts have borne fruit. These internal and regional processes have left their mark on the public discourse and on the vocabulary of the 1967 territories. To some extent, these processes match the division of the period into decades, as each decade has displayed a linguistic characteristic based on the prevailing social and political worldview and the desire to construct a reality by means of words, terms, and phrases.

1967–1977: "WE HAVE RETURNED TO THE WELLS"–THE LANGUAGE OF REDEMPTION

Twenty-two years after the end of the Second World War, when the Jewish nation already had an independent state of its own, a "night shelter"[15] against anti-Semitism and persecution, a homeland and a spiritual and religious center, the Israeli army attained three victories in the theater of war. The sense of suffocation that had accompanied the young state—which had arisen from the concentration camps and gas chambers and moved straight into the flames of the War of Independence, and since then had been engaged in a "dormant war"[16]—dissipated as the State of Israel changed beyond recognition. One of the linguistic expressions of this sense of relief, joy of victory, and happiness in the return to the "ancient biblical spells"[17] was the addition of a verse to the song "Jerusalem of Gold" by Naomi Shemer. The song was composed on the eve of the Six Day War at the request of Teddy Kollek, the Mayor of Jerusalem, and was sung at the Israel Song Festival in May 1967; and after the unification of Jerusalem,[18] Shemer added this verse:[19] "We have returned to the wells/to the market and the square/a *shofar* calls from the Temple Mount/in the Old City./And in the caves in the rock/thousands of suns rise/we shall again descend to the Dead Sea/on the way to Jericho." This addition, and mainly the original lines to the song, such as "How did they dry the wells/the empty market square" and "there is no descent to the Dead Sea/on the way to Jericho," which changed from a song of mourning to become a song of glory, reawakened criticism about the disregard for the Arab public in the mentioned places (*Haaretz*, July 2, 2004, p. 24). With time, the phrase "we have returned to the wells" became a saying used by both sides in the dispute over the 1967 territories, with each side claiming a political significance for the words that matched its specific viewpoint.

In September 1967, the Movement for a Greater Israel produced its manifesto, signed by writers such as Shmuel Yosef Agnon, Uri Zvi Greenberg, Yehuda Burla, Yaakov Orland, Haim Guri, Moshe Shamir, and Nathan Alterman, who was the mainstay of the group and its supporters. A statement published by the movement expressed secular contentions regarding the notion of "the wholeness of the Land" in a language overflowing with florid phrases of redemption: "The victory by the IDF in the Six Day War has entered the people and the State into a new and auspicious period. A Greater Israel is now in the hands of the Jewish people, and just as we do not have the authority to relinquish the State of Israel, so too are we commanded to maintain what we have been given by it—the Land of Israel. We are faithfully obligated to preserve our entire land—regarding the nation's past and its future as one, and no government of Israel has the right to give up this wholeness. The borders of our country today are a guarantee of security and peace, and offer unprecedented prospects for a national all-encompassing intensification of both matter and spirit" (*Davar*, September 22,1967, p. 3).

The more religious parallel to this secular vision of "a Greater Israel" was revealed in the term "the dawn of redemption," which was frequently used during the establishment of the State of Israel. Rabbi Eliezer Melamed, head of the Har Bracha yeshiva, a settlement rabbi, explained in an article titled "The Dawn of Redemption and Sanctification of God": "In establishment of the State the disgrace of exile was lifted...and this was a sanctification by the great and terrible God that was intensified in the Six Day War, when we liberated Jerusalem and the holy cities in Judea and Samaria. This process of ingathering of the exiles and making the wilderness bloom, which received a major impetus during establishment of the State, is the beginning of redemption... and when the end will come, natural processes will begin, accompanied by complications and harsh suffering, which will cause the nation of Israel to return to the land and build it, and thus we shall proceed step by step to the perfect redemption. This suffering that drives the process of redemption is messianic suffering" (http://www.yeshiva.org.il/midrash/shiur.asp?id=3448).

With the increasing pressure during the seventeen months of the War of Attrition (March 1969–August 1970) and the rising number of casualties, public protest arose that reflected the desire to reach a cease-fire at the Suez Canal and halt the waves of terror. The uncompromising stand of the government under the leadership of Golda Meir, including rejection of the UN mediator's "Gunnar Jarring Document" in February 1971, effectively made the Yom Kippur War inevitable (Beilin, 1996, p. 42) In regard to the settlements established in the territories during that period, the Prime Minister adopted severe language, asking rhetorically: "Where is it written that Jews are forbidden to settle in Hebron?... Do we need to take this upon ourselves too just because in 1929 (and I shan't speak of history) they massacred Jews in Hebron?" (Knesset protocol, May 27, 1970). Throughout this speech, Meir scattered symbolism taken from the emergency stock of rhetoric reserved for such prolonged stressful situations[20]: "The whole world is against us"; "our historical rights" to the Land of Israel; "For us even surrender is a luxury"; and "We may be the only ones in the world who after surrender have no life" (ibid.).

One of the songs that reflected the mood of many in the face of the War of Attrition, and that also drew its strength from protest demonstrations against war and from the antiestablishment groups in the United States, was "Song for Peace" ("Shir LaShalom"). The words were composed in 1969 by Ya'akov Rottblit, and the song was performed by the NAHAL army troupe in their show *The NAHAL Outposts in Sinai*. On November 4, 1995, twenty-six years later, a member of that same troupe, Miri Aloni, reprised the song alongside Yitzhak Rabin during a gathering in the municipal square, at the end of which he was assassinated. The "Song for Peace" extols life, love, and peace, and calls not only for hailing peace but also for bringing it about. The song, and similarly the play *Queen of Bathtub*, publicly question the ethos of those who fall in battle, and the place of the dead and the wounded in the national pantheon. The lines "Don't look back, let them go" and "He who has extinguished his candle and is buried in ashes; bitter tears will not wake him, nor return him to here" were perceived by broad sectors of the public not only as unpatriotic and insulting to the injured and dead and to the culture of bereavement, but also as contradicting the basic national values of a state fighting for its existence. They starkly contrasted the "Song for Peace" with the "Song of Comradeship," depicted friendship as "love sanctified in blood."

This defiance of government policy following the Yom Kippur War became great enough to cause a crisis in leadership that deepened in the elections for the Eighth Knesset in December 1973, in which Golda Meir's party again won the support of the electorate. The pressure building up in Israeli society sought an outlet. The ensuing sharp turnabout went far beyond the ordinary differences of opinion prevalent in the country since the end of the 1960s, which had led to mild disquiet. It now shook up the country and reflected a violent outburst of negative energy that had been contained until then due to the insoluble disputes over issues such as Jewish and Israeli identity; the connection to the Land of Israel and the sources of the right to live there; the status of religion in the country's life; and the weight of values, ethos, and symbols that had accumulated over the years. It is not surprising that precisely at this difficult time for the leadership in Israel and a grasping hope for the desired peace, as Rabin had described it,[21] in 1974 the Gush Emunim movement arose, initially as a group from the Mafdal (National Religious Party) and within a few months as a faction fighting for a Greater Israel by establishing settlements in the territory of Judea and Samaria and the Gaza Strip. Three years later, with the aim of encouraging the Begin government to sign Israel's first peace agreement with an Arab state and return to Egypt the territories conquered in 1967, the Peace Now movement arose. Its slogan was "Better peace than a Greater Israel." One of the founders of this movement, Tzaly Reshef, explained in a debate held in 2002: "The breeding ground of 'Gush Emunim' and 'Peace Now' was the Yom Kippur War. This war has shaken up Israeli society, and the question of what we have entrusted to the hands of the political parties and the government has become a highly acute one. Two movements have succeeded in sweeping along with them many people who are prepared to act, to change their perceived reality" (round-table discussion at the Israeli Institute for Democracy, March 12, 2002).

The use of the adverb "now" (in Peace Now) signified the desire for immediate change and an end to the patient wait for the day to come. The name "Peace Now" reveals, on the one hand, a desire for immediate satisfaction, the opposite of patience, and, on the other hand, an objection to the played-out approach of the government, which was still hoping for a telephone call from the Arabs.[22] The value "now" was therefore chosen as an alternative to the value "tomorrow" that is expressed in a song with that title by Naomi Shemer sung in the 1960s by the NAHAL troupe: "Tomorrow when the army will discard its uniform/our hearts will stand still/after every man will build with his own two hands/that which he dreamed today."

1977-1987: "DEVISE YOUR STRATEGY":[23] RIGHTS OVER THE LAND OF ISRAEL

During the term of office of Menachem Begin, the first Prime Minister from the Likud party (1977–1983), there was increased support for the settlements, encouraging their establishment in the 1967 territories. At the same time, sixteen civilian settlements were evacuated in north and south Sinai, including the Yamit area with the township of Yamit at its center, as part of the peace agreement with Egypt. This set a precedent as the first withdrawal from areas conquered in the Six Day War. During this decade, along with the many kilometers of disputed area on the west bank of the Jordan River, stubborn fighting continued with the First Lebanon War, impinging on the main players in the territories. The war badly affected the public and created a rift that divided society into a camp of supporters of the war, defined by the Prime Minister himself as "a tragedy" (Naor, 1993, p. 319), and a camp of objectors of various persuasions.

Already at the beginning of the process, at the end of which Israel evacuated all the Jewish settlements established in the Egyptian arena (in spring 1982), Rabbi Zvi Yehuda Kook, in a letter dated January 19, 1978, expressed his views, which negated any evacuation. The letter, in his particular style, employed a play on words between the terms "autonomy" and "anatomy": "Sinai, and everything connected with it, is the Land of Israel. There is a strict biblical prohibition against giving up something that is part of one to foreigners. Heaven forbid. And the 'anatomy' of the citizens of the lands in Judea and Samaria, which is the Land of Israel just as is Tel Aviv, is an anatomy of our body's essential vitality in the Land of our Life. And the Guardian of Israel will protect and save us from this disgrace of generations of misuse of the word 'peace'-lie, and will protect us within a strong camp of true peace that will obtain in our land throughout the ages" (Tau, 1987, p. 140)

Speakers from the Right, which also had become politically divided with establishment of the Tehiya party in 1979, defined the evacuation of Yamit as "uprooting": "A slap in the face to the naivety of the concept of advancing redemption" (Aran, 1985, p. 2). At the emergency meeting held at the Efrat settlement, in an attempt to gain something from the lessons of the Yamit evacuation (the participants then too employed the terms "expulsion" and "withdrawal"), it was stated: "In order that we shall not have to found yet another movement to stop the withdrawal, we must awake, organize and begin to act immediately" (Har-Noi, 1994, pp. 173–175). Elyakim Haetzni, one of the leaders of the settlement enterprise, quoted from an article he had written regarding the obligation of those loyal to a Greater Israel to all who were ready to evacuate settlements in the future, saying that their path would not be an easy one. Haetzni borrowed his concepts from the fields of physical and mental medicine: "More than a few of our enemies want to see in the evacuation of the Sinai and the dismantling of the settlements a precedent that will spread to Judea and Samaria and the Golan, and also to Jerusalem... to those the bitter war is valuable in stopping the withdrawal from Sinai. We must ensure that this gangrene will not spread to the rest of the body. To do so there must be a bitter struggle for the Sinai, involving agonies and national trauma" (*Nekuda*, 42, "The Sinai Quartet will not arise," April 7, 1982, p. 10).

In early July 1983, in the unrest that occurred a few weeks after the murder of the yeshiva student Aharon Gross in Hebron, MK Amnon Linn of the Ma'arach party, standing in the square that today bears Gross's name, spoke about the proposal on the Knesset agenda regarding "the lack of a clear policy in the territory of Judea and Samaria." The speaker repeatedly used a term borrowed from the reality that Israel had encountered during the fighting in Lebanon—"Lebanonization"[24]: "When thinking about the recent events in Hebron, it seems to me that we are approaching a situation of 'Lebanonization' in the liberated territories—an all-out war, hostility and terror from one side and uncontrolled retaliation from the other, various unidentified groups taking the law into their own hands, and a central government that is losing its authority and its control... it's saddening that when our soldiers are sent to sort things out among the hawks, it's impossible to tell who is fighting whom. Suddenly everybody is battling against the IDF" (Knesset protocol, July 25, 1983).

During Menachem Begin's term of office eighty-two new settlements were established, one after the other; forty-two were developed in Samaria, in the Mount Hebron area (Knesset protocol, January 18, 1984). This widespread activity was based upon his clear declaration during his first visit to Elon Moreh immediately after his election victory: "We shall have many more Elon Moreh" (*HaTzofe*, May 20, 1977, p. 2). The internal struggle among the Israeli public over the right to establish settlements in the territories reached the High Court. In debating the legality of establishing settlements, in connection with Elon Moreh, Rabbi Menachem Reuven Felix, among the leaders of Gush Emunim, claimed that "The act of settlement by the people of Israel in the Land of Israel is the real act of ensuring security, the most effective and true act. But the settlement itself... does not derive from reasons of security and physical needs but from the power of destiny, and the power of the return of Israel to its land." In contrast, General (ret.) Haim Bar-Lev negated Elon Moreh as contributing nothing to the state's security, either in combating terrorist activity or in case of war on the eastern front. In an additional opinion presented to the Court, General (ret.) Mattityahu Peled contended that "Regarding the claim of the security value of Elon Moreh, we contend that this is no innocent and single purpose intention: but is to justify taking land that cannot be justified in any other way" (High Court, October 22, 1979, p. 7). The echoes of this fierce debate in the High Court shook public opinion regarding the absolute security value of the settlements and reflected a turnabout in the public discourse. Not only were alternative voices heard regarding the justification of settlements for security purposes, but the language of redemption that had been widespread during the first decade after the 1967 war made way for a more complex language, less spiritual and florid, and more down-to-earth and nationalist.

Naor (2001) explains that Menachem Begin constructed a system of symbols based on a historical analogy and stated that Israel's strength rested on three components: autonomy in determining policy ("to take our fate into our own hands"), an awareness of justice ("we shall believe in our justification"), and military might ("a renewed Hebrew might"). Faithful to commemorating the Holocaust, in which many members of his family had perished, and adhering to the myth of Masada, Begin stated: "Now the western part of the Land of Israel is in our hands and never again will there be a Masada." (ibid., p. 326).

The settlement enterprise supported the system of creating "facts in the field," which would precede the bureaucracy and the process of obtaining building permits that raised difficulties even when the government supported the settlers and their activities. MK Geula Cohen of the Tehiya party stated in an interview with *Newsweek* her belief that "time is working on the side of the settlers," expressing a then prevalent concept—"creeping annexation": "Even now we have a creeping annexation, I am not in a hurry" (*Ma'ariv*, August 24, 982, p. 3). Israel Harel, the editor of the bulletin *The Believing and Right-wing Public—Nekuda,* wrote: "The pioneering of the 1980s...is doing exactly what the Labour movement did in the days in which they accumulated their large credit in creating and constructing" (*Nekuda 12*, July 11, 1980, p. 15). The settler population often compared the actions of the Israeli government, and the laws enacted by the Knesset, with the pioneering acts in the days when the "Tower and Stockade" kibbutzim were erected against the British Mandatory government, when the slogan "One more dunam and one more goat" directed their actions against the ruling powers.

In his book *Here and There in the Land of Israel* (1982), Amos Oz wrote the following words, which symbolize the desire for a conscious transition from a religious and nationalist ethos to a practical realization: "Perhaps this was a pipedream: to convert, within three generations, so many persecuted, frightened Jews, consumed by love and hate for their countries of birth, into a nation that would constitute a paradigm for the Arab surroundings, an example of salvation for the entire world. Perhaps we have gone too far, perhaps there was here, among both right and left, hidden corruption, a messianic complex. Perhaps less would have been better. Perhaps there was a wild pretension here, beyond our power and beyond human power. Perhaps it is necessary now to draw back and relinquish the array of messianic dreams, with names such as 'restoration of the kingdoms of David and Solomon' or 'establishment of a model society; a light unto the *goyim*,' 'realization of the prophets' vision,' or 'being the heart of the world,' and perhaps we now need to take small steps. To relinquish the Greater Israel for the sake of internal and external peace, to give up the celestial Jerusalem for the good of a Jerusalem comprising Musrara and the Katamon districts" (Oz, 2009, p. 189).

1987–1996: YOU PROMISED A DOVE, AN OLIVE BRANCH, YOU PROMISED PEACE: A DIALOG OF SECURITY AND PEACE

In 1994 Shmuel Hasfari and Uri Vidislavski composed songs for a band in the Educational Corps—"Winter 73." Some of those born that winter had by 1994 already completed their military service, during a period in the army in which they had confronted the first *intifada* and the echoes of the first Gulf War. They were ready to promote the increasing movement toward peace, reflected in the signing in September 1993 of a declaration of principles in regard to an interim arrangement of self-government with the Palestine Liberation Organization (PLO). The words to the song were: "When we were born the old folk blessed us with tears in their eyes/saying if only these children never have to join the army/and your faces in the old photograph prove their words so well/when you promised to do for us everything to turn the enemy into a friend."

Itzhak Rabin, Minister of Defense during the outbreak of the first *intifada*, effectively defined the new reality facing Israel: "The *intifada* is an unfamiliar phenomenon. It isn't terror, but encompasses terrorist acts and is even supported by terrorist organizations" (*Yediot Aharonot*, June 15, 1990, p. 3). The then Prime Minister, Itzhak Shamir, appealed to the Palestinians in the territories as "Arabs of Judea and Samaria," a term parallel to "Israeli Arabs," which refers to Arab citizens of Israel and not part of the Palestinian nation. He declared: "I appeal to the Arabs of Judea, Samaria and Gaza and call upon them not to be dragged after those who incite and preach violence. Disturbances and strikes will not improve their condition or promote their chances in the slightest. Those who enjoy their suffering and exploit it for their own benefit are the PLO terrorists, who rove from capital city to capital city and spread pipedreams that will never come true. It is possible to achieve an honorable dialogue and reach a fair arrangement that will realize a great part of the this population's desires...I wish to bring an end to this chapter by calling once again from the depth of my heart upon the Arab States and the Arabs of Judea, Samaria and Gaza: Come, hold a dialogue with us, for the sake of peace, peace for our children and peace for your children" (Knesset protocol, June 11, 1990).

The Oslo Accords signed with the PLO during the term of Prime Minister Itzhak Rabin led to a severe rupture in the national-religious camp. The language of the 1967 territories during that decade tended toward a political dialogue of peace, blurring the security aspect. Rabin went far in praising peace, incorporating the notion of territorial compromise. He announced to the Knesset the implementation of the Gaza-Jericho agreement at the beginning of May 1994: "It is no coincidence that the territories have not been annexed; even when the government and its Prime Minister supported the notion of a Greater Israel. The Ma'arach government and the Labour party knew then, and still know today, that the annexation of one million and 800,000 Palestinians will deprive the State of Israel of its Jewish and democratic nature. Mr. Speaker, this government went to the polls and returned victorious, having promised to make every effort to achieve peace, to put an end to wars, to try to put an end to one hundred years of enmity...we believe that the two nations can live together in security and peace, side by side, on the same piece of land" (Knesset protocol, May 11, 1994).

In July 1994 Moshe Feiglin, a resident of Karnei Shomron, announced the formation of the This Is Our Land (Zo Artzeinu) movement, whose title expressed protest over the transfer of territories to the Palestinian Authority and sought to secretly establish dozens of new settlements in order to halt the process The roots of the movement were sown a few months before, in December 1993 (*Yediot Aharonot*, December 01, 1993, p. 3). Prime Minister Rabin, recalling the public anger of those who had objected to his course of action, expressed his dismissive attitude to their views in terms such as "propellers" and "they don't budge me." During the debate on the opposition's proposal of a no-confidence vote in the government and its leader, MK Benjamin Netanyahu said, "you don't have a mandate," which served at the time as a claim to negate the legitimacy of the government in continuing the Oslo Accords: "You don't have a mandate from us, that's clear. But for your method, you also don't have a mandate from your electorate, because you didn't receive a mandate for such far-reaching concessions from many sectors of the public that voted for you." MK Rechavam Ze'evi of the Moledet party reacted during this debate to Rabin's use of the term "propellers": "The State of Israel has been given propellers, propellers that pushed it and pushed it, demonstrated and arrested, built and fought, settled and annexed, defended and talked of the nation and of the homeland. Today those of little belief among us, or those who have tired of the continued struggle, try to ridicule the propellers and turn them into mockery. Prime Minister Rabin does so too, even though for many years it was he himself who was a propeller" (Knesset protocol, June 14, 1993). The *halachic* terms *"Din rodef," "Din moser"* and *"Pulsa diNura,"*[25-27] deriving from ancient books of Jewish law, have become part of the vernacular, of street language, like "peace" or "security." Rabbi Shlomo Aviner, the Beth-El settlement rabbi and head of the Ateret-Cohenim yeshiva, wrote in the Judea and Samaria *Rabbinical Bulletin*: "What happens now is destruction... destruction of part of the land, part of Zionism" (*Rabbinical Bulletin*, No. 12, 1993, p. 3). The government of Israel was defined as criminal and as a "malign government" that should be removed from the land (a term borrowed from the prayer-book cycle for the Holy Days—Days of Awe). Rabbi Menachem Felix went even further, in an article titled "They Don't Care about Paving the Way to 'Peace' with Our Bodies," and termed the government a "government of evil" (*Nekuda*, 173, December 1993, p. 3).

In his book *A Hand Raised against a Brother* (2005), Yoram Pery notes that the assassination of Itzhak Rabin, which he perceived as the consequence of a cultural war, was at the heart of this war (ibid., p. 271). In his opinion, there was a struggle between clashing cultures—"retro" and "metro." Each of these cultures subscribes to a different set of beliefs, and there is no necessary identity between either one of them and the political Right or Left, socioeconomic status, or between religious faith and secularism. The dimensions of this diagnosis include "Jews" versus "Israelis"; "ethno-nationalism" versus political nationalism; Land of Israel versus State of Israel; Jewish state versus democratic state; particularism versus universalism; a concept of circular time versus linear time; collectivism versus individualism; preservation versus renewal; dispute orientation versus postdispute orientation; and Jerusalem as a parable/symbol versus Tel Aviv as a parable/symbol (ibid., p. 79).

1996–2005: THINGS THAT ARE SEEN FROM HERE ARE NOT SEEN FROM THERE: THE LANGUAGE OF SEPARATION AND DISENGAGEMENT

Near the end of 1980, when the Ministry of Agriculture had not yet withdrawn from the settlements that were to be evacuated and returned to Egypt in the framework of the peace agreement, the settlers' newsletter, *Nekudah*, stated: "We in the settlements are faced with a difficult and unique tactical question: 'How can we help Arik [Sharon] when he builds worlds, and stop him when he begins to destroy them'" (*Nekudah, 19*, November 14, 1980, p. 8).

After becoming Prime Minister, Ariel Sharon fulfilled the settlers' fear while saying: "To hold three and a half million Palestinians under occupation is a bad thing for Israel, for the Palestinians, and also for Israel's economy" (*Yediot Aharonot*, May 27, 2003, p. 4). Elyakim Rubenstein, Israel's legal adviser to the government, approached the Prime Minister and asked him to substitute the term "disputed territories" for "occupied territories" (*Haaretz*, May 28, 2003, p. 3A) Appearing before the Foreign and Security Committee, Sharon justified his words: "I meant that I do not want to control another nation... things have changed and are not what they were in the past. There are developments now, this is not the situation that existed ten years ago. We don't need to take upon ourselves responsibility for three and a half million Palestinians." The spokesperson of the Ministry of Justice also referred to Sharon's significant innovation. He contended that every government of Israel since 1967 had spoken of territories under dispute and not of occupied territories. According to him, this meant territories that had had no recognized sovereignty prior to 1967 (Jordanian sovereignty was recognized by two countries only—Great Britain and Pakistan). The correct way to legally describe the situation of the territories, said the spokesperson, was "territories under dispute," whose status was still to be determined in the final agreement. "This definition has of course legal relevance in connection with the negotiations held and to be held by the Israeli government," the spokesperson explained in his announcement to the press (*Yediot Aharonot*, May 28, 2003, p. 6).

In an open letter to Ariel Sharon, Manuela Dviri, a peace activist journalist, whose son had been killed in an encounter with terrorists in 1998, wrote: "Dear Prime Minister, you quoted the word 'occupation' from the leftists' underground lexicon and made it acceptable and permitted and even linked the occupation with the economic situation of Israel" ("The Left Bank" Web site, May 30, 2003; http://hagada.org.il/2003/05/30/7%D7%9C%D7%90%D 7%A8%D7%99%D7%90%D7%9C%D7%A9%D7%A8%D7%95%D7%9F%D7% A8%D7%9C%D7%95%D7%9D%D7%A8%D7%91/).

The closer it got to evacuation of the Gush Katif settlements, the greater the anger of the settlers and their supporters. The musician Ariel Zilber composed a song titled "A Jew Doesn't Expel a Jew" (Channel 7, June 10, 2005). The media headlines on the eve of the evacuation foresaw violence, and the vocabulary used was borrowed from the lexicon of war: "Kfar Darom will be the Masada of Gush Katif"; "600 extremists infiltrated the settlement, dictating the agenda in preparation for a siege" (Channel 2 News, August 12, 2005);

"An atmosphere of war" (*Yediot Aharonot*, August 15, 2005, p. 5); "War awaits us in northern Samaria" (*Yediot Aharonot*, August 21, 2005, p. 2); "Preparing for battle" (*Haaretz*, August 23, 2005, p. 3A). Sharon repeated phrases he had already used: "The disengagement plan can pave the way to the beginning of implementing the Road Map, to which we are committed and which we want to implement.... This is the only way to reach two States that will live in peace and quiet alongside one another" (Web site of the Prime Minister's Office, February 8, 2005) To all those who wondered what had happened to "the father of the settlements" in his current support of the evacuation and transfer of land to the Palestinians, Sharon replied: "Things that are seen from here are not seen from there." This expression, in its various foreign-language versions, is attributed, among others, to Richard A. Neustadt,[25] and in Israel it features in the song "Take My Hand in Yours" by Yaakov Rotblit.

At the request of Prime Minister Sharon,[26] the attorney Talia Sasson[27] prepared a report on unauthorized settlements. This report, and the public debate over it, brought to light other nuanced collocations and terms, some of which were familiar only to those in the legal profession, such as "State lands" or "Lands that belong to the State," "Jewish lands," "land declared State land," "survey lands," "lands purchased by Jews after 1967," "Palestinian private lands," "settled lands," and "nonsettled lands," as well as "trailer homes," "caravans," and others.

During this decade, the language of the dispute was enriched with an additional set of concepts and newly minted terms, such as "painful compromises," "significant concessions," "withdrawal," "evacuation," "uprooting," "expulsion," "Jewish transfer," "separation" or "initiated separation," "bilateral disengagement," "unilateral disengagement," "As goes Netzarim so goes Tel Aviv," "separation barrier," "wall," and "no-man's land" (Tsur. 2006). MK Yossi Sarid of the Meretz party stated during the 2001 budget debate: "All the talk on separation, withdrawal, disengagement, and there are those who distinguish between them and confer symbols on each stupid difference—separation, withdrawal, disengagement—all this talk is worthless if we don't understand what is being said...preparation for unilateral disengagement on Israel's borders while withdrawing from the territories of course necessitates moving and removing the settlements. Disengagement is the only answer, and only partitioning is the solution, there is no other solution. And there can be no disengagement with 140 settlements still in place, no disengagement without international aid, without an agreed international presence, for if the two sides by themselves are unable to disengage, responsible international agents will arrive and separate between them" (Knesset protocol, March 28, 2001).

...AND THESE ARE THE NAMES OF THE SETTLEMENTS

On July 14, 1967, one month after the end of the Six Day War, the first Israeli settlement was established on the Golan Heights, becoming a permanent settlement—Merom Golan. On September 27, 1967, three months after the war, the first settlement was established on the West Bank—Kfar Etzion. Less than a year later, during Passover (April 1968), a few families, headed by Rabbi Moshe Levinger, entered the Park Hotel in Hebron, laying the cornerstone for Jewish settlement in Kiryat Arba, and in 1970 Kfar Darom was established in Gaza, later populated by civilians.

As time passed following these initial settlements, the names given the settlements acquired meanings that stressed a link between the linguistic characteristics and the chosen name. For example, the settlements established in the first decade of occupation bore biblical, redemptive names or those that recalled settlements and individuals from Israel's ancient history, such as Ophrah—the first Israeli settlement in Samaria and among the first in Judea and Samaria, which was established in 1975 and named after the biblical city that was headquarters to the Tribe of Benjamin (Joshua 18, 23). This was preceded by Kiryat Arba,[28] the site where Abraham's wife, Sarah, had died (Genesis 23, 2); Mevo Horon, bearing the name of the biblical city of Beth Horon (Chronicles I, 6, 53); and the renewed settlements in Gush Etzion, including Elazar, named for the route between Jerusalem and Hebron, near Efrat[29]; as well as several in the Jordan Valley, including Patzael, established in 1970 and named after the Jewish settlement from the Second Temple, which bore the name of the Governor of Jerusalem, Herod's brother—Patzael. Later, south of Mount Hebron, the settlement of Susya was founded, named after the ancient city of Susya that had existed since the fall of the Second Temple until the Byzantine and early Moslem periods (fourthth to ninth centuries bce).

In the second decade after the Six Day War, there was a clear trend to give the new settlements more nationalist names, such as Shavei Shomron (Return to Samaria), which was founded in 1977 and whose name reflects the return to the Samaria region and the area of the city that had been the capital of the Kingdom of Israel; and Gibeon HaHadasha (the New Gibeon), also founded in 1977 and whose name symbolized the link between the biblical Gibeon and the newly established one on the same land (Joshua 9, 3; Nechemiah 7, 25). In addition, Hebrew names were given to places that previously bore Arabic names, such as Einav—close to Tulkarm, whose name recalls the Arabic name of the nearby village of Anabta—and Kokhav HaShahar—east of the Benjamin mountains, named after the nearby mountain Kubat A-Najma, which in Arabic means "the morning star."

Along with the use of other biblical names in this period, there was a clear trend toward giving theophoric names to the settlements, also reflecting earlier names. These included Elkanah, Beth El, Nahaliel, Peduel, Emmanuel, and Otniel. In one of his public appearances, Itzhak Rabin rejected the settlement enterprise by adding to two of the existing names—Ariel and Emmanuel—the derogatory adjective *schlemiel* ("unlucky person"; (*Davar*, July 05, 1987, p. 3).

In the time that followed another trend could be observed: conferring Jewish names on the settlements, such as Esh Kodesh (Fire of Sacredness) in the Benjamin district, named after the book by Rabbi Klonimus Kalmish Szapira, one of the young Hassidic leaders in Poland who had perished in 1943 in the Budzyn concentration camp in the Lublin region and whose writings were found in the Warsaw Ghetto, and named also for the security guard Esh-Kodesh Gilmore, who was murdered at the beginning of the *intifada* in October 2000 while guarding the entrance to the National Insurance building in East Jerusalem. Modern Israeli names or modern-sounding names also appeared, such as Oranit—on the western slopes of the Samarian mountains, founded in 1985; Negohot—on the western slopes of Mount Hebron, founded in 1982; or Rotem—in the Jordan Valley, founded in 1984 and handed over to civilians in 2001. There were also names that commemorated persons who had perished in terrorist attacks or military operations, such as Maaleh Rechavam—east of Gush Etzion, founded in 2001, commemorating the general (ret.) and government minister Rechavam Ze'evi, who was murdered by terrorists on October 17, 2001; or Shvut Rachel—founded in October 1991, named after Rachela Druk, a resident of Shiloh and a mother of seven, who was killed together with her driver in a shooting attack nearby another settlement, Rechelim.

LINGUISTIC ENCOUNTERS IN THE 1967 TERRITORIES

Three main languages have been used for over a generation from, June 1967 to 2005, in the West Bank and the Gaza Strip: Arabic, Hebrew, and English. The language of the Palestinians inhabiting the territories is Arabic. Israeli settlers speak Hebrew, and so do soldiers moving into and out of military bases and performing policing, civil administration, and antiterrorist tasks. The common language for Israelis and Palestinians, as well as for occasional businessmen and visitors to the territories, is English.

Ever since the Six Day War, Arabic-speaking Palestinians from the territories have been crossing, legally and illegally, the Israeli borders recognized by the armistice accords with Jordan and with Egypt. For many of them Israel is a working place, and they have partially adopted Hebrew in order to communicate with their employers. Religious Palestinians are encouraged to learn and use Hebrew, not only by Hebrew speakers but also by educators and Islamic religious leaders, who consider the acquisition of additional languages as a religious duty (Al Abed Al-Haq and Smadi, 1996). Israelis, on the other hand, are not eager to communicate in Arabic, for various reasons, and learn it reluctantly (Abd-El-Jawad & Al-Abed Al-Haq, 1997, p. 420).

When Israel was founded, it applied Article 82 of The Palestine Order in Council regarding the official languages of the country. Taking into consideration the Arab minority and continuing the colonial heritage, Hebrew, Arabic, and English were selected as official languages. When the reliance on the British Crown was abolished by the Law and Administration Ordinance 1948, English lost its standing in Article 15 (b) of The Palestine Order in Council. Hebrew and Arabic have been used as the official languages of Israel ever since (Salton, 1967). In a 2002 judgment regarding the obligation to use Arabic on road signs of municipalities that include Arab minorities, High Court Judge Aharon Barak wrote: "Israelis speak many languages, but only Arabic, in addition to Hebrew, is an official language in Israel" (High Court of Justice, July, 25, 2002, p. 417). Judge Dov Levin opined in another case: "The Arabic language has its own characteristics, since it is the mother tongue of an important and big part of Israeli society, and a central part of a rich and diverse culture, which fits very well into the colorful cultural mosaic of the State" (High Court of Justice, September 21, 1993, p. 192).

Arabic, which is common to the Arab minority in Israel and to the Palestinian inhabitants of the territories, is seen by a large part of the Israeli-Jewish public as an enemy language, used to order terrorists to carry out attacks against the state and its population. Not all Israeli-Jewish citizens share the view that knowing the languages of linguistic and cultural minorities could moderate conflicts stemming from friction between minorities and majorities in divided societies (Levy, 2000, pp. 40–41). The poet and translator Dori Manor, editor of the literary journal *Ho*, who spent some years in France, said about the standing of Arabic in the Israeli public sphere: "In high school I chose French over Arabic, partly because learning Arabic was intended at the time as a way to understand the enemy's language" (Verbin, 2006, p. 30). Moshe Sakal, his partner in *Ho*, said about the same subject: "I shall be happy to reach Arab culture, but not as a conqueror. I am unable to look an Israeli Arab in the face—I could do it in France, because there I also had Moslem friends. From my place in Israel at this moment it would be a patronizing look, whether I wished it or not. I come from the side of the top-dogs" (ibid.).

There are some who take this attitude even further, believing that protection of the linguistic rights of a cultural minority in a multicultural country could promote a feeling of loyalty to the entire population (Tully, 1997, pp. 197–198). This is not the case in Israel, with a minority torn between loyalty to the state and faithfulness to the Palestinian nationality, including the traditional nationalism based on religious identification with Islam (Kimmerling & Migdal, 1999, pp. 259–268). Various groups within this minority consider themselves layers in the national fabric of Palestinians, some of whom live in the territories and others in the rest of the world while aspiring to return to their land (Sofer & Shalev, 2004). Israelis of all persuasions acknowledge this reality—for instance, exempting Israeli Arabs from national service. At the same time, there are Israelis who object to the fact that Arab citizens support a nation that does not recognize the right of Israel to exist (Sharon, 1992, p. 17).

The reality in the 1967 territories is unique; it does not resemble the one portrayed by the philosopher and psychiatrist Franz Fanon (2008) in his book about life in conquered Algiers, who does not limit his description to the point of view of a National Liberation Front (FLN) activist who strives for its liberation from France. There is no doubt that Israeli control of the territories has also harmed the Palestinian population from the linguistic point of view and has added a Creole dimension to the remnants of English, which was an elite language at the time of the British Mandate. The influence of English has been decreasing during the Jordanian rule in the West Bank and the Egyptian rule in the Gaza Strip. The penetration of Hebrew into the territories as the language of the rulers has further diluted Palestinian Arabic, particularly the vocabulary that joined the fragments of English as well as the Jordanian and Egyptian vocabularies.

Throughout history, conquerors have imposed their language on conquered populations, and have in fact compelled the citizens of subjugated countries to define themselves by vocabulary and linguistic structures, forcing them to make linguistic choices in an alien language. The use of Spanish in the Filipino language is a case in point in a place thousands of miles from Spain (Whinnom, 1954, 1956). A further example is the influence of the Dutch language on the Surinamese (Oostindie & Klinkers, 2003, p. 62). The physical and linguistic conquest turns into a conquest of consciousness, while on the opposite side a language of liberation emerges spoken by the conquered. The poet David Diop, born to a Senegalese father and a mother from Cameroon, divided his life between France, where he was born, Senegal, and Cameroon. For him, the language of the conqueror can be used by oppressed populations in the fight for independence, while the natural language should serve for creative purposes and the expressions of protest (Ogede, 1998, p. 130).

The scale and power of the Israeli linguistic penetration differ from these and other cases—for instance, that of conquered Algiers. This is clearly seen in the descriptions of literary works that respond to the models of intercultural relationship based on dialogue or the rejection of "the other" and his strangeness (Bhabha, 1994). This happens despite the alienation between the Israeli and Palestinian cultures, stemming from conflicts between nations, tense relationships within the State of Israel, and the affiliation of the Hebrew culture with the West, while the Palestinians lean toward the Arabic one (Kayyal, 2006).

The exiled Palestinian writer and poet Mohammed Al-Assad points out in his book *Yaldei Hatal* (*Children of Dew*, 2005) that the language of the conqueror distorts the consciousness of the conquered, who try to adapt their identity to the new situation, as compared to the past, when they were free. Al-Assad, who became a refugee at the age of four and wandered from Umm al-Zinat, the village of his birth on the southern slopes of the Carmel, to Jenin and then to Iraq, Jordan, Cyprus, Bulgaria, and Kuwait, describes through characters of his own family the relationship between language and consciousness, and between that and the feeling of the son of an oppressed people. A similar dialogue between languages in the context of the Israeli-Palestinian conflict appears in the book *Sarayet Bint el-Ghoul* (*Saraya, the Orge's Daughter*, 1993) by the writer and activist Emile Habibi. These descriptions do not impute elements of linguistic compulsion to the conquest and consequent uprooting; but since language is an important cultural component, it is not possible to ignore the influence of the conquerors' language on the indigenous minorities in the conquered land or on the minority that left the country and became refugees (Kymlicka, 1995, pp. 79, 89), since the language reflects the world through historical heritage and common memories (Chen, 1998).

The linguistic conquest has affected more than the subjugated people; in the Israeli- Palestinian reality; it has also affected the Israeli conquerors. New words and expressions, some politically correct and others responding to competing ideologies in the public sphere, have emerged over the years, reflecting political and social trends in Israel.

IN PLACE OF A SUMMARY-WE ARE SOMETIMES LURED BY WORDS, DRAGGED AFTER THEM

Menachem Begin, speaking in the Knesset six years after the Six Day War, asked his opponents from the Ma'arach: "How is it possible to justify our interests, if even today you employ the term 'occupied territories' and have committed yourselves to withdrawing from them? If, in your opinion, they are occupied, we ask you: 'For how much longer will they be occupied? Our right—our homeland, our country, it cannot be partitioned, without it we have no security" (Knesset protocol, November 13, 1973). With these words, directed at the government headed by Golda Meir, from which the Gahal party leader had parted, Begin incorporated the basic terminology of the 1967 territories. In using the terms "our homeland, "our country" he spoke in the language of the promise of redemption, as reflected in the biblical Abraham's request to Eliezer, his farm manager, to help him find a bride for his son Isaac: "The LORD, the God of heaven, who brought me out of my father's household and my native land and who spoke to me and promised me on oath, saying, 'To your offspring I will give this land'—he will send his angel before you so that you can get a wife for my son from there" (Genesis 24, 7). Begin also employed a term borrowed from the field of ethics when he used "our right," a political term linked to the possible political arrangement: "It cannot be partitioned"; nor did he forget the rhetoric of security in saying that "without it we have no security."

The programmatic void in regard to the future of the territories—and thus also in regard to a partial or total withdrawal, whether by agreement or by unilateral evacuation—was filled after 1967 by the settlement initiative, accompanied by enthusiastic sweeping statements and acts of purposeful settlement on the land. The elected leadership was effectively taken over by the activists, with help from the settlement supporters in the Knesset and government and from silent supporters. Throughout the four decades in which Israeli society was subjected to changes and reversals among the various standpoints on the territories' future, the political discourse grew increasingly extremist, becoming more strident and transmitted by professionally trained individuals who blurred the messages and muted the public discourse.

During the first decade, between 1967 and 1977, the language of redemption was prominent, employed by both those who supported settlement and those who rejected it. This was a language used not only by those who wore the yarmulke (religious head covering) and carried out the commandments, but also by the broad public who recognized the Bible as Israel's mandate, as claimed by Schweid (1979, p. 210). During the second decade, between 1977 and 1987, the language of historical justification predominated, along with a discourse on the right to the land. The third decade, between 1987 and 1996, saw the use of a language mainly of conciliation and peace as a guarantee of security. The fourth decade, between 1996 and 2005, was characterized by a language of separation, disengagement, and the creation of separate mechanisms for peace and security. Throughout the decades, however, the public discourse had been accompanied by terms borrowed from the field of security. For example, the government during Begin's second term of office as Prime Minister (August 1981–October 1983) incorporated within its guidelines the language of rights and security: "Settlement in the Land of Israel is a right and an inseparable part of the national security" (Knesset protocol, August 5, 1981).

The language of redemption expressed the belief in the 1967 "Return to Zion"; delivery of Israel from the state of siege that had preceded the war; and liberation of the land of the forefathers and its settlements, a place where the kings of Israel and Judah had walked and the prophets had spoken. There was to be a realization of Jeremiah's prophecy (Jeremiah 31) and of thesr verses: "Yet again will I rebuild you, then you shall be built, O virgin of Israel." "Yet again shall you plant vineyards on the mountains of Samaria"; "For the LORD has redeemed Jacob and has saved him out of the hand of him who is stronger than he." "They shall come back from the land of the enemy"; "And the children shall return to their own border." On the eve of the Six Day War, Rabbi Yaakov Halevi Filver wrote in his book *The Morning Star* (1975): "The train of redemption has started on its journey to the next station, and there is no-one in the world who can stop it" (p. 32).

Just as in the first decade, in the second decade various otherworldly notions were heard, such as "We have no-one to rely on other than our Father in Heaven." In this decade, with the Likud in power, biblical notions were used to justify nationalist messages. For example, in a message sent to U.S. President Ronald Reagan, Prime Minister Menachem Begin wrote: "I stick by the truth. And the truth is, that thousands of years ago there was a Jewish kingdom in Judea-Samaria. There our kings bowed down before our God. There our prophets saw a vision of eternal peace. There we developed a rich culture. We took it with us, in our hearts and our thoughts, in our long wanderings through the world for over one thousand and eight hundred years; and with this we returned home.... After we were attacked by King Hussein, we liberated, with the grace of God, part of our homeland, Judea and Samaria, and there shall nevermore be a 'Left Bank' of the Hashemite Kingdom of Jordan" (Government Press Office bulletin, February 19, 1982).

This message embodies the language of historical justification, which was also often used in that period by various religious factions. For example, Rabbi Moshe Levinger, among the founders of Gush Emunim and the Judea and Samaria Council, and father of the Jewish settlement in Hebron after 1967, stated: "The Land of Israel is not only a night shelter or security support. It is indivisibly linked with the moral and eternal destiny of the nation of Israel" (*Nekudah, 49*, October 22, 1982, p. 7).

The third decade was witness to the language of peace. The new Jew, who had already experienced several wars and other hostile actions, confronted a new type of war: the *intifada*. Eitan Haber, former Director of Prime

Minister Itzhak Rabin's office, evaluated the place of this "populist protest" in guiding Rabin's decision to move within a few years toward peace with the Palestinians: "I believe that there has been a combination here of several things. The prolonged *intifada* and the lack of ability to suppress it by force, and the knowledge that has been acquired that it is not possible to continue to rule over two and a half million Palestinians" (*Yediot Aharonot*, November 10, 1995, p. 9).

In an article titled "Tomorrow Is Already Here" (written shortly after SCUD rockets launched by Iraq in the First Gulf War had ceased to fall on Israel), appearing in the book *The Vocabulary of Peace*, by Shulamith Hareven, still during the period of the *intifada*, the author stated: "Between mid-January to the beginning of March 1991 that tomorrow has already arrived, it already sits among us, inside the home. And our politicians have no choice, if they are not staring somewhere into yesterday, but to rise toward it, and to say what must be said: 'Peace'" (Hareven, 1996, p. 169).

In the fourth decade, mainly against the background of the second *intifada* and the disappointment at the failure of the Oslo Accords' conciliation effort, emphasis moved from a perception of peace as the essence of security to a perception that, while peace and security are separate needs, they will both be achieved by separation, withdrawal, or disengagement. When presenting his amended disengagement plan to the Knesset, Ariel Sharon stated: "I am deeply convinced, and to the best of my knowledge, that this disengagement will strengthen Israel in retaining the territory essential to its existence and that this will receive the blessing and recognition of those both near and far, will reduce hostility, end boycott and siege, and advance us in the path to peace with the Palestinians and our other neighbors" (Web site of the Prime Minister's Office, October 25, 2004; http://www.pmo.gov.il/pmo; http://www.pmo.gov.il/PMO/Archive/Speeches/2004/10/speech2510.htm). Later, several months before the withdrawal from Gaza and evacuation of its Jewish towns, he honed this message: "The year 2005 is a year of great possibility. This can be the year that terror is defeated and ceases to be a significant threat to Israel and its security, ceases to be a threat to peace. This can be the year in which we lay the foundations for an Israeli-Palestinian accord for many years to come. We shall act with all our power so that this year of opportunity does not become a year of missed opportunity" (ibid., December 16, 2004; http://www.pmo.gov.il/PMO/Archive/Speeches/2004/12/speech+1612.htm).

Today, in the fifth decade, against the background of a linguistic "spin" that arose during the "Cast-Lead Campaign,"[30] and the rise too of the legal-moral discourse in Israel and worldwide, the words of the sociologist Baruch Kimmerling ring out. Kimmerling died during this decade, but in early 1996 he opined in a newspaper interview that "The Israeli public and government are ready to 'disengage' from the Palestinians, but not from the majority of the territories" (*Haaretz*, February 9, 1996, p. 37).

In another interview with the same newspaper, Amnon Rubenstein, the then Minister of Education in Rabin's government and Israel Prize recipient, spoke with Faisal Husseini, son of Abd al-Qader al-Husseini, who had been commander of the Arab forces in the Jerusalem area and was killed in 1948 in the battle for the Castel. Faisal Husseini, a relative of the Mufti, had been sentenced to one year in prison for possession of a weapon, and in the interview in prison he told Rubenstein: "That's one of our things. We are sometimes lured by words, dragged after them. In fact we should change many of our entrenched habits. If we want to stop being held back, we must change these habits" (*Haaretz*, March 3, 1969, p. 3). This is as true today for the Israeli public as it is for the Palestinian public.

NOTES

1. This phrase is usually used whenever an Israeli politician wants to come over as wittily plain-spoken to English-speaking audiences—the duck analogy.
2. See the chapter by Magal, Oren, Bar-Tal, and Halperin in this book, which discusses how the territories are perceived by Israeli Jews.
3. The Road Map is a plan introduced by U.S. President George W. Bush on June 24, 2002. It is based on a two-state solution, urging the Palestinians to elect a new leadership and carry out broad reforms in the existing leadership in order to create a democracy. The United States and the international community expressed a commitment to assist the Palestinians' efforts to form a state "based on tolerance and freedom." The American President called upon Israel to withdraw from the Palestinian towns to the pre-intifada Al-Aqsa lines, to take concrete steps to help create a Palestinian state, to apply the conclusions of the Mitchell Report (a document written by an American committee, led by former U.S. Senator George Mitchell, on the state of the Middle East conflict after the failure of the Camp David 2000 summit and following the al-Aqsa intifada) of May 22, 2001, and to cease settlement expansion and enable the Palestinians to develop their economy (Maariv, June 24, 2002, p. 3).
4. The term "1967 territories" that appears in this chapter, unless specified otherwise, refers to the territories conquered in the Six Day War from the Jordanian kingdom, as well as the territory of the Gaza Strip conquered from Egypt.
5. According to the Austrian philosopher Ludwig Wittgenstein (1889–1951), language is what constructs the world around us and sets its borders (Wittgenstein, 2009, p. 88). A similar idea is raised by the linguist Benjamin Whorf (1897–1941), who stated that language shapes the way human beings think about and

look at the world (Whorf ,1956). Thus, language mediates between mankind and between mankind and reality.
6. See Goffman (1974, p. 21).
7. The term "uncontrolled dispute" in referring to the Middle East conflict was developed by Bar-Tal (2007). See ibid., p. 25.
8. "Free-held territories" is a term of ridicule used by the public that combined two adjectives for the 1967 territories—"held territories" and "liberated/freed territories." See Sapan (1971). See also Levy (2007).
9. See Goren (1996).
10. The lack of the word "the" before the term "territories" in the British version of the Security Council decision 242 of November 20, 1967, and, in contrast, its appearance in the French version, created a variety of interpretations about the significance of the decision. While the British version appears in clause 1a, demanding that Israel withdraw from "territories" (i.e., from part of the territories) occupied in the recent conflict, the same clause in French demands withdrawal from "the territories" (i.e., from all the territories). See the evaluation by Yosef Tekoah, Israeli ambassador to the United Nations (1968–1975), in his book (Tekoah, 1976, p. 257).
11. See Saeb Arikat's statement: "Israel's plan is to eliminate the territorial unity of the Palestinian occupied territories by severing Gaza from the Palestinian administrative and political centers in the West Bank, including East Jerusalem" (Channel 2 News, August 22, 2005).
12. A belligerent occupation. See, for example, High Court ruling 393/82 concerning G`ama'at Askan, an official cooperative association working against the IDF military command in the area of Judea and Samaria. (High Court of Justice, July 25, 1982).
13. "...Emphasizing the inadmissibility of the acquisition of territory by war..."
14. The region occupied by the Tribe of Ephraim encompassed the towns of Nablus, Beth El, and the biblical Shiloh: "In majesty he is like a firstborn bull; his horns are the horns of a wild ox. With them he will gore the nations, even those at the ends of the earth. Such are the ten thousands of Ephraim; such are the thousands of Manasseh" (Deuteronomy 33, 17).
15. "Night shelter" is a term coined by Max Nordau at the Sixth Zionist Congress in 1903 in reference to the proposal of Jewish settlement in Uganda under British auspices ("The Uganda Plan"); see Knesset protocol, May 9, 1960, on the 100th anniversary of the birth of Benjamin Zeev Herzl.
16. The term "dormant war" appears in an essay by Dan Horowitz (1982, p. 5; 1996, p. 73)
17. On "the spells of the biblical ancients" and "the spell of the biblical landscape," see Oz (2009): "Where will all this ancient biblical nostalgia lead if Samaria will be filled with pre-fabricated houses? Will we set off to chase the wells and the planted fields and the flocks and the orchards as far as the Mountains of Moab? As far as Gila'ad and the Horan? To the bitter end? To death?" (p. 99).

18. On June 27, 1967, the Knesset approved three proposals presented by the government. These enacted the unification of Jerusalem and validated the application of Israel law to the entire city. On July 30, 1980, the Basic Law: Jerusalem was enacted, determining that "The unified Jerusalem is the capital of Israel."
19. See Kaminer (1997) and Rabinovich (1987, p. 403).
20. See Tsur (2004, pp. 172–173).
21. Itzhak Rabin: "A tired nation—mourning its victims, has difficulty in absorbing the events and understanding their significance—behaved mercifully with the Labor party, not because it tended to forgive it and its leaders and exempt them from the burden of guilt of the blunders, but because it fell under the spell of the Geneva Convention and clung desperately to the hope that from there would spring the yearned for peace" (Rabin, 1979, p. 410).
22. The saying "Waiting for a phone call from the Arabs" was coined by Moshe Dayan, Minister of Defense, in an interview with the BBC (June 13, 1967) and referred to the spiritual process according to which the states that had been defeated in the war would be the first to turn to Israel with a peace initiative' further, said Dayan, "We are well placed where we are standing today." See also Oz (1988, p. 69).
23. "Take counsel and it will be foiled; speak a word and it will not succeed, for God is with us" (Isaiah 8, 10). In Hagai Segal's The Incomplete Settlers' Dictionary this appears as a slogan about the "evacuation of settlements." Retrieved August 22, 2000, from http://myesha.org.il/?CategoryID=178&ArticleID=332&Page=2
24. "Lebanonization," the internal weakness in Lebanon, led to a historical pattern in which each of the internal forces was assisted by an external force in order to overcome its rivals and enforce a political order suited to its interests and those of its leaders. See Sobelman (2007).
25. "Din rodef" ("law of the pursuer"): "He who threatens to kill his friend even though that threat be small, all of Israel is commanded to save he who is threatened and even to kill he who threatens" (Maimonides, "Laws of Murder and Preservation of the Soul," Halacha 1, 6).
26. "Din moser" is a Halachic term prohibiting one from handing over (extraditing) a friend to a powerful foreign entity or from informing on him
27. "Pulsa diNura" ("lashes of fire").
28. Richard E. Neustadt, who researches leadership, was an adviser to U.S. Presidents Truman, Kennedy, Johnson and Clinton. See Neustadt (1960).
29. Government decision, March 13, 2005, in response to the request that Israel respond to the Road Map.
30. Attorney Talia Sasson, former head of the criminal investigation division of the Attorney General's office.
31. Kiryat Arba was the ancient name of Hebron (Judges, 1, 10; Joshua, 14, 15).
32. Elazar was founded in October 1975 and named after Elazar the Hasmonean, who, according to the sources, was killed near the location of the settlement, in Beth Zachariah, during the Maccabee revolt in the second century bce.

33. "The Cast-Lead Campaign" was the name chosen from a children's song written by Hayim Nahman Bialik. The song is sung during the festival of Hannuka and its original wording is: "My teacher brought me a gyrate/it was made of cast lead/do you know why?/for Hannuka!" The word "gyrate" was later replaced by the word "dreidel."

REFERENCES

Abd-El-Jawad, H., & Al-Abed Al-Haq, F. (1997). The impact of the peace process in the Middle-East on Arabic. In M. Clyne (Ed.),*Undoing and redoing corpus planning* (pp. 415–445). Berlin and New York: Mouton de Gruyter.

Al-Abed Al-Haq, F., & Smadi, O. (1996). The status of English in the Kingdom of Saudi Arabia (KSA) from 1940–1990. In J. A. Fishman, A. W. Conrad, & A. Rubal-Lopez (Eds.), *Post-imperial English: Status change in former British and American colonies, 1940–1990* (pp. 457–485). Berlin and New-York: Mouton de Gruyter.

Al-Assad, M. (2005). *Yaldei Hatal* (*The children of the dew*; Y. Meron, Trans.). Haifa: Pardes.

Aran, G. (1985). *The land of Israel between religion and politics: The movement to halt the withdrawal from the Sinai and its lessons.* Jerusalem: Jerusalem Institute for Research of Israel.

Aristotle, (2002). *Rhetoric* (G. Zoran, Trans.). Tel Aviv: Sifriat Hapoalim.

Bar-Tal, D. (2007). *Living with the dispute: Socio-psychological analysis of Israeli-Jewish society.* Jerusalem: Carmel.

Bhabha, Homi K. (1994). The other question: Stereotype, discrimination and the discourse of colonialism. *Theory and Criticism*, 5, 144–159.

Begin, M. (1978). *The revolt*. Tel Aviv: Achiassaf.

Beilin, Y. (1996). *Shaike Ben-Porat—Conversatons with Yossi Beilin*. Tel Aviv: HaKibbutz HaMeuchad-Red Line.

Bronovsky, Y. (1975). *A journey to language*. Tel Aviv: Sifriat Hapoalim.

Civil Appeal. (1993). 105/92..*Re'em Contracting Engineers Ltd v. Upper Nazareth Municipality*. IsrSC 47(5) 189 (1993).

Chen Albert Hung, Y. (1998). The philosophy of language rights. *Language Science*, 20, 45, 47.

Dayan, M. (1969). *New map, other relationships*. Tel Aviv: Sifriat Ma'ariv.

Fanon, F. (2008). *Black skin, white masks* (R. Philcox, Trans.). New York: Grove Press.

Filver, Y. (1975). *The morning star: Studies and sources regarding Israel, its laws and its redemption in its land*. Jerusalem: Torah L'Am, Harry Fischel Institute.

Gazit, S. (1999). *The gullible in a trap*. Tel Aviv: Zmora Bitan.

Goffman, E. (1974). *Frame analysis*. Cambridge, MA: Harvard University Press.

Goren, S. (1996). The wholeness of the land according to the Halacha. In S. Goren (Ed.), *The law of the state* (pp. 68–102). Jerusalem: HaIdra Raba.

Grossman, D. (1987). *The yellow time*. Tel Aviv: HaKibbutz HaMeuchad.

Habermas, J. (1998). *Between facts and norms.* Cambridge, MA: MIT Press.
Habibi, E. (1993). *Sarayet Bint el-Ghoul (Saraya, the orge's daughter;* A. Shammas, Trans.). Tel-Aviv, Hakibbutz Hameuchad.
Hareven, S. (1996). *The vocabulary of peace.* Tel Aviv: Zmora Bitan.
Har-Noi, M. (1994). *The settlers.* Tel Aviv: Sifriat Ma'ariv.
High Court of Justice. (September, 21, 1993). HCJ 105/92.
High Court of Justice. (2002). HCJ 4112/99—*Adalah Legal Centre for Arab Minority Rights in Israel v. Tel-Aviv-Jaffa Municipality,* PD 56(5) 393.
Hoffer, E. (1951). *The true believer.* New York: Harper & Row.
Horowitz, D. (1982). *The fixed and the changing in perceptions of Israeli security.* Publications of State Policy 4. Jerusalem: Leonard Davis Institute for International Relations.
Horowitz, D. & M. Lisk (1996). "Democracy and National Security in a Prolonged Dispute. In: Neuberger B. & A. Ben-Ami. (eds.) (1996). *Democracy and National Security in Israel.* Ramat Aviv: Open University Publications: 73–113.
Kaminer, A. (1997, May 5). Sing happy birthday to the state. *Yediot Aharonot,* pp. 6–8.
Kayyal, M. (2006). *Translation in the shadow of confrontation.* Jerusalem: Hebrew University Magnes Press.
Kimmerling, B., & and Migdal, J. S. (1999). *Palestinians: The making of a people.,* Jerusalem: Keter.
Kymlicka, W. (1995). *Multicultural citizenship: A liberal theory of minority rights.* Oxford: Oxford University Press.
Levy, G. (2007, June 23). The occupied language of the occupier. *Ofakim Hadashim (New Horizons),* 37; available at http://ofakim.org.il/zope/home/he/1181463089/1182001668
Levy, Jacob T. (2000). *The multiculturalism of fear.* Oxford: Oxford University Press.
Naor, A. (1993). *Begin in power.* Tel Aviv: Yediot Aharonot.
Naor, A. (2001). *The greater Israel—Faith and policy.* Haifa and Lod: University of Haifa Publications and Zmora Bitan.
Neustadt, R. E. (1960). *Presidential power: The politics of leadership.* New York: Wiley.
Nir, R. (1998). Political correctness—A clean language and balancing the language. *Panim,* 7, 19–26.
Ogede Ode, S. (1998). David Mandessi Diop. In P. P. Naidu & J. S. Fatima (Eds.), *Postcolonial African writers: A bio-bibliographical critical sourcebook* (pp. 128–134). Westport, CT: Greenwood Press.
Oostindie, G., & Klinkers, I. (2003). *Decolonising the Carribbean Duch policies in a comparative perspective.* Amsterdam: Amsterdam University Press.
Orwell, G. (1949). *Nineteen eighty-four.* London: Secker and Warburg.
Oz, A. (1988). *On the foothills of Lebanon.* Jerusalem: Keter.
Oz, A. (2009). *Here and there in the land of Israel in autumn 1982* (6th ed.). Jerusalem: Keter. (Originally published in 1983)
Pedatzur, R. (1996). *The victory of embarrassment.* Tel Aviv: Bitan.
Perlmutter A. (1987). *Life and times of Menachem Begin.* New York: Doubleday.

Pery, Y. (2005). *A hand raised against his brother*. Tel Aviv: Babel.
Rabin, I. (1979). *Service record*, Vols 1 and 2. Tel Aviv: Sifriat Ma'ariv.
Rabinovich, A. (1987). *The battle for Jerusalem*. Philadelphia: Jewish Publication Society.
Salton, A. (1967). The official languages in Israel. *Hapraklit*, 23, 387.
Sapan, R. (1971). *The Israeli dictionary of slang*. Jerusalem: Kiriat Sefer.
Schweid, E. (1979). *Homeland and a land of promise*. Tel Aviv: Am Oved.
Segal, H. (2001) *Terms—The Channel 7 dictionary of spoken Hebrew*. Ofra: Arutz Sheva.
Shamir, I. (1994). *In summary*. Jerusalem: Idanim.
Sharon, M. (1992). The Islamic dimension in the Middle-Eastern politics. *Nativ*, 3, 15–18.
Sobelmann, D. (2007). Lebanon in the shadow of an internal crisis. *Strategic Update*, 10(3), 27.
Sofer, A., & Shalev, G. (2004). *Realization of the Palestinian homecoming claim*. Monograph 7/2004. Haifa: Israel National Defense College, IDF with the partnership of the Reuven Chaikin Chair in Geostrategy, University of Haifa.
Tau, Z. I. (Ed.). (1987). *Public laws—Notes on matters concerning the public*. Jerusalem: Rabbi Centre.
Tekoah, Y. (1976). *In the face of the nations: Israel's struggle for peace* (D. Aphek, Ed.). New York: Simon & Schuster.
Tsur, N. (2004). *Political rhetoric*. Tel Aviv: HaKibbutz HaMeuchad..
Tsur, N. (2006). *Disengaging from the strip—Ariel Sharon and Israel's withdrawal from the Gaza Strip 2006*. Jerusalem: Tzivonim.
Tsur, Y. A. (1973). *Rules of War and the legal system in the territories held by the IDF*. Jerusalem: Academon.
Tully, J. (1997). *Strange multiplicity: Constitutionalism in an age of diversity*. Cambridge: Cambridge University Press.
Verbin, R. (2006, May 30). I am a cultural activist in the post of periodical editor. *Ofakim Hadashim (New Horizons)*; available at http://ofakim.org.il/zope/home/he/1138194787/1146909118
Whinnom, K. (1954). Spanish in the Philippines. *Journal of Oriental Studies*, 1, 129–194.
Whinnom, K. (1956). *Spanish contact vernaculars in the Philippines*. Hong Kong: Hong Kong University Press.
Wittgenstein, L. (1995). *Philosophical investigations* (E. Ullman-Margalit, Trans.). Jerusalem: Magnus.
Wittgenstein, L. (2009). *Tractatus logico-philosophicus* (C. K. Ogden, Trans.). New York: Cosimo...
Whorf, B. (1956). *Language, thought, and reality*. New-Jersey, Wiley.
Yizhar, S. (2006). The poets of the annexation. In Menuchin (Ed.), *Occupation and objection* (pp. 8–12). Jerusalem: November Books.

Conclusion: The Occupied Territories as a Cornerstone in the Reconstruction of Israeli Society

Izhak Schnell and Daniel Bar-Tal

The Israeli-Palestinian conflict is a dispute between two national movements that lay claims to the same territory. It has been ongoing for over 100 years and has been going through different phases throughout the years. In this respect, the Six Day War signified the beginning of the new stage in managing the conflict, in which the occupied-occupier relations have come to play a formative role in the Israeli reality and have become a primary factor in constructing Israeli society (Ram, 1993). From 1967 to 1977, until the rise of the Likud party to power, one could still speak of the occupation as a temporary phenomenon.

Following the change of government, however, the nature of the occupation altered from the establishment of a limited number of military-backed settlements to a massive expropriation of lands, extended Jewish settlement even in the midst of Palestinian-populated areas, repression of the Palestinian population, and its extensive military control. This process resulted not only in the appropriation of the occupied territory but also in the construction of a new national identity. The chapters in this book have revealed how the initial control of the territories has gradually developed into an established norm of Palestinian domination by Jews in Israel, which, in turn, led to dramatic changes in the entire Israel society and the state.

The question of determining the borders of the State of Israel has surfaced from time to time, but no consensus has been achieved. Nevertheless, the discourse about the territories has touched not only upon the borders and the limits of Israeli control of the territories and the Palestinian residing in them, but also upon fundamental questions of identity in Israeli society and the structure of its regime, which have changed beyond recognition during the years of the occupation. This is a political discourse with both ideological and practical aspects. It expresses a variety of social forces, not all of which act openly. The chapters in this book have shed light on some of these forces that are activated in the prolonged situation of occupation, and on some that are even acting to entrench it. In identifying these forces, the different chapters have considered the effect of the prolonged control of the territories on Israeli society, beginning with the spheres of law and politics, through the economy, psychology, media communications and linguistics, and up to the arts and morality.

To a large extent, most of the writers present the Israeli case as a particular one, and we have avoided any attempt to place it in the context of a priori theoretical generalizations such as those suggested by postcolonial theory. We agree with Memmi's (1985) introduction to his Hebrew translation of his book on relations between colonizers and colonized: the Israeli case differs significantly from colonial occupations. Although the scope of the discussion here is too narrow to enter this debate, we do believe that occupation and succession of territories are common to human history, and that all occupations share some basic commonalities that justify comparison to colonial occupations, as several of the chapters suggest.

The historian David Day (2008) argues that occupation and succession of civilizations by other civilizations is one of the most common practices in human history from antiquity to modern time. He states that some basic principles can be found in all of these cases. First, conquerors need to invent an ideological system to legitimatize territorial claims and disseminate these beliefs in society at large to mobilize it into action. In addition, they have to gain control over the claimed territories. Then conquerors must use the lands and the resources effectively to empower their own economy. Settlement of the occupied territories is the main means for colonizing these territories. These steps cannot take place without suppressing the occupied society, either by expelling, marginalizing, or assimilating its members. Once the occupation has been achieved, the occupier has to invent a moral justification for the occupation.

The first example that comes to mind is the Irish one, which became the basic model for the British colonial occupation of its empire (Ferguson, 2002, pp. 46–49). Ferguson describes how Britain, since the mid-sixteenth century, defined Catholic Ireland as the vulnerable back door of England in its long struggle with Spain for the domination of Europe to justify the occupation of Ireland. The British initiated the practice of filling the desolated lands of Ireland with an English Protestant population that would bring progress and prosperity to the local inhabitants. They founded Protestant settlements in the occupied territories of Ireland, confiscating Irish lands for these settlements and hoping to gain the support of the occupied Irish, to whom they promised to bring prosperity. However, growing Irish revolts forced the British to increase their suppression of the occupied population, leading to a vicious circle of violence and aggression.

In the same line, one of the last colonial regimes, the one in Algeria, may be of interest, especially in terms of the vicious circle of aggression and suppression that characterized the occupation of Algeria after World War II, when colonial occupations lost international legitimacy and most national movements succeeded in gaining independence from colonial control (Roberts, 1990). Scholars like Memmi (1990) and Gallagner (2002), as well as many others, have extensively analyzed the dynamic of occupation and resistance that tragically lead to an unavoidable vicious circle of suppression and aggression until the interests of the settlers and the mother land diverge. Aron (in Mack, 2002) compared two types of colonial regimes: those that failed to impose their rule over the occupied and those that refused to integrate them into the occupying society. Under these conditions, the political, economic, and social costs of the occupation increased to a level that risked (undermining)? social stability. Mack (2002) asked whether the Israeli leadership has the vision and the power to draw the same conclusions that Charles De Gaulle did.

Our evidence shows that the time to answer this question has arrived. In this volume, Hever shows how the economic price of the occupation increased from a negligible level to one that puts a heavy burden on the Israeli economy. Several chapters, but mainly the one by Ezrahi, analyze the deteriorating quality of Israeli democracy in response to the occupation. Several chapters stress the impacts of the occupation on strengthening fragmenting forces in Israeli society. Lastly, Pedatzur's comparison with Algeria considers the increasing involvement of the French army in politics as well as moral corruption of the military that included the justification of torture and, through it, the corruption of the French courts (Gallagher, 2002; Menard, 1964; Sutton & Lawless, 1978). Horne states that these impacts on French society continued for several decades after the end of the occupation.

Most of the Israeli Prime Ministers apparently realized, during the last decade, the need to end the occupation, but they failed to bring the political system to act The strongest example is the hawkish Prime Minister Ariel Sharon, who was quoted as justifying the change in his political opinion of the occupation with the statement: "What I see from here [my position as Prime Minister] I could not see from there [before I was the Prime Minister]."

One lesson that can be learned from the post–World War II examples of occupations is that the delegitimization of occupation by the international community, though sweeping, occurs only when the occupying country loses control over the occupied society. This is the case of Israel. While the international community never legitimized the occupation, including that of Jerusalem, international pressure on Israel started only after the Palestinian uprisings, which led to increasing bloodshed. At the same time, the international community does not put pressure on China or Turkey to end their occupations of Tibet and Cyprus.

Beyond the aforementioned similarities, the chapters in this book highlight many of the unique aspects of the Israeli occupation. However, our main concern is the impacts of the occupation on Israeli society itself. We believe that an occupation is part of the collective life of the occupying society, which creates a Gordian knot with the occupied society that can be eliminated only when the occupation ends. This knot is reflected in the reciprocal strong influences that both societies have on each other during the occupation. The occupying society affects every domain of life of the occupied society, but at the same time, the occupied society and the occupation itself affect the occupiers. These effects are destructive for both societies; thus, the occupation harms both societies in a prolonged process.

The strength and the extent of these reciprocal effects depend on a number of factors. Among the most salient ones are the physical distance between the occupied and occupying states; the extent to which the justifying ideology of the occupation assign formative power to the territories in constituting collective identities; the means used to oppress the occupied society and the determination of the occupied to resist; the political culture of the occupier; and the position of the international community—pressure and sensitivity. Israel's difficulties in ending its occupation stem, first of all, from the historic ties of the people of Israel to the territories of the biblical land as the cradle of Israeli national and religious identity. The proximity of the occupied territories to the State of Israel—especially along the narrow boundaries with the West Bank, which poses a high risk to Israel security—strengthens the resistance of Israeli society to any territorial concession. In the situation of conflict with the Arab world, for many Israelis, the control of the occupied territories is essential for the state's survival. Nevertheless, Israel maintains its democratic system and an active civil society that leaves room for open public debate over the occupation, including peace and human rights movements that act to mobilize the society to end the occupation and to restrain violence.

Our attempt to generalize the academic debate presented in this volume focused on three main impacts of the occupation on Israeli society. These issues are raised, either directly or indirectly, in the various chapters:

1. The first issue is the fundamental question of the essence of Israeli society. Specifically, it concerns the identity and structure of the regime in Israel that evolved as a consequence of the occupation of the territories, the attitudes and treatment of the Palestinian inhabitants, and the establishment of Jewish settlements in these territories. It is our contention

that the Israeli model of prolonged occupation has been characterized especially by a policy of creeping annexation, that is, a long-term process of Judaization, with the purpose of changing the ethnic character of the occupied territories. In fact, we suggest that during this process, the territories have become a central component in the reconstruction of Jewish identity and of the Israeli regime.
2. The second issue relates to the particular domains in the State of Israel and Israeli society that have been affected by the occupation. We realize that it is difficult to uncover the entire spectrum of effects and to prove beyond doubt the extent to which the occupation has played an exclusive or central role in affecting the different social processes in Israeli society. Nonetheless, in this book, we have attempted to identify a number of general processes that have been influenced by the reality of the prolonged occupation.
3. The third issue is the establishment of mechanisms that manage and contribute to the policy of creeping annexation. The chapters in this book have revealed at least three complementary mechanisms: the consolidation of a specific worldview among the leaders of the elite sector of society following the Six Day War; an institutionalized and complex governmental structure that hinders any change of direction or policy aimed at ending the occupation; and bureaucratic mechanisms that have vested interests in continuing the creeping annexation. These mechanisms maintain creeping annexation through bureaucratic decisions accepted by various levels of authority, including the government itself, regardless of the context in which the annexation was created.

We begin the analysis with the first issue.

IDENTITY AND REGIME

Reconstruction of the Jewish-Israeli Identity

The contention that identity and territory are interwoven is the basis of nationalist ideology (Anderson, 1991). In the process of constructing their identity, people fashion the aesthetic space in a way that converts it into a territory representing their national identity; at the same time, this identity is transmitted to the imagined community through the power of its concrete material presence (David & Bar-Tal, 2009; Redfield, 2003; Relph, 1976). The territories, in possessing a mythic significance as the cradle of Jewish culture and a future promise to the Jewish people, became an incubator of "Jewish" identity that replaced the "Hebrew" identity that traditional Zionism had attempted to establish. From the very beginning of the state, Israeli identity was characterized by a tension between an ethnic nationalism that sought to create a homogeneous nationalist society and a democratic society that confers equal rights on all of its citizens, as set out in the Declaration of Independence. The Jewish component is mentioned in the Declaration in connection with "freedom, justice and peace according to the vision of the Prophets of Israel," and the paragraph goes on to stress the equal rights of all of its citizens regardless of religion, sex, or nationality. Thus, the Declaration, like Ben-Gurion's legacy, emphasizes the prophetic legacy of universal morality that the Jewish people had bestowed upon Western culture, and not the particularistic aspects of Judaism found in the religious commandments and rituals. The Declaration begins with reference to the link with the land, but this is phrased in a general way, without demanding ownership of the land within any specific borders. The hegemonic elite of the Labor movement gave practical expression to these principles in the socialist-democratic vision that it sought to apply to Israeli society. According to this view, the territory, rebuilt and organized as part of the daily lives of its citizens, was supposed to engender the New Human, with a renewed Hebrew culture. This was a culture that sought to disconnect itself from the particularistic Judaism of the commandments and rituals that had consolidated in the Diaspora. From the rebuilt territory, it aspired to engender the New Jew—the *tsabar*—whose secular Hebrew culture would be expressed in Israeli art and literature and celebration of the Israeli festivals as they were practiced in the collective Jewish labor settlements (Almog, 1990). Even though not all sectors of Israeli society were partners to this vision, and not always was it translated into practice, this vision was nonetheless accepted as a social consensus through the power of the hegemonic Labor movement. In reality, Israeli society produced a stratified citizenship that formally conferred basic rights upon all of its citizens, but with privileged rights to Jews, and among Jews mainly to the veteran Ashkenazi population (Shafir & Peled, 2002).

An upheaval in reestablishing the Jewish component in the Israeli identity could already be seen in the 1960s among members of the Bnei Akiva youth movement, who despised the marginal and servile stance of the national-religious Zionist leaders in confronting the leaders of the Labor movement. However, this trend remained on the fringes until the occupation of the biblical Land of Israel in 1967 and the Yom Kippur War of 1973 that symbolized the weakening of the Labor movement's hegemony (Peleg, 1997). Gush Emunim, with its messianic vision, led the camp that swept along with it a broader social and political spectrum, including all the religious-Zionist sectors and the ultra-Orthodox public, the Greater Israel group—which established activism in the Labor movement—and the secular right wing (Schnell, 2009). The occupation of territories belonging to the biblical Land of Israel, with their mythic significance, provided the young religious Zionists with the opportunity to free themselves from what they saw as the flawed reality of a Jewish society controlled by the secular hegemony. Instead, they strived to establish an Israeli society that included a national renewal focused on the messianic premises announced by Rabbi Abraham Itzhak Hacohen Kook—that of uniting the Land of Israel, the Torah of Israel, with the people of Israel (Don-Yehiya, 1987; Newman, 1985; Rubinstein, 1984).

The Neo-Zionist vision was accompanied by the adoption of a pantheistic worldview that sanctified the land through the power of the divine presence in the very nature of the land. According to this vision, nourished by the teachings of the Ramban and differing from the teachings of the Rambam (according to which the sacred is not a given for the land itself), every single clod of earth of the land enjoys sanctity. Thus, it is a *mitzva* (holy commandment) for every Jew to settle every clod of earth in the Promised Land, and it is forbidden to relinquish control of any territory within it (Naor, 2001; Sheleg, 2000). The territory is thus perceived as filled with sacred places, which become the focus of Jewish ritual in which the "priestly" Jewish commandments and rituals are practiced, with the intention of fulfilling the messianic promise. This alternative vision emphasizes the particularistic foundations of the Jewish identity, focused upon the holy commandment to return to the land, and a willingness at the same time to enter into conflict with broad sectors of Israel society and the international community over the issue of settlement.

The territories thereby became not only an objective for territorial expansion under Israeli control, but also the cradle of a new settlement attempt to establish the new Jewish identity under the guidance of the national-religious sector, based on a particularistic Jewish identity (Don-Yehiya, 1987; Gurevitch, 2007). Those with this objective were willing to restrict the rights of the Palestinian residents who threatened the creation of a homogeneous Jewish territory in a space entirely under Jewish control. This was actually a return to the priestly Judaism established in the Diaspora, along with recognition of the importance of political and military power in achieving nationalist-religious goals. This belligerent awareness had developed at the very beginning of Zionism (Shapira, 1992), and it became less restrained with the progressive dehumanization of the Palestinians and the presentation of the Jewish people in Israel as victims throughout the years of struggle between the Jewish and Palestinian national movements (Bar-Tal, 1998, 2007). The effects of these processes were primarily expressed in expansion of the territories under control of the state, but also in two additional ways: the legacy of the territories was converted into the construction of a Jewish identity that differed from that of early Zionism; and the uncompromising territorial conflict intensified with both the Palestinians who lived inside the state and those in the territories, all in the name of particularistic national-religious values.

The 1980s were characterized by an erosion of the traditional Zionist discourse and competition between the post-Zionist and neo-Zionist discourses, as described previously. While the post-Zionist discourse consolidated around "Shenkin Street" in the inner zone of Tel Aviv as a focus of mingling in a Soho-type place for many young secular Jews, the neo-Zionist discourse consolidated around the settlement project in the territories. The settler became a symbol of Israeli rootedness that reawakened the youthful power of the *palmachnik* (the early pioneering fighter): he who had tired of the struggle in the "wilderness," the sandals-and-khaki-shorts-wearing youth, forelock blowing in the wind, but this time also wearing a skullcap and ritual fringed garment. For the settler—the new pioneer—the term "Shenkin-ite" became a derogatory concept, referring to those who betrayed the particularistic Jewish heritage for the sake of integrating into the globalized world and who stressed values of individualism, universality, creativity, and self-expression (Newman, 2001; Schnell, 2001). Intensification of the armed struggle and the sense of existential threat in the third millennium led to the victory of the neo-Zionist identity, which acquired a consensus among the majority of the Israeli public.

The particularistic Jewish identity—which sees the Jewish nation as having the sole right to the promised land, the very heart of which lies in Judea and Samaria—along with the intensified Palestinian resistance over the last two decades began to produce a pragmatic decision to maintain continued control of the territories. This decision was strengthened by the prediction that the Palestinians would in the very near future constitute a majority in the territory. This demographic forecast was considered an existential threat to Israel by Bistrov and Sofer (2007), who concluded that Israel needs to entrench behind closed borders in restricted areas in which the Jewish majority could remain secure for the long term. There is reason to believe that the perception of a demographic existential threat to Israel's future was a factor affecting the increasing demonization of the Palestinians, but was also a factor that led to compromising political decisions such as establishing the separation wall and withdrawing unilaterally from the Gaza Strip, as well as the planning for further withdrawal from additional territories in the West Bank (Kartin & Schnell 2008). In addition, the sense of an existential threat to a Jewish presence in the Land of Israel nourished the myth of "the people that shall dwell alone," persecuted by a world hostile to Judaism, and of the exclusive nature of the Jewish identity, as well as a lack of consideration for the rights of any social or political group that might threaten the vision of a Greater Israel (Bar-Tal, 2007; Bar-Tal & Antebi, 1992).

This perception has far-reaching moral ramifications. Dascal, in his chapter in this book, has revealed the shift in Israeli society from an identity emphasizing universal values, based on the legacy of the prophets and of Jewish principles such as "Love thy neighbor as thyself" and "Do not unto others what you would not have them do unto you"—declarations that had become a cornerstone in the modern philosophy of universal morality—to an identity reflecting a relative and extremist ethnocentric morality. Neo-Zionism barricades itself behind moral-historical and religious justifications of the exclusive right to the land while ignoring similar claims by the Palestinians. Consequently, the standpoints have become fixed and the claims of the other side have become delegitimized. It is only a short step from there to dehumanization of the Palestinians and pseudorationalization of the injuries inflicted on them (Halperin, Bar-Tal, Sharvit, Rosler, & Raviv, 2010). Statements made by nationalist leaders, mainly among former high-ranking military officers, such as "I don't care about what's good for the Palestinians but only what's good for the Israeli people," are the result of establishing a particularistic identity—which refuses to recognize the legitimacy of some of the claims of the other side and leads to the disregard of universal general moral values.

Reconstruction of the Regime

Regarding the structure of the regime, it appears that Israel has avoided an unequivocal decision concerning the legal and political status of the territories. On the one hand, officially with the exception of Jerusalem, the State of Israel has avoided annexing the territories to Israel proper. On the other hand, in many ways the state has acted as if they are Israeli territories. Beyond this, Israel has declared that, in its approach to the Palestinians, it accepts the international protocols pertaining to occupied territories. The status of occupied territory was confirmed in a series of decisions by the High Court, as revealed in the chapter by Krezmer. The reservations expressed by Justice Meir Shamgar, in his ruling in the 1970s, firmly establish this, noting that Israel is a signatory to the Fourth Geneva Convention, which determines the permitted patterns of activity in occupied territories, and thus also with regard to the Palestinian population. According to Gold and Gerstenfeld (2002), even the attempts by right-wing groups to define the territories as under dispute are based on the assumption that Israel is obligated to treat the Palestinians as an occupied population. This definition, however, has failed to obtain international recognition.

At the same time, the state has established various practices that define the territories as a product of Jewish-Zionist nationalism and as an integral part of Israeli territory. First and foremost has been the policy of taking control of over half of the lands of the West Bank and transferring them to the authority of the intensive Jewish settlement process, contradicting the state's obligation to treat the territories and their population as occupied (Sivel, 2009). In addition, the territories have been defined in public discourse and consciousness as an integral part of the Jewish national state. In order to understand these practices, it is important to know that their purpose was to provide the time needed to change the status of the territory to one of active annexation. After that happened, the political elite hoped that the legitimacy of Israeli control would become recognized by the international community. This hope was expressed in 2009 by Robbie Sivel (2009), a legal counsellor of the Foreign Ministry. He claimed that the international conventions do not ignore existing realities in the field, including occupied territories, and it was reasonable to assume that Israel would not be required, in the name of these conventions, to evacuate hundreds of thousands of settlers in order to turn back the clock.

An analysis of this process reveals the separation in thinking between two entities: the territories that have been accepted as a new part of Israel for development and settlement, and the Palestinian residents of these territories, who have not been recognized in the public discourse in Israel but instead have been defined by the regime as being occupied. In the process of settling the occupied territories, the Jewish settlers have preserved their civil status as Israelis, while the Palestinians in these territories have been deprived of civil rights and subjected to the occupation regime. The duality of this situation—referring, on the one hand, to the territories as a "wilderness" awaiting settlement, and to the Palestinian people as subject to a temporary occupation, and, on the other hand, referring to the settlers in the territories as full citizens of the state and to the Palestinians as lacking citizenship—has created a unique political regime for the State of Israel, a regime that is difficult to define as democratic but is also difficult to define as not undemocratic, as Azulai and Ophir (2008) effectively characterize it. Defining the regime as undemocratic derives from the denial of civil rights to the Palestinians in the territories; but such a definition is simplistic and ignores the reality in many democratic societies. Even modern democratic countries have a "backyard" containing many large groups who have no civil rights and who are not allowed to run their own lives. A current example of this situation is that of the millions of migrant workers found in many democratic countries (Azoulai & Ophir, 2008). The existence of millions of individuals with no rights in the backyards of such countries as the United

States, Switzerland, and the Netherlands does not prevent us from referring to these countries as democratic. However, it is the indigenous status of the Palestinian population deprived of rights, in contrast to the migrant populations in the other countries, and the ideology that justifies this practice, that differentiates between Israel and those other countries.

An analysis of the regime is important. The nature of a regime is expressed by more than the structure of the various authorities, their interrelations, the nature of their activities, and their electoral procedures or decision-making processes. First and foremost, the nature of a regime is expressed in the relationship between the majority and minority groups, and in general also in the extent to which democratic values are internalized in the political culture of the country and by its various authorities. In evaluating the democratic status of Israel up to 1967, there is broad agreement that it was far from a liberal democracy. Severe restrictions were imposed on the Arab minority, who were citizens of the State of Israel, and on freedom of expression, as part of the political culture of the state, in addition to other phenomena that impacted democracy and were common in the first two decades of Israel's existence (Hoffnung, 1991; Smooha 2000). Nonetheless, prior to the 1967 war, there was a trend toward reinforcing democratic values and equality among all sectors of the Israeli population. In the second half of the 1960s, under Prime Minister Levi Eshkol, processes of democratization were underway in Israeli society. The most prominent step in this direction was the ending of military rule over Israeli-Arab citizens. In addition, the right-wing Herut and Communist Maki parties were legitimized and included within the political system. This was achieved both by symbolic steps, such as the transfer to Israel of Ze'ev Jabotinsky's bones, and also by more concrete means such as Herut's joining the national unity government on the eve of the Six Day War, as well as the halt of security surveillance of Mapam and Maki Marxist members of the Knesset.

With these changes, occupation of the territories in 1967 created a new reality that left its stamp on the nature of the Israeli regime. In the early years after 1967 it had been possible to consider the occupation as a temporary reality that responded to the requirements of the Fourth Geneva Convention; forty-three years later this is no longer valid. The increasing Palestinian resistance against the occupation has stirred the international community to act firmly to end it and establish a Palestinian state alongside the State of Israel, according to the United Nations decisions taken in 1947. As a consequence, the hope for a post facto recognition by the international community of the creeping annexation of the territories has been fading. By contrast, the isolation of the State of Israel from the international community has been intensifying.

In evaluating the nature of the Israeli regime, one should take into account not only the prolonged occupation, with its slowly eroding effect on the areas beyond the Green Line and the increasing suppression of Palestinian resistance, but first and foremost the expanding settlement of Jews in the occupied territories. The settler Jewish population has increased in number, as has the political influence of their supporters on decisions regarding the nature of the state and their ideological influence on the social discourse concerning the identity of Israeli society. It is no longer possible to evaluate the regime in Israel by focusing on the borders of the Green Line; rather, it is now necessary to consider the entire territory controlled by Israel as a single entity. Furthermore, the relationships between Palestinians and Jews in this territory are shaped in a synergetic process in which one entity can be understood only with reference to the conflict in which it is engaged with the other entity (Portugali, 1996; Ram, 1993). The Israeli regime is primarily characterized by the differential relationship between the various governmental authorities, institutions, and security organizations, on the one hand, and the different populations that also enjoy different rights, on the other hand. It is very clear that within this regime the Jews enjoy greater rights, derived from their greater accessibility to power, prestige, and resources. To preserve these greater rights, they pass laws that discriminate against the Arab citizens within the Green Line, such as the law that refuses unification of non-Israeli Arabs with Israeli Arabs. Another form of discrimination consists of practices such as denying non-Jews access to certain resources and opportunities, such as preventing them from holding public service positions. The political process of exclusion, of denying access to economic resources and certain residential areas, has also become established in the attitudes and behaviors of broad sectors of the Israeli Jewish public. Consequently, five different populations have crystallized in the Israeli regime: (1) Jewish settlers who live in the occupied territories, with greater rights than Jews living within the Green Line; (2) Jews living within the Green Line with full civil rights; (3) Arab citizens of Israel with full civil rights but institutionalized discrimination, surveillance, and exclusion; (4) East-Jerusalem Arabs with restricted civil rights Being defined residence instead of citizens of the state of israel; and (5) Palestinians in the occupied territories with no civil rights, under full surveillance and control, and legally discriminated against in comparison with the Jews living in those same territories who are defined full citizens of the state of israel. This regime, characterized especially by different levels of rights conferred upon different populations, has relied on different rationales for rights—from rescinding the rights of Palestinians in the territories, under what was presented as a temporary occupation, through rights conferred according to the liberal rationale on all citizens; preferential rights to specific communities according to the republican rationale; and privileged rights to the settlers along with restricted rights to Arab-Israeli citizens—all in the name of nationalist values (Azulai & Ophir, 2008; Benvenisti, 1988; Shafir & Peled, 2002).

Consequently, we propose characterizing the political reality created in Israel in the area between the River Jordan and the Mediterranean Sea as a process of creeping annexation, effected by means of "ethnization" or "Judaization" the territories. The closest example of such a regime would seem to be the occupation of Tibet by China, although the Tibetan local population has received full civil rights. For Israel, annexation is a gradual process that seeks to marginalize the Palestinian population in the territories under a regime that denies them their rights while controlling their land under a one-sided legal system and, in many cases, even violating Israeli law. The regime subsidizes and privileges Jews in order to encourage large Jewish populations to migrate to the territories, while at the same time preserving the internationally defined status of occupied territory and declaring its readiness for peace and compromise, in order to attain international legitimacy for this creeping annexation. More precisely, this is a process of reinforcing the Jewish nature of the territories while employing means of control, exclusion, surveillance, separation, and discrimination against the Palestinian population. The process takes place in a territorial, political, economic, social, religious, and cultural space, differentiating between democratic procedures, including the mechanisms of control and discrimination between different populations inhabiting the same space. An imbalance is thus created between the Jewish and democratic characteristics that are supposed to define the essence of the State of Israel; and tension heightens between the national project of homogenizing the space and providing rights to all citizens. In this tension, the democratic component is overwhelmed by the national-religious component. The sense of an existential threat from the Palestinians, and the feeling of collective victimhood by the Jews, increase the legitimacy of denying rights to anyone who seems to resist the national-religious project of creeping annexation.

THE RAMIFICATIONS OF TERRITORIAL CONTROL FOR ISRAELI SOCIETY

The second question examines the ramifications of constructing a Jewish identity in Israel and the structure of the regime. The relevant chapters have emphasized the issue in relation to several social domains, including the quality of Israeli democracy; depth of the social polarizations; adoption of a short-sighted security narrative in neglecting various social problems; harm to the economy and public administration; mischief to national security; damage to the public's mental health; deterioration of social morality; and increased discrimination against Arab-Israeli citizens (see also *Israeli Sociology*, 2008). All of these consequences have a common background: the impact of the prolonged control of a Palestinian people deprived of their basic rights, the creeping annexation project, and the increasing Palestinian resistance to occupation. In the following sections, we briefly indicate just a few of the central effects.

The Quality of Israeli Democracy and the Deepening of Social Divides

The first ramification can be seen in the weakening of Israeli democracy and the deepening of social divides. The greatest danger to Israeli democracy involves the increasing questioning of the legitimacy of Israel's control over a large and expanding population. The struggle over the territories seems to intensify the deepest divides in the state over questions of ideology and power, leading to an undermining of the state's authority. Yaron Ezrachi has identified a systematic deterioration in democratic values as a result of the occupation, which has led to the massive violation of Palestinians' civil rights, illegal Jewish settlements in the occupied territories, and repressive acts of the security forces and the Jewish settlers against the Palestinians. In this reality, it is hard to arrive at a consensus on the democratic values intended to apply to the entire Israeli population. The deepening polarization, mainly between Right and Left, between religious and secular, and between Arab and Jewish citizens of the State of Israel around issues related to the occupation has undermined the solidarity of the society. According to Mautner (2008), the two deepest divides, on the national and religious issues, constitute the most basic polarizations, because they are accompanied by divisions regarding status, ideology, and territory (Smooha, 2000). Some sociologists are convinced that the conflict could lead to civil war in the absence of any cooperative ethics or a common past or future vision concerning these divisions (Kimmerling, 2004; Mautner, 2008; Ram, 2005).

Reflecting this analysis, a deep division between secular and religious Jews has emerged within Israel. This division has become great enough to arouse the extremists among them to question the legitimacy of the government's control of state institutions. The government's decision to withdraw from the Gaza Strip and northern Samaria severely tested the neo-Zionist veto stand in Israeli politics; on the other hand, the separation plan proposed by the Kadima government under Prime Minister Sharon tested the settlement rabbis, who questioned the legitimacy of the government in taking political decisions. From the rabbinical extremism in the political assassination of

Prime Minister Rabin, through the call to challenge the sovereignty of the state in deciding to withdraw from Gaza, to the organized mass rabbinical support of army officers who threatened to refuse to obey commands if ordered to evacuate settlements, the authority of certain state institutions to make political decisions has been undermined, and the argument between religious and secular sectors has become a struggle over the legitimacy of the democratic institutions of the state. This struggle also includes groups on the left who refuse to serve in the occupied territories, who challenge the government and the security forces with demonstrations against the wall of separation and/or Jewish settlement in East Jerusalem, and who challenge the right to create illegal settlements by building outposts and by extending existing Jewish settlements.

The challenging of the government's legitimacy has also intensified among the Arab-Palestinian elite in Israel following the occupation and discrimination against the native Palestinian population. In their chapter in this book, Amara and Mustafa have revealed that the Arabs in Israel have redefined the patterns of their political involvement in the state as well as their identity. The national component has become more central in their political platforms, and the struggle for equal civil rights is linked to the national struggle at a time when the government is justifying the denial of equal rights and of equality in economic development by the continuous Palestinian conflict with the prolonged occupation. The Palestinian civil uprisings in the territories have fired the imagination of young Arabs in Israel and reinforced their identification with their Palestinian identity (Schnell, 1994). Following the failure of the Camp David meeting in 2000 and the violent suppression of the Israeli-Arab demonstrations, the struggle for the national interests of Arab-Israeli citizens increased. Their documented platforms (called "visions") call for a change in the nature of the State of Israel from a Jewish state to a state for all of its citizens or the establishment of a binational state. At the same time, the Jewish public's trust in Arab citizens of Israel has eroded. Israeli Arabs are perceived as part of the Palestinian population in the territories and thus as deserving the same delegitimization applied to that population. This attitude was expressed in the violent events of October 2000, in which the struggle between the nationalist groups escalated while the minority group lost faith in the state institutions, a faith that is indispensable for any democratic regime. And just as the documented platform of the Arab elite in the state defined the Israeli regime as racist and sought to change its nature, Jewish political groups suggested restricting the rights of the Arabs, who are Israeli citizens. A proposal to transfer the areas settled by Arab citizens of Israel along the Green Line to the Palestinian Authority in exchange for transferring areas settled by Jews in the territories to within the realm of the State of Israel further damaged Jewish-Arab relations in Israel.

The legitimacy of the authorities and the rule of law in the Israeli political system have been undermined most dramatically by one decision: the decision to assign the main task of controlling the territories to the Israel Defence Forces (IDF) as a function of their official status as occupied territories. In his chapter in this book, Pedatzur has shown how the army became a lead player in the political agenda in the territories, independent of government decisions and sometimes even in contradiction to them. The IDF became a central player in promoting the settlement process. In the early years of the occupation, the IDF was used as a settlement tool to prevent a flagrant breach of the ban on permanent civilian settlements in the occupied territories. On the basis of these acts, the army was forced to provide false claims in court cases that the settlements established as civilian settlements had been constructed for security considerations (Zertal & Eldar, 2007). Quite the opposite was true; the settlements impeded the army's strategic approach since, if the territories were empty of Jewish settlements, they would have given Israel more space for military maneuvers and eliminated the need to guard the Jewish settlements and the settlers.

Over the years, the settlers have become an influential political factor that has succeeded in biasing the judgment of military personnel in the field. The *Karp Report* (1982) revealed how the army justified the expropriation of land for security purposes despite the fact that these expropriations had no real security justification. The report also indicated soldiers' disregard of the repeated law-breaking by the Jewish settlers against Palestinians in the territories. Later, the *Sasson Report* (2005) revealed how the army supported dozens of illegal settlements and, instead of evacuating them, it sent soldiers to protect them. Pedatzur notes that officers up to the rank of general discovered that military promotion depended on recommendations by settler leaders, and they therefore preferred to ignore law-breaking by the settlers and even to support such acts. Over time, the settlers have been assigned to army units in the territories, effectively creating a militia of settler-soldiers that serves the settler leadership no less than it does the State of Israel. Many cases of settlers attacking the Palestinians or even the soldiers were not reported by the soldiers who identified with the settlement project.

In his chapter in this book, Ezrahi has contended that civic education has been harmed by the blurred messages of the Israeli democratic regime and the lack of consensus regarding basic questions such as state borders, civil rights, and others. Teachers have been wary of considering issues connected to the basic values and principles of Israeli society, and have tended to avoid discussing questions reflecting deep polarization that pertain to civic education (Hofman, Alpert, & Schnell, 2007). Moreover, the human rights of the Palestinians in the occupied territories have systematically eroded, as reported by organizations such as B'tselem. Kaufman, in his chapter in this book, has perceived this trend as also filtering into areas within the Green Line. It is thus no wonder that, in this atmosphere, the discussion of human rights has been marginalized in the public discourse and the human rights organizations in Israel are frequently presented as traitors to the national interest.

The last right-wing coalition, established in 2009, started a new attempt by Prime Minister Benjamin Netenyahu and some of his supporters to limit the power of democratic institutions that criticize his aggressive policies toward the Palestinians. A group of Knesset members from the key parties in the coalition—Likud and Israel Beitenu—took the lead in promoting, in the name of the Prime Minister and the Minister of Justice, Jacob Ne'eman, a set of laws and steps against the Supreme Court of Israel, pro-peace and human rights nongovernment organizations (NGOs), and the media. To secure support for controversial settlements, they suggested changing the procedure for electing judges for the Supreme Court and forcing them to get the approval of the Knesset, steps that could have led to parliamentary control over the Supreme Court. Concerning the NGOs, they suggested prohibiting donations to leftist groups from foreign governments and avoiding public money from organizations that mention the *Nakba* day (the memorial day for the defeat of the Palestinians in the 1948 war, which led to the expulsion of about 700,000 Palestinians, who became refugees). Concerning the media, Netenyahu attempted to gain control over public television, and his supporters threatened a television channel with economic reprisal in response to their criticism of the Prime Minister. Fortunately, almost all of the initiatives failed due to the resistance of the opposition and some of the ministers from the Likud party itself. However, the challenge to democratic values by leading politicians from the center of the political spectrum are alarming.

Beyond these steps, two others ones stand out. The first was the attempt to rehabilitate illegal outposts in the occupied territories according to Israeli law and to avoid their evacuation in defiance of the Supreme Court's decision. The second was the introduction of controversial educational programs presenting the occupied territories as part of Israel, thus promoting uncritical patriotic emotions. Such programs include required field trips to Hebron and other biblical places in the occupied territories as well as tours that emphasis the neo-Zionist national religious ideology of the settlers.

*Locating a Shortsighted Security Narrative at the Center
of the Political Discourse*

Another effect of the occupation on Israeli society is that a short-sighted security narrative has been located at the center of the political discourse, as revealed in the chapter by Herzog. The enormous security challenge, deriving from the occupation and the Palestinian uprisings against it, has marginalized the public discourse on questions of security and prevented a broader understanding of this concept. The increasingly militaristic approach that took over the public discourse in Israel led to the neglect of questions of security, focusing instead on the crimes and internal violence occurring along the borders of the Green Line. Questions of social security were also marginalized, eroding Israel's welfare society and creating a culture of intolerance toward demands to widen social services. This worldview placed men of experience and knowledge in the field of security at the center of the public space. Women were relegated to the home, and discrimination and violence against women were ignored (see also Mayer, 1994). In Israel today there is a great economic gap between rich and poor, and women are generalized marginalized.

The occupation has also led to greater public violence. The chapter by Greenbaum and Elizur has shown how the violence carried by soldiers and settlers into the territories has left long-term scars on them that have continued to affect the quality of their lives and their behavior; and how the violence toward the Palestinians in the territories has permeated the State of Israel and the lives of its citizens. A correlation has been found between the waves of violent outbursts following the occupation and the rise in violence in Israeli society. This violence was not confronted by the state authorities due to the narrow definition of security by those in charge of public safety. In this situation such waves of violence have increased, mainly since the outbreak of the *intifadas*. The overall reasons for this trend may be more complex, but Greenbaum and Elizur have nonetheless shown that an occupation has a significant connection to increasing violence.

The occupation helps to impair the personal safety of citizens within the Green Line in three ways. First, the violence of the occupation has penetrated Israeli society itself, as demonstrated by Greenbaum and Elizur. Second, the narrow perception of security has weakened the law enforcement policy and public order, as revealed by Herzog. Third, the infiltration of terror or Palestinian resistance into areas inside Israel has made the Israeli citizen's life less secure. Dascal has emphasized the contribution of all these factors to the existence of a constant threat of terror: security guards posted at the entrances to every public building or site, increasingly aggressive security checks, education of children to avoid trusting others, both Jews and non-Jews, and severe damage to both the fabric of society and moral assumptions—all of which are internalized by young Israelis as part of their overall worldview.

Economics of the Occupation

The economic costs of control of the territories are twofold, greatly burdening the Israeli economy and indirectly causing deterioration in public services. The settler project and control of the Palestinians has become the largest and most important national project of the State of Israel. Vast economic resources are invested in it, raising an important question: how significant is this project for economic growth and for the deepening economic inequality in Israel? Hever's chapter has revealed that the cost of the occupation was negligible in the early years, when little military force was required for control and the economic advantages of creating Palestinian markets for Israeli products and exploiting a cheap work force were significant. However, the cost of occupation and settlement has greatly increased. As a rough estimate, Israel spent about 380 billion shekels on the occupation by the end of 2008 and 440 billion shekels by the end of 2010. This sum has grown annually, reflecting the increase in the number of settlers who benefit from subsidies and the increased investment in ensuring the security of these settlers. On average, the State of Israel invests about 26 billion shekels, or 7 billion dollars, each year in the settlements, a sum that has grown exponentially since the 1980s. The cost of a settler in the territories is two times higher than the cost of an Israeli citizen in central Israel and is even higher for settlers on the periphery (see also Swirski, 2008).

The cost of the occupation will be even higher if we assume that, in a peaceful settlement of the Israeli-Palestinian conflict, at least some of the settlements will be dismantled and the evacuated settlers will be dispersed by the state, following the pattern of the evacuation from Gaza and northern Samaria. Compensation of about 1 million shekels per household, and the loss of the infrastructure created for it in the territories, will significantly increase the cost of occupation. The evacuation of 100,000 settlers or 20,000 households could reach a cost of 30 billion shekels, constituting a dead-end trap. With the constant rise in the cost of occupation, its continuation for one year will cost the same as the immediate evacuation of about 100,000 settlers in 2010. These sums are an increasing burden on the Israeli economy and may lead to a significant reduction in economic growth.

Beyond the effect of the occupation on potential economic growth there is also a social cost. Because of the burden of the security budget and the cost of the occupation, the government must allot many resources to security. To compensate for these increasing costs, the government systematically and constantly reduces the wages of those in the public services, who have become among the lowest-paid workers in the developed world. The consequence is a decline in public services, including the educational, welfare, and personal security systems. Israel also spends far less money on environmental protection than other developed countries. In addition, the settlement project, which demands a vastly greater economic investment today than in 1967, reduces the possibility of investing in alternative development projects, such as developing the periphery in the Negev and Galilee. A public debate in the media held in early 2010, following the enactment of a Knesset law to encourage investment in the country, clearly presents the contrast between national support for developing the periphery and support for the settlements.

The Cost of Security

The occupation also exerts a significant cost on security, as explained by Pedatzur. The IDF had become increasingly mired in the attempt to suppress the escalating uprising of the Palestinians in the territories, to the extent of neglecting its preparedness for regular war. The Chief of Staff found that the mass acts of terrorism in the second *intifada* could have a potentially strategic outcome; consequently, the majority of resources and military personnel should be assigned to the fight against terrorism. As a result, according to Pedatzur, the army's preparedness to fight an all-out regular war declined, a situation that came back to haunt the military during the Second Lebanon War. Pedatzur noted, furthermore, that the IDF, bogged down in its role of military government in the territories, in the war on terror, and in the support of the settlements, had difficulty consolidating a new security strategy for Israel.

Israel's Status in the World

The change in Israel's international status following the occupation was dramatic. In the early years after the 1967 war, when the occupation led to no significant Palestinian resistance, support for Israel rose among the European countries and in North America as a small, vulnerable state that had proved its ability to survive in the face of a severe external threat. The Six Day War was particularly effective in firing the Jewish imagination in regard to the centrality of the State of Israel to the Jewish people, as well as awareness of the need to encourage the immigration of Soviet Russian Jews to Israel. As time passed and the occupation continued, the Palestine Liberation Organization (PLO) developed and Palestinian resistance increased. In addition, the international legitimization of the occupation eroded, and delegitimization of the occupation began to be extended to delegitimization of the Israeli regime. The prolonged occupation undoubtedly influences the attitude of many countries toward the State of Israel. Furthermore, the occupation affects Israel's image in the world media and, consequently, public opinion in many states. Added to this is the criticism by various international and national organizations created to improve or supervise the status of human rights in the world; this includes certain progressive Jewish sectors worldwide that have begun to distance themselves from the State of Israel. Israel is mired in the national project of creeping annexation while slowly but surely disregarding the discourse on human rights. It finds itself in a situation that is hard to explain to the international community in the face of its actions in the territories concerning the Jewish settlements and its attitude toward the occupied Palestinian population.

MECHANISMS OF THE POLICY OF CREEPING ANNEXATION

The policy of creeping annexation, with all of its consequences, has been enabled by three mechanisms that act in parallel and support each other. The first is the establishment of broad public support for the belief that the occupied territories are part of the Jewish homeland, deeply interwoven with the Jewish-Zionist identity, and/or are a security asset without which the State of Israel would not continue to exist. Therefore, continued control of the territories is of central national security interest to the state (see also Bar-Tal, Halperin, & Oren, 2010. This idea has produced support for the political parties and institutions that have acted to continue the policy of creeping annexation. The second mechanism is the political system and its dependence on the right-wing parties for a coalition. The third mechanism is the institutionalization of those interests and means of control that function within the bureaucracy and possess their own inertia.

The Mechanism of Creating Public Opinion

The operations of the first mechanism during the prolonged occupation, together with the policy of creeping annexation and increasing Palestinian resistance, have deeply influenced the political discourse in Israel. Over time, the public discourse has come to support, to various degrees, the continuation of this creeping annexation (Oren, 2005, 2009; see also the chapter by Magal and his colleagues in this book). It has become a discourse on the image of the State of Israel and Israeli society, with control of the territories located at its center. In order to understand the mechanism behind the creation of public support, it is necessary to return to the first weeks following the Six Day War. Within the shortest possible time nearly all the political leadership, with the help of the media, had reframed reality: "liberating the territories and return to the homeland" (Segev, 2007). This was achieved by speeches by the leaders, articles in newspapers, news reports, songs, victory albums, and, of course, educational activities in the schools, the army, and other institutions (see, e.g., Sheffi, 2009). Furthermore, the various Israeli governments managed an active policy of erasing the Green Line from public consciousness by means of education, map-drawing, archaeological research, and "Judaization" of the area, as described in Schnell's chapter. Even the language adopted a jargon appropriating the new areas into the national territory, as noted in Tsur's chapter. The majority of Israelis, who before the 1967 war had come to terms with the nation's sovereignty over only part of the land, accepted and internalized the new reality after this war in response to the massive reframing. It is important to note that this reframing of reality is deeply rooted in the Jewish heritage, in which Judea and Samaria constitute the cradle of the ancient Jewish identity. Moreover, in the 1950s and 1960s, there were political groups on the Right (the Herut party) and Left (e.g., among the Ahdut Avoda circles) that openly dreamed of expanding Israel's borders in order to incorporate those parts of the Land of Israel that had remained outside the state borders (Naor, 2001).

The reframing process was successful; by the 1990s, the Green Line had been erased from the spatial awareness of younger Israelis (Portugali, 1996). Almost every major Israeli leader, including Yitzhak Rabin, Shimon Peres, and Ehud Barak from the Labor party, considered the occupied territories as the homeland of Israel, as shown in the chapter by Magal and colleagues. In order to understand this mechanism, one must also include in the analysis the construction of the Palestinian image. Palestinians were defined as a strategic threat to the existence of the State of Israel; Therefore, the territories, or part of them, had to be retained in order to prevent the existential danger, as noted by Magal et al. The Palestinians' continuing violence has undoubtedly reinforced this perception (see also Bar-Tal & Teichman, 2005; Oren & Bar-Tal, 2007).

The status of the territories as part of Israel's national territory, and the delegitimization of the Palestinians' rights to the territories was thus reframed. It was then necessary to preserve a positive self-image while managing the conflict linked to the policy of creeping annexation. This has become an additional mechanism of institutionalizing the state's new identity and regime (Halperin et al., 2010). Magal et al. systematically surveyed the beliefs and understandings that justified the occupation and creeping annexation among the leadership and the broad public, which remained dominant for several decades. In discussing this mechanism, which was socially constructed in order to preserve Israelis' positive self-image in managing the dispute with the Palestinians, it is necessary to understand how the mechanism functioned to block out information on the problems connected with the occupation and creeping annexation (Bar-Tal et al., 2010). This has involved selective, biased, and distorted information processing that prevented Israelis from knowing the costs to both the Palestinian and Israeli societies. This reframing of reality also functioned as a defense mechanism that made the problems connected with the occupation appear to be less serious than they actually were. This was achieved by repression, avoidance, pseudointellectualism, transference, or pseudorationalism, all of which helped to reinforce the collective positive self-image (Halperin et al., 2010). Finally, mainstream Israeli-Jewish society rejected any criticism of the occupation and creeping annexation, seeing it as an expression of lack of patriotism and/or self-hatred. The system was thus set in to motion to delegitimize any information or sources of information that displayed criticism within Israel or abroad. Many of the established Jewish communities worldwide also joined the cause to block any criticism of Israel's policy of occupation and annexation.

Nonetheless, despite the widespread belief that the territories were part of the homeland, by the second half of the 1970s an alternative concept was beginning to develop: the need to make peace in return for withdrawal from the territories. Within this discourse, a small minority pointed out the moral cost that Israel was paying for the continued occupation. The peace dialogue intensified in the 1980s and in the first half of 1990s (with the signing of the Oslo Accords in 1993), dominating the discourse until 2000. This happened because the public had accepted the new idea that the existential threat to Israel had lessened as a result of the peace agreements with Egypt and Jordan and the Oslo Accords signed with the Palestinian Authority. This belief, however, weakened once more due to the increased terror activities against Israel that followed the failure of the Camp David meeting and the withdrawal from Lebanon and the Gaza Strip, which led to the intensification of terror and renewal of the existential threat to Israel by Iran. In this connection, Tsur has stressed the lack of agreement among the main segments of Israeli society with regard to a common language. Tsur concurs with Kimmerling's (2004) observation regarding the lost possibility of achieving an Israeli society in which different worldviews could be openly discussed. Both Magal et al. and Tsur point to the change in viewpoints that took place nonetheless in the public discourse, and they have drawn a picture of the pragmatic change in ideology among the political elite as well as the broad public. In other words, since the intensification of Palestinian resistance against the occupation at the end of the 1980s, and mainly since the Oslo Accords, the pragmatic approach has located Israel's security needs at the center of the discourse, with the threat of a demographic imbalance perceived as a danger to a Jewish and democratic state. This threat has increasingly been seen as an internal one, undermining the essence of the state, and not as an external threat to control of the occupied territories. As a result, there has been increasing agreement on territorial compromise. Tsur defines four phases in the dominant discourse, each lasting for about a decade: a religious-messianic phase, a phase emphasizing the historical-national rights of the Jews, a phase of conciliation and compromise, and a separation phase. He suggests that Israel is currently in the fourth phase: ready to separate from the Palestinians without separating from the territories or, alternatively, annexing Area C and conferring less status than that of an independent state on Areas A and B. Neither of these solutions provides a basis for any reasonable agreement on territorial compromise with the Palestinians (see also Bar-Tal et al., 2010; Ben-Meir, 2009).

The critical artistic discourse on the occupation, reflecting the pragmatic approach, emerged at the beginning of the 1980s. Art and literature represent a particular perception of reality and engage in a sensitive dialogue with it. On the one hand, they are fed by the public discourse; on the other hand, they themselves become active in shaping this discourse (Hooks, 1995). With the end of the war in 1967, art, together with other social agents, became actively engaged in a dialogue of liberation and redemption with the broad public. In the 1970s, however, a discourse presenting an alternative perception of the occupation—a negative one—began to appear, and by the 1980s this discourse had broadened. The chapter by Urian has described the changes in Israeli playwriting that have taken place between the 1970s and the new millennium. This trend, like the one involving the use of language and academic criticism of the occupation, should be perceived as an expression of the pragmatic approach to the occupation by at least part of the public. Although this artistic criticism stressed mainly the moral aspects of the occupation, its major effect on the public was in the utalitarian-practical aspects; criticism of the moral implications of the occupation was restricted to the narrowest social circles. There is at least one bright spot in this scenario: although Israelis tend to block critics by claiming that they are unpatriotic, Israel has succeeded in holding a democratic and open cultural discourse on the society's existential questions.

Mechanism of Dependence on the Right-Wing Parties

The second mechanism of the policy of creeping annexation is connected to the composition of every Israeli government since the political change in 1977, which included right-wing parties and sometimes even those of the extreme right. During most of these years the government was headed by the Likud party, which, despite its pragmatic approach, still adhered to the right-wing ideology that supported creeping annexation, with all the consequences of the occupation. The coalitions since 1977 were based either on right-wing parties or on a national unity government including these parties. The exceptional governments headed by Yitzhak Rabin and Ehud Barak, leaders of the Labor party that governed for six years in the 1990s, were forced to participate in a coalition with such right-wing parties as Shas. Thus, despite the contention of Doron and Rosenthal in their chapter that the political representation of the settlers was marginal, the right-wing parties that have been in power, backed by strong public support for continuing the Israeli occupation of the territories, acted to intensify the control and creeping annexation and to prevent any attempt to end the occupation. It was under the Labor government, however, that the settlement project gained momentum, along with attempts to promote peace plans with the Palestinians. In this setting, it is helpful to understand how the lobby represented by the small extremist right-wing parties and the Judea and Samaria Council, by supporting the pragmatic right-wing party (Likud), succeeded in forcing the entire political system to promote the policy of creeping annexation (Gorenberg, 2006; Zertal & Eldar, 2007).

Determined and committed groups sometimes succeed in diverting government policy in the face of political and public apathy, a phenomenon familiar in other democratic regimes (Freeman 1995) and as shown by Doron and Rosenthal. But in our view, in the case of Israel, the government policy of creeping annexation gained broad public support by the pragmatic majority. For this group, the Jewish settlement of the occupied territories was not the main issue due to the prevailing belief that peace was in any case not possible.

The Mechanism of Bureaucratic Inertia

The third mechanism in the policy of creeping annexation involves the inertia within the state bureaucracy. There, as indicated by Doron and Rosenthal, institutionalized department and interests strive to maintain the policy regardless of any decisions taken by the government. These departments include government offices such as the Ministry of Justice, which permitted the expropriation of land in the territories; the Ministry of the Interior, which authorized the construction and development plan; the Ministry of Public Works, which built the Jewish settlements beyond the Green Line; the Ministry of Transport, which built the many roads there (some for the sole use of Jews); and the Ministries of Welfare and Education, which supported the local authorities established beyond the Green Line. One should also mention the Jewish Agency and the Jewish National Fund, which supported the settlement activities, and the law courts, which in the majority of cases permitted the expropriations or construction of the settlements, at no small cost to the Palestinian population in the territories. Finally, one should note the IDF's unfounded support of the settlements in its readiness to divert valuable resources to their construction, to protect them from the authority of the law, guard them, and overlook the law-breaking of the settlers. Two examples in the book have demonstrated the institutionalization of these mechanisms: the use of the IDF to control the territories and the behavior of the Israeli media. As we have already noted, an example of the bureaucratic activity was analyzed by Pedatzur, who showed how the military became a central agent of the policy of creeping annexation and how the settler leadership established a powerful influence over the army commanders and soldiers irrespective of the various governments' policies (see also Zertal & Eldar, 2007). He has shown how the army, certain that its control of the territories was important for state security, supported the settlements in order to ensure that the territories would not come under foreign sovereignty within the framework of political agreements. In addition, it is necessary to point out that the Judea and Samaria Council more than once pushed the state into accepting settlements unauthorized by the government, in contradiction to government policy but with the aid of the army and some of the ministries. These factors helped to promote the settlement project independently of the government leadership, but with the support of public opinion and in the face of governments that sometimes supported the settlement project and sometimes were so divided and weakened that they were unable to halt the process of creeping annexation.

The second institution that has aided the continued creeping annexation is the media, which play a central role in maintaining a consolidated public discourse. This discourse justified the Jewish settlements in the territories and presented Israeli society as a victim of the Palestinians—who in fact have been delegitimized—while ignoring the massive harm done to them. The chapter by Caspi and Rubenstein has shown how the media created an "information barrier" that neutralized the transfer of any information differing from the established narrative. The information barrier has both physical and cognitive components. In the early years, the physical barriers were more effective. They included blocking or disrupting anti-Israel media channels and firing journalists who raised issues concerning the territories. In this new era of globalization of information, however, it is mainly the cognitive mechanisms that function. Caspi and Rubenstein have presented the Israeli media as controlled by security sources and journalists, many of whom have a security background. These journalists view the Arab world and the Palestinians mainly through a narrative that defines them as a security threat and not as of potential neighbors, with whom it is necessary to solve the dispute by peaceful means. The public too, interested in reinforcing its positive self-image, prefers to maintain the narrative that defines the Palestinian as a cruel enemy rather than a neighbor. The journalists who surveyed the Palestinian population in the territories have been marginalized, and many of those who maintained direct connections with the daily life of the Palestinians were neutralized by questioning their loyalty to the homeland. The Arab media, using a language unacceptable to the Jewish-Israeli public and focused on blind incitement, simply eased the work of constructing an information barrier to the Arab world. The Israeli media have thus formed an additional layer preventing an open and critical public discussion of the patriotic-security narrative that has dominated the public discourse and thereby have cleared the way for the settlers' lobby.

AFTERWORD

The central claim of this book is that control over the territories and the Palestinian people, as a new phase in managing the conflict, has functioned as an accelerating factor, impelling social, political, economic, and cultural developments in Israeli society on both sides of the Green Line. These developments have become institutionalized in the political system, the bureaucracy, among the ruling powers, and in the public discourse to an extent that has led to a reconstruction of Israeli society. Control of the territories has affected developments in a variety of ways: the territories have been presented as new areas for control and as a "wilderness" that needs to be occupied; as an encounter with the sacred space of the cradle of the Jewish experience; as a liberated territory whose present residents use violence to resist the return of Jews to their homeland; and as a space that challenges the demographic majority of the Jewish people in the territories. These ideas have been expressed on both sides of the Green Line, converting the occupation of the territories and domination of the Palestinians into an internal and structural characteristic of Israeli Jewish society. All these factors together influenced Israeli-Jewish society to an extent that was not predicted by the Israeli leadership immediately following the Six Day War—a leadership that was unable to understand the full significance of the developments that accompany the domination of another nation against its will and unable to comprehend how the codes and mores of the international community would develop. We thus close the account begun in the introductory chapter to this book, where we contended that both the occupier and the occupied become engaged in an endless series of mutually disruptive acts and reprisals, and that the occupation fundamentally affects the occupying society too. This effect, both direct and indirect, open and concealed, is extremely powerful, to the extent of having reconstructed Israeli-Jewish society.

Indeed, the occupation of the territories, their domination, and the national struggle with the Palestinians have reconstructed Israeli-Jewish society to the point where it has developed a new identity and regime. This new Jewish identity emphasizes the connection to the particularistic components of the Jewish identity alongside a nationalism that emphasizes the connection between the Jewish nation, the biblical Land of Israel, and the religion of Israel. This identity is replacing the Jewish-Hebrew identity rooted in the new practices of independent Jews in the new-old land that also emphasized universal values and strove to consolidate a Hebrew culture within the new reality in the country. In parallel, a regime has developed that undermines the law and order established by the Israeli regime prior to 1967, diverting the main national struggle to achieving a creeping domination of the territories while contravening the international obligations of a state that controls occupied territories. There is no agreed-upon interpretation of the laws pertaining to the status of land in the territories and the importance of the settlement project to Israel's security. As a result of this diversion of the national struggle, the balance among those who guide Israeli democracy has been disturbed. The progressive promise of basic rights to all has been eroded in favor of emphasizing the national perception that justifies privileging the "pioneering" communities that serve the policy of "ethnicizing" the territories and withholding rights from those minorities that threaten this policy. These processes have helped to weaken democracy, corrupt moral behaviour, and cripple the discourse on human rights in Israeli society. This is one of the reason the Jews in Israel do not comprehend the dominating discourse in the world, which demands observance of human rights, and monitors and criticizes their violations. Today, prolonged occupation is unacceptable.

Beyond the imbalance created between the Jewish state and democracy, several of the authors have noted the socioeconomic consequences of the occupation. These include the threat to Israel's economic growth; a decline in the standard of public services, personal security, and the social status of women; and neglect of the periphery and of minority groups. The structural changes in the Israeli identity and regime have become institutionalized in the political structure, in the public discourse, and in the mechanisms of control. This reveals that these changes are deeply ingrained and reflect strong sociopolitical inertia. This inertia has perpetuated the entrenchment of the Israeli mindset to successfully survive while managing the conflict, but at the same time it hinders the ability to achieve any compromise with the Palestinian people through a readiness to give up control of the territories. Our conclusion is that Israeli society contains powerful institutionalized forces that drive the policy of creeping annexation. To exchange this policy for one of compromise with the Palestinian people would mean a deep social-political crisis together with a reconstruction of a new Israeli identity and a new regime that is more sensitive to democratic values. For a society that finds itself in "overload" and being constantly mobilized, this is a harsh challenge. In addition, raising public awareness of the issue merely reinforces support for the conservative forces, since society prefers to deal with difficulties stemming from the familiar reality rather than exchanging them for an unknown and deeply unacknowledged reality.

However, we observe some signs of hope for a critical transition of the kind De Gaulle initiated in France concerning the occupation of Algeria. At least three of the last four Prime Ministers of Israel, although they came from an activist background, understood the need to reach a political compromise with the Palestinians, even though they failed or did not try to mobilize sufficient political support to do so. The rise of pragmatic voices in the general public and of a moral debate among intellectuals are hopeful signs. Wishing to conclude the argument with some sense of optimism, we believe that Israel will be pushed to end the occupation, thus providing an opportunity to rebuild the Israeli identity, regime, state apparatus, and society. We hope that this process will begin as early as possible.

NOTES

1. Theodor Miron, who served as legal adviser to the Israeli Foreign Ministry in 1967, in September 1967 presented an opinion at the request of the Israeli government, stating that the settlement of Israeli citizens in the territories contradicted international law (Gorenberg, 2006).
2. Following the Six Day War and the annexation of East Jerusalem in 1967, its inhabitants received the civil status of "permanent resident" of the State of Israel. The main right of a permanent resident is the right to live and work in Israel without requiring special permits. Moreover, permanent residents are entitled to social benefits according to the National Insurance and Health Insurance laws, and are allowed to vote in municipal elections but not in elections to the Knesset. Permanent residency, unlike citizenship, is transferable to the resident's children only under certain conditions. Residents married to someone who is not a resident or citizen of Israel need to apply for a family unification permit for their partner.
3. According to the Association for Civil Rights in Israel, the Palestinians in the occupied territories live under an occupying regime and are denied their basic rights promised by a democratic regime. They are also denied partnership in those processes that affect their fate. Establishment of the Palestinian Authority

and the holding of elections did not essentially alter their civil status. In the West Bank the Palestinian Authority enjoys jurisdiction on very few issues and in very small enclaves. In the Gaza Strip, Israel has continued to control all matters crucial to the lives of the inhabitants, even after the disengagement.

REFERENCES

Almog, S. (1990). The redemption in Zionist rhetoric. In R. Kark (Ed.), *Redeeming the land in Israel* (pp. 13–32). Jerusalem: Yad Ben-Zvi.

Anderson, B. (1991). *Imagined communities*. London: Verso.

Azulai, A., & Ophir, A. (2008). *This regime is not one*. Tel Aviv: Resling (in Hebrew).

Barrier Watch. Organization Web site: Machsomwatch.org (reports during the years 2009–2010).

Bar-Tal, D. (1998). Societal beliefs in times of intractable conflict: The Israeli case. *International Journal of Conflict Management, 9*, 22–50.

Bar-Tal, D. (2007). *Living with the conflict: Socio-psychological analysis of the Israeli-Jewish society*. Jerusalem: Carmel (in Hebrew).

Bar-Tal, D., & Antebi, D. (1992). Siege mentality in Israel. *International Journal of Intercultural Relations, 16*, 251–275.

Bar-Tal, D., Halperin, E., & Oren, N. (2010). Socio-psychological barriers to peace making: The case of the Israeli Jewish society. *Social Issues and Policy Review, 4*, 63–109.

Bar-Tal, D., & Teichman Y. (2005). *Stereotypes and prejudice in conflict: Representations of Arabs in Israeli Jewish society*. Cambridge: Cambridge University Press.

Ben-Meir, Y. (2009). The political arena and audience opinion. In S. Barom & A. Kurtz (Eds.), *Strategic evaluation for Israel 2009* (pp. 123–137). Tel Aviv: Institute for National Security Research.

Benvenisti, M. (1988). *The sniper and the goddess: Territories, Jews and Arabs*. Jerusalem: Keter (in Hebrew).

Bistrov, Y., & Sofer, A. (2007). *Israel 2007–2020—demography and crowding*. The Haikin Chair in Geostrategy: Haifa: Haifa University (in Hebrew).

B'Tselem Web site: www.btselem.org. Retrieved July 23, 2010.

David, O., & Bar-Tal, D. (2009). A socio-psychological conception of collective identity: The case of national identity. *Personality and Social Psychology Review, 13*, 354–379.

Day, D. (2008). *Conquest: How societies overwhelm others*. Oxford: Oxford University Press.

Don-Yehiya, E. (1987). Jewish messianism, religious Zionism and Israeli politics: The impact and origins of Gush Emunim. *Middle Eastern Studies, 23*, 215–234.

Ferguson, N. (2002). *Empire: The rise and demise of the British world order and the lessons for global power*. New York: Basic Books.

Freeman, G. P. (1995). Modes of immigration policies in liberal democratic states, *International Migration Review, 24*(4), 881–902.

Gallagher, N.(2002). Learning lessons from the Algerian war of independence. *Middle East Report*, 225, 44–49.

Gold, D., & Gerstenfeld, M. (2002). *From occupied territories to disputed territories.* Jerusalem: Jerusalem Institute for Public Policy

Gorenberg, G. (2006). *The accidental empire: Israel and the birth of the settlements—1967–1977.* New York: Times Books.

Gurevitch, Z. (2007). *On the place.* Tel Aviv: Am Oved (in Hebrew).

Halperin, E., Bar-Tal, D., Sharvit, K., Rosler, N., & Raviv, A. (2010). Social psychological implications for an occupying society: The case of Israel. *Journal of Peace Research*, 47, 59–70.

Hoffnung, M. (1991). *Israel—State security versus the rule of law 1948–1991.* Jerusalem: Nevo (in Hebrew).

Hofman, A., Alpert, B., & Schnell, I. (2007). Education and social change: The case of Israel's state curriculum. *Curriculum Inquiry*, 37(4), 303–328.

Hooks, B. (1995). *Art on my mind: Visual politics.* New York: New Press.

Israeli Sociology. (2008). Volume 9, Whole Issue No. 2 (in Hebrew).

Karp, Y. (1982). "Karp Report" to the legal advisor, A. Zamir-Ravitzky, 1997. *Religious and secular: A culture war?* Jerusalem: Israeli Institute for Democracy (in Hebrew).

Kartin, A., & Schnell, I. (2008). The demographic rogue and borders in the Land of Israel. *Space, Populations, Societies*, 3, 411–422.

Kimmerling, B. (1989). Boundaries and frontiers of the Israeli control system. In B. Kimmerling (Ed.), *The Israeli state and society: Boundaries and frontiers* (pp. 265–286). Albany: State University of New York Press.

Kimmerling, B. (2004). *Migrants, settlers, children—The state and society in Israel between multiculturalism and culture war.* Tel Aviv: Am Oved (in Hebrew).

Mack, A. (2002). Sharon's Algerian shhadow. *Globe and Mail*, p. 27.

Mautner, M. (2008). *Law and culture in Israel at the beginning of the twenty-first century.* Tel Aviv: Am Oved (in Hebrew).

Mayer, T. (Ed.). (1994). *Women and the Israeli occupation—The politics of change.* London and New York: Rutledge.

Memmi, A. (1985). *Portrait of the conquered and portrait of the conqueror.* Jerusalem: Carmel.

Menard, O. (1964). The French army above the state. *Military Affairs*, 28(3), 123–129.

Naor, A. (2001). *The greater Israel: Theology and policy.* Haifa: Haifa University Press (in Hebrew).

Newman, D. (Ed.). (1985). *Impact of Gush Emunim: Politics and settlement in the West Bank.* Sydney: Croom Helm.

Newman, D. (2001). From national to postnational territorial identities in Israel-Palestine. *Geojournal*, 3, 235–246.

Oren, N. (2005). *The Israeli ethos of the Arab-Israeli conflict 1967–2000: The effects of major events.* Dissertation, Tel Aviv University (in Hebrew).

Oren, N. (2009). *The Israeli ethos of conflict 1967–2005*. Working Paper #27. Fairfax, VA: Institute for Conflict Analysis and Resolution, George Mason University. Retrieved November 20, 2009, from http://icar.gmu.edu/wp_27oren.pdf

Oren, N., & Bar-Tal, D. (2007). The detrimental dynamics of delegitimization in intractable conflicts: The Israeli-Palestinian case. *International Journal of Intercultural Relations, 31*, 111–126.

Peleg, M. (1997). *Dissemination of the wrath of God*. Tel Aviv: HaKibbutz HaMeuchad (in Hebrew).

Portugali, Y. (1996). *Implicate relations: Society and space in the Israeli-Palestinian dispute*. Tel Aviv: HaKibbutz HaMeuchad (in Hebrew).

Ram, A. (1993). *Israeli society: Critical aspects*. Tel Aviv: Brerot (in Hebrew).

Ram, A. (2005). *The globalization of Israel*. Tel Aviv: Ressling (in Hebrew).

Redfield, M. (2003). *The politics of aesthetics*. Stanford, CA: Stanford University Press.

Relph, E. (1976). *Place and placenessness* London: Pion.

Roberts A. (1990). *Moments of colonial Africa*. Cambridge: Cambridge University Press.

Rubinstein, A. (1984). *The Zionist dream revisited: From Herzl to Gush Emunim and back*. New York: Schocken Books.

Sasson, D. (2005). *Report on the illegal settlements*. Report submitted to the Prime Minister's Office. Retrieved July 21, 2009, from http://www.planetnana.co.il (in Hebrew)

Schnell, I. (1994). *Perceptions of Israeli Arabs: Territoriality and identity*. Beit Berl: Centre for Research of Arab Society (in Hebrew).

Schnell, I. (2001). Transformations in territorial concepts: From nation building to concessions. *Geojournal, 53*(3), 221–234.

Schnell, I. (2009). The territorial strategy of the occupation. In A. Lavie (Ed.), *Settlement and defining Israel's borders* (pp. 49–54). Tel Aviv: Tami Steinmetz Centre for Peace Research, Tel Aviv University (in Hebrew).

Segev, T. (2007). *1967: Israel, the war, and the year that transformed the Middle East*. New York: Metropolitan Books.

Shafir, G., & Peled, Y. (2002). *Being Israeli: The dynamics of multiple citizenship*. New York: Cambridge University Press.

Shapira, A. (1992). *Land and power: The Zionist resort to force, 1881–1948*. Oxford: Oxford University Press.

Sheffi, N. (2009). Shifting boundaries: The 1967 war in Israeli children's magazines. *The Journal of Israeli History, 28*(2), 137–154.

Sheleg, Y. (2000). *The new religious*. Jerusalem: Keter (in Hebrew).

Sivel, R. (2009, March 19). *The State of Israel and territorial control*. Paper presented at the Conference of the Jerusalem Institute and Slifka Fund. Jerusalem: Jerusalem Institute for Israeli Research.

Smooha, S. (2000). The State of Israel's regime: Civilian democracy, no democracy or ethnic democracy? *Israel Sociology, 2*, 565–630.

Sutton, K., & Lawless, R. I. (1978). Population regrouping in Algeria: Traumatic change and the rural settlement pattern. *Transactions, Institute of British Geographers, 3,* 243–270.

Swirski, S. (2008). *The price of occupation.* Tel Aviv: Adva Center (in Hebrew).

Zertal, I., & Eldar, A. (2007). *Lords of the land: The war over Israel's settlements in the occupied territories, 1967–2007.* New York: Nation Books.

Contributors

Muhammad Amara is Associate Professor and head of the English Department at Beit Berl Academic College. His academic interests include language education, language policy, sociolinguistics, language and politics, collective identities, and the Arab-Jewish divide in Israel. His publications include *Politics and Sociolinguistics Reflexes: Palestinian Border Villages* (Philadelphia and Amsterdam: John Benjamins, 1999); *Language Education Policy: The Arab Minority in Israel*, with Abd Al-Rahman Mar'I (London: Kluwer Academic Publishers, 2002); *Languages in Conflict: A Study of Linguistic Terms in the Arab-Israeli Conflict*, with Abd Al-Rahman Mar'i, Dar-Al-Huda, and Dar Al-Fiker published in 2008, Amman; and the edited book *Language and Identity in Israel* (Ramallah: The Palestinian Forum for Israeli Studies [Madar], 2002).

Daniel Bar-Tal is Branco Weiss Professor of Research in Child Development and Education at the School of Education, Tel Aviv University. His research interest is in political and social psychology, studying the sociopsychological foundations of intractable conflicts and peacemaking, as well as the development of political understanding among children and peace education. He has published over 20 books and over 200 articles and chapters in major social and political psychology journals and books. He served as President of the International Society of Political Psychology and received various awards for his work. In 1991 and 2009, he was awarded the Otto Klineberg Intercultural and International Relations Prize of the Psychological Study of Social Issues (SPSSI), and in 2000–2001 he was awarded the Golestan Fellowship at the Netherlands Institute for Advanced Study in the Humanities and Social Science. In 2006 his book *Stereotypes and Prejudice in Conflict*, coauthored with Yona Teichman (Cambridge University Press, 2005), received the Alexander George Award of the International Society of Political Psychology for the best book in political psychology. In 2006 he also received the Peace Scholar Award of the Peace and Justice Studies Association for great scholarship and hard work in studying conflicts and peacemaking. In 2011 he received the Lasswell Award of the International Society of Political Psychology for "distinguished scientific contribution in the field of political psychology." In 2012 he received the Nevitt Sanford Award of the International Society of Political Psychology for engaging in the practical application of political psychological principles and for creating knowledge that is accessible to and used by practitioners to make a positive difference in the way politics is practiced.

Dan Caspi is Professor and former Chair of the Department of Communications Studies, Ben-Gurion University of the Negev (2004–2009). He is also the Founding Chair of the Israel Communication Association (ISCA) and has filled several public roles, including Consultant for a communications program at Israeli Educational Television (1991–1993); Member of the Committee on Public Broadcasting of the Ministry of Science, Culture and Sports; and Board Member of the Israeli Broadcasting Authority (2000–2003). He has written and coauthored several books: *Media, Minorities, and Hybrid Identities: The Arab and Russian Communities in Israel* (2006); with Hanna Adoni and Akiba A. Cohen, *Due to Technical Difficulties: The Fall of the Israeli Broadcasting Authority* (2005); in Hebrew, *The In/Outsiders: The Mass Media in Israel* (1999); with Yehiel Limor, *Media Decentralization: The Case of Israel's Local Newspapers* (1986); and has coedited, with Avraham Diskin and Emanuel Gutmann, *The Roots of Begin's Success: The 1981 Elections* (1984).

Marcelo Dascal is Professor of Philosophy and former Dean of Humanities at Tel Aviv University, Israel. He was a Fellow of the Netherlands Institute of Advanced Studies (NIAS), of the Institute for Advanced Studies of Jerusalem (Israel), and of the Institute of Advanced Studies of the University of Leipzig (Germany). In the last position, he held the Leibniz Professor Chair. He also held the Gulbenkian Professorship at Lisbon University (Portugal). Dascal is President of the New Israeli Philosophical Association and of the International Association for the Study of Controversies, as well as a member of the Steering Committee of the Fédération Internationale des Sociétés de Philosophie (FISP). His research domains include pragmatics and the philosophy of language, epistemology and the philosophy of science, cognitive sciences and the philosophy of mind, the study of controversies, and the history of ideas, with special emphasis on early modern thought. He has authored and edited more than 30 books, including *La Sémiologie de Leibniz* (1978), *Pragmatics and the Philosophy of Mind* (1983), *Leibniz: Language, Signs, and Thought* (1987), *Philosophy of Language: Handbook of Contemporary Research* (1995–1996), *Negotiation and Power in Dialogic Interaction* (2001), *Interpretation and Understanding* (2003), *The Gust of the Wind: Humanities in a New-Old World* (2004; in Hebrew), *Controversies and Subjectivity* (2005), *G. W. Leibniz: The Art of Controversies* (2006, 2008 paperback edition), *Traditions of Controversy* (2007), *Leibniz: What Kind of Rationalist?* (2008), and *The Practice of Reason: Leibniz and His Controversies* (2010). He is the founder and Editor of the journal *Pragmatics & Cognition* and of the book series "Controversies" and *Ma?Da?* (in Hebrew). A "Marcelo Dascal Prize" is awarded every three years by the Brazilian Society of Cognitive Science for the best submitted monograph in the field. For his research achievements, Dascal was awarded the Humboldt Prize (2002) and the Argumentation Award of the International Society for the Study of Argumentation (2004).

Gideon Doron † was Professor in the Department of Political Science at Tel Aviv University. He served as a Chair of the Israeli Association of Political Science and served as the Chair of the Board of the Second Authority for Television and Regional Radio, and as a Chair and member of the board of several academic and public councils. He specialized in the study of political economy, public policy, methods of social choice, and Israeli politics. He has published 17 books and dozens and articles in English and Hebrew in the above-mentioned areas. His edited volume, *Law and Politics in Israel*, with Arey Naor and Assaf Maydani, was published in 2010.

Yoel Elizur is an Associate Professor at the Hebrew University of Jerusalem, School of Education, Division of Child Clinical and School Psychology and the Chairperson of the Israeli Council of Psychologists. He is the former Director of the Kibbutz Child and Family Clinics in Hedera and Yoav, and the Kibbutz Clinics' Medical Psychology Center. He coauthored *Institutionalizing Madness: Families, Therapy and Society* (1989), which was awarded the Esther Haar Award of the Jerusalem Foundation for an original contribution to social psychiatry in Israel, *Holding Their Own: Self/Mutual Help, Therapy, and Society* (2003), which received the Bahat Award for best nonfiction work in 2002, and The Blot of a Light Cloud: Israeli Soldiers, Army, and Society in the Intifada (2012).

Yaron Ezrahi is Emeritus Professor of Political Science at the Hebrew University of Jerusalem and a Senior Fellow Emeritus at the Israel Democracy Institute in Jerusalem, Israel. He was a Fellow at the Center for Advanced Study in the Behavioral Sciences at Stanford University and served as a Visiting Professor at Pennsylvania, Harvard, and Duke Universities. He also served as consultant to a variety of institutions, including the White House, the Organization for Economic Cooperation and Development (OECD), the Israel National Academy of Science, and, more recently, the Carnegie Commission on Science and Government. His research focused on the impact of modern science and technology on democratic governments and the conduct of public affairs. He is also interested in comparative politics and democracies; science policy and cultural policy; and culture and democracy. He has also written extensively on Israeli democracy, and through his activities at the Israel Democracy Institute, he has taken part in the effort to draft a written Israeli constitution. He is the winner of the 1997 National Jewish book Award in the category of Israel and

Zionism. His publications include *Israel Towards a Constitutional Democracy*, with Mordechai Kremnitzer and the assistance of Margit Cohen and Eytan Alimi (The Israel Democracy Institute, 2001, in Hebrew); *Rubber Bullets, Power and Conscience in Modern Israel* (Farrar, Straus Giroux, 1997); *Of Technology, Pessimism and Postmodernism*, coedited with Everett Mendelsohn and Howard Siegal (Kluwer Academic Publishers, 1994); and *The Descent of Icarus: Science and the Transformation of Contemporary Democracy* (Harvard University Press, 1990); *IMAGINED DEMOCRACIES: Necessary Political Fictions* (Cambridge-New York: Cambridge University Press, Forthcoming 2012).

Charles W. Greenbaum is the James Marshall Emeritus Professor of Social Psychology at the Hebrew University of Jerusalem. He taught and performed research at Duke University and Tufts University in the United States. His research interests are in social development, the child at risk, children's rights, child adoption, and social policy toward children, particularly the prevention of exposure of children to risk. He was granted the Volunteer of the Year award of the Israel Association for Civil Rights in 1991, and was the 2007 Visiting Scholar at the University of Minnesota in its Harris Foundation Visiting Scholars Program in Early Education and Development.

Eran Halperin is a Senior Lecture and Deputy Director of the Political Psychology Program at the Lauder School of Government, Interdisciplinary Center, Herzliya, Israel. His studies concentrate on the role of emotions and emotion regulation in determining public opinion toward peace and equality, on the one hand, and war and discrimination, on the other. He serves as an associate editor of *Political Psychology*. He has published papers in the *Journal of Conflict Resolution*, the *Journal of Peace Research*, and the *Journal of Social Issues and Political Psychology*.

Hanna Herzog is Professor of Sociology at Tel Aviv University, Department of Sociology and Anthropology. She is one of the founders of the Gender Studies Program and is currently the Head of the program. She is also the Academic Director of the Civil Society Program at Van Leer Jerusalem Institute and Codirector with Prof. Naomi Chazan of the Center for Advancement of Women in the Public Sphere (WIPS) at the Van Leer Jerusalem Institute. She specializes in political sociology, sociology of gender, ethnicity, religion, sociology of knowledge, and generation. She has published many academic articles with a strong emphasis on women's issues. Among her books are *Political Ethnicity: The Image and the Reality* (1986, in Hebrew); *Realistic Women: Women in Israeli Local Politics* (1994, in Hebrew); *Gendering Politics: Women in Israel* (University of Michigan Press, 1999). She is the coauthor of *Sex Gender Politics: Women in Israel* (1999, in

Hebrew) and has published an edited book with Ann Braude, *Gendering Religion and Politics: Untangling Modernities* (Palgrave/Macmillan, 2009).

Shir Hever is an economic researcher in the Alternative Information Center, a Palestinian-Israeli organization active in Jerusalem and Beit-Sahour. Hever researches the economic aspect of the Israeli occupation of the Palestinian territories, some of his research topics include the international aid to the Palestinians and to Israel, the effects of the Israeli occupation of the Palestinian territories on the Israeli economy, and the boycott, divestment and sanctions campaigns against Israel. His work also includes giving lectures and presentations on the economy of the occupation. His first book: *Political Economy of Israel's Occupation: Repression Beyond Exploitation*, was published by Pluto Press.

Edward (Edy) Kaufman is a Senior Researcher and former Director of the Center for International Development and Conflict Management at the University of Maryland (UMD), and held earlier similar positions in the Harry S. Truman Research Institute for the Advancement of Peace at the Hebrew University of Jerusalem. He is currently teaching at UMD's Department of Government and Politics and in the Government and Diplomacy Program of the Interdisciplinary Center, Herzliya, as well as at Haifa University's International School. His relevant books include the *Human Rights in World Politics* (Tel Aviv: Defense Ministry Publishing House, 2001, in Hebrew) and the coedited volume, with Shukri B. Abed and Robert. L. Rothstein, *Democracy, Peace and the Israeli-Palestinian Conflict* (Boulder, CO: Lynne Rienner, 1993). Among his many relevant contributions are "Introducing Human Rights into Conflict Resolution: The Relevance for the Israeli-Palestinian Peace Process" (with Ibrahim Bisharat), *Journal of Human Rights*, 1(1), March 2002), 71–92; and the chapter "Bridging Conflict Transformation and Human Rights: Lessons from the Israeli/Palestinian Peace Process" (with Mohammed Abu Nimer), in J. Mertus and J. W. Helsing (Eds.), *Human Rights and Conflict* (Washington, DC: United States Institute for Peace Press, 2006).

David Kretzmer is Professor Emeritus of International Law at the Hebrew University of Jerusalem and Professor of Law at Sapir Academic College, Sderot. He has also been Professor of Law at the Transitional Justice Institute, University of Ulster; a Visiting Professor at Columbia Law School, the Fletcher School of Tufts University, the University of Southern California, and Bar Ilan University; and an Inaugural Fellow at the Straus Institute for the Advanced Study of Law and Justice of New York University School of Law. From 1995 to 2002 he was a member of the United Nations Human Rights Committee. His main fields of research are constitutional law, international human rights, and the law of armed conflict. His books include The *Legal Status of the Arabs in Israel* (1990 and 2002), *The Occupation of Justice: The Supreme Court of Israel and the Occupied Territories* (2002), and *The Concept of Human Dignity in Human Rights Discourse* (edited with E. Klein, 2002).

Tamir Magal is a PhD candidate at the School for Political Science at Haifa University. He also serves as a Research Fellow at the Institute for National Security Studies at Tel Aviv University. His doctoral dissertation is an investigation of the role of dissent and entrepreneurship in peace organizations in Israel and the strategies of these organizations for challenging societal beliefs concerning the Israeli-Palestinian conflict. Other areas of interest include social movements, political deviance, nuclear nonproliferation, and peace and reconciliation. He was awarded the Yad-Tabenkin Scholarship for 2007.

Mohanad Mostafa is a PhD candidate in the department of Political Science at Haifa University. He is studying Arab society in Israel, as well as political Islam and democratization. His doctoral dissertation is an investigation of the impact of political Islam on the development of democratization in the Arab world from both theoretical and practical perspectives. He has published academic articles and books in Arabic, Hebrew, and English on Arab society in Israel and on political Islam.

Neta Oren is a Visiting Scholar at the Institute of Conflict Analysis and Resolution at George Mason University. She was awarded her PhD in Political Science from Tel Aviv University. Her research interests are conflict resolution, political psychology, political communication, public opinion, and the Arab-Israeli conflict. The results of her research were presented at numerous international conferences in Europe and the United States. She has written over 20 journal articles and book chapters.

Reuven Pedatzur is Senior Lecturer in Political Science at Tel Aviv University and the Academic Director of the Daniel Abraham Center for Strategic Dialogue at Netanya Academic College. He is also the Senior Military Affairs Analyst of *Haaretz*. He was a Visiting Scholar (1993–1994) at the Center for Strategic Studies at MIT. His areas of research interest include missile defense, nuclear and other nonconventional weapons, the Israel Defense Forces strategic doctrine, and the Israeli-Palestinian conflict. He has written *Rearming Israel: Defense Procurement Through the 1990's* with Aharon Klieman (1991), *The Arrow Project and Active Defense: Challenges and Questions* (1993), and *The*

Triumph of Embarrassment (Israel and the Territories, 1967–1969) (1996) and has edited *Ballistic Missiles in the Middle East: The Next Challenge* (2001).

Maoz Rosenthal is a Visiting Lecturer at the Lauder School for Government, Diplomacy and Strategy at the Interdisciplinary Center (IDC), Herzliya. He completed his doctoral studies in Tel Aviv University in 2007 and since then has been a Postdoctoral Fellow at the Open University of Israel and a Visiting Scholar at the Betty and Whitney McMillan Center for Interational and Area Studies at Yale University. He specializes in political economy, comparative public policy, and public choice.

Danny Rubinstein teaches at Ben Gurion University and The Hebrew University in Jerusalem. Until 2008, he was a member of the editorial board of *Haaretz*. He is a specialist on Arab and Palestinian affairs. He has written *The People of Nowhere* (Random House, 1991) and *The Mystery of Arafat* (Steerforth Press, 1995).

Izhak Schnell is Professor at the Department of Geography and Human Environment in Tel Aviv University. He has served on several academic committees, such as Head of the Academic Committee of Beit Berl College (1993–1995), Chair of the Department of Geography in Tel Aviv University (2001–2005), President of the Israeli Association of Geographers (2003–2004), and Representative of the Israeli Academy of Science in the International Association of Geographers (beginning in 2010). He is also a member of the editorial boards of several international academic journals and research centers on campus. His research interests are in social and cultural geography. He investigates the structure of networked space in the era of globalization. His work on ethnic segregation and interaction in spaces, migrant workers' adaptation to new places, and ethnic entrepreneurs' embeddedness in sociospatial networks has been published in books and in international academic journals. He has also written sets of articles on Israeli landscapes, on the geographical impacts of environmental issues in Israel, and on the geography of the occupation in Israel.

Nadir Tsur is Affiliated Researcher at the Harry S. Truman Research Institute for the Advancement of Peace, the Hebrew University of Jerusalem, and a Visiting Fellow at the Chaim Herzog Center for Middle East Studies and Diplomacy at Ben-Gurion University. His main fields of research are in the realm of political psychology, influential tools used by leaders in different leadership processes, and national security. His book *The Rhetoric of Israeli Leaders in Stress Situations* (2004) won the Israel Political Science Association's prize for 2005. His book *Disengaging from the Strip: Ariel Sharon and Israel's Withdrawal from the Gaza Strip*, was published in 2006.

Dan Urian is Professor at the Theatre Department, Tel Aviv University and Chair of the Theatre Studies, Western Galilee College. His research concerns sociology of the theater, Israeli theater, drama in education, and television drama. His published books include *The Ethnic Problem in the Israeli Theatre* (The Open University, 2004, in Hebrew), *Television Drama* (Mofet: Ministry of Education, 2004, in Hebrew), and *Theatre in Society* (The Open University, 2008, in Hebrew), as well as *The Arab in Israeli Drama and Theatre* (Routledge Harwood, 1997) and *The Judaic Nature of Israeli Theatre: A Search for Identity* (Routledge Harwood, 2000). He is also co-editor, with Maria Shevtsova, of *The Sociology of Theatre* (Routledge Harwood, 2002).

Index

Page numbers followed by f, t, or n refer to figures, tables, or notes, respectively.

Abir (Yaari), 457–458
Abna' al-balad (Sons of the Village), 284–285, 286
Absentee Property Act, 98
absolutism/absolutist approach, 75–78, 84
Abu Al-Ayash, Dr., 319
Abu Shakra, Asim, 447
Abu-Shalabiya, Muhammad, 309–310
Achdut Avoda party, 117, 176–177n7. *See also* Labor Party
Acre Festival for Alternative Theatre, 453, 455, 458
Act of State 1967–2007 (exhibition), 464, 468
administrative detention/detainees, 16
Adva Center, 331, 347
Adwan, S., 399
Afghanistan, occupation of, ix, 11, 124, 349, 416
Agamben, G., 118
aggression
 effects on aggressors, 391–392
 intifada and, 386
 learned aggression, 384–386
 social norms for, 384, 390
 theoretical views on, 383–385
 toward civilians, 392–393
agricultural subsidies, 336–337
Ai, location of, 110
aid agencies, 329

Ajuri case, 33
Al-Aksa *intifada*, 386. *See also intifada*
Al-Anba (The News), 309
Albeck, Plia, 40
Alberstein, Chava, 459
Algeria, French occupation of, viii–ix, 243–247, 316–319, 350, 441, 509, 535
Al-Haraka Al-taqadumiyya Lilsalam (Progressive List for Peace), 285
Al-jabha Al-demokratiya lilsalm wa-almusawa (Democratic Front for Peace and Equality), 285
Al-jabha al-sha'biya (the Democratic Front), 277
Al-Jazeera, 306, 308
Al Majdal, 349
al-Naazer case, 41
Al-nakba ("the catastrophe"), 275–276
Al-nakba (the catastrophe), 278
Alon, Nitzan, 230
Alon, Yigal
 mapping/border actions by, 102–103
 on non-decision, 211
 plan implementation by Labor, 98
 political views of, 135–136
 on security borders, 212
 Suez Canal defense and, 218
Alon/Alon Plus Plan, 98, 100, 156
Aloni, Shulamit, 149

Al-Shams, Iman, 391–392
Alterman, Ella, 449
Alternative Information Center, 341
alternative media, 302, 304, 319
Amara, Muhammad, 21, 521, 540
Amir, Yigal, 423
Amiran, David, 103
Amnesty International, 16, 415
Anderson, B., 94, 115
annexation, creeping
   bureaucratic inertia and, 531–533
   dependence on Right-Wing parties, 530–531
   international community and, 517
   media's role in, 532–533
   policy/process of, 511, 519–520
   public opinion and, 527–530
An-Sky, S., 454
appearance, of settlements, 112
Arab affairs
   experts on, 311, 315, 454
   reporters/commentators, 303–304, 314
Arab duality, 445
"Arab Higher Committee," 312, 322n19
Arabic-language, fluency in, 307–308
Arabic-language broadcasts, 301, 306, 312
Arab Lists, 277–278, 279t, 284, 291n5, 291n6
Arab minority
   arts, representation in, 438
   discriminatory practices directed at, 418–420
   human rights and, 416
   in Israeli democracy, 199–200
   official languages and, 495
   restrictions on, 517
"Arab question," 413, 442–443
Arabs. *See* Israeli Arabs
Arab schools, 419
archaeological sites, significance of, 108–111

Archer, D., 394
argumentation
   economic, 329
   probable, 89n12
Arian, Asher, 161
Ariel College, 109–110, 196
Aristotle, 70–71, 89n9
army. *See also* Israel Defense Forces (IDF)
   gendered division of labor in, 367
   religious soldiers, 206n1
   settler relationship, 229–234
   training in, 399
   use/purpose of, 194–196
Arnon, A., 330
Aron, Raymond, 243
Article 55 (Hague Regulations), 41
Articles, of Geneva Convention IV
   "assigned residence," 51
   on deportations, 48
   funds transfers, 333
   on house demolitions, 49
   Israel's position on, 12–13, 33–34, 222
   occupier as trustee, 8
   protected persons, 34–35, 42, 48
   separation barrier and, 42
   settlement as violation of, 37
   settlement legality and, 38
   status of occupied territories, 515, 517
arts, representation in. *See also specific artists; specific works*
   Arab characters, portrayal of, 453
   audience characteristics, 440–441
   censorship laws, 443
   collaborating with Palestinian artists, 447
   of conflict, 439–440
   critical discourse, 530
   documentaries, 459–460
   ideological component, 441
   intifada and, 447–449, 459, 463, 465–466, 552–557

from 1967–1982, 442–446
from 1982–1995, 446–459
from 1995, 459–465
occupation as subject, 465–468
opposition to right-wing policy, 446
"Palestinian question" in, 446–447
protest and, 447
protest songs, 459
public debate on, 443
refugee issue, 445
repertoire, 438
Arutz 7, 302
"assigned residence," 51
Association for Civil Rights in Israel, 333
attack methods (Palestinian), 19
Auerbuch, Ephraim, 105
authoritarian states/regimes, ix, 175, 266, 424
Autonomy plan, 144
Avoda (Labor), 117, 176–177n7. *See also* Labor Party
Awa, Fuad, 455
Azariyahu, Joseph, 105
Azoulay, Ariella, 115, 194, 464, 465, 516

Baharav, Motti, 455
Balad (political party), 426
Balkan War. *See* Croatian settlements
Banai, Ehud, 454
Bandura, A., 384–385, 390
"banking" model, 67–68, 88n6
Bank of Israel, 335
Barabash, Uri, 450
Barak, Aharon, 34
Barak, Ehud
 coalition government of, 259
 political views of, 158–159, 169
 settler movement and, 193–194
 settlers' university and, 196
Bardala, lands in, 226
Barenboim, Daniel, 422
Bar-Gal, Y., 106

Bar-Lev, Haim, 213–216, 218–219, 227
Bar-Lev line, 218–220, 241
Bar-On, D., 387–388, 390, 396–397, 399
Bar-Tal, Daniel, 20, 22, 114–115, 385, 540
La Battaglia di Algeri (The Battle for Algeria), 441
"Battering Ram" exercise, 219–220
BDS (boycott/divestment/sanction) campaigns, 349, 351
Bedouins, removal of, 227–228
Begin, Menachem
 border determination by, 475
 political views of, 131, 144
 on West Bank, 479
 women's status and, 363
Behind the Bars (film), 450
Beilin, Yossi, 148–149
Beinisch, Dorit, 433n10
Beit Sourik case, 53
belligerent occupation
 "held territories" and, 477
 law of, 31, 44, 50
 norms of, 32
 as system of control, 34–36, 39, 53
Ben Ari, Michael, 427
Ben-David, Arnon, 448
Ben-David, D., 330
Ben-Gurion, David, 96, 98, 191, 208, 210, 300
"benign occupation," 14
Ben-Ner, Yitzhak, 456–457
Benvenisti, Eyal, 7
Benyamini, K., 447
Bereaved Families Forum, 423
Berger, T., 102
Berglas, E., 330
Beth El case, 34, 38
Bible, archaeological studies and, 109–110
biblical names, of settlements, 104–105, 105t

Bichler, S., 336, 346
bigotry, casual, 418–419
Bin-Nun, Yoel, 302
Bir Zeit University, 283
Bistrov, Y., 514
Bleich, A., 371
"Blue Box" map, 102
Blum, Yehuda, 53
Bnei Akiva youth movement, 105, 512
Border Police, 429
borders, determining, 507. *See also* "defensible borders," construction of
Bowins, B., 384
boycott/divestment/sanction (BDS) campaigns, 349, 351
Bracha Report, 440
Braver, Moshe, 103
"Breaking the Silence—Fighters Talk about Hebron" (exhibition), 464
Breaking the Silence movement, 361, 423
Britain, in Northern Ireland, 246, 508
British colonial occupation, 508
British Mandate, resistance to, 193, 199, 203–204
B'Tselem (website)
    on deaths/casualties, 16, 18–19, 386, 387
    on deportations, 18
    on human rights erosion, 523
    on IDF and settler violence, 232–233
    on interrogation and torture, 17
    on settlements, 15
bureaucratic inertia, 531–533
Burg, Yossef, 255
Bush, George W., 260
Buton, Yitzak, 455
Buzaglo, Haim, 450

Cameri Theatre, 442
Campbell, J. D., 246–247
Camp David Accords, 142, 144, 259–260
Carambo in Enemy Territory (Niv), 454
Caspi, Dan, 21, 532, 541
casualties, 16, 18–19, 386, 387
censorship laws, 443
Certeau, Michel de, 94
child poverty, 370
children's theater, 453, 458
Chilton, Nola, 438, 439*f*, 464
Chinese rule, in Tibet, viii, ix, 115, 316, 519
Chomsky, Noam, 427
Christian Society case, 33
"Christian Zionists," 423
cinema, representations in, 449–450. *See also* arts, representation in
civic education, 203–204, 430, 522–523
Civil Administration, in Israeli democracy, 196–199
civil disorder, 422–423
civilian matters, military government and, 235–237
civilians
    aggression toward, 392–393
    criminal behavior and, 393–396
    deaths of, 385
Clinton, Bill, 259
Clouds Over Samaria (Steinberg), 458–459
coalitions, 251, 257–258, 264, 267
Co-existence (Watad), 438
cognitive dissonance, 85–86
Cohen, Guy, 462
Cohen, R., 284
Cohen, S. B., 104
"collective consciousness," 439
collective punishment, house demolitions as, 48–49
colonialism
    effect on colonizers, 3, 508
    "internal colonialism," 275

regime comparison, 509
settlement policy as, 44
"colonial system," 69
The Colonized and the Colonizer (Memmi), 69
commemorative names, of settlements, 105t
commentators, on Arab affairs, 303–304, 314
communication. *See* media (Israeli)
Communist party. *See* Israeli Communist party
compensation
  to civilians, 339
  to settlers, 344–345
confounding factors, in studies, 399–400
Conquest (Day), 54
conquest, dynamics of, 114
conscription rates, 354n11
"conspiracy of silence," 415
constitution, Israel's failure to establish, 192, 194
Contained Relationships (Portugali), 280
control, belligerent occupation as system of, 34–36, 39, 53
controversies, role of, 82–87
controversy model, 64. *See also* occupation, morality and
corruption, in Civil Administration, 196–198
cost of occupation (to Israel)
  BDS campaigns, 349
  calculation method, 333–334
  comparisons of, 343–344
  compensation to settlers, 344–345
  data availability, 331–333
  economists' discourse on, 329–331
  funds transfers, 333
  growing awareness of, 330–331
  historical overview, 327–329
  income generated, 335–336
  interest calculation, 334–335
  international comparisons, 349–350
  international support, 352–353
  to Israeli society, 18–19, 346–349
  jobs/labor market, 348
  macroeconomic indicators, 347
  to Palestinians, 14–18
  profits and, 345–346
  of security, 338–341, 526
  security implications, 342–343
  settlement subsidies, 336–338
  sum of costs, 341, 342f, 343f
  terms, use of, 326–327
  for territorial control, 525–526
Council for Films and Plays, 456
Council of Settlements, 302
Courriere, Yves, 441
Covenant on Civil and Political Rights, 10
Covenant on Economic, Social and Cultural Rights, 10
creeping annexation, mechanisms of
  bureaucratic inertia, 531–533
  dependence on Right-Wing parties, 530–531
  international community and, 517
  media's role in, 532–533
  policy/process of, 511, 519–520
  public opinion, 527–530
crime, civilian, 393–396
Croatian settlements, 264–268
Cup Final (film), 450
curfews, roadblocks and, 17
Custodian of Government Property, 39–40
Cypress/Cypriots, 9, 115, 290

daily life, under occupation, 111–114
Dancy, J., 75–76
Dao, Salim, 453
Dascal, Marcelo, 19–20, 515, 524, 541
Day, David, 54, 114, 508
Dayan, Ilana, 391–392

Dayan, Moshe
  case for occupation, 125
  on defense of Suez Canal line, 220
  on defensible borders, 212
  Levinger group and, 224–225
  military government appointments, 236–237
  on *Nahal* outposts, 223
  political views of, 130, 131, 132–133, 144–145
  post-1967 war protocol, 12
  on *Queen of Bathtub*, 443
  Six Day War and, 208
deaths, of soldiers/civilians, 385. *See also* casualties
debate, typology of, 83
Debré, Michel Jean-Pierre, 245–246
Deception (Ben-Ner), 456–457
"decision not to decide," 211–213
Declaration of Independence (Israel's), 191, 512
decolonization movement, 68–69
Deconstruction (Pinkovsky), 460–461, 464
defense budget, 339
Defense Regulations, 48
"defensible borders," construction of
  military doctrine and, 210–211, 217
  political issues, 213–219
  as "security borders," 212
  withdrawal from territories, 213–219
dehumanization, 111
delegitimization
  of information sources, 529
  of Israeli Arabs, 521
  of occupation, 115, 509, 526–527
  of Palestinians, 532
  of victims/"other," 385, 394, 515
deliberation
  Aristotelian notion of, 89n9
  reason in, 71
Delouvrier, Paul, 245

democracies, belligerent occupation and, 36
democracy, Israeli
  army, use of, 194–196
  civic education in, 203–204
  Civil Administration in, 196–199
  extralegal force in, 190–194
  international legitimacy and, 204–205
  Israeli Arabs in, 199–200
  religion in, 200–203
  weakening of, 520–523
Democratic Front for Peace and Equality (*Al-jabha Al-demokratiya lilsalm wa-almusawa*), 285
"demographic bomb," 419
demographic equilibrium, 117–118
demonstrations, of October 2000, 114
deportations, 18, 48, 50–51
Derrida, J., 118
deviant norms, violent behavior and, 384
dialectical process, peacemaking as, 87
dichotomization, 77, 90n19
discrimination, Arab minority and, 418–420
discussion model, 64, 83, 84. *See also* occupation, morality and
Disengagement Plan, 1, 32, 261, 341, 492, 500
disengagement theory. *See* self-disengagement theory
disillusionment, process of, 441
Diskin, Yuval, 429
dispute model, 64, 83–84. *See also* occupation, morality and
dissociation process, 384–385, 390, 394, 397
dissonance, cognitive, 85–87
dissonance reduction, 385, 391, 393, 396, 403
dissonant nonnormative acts, 390
Ditzani, Rami, 459

diversity, 393
divestments. *See* BDS (boycott/
    divestment/sanction) campaigns
documentaries, 459–460
domestic violence, 372–373
Doron, Gideon, 21, 531, 542
Dotan, Shimon, 450
draft, military, 354n11
Drobless, M., 101
Drobless Plan, 40
duality, Arab, 445
dual regime, creation of, 115–116
"dunam by dunam," ideology of, 97
The Dybbuk (An-Sky), 454

Eastern Europe, Soviet Union in, ix
East Jerusalem
    annexation of, 535n2
    HR policies in, 412
    Palestinians in Israel, 420
Eating (Shabtai), 445
Eban, Abba, 223, 224
Ecce Hommo (Laor), 459
economic cost of occupation (to Israel)
    BDS campaigns, 349
    calculation method, 333–334
    comparisons of, 343–344
    compensation to settlers, 344–345
    data availability, 331–333
    economists' discourse on, 329–331
    funds transfers, 333
    growing awareness of, 330–331
    historical overview, 327–329
    income generated, 335–336
    interest calculation, 334–335
    international comparisons, 349–350
    international support, 352–353
    to Israeli society, 18–19, 346–349
    jobs/labor market, 348
    macroeconomic indicators, 347
    profits and, 345–346
    of security, 338–341, 526
    security implications, 342–343

settlement subsidies, 336–338
sum of costs, 341, 342*f*, 343*f*
terms, use of, 326–327
of territorial control, 525–526
economic cost of occupation (to
    Palestinians), 14–18
economic exploitation, 336
economic recessions, gendered effects
    of, 372
economic stress, violent crime and,
    394
The Economist, 347, 353
economy, strength of Israeli, 347
Edelstein, D. M., 7
Edingen, Angelica, 454
education
    banking concept in, 88n6
    human rights and, 430
    national heritage and, 105–108
    spending on, 349
    subsidies for, 337
    theater production and, 458
Educational Television channel, 107
"effective morality," 70
ego defenses, 384–385
Egypt
    Palestinian people and, viii
    peace agreement proposals, 216–217
    Suez Canal defense and, 218
Egyptian-Israeli peace negotiations,
    66–67
Eichmann, Adolf, 205
Eitan, Raphael, 143, 227, 231
Elazar, David, 220, 224
Elbak, Pelia, 99
Eldar, A., 230
electoral politics/power, of radical
    right-wing parties, 257–261
Elitzur, Yosef, 433n7
Elizur, Yoel, 22, 389–390, 396, 524, 542
Elon Moreh case
    private land requisition, 39, 427
    Supreme Court judgment, 31, 38

Emergency Regulations of 1945, 48, 55–56n14
The Emperor's New Clothes, 453
empirical studies, of psychological legitimization, 173–174
"enlightened occupation," 438
enlightened self-interest. *See* human rights/human rights practices
enlistment, military, 354n11
Ephraim Returns to the Army (Laor), 456
epistemic authority, 68–69
Epstein, Yitzhak, 442
Eshkol, Levi
   democratization under, 517
   on Golan Heights settlements, 222–223
   Gush Etzion settlement, 224–225
   political views of, 129–130
   on "security borders," 212, 213
   Six Day War and, 208
ethnic groups, in Israeli society, 380
"ethos of conflict," 13
Euripides, 441, 454
European Union (EU), trade relations with Israel, 349
expenditure on occupation. *See* economic cost of occupation (to Israel)
expropriation, of land, 15, 45–46, 95*f*, 98–99, 107, 226–227, 444–445, 460, 465, 507, 522, 531–532
extralegal force, in Israeli democracy, 190–194
Ezrahi, Yaron, 20, 509, 520, 522, 542–543

family, importance of, 368
family reunifications, 18
Famir, Tali, 447
Fanon, Franz, 317
fear, role of, 457
feminism, occupation and, 362–365. *See also* gender perspective; women

Ferguson, N., 508
fertility, promotion of, 368–369
Festinger, L., 85–86, 385
Fictitious Marriage (film), 450
"50% rule," 55n10, 55n11
filmmakers, 450
Finkelstein, I., 109
Finkelstein, Norman, 427
FLN (National Liberation Front), 318
foreign rule, acceptance of, 123–124
Fourth Geneva Convention
   "assigned residence," 51
   on deportations, 48
   funds transfers, 333
   on house demolitions, 49
   Israel's position on, 12–13, 33–34, 222
   occupier as trustee, 8
   protected persons, 34–35, 42, 48
   separation barrier and, 42
   settlement as violation of, 37
   settlement legality and, 38
   status of occupied territories, 515, 517
France
   Algerian occupation by, viii–ix, 243–247, 316–319, 350, 441, 509, 535
   Germany's occupation of, 403
Freedman, Marsha, 362
Freire, Paulo, 67–68
Freud, Anna, 384
"The Future Vision of the Palestinians in Israel," 289

Gal, Meir, 459
Galei Zahal (IDF Radio), 311–312
Galili, Israel
   on *Nahal* outposts, 222–224
   Suez Canal defense and, 218
Gallagher, N., 509
Gamliel, N., 331
Gantz, Benny, 230
Gartner, R. A., 394

Gaulle, Charles de, 244
Gavish, Yishayahu, 216
Gaza. *See* West Bank and Gaza
Gazans (Baharav), 455
Gaza War, 427. *See also* Operation Cast Lead
Gazit, Shlomo, 226, 236
GDP growth, 347, 350
gender perspective
  feminist voices, 362–365
  gender security, 371
  long-term stress and, 386
  national security and, 365–369
  on protracted conflict's effects, 371–373
  security paradigm in, 369–371
  UN Security Council Resolution 1325, 359, 371
generalism, 75
General Security Service (GSS), 17, 313
generational analysis, 360–361
Geneva Convention IV
  on "assigned residence," 51
  civilian protection focus of, 36
  departure of military authorities from, 33–34
  on deportations, 48
  on funds transfers, 333
  on house demolitions, 49
  Israel's position on, 12–13, 33–34, 222
  occupier as trustee, 8
  protected persons, 34–35, 42, 48
  Security Provisions Order and, 33
  separation barrier and, 42
  settlement legality and, 37–38
  status of occupied territories, 515, 517
Geneva Protocol (1977), 10
geographical influence, mechanisms of
  archaeology, 108–111
  daily life, 111–114
  land acquisition, 97–99
  maps, 102–103

  national education, 105–108
  place names, 103–105
  settlements, 100–102
  territorial identity and, 93–97, 116
Geography of the Middle East (Sofer), 107
geography textbooks, 105–107
Germany, occupation of France, 403
Gerstenfeld, M., 515
Gertz, Nurit, 441
Geva, Tsibi, 448
Ghanem, A., 275
Gilo, Roni, 231
God's legacy, 66
Golan, Yair, 354n7
Golan Heights
  HR policy/violations in, 412, 416–417
  as line of defense, 220–221
  settlement initiation in, 222–223, 225
Gold, D., 515
"golden rule," 73
Goldmann, Lucien, 439
Goldstein, C. S., 403
Goldstone Report, 205
Good Arab (Kaniuk), 448
Gordon, Neve, 425
Goren, Amit, 460
government coalitions, 257–258, 264, 267
The Governor of Jericho (Mundi), 444
Green, Dror, 448
Greenbaum, Charles, 22, 387–388, 390, 396–397, 524, 543
Greenberg, Tamir, 467
Green Line
  conquest of territories beyond, 125
  Jewish acceptance of, 122
  omission of, 102–103
Grossman, David, 448–449, 455
group solidarity, 393
Grunzweig, Emil, 422
GSS (General Security Service), 17, 313
La Guerre d'Algerie (film), 441

guilt (feelings of), of Israeli Jews, 382
Gush Emunim
　land acquisition and, 98, 100–101
　media struggle of, 302
　national identity and, 96
　settlement movement of, 191
　settlement promotion, 254
　state institutions and, 116
　vision of, 512–513
Gutwein, D., 370

Ha'aretz
　economic cost of occupation, 331, 343
　on Israeli deaths, 18–19
　subsidy estimates, 338
habituation-depreciation hypothesis, 394
Hadari-Rammage, Yona, 443
Hague Convention of 1907, 8
Hague Regulations, 8, 41
Haifa Municipal Theatre, 452
Haiti, U.S. occupation of, 402–403
"Halalim" (Shmueli), 465–466
Haleumni, Haichud, 260–261
Halperin, Eran, 20, 173, 385, 393, 543
Hamdu and Son (Buton), 455
Hampshire, Stuart, 89n9
HaOlam HaZez–Koah Hadash (This World–New Force), 177n11
HaOlam HaZez party (MERI), 139
Harakat al-arad (the Land Movement), 277, 291n4
Harel, Amos, 229
Hasmonean Tunnel, 231–232
Hatechia (Revival) party, 255–256
Hatzor, Ilan, 457
Hazlitt, William, 299
health care, subsidies for, 337
Hebraized names, of settlements, 105*t*
Hebrew University, 283
Hebron (Greenberg), 467
hegemonic orientation, 125, 172–173

Heiman, G., 425
Heiman, Yossi, 230
Heimatkunde (home studies) model, 105–106
Heller, Gur, 450
"here" and "there" dichotomy, 359, 364
Herut party, 117, 517
Herzog, Hanna, 21, 524, 543
Hever, Shir, 21, 525–526, 544
Hey Rimona (Hatzor & Sheinfeld), 457
High Court of Justice, 118, 427
Higher Follow-Up Committee for the Palestinians, 280, 282
highways, 45–47. *See also* roads/roadblocks
historicism, 77–79
Hizbullah, 237, 239–240
Hoffman, I., 105
holism, 75
Holocaust, 414, 432
"homeland security"
　development of, 330
　exportable technologies and, 350
　profits from, 346
homicide, 393–394
Horne, A., 247
house demolitions, 17, 48–49
housing, subsidies for, 337
humanitarian provisions, of Geneva Convention, 33
human rights/human rights practices
　accountability, absence of, 430
　education, implications of, 430
　impact of occupation on, 417–418, 431–432
　institutional impact on, 425–430
　legislative branch and, 426–427
　in OPT, 416–417
　policies toward, 411–13
　societal trends and, 420–423
　violations following Six Day War, 413–414

vulnerable populations and, 423–425
in world politics, 414–416
Hussein, Sadam, 415
Huysmans, J., 365

IBH (Israel Broadcasting House), 312
identity
Gush Enunim and, 96
reconstruction of Jewish-Israeli, 511–515
religious, 117
identity, geographical mechanisms of
archaeology, 108–111
daily life, 111–114
land acquisition, 97–99
maps, 102–103
national education, 105–108
place names, 103–105
settlements, 100–102
territorial identity and, 93–97, 116
ideological elements, in studies, 399
IDF (Israel Defense Forces). *See also* "defensible borders," construction of
as army of occupation, 194–196
civil disorder and, 422
civilian matter and, 235–237
HR policy/violations and, 417, 428–429
Information Wall (IW) and, 310–312, 314, 319
on Israeli deaths, 18–19
legal issues and, 226–228
military policy implications, 389
military thinking and, 221, 237, 240–241
moral behavior of soldiers, 390, 393
names used for OT, 382
occupation's effect on, 208–210
Palestinian casualties and, 16
politics of settlements and, 221–226
power taking by, 32–33
replacement of, 191

roadblocks and curfews, 17
settlement support/promotion, 522, 532
settlers, relationship with, 229–234
terror, fight against, 237–240
uniforms/insignias of, 424
violence reports, reaction to, 388–389
IDF Radio (*Galei Zahal*), 311–312
Ihud Lehumi (National Union)
description of, 178n17
political views of, 151–152, 162
immigrants, from Soviet Union, 424
imprisonment, of Palestinians, 16–17
Im Tirzu movement, 423
India, occupation of Kashmir, 289
individual rights, as entitlements, 415–416
industry, subsidies for, 337
information, sources of, 71–72
Information Wall (IW), 299–300, 305, 315–316, 320. *See also* media
infrastructure requirements, highways, 45–47
"inner debate," 85
innocence, presumption of, 50
institutions, control of state, 116
"internal colonialism," 275
international community, perspective of, 9–10
international companies, profits to, 346
International Court of Justice, 36, 41–42
International Criminal Court, 8, 415
international law
of belligerent occupation, 35–36
Geneva Convention IV in, 34
vs. government action in OT, 32
house demolitions, 48–51
international legitimacy, Israeli democracy and, 204–205
international pressure, to withdraw, 251
international status, of Israel, 526–527

International Women's Year Conference, 363
interpersonal communication, restriction/prohibition of, 306–307. *See also* media (Israeli)
interrogation/torture methods, 16–17
intifada
  casualty data, 16
  domestic/sexual violence and, 372–373
  economic impacts on Israel, 328, 329–330
  effects on soldiers, 387–390
  as generational turning point, 363–364
  HR support and, 419
  outbreak of, 143, 162
  Palestinian state opposition and, 151
  Palestinian support and, 171, 176n2
  political aggression and, 386
  representation in arts, 447–449, 459, 463, 465–466, 552–557
  security concerns and, 145
"*intifada* grants," 332
Intifada Legends (Green), 448
intradomestic bargaining. *See* radical right-wing parties
Iraq, U. S. occupation of, 403
Ireland, occupation of, 246, 508
ISA (Israel Security Agency), 313, 322n18
Isha L'Isha (Woman to Woman), 371–372, 374
Islamic Movement, 285, 426
IsraCampus, 425
Israel Academia, 425
Israel Academy, 109
"Israel and Palestinian Artists against the Occupation," 447
Israel Atlas (Amiran), 103
Israel Baaliya, 260
Israel Beytenu (Israel is our home)
  coalition government and, 260–261
  description of, 178n19
  motto of, 426
  political views of, 155, 163–166
  settlement support, 523
Israel Broadcasting House (IBH), 306, 307, 312
Israel Committee Against House Demolitions (ICAHD), 17
Israel Defense Forces (IDF). *See also* "defensible borders," construction of
  as army of occupation, 194–196
  civil disorder and, 422
  civilian matter and, 235–237
  HR policy/violations and, 417, 428–429
  Information Wall (IW) and, 310–312, 314, 319
  on Israeli deaths, 18–19
  legal issues and, 226–228
  military policy implications, 389
  military thinking and, 221, 237, 240–241
  moral behavior of soldiers, 390, 393
  names used for OT, 382
  occupation's effect on, 208–210
  Palestinian casualties and, 16
  politics of settlements and, 221–226
  power taking by, 32–33
  replacement of, 191
  roadblocks and curfews, 17
  settlement support/promotion, 522, 532
  settlers, relationship with, 229–234
  terror, fight against, 237–240
  uniforms/insignias of, 424
  violence reports, reaction to, 388–389
Israeli Arabs
  in Israeli democracy, 199–200
  occupation and, 199–200
Israeli Civil Administration, 15
Israeli claim, legitimacy of. *See* political system, views of

Israeli Communist party, 277, 279t, 282, 284
Israeli Council for Higher Education, 196
Israeli courts, human rights and, 427–428. *See also* Supreme Court of Israel
Israeli democracy
 army, use of, 194–196
 civic education in, 203–204
 Civil Administration in, 196–199
 extralegal force in, 190–194
 international legitimacy and, 204–205
 Israeli Arabs in, 199–200
 religion in, 200–203
 weakening of, 520–523
Israeli Jewish public, sectors of, 518–519
Israel Intelligence Heritage & Commemoration Center (IICC), 18, 19
"Israelization," 273
Israel Prison Service, 16
Israel Radio, 301
Israel Security Agency (ISA), 313, 322n18
Israel Television, 300, 309, 313

Jabbar's Head (Vanus), 455
Jabotinsky, Ze'ev, 517
Jabotinsky approach, 96, 97
Jakobi, Danny, 106
Jamait Ascan case, 31, 34, 46
Jamal, A., 288
The Jerusalem Syndrome (Sobol), 451, 452–453, 462, 467
Jewish appearance, of settlements, 112
Jewish-Israeli Identity, reconstruction of, 511–515
Jewish public, political views of, 160–162, 170–171
Jewish superiority, in subduing nature, 107–108

"Jewish traitors," 422
"Jewish underground," 231
jobs/labor market, 348
Jordan River
 as line of defense, 132, 214–215
 as security border, 148, 159, 172, 213
journalists. *See* media
"Judaization," process of, 511, 528
Judea and Samaria Council
 Israel Atlas and, 103
 land acquisition and, 98
 settlement support, 532
 state institutions and, 116
 tourist map distribution, 110
justification, of behavior, 385
justified preemption, vii
"just peace," 81

Kach (political party), 256–257, 447
Kadima (Forward)
 description of, 179n24
 political views of, 166–168, 171
Kahana Chai, 433 n6
Kahane, Meir, 256, 447
Kalkiliya (photo), 467f
Kaniuk, Yoram, 448
Kaplinsky, Moshe, 239
Karp Report, 193, 230, 522
Kashmir, Indian occupation of, 289
Kastel, Moshe, 442
Kaufman, Edward (Edy), 22, 523, 544
Kav Laoved, 335
keffiyot, 448, 457
Kelly, G. A., 244–245
Keshev Association–The Center for Protection Democracy in Israel, 302–303, 304, 321n7
Keynesian policies, 350
Kfar Etzion field school, 110
"Khirbet Kizha" (Yizhar), 445–446
Kibbutz Artzi movement, 212
Kibbutz Seminary, 464
Kimhi, S., 390

Kimmerling, Baruch, 276, 428, 456
Klezmer, Gaby, 447
Kliot, N., 104
Knesset. *See also* radical right-wing parties
  human rights and, 426–427
  silencing statements in, 362
knowledge, sociology of, 360
Kochavi, E., 108
Kook, Abraham Itzhak Hacohen, 513
Kook, Zevi Jehuda, Jr., 96
Kook, Zvi Yehuda Hacohen, 480, 485
Kotel Tunnel Incident, 231–232
koushan (certificate of title), 40
Krajina (Balkan region), 264–268
Kretzmer, David, 19, 515, 544–545
Kultuum, Um, 455

labor, exploitation of, 336
labor law, 44
labor market, 348, 368
Labor Party
  annexation of territories and, 117
  description of, 176–177n7
  national religious party and, 201
  political views (1967–1977), 131, 133–134
  political views (1977–1992), 145–147
  political views (1992–2000), 151, 157, 158, 160
  political views (2000 - 2009), 168–169
  settlement process and, 100
  settler movement and, 193–194
  socialist-democratic vision of, 512
land
  acquisition of, 97–99
  categories of, 55n7
  expropriation of, 15, 45–47, 95f, 98–99, 107, 226–227, 444–445, 460, 465, 507, 522, 531–532
  public use of, 39–40
Landau, J., 284
Landau, Moshe, 17, 34

Landau, S. F., 394
Landau, Simha, 393
Landau Commission, 17
Land Day, 281
"Land Exchange," 444
language. *See also* Arabic-language broadcasts
  Arabic-language fluency, 307–308
  deliberation capacity and, 71
  legal, 192
  official languages, 495
Lanner, Dan, 219–220, 224
Laor, Yitzhak, 456, 459
latent violence, under occupation, 112
Law for the Extension of Emergency Regulations, 55–56n14.
law/law enforcement
  dual system of, 193
  human rights and, 428–430
Lawless, R. I., 244
law of belligerent occupation, 34–36, 39, 53
Law of Permanent Residency, 420
learned aggression, stress and, 384–386
Lebanon, 346, 446, 447
left-wing generational unit, 361
left-wing point of view, 253, 381–382
legal aspects, of settlement policy
  foreign ministry, advice to, 37–38
  highway cases, 45–47
  legal system, separate nature of, 52
  public land use, 39–41
  security measures, 47–52
  separation barrier, 41–43, 52–53
  settlers' status in OT, 43–45
  Supreme Court cases, 38–39
"legal hypocrisy," 32
legal language, use of, 192
legal view, of occupation, 6–8
legislative branch, human rights and, 426–427
Leibniz, G. W., 73–74, 83–84, 89n12

Letters of the Sun and Letters of the Moon (Levy), 448
Leviathan, Shlomo, 231
Levin, Honoch, 442, 445, 460, 462–464, 463f, 467
Levinger, Moshe, 224–225
Levy, David, 103
Levy, Ittamar, 448
Levy, Ram, 446
Liberal party, annexation of territories and, 117
"liberation," occupation as, 11
Lieberman, Avigdor, 155–156, 165–166, 260, 426
Likud (The Union). *See also* radical right-wing parties
　description of, 176n5
　land acquisition and, 98–101
　nationalistic-ideological orientation of, 130, 131
　National Religious Zionists and, 201–202
　political views (1977–1992), 141–145
　political views (1992–2000), 151, 153–155, 158
　political views (2000 - 2009), 163–164, 168
　settlement policy of, 40
　settlement support, 523
literature/poetry, 448–449
Livnat, Limor, 103
Luski, I., 330
Lustick, I., 275

Machsom Watch reports, 112
Mack, A., 244, 509
macroeconomic indicators, 347
Madrid Talks, 257
Mafdal (National Religious Party)
　in coalition politics, 255–256
　nationalistic-ideological orientation of, 130

　political views of, 142–143, 151–152, 162–163, 176n4
Magal, Tamir, 20, 528, 545
Mammy (Mittelpunkt), 454, 455
Mandatory Palestine, 52
Mannheim, K., 360
Map (film), 460
MAPAI party, 117, 278, 279t
Mapam (Workers' Union party)
　in coalition politics, 278
　description of, 177n8
　political views of, 137, 148
maps, in national identity construction, 102–103. *See also* geographical influence, mechanisms of
Margalit, Avishai, 81–82
Mar-Him, Yossi, 454
Mar'i, S., 280
Martyr (Valentine), 448
Masked (Hatzor), 457
"Massada syndrome," 371
Massarweh, Riad, 443
mass media. *See* media (Israeli)
Matalon, Ronit, 388
Mautner, M., 520
Mayer, Tamar, 364
McKeever, S., 75
media (Israeli)
　alternative media, 302
　Arabic-language fluency and, 307–308
　blocking sources/channels, 305–6
　cognitive layer in, 308–310
　credibility and, 308–310
　disruption of broadcasts/information, 305, 309, 316
　dual role system, 310–313
　French government comparison, 316–319
　Information Wall (IW), 299–300, 305, 310, 315–316, 320
　interpersonal communication, restriction/prohibition of, 306–307

media (Israeli) (*Continued*)
  monitoring organizations, 302–303
  Netanyahu and, 523
  new media role, 303–304
  Operation Cast Lead, 319
  propagandists and, 308–310
  role in creeping annexation, 532–533
  routine operation of, 313–315
  settlers' media activity effects, 304–305
  television, introduction of, 300–302
Media Watch, 302, 304, 321n6
Megged, Aharon, 445
Meimad (political party), 423
Meir, Golda, 218, 414
Melamed, Zalman, 432n4
Memmi, A.
  on colonial regimes, 3, 509
  on colonizer/colonized relations, 69–70, 94, 508
  on daily life under occupation, 111
  on violence and suppression, 115
Menard, O., 245–246
Meretz (Vigor)
  description of, 178n20
  political views of, 160
MERI (HaOlam HaZez party), 139
Meron, Theodor, 13, 37–38, 39
Michael, Sami, 450
Middle East Media Research Institute (MEMRI), 303, 321n8
Migdal, J. S., 276
military doctrine. *See* "defensible borders," construction of
"military Keynesianism," 350
military/military government. *See* Israel Defense Forces (IDF)
military occupation, types of, 7–8
military rule
  belligerent occupation and, 35–36
  period of, 276–279, 279t, 282, 287t
military spending, 350
mind colonization, 67–69

Ministry of Defense, data on deaths, 385
Ministry of Education, 106, 110–111
miri land, 41, 55n7, 55n10
Miron, Theodor, 222
Mishna names, of settlements, 104, 105t
Mittelpunkt, Hillel, 454
Mitzna, Amram, 230
modernization theory, 283
Moledet party, 151, 256, 259–260
Monnier, Philippe, 441
moral absolutism, 75–78, 84
moral authority, 68–69
moral behavior, of soldiers, 390, 393
moral disengagement, 384, 390, 394
morality, occupation and
  "colonization of mind," 67–70
  context-sensitivity, 75–82
  interrelation between, 62–63
  Palestine Partition Plan, 65
  pragma-morality, 63–64, 70–75
  pragmatic/moral dissociation, 64–67
  rhetorical interpretation, 61–62
  territorial arrangements and, 66
moral justification, need for, 114–115
moral presumption, 63, 79–82
moral/psychological consequences
  of aggression, 391–392
  civilian crime, 393–396
  definitions/measurements of, 381–383
  limitations to studies, 399–403
  policy approaches, 398–399
  processes related to, 396–397
  social-psychological effects, 383–385
  for soldiers, 387–390, 393
  stress/stressful situations, 385–386
moral relativism, 75–79, 84
"mothers of the nation," 366
Movement for a Greater Israel
  annexation of territories and, 117
  Eshkol and, 213

movement restrictions, 17–18, 51
Mundi, Yosef, 444
municipalities, subsidies for, 337
Murder (Levin), 445, 460, 462–464, 463*f*
Mustafa, Mohanad, 21, 521, 545
And with My Spirit, My Corpse (Laor), 459

Nahal/Nachal outposts, 38, 101, 221–227
Nakba Day, 426, 523
Nakkah Law, 426
names
 of military sites, 220
 of settlements, 103–104, 105*t*
Naqba, 81–82
Narkiss, Uzi, 218, 224
narrative histories, teaching of, 399
Natal (Israel Trauma Center for Victims of Terror and War), 370–371
National Committee for the Heads of the Arab Local Authorities in Israel, 281, 289
national education, 105–108. *See also* education
national identity, as religious identity, 117
national identity construction. *See* geographical influence, mechanisms of
national ideology, foundations of, 13
National Insurance Institute (NII), 327, 370, 372
nationalism, as ideology, 96
nationalistic-ideological orientation, 127, 130, 139, 141, 153, 162, 172
nationalistic-pragmatic orientation, 128, 131, 141, 151, 152–156, 163, 172
National Liberation Front (FLN), 318
National Liberation League, 282
National Religious Party (NRP), 201–202, 255–256
national security, as gendering mechanism, 365–369

"natural growth," 197
natural right, 77
nature
 Jewish superiority in subduing, 107
 settlement names from, 105*t*
Naturei Karta, 426
Naveh, Eyal, 106
Nazi genocide, 205
Ne'eman, Jacob, 523
Ne'eman, Yehuda (Judd), 450
Nekuda, 302
Neo-Zionist vision, 513–515
Netanyahu, Benjamin
 coalition government of, 259
 democratic institutions and, 523
 on Holocaust's lessons, 414
 on 9/11 attacks, 353n2
 political views of, 153–155, 164–165
 on two-state solution, 345
New Profile movement, 361
news sites/sources, 302
New York Times, 222–223
NGO Monitor, 303, 321n8
NGOs (nongovernmental organizations)
 criticism by, 10
 human rights campaigns and, 423
 political views and, 160
 restrictions on, 426
 settlement supporters and, 523
Nichomachean Ethics (Aristotle), 70–71
Night Movie (film), 450
nihilism, 77
9/11 attacks, 353n2, 415–416
1967 war. *See* Six Day War
The Ninth Wave (Massarweh), 443
Nir, Dov, 106
Nirgad, Lia, 439*f*, 464
Nitzan, J., 336, 346
Niv, Kobi, 454
nondecision, as official stance, 211–213
norms. *See* social norms

"not one millimeter" approach, 216, 218, 220
novels, 448–449. *See also* arts, representation in
NRP (National Religious Party), 201–202, 255–256

occupation. *See also* belligerent occupation
　as commodity, 350
　economics of, 525–526
　interactive features of, 3–4
　international legitimacy and, 509–510
　Israeli case for, 125–127
　Israeli feminism and, 362–365
　legal view of, 6–8
　as "liberation," 11
　meaning of, 123–125
　profits of, 345–346
　psychological processes and, 396–397
　rationales for, 11, 124–125
　service provision under, 4–5
　social-psychological effects of, 383–385
　socio-economic cost of, 346–349
　sociology of, 360–362
　succession of civilizations and, 508
　term definition, 6–7, 381–382
occupation, morality and
　"colonization of mind," 67–70
　context-sensitivity, 75–82
　interrelation between, 62–63
　Palestine Partition Plan, 65
　pragma-morality, 63–64, 70–75
　pragmatic/moral dissociation, 64–67
　rhetorical interpretation, 61–62
　territorial arrangements and, 66
occupation, views of
　basic orientations, 127t
　competing declarations, 125–126
　nationalistic-ideological orientation, 127, 130

nationalistic-pragmatic orientation, 128
　nature of the worldview, 126–127
　universal-ideological orientation, 129
　universal-pragmatic orientation, 128–129
　value orientation, 126
occupations, lack of comparability in, 400–403
occupied society
　acceptance of foreign rule, 123–124
　international society and, 2
　perspective of, 8–9
　resistance/oppression cycles, 4
　violent acts of, 5
occupied territories (OT). *See also* "defensible borders," construction of
　government action vs. international law, 32
　human rights practices in, 416–417
　legal system in, 32–35
　as national territory, 95f
occupying society
　decision to annex/settle, 4–5
　impact of occupation on, 510–511
　neglect of effects on, 2
　occupation's effect on, 3–4
　perspective of, 10–11
　responsibility to react, 4
October 2000 demonstrations, 114
oil, price/profits of, 346
Olmert, Ehud, 1, 167–168, 419
One of Ours (Barabash), 450, 456
one-state solution, ix
Operation Cast Lead, 319, 389, 428
Ophir, A., 115, 194, 516
Or, Theodor, 419
Oren, Neta, 20, 545
Organization of Families Victims, 18–19
Orli, Abraham, 226–227

Orthodox Jews
  founding liberal ideals and, 423–424
  settlements, position/stance on, 253
Oslo Accords, 98–99, 100, 151–154, 158, 162, 287, 529–530
"Oslo grants," 332
OT. *See* occupied territories (OT)
"other's place," principle of, 73–74
Ottoman Land Law, 55n7, 55n8, 55n10
outpost ("stronghold"), 23n5. *See also Nahal/Nachal* outposts
Oz, Amos, 61

Palestine Liberation Organization (PLO)
  in film, 450
  Israeli security responses to, 418
  Palestinians in Israel, contact with, 285
  political status consolidation of, 307
  recognition of, 132–133
Palestinian attacks, compensation to victims of, 339
Palestinian Authority (PA), 153–155, 157, 163, 168–169, 171, 336
Palestinian Authority Areas (PAA), 313–315
Palestinian claim, legitimacy of. *See* political system, views of
The Palestinian Girl (Sobol), 451, 454
Palestinian Media Watch (PMW), 303, 321n8, 321n9
Palestinians
  armed struggle, participation in, 280–281
  Document of June 6, 1980, 286–287
  in East Jerusalem, 420
  education, emphasis on, 281–282
  effect on Israel's economy, 328, 331
  identify/affiliation of, 273–274, 280, 290
  Israeli citizenship of, 281
  national institutions of, 280
  Partition Plan rejection, 65
  permit requirements for, 113
  political leadership, 282
  political organization of, 274
  population in West Bank/Gaza Strip, 14
  rising expectations of, 283–284
  socio-economic situation of, 274
  student movements, 283
  voting distribution of, 279*t*
Palestinians, political discourse of
  before 1967 war, 275–279
  after 1967 war, 279–283
  characteristics of, 288
  "future visions," 288–289
  periods of development, 274–275
  political-ideological movements, 283–289
  pre/post war differences in, 287*t*
Palestinian society, costs of occupation to, 14
Palestinian state/statehood, ix, 128, 214–215, 285, 287, 501, 517. *See also* political system, views of
Palestinian women, 457–458
"Palestinization," 273
palmachnik, 514
particularism, 75–76, 514–515
Pathways of Peace, 423
"Peace and Security" List, 137–138
Peace and Security Movement, 177n10
Peace Index, 161, 170, 173, 174, 179n28
peacemaking, as ongoing dialectic process, 87
Peace Now, 41, 353–354n5, 422
Pedatzur, Reuven, 12, 20–21, 388, 509, 522, 526, 532, 545
Peel Commission, 98
Pelach, Dalia, 438
Peled, Matti, 213–314
Peres, Shimon
  political views of, 136–137, 147–148
  Shamir government and, 202–203

"permanent resident" civil status of, 535n2
permit requirements, for Palestinians, 113
personal safety/security, 369, 370–373, 524–525. *See also* violence
personal-social insecurity, 364–365
persuasion, rationality and, 71
Philippines, United States in, viii
photography, 465. *See also* arts, representation in
physical violence. *See also* violence
  soldiers' views on, 388
  stress and, 384
Physicians for Human Rights, 16–17
pieds noirs (black feet), 317, 322n20
Pinkovsky, Roni, 460
Pisker, Roni, 451
place names, 103–105
Planning Authority, 197
"Play, Play on the Dreams" (Tchernikovsky), 448
PMW (Palestinian Media Watch), 303, 321n8, 321n9
poetry, 448–449
polarization, 77
polemic exchanges, 83
police/internal security costs, 339–340
polis, 71
political aggression, *intifada* and, 386
political coalitions, 251, 257–258, 264, 267
political discourse, 524–525. *See also* Palestinians, political discourse of
political killings, 395
political system, views of (1967–1977)
  Alon, 135–136
  Begin, 131
  Dayan, 130, 131, 132–133
  Eshkol, 129–130
  HaOlam HaZez party, 139
  on Israeli claim, 130, 133, 135, 136–138, 140
  of Jewish public, 139–141
  Labor Party, 131, 133–134
  Likud government, 130–131
  Mafdal, 130
  nationalistic-ideological orientation, 139, 141
  nationalistic-pragmatic orientation, 131, 141
  on Palestinian claim, 130–132, 133–136
  Peres, 136–137
  practical-nationalistic-pragmatic orientation, 133
  Rabin, 135
  Sapir, 134–135
  on security concerns, 132–134, 136–139, 141*f*
  Sharon, 131–132
  Shelomzion, 131–132
  universal-ideological orientation, 139
  universal-pragmatic orientation, 137
  on withdrawal from territories, 131, 136, 139, 140*f*
political system, views of (1977–1992)
  Aloni, 149
  Begin, 144
  Beilin, 148–149
  Dayan, 144–145
  Eitan, 143
  on Israeli claim, 142, 144–145, 150*f*
  of Jewish public, 142*f*, 149–151, 150*f*
  Labor Party, 145–147
  Likud party, 141–145
  Mafdal party, 142–143
  Mapam party, 148
  nationalistic-ideological orientation, 142–143, 150
  nationalistic-pragmatic orientation, 142, 144–145, 151
  on Palestinian claim, 143–144, 146–149

on Palestinian statehood, 142f
Peres, 147–148
Rabin, 148
Ratz party, 148, 149
on security concerns, 143–144, 146, 148
Shamir, 143
Sharon, 145
SHELI party, 149
Tehiya party, 142
Tzomet party, 142, 143
on withdrawal from territories, 144, 146–149
political system, views of (1992–2000)
Alon Plus plan, 156
Barak, 158–159
Ihud Lehumi party, 151–152
Israel Beytenu, 155
on Israeli claim, 152–153, 156, 158
of Jewish public, 160–162
Labor Party, 151, 153, 157, 158, 160
Liberman, 155–156
Likud Party, 151, 153–155, 158
Mafdal party, 151–152
Meretz party, 160
Moledet party, 151
nationalistic-ideological orientation, 153
nationalistic-pragmatic orientation, 151, 152–156
Netanyahu, 153–155
Oslo Accords and, 151–154, 158
on Palestinian claim, 152, 154, 155–160
Rabin, 158
security concerns and, 152, 154–159
Sharon, 155
Tzomet party, 151
universal-pragmatic orientation, 160
withdrawal from territories, 156, 160
political system, views of (2000–2009)
Barak, 169
Ihud Lehumi party, 162

Israel Beytenu, 163–166
of Jewish public, 170–171, 174–175
Kadima party, 166–168, 171
Labor Party, 168–169
of Liberman, 165–166
Likud party, 163–164, 168
Mafdal party, 162–163
nationalist-ideological orientation, 162
nationalist-pragmatic orientation, 163
of Netanyahu, 164–165
Olmert, 167–168
Oslo Accords and, 162
security concerns and, 162–170
on self-determination, 169, 172
Sharon, 167
on territorial compromise, 163–164
on two-state solution, 166, 168
withdrawal from territories, 166, 169, 171
political violence, 372, 385–386
Politics (Aristotle), 70–71
"politics of insecurity," 365
Pontecorvo, Gillo, 441
population
of Palestinians, 14
of settlers, 334f
Portugali, Y., 280
postdecision dissonance, 86–87
posttraumatic stress disorder (PTSD), 386
posttraumatic stress syndrome (PTS), 370–371
poverty/income gaps, 348, 370, 372
power, felt by soldiers, 392–393
practical-nationalistic-pragmatic orientation, 133
"pragma-morality," 63–64, 70–75
preemption, justified, vii
Present Absentees (Grossman), 448, 449
presumption
reliance on, 72–73
role in cognition, 89n12
trust/mistrust and, 79–81

"preventive" violence, 392
preventive vs. preemptive wars, vii
private security companies, 328–329
privatization, of welfare state, 370
"probable argumentation," 89n12
Progressive List for Peace (PLP), 285
protected persons, 34–35, 42, 48
protest songs, 459
psychoanalytic theory, ego-defenses and, 384–385
psychological consequences
  of aggression, 391–392
  civilian crime, 393–396
  definitions/measurements of, 381–383
  limitations to studies, 399–403
  policy approaches, 398–399
  processes related to, 396–397
  social-psychological effects, 383–385
  for soldiers, 387–390, 393
  stress/stressful situations, 385–386
psychological legitimization. *See* political system, views of
PTS (posttraumatic stress syndrome), 370–371
PTSD (posttraumatic stress disorder), 386
"public emissary," artists' role as, 439–440
public land, use of, 39–40
public opinion
  creeping annexation and, 527–530
  on human rights, 421
public services, spending on, 348–349
punishment, collective, 48–49
Putin, Vladimir, ix

Queen of Bathtub (Levin), 442–443, 464, 467

Rabbis for Human Rights, 423
Rabin, Yitzhak
  assassination of, 395, 422, 423, 463
  case for occupation, 125
  on civilian matters, 235–236
  Egypt/Syrian peace agreements and, 216–217
  intifada and, 387
  on Jordan River as security border, 213
  political views of, 135, 148, 158
  post-1967 war protocol, 12
  settler movement and, 193–194
  on withdrawal from territories, 214–215
  women's status and, 363
racism, in arts, 447
radical right-wing parties
  comparative analysis, 263–265
  formation of, 253–255
  parliamentary seats, 255–257
  as partisan veto player, 257–261
  settlement policies, effect on, 261–263, 262t
radio broadcasts, 301, 306, 309, 311, 315, 318
Rafah Approach case, 34, 38
Rambam (Rabbi Moses Maimonides), 96
Ramban vs. Rambam teachings, 513
rationality, persuasion and, 71
rationalization process, violent behavior and, 384–386, 390, 393, 396
Ratz (Runner–Civil Rights and Peace Movement)
  description of, 177n9
  political views of, 137–138, 148, 149
Raviv, A., 385
Raviv, Moshe, 223
Raz, Joseph, 75–76
Redfield, M., 94
refugee issue, in arts, 445
regime
  analysis/nature of, 517
  dual regime creation, 115–116

nationalist ideology and, 515
populations in, 518–519
reconstruction of, 515–519
regional geography, 105–107
Rekhess, E., 280, 283–284
relativism, moral, 75–79, 84
religion
  in Israeli democracy, 200–203
  military force and, 206n1
religious commandment, 66
religious extremists, 395. *See also*
  radical right-wing parties
religious identity, national identity as, 117
religious vs. state education, 105–106
Renda, M.A., 402
reporters, on Arab affairs, 303–304, 314
repression
  as defense mechanism, 393
  as psychological process, 396
residency, revocations/restrictions, 18, 420
Resolution 1325, 359, 371
return of territories, 140f. *See also*
  political system, views of
reunifications, of families, 18
revocations of residency, 18
Rhetoric (Aristotle), 70–71
Rice, Condoleezza, 165
Ridge, M., 75
right, natural, 77
right of return, 66, 414
right-wing, violence and, 395
right-wing generational unit, 361
right-wing parties. *See also* radical
  right-wing parties
  dependence on, 530–531
  settlements, position/stance on, 253
right-wing theorists, arguments of, 381–382
Riklin, Shimon, 110
Riklis, Eran, 450
Riv, David, 447, 459

roads/roadblocks
  curfews, 17
  image of, 466f
  security checks, 112
  soldiers' stress and, 390
  subsidies for, 337–338
robbery, 393–394
Roberts, A., 7–8
rocket fire/mortar shelling, 19
Rome Statute of the International
  Criminal Court, 8
Rontzki, Avichai, 206n1
Rosenthal, Maoz, 21, 531, 545–546
Rosler, N., 173, 385
Rouhana, N., 275
Rousseau, Jean Jacques, 204
Rubinger, David, 459
Rubinstein, A., 330
Rubinstein, Danny, 21, 532, 546
Rubinstein, Elyakim, 22n1
Russian Jews, 424

Saar, R., 337
Sachs, D., 372
Sadat, Anwar, 255
Sagy, S., 390
Samara (Mittelpunkt), 454
"Samatocha," 442, 444–445, 463
sanctions. *See* BDS (boycott/
  divestment/sanction) campaigns
Sapir, Pinhas, 134–135
Sartre, Jean Paul, 441, 454
Sasson, Talia, 228, 232, 233–234
Sasson Report, 430, 522
"Satellite Lists," 291n3
Sawt al-Arab (Voice of Arabia), 309
Schiff, Zeev, 456
Schloss, Ruth, 442
Schnell, Izhak, 20, 22, 106, 114, 528, 546
Schofield, N., 260
School of Theatre Arts (Kibbutz
  Seminary), 464

schools, Arab, 419
security
　cost of, 338–341, 526
　personal and human, 369–371
　political views on, 162–170
　Supreme Court decisions on, 51–52
"security borders," 212, 213. *See also* "defensible borders," construction of
security checks, 112
security measures, legal aspects of, 47–52
security narrative, in territorial control, 524–525
security paradigm, renewed definition of, 369–371
security policy, Six Day war and, 208–210
Security Provisions Order, 32–33
Security Services (Shin Bet), 429
"security tax," 335
security threat(s), 364–365, 369–371. *See also* political system, views of
Segev, Tom, 277
Sela-Shayovitz, R., 394
self-defense mechanisms, 384, 389, 390
self-determination, 169, 172
self-disengagement theory, 390
self-image, of occupiers, 111
self-interest. *See* human rights/human rights practices
self-justification, 391
separation barrier
　cases dealing with, 33
　legal opinions on, 41–43
　reason for, 354n7
　route legality, 52–53
　as security cost, 340–341
September 11, 2001 attacks, 353n2, 415–416
settlement policy (legal aspects)
　foreign ministry, advice to, 37–38
　highway cases, 45–47
　legal system, separate nature of, 52
　public land use, 39–41
　security measures, 47–52
　separation barrier, 41–43, 52–53
　settlers' status in OT, 43–45
　Supreme Court cases, 38–39
settlements/settlement movement. *See also* Geneva Convention IV; Gush Emunim
　economic investment in, 334–335
　land acquisition and, 100–102
　occupation and, vii–viii
　population growth, 334f
　profits of, 345–346
　secular-religious positions on, 253
　subsidies to, 336–338
settlers
　IDF relationship with, 229–234
　media activity of, 304–305
Shabtai, Yaakov, 445
Shalev, Mordechai, 448
Shamgar, Meir
　al-Naazer case, 41
　on Fourth Geneva Convention, 515
　on international law compliance, 13
　Vat case, 34
Shamir, Yitzhak, 143–144, 202–203, 257
Shapira, Arik, 448
Shapira, Yaakov Shimshon, 54n2, 222
Shapira, Yitzhak, 433n7
Sharon, Ariel
　Bedouin removal by, 227
　coalition government of, 260–261
　"disengagement plan," 1
　on peace agreement conditions, 214
　political opinion of, 509
　political views of, 131–132, 142, 145, 155, 167, 173
　settlement expansion and, 100–101
　on withdrawal from territories, 216

Sharon, Roi, 422
Sharvit, K., 385
Sheef, Ze'ev, 337–338
Sheinfeld, Ilan, 457
SHELI (Peace for Israel)
  description of, 178n15
  political views of, 149
Shelomzion (Security for Israel)
  description of, 176n6
  political views of, 131–132
Shilon, Avi, 464–465
Shinar, O., 428
Shin Bet (security service), 17, 19, 429
S H I T (Self Hating Israeli Traitors), 433 n6
Shmueli, Itzhak, 465–466
Shohat, Ella, 449
Shomron, Dan, 388
Shuvi organization, on Israeli deaths, 18–19
Siedler-Feller, Haim, 432
Silberman, N.A., 109
"Silent Witness" (Sachs), 372
Sinai Peninsula, as defensive space, 219
situation-depreciation hypothesis, 395
Sivel, Robbie, 516
Six Day War. *See also* "defensible borders," construction of
  consequences for IDF, 208–210
  crime levels after, 394
  effect on military thinking, 221
  generational analysis and, 361, 363
  HR violations following, 413–414
  as just war, vii
  political space, effects on, 252–253
  religious meaning to, 201
  results of, 122
  as subject of plays, 444
  television after, 313
"Slave Square," 443
Smilansky, Yizhar, 445–446
Smile of the Lamb (Grossman), 448–449, 450

Smooha, S., 366
Sobol, Yehoshua, 451, 452, 454, 467
social authority, 68
social divides, 520–523
social learning theory, 383
social norms
  permitting aggression, 384, 390
  physical violence and, 388
social-psychological effects, of occupation, 383–385
social security payments, 335
societal events, in studies, 399
societal trends
  civil disorder, 422
  public opinion, 421
  tolerance, erosion of, 423
  violent acts/threats, 421–422
socio-economic cost, of occupation, 346–349
sociology, of occupation, 360–362
Sofer, Arnon, 107, 514
soldiers. *See also* Israel Defense Forces (IDF)
  deaths of, 385
  effects of violence on, 387–390
  participation in violence, 389
  power felt by, 392–393
  training of, 399
Somer, E., 370–371
songs, of protest, 459
Sons of the Village (*Abna' al-balad*), 284–285
sources, of information, 71–72
South African comparison, 351
Soviet Union
  in Eastern Europe, ix
  immigrants from, 424
Spivak, A., 330
State Controller's Report (1994), 17
statehood, Palestinian, ix, 128, 214, 285, 287, 501, 517. *See also* political system, views of
state institutions, control of, 116

state vs. religious education, 105–106
Steinberg, David, 458
Stern, Alfred, 77–78
Sternhell, Zeev, 422
"Stop the Occupation," 447
Strauss, Leo, 77–78
stress
    learned aggressions and, 384–386
    prevalence of, 397
    symptoms associated with, 386
    violent crime and, 394
Suez Canal
    as line of defense, 215, 218, 219
    War of Attrition and, 220
suicide bombings, 395
summud (steadfastness), 14
Supreme Court of Israel
    on deportations, 48, 50–51
    on freedom of movement, 51
    on Geneva Convention IV, 33
    highway cases, 45–47
    on house demolitions, 48–51
    human rights, defense of, 426
    judgments/precedents of, 31–32
    on land policy, 41
    presumption of innocence and, 50
    security matter decisions, 51–52
    on security measures, 48–52
    separation barrier and, 41–43, 52–53
    settlement cases before, 38–39, 198
    settlement supporters and, 523
Sutton, K., 244
Swirski, Shlomo, 330, 331, 332, 337, 339, 370
symbolic names, of settlements, 105*t*
Syria
    defense plans against, 221
    peace agreement proposals, 216–217

Taba negotiations, 66, 88n4
Tal, Israel, 213, 220, 227–228
Talmud names, of settlements, 105*t*

Tartakover, David, 459
Taub, Gadi, 460
tax benefits/breaks, 337–338
Tchernikovsky, Shaul, 448
technology exports, "homeland security" and, 350
Tehiya (Resurrection)
    description of, 177–178n13
    political views of, 142
Teitel, Yaakov, 423
Tel Aviv Research Center, 423
television, introduction of, 300–302
tentative cognition, 89n12
territorial compromise, 163–164
territorial control, ramifications of
    economic costs, 525–526
    Israel's world status and, 526–527
    security narrative and, 524–525
    social divides, 520–523
    weakening of democracy, 520–523
territories, Jewish identity and, 513–514
territory construction, mechanisms of
    archaeology, 108–111
    daily life, 111–114
    identity and, 93–97
    land acquisition, 97–99
    maps, 102–103
    national education, 105–108
    place names, 103–105
    settlements, 100–102
terror, fight against, 237–240
textbooks, 106–107
theater. *See* arts, representation in
theatergoers, 440
Tibet
    Chinese rule in, viii, ix, 115, 316, 519
    civil rights in, 11
tolerance, erosion of, 423
Tori, Meir, 110
torture, interrogation and, 16–17
Toufik, Suleiman, 226
tourist maps, 110

Tozomet party, 256
Trabshe, Adnan, 455
The Trojan Women/Les Troyennes (Euripides), 441, 454
Tsaban, D., 331, 337
tsabar, 447, 512
tsumud, 447
Tsur, Nadir, 22, 528, 529–530, 546
Turkey/Turkish Cypriots, 9, 115, 290
The 20th Century on the Threshold of Tomorrow (Naveh), 106
two-state solution, 166, 168. *See also* Palestinian state/statehood
Tzomet (Junction)
　in coalition politics, 256
　description of, 177n12
　political views of, 142, 143, 151

Uganda proposal, 82
Ullman, Micha, 444
"under dispute," vs. "occupied" term, 22n1
unemployment, 348
union fees, 335–336
United Nations
　OPT name use, 382
　Palestine Partition Plan and, 65
　Security Council Resolution 1325, 359, 371
　on Zionism, 363
United Nations Office for the Coordination of Humanitarian Affairs in the Occupied Palestinian Territory (OCHA), 17–18
United States
　occupation of Haiti, 402–403
　occupation of Iraq, 403
　in Philippines, viii
　withdrawal pressure from, 251
Universal Declaration of Human Rights (UDHR), 10, 414, 421
universal-ideological orientation, 129, 139

universal-pragmatic orientation, 128–129, 137, 160
university community, 424–425
Urian, Dan, 22, 530, 546–547
Ushpiz, Jakob, 106

Valentine, Avi, 448
"vanished question," 442
Vanus, Sa'ad Allah, 455
Verdiger, Abraham, 202–203
Vinograd Committee, 238
violence
　carried out by soldiers, 524
　continuation of, 346
　domestic, 372–373
　economic hardship and, 342
　latent, 112
　in October 2000 demonstrations, 114
　oppositions to, 396–397
　participation in, 389
　political, 372, 385–386
　"preventive," 392
　verbal disrespect and, 419
violent acts/threats, 421–422
violent behavior, in deviant norm-setting process, 384
violent crime, stress and, 394
vulnerable populations, 423–425

wage additions, 335
Wainstein, B., 390
"Wallkeepers." *See* media (Israeli)
war, preparation for, 237–240
war crime. *See also* human rights
War of Attrition, 220
Watad, Muhammed, 438
Watch (Women against the Occupation and for Human Rights), 464
water infrastructure, 338
Wax, Adrian, 452
weapon companies, profits of, 346
web sites, 302
Weinblatt, J., 330

Weizmann, Ezer, 142, 214, 216
welfare state, privatization of, 370
West Bank and Gaza
  annexation of, 214–215
  HR policy/violations in, 412, 416
  legal status of, 34, 35
  Palestinian's as protected persons in, 35
Western Wall tunnel incident, 231–232
Wieseltier, Meir, 459
Winter in Kalandia (Nirgad), 438, 439f, 464, 468
withdrawal from territories. *See also* political system, views of
  decline in support for, 171
  in peace agreement proposal, 217
  Peled on, 214
  Rabin on, 215
  security considerations, 166, 169
  Sharon on, 216
  War of Attrition and, 220
  Weizmann on, 216
Witkon, Justice, 54n3
Woman to Woman (Isha L'Isha), 371–372
women. *See also* gender perspective
  Begin on status of, 363
  Palestinian, 457–458
  violence against, 524
Women against the Occupation and for Human Rights (Watch), 464
Women's Coalition for Peace, 374
A World of Exchanges (Jakobi), 106
World Zionist Organization (WZO), 45, 336–337
Wye Plantation Agreement, 259

Ya'alon, Moshe, 237
Ya'ari, Ehud, 456
Yaari, Hagit, 457
Yafeh, Adi, 223
Yamit evacuation, 255
Yaniv, Avner, 240
Yaring, Gunnar, 214
The Yellow Time (Grossman), 448–449, 455
Yesha Settlements Council, on Israeli deaths, 18–19
Yesh Gvul movement, 361
yeshivas, 105
Yishay-Krien, Nufar, 389–390, 396
Yizhar, S., 445–446
Yom Kippur War
  military aims of, 220–221
  national religious movement and, 96
  women and, 362
youth, intolerance of, 424

Zahdeh, Abed al-Wahab, 309–310
Zartal, I., 230
Zeevi, Rehavam, 221
Ze'evi, Rehavam, 225, 237, 260
Ziad, Tawfiq, 282
Zionism/Zionist movement
  land acquisition, 97–98
  nationalism and, 96
  as national liberation movement, 413
  occupied territories and, 13
  Uganda proposal and, 82
Zionist Left, 66
Zoubi, Seef Al-Din, 282
Zureik, E. T., 275